Lead, Follow, or Move Out of the Way

Global Perspectives in Literature

Monique Ferrell
Julian Williams
New York City College of Technology

KENDALL/HUNT PUBLISHING COMPANY
4050 Westmark Drive Dubuque, Iowa 52002

All photographs by Al Vargas, senior graphic designer at New York City College
of Technology, City University of New York

All photographed students are attendees at New York City College of Technology

Copyright © 2006 by Monique Ferrell and Julian Williams

ISBN: 978-0-7575-5447-6

Kendall/Hunt Publishing Company has the exclusive rights to reproduce this work,
to prepare derivative works from this work, to publicly distribute this work,
to publicly perform this work and to publicly display this work.

All rights reserved. No part of this publication may be reproduced,
stored in a retrieval system, or transmitted, in any form or by any
means, electronic, mechanical, photocopying, recording, or otherwise,
without the prior written permission of the copyright owner.

Printed in the United States of America
10 9 8 7 6 5 4 3 2

Contents

Three Racial Matters

Four Class and the Culture of Power

Twain's "experiments" provide cynical views of mankind that, interestingly enough, are just as distressing today as they have ever been.

On July 5, 1852, Douglass gave a speech commemorating the signing of the Declaration of Independence. During the speech, Douglass pointed out that this celebratory holiday is a "sham" to the enslaved American and asserted that America was guilty of the most shocking and bloody crimes imaginable.

Neusner ponders the consequences and the importance of empowering students by allowing them to grade their college professors.

The British policy of Kenyans speaking only English in classrooms after the first three years of study is seen as a major factor regarding the native speakers' self-image.

This article examines a case of sexual harassment and seeks to determine what the proper etiquette is for a college professor and students.

A poor college student determines she must steal in order to pursue her education.

A supposed member of the weaker sex sets out to determine whether or not she can manipulate a man into thinking she is several different women.

A poor taxi driver, who works part-time at a doctor's office, picks up a wealthy Indian-American family having an obnoxious and, as he soon learns, revealing visit.

After successfully "passing" in the White world, a man returns home to visit the women he left behind.

LA Times article that looks at the tragedy and devastation that remains after the most horrific natural disaster in American history.

Five Religion

An examination of the notion of good and the determination that the concept of "goodness" is almost without meaning.

The author attempts to examine the ways in which religion has been used to subjugate oppressed people as opposed to being used as an expression of faith.

Reflections of an author who feels that her faith has both exalted her and damned her as a woman.

A father, who is a practicing Hindi, feels that the women in his family are "too" American and that this will, and does, bring about disastrous consequences.

Six Gender, Sex, and Sexuality

Seven Fork in the Road

Eight Comprehension through Charts and Graphs

Films

Our students, like the majority of the world's population, love movies. Whether it's drama or action/adventure or mystery or comedy or the love story or, with ever increasing audiences, the documentary, film has proven that it is arguably the main vehicle used to both express sentiment and entertain viewers. Even though this point is virtually inarguable, literary materials still remain the core for most classrooms. However, books are now, more than ever, forced to compete with our growing technological societies. Let's be honest: today's students relate more readily to wireless communication devices and the internet than they do with paper texts. Amazon recently released the Amazon Kindle—a wireless portable reading device with access to 190,000 books, magazines, newspapers, and blogs—providing further proof that the texts-only based classroom must adjust to this new techno world or get left behind the times. As such, we strongly promote a blending of what the student's love with what they need. Alongside our written works we strongly encourage that selected films—movies, like the chosen literature, from around the globe—be incorporated into the classroom curriculum. The infusion of these two impacting mediums allows the students to not only read and discuss texts but, also, to visualize the topics and themes that come out of classroom examinations.

We have carefully selected the following films. In an attempt to help both professor and students choose which film goes best with what written work, we have placed specific films in chapter sections and provided a brief review that provides insight into who, what, when, and where for each film.

Note to Professors/Instructors

*Please review each film before showing it to the classrooms. Some films contain serious, adult content.

CHAPTER ONE: SOCIAL RESPONSIBILITY

The Agronomist: A documentary on the assassination of Haitian political activist Jean Dominique.

Dead Poet's Society: In the spirit of Emerson, a prep-school teacher challenges his male students to be nonconformists and tap into their inner genius.

Fight Club: Looking at the duality that resides within men—males who prove themselves by fighting bare knuckled—the film examines a specific question: Does a man belong to himself or is maleness a societal construct that he inevitably falls prey to?

Hotel Rwanda: An examination of a man who stands up to be counted when the "new" norm in his African homeland is violence and warfare.

I Am Because We Are: Writer-producer Madonna exposes the tragic stories of the millions of Malawi children orphaned by AIDS.

In the Year of the Pig: Emile de Antonio's ground breaking 1968 protest documentary against the Vietnam War, where he reveals the American government's lies; moreover, the director calls into question all versions of the war released to the public.

Jump Tomorrow: A Nigerian pledged in an arranged marriage questions "his situation."

Juno: Two adolescent outcasts find themselves expecting a child in a reserved Minnesota community. Film examines abortion, adoption, and the growing pains of the protagonists and everyone around them.

Keane: A film dedicated to unearthing the reality of what it means to live with mental illness.

The Business of Being Born: Documentary that explores issues surrounding child birthing, noting that the U.S. spends twice as much per birth than any other industrialized country, while, interestingly, having the second worst mortality rate for both mothers and infants.

The Kite Runner: The subtitled film adaptation to Khalid Hosseini's best selling novel on Afghanistan, lost childhoods, betrayal, and redemption.

The Last Supper: Five midwestern graduate students decide to rid the world of those who hold opposing political ideas, by offering them dinners and a very special glass of wine.

Moolaaddé: A mother who experienced female circumcision as a child attempts to prevent her daughter from being forced to take part in the ceremony.

School Ties: In the 1950s, an all-male school is challenged to open the prejudiced minds and hearts of its privileged students after one of their own admits he is Jewish.

Twilight Zone: Eye of the Beholder: A woman struggles to change her face so that she can look like everyone else in order to avoid being evicted from her community.

Young Rebels: A documentary on young Cuban revolutionaries who use Hip-Hop music as a forum to discuss race and class issues in their native Cuba.

Weatherman: Local weatherman's convoluted journey to find his place in the world while dealing with the disintegration of his family.

Without the King: This lively documentary looks at the tiny African nation of Swaziland, one of the last existing absolute monarchies. This look at the African kingdom exposes a life expectancy that is one of the shortest in the world—the rate of HIV infection is the globe's highest—as well as thousands of citizens who subsist on some of the most revolting food imaginable.

CHAPTER TWO: DEATH AND VIOLENCE

American Gun: **Vignettes on gun violence and how this epidemic is devastating American families.**

An Omar Broadway Film: **Using a contraband video camera inside the gang unit at Newark's Northern State Prison, a jailed Bloods member puts his life on the line to document guards' corruption and excessive force. Documentary exposes the often corrupt and violent world behind bars.**

Apocalypse Now: **Francis Ford Coppola's surrealistic and symbolic film details the confusion, violence, fear, and madness that encompassed the Vietnam War.**

Bowling for Columbine: **Documentary filmmaker Michael Moore examines how the culture of fear, class, racism, and violence may have led to America's most horrific school shooting.**

Crying Ladies: **Comedy that follows the lives of three women who cry at funerals— professionally.**

Freak: **Told with seamless comic flare, comedian John Leguizamo's stand-up show explores what it means to grow up in a house of domestic abuse.**

How I Killed a Saint: **A woman living abroad in America returns to her native war-torn Balkans and discovers that both her family and country are in utter turmoil.**

Kassim the Dream: **Documentary that follows Kassim "The Dream" Ouma, who went from Ugandan child soldier to world champion boxer.**

Love Story: **Harvard rich kid meets Radcliffe musician. They fall in love and then discover that she is terminally ill. (Original, 1970)**

Munyurangabo: **Following the relationship between two boys traveling on a vengeance mission across Rwanda's countryside, the film, which has a completely nonprofessional cast, takes a potent look at genocide, as it depicts friendships and familial betrayals.**

Mystic River: **Boston community implodes as the death of a teenage girl puts her father at odds with his childhood friends—men bonded through a horrible childhood experience.**

Nanking: **Powerful documentary that provides first person recollections of the near-total destruction of the Chinese city and its inhabitants by imperial Japanese troops in 1937.**

Ordinary People: **The accidental death of an older son from an affluent family deeply strains the relationships between the bitter mother, the good-natured father, and the guilt-ridden son. (Original, 1980)**

Paradise Now: **After a horrific experience, two Palestinian friends decide to become suicide bombers in Tel Aviv.**

The Passion of the Christ: **An exploration of the violence Christ endured during his last days.**

Raging Bull: **The story details the main stages of temperamental, paranoid, and abusive boxer Jake Lamotta: his rise, fall, and in-between life.**

Sleepers: **Supposedly based on a true crime, four teenage pranksters are sent to a juvenile detention center where they are physically and sexually abused by the guards. Ten years later, two of the boys murder the ringleader, leading to a highly publicized trial.**

State of Fear: **Documentary that offers a balanced view of the atrocities occurring during Peru's sordid twenty-year cycle of violence and corruption.**

Taxi Driver: **The quintessential average man is compelled to seek social validation through the only means available: violence.**

Terms of Endearment: **Movie traces the lives of mother and daughter, women always trying to find happiness, who march to the beat of different drummers—women reunited when one becomes stricken with cancer.**

The 3 Rooms of Melancholia: **Documentary that deals with the ongoing Russia/ Chechnya conflict, examining how children become collateral damage on the Eastern front.**

United 93: **Reenactment of the final hours of the doomed flight that plunged out of the Pennsylvania sky on September 11, 2001.**

The War of the Roses: **A married couple turns to horrendous acts of violence after the collapse of their "ideal" marriage.**

We Were Soldiers: **Story of the first major battle of the American phase of the Vietnam War and the soldiers on both sides who fought.**

Winter Soldier: **True-life accounts from actual soldiers who returned from Vietnam—men physically and mentally left too scarred to rejoin society.**

Wit: **Literary scholar faced with cancer discovers human kindness.**

CHAPTER THREE: RACIAL MATTERS

Arranged: **Movie revolves around the friendship of two young teachers in Brooklyn—one Muslim, one an Orthodox Jew—who meet at a racially and culturally diverse Brooklyn grade school. The film tackles arranged marriages, faith, secular Americanism, and the boundaries of family tolerance.**

The Boy Who Played on the Buddhas of Bamiyan: **Family of Afghani refugees lives among the ruins of a tourist attraction that was destroyed by the Taliban.**

Color of the Cross: **An examination of the last forty-eight hours of Jesus Christ as a Black man.**

C.S.A.: The Confederate States of America: **An alternate historical society where the South won the Revolutionary War and America has embraced racism as a part of life.**

The Defiant Ones: **Two escaped convicts—one White, the other Black—must overcome their own prejudices in an attempt to evade their pursuers, survive in a racist society, and, most of all, overcome their own social conditioning.** (Original, 1958)

Donkey in Lahore: **An unusual love story style documentary of an Australian puppeteer who falls in love with a Muslim woman he met in Pakistan. Can this unlikely couple survive the challenges they are about to face?**

Freedomland: **A portrait of a White mother who claims her child was abducted by a Black male and how this accusation fuels negative race relations in a segregated, racially charged community.**

The Goebbels Experiment: **A documentary about the anti-Jewish propaganda perpetuated during World War II.**

In the Heat of the Night: **Black Philadelphia police detective reluctantly becomes embroiled in a murder investigation in racially hostile 1960s Mississippi.** (Original, 1967)

Kippur: **Portrait of the 1973 Yom Kippur between Syria and Israel, told from the perspective of a skeptical soldier.**

La Vita e Bella (Life Is Beautiful): **Man uses humor and fantasy to protect his son in a Nazi death camp.**

Michael Collins: **Leader fights to establish Irish Free State in the 1920s while becoming vilified by those hoping to create a completely independent Irish Republic.**

Mississippi Burning: **Two FBI agents are sent to Mississippi to investigate the disappearance of missing civil rights workers. The film is an exploration of one of the ugliest chapters in American history, examining White supremacy, corruption, and extreme conflicts of social conscience.**

My Life Inside: **Film follows the tragic life of Rosa Jimenez who, at seventeen, came to the U.S. to provide a better life for her family back in Mexico. This heartbreaking documentary examines how she came to stand accused of murder in a Texas courtroom.**

Occupation: Dreamland: **Documentary filmmakers record soldiers who are stationed in Iraq and gain insight about how and why they are perceived as invaders.**

The Order of Myths: **Based on Alabama's 2007 Mardi Gras, an annual event that has existed since the 1700s, this documentary examines Mobile's first ethnically blended events, where the African-American community's regents attended their White counterparts' coronation and vice-versa. The result is a microcosmic look at race relations that proves how largely divided this nation still remains.**

Planet of the Apes: **An astronaut crew crash-lands on a planet in the distant future where talking apes are the dominant species and humans are oppressed and enslaved.** (Original, 1968)

The Price of the Ticket: **Documentary on the life and literary career of one of America's most prolific writers, James Baldwin. This is an American Masters Series.**

Protocols of Zion: **Documentary about anti-Semitism in America and the rise of anti-Jewish sentiment after 9/11.**

Rosewood: **Based on the actual massacre of Black townspeople in Rosewood Florida, this film gives an account of the events that led to White town's people attacking the Black community over several days.**

Some Mother's Son: **Based on the true story of IRA prisoner Bobby Sands's 1981 hunger strike in a British prison.**

Street Fight: **Documentary that chronicles the racist overtones involved in the 2002 mayoral race in Newark, New Jersey, between Sharpe James—the "average-Joe," darker skinned incumbent—and Cory Booker—the fair-skinned, Yale Law School graduate.**

Twilight Zone: Maple Street: **After the power goes out in a small middle-America neighborhood, all hell breaks loose as neighbors and friends turn against one another.**

What's Cooking?: **Tensions mount amidst four families of different ethnic and economic backgrounds living in contemporary Los Angeles as they prepare dinner for family and guests.**

White Man's Burden: **The film takes an alternative view on Black/White race relations by constructing a world where Blacks hold all of the power.**

Zoned In: **Filmed over the course of nine years, this documentary traces the remarkable journey of sixteen-year-old Daniel who, beginning at a Bronx high school, goes to an Ivy League university. At the same time, this film explores the role of race and class in the American educational system.**

CHAPTER FOUR: CLASS AND THE CULTURE OF POWER

4 Months, 3 Weeks and 2 Days: **Set in 1980s Bucharest, while still behind the Iron Curtain, movie concerns two friends—one pregnant, one supportive—as they attempt to have an** illegal procedure with a black-market abortionist. The film is centered mainly in the hotel room where the negotiations are discussed, revealing to the audience the hellish dynamics of economics, power games, and sex.

Alexandra: Story of an elderly woman who visits a remote military outpost in implied Chechnya and observes various degrees of soldiering: banality of barrack life and machinery placement over human beings. This moving film also provides a face and voice to the enemy, as well as the difficulties of politics and the bond of the woman and her ward.

Amores Perros: Three interconnected stories about the different strata of life in Mexico City, revolving around a fatal car crash.

A Walk to Beautiful: This documentary follows five Ethiopian women from isolated rural communities who developed obstetric fistulas after prolonged obstructed deliveries. These women are ostracized and abandoned, even though a simple surgery can correct their condition. This film is an unabashed humanitarian call to action, as it examines how superstition, poverty, and hundreds of miles to medical care all stand in the way of these women's survival.

Ballast: A cryptic and intimate tale of three people dealing with a tragedy in the Deep South. Film brilliantly handles people living below the poverty line with poetic sensitivity.

Beaufort: Well crafted movie that looks at various soldiers in Lebanon guarding the highly symbolic Beaufort Castle from Hezbollah forces in the last remaining days of Israel's occupation.

A Bronx Tale: The protagonist struggles to come to terms with his growing affinity for a neighborhood gangster, who treats him like a son, and his father, a working-class bus driver.

Bubble: Set in small-town Ohio and West Virginia, the movie examines the lives of three paycheck-to-paycheck wage earners—individuals who have lived this way for so long they have forgotten how to imagine a future. Film also contains a murder mystery twist.

Claudine: A classic "dramadey" that examines America's welfare system and the ways in which it forces a wedge between a mother and her garbage-man boyfriend in 1970s New York.

The Constant Gardner: In an attempt to expose the corporate and political AIDS drug racket in Kenya, a couple risks their lives.

Duck Season: Adolescents spend a lazy Sunday afternoon together. Melancholy film that examines loneliness, togetherness, and the end of family in a small Mexico City apartment.

El Inmortal: Mercedes Moncarda Rodriguez follows the plight of a woman and her four children living in Nicaragua.

Enron: The Smartest Guys in the Room: Based on the 2003 investigative digest, this documentary is a methodical look at the men who became known as the largest white-collar crooks ever taken to trial in American history.

Goodwill Hunting: the main character, a poor street kid from Boston's low-end—who just happens to be genius—attempts to work out his issues about who he is in relation to where he lives and the expectations of those around him.

Hustle and Flow: Sympathetic southern pimp attempts to better his station in life—involving everyone in his limited world—through Hip-Hop.

In America: Irish immigrants struggle to survive and maintain their sanity in New York City's Hell's Kitchen.

The Joy Luck Club: Chinese mothers and daughters reflect on the roles they played in the culture clash between the mothers' traditional Chinese values and their Americanized children.

Mardi Gras: Made in China: **Conscience-stirring documentary examines the life cycle of the bead necklaces used during this New Orleans' event, alongside the millionaires who own the Tai Kuen bead factory in China and their employees—individuals who work fourteen hour days, six days a week under horrendous conditions.**

Pray the Devil Back to Hell: **After more than a decade of civil wars leading to more than 250,000 deaths and one million refugees, the documentary looks at a group of courageous Liberian women who rose up and propelled to victory the first female head of state on the African continent.**

The Oil Factor: Behind the War on Terror: **Film chronicles the major events surrounding U.S. politics of the past quarter-century.**

A Raisin in the Sun: **Desperate to be seen as the breadwinner in his family, a Black man—a son, husband, and father—blames himself, his mother, and his wife for what he sees as his personal failure with regard to not being able to provide as a "man."** (Original, 1961)

Return to the Land of Wonders: **Documentary where the filmmaker—having lived thirty-five years abroad—walks the streets in Iraq, her homeland, and interviews everyday citizens about what they have been through—both under Saddam Hussein's regime and during U.S. occupation.**

Rocky: **In this classic "underdog" tale, the self-titled main character boxes his way out of Philadelphia's underbelly, training his way to a heavyweight championship fight.**

Sarafina: **A young girl struggles to break the racial and class barriers while living in apartheid South Africa.**

Sicko: **Michael Moor's compelling documentary is a scathing indictment of America's failing health care system. He travels to Canada, England, France, and Cuba—where free universal health care is the norm—and finds himself asking, "Why can't this happen in America?"**

SlumDog Millionaire: **While consistently winning India's most popular game show, an impoverished teen who has no desire for wealth comes face to face with the social pressures associated with instant wealth; at the same time, the police suspect him of cheating because they cannot figure out how he, a street kid, continues to do so well.**

The Squid and the Whale: **A failed novelist and his successful-writer wife split and the ugliness of divorce forces their sons to choose sides.**

Wal-Mart: The High Cost of Low Price: **Documentary that chronicles the corporation's ruthless policies.**

The Weeping Meadow: **A romantic Greek tragedy. Film tracks two runaway lovers from the 1919 incursion of Bolshevism to the bitter end of World War II.**

Young and Restless in China: **Documentary follows the lives of nine youngish Chinese citizens over the course of a few years, ranging from a Western-educated entrepreneur struggling with the ethical challenges of doing business in his home country, to a young factory worker contemplating breaking off the engagement arranged by her rural family. Film illustrates the profound changes that China's double-digit economic growth has instigated in every area of life.**

CHAPTER FIVE: RELIGION

Agnes of God: **When a nun is discovered in her quarters with a dead newborn, a court-appointed psychiatrist investigates.**

Constantine's Sword: **Based on the 2001 book of the same name, this documentary follows James Carroll—a former Catholic priest whose faith was rocked by Christianity's** militancy and anti-Semitism—as he examines the Crusades, the infamous treaty between Pope Pius XII and Adolf Hitler, and the rise of Mega Churches and evangelical fervor.

The Dali Lama: **Peace and Prosperity: A visual record of the Dali Lama's sold out Radio City Music Hall visit and presentation.**

Destiny: **Examines the historic battle between Islamic fundamentalists and liberals through the story of the enlightened 12th-century Andalusian philosopher and Quranic scholar Averroes.**

The Dhamma Brothers: **Documentary looks at a group of inmates sentenced to Alabama's maximum-security prison who began practicing meditation following a ten-day course in the Buddhist technique of vipassana.**

Dogma: **Two renegade angels try to exploit a religious loophole that could bring an end to humanity.**

A Door to the Sky: **Father's death forces Moroccan woman to return from her expatriate life in Paris to the constrained Muslim customs of her homeland.**

The Excorcist: **Teen is possessed by the devil and priests are forced to perform a dangerous religious ceremony.** (Original, 1973)

Guyana Tragedy—The Story of Jim Jones: **This made for TV film is based on the cult-like world of charismatic leader Jim Jones and the 1978 mass suicide of the People's Temple in Jonestown, Guyana. Not only does this real life event—one that took the lives of over 900 people—serve as one of the largest mass suicides in world history, it also serves as the greatest single loss of American civilian life in a non-natural disaster until the events of September 11th, 2001.** (Original, 1980)

History of the World: **Mel Brooks's satire where we learn what "really happened" at the last supper.**

The Last Temptation of Christ: **At his execution, Jesus is tempted by an alluring image of a blissful life with Mary Magdelene—a temptation that tries to sway him from the sacrifice he must make.**

The Omen: **Diplomat learns that his son is the literal anti-Christ.** (Original, 1976)

Orthodox Stance: **Documentary that looks at 25-year old Orthodox Jewish prizefighter Dmitry Salita who literally won't fight after Sundown of Friday.**

Religulous: **Bill Mahr's hilarious documentary on the current state of world religion.**

Rosemary's Baby: **Woman learns that her pregnancy is actually part of a satanic ritual.** (Original, 1968)

Saint Ralph: **A young man is forced to join his Catholic school track team after it is discovered that he has committed twenty-two sins against the flesh—his own flesh.**

Saved: **This satire looks at how religious beliefs can lead to extreme intolerance, when a girl finds herself pregnant at a Baptist high school.**

Twist of Faith: **Documentary that looks at a man who confronts his past sexual abuse at the hands of a Catholic priest, only to discover how this shatters his relationships with his family, community, and faith.**

West Beirut: **Follows two teenagers during the beginning of the civil war between Christians and Muslims that devastated Lebanon between 1975 and 1990 and turned cosmopolitan Beirut into a bombed-out ruin.**

Witness to Jonestown: **A powerful and extremely revealing documentary that explores the social and political worlds that allowed Jim Jones to successfully seduce the city of**

San Francisco. The film interviews survivors and family members on the thirty year anniversary of the Jones Town massacre—tracing Jones' unstoppable rise as reverend and community activist to this tragic last days in the jungle of Guyana.

CHAPTER SIX: GENDER, SEX, AND SEXUALITY

12 Angry Men: **This 1957 classic introduces viewers to a jury of various male personalities who, during deliberation, are prevented from sentencing a Latino male when one of the men refuses to vote guilty. The result is a tense contrast in racist, bullying, often apathetic personas that boil to a head, leading to the films dramatic conclusion.** (Original, 1957)

American Beauty: **A depressed suburban father in the midst of a midlife crisis decides to change his life—most notably through the pursuit of his teenage daughter's friend.**

Antwone Fisher: **An abused societal outcast attempts to understand what it means to be a man by exploring the institutions and determining factors that shaped him as a boy.**

Beneath the Veil: **Examines women rebelling against the treatment they receive under the Taliban in Afghanistan.**

Born into Brothels: **Documentary that focuses on the children existing in Calcutta's inherently abusive red-light district.**

Boys Don't Cry: **The true story of Teena Brandon, who chose to live her short life as her male alter-ego, Brandon Teena.**

Boys in the Hood: **Coming-of-age tale about three friends—young males trying to grasp manhood in various ways—living in violent South Central, Los Angeles.**

A Boy's Life: **Documentary that follows a Mississippi family's struggle—according to the obviously disturbed grandmother—with an increasingly violent and erratic child.**

Bridget Jones' Diary: **A thirty-something woman struggles with the notion of becoming a spinster.**

Brokeback Mountain: **Love story that examines the forbidden love between two modern-day cowboys.**

The Business of Fancy Dancing: **Gay Indian poet from Spokane confronts his past when he returns to his childhood home, on the reservation, to attend a friend's funeral.**

The Circle: **Tracks the hopeless situation of a half-dozen Iranian women, including three who have escaped from jail.**

The Day I Became a Woman: **A trio of tales that simply, yet evocatively, lays out the problems of being a woman in Iran.**

Disney's Beauty and the Beast: **Young maiden offers herself to the beast—a raging and abusive male—and eventually discovers the prince inside.**

Eat Drink Man Woman: **Living in Tai Pei, a senior chef lives with his three unmarried adult daughters. Film revolves around everyone's relationships and the elaborate Sunday dinners.**

How to Murder Your Wife: **When a nationally syndicated cartoonist—one so successful he lives in a luxurious penthouse with his man-servant, Charles—attends a stag party and awakens the next day married to a young woman who barely speaks English, he finds that this mistake turns his life upside down. The end result is as complex as it is hilarious when he begins to plot his wife's murder within the pages of his cartoon. When she suddenly disappears, the cartoon is used as evidence at his trial.** (Original, 1965)

A League of Their Own: **Women grow and stand up to oppression when they start their own baseball league.**

Like Water for Chocolate: **Living in Mexico, a woman, prevented from marrying the man she loves, discovers she can do amazing things through her cooking.**

Love Actually: **Follows the lives of eight very different London couples dealing with their love lives in various interrelated tales.**

Mona Lisa Smile: **Feminist-thinking art professor challenges the conditioned lives of her students at an all-female college.**

No Secret Anymore: **Documentary that tackles—through the attempts of the filmmakers to develop a coalition—the prevailing belief that lesbians are illegal, immoral, and sick.**

On the Outs: **Three different Latinas and their crack-laced lives face the horrors and ravages of inner-city life.**

Paris Is Burning: **Documentary on "drag nights" among New York's underclass.**

Pretty Woman: **Prostitute elevates her social standing when a wealthy businessman decides to teach her how to be a proper woman.**

Real Women Have Curves: **Young L.A. Mexican butts heads with her matriarchal mother after expressing that she wants more out of life—namely a quality education—than simply being supportive of her family.**

Same Sex in America: **Documentary looks at same-sex marriage, as seen through several couples experiencing dilemmas.**

Second Hand Lions: **Two set-in-their-ways veterans, men who have lived full and active lives, reluctantly teach their young nephew what manhood is all about.**

The Sisterhood of the Traveling Pants: **A group of teenage friends from different backgrounds separate for the summer and have life-changing experiences—but not before discovering that they all can share a very special pair of jeans.**

Thelma & Louise: **Two women take a road trip and become wanted fugitives, all while embracing life, womanhood, and friendship.**

Thirteen: **A thirteen-year-old girl's relationship with her mother is put to the test as she discovers drugs, petty crime, and sex.**

The Three Burials of Melquiades Estrada: **Ranch hand attempts to fulfill two promises: bury his friend in his home in Mexico and punish the man who killed him.**

The World According the Garp: **Young man, who sees himself as a serious writer, is overwhelmed by his famous feminist mother and the variously distressed women that come into his life.**

Y Tu Mama Tambien: **In Mexico, two teenage boys and an attractive older woman embark on a road trip and learn about life, friendship, sex, and each other.**

CHAPTER SEVEN: FORK IN THE ROAD

The Big One: **On his book tour, Michael Moore exposes wrongdoings by greedy big businesses and callous politicians.**

Bigger, Stronger, Faster: **Documentary that examines America's fascination—athletes and amateurs—with being the biggest, strongest, and the fastest.**

Billy the Kid: **Documentary on teenager Billy Price and his dignified coping with Asperger's syndrome.**

Boli Zhi Cheng (City of Glass): **Twenty years after a college couple's break-up and marriage to other people, their children—from respective marriages—meet and join forces to help them live out a dream.**

Changing Lanes: **Road rage spirals into a all-consuming feud between two men who both find they are at crossroads in their lives.**

City of God: **Poor Brazilian youth decides to pick up a camera and abandon his life of crime and embrace his new hobby: recording the violence and disparity of his world on film.**

Dorian Blues: **One night, a closeted high school senior—saddled with a domineering father, an athletic brother, and a loopy mother—challenges his father's conservative views and, during their argument, has an epiphany: he is gay.**

The English Sheik and the Yemeni Gentleman: **Follows a British filmmaker who returns to Yemen—the home of his father—and meets a British expatriate. Together they roam the land and discover a true sense of belonging.**

Fame: **Students at NYC's School for the Performing Arts attempt to overcome social and personal barriers and fulfill their artistic dreams.** (Original, 1980)

Flight of the Red Balloon: **Film deals with a Parisian summer filled with uncertainty, with each of the characters—mother, son, and Chinese au pair—expressing loss and pain.**

Imitation of Life: **Explores the practice of passing by a young Black woman attempting to prosper in segregated America.** (Original, 1934)

Look at Me: **A Parisian choral student lives in a world of disconnectedness. Notably, there is a subplot on weight obsession after the father marries a rail-thin trophy wife, leaving his heavyset daughter feeling threatened.**

Mildred Pierce: **After her cheating husband leaves her, title character proves she can thrive independently.** (Original, 1945)

My Brother is an Only Child: **A coming of age story that chronicles the political awakening of a rural Italian boy in the 1960s and 70s. The film follows the contentious protagonist as he drifts from a seminary stint to Fascist party membership to Communist activism in search of a purpose.**

The Reception: **Frenchwoman, her daughter, and new son-in-law, along with a gay African American painter, drink and unleash a torrent of frank talk about sex, race, class, and hopelessly damaged family relationships.**

Thumbsucker: **Whenever the teenage protagonist feels overwhelmed, he indulges in the infantile oral fixation of sucking his thumb. Once teen discovers Ritalin, he goes from vulnerable to being overly aggressive.**

Trudell: **Documentary that examines Native American activist, actor, and poet John Trudell's political life, which changed drastically and tragically twelve hours after he burned an American flag on the steps of FBI's Washington, D.C., headquarters in 1979.**

Tsotsi: **Set in postapartheid Johannesburg, film follows the moral rehabilitation of a street thug who, after carjacking an affluent woman, decides to nurture her baby as his own.**

Two for the Road: **Couple drives across Europe at three different, precarious points in their relationship. Film focuses on specific questions: Are they a happy twosome facing a rough road, or a mismatch finally realizing their mutual error; or, is marriage just about the journey itself?** (Original, 1967)

Where in the World is Osama bin Laden?: **Morgan Spurlock, the director of the documentary** *Super Size Me,* **chronicles his search for Osama bin Laden and other high ranking Al Qaeda officials. Film travels through Egypt, Morocco, Israel, Jordan, Saudi Arabia, Afghanistan, and Pakistan. While comedic in many ways, the film reveals rampant poverty and people who would love to have some semblance of justice and peace.**

Winter Passing: **East Village young woman, eventually joined by other lost souls desperately trying to stay numb by any means necessary, attempt to heal.**

Foreword

Lee Knefelkamp, professor of Higher Education at Teachers College, Columbia University once said, ". . . the curriculum is the autobiography of the faculty." These very powerful words come to mind when I peruse the Contents for the anthology entitled *Lead, Follow, or Move Out of the Way: Global Perspectives in Literature,* edited by authors Monique Ferrell and Julian Williams. I believe Dr. Knefelkamp's words punctuate the idea that faculty are the designers of the curriculum. In so doing, faculty have the responsibility to not only own the content that appears in the pages of a course's syllabus but, more importantly, to ensure that the material presented to students, especially given today's classroom dynamic, is globally broad, socially impacting, and—just as significant—facilitates their engagement. Looking at this book, Knefelkamp's message appears to have been received loud and clear.

Doctors Monique Ferrell and Julian Williams have compiled an anthology that honors the social, racial, class, and ethnic backgrounds of the students they teach. In a broadening academic world, the insight toward teaching that these professors share—one that speaks to making professors and students engage issues that they not only want but need to discuss—is what inspired them to develop a truly active reader. At just a glance, you are instantly impressed with how the reading selections address debatable issues that cut across a number of stimulating topics: sexuality, war, crime, music, God, immigrants, and racial inequality—naming just a few. Interestingly—and purposefully—Monique and Julian have assembled works by famous authors like James Baldwin, Ralph Waldo Emerson, Toni Morrison, Elie Wiesel, and Mark Twain within the same intellectual space of lesser-known authors such as Ngũgõ Wa Thiong'o, Américo Paredes, Anna Lisa Raya, and Angela Nissel. If their intention was to create a text that would not seem repetitive regarding the works that they offered, they have succeeded. If Monique and Julian were seeking to assemble writings that would not be received as boring—selecting pieces that would make students not only want to participate in classroom discussions but lead them—then, again, this book is right on target.

Not to be overlooked in this visual age in which we all live, the movie selections are a refreshing teaching tool that is sorely needed in today's classrooms. The linking of literature and film has always been joined at the hip. Thankfully, this text understands these communicative connectors and encourages both instructors and students to combine the two worlds.

There is much educational rhetoric these days about creating opportunities for college students to think critically. This notion becomes a high-stakes challenge for teachers as they face the complexities associated with student academic preparedness. I believe that a text like *Lead, Follow, or Move Out of the Way: Global Perspectives in Literature* represents an exciting response to these challenges.

Invested educators enter the classroom with a mission. As such, we must all remember that diverse curriculum content coupled with an engaging pedagogical framework can set the stage for enriched classroom discussions, thoughtful written expression, and, most meaningfully, whetting the students' academic appetites for more. Looking at this book, I see how these two educators have truly embraced these ideas.

Bravo, Monique and Julian.

Sonja Jackson
Dean, Curriculum and Instruction
New York City College of Technology, CUNY

Preface

Perhaps the easiest part of this text was creating the title. We are hoping that the words "Lead, Follow, or Move Out of the Way" will become a new mantra that students will carry with them alongside all their other social and cultural interests. It is our greatest desire and belief that the works within this anthology will also pique their academic interest in such a way that these varied articles, essays, short stories, and films will become part of their everyday discussions outside of the classroom.

Some would have us believe that today's students are apathetic or unaware of the world's ever-changing social, cultural, and political landscapes; moreover, that they are unable to create well-informed, articulate written works that address such issues. *Lead, Follow, or Move Out of the Way* takes the position that students are not only able to engage in critical discussions and writing, but that they are also looking forward to it.

We believe that we have compiled a selection of texts that can create a dynamic atmosphere for classroom discussion and build bridges from one country to another, turning our rather large global world into a small-town community of shared learning and experience.

The authors included within this anthology differ in ethnicity, faith, gender, sexual orientation, political assertions, and overall life ideology, but the point we believe the texts make is that no matter where we fall on the battlefield that is life, we are all, at the very core, intrinsically the same. Our world is changing; our students get that. Perhaps what we take for apathy is in fact an uncertainty about how best to navigate their process. *Lead, Follow, or Move out of the Way* is perhaps a tool for providing a safe space to learn, express, and develop a clearer picture of who our students wish to become.

Outside of the diverse texts, professors will find annotated film selections that will provide students with a visual companion to better digest written texts. Furthermore, each reading selection—divided into three parts—is followed by what we have termed the Critical Eye, which includes For Discussion, Reapproaching the Literature, and Writing Assignment features. These Critical Eye components are designed to facilitate classroom discussions and, in many cases, ask the student to examine the text alongside other works, different historical perspectives, and other outside texts. *Lead, Follow, or Move Out of the Way* also includes a section of readings that are accompanied by charts and graphs. This section adds a new dimension to reading comprehension and classroom learning.

All in all, we believe the anthology makes for a positive learning experience for the professor and the student. This is *Lead, Follow, or Move Out of the Way*. Welcome!

1 2 3 4 5

Social Responsibility

> Never in the field of human conflict has
> so much been owed by so many to so few.
> *Winston Churchill*

Today's world is one in which the threat of war and natural disasters looms over the heads of all persons everywhere. The ravages of a world involved in manmade combat have now been equaled by nature's vengeful forces affecting our ocean shores—issues that must be watched closely. With worry and fear becoming the call of the day, our need to be more socially conscious has become insistent. No longer can the citizens of the world ignore or exclude their brethren, no matter where they reside or what their ethnic, gender, class, or religious backgrounds may be. The world has awoken in peril, and we, as a world community, must demonstrate an unprecedented sense of communal responsibility. And, for those who ask, "what is my role to be?" the reality is that social responsibility in our world community might be more than just a little perplexing.

Because our human role is ever-evolving—a result of culture, technology, and policy—human beings, indeed, find themselves puzzled as to where they fit in, let alone how to accommodate or support others outside of their immediate surroundings. At the same time, citizens may find themselves questioning the ethical weight of whether or not their first allegiance is to their individual surroundings as opposed to the wide embrace of humankind. On the other hand, a large section of our population recognizes that humanity's plights and responses are the clearly defined moral obligations of everyone.

The texts in this section explore the various ways that people from all walks of life interpret the notion of social responsibility. Hopefully, the authors and their writings provide us ways to examine and articulate these ideas to their communities, their families, their enemies, and themselves.

Stanley Crouch

Taking Back the Music

They're smart, they're black and they're gonna change rap's image of women

When Bill and Camille Cosby donated $20 million to the historically black Spelman College in 1988, consternation went through the black community because the size of the check was so shocking. No one, even Bill Cosby himself, could have imagined that within two decades the young black women at Spelman would spark what is easily the most important American cultural movement in this new century.

In April of last year, under the leadership of Asha Jennings, who now attends New York University as a law major, the Spelman women gave voice to the fact that they had had enough of the dehumanizing images of black women in rap. They went after the rapper Nelly, who was scheduled to appear on campus, for the images in his "Tip-Drill" video.

Nelly hid under his bed and chose to stay away from that female ire. Maybe it would blow away. It did not.

On Friday, Atlanta was set afire by the emotion and the hard thinking of black women. Spelman and Essence magazine presented a hip hop town meeting at the Cosby Academic Center Auditorium as part of their Take Back the Music campaign. The campaign is a response across generations that Essence has covered in its last two issues and will continue to address as long as necessary. One can easily see that many women find the overt hatred of females and the reductive, pornographic images of the worst hip hop quite disturbing.

The overflow audience filled three additional rooms. Michaela Angela Davis, an editor at Essence, was the moderator. The panelists were Tarshia Stanley, assistant professor of English at Spelman; Moya Bailey, Spelman senior; Kevin Powell, author and activist; Michael Lewellen, vice president of BET public relations; Brian Leach, vice president of A&R, TVT Records, and hip hop artist and actress MC Lyte.

"Taking Back the Music" by Stanley Crouch, New York Daily News, February 27, 2005. © New York Daily News, L.P., reprinted with permission.

The event lasted three hours. Said Davis: "It was most heated and most uncomfortable for those representing the companies. Lewellen and Leach received the most fire from the audience. These women are in pain and are confused. One woman asked, 'What did we do to make you all seemingly hate us so much?' There was a great silence, and a feeling of collective pain filled the air."

This mysogynistic and brutal turn in music is damaging the image of black American women to the point that they are approached outside of the U.S. like freelance prostitutes.

The Spelman women made their voices heard and have inspired thinking young men to fight the stereotypes and question the images. This is no less than an extension of the civil rights movement. But true change will only come when white females begin to identify with the dues their black sisters must pay as this hostility and exploitation continues to be splattered through radio and television. White women have to open up on white men, who buy four out of five rap recordings. Once they declare it uncool for white guys to support the dehumanization of black women, we will see much more than a sea change.

I'm an optimist. I think the tide is about to turn.

Critical Eye

FOR DISCUSSION

a. Is Hip-Hop music responsible for the decline of America's youth?

b. More Hip-Hop records are bought by White males than Black males. According to the article, White women should speak to "their" men about the negative images of women in the music. Do you agree?

c. Is it true that Hip-Hop music is causing nations around the globe to view all Black women as prostitutes?

d. Are the arguments against Rap any different from those made about Rock 'n' Roll during the 1950s?

REAPPROACHING THE LITERATURE

Feminist writer Naomi Wolf asserts that our society creates "bad girls" so that women without reputations can feel safe. Are the women in these Hip-Hop videos any different from everyday women?

WRITING ASSIGNMENT

To imply that one form of music is creating a problematic gender structure among American youth is an astounding assertion. Have today's parents lost control over their children?

Nella Larsen

From
Passing

The next morning brought with it a snowstorm that lasted throughout the day.

After a breakfast which had been eaten almost in silence and which she was relieved to have done with, Irene Redfield lingered for a little while in the downstairs hall, looking out at the soft flakes fluttering down. She was watching them immediately fill some ugly irregular gaps left by the feet of hurrying pedestrians when Zulena came to her, saying: "The telephone, Mrs. Redfield. It's Mrs. Bellew."

"Take the message, Zulena, please."

Though she continued to stare out of the window, Irene saw nothing now, stabbed as she was by fear—and hope. Had anything happened between Clare and Bellew? And if so, what? And was she to be freed at last from the aching anxiety of the past weeks? Or was there to be more, and worse? She had a wrestling moment in which it seemed that she must rush after Zulena and hear for herself what it was that Clare had to say. But she waited.

Zulena, when she came back, said: "She says, ma'am, that she'll be able to go to Mrs. Freeland's tonight. She'll be here sometime between eight and nine."

"Thank you, Zulena."

The day dragged on to its end.

At dinner Brian spoke bitterly of a lynching that he had been reading about in the evening paper.

"Dad, why is it that they only lynch, colored people?" Ted asked.

"Because they hate 'em, son."

"Brian!" Irene's voice was a plea and a rebuke.

Ted said: "Oh! And why do they hate 'em?"

"Because they are afraid of them."

"But what makes them afraid of 'em?"

"Because—"

"Brian!"

"It seems, son, that is a subject we can't go into at the moment without distressing the ladies of our family," he told the boy with mock seriousness, "but we'll take it up sometime when we're alone together."

Ted nodded in his engaging grave way. "I see. Maybe we can talk about it tomorrow on the way to school."

"That'll be fine."

"Brian!"

"Mother," Junior remarked, "that's the third time you've said 'Brian' like that."

"But not the last, Junior, never you fear," his father told him.

After the boys had gone up to their own floor, Irene said suavely: "I do wish, Brian, that you wouldn't talk about lynching before Ted and Junior. It was really inexcusable for you to bring up a thing like that at dinner. There'll be time enough for them to learn about such horrible things when they're older."

"You're absolutely wrong! If, as you're so determined, they've got to live in this damned country, they'd better find out what sort of thing they're up against as soon as possible. The earlier they learn it, the better prepared they'll be."

"I don't agree. I want their childhood to be happy and as free from the knowledge of such things as it possibly can be."

"Very laudable," was Brian's sarcastic answer. "Very laudable indeed, all things considered. But can it?"

"Certainly it can. If you'll only do your part."

"Stuff! You know as well as I do, Irene, that it can't. What was the use of our trying to keep them from learning the word 'nigger' and its connotation? They found out, didn't they? And how? Because somebody called Junior a dirty nigger."

"Just the same, you're not to talk to them about the race problem. I won't have it."

They glared at each other.

"I tell you, Irene, they've got to know these things, and it might as well be now as later."

"They do not!" she insisted, forcing back the tears of anger that were threatening to fall.

Brian growled: "I can't understand how anybody as intelligent as you like to think you are can show evidences of such stupidity." He looked at her in a puzzled harassed way.

"Stupid!" she cried. "Is it stupid to want my children to be happy?" Her lips were quivering.

"At the expense of proper preparation for life and their future happiness, yes. And I'd feel I hadn't done my duty by them if I didn't give them some inkling of what's before them. It's the least I can do. I wanted to get them out of this hellish place years ago. You wouldn't let me. I gave up the idea, because you objected. Don't expect me to give up everything."

Under the lash of his words she was silent. Before any answer came to her, he had turned and gone from the room.

Sitting there alone in the forsaken dining room, unconsciously pressing the hands lying in her lap tightly together, she was seized by a convulsion of shivering. For, to her, there had been something ominous in the scene that she had just had with her husband. Over and over in her mind his last words: "Don't expect me to give up everything," repeated themselves. What had they meant? What could they mean? Clare Kendry?

Surely she was going mad with fear and suspicion. She must not work herself up. She must not! Where were all the self-control, the common sense, that she was so proud of? Now, if ever, was the time for it.

Critical Eye

FOR DISCUSSION

a. The Father says that he is preparing his children for "what's before them." Should parents expose children to the harsh realities of racism?

b. What is the danger of not discussing social intolerance with children?

REAPPROACHING THE LITERATURE

What, exactly, is a nigger?

WRITING ASSIGNMENT

Consider the father in the story. Is he preparing his son for "manhood?" What exactly does that mean these days, and how crucial is it?

Ralph Waldo Emerson

Self-Reliance

from Essays: First Series (1841)

"Ne te quaesiveris extra."
"Man is his own star; and the soul that can
Render an honest and a perfect man,
Commands all light, all influence, all fate;
Nothing to him falls early or too late.
Our acts our angels are, or good or ill,
Our fatal shadows that walk by us still."
Epilogue to Beaumont and Fletcher's Honest Man's Fortune

Cast the bantling on the rocks,
Suckle him with the she-wolf's teat;
Wintered with the hawk and fox,
Power and speed be hands and feet.

essay II self-reliance

I read the other day some verses written by an eminent painter which were original and not conventional. The soul always hears an admonition in such lines, let the subject be what it may. The sentiment they instill is of more value than any thought they may contain. To believe your own thought, to believe that what is true for you in your private heart is true for all men,—that is genius. Speak your latent conviction, and it shall be the universal sense; for the inmost in due time becomes the outmost,—and our first thought is rendered back to us by the trumpets of the Last Judgment. Familiar as the voice of the mind is to each, the highest merit we ascribe to Moses, Plato, and Milton is, that they set at naught books and traditions, and spoke not what men but what they thought. A man should learn to detect and watch that gleam of light which flashes across his mind from within, more than the lustre of the firmament of bards and sages. Yet he dismisses without notice his thought, because it is his. In every work of genius we recognize our own rejected thoughts: they come back to us with a certain alienated majesty. Great works of art have no more affecting lesson for us than this. They teach us to abide by our spontaneous impression with good-humored inflexibility then most when the whole cry of voices is on the other side. Else, to-morrow a stranger will say with masterly good sense precisely what we have thought and felt all

From *The House Behind the Cedars* by Charles Chestnut, Houghton Mifflin 1990.

the time, and we shall be forced to take with shame our own opinion from another.

There is a time in every man's education when he arrives at the conviction that envy is ignorance; that imitation is suicide; that he must take himself for better, for worse, as his portion; that though the wide universe is full of good, no kernel of nourishing corn can come to him but through his toil bestowed on that plot of ground which is given to him to till. The power which resides in him is new in nature, and none but he knows what that is which he can do, nor does he know until he has tried. Not for nothing one face, one character, one fact, makes much impression on him, and another none. This sculpture in the memory is not without preestablished harmony. The eye was placed where one ray should fall, that it might testify of that particular ray. We but half express ourselves, and are ashamed of that divine idea which each of us represents. It may be safely trusted as proportionate and of good issues, so it be faithfully imparted, but God will not have his work made manifest by cowards. A man is relieved and gay when he has put his heart into his work and done his best; but what he has said or done otherwise, shall give him no peace. It is a deliverance which does not deliver. In the attempt his genius deserts him; no muse befriends; no invention, no hope.

Trust thyself: every heart vibrates to that iron string. Accept the place the divine providence has found for you, the society of your contemporaries, the connection of events. Great men have always done so, and confided themselves childlike to the genius of their age, betraying their perception that the absolutely trustworthy was seated at their heart, working through their hands, predominating in all their being. And we are now men, and must accept in the highest mind the same transcendent destiny; and not minors and invalids in a protected corner, not cowards fleeing before a revolution, but guides, redeemers, and benefactors, obeying the Almighty effort, and advancing on Chaos and the Dark.

What pretty oracles nature yields us on this text, in the face and behaviour of children, babes, and even brutes! That divided and rebel mind, that distrust of a sentiment because our arithmetic has computed the strength and means opposed to our purpose, these have not. Their mind being whole, their eye is as yet unconquered, and when we look in their faces, we are disconcerted. Infancy conforms to nobody: all conform to it, so that one babe commonly makes four or five out of the adults who prattle and play to it. So God has armed youth and puberty and manhood no less with its own piquancy and charm, and made it enviable and gracious and its claims not to be put by, if it will stand by itself. Do not think the youth has no force, because he cannot speak to you and me. Hark! in the next room his voice is sufficiently clear and emphatic. It seems he knows how to speak to his contemporaries. Bashful or bold, then, he will know how to make us seniors very unnecessary.

The nonchalance of boys who are sure of a dinner, and would disdain as much as a lord to do or say aught to conciliate one, is the healthy attitude of human nature. A boy is in the parlour what the pit is in the playhouse; independent, irresponsible, looking out from his corner on such people and facts as pass by, he tries and sentences them on their merits, in the swift, summary way of boys, as good, bad, interesting, silly, eloquent, troublesome. He cumbers himself never about consequences, about interests: he gives an independent, genuine verdict. You must court him: he does not court you. But the man is, as it were, clapped into jail by his consciousness. As soon as he has once acted or spoken with eclat, he is a committed person, watched by the sympathy or the hatred of hundreds, whose affections must now enter into his account. There is no Lethe for this. Ah, that he could pass again into his neutrality! Who can thus avoid all pledges, and having observed, observe again from the same unaffected, unbiased, unbribable, unaffrighted innocence, must always be formidable. He would utter opinions on all passing affairs, which being seen to be not private, but necessary, would sink like darts into the ear of men, and put them in fear.

These are the voices which we hear in solitude, but they grow faint and inaudible as we enter into the world. Society everywhere is in conspiracy against the manhood of every one of its members. Society is a joint-stock company, in which the members agree, for the better securing of his bread to each shareholder, to surrender the liberty and culture of the eater. The virtue in most request is conformity. Self-reliance is its aversion. It loves not realities and creators, but names and customs.

Whoso would be a man must be a nonconformist. He who would gather immortal palms must not be hindered by the name of goodness, but must explore if it be goodness. Nothing is at last sacred but the integrity of your own mind. Absolve you to yourself, and you shall have the suffrage of the world. I remember an answer which when quite young I was prompted to make to a valued adviser, who was wont to importune me with the dear old doctrines of the church. On my saying, What have I to do with the sacredness of traditions, if I live wholly from within? my friend suggested,—"But these impulses may be from below, not from above." I replied, "They do not seem to me to be such; but if I am the Devil's child, I will live then from the Devil." No law can be sacred to me but that of my nature. Good and bad are but names very readily transferable to that or this; the only right is what is after my constitution, the only wrong what is against it. A man is to carry himself in the presence of all opposition, as if every thing were titular and ephemeral but he. I am ashamed to think how easily we capitulate to badges and names, to large societies and dead institutions. Every decent and well-spoken individual affects and sways me more than is right. I ought to go upright and vital, and speak the rude truth in all ways. If malice and vanity wear the coat of philanthropy, shall that pass? If an angry bigot assumes this bountiful cause of Abolition, and comes to me with his last news from Barbadoes, why should I not say to him, 'Go love thy infant; love thy wood-chopper: be good-natured and modest: have that grace; and never varnish your hard, uncharitable ambition with this incredible tenderness for black folk a thousand miles off. Thy love afar is spite at home.' Rough and graceless would be such greeting, but truth is handsomer than the affectation of love. Your goodness must have some edge to it,—else it is none. The doctrine of hatred must be preached as the counteraction of the doctrine of love when that pules and whines. I shun father and mother and wife and brother, when my genius calls me. I would write on the lintels of the door-post, *Whim.* I hope it is somewhat better than whim at last, but we cannot spend the day in explanation. Expect me not to show cause why I seek or why I exclude company. Then, again, do not tell me, as a good man did to-day, of my obligation to put all poor men in good situations. Are they *my* poor? I tell thee, thou foolish philanthropist, that I grudge the dollar, the dime, the cent, I give to such men as do not belong to me and to whom I do not belong. There is a class of persons to whom by all spiritual affinity I am bought and sold; for them I will go to prison, if need be; but your miscellaneous popular charities; the education at college of fools; the building of meeting-houses to the vain end to which many now stand; alms to sots; and the thousandfold Relief Societies;—though I confess with shame I sometimes succumb and give the dollar, it is a wicked dollar which by and by I shall have the manhood to withhold.

Virtues are, in the popular estimate, rather the exception than the rule. There is the man *and* his virtues. Men do what is called a good action, as some piece of courage or charity, much as they would pay a fine in expiation of daily non-appearance on parade. Their works are done as an apology or extenuation of their living in the world,—as invalids and the insane pay a high board. Their virtues are penances. I do not wish to expiate, but to live. My life is for itself and not for a spectacle. I much prefer that it should be of a lower strain, so it be genuine and equal, than that it should be glittering and unsteady. I wish it to be sound and sweet, and not to need diet and bleeding. I ask primary evidence that you are a man, and refuse this appeal from the man to his actions. I know that for myself it makes no difference whether I do or forbear those actions which are reckoned excellent. I cannot consent to pay for a privilege where I have intrinsic right. Few and mean as my gifts may be, I actually am, and do not need for my own assurance or the assurance of my fellows any secondary testimony.

What I must do is all that concerns me, not what the people think. This rule, equally arduous in actual and in intellectual life, may serve for the whole distinction between greatness and meanness. It is the harder, because you will always find those who think they know what is your duty better than you know it. It is easy in the world to live after the world's opinion; it is easy in solitude to live after our own; but the great man is he who in the midst of the crowd keeps with perfect sweetness the independence of solitude.

The objection to conforming to usages that have become dead to you is, that it scatters your force. It loses your time and blurs the impression of your character. If you maintain a dead church, contribute to a dead Bible-society, vote with a great party either for the government or against it, spread your table like base housekeepers,—under all these screens I have difficulty to detect the precise man you are. And, of course, so much force is withdrawn from your proper life. But do your work, and I shall know you. Do your work, and you shall reinforce yourself. A man must consider what a blindman's-buff is this game of conformity. If I know your sect, I anticipate your argument. I hear a preacher announce for his text and topic the expediency of one of the institutions of his church. Do I not know beforehand that not possibly can he say a new and spontaneous word? Do I not know that, with all this ostentation of examining the grounds of the institution, he will do no such thing? Do I not know that he is pledged to himself not to look but at one side,—the permitted side, not as a man, but as a parish minister? He is a retained attorney, and these airs of the bench are the emptiest affectation. Well, most men have bound their eyes with one or another handkerchief, and attached themselves to some one of these communities of opinion. This conformity makes them not false in a few particulars, authors of a few lies, but false in all particulars. Their every truth is not quite true. Their two is not the real two, their four not the real four; so that every word they say chagrins us, and we know not where to begin to set them right. Meantime nature is not slow to equip us in the prison-uniform of the party to which we adhere. We come to wear one cut of lace and figure, and acquire by degrees the gentlest asinine expression. There is a mortifying experience in particular, which does not fail to wreak itself also in the general history; I mean "the foolish face of praise," the forced smile which we put on in company where we do not feel at ease in answer to conversation which does not interest us. The muscles, not spontaneously moved, but moved by a low usurping wilfulness, grow tight about the outline of the face with the most disagreeable sensation.

For nonconformity the world whips you with its displeasure. And therefore a man must know how to estimate a sour face. The by-standers look askance on him in the public street or in the friend's parlour. If this aversion had its origin in contempt and resistance like his own, he might well go home with a sad countenance; but the sour faces of the multitude, like their sweet faces, have no deep cause, but are put on and off as the wind blows and a newspaper directs. Yet is the discontent of the multitude more formidable than that of the senate and the college. It is easy enough for a firm man who knows the world to brook the rage of the cultivated classes. Their rage is decorous and prudent, for they are timid as being very vulnerable themselves. But when to their feminine rage the indignation of the people is added, when the ignorant and the poor are aroused, when the unintelligent brute force that lies at the bottom of society is made to growl and mow, it needs the habit of magnanimity and religion to treat it godlike as a trifle of no concernment.

The other terror that scares us from self-trust is our consistency; a reverence for our past act or word, because the eyes of others have no other data for computing our orbit than our past acts, and we are loath to disappoint them.

But why should you keep your head over your shoulder? Why drag about this corpse of your memory, lest you contradict somewhat you have stated in this or that public place? Suppose you should contradict yourself; what then? It seems to be a rule of wisdom never to rely on your memory alone, scarcely even in acts of pure memory, but to bring the past for judgment into the thousand-eyed present, and live ever in a new day. In your metaphysics you have denied personality to the Deity: yet when the devout motions of the soul come, yield to them heart and life, though they should clothe God with shape and color. Leave your theory, as Joseph his coat in the hand of the harlot, and flee.

A foolish consistency is the hobgoblin of little minds, adored by little statesmen and philosophers and divines. With consistency a great soul has simply nothing to do. He may as well concern himself with his shadow on the wall. Speak what you think now in hard words, and to-morrow speak what to-morrow thinks in hard words again, though it contradict every thing you said to-day.—'Ah, so you shall be sure to be misunderstood.'— Is it so bad, then, to be misunderstood? Pythagoras was misunderstood, and Socrates, and Jesus, and Luther, and Copernicus, and Galileo, and Newton, and every pure and wise spirit that ever took flesh. To be great is to be misunderstood.

I suppose no man can violate his nature. All the sallies of his will are rounded in by the law of his being, as the inequalities of Andes and Himmaleh are insignificant to the curve of the sphere. Nor does it matter how you gauge and try him. A character is like an acrostic or Alexandrian stanza;—read it forward, backward, or across, it still spells the same thing. In this pleasing, contrite wood-life which God allows me, let me record day by day my honest thought without prospect or retrospect, and, I cannot doubt, it will be found symmetrical, though I mean it not, and see it not. My book should smell of pines and resound with the hum of insects. The swallow over my window should interweave that thread or straw he carries in his bill into my web also. We pass for what we are. Character teaches above our wills. Men imagine that they communicate their virtue or vice only by overt actions, and do not see that virtue or vice emit a breath every moment.

There will be an agreement in whatever variety of actions, so they be each honest and natural in their hour. For of one will, the actions will be harmonious, however unlike they seem. These varieties are lost sight of at a little distance, at a little height of thought. One tendency unites them all. The voyage of the best ship is a zigzag line of a hundred tacks. See the line from a sufficient distance, and it straightens itself to the average tendency. Your genuine action will explain itself, and will explain your other genuine actions. Your conformity explains nothing. Act singly, and what you have already done singly will justify you now. Greatness appeals to the future. If I can be firm enough to-day to do right, and scorn eyes, I must have done so much right before as to defend me now. Be it how it will, do right now. Always scorn appearances, and you always may. The force of character is cumulative. All the foregone days of virtue work their health into this. What makes the majesty of the heroes of the senate and the field, which so fills the imagination? The consciousness of a train of great days and victories behind. They shed an united light on the advancing actor. He is attended as by a visible escort of angels. That is it which throws thunder into Chatham's voice, and dignity into Washington's port, and America into Adams's eye. Honor is venerable to us because it is no ephemeris. It is always ancient virtue. We worship it to-day because it is not of to-day. We love it and pay it homage, because it is not a trap for our love and homage, but is self-dependent, self-derived, and therefore of an old immaculate pedigree, even if shown in a young person.

I hope in these days we have heard the last of conformity and consistency. Let the words be gazetted and ridiculous henceforward. Instead of the gong for dinner, let us hear a whistle from the Spartan fife. Let us never bow and apologize more. A great man is coming to eat at my house. I do not wish to please him; I wish that he should wish to please me. I will stand here for humanity, and though I would make it kind, I would make it true. Let us affront and reprimand the smooth mediocrity and squalid contentment of the times, and hurl in the face of custom, and trade, and office, the fact which is the upshot of all history, that there is a great responsible Thinker and Actor working wherever a man works; that a true man belongs to no other time or place, but is the centre of things. Where he is, there is nature. He measures you, and all men, and all events. Ordinarily, every body in society reminds us of somewhat else, or of some other person. Character, reality, reminds you of nothing else; it takes place of the whole creation. The man must be so much, that he must make all circumstances indifferent. Every true man is a cause, a country, and an age; requires infinite spaces and numbers and time fully to accomplish his design;—and posterity seem to follow his steps as a train of clients. A man Caesar is born, and for ages after we have a Roman Empire. Christ is born, and millions of minds so grow and cleave to his genius, that he is confounded with virtue and the possible of man. An institution is the lengthened shadow of one man; as, Monachism, of the Hermit Antony; the Reformation, of Luther; Quakerism, of Fox; Methodism, of Wesley; Abolition, of Clarkson. Scipio, Milton called "the height of Rome"; and all history resolves itself very easily into the biography of a few stout and earnest persons.

Let a man then know his worth, and keep things under his feet. Let him not peep or steal, or skulk up and down with the air of a charity-boy, a bastard, or an interloper, in the world which exists for him. But the man in the street, finding no worth in himself which corresponds to the force which built a tower or sculptured a marble god, feels poor when he looks on these. To him a palace, a statue, or a costly book have an alien and forbidding air, much like a gay equipage, and seem to say like that, 'Who are you, Sir?' Yet they all are his, suitors for his notice, petitioners to his faculties that they will come out and take possession. The picture waits for my verdict: it is not to command me, but I am to settle its claims to praise. That popular fable of the sot who was picked up dead drunk in the street, carried to the duke's house, washed and dressed and laid in the duke's bed, and, on his waking, treated with all obsequious ceremony like the duke, and assured that he had been insane, owes its popularity to the fact, that it symbolizes so well the state of man, who is in the world a sort of sot, but now and then wakes up, exercises his reason, and finds himself a true prince.

Our reading is mendicant and sycophantic. In history, our imagination plays us false. Kingdom and lordship, power and estate, are a gaudier vocabulary than private John and Edward in a small house and common day's work; but the things of life are the same to both; the sum total of both is the same. Why all this deference to Alfred, and Scanderbeg, and Gustavus? Suppose they were virtuous; did they wear out virtue? As great a stake depends on your private act to-day, as followed their public and renowned steps. When private men shall act with original views, the lustre will be transferred from the actions of kings to those of gentlemen.

The world has been instructed by its kings, who have so magnetized the eyes of nations. It has been taught by this colossal symbol the mutual reverence that is due from man to man. The joyful loyalty with which men have everywhere suffered the king, the noble, or the great proprietor to walk among them by a law of his own, make his own scale of men and things, and reverse theirs, pay for benefits not with money but with honor, and represent the law in his person, was the hieroglyphic by which they obscurely signified their consciousness of their own right and comeliness, the right of every man.

The magnetism which all original action exerts is explained when we inquire the reason of self-trust. Who is the Trustee? What is the aboriginal Self, on which a universal reliance may be grounded? What is the nature and power of that science-baffling star, without parallax, without calculable elements, which shoots a ray of beauty even into trivial and impure actions, if the least mark of independence appear? The inquiry leads us to that source, at once the essence of genius, of virtue, and of life, which we call Spontaneity or Instinct. We denote this primary wisdom as Intuition, whilst all later teachings are tuitions. In that deep force, the last fact behind which analysis cannot go, all things find their common origin. For, the sense of being which in calm hours rises, we know not how, in the soul, is not diverse from things, from space, from light, from time, from man, but one with them, and proceeds obviously from the same source whence their life and being also proceed. We first share the life by which things exist, and afterwards see them as appearances in nature, and forget that we have shared their cause. Here is the fountain of action and of thought. Here are the lungs of that inspiration which giveth man wisdom, and which cannot be denied without impiety and atheism. We lie in the lap of immense intelligence, which makes us receivers of its truth and organs of its activity. When we discern justice, when we discern truth, we do nothing of ourselves, but allow a passage to its beams. If we ask whence this comes, if we seek to pry into the soul that causes, all philosophy is at fault. Its presence or its absence is all we can affirm. Every man discriminates between the voluntary acts of his mind, and his involuntary perceptions, and knows that to his involuntary perceptions a perfect faith is due. He may err in the expression of them, but he knows that these things are so, like day and night, not to be disputed. My wilful actions and acquisitions are but roving;—the idlest reverie, the faintest native emotion, command my curiosity and respect. Thoughtless people contradict as readily the statement of perceptions as of opinions, or rather much more readily; for, they do not distinguish between perception and notion. They fancy that I choose to see this or that thing. But perception is not whimsical, but fatal. If I see a trait, my children will see it after me, and in course of time, all mankind,—although it may chance that no one has seen it before me. For my perception of it is as much a fact as the sun.

The relations of the soul to the divine spirit are so pure, that it is profane to seek to interpose helps. It must be that when God speaketh he should communicate, not one thing, but all things; should fill the world with his voice; should scatter forth light, nature, time, souls, from the centre of the present thought; and new date and new create the whole. Whenever a mind is simple, and receives a divine wisdom, old things pass away,—means, teachers, texts, temples fall; it lives now, and absorbs past and future into the present hour. All things are made sacred by relation to it,—one as much as another. All things are dissolved to their centre by their cause, and, in the universal miracle, petty and particular miracles disappear. If, therefore, a man claims to know and speak of God, and carries you backward to the phraseology of some old mouldered nation in another country, in another world, believe him not. Is the acorn better than the oak which is its fulness and completion? Is the parent better than the child into whom he has cast his ripened being? Whence, then, this worship of the past? The centuries are conspirators against the sanity and authority of the soul. Time and space are but physiological colors which the eye makes, but the soul is light; where it is, is day; where it was, is night; and history is an impertinence and an injury, if it be any thing more than a cheerful apologue or parable of my being and becoming.

Man is timid and apologetic; he is no longer upright; he dares not say 'I think,' 'I am,' but quotes some saint or sage. He is ashamed before the blade of grass or the blowing rose. These roses under my window make no reference to former roses or to better ones; they are for what they are; they exist with God to-day. There is no time to them. There is simply the rose; it is perfect in every moment of its existence. Before a leaf-bud has burst, its whole life acts; in the full-blown flower there is no more; in the leafless root there is no less. Its nature is satisfied, and it satisfies nature, in all moments alike. But man postpones or remembers; he does not live in the present, but with reverted eye laments the past, or, heedless of the riches that surround him, stands on tiptoe to foresee the future. He cannot be happy and strong until he too lives with nature in the present, above time.

This should be plain enough. Yet see what strong intellects dare not yet hear God himself, unless he speak the phraseology of I know not what David, or Jeremiah, or Paul. We shall not always set so great a price on a few texts, on a few lives. We are like children who repeat by rote the sentences of grandames and tutors, and, as they grow older, of the men of talents and character they chance to see,—painfully recollecting the exact words they spoke; afterwards, when they come into the point of view which those had who uttered these sayings, they understand them, and are willing to let the words go; for, at any time, they can use words as good when occasion comes. If we live truly, we shall see truly. It is as easy for the strong man to be strong, as it is for the weak to be weak. When we have new perception, we shall gladly disburden the memory of its hoarded treasures as old rubbish. When a man lives with God, his voice shall be as sweet as the murmur of the brook and the rustle of the corn.

And now at last the highest truth on this subject remains unsaid; probably cannot be said; for all that we say is the far-off remembering of the intuition. That thought, by what I can now nearest approach to say it, is this. When good is near you, when you have life in yourself, it is not by any known or accustomed way; you shall not discern the foot-prints of any other; you shall not see the face of man; you shall not hear any name;— the way, the thought, the good, shall be wholly strange and new. It shall exclude example and experience. You take the way from man, not to man. All persons that ever existed are its forgotten ministers. Fear and hope are alike beneath it. There is somewhat low even in hope. In the hour of vision, there is nothing that can be called gratitude, nor properly joy. The soul raised over passion beholds identity and eternal causation, perceives the self-existence of Truth and Right, and calms itself with knowing that all things go well. Vast spaces of nature, the Atlantic Ocean, the South Sea,— long intervals of time, years, centuries,—are of no account. This which I think and feel underlay every former state of life and circumstances, as it does underlie my present, and what is called life, and what is called death.

Life only avails, not the having lived. Power ceases in the instant of repose; it resides in the moment of transition from a past to a new state, in the shooting of the gulf, in the darting to an aim. This one fact the world hates, that the soul *becomes;* for that for ever degrades the past, turns all riches to poverty, all reputation to a shame, confounds the saint with the rogue, shoves Jesus and Judas equally aside. Why, then, do we prate of self-reliance? Inasmuch as the soul is present, there will be power not confident but agent. To talk of reliance is a poor external way of speaking. Speak rather of that which relies, because it works and is. Who has more obedience than I masters me, though he should not raise his finger. Round him I must revolve by the gravitation of spirits. We fancy it rhetoric, when we speak of eminent virtue. We do not yet see that virtue is Height, and that a man or a company of men, plastic and permeable to principles, by the law of nature must overpower and ride all cities, nations, kings, rich men, poets, who are not.

This is the ultimate fact which we so quickly reach on this, as on every topic, the resolution of all into the ever-blessed ONE. Self-existence is the attribute of the Supreme Cause, and it constitutes the measure of good by the degree in which it enters into all lower forms. All things real are so by so much virtue as they contain. Commerce, husbandry, hunting, whaling, war, eloquence, personal weight, are somewhat, and engage my respect as examples of its presence and impure action. I see the same law working in nature for conservation and growth. Power is in nature the essential measure of right. Nature suffers nothing to remain in her kingdoms which cannot help itself. The genesis and maturation of a planet, its poise and orbit, the bended tree recovering itself from the strong wind, the vital resources of every animal and vegetable, are demonstrations of the self-sufficing, and therefore self-relying soul.

Thus all concentrates: let us not rove; let us sit at home with the cause. Let us stun and astonish the intruding rabble of men and books and institutions, by a simple declaration of the divine fact. Bid the invaders take the shoes from off their feet, for God is here within. Let our simplicity judge them, and our docility to our own law demonstrate the poverty of nature and fortune beside our native riches.

But now we are a mob. Man does not stand in awe of man, nor is his genius admonished to stay at home, to put itself in communication with the internal ocean, but it goes abroad to beg a cup of water of the urns of other men. We must go alone. I like the silent church before the service begins, better than any preaching. How far off, how cool, how chaste the persons look, begirt each one with a precinct or sanctuary! So let us always sit. Why should we assume the faults of our friend, or wife, or father, or child, because they sit around our hearth, or are said to have the same blood? All men have my blood, and I have all men's. Not for that will I adopt their petulance or folly, even to the extent of being ashamed of it. But your isolation must not be mechanical, but spiritual, that is, must be elevation. At times the whole world seems to be in conspiracy to importune you with emphatic trifles. Friend, client, child, sickness, fear, want, charity, all knock at once at thy closet door, and say,—'Come out unto us.' But keep thy state; come not into their confusion. The power men possess to annoy me, I give them by a weak curiosity. No man can come near me but through my act. "What we love that we have, but by desire we bereave ourselves of the love."

If we cannot at once rise to the sanctities of obedience and faith, let us at least resist our temptations; let us enter into the state of war, and wake Thor and Woden, courage and constancy, in our Saxon breasts. This is to be done in our smooth times by speaking the truth. Check this lying hospitality and lying affection. Live no longer to the expectation of these deceived and deceiving people with whom we converse. Say to them, O father, O mother, O wife, O brother, O friend, I have lived with you after appearances hitherto. Henceforward I am the truth's. Be it known unto you that henceforward I obey no law less than the eternal law. I will have no covenants but proximities. I shall endeavour to nourish my parents, to support my family, to be the chaste husband of one wife,—but these relations I must fill after a new and unprecedented way. I appeal from your customs. I must be myself. I cannot break myself any longer for you, or you. If you can love me for what I am, we shall be the happier. If you cannot, I will still seek to deserve that you should. I will not hide my tastes or aversions. I will so trust that what is deep is holy, that I will do strongly before the sun and moon whatever inly rejoices me, and the heart appoints. If you are noble, I will love you; if you are not, I will not hurt you and myself by hypocritical attentions. If you are true, but not in the same truth with me, cleave to your companions; I will seek my own. I do this not selfishly, but humbly and truly. It is alike your interest, and mine, and all men's, however long we have dwelt in lies, to live in truth. Does this sound harsh today? You will soon love what is dictated by your nature as well as mine, and, if we follow the truth, it will bring us out safe at last.—But so you may give these friends pain. Yes, but I cannot sell my liberty and my power, to save their sensibility. Besides, all persons have their moments of reason, when they look out into the region of absolute truth; then will they justify me, and do the same thing.

The populace think that your rejection of popular standards is a rejection of all standard, and mere antinomianism; and the bold sensualist will use the name of philosophy to gild his crimes. But the law of consciousness abides. There are two confessionals, in one or the other of which we must be shriven. You may fulfil your round of duties by clearing yourself in the *direct,* or in the *reflex* way. Consider whether you have satisfied your relations to father, mother, cousin, neighbour, town, cat, and dog; whether any of these can upbraid you. But I may also neglect this reflex standard, and absolve me to myself. I have my own stern claims and perfect circle. It denies the name of duty to many offices that are called duties. But if I can discharge its debts, it enables me to dispense with the popular code. If any one imagines that this law is lax, let him keep its commandment one day.

And truly it demands something godlike in him who has cast off the common motives of humanity, and has ventured to trust himself for a taskmaster. High be his heart, faithful his will, clear his sight, that he may in good earnest be doctrine, society, law, to himself, that a simple purpose may be to him as strong as iron necessity is to others!

If any man consider the present aspects of what is called by distinction *society*, he will see the need of these ethics. The sinew and heart of man seem to be drawn out, and we are become timorous, desponding whimperers. We are afraid of truth, afraid of fortune, afraid of death, and afraid of each other. Our age yields no great and perfect persons. We want men and women who shall renovate life and our social state, but we see that most natures are insolvent, cannot satisfy their own wants, have an ambition out of all proportion to their practical force, and do lean and beg day and night continually. Our housekeeping is mendicant, our arts, our occupations, our marriages, our religion, we have not chosen, but society has chosen for us. We are parlour soldiers. We shun the rugged battle of fate, where strength is born.

If our young men miscarry in their first enterprises, they lose all heart. If the young merchant fails, men say he is *ruined.* If the finest genius studies at one of our colleges, and is not installed in an office within one year afterwards in the cities or suburbs of Boston or New York, it seems to his friends and to himself that he is right in being disheartened, and in complaining the rest of his life. A sturdy lad from New Hampshire or Vermont, who in turn tries all the professions, who *teams it, farms it, peddles,* keeps a school, preaches, edits a newspaper, goes to Congress, buys a township, and so forth, in successive years, and always, like a cat, falls on his feet, is worth a hundred of these city dolls. He walks abreast with his days, and feels no shame in not 'studying a profession,' for he does not postpone his life, but lives already. He has not one chance, but a hundred chances. Let a Stoic open the resources of man, and tell men they are not leaning willows, but can and must detach themselves; that with the exercise of self-trust, new powers shall appear; that a man is the word made flesh, born to shed healing to the nations, that he should be ashamed of our compassion, and that the moment he acts from himself, tossing the laws, the books, idolatries, and customs out of the window, we pity him no more, but thank and revere him,—and that teacher shall restore the life of man to splendor, and make his name dear to all history.

It is easy to see that a greater self-reliance must work a revolution in all the offices and relations of men; in their religion; in their education; in their pursuits; their modes of living; their association; in their property; in their speculative views.

1. In what prayers do men allow themselves! That which they call a holy office is not so much as brave and manly. Prayer looks abroad and

asks for some foreign addition to come through some foreign virtue, and loses itself in endless mazes of natural and supernatural, and mediatorial and miraculous. Prayer that craves a particular commodity,—any thing less than all good,—is vicious. Prayer is the contemplation of the facts of life from the highest point of view. It is the soliloquy of a beholding and jubilant soul. It is the spirit of God pronouncing his works good. But prayer as a means to effect a private end is meanness and theft. It supposes dualism and not unity in nature and consciousness. As soon as the man is at one with God, he will not beg. He will then see prayer in all action. The prayer of the farmer kneeling in his field to weed it, the prayer of the rower kneeling with the stroke of his oar, are true prayers heard throughout nature, though for cheap ends. Caratach, in Fletcher's Bonduca, when admonished to inquire the mind of the god Audate, replies,—

"His hidden meaning lies in our endeavours;
    Our valors are our best gods."

Another sort of false prayers are our regrets. Discontent is the want of self-reliance: it is infirmity of will. Regret calamities, if you can thereby help the sufferer; if not, attend your own work, and already the evil begins to be repaired. Our sympathy is just as base. We come to them who weep foolishly, and sit down and cry for company, instead of imparting to them truth and health in rough electric shocks, putting them once more in communication with their own reason. The secret of fortune is joy in our hands. Welcome evermore to gods and men is the self-helping man. For him all doors are flung wide: him all tongues greet, all honors crown, all eyes follow with desire. Our love goes out to him and embraces him, because he did not need it. We solicitously and apologetically caress and celebrate him, because he held on his way and scorned our disapprobation. The gods love him because men hated him. "To the persevering mortal," said Zoroaster, "the blessed Immortals are swift."

As men's prayers are a disease of the will, so are their creeds a disease of the intellect. They say with those foolish Israelites, 'Let not God speak to us, lest we die. Speak thou, speak any man with us, and we will obey.' Everywhere I am hindered of meeting God in my brother, because he has shut his own temple doors, and recites fables merely of his brother's, or his brother's brother's God. Every new mind is a new classification. If it prove a mind of uncommon activity and power, a Locke, a Lavoisier, a Hutton, a Bentham, a Fourier, it imposes its classification on other men, and lo! a new system. In proportion to the depth of the thought, and so to the number of the objects it touches and brings within reach of the pupil, is his complacency. But chiefly is this apparent in creeds and churches, which are also classifications of some powerful mind acting on the elemental thought of duty, and man's relation to the Highest. Such is Calvinism, Quakerism, Swedenborgism. The pupil takes the same delight in subordinating every thing to the new terminology, as a girl who has just learned botany in seeing a new earth and new seasons thereby. It will happen for a time, that the pupil will find his intellectual power has grown by the study of his master's mind. But in all unbalanced minds, the classification is idolized, passes for the end, and not for a speedily exhaustible means, so that the walls of the system blend to their eye in the remote horizon with the walls of the universe; the luminaries of heaven seem to them hung on the arch their master built. They cannot imagine how you aliens have any right to see,—how you can see; 'It must be somehow that you stole the light from us.' They do not yet perceive, that light, unsystematic, indomitable, will break into any cabin, even into theirs. Let them chirp awhile and call it their own. If they are honest and do well, presently their neat new pinfold will be too strait and low, will crack, will lean, will rot and vanish, and the immortal light, all young and joyful, million-orbed, million-colored, will beam over the universe as on the first morning.

2. It is for want of self-culture that the superstition of Travelling, whose idols are Italy, England, Egypt, retains its fascination for all educated Americans. They who made England, Italy, or Greece venerable in the imagination did so by sticking fast where they were, like an axis of the earth. In manly hours, we feel that duty is our place. The soul is no traveller; the wise man stays at home, and when his necessities, his duties, on any occasion call him from his house, or into foreign lands, he is at home still, and shall make men sensible by the expression of his countenance, that he goes the missionary of wisdom and virtue, and visits cities and men like a sovereign, and not like an interloper or a valet.

I have no churlish objection to the circumnavigation of the globe, for the purposes of art, of study, and benevolence, so that the man is first domesticated, or does not go abroad with the hope of finding somewhat greater than he knows. He who travels to be amused, or to get somewhat which he does not carry, travels away from himself, and grows old even in youth among old things. In Thebes, in Palmyra, his will and mind have become old and dilapidated as they. He carries ruins to ruins.

Travelling is a fool's paradise. Our first journeys discover to us the indifference of places. At home I dream that at Naples, at Rome, I can be intoxicated with beauty, and lose my sadness. I pack my trunk, embrace my friends, embark on the sea, and at last wake up in Naples, and there beside me is the stern fact, the sad self, unrelenting, identical, that I fled from. I seek the Vatican, and the palaces. I affect to be intoxicated with sights and suggestions, but I am not intoxicated. My giant goes with me wherever I go.

3. But the rage of travelling is a symptom of a deeper unsoundness affecting the whole intellectual action. The intellect is vagabond, and our system of education fosters restlessness. Our minds travel when our bodies are forced to stay at home. We imitate; and what is imitation but the travelling of the mind? Our houses are built with foreign taste; our shelves are garnished with foreign ornaments; our opinions, our tastes, our faculties, lean, and follow the Past and the Distant. The soul created the arts wherever they have flourished. It was in his own mind that the artist sought his model. It was an application of his own thought to the thing to be done and the conditions to be observed. And why need we copy the Doric or the Gothic model? Beauty, convenience, grandeur of thought, and quaint expression are as near to us as to any, and if the American artist will study with hope and love the precise thing to be done by him, considering the climate, the soil, the length of the day, the wants of the people, the habit and form of the government, he will create a house in which all these will find themselves fitted, and taste and sentiment will be satisfied also.

Insist on yourself; never imitate. Your own gift you can present every moment with the cumulative force of a whole life's cultivation; but of the adopted talent of another, you have only an extemporaneous, half possession. That which each can do best, none but his Maker can teach him. No man yet knows what it is, nor can, till that person has exhibited it. Where is the master who could have taught Shakspeare? Where is the master who could have instructed Franklin, or Washington, or Bacon, or Newton? Every great man is a unique. The Scipionism of Scipio is precisely that part he could not borrow. Shakspeare will never be made by the study of Shakspeare. Do that which is assigned you, and you cannot hope too much or dare too much. There is at this moment for you an utterance brave and grand as that of the colossal chisel of Phidias, or trowel of the Egyptians, or the pen of Moses, or Dante, but different from all these. Not possibly will the soul all rich, all eloquent, with thousand-cloven tongue, deign to repeat itself; but if you can hear what these patriarchs say, surely you can reply to them in the same pitch of voice; for the ear and the tongue are two organs of one nature. Abide in the simple and noble regions of thy life, obey thy heart, and thou shalt reproduce the Foreworld again.

4. As our Religion, our Education, our Art look abroad, so does our spirit of society. All men plume themselves on the improvement of society, and no man improves.

Society never advances. It recedes as fast on one side as it gains on the other. It undergoes continual changes; it is barbarous, it is civilized, it is christianized, it is rich, it is scientific; but this change is not amelioration. For every thing that is given, something is taken. Society acquires new arts, and loses old instincts. What a contrast between the well-clad, reading, writing, thinking American, with a watch, a pencil, and a bill of exchange in his pocket, and the naked New Zealander, whose property is a club, a spear, a mat, and an undivided twentieth of a shed to sleep under! But compare the health of the two men, and you shall see that the white man has lost his aboriginal strength. If the traveller tell us truly, strike the savage with a broad axe, and in a day or two the flesh shall unite and heal as if you struck the blow into soft pitch, and the same blow shall send the white to his grave.

The civilized man has built a coach, but has lost the use of his feet. He is supported on crutches, but lacks so much support of muscle. He has a fine Geneva watch, but he fails of the skill to tell the hour by the sun. A Greenwich nautical almanac he has, and so being sure of the information when he wants it, the man in the street does not know a star in the sky. The solstice he does not observe; the equinox he knows as little; and the whole bright calendar of the year is without a dial in his mind. His note-books impair his memory; his libraries overload his wit; the insurance-office increases the number of accidents; and it may be a question whether machinery does not encumber; whether we have not lost by refinement some energy, by a Christianity entrenched in establishments and forms, some vigor of wild virtue. For every Stoic was a Stoic; but in Christendom where is the Christian?

There is no more deviation in the moral standard than in the standard of height or bulk. No greater men are now than ever were. A singular equality may be observed between the great men of the first and of the last ages; nor can all the science, art, religion, and philosophy of the nineteenth century avail to educate greater men than Plutarch's heroes, three or four and twenty centuries ago. Not in time is the race progressive. Phocion, Socrates, Anaxagoras, Diogenes, are great men, but they leave no class. He who is really of their class will not be called by their name, but will be his own man, and, in his turn, the founder of a sect. The arts and inventions of each period are only its costume, and do not invigorate men. The harm of the improved machinery may compensate its good. Hudson and Behring accomplished so much in their fishing-boats, as to astonish Parry and Franklin, whose equipment exhausted the resources of science and art. Galileo, with an opera-glass, discovered a more splendid series of celestial phenomena than any one since. Columbus found the New World in an undecked boat. It is curious to see the periodical disuse and perishing of means and machinery, which were introduced with loud laudation a few years or centuries before. The great genius returns to essential man. We reckoned the improvements of the art of war among the triumphs of science, and yet Napoleon conquered Europe by the bivouac, which consisted of falling back on naked valor, and disencumbering it of all aids. The Emperor held it impossible to make a perfect army, says Las Casas, "without abolishing our arms, magazines, commissaries, and carriages, until, in imitation of the Roman custom, the soldier should receive his supply of corn, grind it in his hand-mill, and bake his bread himself."

Society is a wave. The wave moves onward, but the water of which it is composed does not. The same particle does not rise from the valley to the ridge. Its unity is only phenomenal. The persons who make up a nation to-day, next year die, and their experience with them.

And so the reliance on Property, including the reliance on governments which protect it, is the want of self-reliance. Men have looked away from themselves and at things so long, that they have come to esteem the religious, learned, and civil institutions as guards of property, and they deprecate assaults on these, because they feel them to be assaults on property. They measure their esteem of each other by what each has, and not by what each is. But a cultivated man becomes ashamed of his property, out of new respect for his nature. Especially he hates what he has, if he see that it is accidental,—came to him by inheritance, or gift, or crime; then he feels that it is not having; it does not belong to him, has no root in him, and merely lies there, because no revolution or no robber takes it away. But that which a man is does always by necessity acquire, and what the man acquires is living property, which does not wait the beck of rulers, or mobs, or revolutions, or fire, or storm, or bankruptcies, but perpetually renews itself wherever the man breathes. "Thy lot or portion of life," said the Caliph Ali, "is seeking after thee; therefore be at rest from seeking after it." Our dependence on these foreign goods leads us to our slavish respect for numbers. The political parties meet in numerous conventions; the greater the concourse, and with each new uproar of announcement, The delegation from Essex! The Democrats from New Hampshire! The Whigs of Maine! the young patriot feels himself stronger than before by a new thousand of eyes and arms. In like manner the reformers summon conventions, and vote and resolve in multitude. Not so, O friends! will the God deign to enter and inhabit you, but by a method precisely the reverse. It is only as a man puts off all foreign support, and stands alone, that I see him to be strong and to prevail. He is weaker by every recruit to his banner. Is not a man better than a town? Ask nothing of men, and in the endless mutation, thou only firm column must presently appear the upholder of all that surrounds thee. He who knows that power is inborn, that he is weak because he has looked for good out of him and elsewhere, and so perceiving, throws himself unhesitatingly on his thought, instantly rights himself, stands in the erect position, commands his limbs, works miracles; just as a man who stands on his feet is stronger than a man who stands on his head.

So use all that is called Fortune. Most men gamble with her, and gain all, and lose all, as her wheel rolls. But do thou leave as unlawful these winnings, and deal with Cause and Effect, the chancellors of God. In the Will work and acquire, and thou hast chained the wheel of Chance, and shalt sit hereafter out of fear from her rotations. A political victory, a rise of rents, the recovery of your sick, or the return of your absent friend, or some other favorable event, raises your spirits, and you think good days are preparing for you. Do not believe it. Nothing can bring you peace but yourself. Nothing can bring you peace but the triumph of principles.

Critical Eye

FOR DISCUSSION

a. Emerson asserts that every individual has an inner genius and that it is our responsibility to honor it. Do you agree with this sentiment?

b. According to Emerson, we have all become conformists because we refuse to speak what we believe is true because it is seen as "rude." In your opinion, is his assessment accurate?

REAPPROACHING THE LITERATURE

Rap music has been called a kind of poetry that speaks to the youth of today. Are rap artists following their "inner genius" or are they conformists?

WRITING ASSIGNMENT

Why is conformity dangerous? How does this conformity speak to Emerson's notions of self-trust and foolish consistency?

Khaled Hosseini

From
The Kite Runner

five

Something roared like thunder. The earth shook a little and we heard the *rat-a-tat-tat* of gunfire. "Father!" Hassan cried. We sprung to our feet and raced out of the living room. We found Ali hobbling frantically across the foyer.

"Father! What's that sound?" Hassan yelped, his hands out-stretched toward Ali. Ali wrapped his arms around us. A white light flashed, lit the sky in silver. It flashed again and was followed by a rapid staccato of gunfire.

"They're hunting ducks," Ali said in a hoarse voice. "They hunt ducks at night, you know. Don't be afraid."

A siren went off in the distance. Somewhere glass shattered and someone shouted. I heard people on the street, jolted from sleep and probably still in their pajamas, with ruffled hair and puffy eyes. Hassan was crying. Ali pulled him close, clutched him with tenderness. Later, I would tell myself I hadn't felt envious of Hassan. Not at all.

We stayed huddled that way until the early hours of the morning. The shootings and explosions had lasted less than an hour, but they had frightened us badly, because none of us had ever heard gunshots in the streets. They were foreign sounds to us then. The generation of Afghan children whose ears would know nothing but the sounds of bombs and gunfire was not yet born. Huddled together in the dining room and waiting for the sun to rise, none of us had any notion that a way of life had ended. *Our* way of life. If not quite yet, then at least it was the beginning of the end. The end, the *official* end, would come first in April 1978 with the communist coup d'état, and then in December 1979, when Russian tanks would roll into the very same streets where Hassan and I played, bringing the death of the Afghanistan I knew and marking the start of a still ongoing era of bloodletting.

"Fremont, California. 1980s," from *The Kite Runner* by Khaled Hosseini, copyright © 2003 by Khaled Hosseini. Used by permission of Riverhead Books, an imprint of Penguin Group (USA) Inc.

Just before sunrise, Baba's car peeled into the driveway. His door slammed shut and his running footsteps pounded the stairs. Then he appeared in the doorway and I saw something on his face. Something I didn't recognize right away because I'd never seen it before: fear. "Amir! Hassan!" he exclaimed as he ran to us, opening his arms wide. "They blocked all the roads and the telephone didn't work. I was so worried!"

We let him wrap us in his arms and, for a brief insane moment, I was glad about whatever had happened that night.

They weren't shooting ducks after all. As it turned out, they hadn't shot much of anything that night of July 17, 1973. Kabul awoke the next morning to find that the monarchy was a thing of the past. The king, Zahir Shah, was away in Italy. In his absence, his cousin Daoud Khan had ended the king's forty-year reign with a bloodless coup.

I remember Hassan and I crouching that next morning outside my father's study, as Baba and Rahim Khan sipped black tea and listened to breaking news of the coup on Radio Kabul.

"Amir agha?" Hassan whispered.

"What?"

"What's a 'republic'?"

I shrugged. "I don't know." On Baba's radio, they were saying that word, "republic," over and over again.

"Amir agha?"

"What?"

"Does 'republic' mean Father and I will have to move away?"

"I don't think so," I whispered back.

Hassan considered this. "Amir agha?"

"What?"

"I don't want them to send me and Father away."

I smiled. "*Bas,* you donkey. No one's sending you away."

"Amir agha?"

"What?"

"Do you want to go climb our tree?"

My smile broadened. That was another thing about Hassan. He always knew when to say the right thing—the news on the radio was getting pretty boring. Hassan went to his shack to get ready and I ran upstairs to grab a book. Then I went to the kitchen, stuffed my pockets with handfuls of pine nuts, and ran outside to find Hassan waiting for me. We burst through the front gates and headed for the hill.

We crossed the residential street and were trekking through a barren patch of rough land that led to the hill when, suddenly, a rock struck Hassan in the back. We whirled around and my heart dropped. Assef and two of his friends, Wali and Kamal, were approaching us.

Assef was the son of one of my father's friends, Mahmood, an airline pilot. His family lived a few streets south of our home, in a posh, high-walled compound with palm trees. If you were a kid living in the Wazir Akbar Khan section of Kabul, you knew about Assef and his famous stainless-steel brass knuckles, hopefully not through personal experience. Born to a German mother and Afghan father, the blond, blue-eyed Assef towered over the other kids. His well-earned reputation for savagery preceded him on the streets. Flanked by his obeying friends, he walked the neighborhood like a Khan strolling through his land with his eager-to-please entourage. His word was law, and if you needed a little legal education, then those brass knuckles were just the right teaching tool. I saw him use those knuckles once on a kid from the Karteh-Char district. I will never forget how Assef's blue eyes glinted with a light not entirely sane and how he grinned, how he *grinned,* as he pummeled that poor kid unconscious. Some of the boys in Wazir Akbar Khan had nicknamed him Assef *Goshkhor,* or Assef "the Ear Eater." Of course, none of them dared utter it to his face unless they wished to suffer the same fate as the poor kid who had unwittingly inspired that nickname when he had fought Assef over a kite and ended up fishing his right ear from a muddy gutter. Years later, I learned an English word for the creature that Assef was, a word for which a good Farsi equivalent does not exist: "sociopath."

Of all the neighborhood boys who tortured Ali, Assef was by far the most relentless. He was, in fact, the originator of the Babalu jeer, *Hey, Babalu, who did you eat today? Huh? Come on, Babalu, give us a smile!* And on days when he felt particularly inspired, he spiced up his badgering a little, *Hey, you flat-nosed Babalu, who did you eat today? Tell us, you slant-eyed donkey!*

Now he was walking toward us, hands on his hips, his sneakers kicking up little puffs of dust.

"Good morning, *kunis!*" Assef exclaimed, waving. "Fag," that was another of his favorite insults. Hassan retreated behind me as the three older boys closed in. They stood before us, three tall boys dressed in jeans and T-shirts. Towering over us all, Assef crossed his thick arms on his chest, a savage sort of grin on his lips. Not for the first time, it occurred to me that Assef might not be entirely sane. It also occurred to me how lucky I was to have Baba as my father, the sole reason, I believe, Assef had mostly refrained from harassing me too much.

He tipped his chin to Hassan. "Hey, Flat-Nose," he said. "How is Babalu?"

Hassan said nothing and crept another step behind me.

"Have you heard the news, boys?" Assef said, his grin never faltering. "The king is gone. Good riddance. Long live the president! My father knows Daoud Khan, did you know that, Amir?"

"So does my father," I said. In reality, I had no idea if that was true or not.

"'So does my father,'" Assef mimicked me in a whining voice. Kamal and Wali cackled in unison. I wished Baba were here.

"Well, Daoud Khan dined at our house last year," Assef went on. "How do you like that, Amir?"

I wondered if anyone would hear us scream in this remote patch of land. Baba's house was a good kilometer away, I wished we'd stayed at the house.

"Do you know what I will tell Daoud Khan the next time he comes to our house for dinner?" Assef said. "I'm going to have a little chat with him, man to man, *mard* to *mard*. Tell him what I told my mother. About Hitler. Now, there was a leader. A great leader. A man with vision. I'll tell Daoud Khan to remember that if they had let Hitter finish what he had started, the world be a better place now."

"Baba says Hitler was crazy, that he ordered a lot of innocent people killed," I heard myself say before I could clamp a hand on my mouth.

Assef snickered. "He sounds like my mother, and she's German; she should know better. But then they want you to believe that, don't they? They don't want you to know the truth."

I didn't know who "they" were, or what truth they were hiding, and I didn't want to find out. I wished I hadn't said anything. I wished again I'd look up and see Baba coming up the hill.

"But you have to read books they don't give out in school," Assef said. "I have. And my eyes have been opened. Now I have a vision, and I'm going to share it with our new president. Do you know what it is?"

I shook my head. He'd tell me anyway; Assef always answered his own questions.

His blue eyes flicked to Hassan. "Afghanistan is the land of Pashtuns. It always has been, always will be. We are the true Afghans, the pure Afghans, not this Flat-Nose here. His people pollute our homeland, our *watan*. They dirty our blood." He made a sweeping, grandiose gesture with his hands. "Afghanistan for Pashtuns, I say. That's my vision."

Assef shifted his gaze to me again. He looked like someone coming out of a good dream. "Too late for Hitler," he said. "But not for us."

He reached for something from the back pocket of his jeans. "I'll ask the president to do what the king didn't have the *quwat* to do. To rid Afghanistan of all the dirty, *kasseef* Hazaras."

"Just let us go, Assef", I said, hating the way my voice trembled. "We're not bothering you."

"Oh, you're bothering me," Assef said. And I saw with a sinking heart what he had fished out of his pocket. Of course. His stainless-steel brass knuckles sparkled in the sun. "You're bothering me very much. In fact, you bother me more than this Hazara here. How can you talk to him, play with him, let him touch you?" he said, his voice dripping with disgust. Wali and Kamal nodded and grunted in agreement. Assef narrowed his eyes. Shook his head. When he spoke again, he sounded as baffled as he looked. "How can you call him your 'friend'?"

But he's not my friend! I almost blurted. *He's my servant!* Had I really thought that? Of course I hadn't. I hadn't. I treated Hassan well, just like a friend, better even, more like a brother. But if so, then why, when Baba's friends came to visit with their kids, didn't I ever include Hassan in our games? Why did I play with Hassan only when no one else was around?

Assef slipped on the brass knuckles. Gave me an icy look. "You're part of the problem, Amir. If idiots like you and your father didn't take these people in, we'd be rid of them by now. They'd all just go rot in Hazarajat where they belong. You're a disgrace to Afghanistan."

I looked in his crazy eyes and saw that he meant it. He *really* meant to hurt me. Assef raised his fist and came for me.

There was a flurry of rapid movement behind me. Out of the corner of my eye, I saw Hassan bend down and stand up quickly. Assef's eyes flicked to something behind me and widened with surprise. I saw that same look of astonishment on Kamal and Wali's faces as they too saw what had happened behind me.

I turned and came face to face with Hassan's slingshot. Hassan had pulled the wide elastic band all the way back. In the cup was a rock the size of a walnut. Hassan held the slingshot pointed directly at Assef's face. His hand trembled with the strain of the pulled elastic band and beads of sweat had erupted on his brow.

"Please leave us alone, Agha," Hassan said in a flat tone. He'd referred to Assef as "Agha," and I wondered briefly what it must be like to live with such an ingrained sense of one's place in a hierarchy.

Assef gritted his teeth. "Put it down, you motherless Hazara."

"Please leave us be, Agha," Hassan said.

Assef smiled. "Maybe you didn't notice, but there are three of us and two of you."

Hassan shrugged. To an outsider, he didn't look scared. But Hassan's face was my earliest memory and I knew all of its subtle nuances, knew each and every twitch and flicker that ever rippled across it. And I saw that he was scared. He was scared plenty.

"You are right, Agha. But perhaps you didn't notice that I'm the one holding the slingshot. If you make a move, they'll have to change your nickname from Assef 'the Ear Eater' to 'One-Eyed Assef,' because I have this rock pointed at your left eye." He said this so flatly that even I had to strain to hear the fear that I knew hid under that calm voice.

Assef's mouth twitched. Wali and Kamal watched this exchange with something akin to fascination. Someone had challenged their god. Humiliated him. And, worst of all, that someone was a skinny Hazara. Assef looked from the rock to Hassan. He searched Hassan's face intently. What he found in it must have convinced him of the seriousness of Hassan's intentions, because he lowered his fist.

"You should know something about me, Hazara," Assef said gravely. "I'm a very patient person. This doesn't end today, believe me." He turned to me. "This isn't the end for you either, Amir. Someday, I'll make you face me one on one." Assef retreated a step. His disciples followed.

"Your Hazara made a big mistake today, Amir," he said. They then turned around, walked away. I watched them walk down the hill and disappear behind a wall.

Hassan was trying to tuck the slingshot in his waist with a pair of trembling hands. His mouth curled up into something that was supposed to be a reassuring smile. It took him five tries to tie the string of his trousers. Neither one of us said much of anything as we walked home in trepidation, certain that Assef and his friends would ambush us every time we turned a corner. They didn't and that should have comforted us a little. But it didn't. Not at all.

six

Winter.

Here is what I do on the first day of snowfall every year: I step out of the house early in the morning, still in my pajamas, hugging my arms against the chill. I find the driveway, my father's car, the walls, the trees, the rooftops, and the hills buried under a foot of snow. I smile. The sky is seamless and blue, the snow so white my eyes burn. I shovel a handful of the fresh snow into my mouth, listen to the muffled stillness broken only by the cawing of crows. I walk down the front steps, barefoot, and call for Hassan to come out and see.

Winter was every kid's favorite season in Kabul, at least those whose fathers could afford to buy a good iron stove. The reason was simple: They shut down school for the icy season. Winter to me was the end of long division and naming the capital of Bulgaria, and the start of three months of playing cards by the stove with Hassan, free Russian movies on Tuesday mornings at Cinema Park, sweet turnip *qurma* over rice for a lunch after a morning of building snowmen.

And kites, of course. Flying kites. And running them.

For a few unfortunate kids, winter did not spell the end of the school year. There were the so-called voluntary winter courses. No kid I knew ever volunteered to go to these classes; parents, of course, did the volunteering for them. Fortunately for me, Baba was not one of them. I remember one kid, Ahmad, who lived across the street from us. His father was some kind of doctor, I think. Ahmad had epilepsy and always wore a wool vest and thick black-rimmed glasses—he was one of Assef's regular victims. Every morning, I watched from my bedroom window as their Hazara servant shoveled snow from the driveway, cleared the way for the black Opel. I made a point of watching Ahmad and his father get into the car, Ahmad in his wool vest and winter coat, his schoolbag filled with books and pencils. I waited until they pulled away, turned the corner, then I slipped back into bed in my flannel pajamas. I pulled the blanket to my chin and watched the snowcapped hills in the north through the window. Watched them until I drifted back to sleep.

I loved wintertime in Kabul. I loved it for the soft pattering of snow against my window at night, for the way fresh snow crunched under my black rubber boots, for the warmth of the cast-iron stove as the wind screeched through the yards, the streets. But mostly because, as the trees froze and ice sheathed the roads, the chill between Baba and me thawed a little. And the reason for that was the kites. Baba and I lived in the same house, but in different spheres of existence. Kites were the one paper-thin slice of intersection between those spheres.

Every winter, districts in Kabul held a kite-fighting tournament. And if you were a boy living in Kabul, the day of the tournament was undeniably the highlight of the cold season. I never slept the night before the tournament. I'd roll from side to side, make shadow animals on the wall, even sit on the balcony in the dark, a blanket wrapped around me. I felt like a soldier trying to sleep in the trenches the night before a major battle. And that wasn't so far off. In Kabul, fighting kites *was* a little like going to war.

As with any war, you had to ready yourself for battle. For a while, Hassan and I used to build our own kites. We saved our weekly allowances in the fall, dropped the money in a little porcelain horse Baba had brought one time from Herat. When the winds of winter began to blow and snow fell in chunks, we undid the snap under the horse's belly. We went to the bazaar and bought bamboo, glue, string, and paper. We spent hours every day shaving bamboo for the center and cross spars, cutting the thin tissue paper which made for easy dipping and recovery. And then, of course, we had to make our own string, or *tar.* If the kite was the gun, then *tar,* the glass-coated cutting line, was the bullet in the chamber. We'd go out in the yard and feed up to five hundred feet of string through a mixture of ground glass and glue. We'd then hang the line between the trees, leave it to dry. The next day, we'd wind the battle-ready line around a wooden spool. By the time the snow melted and the rains of spring swept in, every boy in Kabul bore telltale horizontal gashes on his fingers from a whole winter of fighting kites. I remember how my classmates and I used to huddle, compare our battle scars on the first day of school. The cuts stung and didn't heal for a couple of weeks, but I didn't mind. They were reminders of a beloved season that had once again passed too quickly. Then the class captain would blow his whistle and we'd march in a single file to our classrooms, longing for winter already, greeted instead by the specter of yet another long school year.

But it quickly became apparent that Hassan and I were better kite fighters than kite makers. Some flaw or other in our design always spelled its doom. So Baba started taking us to Saifo's to buy our kites. Saifo was a nearly blind old man who was a *moochi* by profession—a shoe repairman. But he was also the city's most famous kite maker, working out of a tiny hovel on Jadeh Maywand, the crowded street south of the muddy banks of the Kabul River. I remember you had to crouch to enter the prison cell–sized store, and then had to lift a trapdoor to creep down a set of wooden steps to the dank basement where Saifo stored his coveted kites.

Baba would buy us each three identical kites and spools of glass string. If I changed my mind and asked for a bigger and fancier kite, Baba would buy it for me—but then he'd buy it for Hassan too. Sometimes I wished he wouldn't do that. Wished he'd let me be the favorite.

The kite-fighting tournament was an old winter tradition in Afghanistan. It started early in the morning on the day of the contest and didn't end until only the winning kite flew in the sky—I remember one year the tournament outlasted daylight. People gathered on sidewalks and roofs to cheer for their kids. The streets filled with kite fighters, jerking and tugging on their lines, squinting up to the sky, trying to gain position to cut the opponent's line. Every kite fighter had an assistant—in my case, Hassan—who held the spool and fed the line.

One time, a bratty Hindi kid whose family had recently moved into the neighborhood told us that in his hometown, kite fighting had strict rules and regulations. "You have to play in a boxed area and you have to stand at a right angle to the wind," he said proudly. "And you can't use aluminum to make your glass string."

Hassan and I looked at each other. Cracked up. The Hindi kid would soon learn what the British learned earlier in the century, and what the Russians would eventually learn by the late 1980s: the Afghans are an independent people. Afghans cherish custom but abhor rules. And so it was with kite fighting. The rules were simple: No rules. Fly your kite. Cut the opponents. Good luck.

Except that wasn't all. The real fun began when a kite was cut. That was where the kite runners came in, those kids who chased the windblown kite drifting through the neighborhoods until it came spiraling down in a field, dropping in someone's yard, on a tree, or a rooftop. The chase got pretty fierce; hordes of kite runners swarmed the streets, shoved past each other like those people from Spain I'd read about once, the ones who ran from the bulls. One year a neighborhood kid climbed a pine tree for a kite. A branch snapped under his weight and he fell thirty feet. Broke his back and never walked again. But he fell with the kite still in his hands. And when a kite runner had his hands on a kite, no one could take it from him. That wasn't a rule. That was custom.

For kite runners, the most coveted prize was the last fallen kite of a winter tournament. It was a trophy of honor, something to be displayed on a mantle for guests to admire. When the sky cleared of kites and only the final two remained, every kite runner readied himself for the chance to land this prize. He positioned himself at a spot that he thought would give him a head start. Tense muscles readied themselves to uncoil. Necks craned. Eyes crinkled. Fights broke out. And when the last kite was cut, all hell broke loose.

Over the years, I had seen a lot of guys run kites. But Hassan was by far the greatest kite runner I'd ever seen. It was downright eerie the way he always got to the spot the kite would land *before* the kite did, as if he had some sort of inner compass.

I remember one overcast winter day, Hassan and I were running a kite. I was chasing him through neighborhoods, hopping gutters, weaving through narrow streets. I was a year older than him, but Hassan ran faster than I did, and I was falling behind.

"Hassan! Wait!" I yelled, my breathing hot and ragged.

He whirled around, motioned with his hand. "This way!" he called before dashing around another corner. I looked up, saw that the direction we were running was opposite to the one the kite was drifting.

"We're losing it! We're going the wrong way!" I cried out.

"Trust me!" I heard him call up ahead. I reached the corner and saw Hassan bolting along, his head down, not even looking at the sky, sweat soaking through the back of his shirt. I tripped over a rock and fell—I wasn't just slower than Hassan but clumsier too; I'd always envied his natural athleticism. When I staggered to my feet, I caught a glimpse of Hassan disappearing around another street corner. I hobbled after him, spikes of pain battering my scraped knees.

I saw we had ended up on a rutted dirt road near Isteqlal Middle School. There was a field on one side where lettuce grew in the summer, and a row of sour cherry trees on the other. I found Hassan sitting cross-legged at the foot of one of the trees, eating from a fistful of dried mulberries.

"What are we doing here?" I panted, my stomach roiling with nausea.

He smiled. "Sit with me, Amir agha."

I dropped next to him, lay on a thin patch of snow, wheezing. "You're wasting our time. It was going the other way, didn't you see?"

Hassan popped a mulberry in his mouth. "It's coming," he said. I could hardly breathe and he didn't even sound tired.

"How do you know?" I said.

"I know."

"How can you *know?*"

He turned to me. A few sweat beads rolled from his bald scalp. "Would I ever lie to you, Amir agha?"

Suddenly I decided to toy with him a little. "I don't know. Would you?"

"I'd sooner eat dirt," he said with a look of indignation.

"Really? You'd do that?"

He threw me a puzzled look. "Do what?"

"Eat dirt if I told you to," I said. I knew I was being cruel, like when I'd taunt him if he didn't know some big word. But there was something fascinating—albeit in a sick way—about teasing Hassan. Kind of like when we used to play insect torture. Except now, he was the ant and I was holding the magnifying glass.

His eyes searched my face for a long time. We sat there, two boys under a sour cherry tree, suddenly looking, *really* looking, at each other. That's when it happened again: Hassan's face changed. Maybe not *changed*, not really, but suddenly I had the feeling I was looking at two faces, the one I knew, the one that was my first memory, and another, a second face, this one lurking just beneath the surface. I'd seen it happen before—it always shook me up a little. It just appeared, this other face, for a fraction of a moment, long enough to leave me with the unsettling feeling that maybe I'd seen it someplace before. Then Hassan blinked and it was just him again. Just Hassan.

"If you asked, I would," he finally said, looking right at me. I dropped my eyes. To this day, I find it hard to gaze directly at people like Hassan, people who mean every word they say.

"But I wonder," he added. "Would you ever ask me to do such a thing, Amir agha?" And, just like that, he had thrown at me his own little test. If I was going to toy with him and challenge his loyalty, then he'd toy with me, test my integrity.

I wished I hadn't started this conversation. I forced a smile. "Don't be stupid, Hassan. You know I wouldn't."

Hassan returned the smile. Except his didn't look forced. "I know," he said. And that's the thing about people who mean everything they say. They think everyone else does too.

"Here it comes," Hassan said, pointing to the sky. He rose to his feet and walked a few paces to his left. I looked up, saw the kite plummeting toward us. I heard footfalls, shouts, an approaching melee of kite runners. But they were wasting their time. Because Hassan stood with his arms wide open, smiling, waiting for the kite. And may God—if He exists, that is—strike me blind if the kite didn't just drop into his outstretched arms.

In the winter of 1975, I saw Hassan run a kite for the last time.

Usually, each neighborhood held its own competition. But that year, the tournament was going to be held in my neighborhood, Wazir Akbar Khan, and several other districts—Karteh-Char, Karteh-Parwan, Mekro-Rayan, and Koteh-Sangi—had been invited. You could hardly go anywhere without hearing talk of the upcoming tournament. Word had it this was going to be the biggest tournament in twenty-five years.

One night that winter, with the big contest only four days away, Baba and I sat in his study in overstuffed leather chairs by the glow of the fireplace. We were sipping tea, talking. Ali had served dinner earlier—potatoes and curried cauliflower over rice—and had retired for the night with Hassan. Baba was fattening his pipe and I was asking him to tell the story about the winter a pack of wolves had descended from the mountains in Herat and forced everyone to stay indoors for a week, when he lit a match and said, casually, "I think maybe you'll win the tournament this year. What do you think?"

I didn't know what to think. Or what to say. Was that what it would take? Had he just slipped me a key? I was a good kite fighter. Actually, a very good one. A few times, I'd even come close to winning the winter tournament—once, I'd made it to the final three. But coming close wasn't the same as winning, was it? Baba hadn't *come close*. He had won because winners won and everyone else just went home. Baba was used to winning, winning at everything he set his mind to. Didn't he have a right to expect the same from his son? And just imagine. If I did win . . .

Baba smoked his pipe and talked. I pretended to listen. But I couldn't listen, not really, because Baba's casual little comment had planted a seed in my head: the resolution that I would win that winter's tournament. I was going to win. There was no other viable option. I was going to win, and I was going to run that last kite. Then I'd bring it home and show it to Baba. Show him once and for all that his son was worthy. Then maybe my life as a ghost in this house would finally be over. I let myself dream: I imagined conversation and laughter over dinner instead of silence broken only by the clinking of silverware and the occasional grunt. I envisioned us taking a Friday drive in Baba's car to Paghman, stopping on the way at Ghargha Lake for some fried trout and potatoes. We'd go to the zoo to see Marjan the lion, and maybe Baba wouldn't yawn and steal looks at his wristwatch all the time. Maybe Baba would read one of my stories. I'd write him a hundred if I thought he'd read one. Maybe he'd call me

Amir jan like Rahim Khan did. And maybe, just maybe, I would finally be pardoned for killing my mother.

Baba was telling me about the time he'd cut fourteen kites on the same day. I smiled, nodded, laughed at all the right places, but I hardly heard a word he said. I had a mission now. And I wasn't going to fail Baba. Not this time.

It snowed heavily the night before the tournament. Hassan and I sat under the *kursi* and played panjpar as wind-rattled tree branches tapped on the window. Earlier that day, I'd asked Ali to set up the *kursi* for us—which was basically an electric heater under a low table covered with a thick, quilted blanket. Around the table, he arranged mattresses and cushions, so as many as twenty people could sit and slip their legs under. Hassan and I used to spend entire snowy days snug under the *kursi,* playing chess, cards—mostly panjpar.

I killed Hassan's ten of diamonds, played him two jacks and a six. Next door, in Baba's study, Baba and Rahim Khan were discussing business with a couple of other men—one of them I recognized as Assef's father. Through the wall, I could hear the scratchy sound of Radio Kabul News.

Hassan killed the six and picked up the jacks. On the radio, Daoud Khan was announcing something about foreign investments.

"He says someday we'll have television in Kabul," I said.

"Who?"

"Daoud Khan, you ass, the president."

Hassan giggled. "I heard they already have it in Iran," he said.

I sighed. "Those Iranians . . ." For a lot of Hazaras, Iran represented a sanctuary of sorts—I guess because, like Hazaras, most Iranians were Shi'a Muslims. But I remembered something my teacher had said that summer about Iranians, that they were grinning smooth talkers who patted you on the back with one hand and picked your pocket with the other. I told Baba about that and he said my teacher was one of those jealous Afghans, jealous because Iran was a rising power in Asia and most people around the world couldn't even find Afghanistan on a world map. "It hurts to say that," he said, shrugging. "But better to get hurt by the truth than comforted with a lie."

"I'll buy you one someday," I said.

Hassan's face brightened. "A television? In truth?"

"Sure. And not the black-and-white kind either. We'll probably be grown-ups by then, but I'll get us two. One for you and one for me."

"I'll put it on my table, where I keep my drawings," Hassan said.

His saying that made me kind of sad. Sad for who Hassan was, where he lived. For how he'd accepted the fact that he'd grow old in the mud shack in the yard, the way his father had. I drew the last card, played him a pair of queens and a ten.

Hassan picked up the queens. "You know, I think you're going to make Agha sahib very proud tomorrow."

"You think so?"

"*Inshallah*," he said.

"*Inshallah*," I echoed, though the "God willing" qualifier didn't sound as sincere coming from my lips. That was the thing with Hassan. He was so goddamn pure, you always felt like a phony around him.

I killed his king and played him my final card, the ace of spades. He had to pick it up, I'd won, but as I shuffled for a new game, I had the distinct suspicion that Hassan had *let* me win.

"Amir agha?"

"What?"

"You know . . . I *like* where I live." He was always doing that, reading my mind. "It's my home."

"Whatever," I said. "Get ready to lose again."

seven

The next morning, as he brewed black tea for breakfast, Hassan told me he'd had a dream. "We were at Ghargha Lake, you, me, Father, Agha sahib, Rahim Khan, and thousands of other people," he said. "It was warm and sunny, and the lake was clear like a mirror. But no one was swimming because they said a monster had come to the lake. It was swimming at the bottom, waiting."

He poured me a cup and added sugar, blew on it a few times. Put it before me, "So everyone is scared to get in the water, and suddenly you kick off your shoes, Amir agha, and take off your shirt. 'There's no monster,' you say. 'I'll show you all.' And before anyone can stop you, you dive into the water, start swimming away. I follow you in and we're both swimming."

"But you can't swim."

Hassan laughed. "It's a dream, Amir agha, you can do anything. Anyway, everyone is screaming, 'Get out! Get out!' but we just swim in the cold water. We make it way out to the middle of the lake and we stop swimming. We turn toward the shore and wave to the people. They look small like ants, but we can hear them clapping. They see now. There is no monster, just water. They change the name of the lake after that, and call it the 'Lake of Amir and Hassan, Sultans of Kabul,' and we get to charge people money for swimming in it."

"So what does it mean?" I said.

He coated my *naan* with marmalade, placed it on a plate. "I don't know. I was hoping you could tell me."

"Well, it's a dumb dream. Nothing happens in it."

"Father says dreams always mean something."

I sipped some tea. "Why don't you ask him, then? He's so smart," I said, more curtly than I had intended. I hadn't slept all night. My neck and back were like coiled springs, and my eyes stung. Still, I had been mean to Hassan. I almost apologized, then didn't. Hassan understood I was just nervous. Hassan always understood about me.

Upstairs, I could hear the water running in Baba's bathroom.

The streets glistened with fresh snow and the sky was a blameless blue. Snow blanketed every rooftop and weighed on the branches of the stunted mulberry trees that lined our street. Overnight, snow had nudged its way into every crack and gutter. I squinted against the blinding white when Hassan and I stepped through the wrought-iron gates. Ali shut the gates behind us. I heard him mutter a prayer under his breath—he always said a prayer when his son left the house.

I had never seen so many people on our street. Kids were flinging snowballs, squabbling, chasing one another, giggling. Kite fighters were huddling with their spool holders, making last-minute preparations. From adjacent streets, I could hear laughter and chatter. Already, rooftops were jammed with spectators reclining in lawn chairs, hot tea steaming from thermoses, and the music of Ahmad Zahir blaring from cassette players. The immensely popular Ahmad Zahir had revolutionized Afghan music and outraged the purists by adding electric guitars, drums, and horns to the traditional tabla and harmonium; on stage or at parties, he shirked the austere and nearly morose stance of older singers and actually smiled when he sang—sometimes even at women. I turned my gaze to our rooftop, found Baba and Rahim Khan sitting on a bench, both dressed in wool sweaters, sipping tea. Baba waved. I couldn't tell if he was waving at me or Hassan.

"We should get started," Hassan said. He wore black rubber snow boots and a bright green *chapan* over a thick sweater and faded corduroy pants. Sunlight washed over his face, and, in it, I saw how well the pink sear above his lip had healed.

Suddenly I wanted to withdraw. Pack it all in, go back home. What was I thinking? Why was I putting myself through this, when I already knew the outcome? Baba was on the roof, watching me. I felt his glare on me like the heat of a blistering sun. This would be failure on a grand scale, even for me.

"I'm not sure I want to fly a kite today," I said.

"It's a beautiful day," Hassan said.

I shifted on my feet. Tried to peel my gaze away from our rooftop. "I don't know. Maybe we should go home."

Then he stepped toward me and, in a low voice, said something that scared me a little. "Remember, Amir agha. There's no monster, just a beautiful day." How could I be such an open book to him when, half the time, I had no idea what was milling around in his head? I was the one who went to school, the one who could read, write. I was the smart one. Hassan couldn't read a first-grade textbook but he'd read me plenty. That was a little unsettling, but also sort of comfortable to have someone who always knew what you needed.

"No monster," I said, feeling a little better, to my own surprise.

He smiled, "No monster."

"Are you sure?"

He closed his eyes. Nodded.

I looked to the kids scampering down the street, flinging snowballs. "It is a beautiful day, isn't it?"

"Let's fly," he said.

It occurred to me then that maybe Hassan had made up his dream. Was that possible? I decided it wasn't. Hassan wasn't that smart. *I* wasn't that smart. But made up or not, the silly dream had lifted some of my anxiety. Maybe I *should* take off my shirt, take a swim in the lake. Why not?

"Let's do it," I said.

Hassan's face brightened. "Good," he said. He lifted our kite, red with yellow borders, and, just beneath where the central and cross spars met, marked with Saifo's unmistakable signature. He licked his finger and held it up, tested the wind, then ran in its direction—on those rare occasions we flew kites in the summer, he'd kick up dust to see which way the wind blew it. The spool rolled in my hands until Hassan stopped, about fifty feet away. He held the kite high over his head, like an Olympic athlete showing his gold medal. I jerked the string twice, our usual signal, and Hassan tossed the kite.

Caught between Baba and the mullahs at school, I still hadn't made up my mind about God. But when a Koran *ayat* I had learned in my *diniyat* class rose to my lips, I muttered it. I took a deep breath, exhaled, and pulled on the string. Within a minute, my kite was rocketing to the sky. It made a sound like a paper bird flapping its wings. Hassan clapped his hands, whistled, and ran back to me. I handed him the spool, holding on to the string, and he spun it quickly to roll the loose string back on.

At least two dozen kites already hung in the sky, like paper sharks roaming for prey. Within an hour, the number doubled, and red, blue, and yellow kites glided and spun in the sky. A cold breeze wafted through my hair. The wind was perfect for kite flying, blowing just hard enough to give some lift, make the sweeps easier. Next to me, Hassan held the spool, his hands already bloodied by the string.

Soon, the cutting started and the first of the defeated kites whirled out of control. They fell from the sky like shooting stars with brilliant, rippling tails, showering the neighborhoods below with prizes for the kite runners. I could hear the runners now, hollering as they ran the streets. Someone shouted reports of a fight breaking out two streets down.

I kept stealing glances at Baba sitting with Rahim Khan on the roof, wondered what he was thinking. Was he cheering for me? Or did a part of him enjoy watching me fail? That was the thing about kite flying: Your mind drifted with the kite.

They were coming down all over the place now, the kites, and I was still flying. I was still flying. My eyes keep wandering over to Baba, bundled up in his wool sweater. Was he surprised I had lasted as long as I had? *You don't keep your eyes to the sky, you won't last much longer.* I snapped my gaze back to the sky. A red kite was closing in on me—I'd caught it just in time. I tangled a bit with it, ended up besting him when he became impatient and tried to cut me from below.

Up and down the streets, kite runners were returning triumphantly, their captured kites held high. They showed them off to their parents, their friends. But they all knew the best was yet to come. The biggest prize of all was still flying. I sliced a bright yellow kite with a coiled white tail. It cost me another gash on the index finger and blood trickled down into my palm. I had Hassan hold the string and sucked the blood dry, blotted my finger against my jeans.

Within another hour, the number of surviving kites dwindled from maybe fifty to a dozen. I was one of them. I'd made it to the last dozen. I knew this part of the tournament would take a while, because the guys who had lasted this long were good—they wouldn't easily fall into simple traps like the old lift-and-dive, Hassan's favorite trick.

By three o'clock that afternoon, tufts of clouds had drifted in and the sun had slipped behind them. Shadows started to lengthen. The spectators on the roofs bundled up in scarves and thick coats. We were down to a half dozen and I was still flying. My legs ached and my neck was stiff. But with each defeated kite, hope grew in my heart, like snow collecting on a wall, one flake at a time.

My eyes kept returning to a blue kite that had been wreaking havoc for the last hour.

"How many has he cut?" I asked.

"I counted eleven," Hassan said.

"Do you know whose it might be?"

Hassan clucked his tongue and tipped his chin. That was a trademark Hassan gesture, meant he had no idea. The blue kite sliced a big purple one and swept twice in big loops. Ten minutes later, he'd cut another two, sending hordes of kite runners racing after them.

After another thirty minutes, only four kites remained. And I was still flying. It seemed I could hardly make a wrong move, as if every gust of wind blew in my favor. I'd never felt so in command, so lucky. It felt intoxicating. I didn't dare look up to the roof. Didn't dare take my eyes off the sky. I had to concentrate, play it smart. Another fifteen minutes and what had seemed like a laughable dream that morning had suddenly become reality: It was just me and the other guy. The blue kite.

The tension in the air was as taut as the glass string I was tugging with my bloody hands. People were stomping their feet, clapping, whistling, chanting, *"Boboresh! Boboresh!" Cut him! Cut him!* I wondered if Baba's voice was one of them. Music blasted. The smell of steamed *mantu* and fried *pakora* drifted from rooftops and open doors.

But all I heard—all I willed myself to hear—was the thudding of blood in my head. All I saw was the blue kite. All I smelled was victory. Salvation. Redemption. If Baba was wrong and there *was* a God like they said in school, then He'd let me win. I didn't know what the other guy was playing for, maybe just bragging rights. But this was my one chance to become someone who was looked at, not seen, listened to, not heard. If there was a God, He guide the winds, let them blow for me so that, with a tug of my string, I'd cut loose my pain, my longing. I'd endured too much, come too far. And suddenly, just like that, hope became knowledge. I was going to win. It was just a matter of when.

It turned out to be sooner than later. A gust of wind lifted my kite and I took advantage. Fed the string, pulled up. Looped my kite on top of the blue one. I held position. The blue kite knew it was in trouble. It was trying desperately to maneuver out of the jam, but I didn't let go. I held position. The crowd sensed the end was at hand. The chorus of "Cut him! Cut him!" grew louder, like Romans chanting for the gladiators to kill, kill!

"You're almost there, Amir agha! Almost there!" Hassan was panting.

Then the moment came. I closed my eyes and loosened my grip on the string. It sliced my fingers again as the wind dragged it. And then . . . I didn't need to hear the crowd's roar to know. I didn't need to see either. Hassan was screaming and his arm was wrapped around my neck.

"Bravo! Bravo, Amir agha!"

I opened my eyes, saw the blue kite spinning wildly like a tire come loose from a speeding car. I blinked, tried to say something. Nothing came out. Suddenly I was hovering, looking down on myself from above. Black leather coat, red scarf, faded jeans. A thin boy, a little sallow, and a tad short of his twelve years. He had narrow shoulders and a hint of dark circles around his pale hazel eyes. The breeze rustled his light brown hair. He looked up to me and we smiled at each other.

Then I was screaming, and everything was color and sound, everything was alive and good. I was throwing my free arm around Hassan and we were hopping up and down, both of us laughing, both of us weeping. "You won, Amir agha! You won!"

"*We* won! *We* won!" was all I could say. This wasn't happening. In a moment, I'd blink and rouse from this beautiful dream, get out of bed, march down to the kitchen to eat breakfast with no one to talk to but Hassan. Get dressed. Wait for Baba. Give up. Back to my old life. Then I saw Baba on our roof. He was standing on the edge, pumping both of his fists. Hollering and clapping. And that right there was the single greatest moment of my twelve years of life, seeing Baba on that roof, proud of me at last.

But he was doing something now, motioning with his hands in an urgent way. Then I understood. "Hassan, we—"

"I know," he said, breaking our embrace. "*Inshallah*, we'll celebrate later. Right now, I'm going to run that blue kite for you," he said. He dropped the spool and took off running, the hem of his green *chapan* dragging in the snow behind him.

"Hassan!" I called. "Come back with it!"

He was already turning the street corner, his rubber boots kicking up snow. He stopped, turned. He cupped his hands around his mouth. "For you a thousand times over!" he said. Then he smiled his Hassan smile and disappeared around the corner. The next time I saw him smile unabashedly like that was twenty-six years later, in a faded Polaroid photograph.

I began to pull my kite back as people rushed to congratulate me. I shook hands with them, said my thanks. The younger kids looked at me with an awestruck twinkle in their eyes; I was a hero. Hands patted my back and tousled my hair. I pulled on the string and returned every smile, but my mind was on the blue kite.

Finally, I had my kite in hand. I wrapped the loose string that had collected at my feet around the spool, shook a few more hands, and trotted home. When I reached the wrought-iron gates, Ali was waiting on the other side. He stuck his hand through the bars. "Congratulations," he said.

I gave him my kite and spool, shook his hand, "*Tashakor,* Ali jan."

"I was praying for you the whole time."

"Then keep praying. We're not done yet."

I hurried back to the street. I didn't ask Ali about Baba. I didn't want to see him yet. In my head, I had it all planned: I'd make a grand entrance, a hero, prized trophy in my bloodied hands. Heads would turn and eyes would lock. Rostam and Sohrab sizing each other up. A dramatic moment of silence. Then the old warrior would walk to the young one, embrace him, acknowledge his worthiness. Vindication. Salvation. Redemption. And then? Well . . . happily ever after, of course. What else?

The streets of Wazir Akbar Khan were numbered and set at right angles to each other like a grid. It was a new neighborhood then, still developing, with empty lots of land and half-constructed homes on every street between compounds surrounded by eight-foot walls. I ran up and down every street, looking for Hassan. Everywhere, people were busy folding chairs, packing food and utensils after a long day of partying. Some, still sitting on their rooftops, shouted their congratulations to me.

Four streets south of ours, I saw Omar, the son of an engineer who was a friend of Baba's. He was dribbling a soccer ball with his brother on the front lawn of their house. Omar was a pretty good guy. We'd been classmates in fourth grade, and one time he'd given me a fountain pen, the kind you had to load with a cartridge.

"I heard you won, Amir," he said. "Congratulations."

"Thanks. Have you seen Hassan?"

"Your Hazara?"

I nodded.

Omar headed the ball to his brother. "I hear he's a great kite runner." His brother headed the ball back to him. Omar caught it, tossed it up and down. "Although I've always wondered how he manages. I mean, with those tight little eyes, how does he *see* anything?"

His brother laughed, a short burst, and asked for the ball. Omar ignored him.

"Have you seen him?"

Omar flicked a thumb over his shoulder, pointing southwest. "I saw him running toward the bazaar awhile ago."

"Thanks." I scuttled away.

By the time I reached the marketplace, the sun had almost sunk behind the hills and dusk had painted the sky pink and purple. A few blocks away, from the Haji Yaghoub Mosque, the mullah bellowed *azan*, calling for the faithful to unroll their rugs and bow their heads west in prayer. Hassan never missed any of the five daily prayers. Even when we were out playing, he'd excuse himself, draw water from the well in the yard, wash up, and disappear into the hut. He'd come out a few minutes later, smiling, find me sitting against the wall or perched on a tree. He was going to miss prayer tonight, though, because of me.

The bazaar was emptying quickly, the merchants finishing up their haggling for the day. I trotted in the mud between rows of closely packed cubicles where you could buy a freshly slaughtered pheasant in one stand and a calculator from the adjacent one. I picked my way through the dwindling crowd, the lame beggars dressed in layers of tattered rags, the vendors with rugs on their shoulders, the cloth merchants and butchers closing shop for the day. I found no sign of Hassan.

I stopped by a dried fruit stand, described Hassan to an old merchant loading his mule with crates of pine seeds and raisins. He wore a powder blue turban.

He paused to look at me for a long time before answering. "I might have seen him."

"Which way did he go?"

He eyed me up and down. "What is a boy like you doing here at this time of the day looking for a Hazara?" His glance lingered admiringly on my leather coat and my jeans—*cowboy pants,* we used to call them. In Afghanistan, owning anything American, especially if it wasn't secondhand, was a sign of wealth.

"I need to find him, Agha."

"What is he to you" he said. I didn't see the point of his question, but I reminded myself that impatience wasn't going to make him tell me any faster.

"He's our servant's son," I said.

The old man raised a pepper gray eyebrow. "He is? Lucky Hazara, having such a concerned master. His father should get on his knees, sweep the dust at your feet with his eyelashes."

"Are you going to tell me or not?"

He rested an arm on the mule's back, pointed south. "I think I saw the boy you described running that way. He had a kite in his hand. A blue one."

"He did?" I said. *For you a thousand times over,* he'd promised. Good old Hassan. Good old reliable Hassan. He'd kept his promise and run the last kite for me.

"Of course, they've probably caught him by now," the old merchant said, grunting and loading another box on the mule's back.

"Who?"

"The other boys," he said. "The ones chasing him. They were dressed like you." He glanced to the sky and sighed. "Now, run along, you're making me late for *namaz.*"

But I was already scrambling down the lane.

For the next few minutes, I scoured the bazaar in vain. Maybe the old merchant's eyes had betrayed him. Except he'd seen the blue kite. The thought of getting my hands on that kite . . . I poked my head behind every lane, every shop. No sign of Hassan.

I had begun to worry that darkness would fall before I found Hassan when I heard voices from up ahead. I'd reached a secluded, muddy road. It ran perpendicular to the end of the main thoroughfare bisecting the bazaar. I turned onto the rutted track and followed the voices. My boot squished in mud with every step and my breath puffed out in white clouds before me. The narrow path ran parallel on one side to a snow-filled ravine through which a stream may have tumbled in the spring. To my other side stood rows of snow-burdened cypress trees peppered among flat-topped clay houses—no more than mud shacks in most cases—separated by narrow alleys.

I heard the voices again, louder this time, coming from one of the alleys. I crept close to the mouth of the alley. Held my breath. Peeked around the corner.

Hassan was standing at the blind end of the alley in a defiant stance: fists curled, legs slightly apart. Behind him, sitting on piles of scrap and rubble, was the blue kite. My key to Baba's heart.

Blocking Hassan's way out of the alley were three boys, the same three from that day on the hill, the day after Daoud Khan's coup, when Hassan had saved us with his slingshot. Wali was standing on one side, Kamal on the other, and in the middle, Assef. I felt my body clench up, and something cold rippled up my spine. Assef seemed relaxed, confident. He was twirling his brass knuckles. The other two guys shifted nervously on their feet, looking from Assef to Hassan, like they'd cornered some kind of wild animal that only Assef could tame.

"Where is your slingshot, Hazara?" Assef said, turning the brass knuckles in his hand. "What was it you said? 'They'll have to call you One-Eyed Assef.' That's right. One-Eyed Assef. That was clever. Really clever. Then again, it's easy to be clever when you're holding a loaded weapon."

I realized I still hadn't breathed out. I exhaled, slowly, quietly. I felt paralyzed. I watched them close in on the boy I'd grown up with, the boy whose harelipped face had been my first memory.

"But today is your lucky day, Hazara," Assef said. He had his back to me, but I would have bet he was grinning. "I'm in a mood to forgive. What do you say to that, boys?"

"That's generous," Kamal blurted, "Especially after the rude manners he showed us last time." He was trying to sound like Assef, except there was a tremor in his voice. Then I understood: He wasn't afraid of Hassan, not really. He was afraid because he had no idea what Assef had in mind.

Assef waved a dismissive hand. "*Bakhshida.* Forgiven. It's done." His voice dropped a little. "Of course, nothing is free in this world, and my pardon comes with a small price."

"That's fair," Kamal said.

"Nothing is free," Wali added.

"You're a lucky Hazara," Assef said, taking a step toward Hassan. "Because today, it's only going to cost you that blue kite. A fair deal, boys, isn't it?"

"More than fair," Kamal said.

Even from where I was standing, I could see the fear creeping into Hassan's eyes, but he shook his head. "Amir agha won the tournament and I ran this kite for him. I ran it fairly. This is his kite."

"A loyal Hazara. Loyal as a dog," Assef said.

Kamal's laugh was a shrill, nervous sound.

"But before you sacrifice yourself for him, think about this: Would he do the same for you? Have you ever wondered why he never includes you in games when he has guests? Why he only plays with you when no one else is around? I'll tell you why, Hazara. Because to him, you're nothing but an ugly pet. Something he can play with when he's bored, something he can kick when he's angry. Don't ever fool yourself and think you're something more."

"Amir agha and I are friends," Hassan said. He looked flushed.

"Friends?" Assef said, laughing. "You pathetic fool! Someday you'll wake up from your little fantasy and learn just how good of a friend he is. Now, *bas!* Enough of this. Give us that kite."

Hassan stooped and picked up a rock.

Assef flinched. He began to take a step back, stopped. "Last chance, Hazara."

Hassan's answer was to cock the arm that held the rock.

"Whatever you wish." Assef unbuttoned his winter coat, took it off, folded it slowly and deliberately. He placed it against the wall.

I opened my mouth, almost said something. Almost. The rest of my life might have turned out differently if I had. But I didn't. I just watched. Paralyzed.

Assef motioned with his hand, and the other two boys separated, forming a half circle, trapping Hassan in the alley.

"I've changed my mind," Assef said. "I'm letting you keep the kite, Hazara. I'll let you keep it so it will always remind you of what I'm about to do."

Then he charged. Hassan hurled the rock. It struck Assef in the forehead. Assef yelped as he flung himself at Hassan, knocking him to the ground. Wali and Kamal followed.

I bit on my fist. Shut my eyes.

A memory:

Did you know Hassan and you fed from the same breast? Did you know that, Amir agha? Sakina, her name was. She was a fair, blue-eyed Hazara woman from Bamiyan and she sang you old wedding songs. They say there is a brotherhood between people who've fed from the same breast. Did you know that?

A memory:

"A *rupia* each, children. Just one *rupia* each and I will part the curtain of truth." *The old man sits against a mud wall. His sightless eyes are like molten silver embedded in deep, twin craters. Hunched over his cane, the fortune-teller runs a gnarled hand across the surface of his deflated cheeks. Cups it before us.* "Not much to ask for the truth, is it, a *rupia* each?" *Hassan drops a coin in the leathery palm. I drop mine too.* "In the name of Allah most beneficent, most merciful," *the old fortune-teller whispers. He takes Hassan's hand first, strokes the palm with one hornlike fingernail, round and round, round and round. The finger then floats to Hassan's face and makes a dry, scratchy sound as it slowly traces the curve of his cheeks, the outline of his ears. The calloused pads of his fingers brush against Hassan's eyes. The hand stops there. Lingers. A shadow passes across the old man's face. Hassan and I exchange a glance. The old man takes Hassan's hand and puts the* rupia *back in Hassan's palm. He turns to me.* "How about you, young friend?" *he says. On the other side of the wall, a rooster crows. The old man reaches for my hand and I withdraw it.*

A dream:

I am lost in a snowstorm. The wind shrieks, blows stinging sheets of snow into my eyes. I stagger through layers of shifting white. I call for help but the wind drowns my cries. I fall and lie panting on the snow, lost in the white, the wind wailing in my ears. I watch the snow erase my fresh footprints. I'm a ghost now, *I think,* a ghost with no footprints. *I cry out again, hope fading like my footprints. But this time, a muffled reply. I shield my eyes and manage to sit up. Out of the swaying curtains of snow, I catch a glimpse of movement, a flurry of color. A familiar shape materializes. A hand reaches out for me. I see deep, parallel gashes across the palm, blood dripping, staining the snow. I take the hand and suddenly the snow is gone. We're standing in a field of apple green grass with soft wisps of clouds drifting above. I look up and see the clear sky is filled with kites, green, yellow, red, orange. They shimmer in the afternoon light.*

A havoc of scrap and rubble littered the alley. Worn bicycle tires, bottles with peeled labels, ripped up magazines, yellowed newspapers, all scattered amid a pile of bricks and slabs of cement. A rusted cast-iron stove with a gaping hole on its side tilted against a wall. But there were two things amid the garbage that I couldn't stop looking at: One was the blue kite resting against the wall, close to the cast-iron stove; the other was Hassan's brown corduroy pants thrown on a heap of eroded bricks.

"I don't know," Wali was saying. "My father says it's sinful." He sounded unsure, excited, scared, all at the same time. Hassan lay with his chest pinned to the ground. Kamal and Wali each gripped an arm, twisted and bent at the elbow so that Hassan's hands were pressed to his back. Assef was standing over them, the heel of his snow boots crushing the back of Hassan's neck.

"Your father won't find out," Assef said. "And there's nothing sinful about teaching a lesson to a disrespectful donkey."

"I don't know," Wali muttered.

"Suit yourself," Assef said. He turned to Kamal. "What about you?"

"I . . . well . . ."

"It's just a Hazara," Assef said. But Kamal kept looking away.

"Fine," Assef snapped. "All I want you weaklings to do is hold him down. Can you manage that?"

Wali and Kamal nodded. They looked relieved.

Assef knelt behind Hassan, put his hands on Hassan's hips and lifted his bare buttocks. He kept one hand on Hassan's back and undid his own belt buckle with his free hand. He unzipped his jeans. Dropped his underwear. He positioned himself behind Hassan. Hassan didn't struggle. Didn't even whimper. He moved his head slightly and I caught a glimpse of his face. Saw the resignation in it. It was a look I had seen before. It was the look of the lamb.

Tomorrow is the tenth day of Dhul-Hijjah, *the last month of the Muslim calendar, and the first of three days of* Eid Al-Adha, *or* Eid-e-Qorban, *as Afghans call it—a day to celebrate how the prophet Ibrahim almost sacrificed his own son for God. Baba has handpicked the sheep again this year, a powder white one with crooked black ears.*

We all stand in the backyard, Hassan, Ali, Baba, and I. The mullah recites the prayer, rubs his beard. Baba mutters, Get on with it, *under his breath. He sounds annoyed with the endless praying, the ritual of making the meat* halal. *Baba mocks the story behind this* Eid, *like he mocks everything religious. But he respects the tradition of* Eid-e-Qorban. *The custom is to divide the meat in thirds, one for the family, one for friends, and one for the poor. Every year, Baba gives it all to the poor.* The rich are fat enough already, *he says.*

The mullah finishes the prayer. Ameen. *He picks up the kitchen knife with the long blade. The custom is to not let the sheep see the knife. Ali feeds the animal a cube of sugar—another custom, to make death sweeter. The sheep kicks, but not much. The mullah grabs it under its jaw and places the blade on its neck. Just a second before he slices the throat in one expert motion, I see the sheep's eyes. It is a look that will haunt my dreams for weeks. I don't know why I watch this yearly ritual in our backyard; my nightmares persist long after the bloodstains on the grass have faded. But I always watch. I watch because of that look of acceptance in the animal's eyes. Absurdly, I imagine the animal understands. I imagine the animal sees that its imminent demise is for a higher purpose. This is the look. . .*

I STOPPED WATCHING, turned away from the alley. Something warm was running down my wrist. I blinked, saw I was still biting down on my fist, hard enough to draw blood from the knuckles. I realized something else. I was weeping. From just around the corner, I could hear Assef's quick, rhythmic grunts.

I had one last chance to make a decision. One final opportunity to decide who I was going to be. I could step into that alley, stand up for Hassan—the way he'd stood up for me all those times in the past—and accept whatever would happen to me. Or I could run.

In the end, I ran.

I ran because I was a coward. I was afraid of Assef and what he would do to me. I was afraid of getting hurt. That's what I told myself as I turned my back to the alley, to Hassan. That's what I made myself believe. I actually *aspired* to cowardice, because the alternative, the real reason I was running, was that Assef was right: Nothing was free in this world. Maybe Hassan was the price I had to pay, the lamb I had to slay, to win Baba. Was it a fair price? The answer floated to my conscious mind before I could thwart it: He was just a Hazara, wasn't he?

I ran back the way I'd come. Ran back to the all but deserted bazaar. I lurched to a cubicle and leaned against the padlocked swinging doors. I stood there panting, sweating, wishing things had turned out some other way.

About fifteen minutes later, I heard voices and running footfalls. I crouched behind the cubicle and watched Assef and the other two sprinting by, laughing as they hurried down the deserted lane. I forced myself to wait ten more minutes. Then I walked back to the rutted track that ran along the snow-filled ravine. I squinted in the dimming light and spotted Hassan walking slowly toward me. I met him by a leafless birch tree on the edge of the ravine.

He had the blue kite in his hands; that was the first thing I saw. And I can't lie now and say my eyes didn't scan it for any rips. His *chapan* had mud smudges down the front and his shirt was ripped just below the collar. He stopped. Swayed on his feet like he was going to collapse. Then he steadied himself. Handed me the kite.

"Where were you? I looked for you," I said. Speaking those words was like chewing on a rock.

Hassan dragged a sleeve across his face, wiped snot and tears. I waited for him to say something, but we just stood there in silence, in the fading light. I was grateful for the early-evening shadows that fell on Hassan's face and concealed mine. I was glad I didn't have to return his gaze. Did he know I knew? And if he knew, then what would I see if I *did* look in his eyes? Blame? Indignation? Or, God forbid, what I feared most: guileless devotion? That, most of all, I couldn't bear to see.

He began to say something and his voice cracked. He closed his mouth, opened it, and closed it again. Took a step back. Wiped his face. And that was as close as Hassan and I ever came to discussing what had happened in the alley. I thought he might burst into tears, but, to my relief, he didn't, and I pretended I hadn't heard the crack in his voice. Just like I pretended I hadn't seen the dark stain in the seat of his pants. Or those tiny drops that fell from between his legs and stained the snow black.

"Agha sahib will worry," was all he said. He turned from me and limped away.

It happened just the way I'd imagined. I opened the door to the smoky study and stepped in. Baba and Rahim Khan were drinking tea and listening to the news crackling on the radio. Their heads turned. Then a smile played on my father's lips. He opened his arms. I put the kite down and walked into his thick hairy arms. I buried my face in the warmth of his chest and wept. Baba held me close to him, rocking me back and forth. In his arms, I forgot what I'd done. And that was good.

Critical Eye

FOR DISCUSSION

a. Does every friendship have a more dominant personality?

b. Why is Amir unable to help Hassan?

c. Can a friendship survive if the parties are members of different classes?

d. Is Hassan stronger than Amir? Why?

REAPPROACHING THE LITERATURE

Would the story change if Hassan's character were a girl? Would this make the assault even more tragic? If so, why? If not, why? Pay particular attention to conflict(s) worldwide.

WRITING ASSIGNMENT

Historically/culturally, is there evidence to support the phenomenon of the strong standing up for the weak?

Bidpai

The Camel and His Friends

c. 4th century

Once a merchant was leading a caravan of heavily-laden camels through a jungle when one of them, overcome by fatigue, collapsed. The merchant decided to leave the camel in the jungle and go on his way. Later, when the camel recovered his strength, he realized that he was alone in a strange jungle. Fortunately there was plenty of grass, and he survived.

One day the king of the jungle, a lion, arrived along with his three friends—a leopard, a fox, and a crow. The king lion wondered what the camel was doing in the jungle! He came near the camel and asked how he, a creature of the desert, had ended up in the hostile jungle. The camel tearfully explained what happened. The lion took pity on him and said, "You have nothing to fear now. Henceforth, you are under my protection and can stay with us." The camel began to live happily in the jungle.

Then one day the lion was wounded in a fight with an elephant. He retired to his cave and stayed there for several days. His friends came to offer their sympathy. They tried to catch prey for the hungry lion but failed. The camel had no problem as he lived on grass while the others were starving.

The fox came up with a plan. He secretly went to the lion and suggested that the camel be sacrificed for the good of the others. The lion got furious, "I can never kill an animal who is under my protection."

The fox humbly said, "But Lord, you have provided us food all the time. If any one of us voluntarily offered himself to save your life, I hope you won't mind!" The hungry lion did not object to that and agreed to take the offer.

The fox went back to his companions and said, "Friends, our king is dying of starvation. Let us go and beg him to eat one of us. It is the least we can do for such a noble soul."

"The Camel and His Friends" (originally titled "The Unreliable Friends") by Bidpai, from *Panchatantra* edited by Arundhati Khanwalkar. Reprinted by permission of Arundhati Khanwalkar.

So they went to the king and the crow offered his life. The fox interrupted, and said, "You are a small creature, the master's hunger will hardly be appeased by eating you. May I humbly offer my life to satisfy my master's hunger."

The leopard stepped forward and said, "You are no bigger than the crow, it is me whom our master should eat."

The foolish camel thought, "Everyone has offered to lay down their lives for the king, but he has not hurt any one. It is now my turn to offer myself." So he stepped forward and said, "Stand aside friend leopard, the king and you have close family ties. It is me whom the master must eat."

An ominous silence greeted the camel's offer. Then the king gladly said, "I accept your offer, O noble camel." And in no time he was killed by the three rogues, the false friends.

Moral: Be careful in choosing your friends.

Critical Eye

FOR DISCUSSION

a. Do we live in a society where people are willing to sacrifice themselves?

b. Why are the animals "false friends?"

c. Should the leader of a nation expect its citizens to make sacrifices?

d. Does the story suggest that we cannot place trust in our nation's leaders or its citizens?

REAPPROACHING THE LITERATURE

Imagine the animals of the story are people of different races, faiths, and genders. With these new factors in mind, what would the story be saying about human nature?

WRITING ASSIGNMENT

Why should we feel compelled to sacrifice ourselves for strangers when they need our help? What is gained by doing so?

Margaret Sanger

The Turbid Ebb
and Flow of Misery

> Every night and every morn
> Some to misery are born.
> Every morn and every night
> Some are born to sweet delight.
> Some are born to sweet delight,
> Some are born to endless night.
> *William Blake*

During these years [about 1912] in New York trained nurses were in great demand. Few people wanted to enter hospitals; they were afraid they might be "practiced" upon, and consented to go only in desperate emergencies. Sentiment was especially vehement in the matter of having babies. A woman's own bedroom, no matter how inconveniently arranged, was the usual place for her lying-in. I was not sufficiently free from domestic duties to be a general nurse, but I could ordinarily manage obstetrical cases because I was notified far enough ahead to plan my schedule. And after serving my two weeks I could get home again.

Sometimes I was summoned to small apartments occupied by young clerks, insurance salesmen, or lawyers, just starting out, most of them under thirty and whose wives were having their first or second baby. They were always eager to know the best and latest method in infant care and feeding. In particular, Jewish patients, whose lives centered around the family, welcomed advice and followed it implicitly.

But more and more my calls began to come from the Lower East Side, as though I were being magnetically drawn there by some force outside my control. I hated the wretchedness and hopelessness of the poor, and never experienced that satisfaction in working among them that so many noble women have found. My concern for my patients was now quite different from my earlier hospital attitude. I could see that much was wrong with them which did not appear in the physiological or medical diagnosis. A woman in childbirth was not merely a woman in childbirth. My expanded

Chapter 7 of An *Autobiography* (1938). Sanger has taken her chapter title from a line in Matthew Arnold's poem "Dover Beach" [Editor's note].

outlook included a view of her background, her potentialities as a human being, the kind of children she was bearing, and what was going to happen to them.

The wives of small shopkeepers were my most frequent cases, but I had carpenters, truck drivers, dishwashers, and pushcart vendors. I admired intensely the consideration most of these people had for their own. Money to pay doctor and nurse had been carefully saved months in advance—parents-in-law, grandfathers, grandmothers, all contributing.

As soon as the neighbors learned that a nurse was in the building they came in a friendly way to visit, often carrying fruit, jellies, or gefüllter fish made after a cherished recipe. It was infinitely pathetic to me that they, so poor themselves, should bring me food. Later they drifted in again with the excuse of getting the plate, and sat down for a nice talk; there was no hurry. Always back of the little gift was the question, "I am pregnant (or my daughter, or my sister is). Tell me something to keep from having another baby. We cannot afford another yet."

I tried to explain the only two methods I had ever heard of among the middle classes, both of which were invariably brushed aside as unacceptable. They were of no certain avail to the wife because they placed the burden of responsibility solely upon the husband—a burden which he seldom assumed. What she was seeking was self-protection she could herself use, and there was none.

Below this stratum of society was one in truly desperate circumstances. The men were sullen and unskilled, picking up odd jobs now and then, but more often unemployed, lounging in and out of the house at all hours of the day and night. The women seemed to slink on their way to market and were without neighborliness.

These submerged, untouched classes were beyond the scope of organized charity or religion. No labor union, no church, not even the Salvation Army reached them. They were apprehensive of everyone and rejected help of any kind, ordering all intruders to keep out: both birth and death they considered their own business. Social agents, who were just beginning to appear, were profoundly mistrusted because they pried into homes and lives, asking questions about wages, how many were in the family, had any of them ever been in jail. Often two or three had been there or were now under suspicion of prostitution, shoplifting, purse snatching, petty thievery, and, in consequence, passed furtively by the big blue uniforms on the corner.

The utmost depression came over me as I approached this surreptitious region. Below Fourteenth Street I seemed to be breathing a different air, to be in another world and country where the people had habits and customs alien to anything I had ever heard about.

There were then approximately ten thousand apartments in New York into which no sun ray penetrated directly; such windows as they had opened only on a narrow court from which rose fetid odors. It was seldom cleaned, though garbage and refuse often went down into it. All these dwellings were pervaded by the foul breath of poverty, that moldy, indefinable, indescribable smell which cannot be fumigated out, sickening to me but apparently unnoticed by those who lived there. When I set to work with antiseptics, their pungent sting, at least temporarily, obscured the stench.

I remember one confinement case to which I was called by the doctor of an insurance company. I climbed up the five flights and entered the airless rooms, but the baby had come with too great speed. A boy of ten had been the only assistant. Five flights was a long way; he had wrapped the placenta in a piece of newspaper and dropped it out the window into the court.

Many families took in "boarders," as they were termed, whose small contributions paid the rent. These derelicts, wanderers, alternately working and drinking, were crowded in with the children; a single room sometimes held as many as six sleepers. Little girls were accustomed to dressing and undressing in front of the men, and were often violated, occasionally by their own fathers or brothers, before they reached the age of puberty.

Pregnancy was a chronic condition among the women of this class. Suggestions as to what to do for a girl who was "in trouble" or a married woman who was "caught" passed from mouth to mouth—herb teas, turpentine, steaming, rolling downstairs, inserting slippery elm, knitting needles, shoe-hooks. When they had word of a new remedy they hurried to the drugstore, and if the clerk were inclined to be friendly he might say, "Oh, that won't help you, but here's something that may." The younger druggists usually refused to give advice because, if it were to be known, they would come under the law; midwives were even more fearful. The doomed women implored me to reveal the "secret" rich people had, offering to pay me extra to tell them; many really believed I was holding back information for money. They asked everybody and tried anything, but nothing did them any good. On Saturday nights I have seen groups of from fifty to one hundred with their shawls over their heads waiting outside the office of a five-dollar abortionist.

Each time I returned to this district, which was becoming a recurrent nightmare, I used to hear that Mrs. Cohen "had been carried to a hospital, but had never come back," or that Mrs. Kelly "had sent the children to a neighbor and had put her head into the gas oven." Day after day such tales were poured into my ears—a baby born dead, great relief—the death of an older child, sorrow but again relief of a sort—the story told a thousand times of death from abortion and children going into institutions. I shuddered with horror as I listened to the details and studied the reasons back of them—destitution linked with excessive childbearing. The waste of life seemed utterly senseless. One by one worried, sad, pensive, and aging faces marshaled themselves before me in my dreams, sometimes appealingly, sometimes accusingly.

These were not merely "unfortunate conditions among the poor" such as we read about. I knew the women personally. They were living, breathing, human beings, with hopes, fears, and aspirations like my own, yet the weary, misshapen bodies, "always ailing, never failing," were destined to be thrown on the scrap heap before they were thirty-five. I could not escape from the facts of their wretchedness; neither was I able to see any way out. My own cozy and comfortable family existence was becoming a reproach to me.

Then one stifling mid-July day of 1912 I was summoned to a Grand Street tenement. My patient was a small, slight Russian Jewess, about twenty-eight years old, of the special cast of feature to which suffering lends a madonna-like expression. The cramped three-room apartment was in a sorry state of turmoil. Jake Sachs, a truck driver scarcely older than his wife, had come home to find the three children crying and her unconscious from the effects of a self-induced abortion. He had called the nearest doctor, who in turn had sent for me. Jake's earnings were trifling, and most of them had gone to keep the none-too-strong children clean and properly fed. But his wife's ingenuity had helped them to save a little, and this he was glad to spend on a nurse rather than have her go to a hospital.

The doctor and I settled ourselves to the task of fighting the septicemia. Never had I worked so fast, never so concentratedly. The sultry days and nights were melted into a torpid inferno. It did not seem possible there could be such heat, and every bit of food, ice, and drugs had to be carried up three flights of stairs.

Jake was more kind and thoughtful than many of the husbands I have encountered. He loved his children, and had always helped his wife wash and dress them. He had brought water up and carried garbage down before he left in the morning, and did as much as he could for me while he anxiously watched her progress.

After a fortnight Mrs. Sachs' recovery was in sight. Neighbors, ordinarily fatalistic as to the results of abortion, were genuinely pleased that she had survived. She smiled wanly at all who came to see her and thanked them gently, but she could not respond to their hearty congratulations. She appeared to be more despondent and anxious than she should have been, and spent too much time in meditation.

At the end of three weeks, as I was preparing to leave the fragile patient to take up her difficult life once more, she finally voiced her fears. "Another baby will finish me, I suppose?"

"It's too early to talk about that," I temporized.

But when the doctor came to make his last call, I drew him aside. "Mrs. Sachs is terribly worried about having another baby."

"She well may be," replied the doctor, and then he stood before her and said, "Any more such capers, young woman, and there'll be no need to send for me."

"I know, doctor," she replied timidly, "but," and she hesitated as though it took all her courage to say it, "what can I do to prevent it?"

The doctor was a kindly man, and he had worked hard to save her, but such incidents had become so familiar to him that he had long since lost whatever delicacy he might once have had. He laughed good-naturedly. "You want to have your cake and eat it too, do you? Well, it can't be done."

Then picking up his hat and bag to depart he said, "Tell Jake to sleep on the roof."

I glanced quickly at Mrs. Sachs. Even through my sudden tears I could see stamped on her face an expression of absolute despair. We simply looked at each other, saying no word until the door had closed behind the doctor. Then she lifted her thin, blue-veined hands and clasped them beseechingly. "He can't understand. He's only a man. But you do, don't you? Please tell me the secret, and I'll never breathe it to a soul. *Please!*"

What was I to do? I could not speak the conventionally comforting phrases which would be of no comfort. Instead, I made her as physically easy as I could and promised to come back in a few days to talk with her again. A little later, when she slept, I tiptoed away.

Night after night the wistful image of Mrs. Sachs appeared before me. I made all sorts of excuses to myself for not going back. I was busy on other cases; I really did not know what to say to her or how to convince her of my own ignorance; I was helpless to avert such monstrous atrocities. Time rolled by and I did nothing.

The telephone rang one evening three months later, and Jake Sachs' agitated voice begged me to come at once; his wife was sick again and from the same cause. For a wild moment I thought of sending someone else, but actually, of course, I hurried into my uniform, caught up my bag, and started out. All the way I longed for a subway wreck, an explosion, anything to keep me from having to enter that home again. But nothing happened, even to delay me. I turned into the dingy doorway and climbed the familiar stairs once more. The children were there, young little things.

Mrs. Sachs was in a coma and died within ten minutes. I folded her still hands across her breast, remembering how they had pleaded with me, begging so humbly for the knowledge which was her right. I drew a sheet over her pallid face. Jake was sobbing, running his hands through his hair and pulling it out like an insane person. Over and over again he wailed, "My God! My God! My God!"

I left him pacing desperately back and forth, and for hours I myself walked and walked and walked through the hushed streets. When I finally arrived home and let myself quietly in, all the household was sleeping. I looked out my window and down upon the dimly lighted city. Its pains and griefs crowded in upon me, a moving picture rolled before my eyes with photographic clearness: women writhing in travail to bring forth little babies; the babies themselves naked and hungry, wrapped in newspapers to keep them from the cold; six-year-old children with pinched, pale, wrinkled faces, old in concentrated wretchedness, pushed into gray and fetid cellars, crouching on stone floors, their small scrawny hands scuttling through rags, making lamp shades, artificial flowers; white coffins, black coffins, coffins, coffins interminably passing in never-ending succession. The scenes piled one upon another on another. I could bear it no longer.

As I stood there the darkness faded. The sun came up and threw its reflection over the house tops. It was the dawn of a new day in my life also. The doubt and questioning, the experimenting and trying, were now to be put behind me. I knew I could not go back merely to keeping people alive.

I went to bed, knowing that no matter what it might cost, I was finished with palliatives and superficial cures; I was resolved to seek out the root of evil, to do something to change the destiny of mothers whose reveries were vast as the sky.

Critical Eye

FOR DISCUSSION

a. What is Sanger arguing regarding the notion of poverty and the lack of opportunities it affords women?

b. Was the distribution of birth control the best answer?

c. Does anyone have the right to determine that a segment of the population is overbreeding?

d. Are marriage and childbearing the best options for women?

REAPPROACHING THE LITERATURE

If Sanger were a man, would her story change? How?

WRITING ASSIGNMENT

What would happen in America if *Roe vs. Wade* were overturned?

Naomi Wolf

The Making of a Slut

So much of the debate over issues relating to women and sexuality today is stereotypical, grinding together false dualisms of good and evil, saints and villains. All too often we discuss important issues such as teen pregnancy and date rape with a lot of name-calling but with too little real-life experience providing a background against which to measure myths and distortions.

Because sexual awakening for girls and sexuality for women are almost always complex, contextual and nuanced, I felt a need to "unpack" the statistics and the polemics. As a writer, I have faith in the power of stories to get at truths that numbers and political screeds can't reach. So this is my effort to tell some of the stories that statistics can't and that polemics won't.

Many women of my mother's generation told their stories of sexual coming-of-age in the shadow of the repressive hypocrisy of the fifties, and of "finding themselves" by casting off that era's inhibitions. For a quarter century, their conclusions have shaped our discussions of sex, women, and freedom. Those conclusions no longer fit the experiences of the two generations that have grown into womanhood during and after the sexual and feminist revolutions—generations whose experiences are sometimes so very different from those of their mothers that in some ways their stories are harder to tell, and, consequently, harder to learn from.

It is still more difficult to lay claim to the personal experiences of the slut than to those of the virgin. Women's sexual past is still materially used against them. This can happen in a court of law, a place of business, a congressional hearing, or an intimate negotiation. When someone's past "catches up with her," that woman is scapegoated and separated from the "good girls." But the punishment aimed at her inhibits all of us, and can keep us from actions ranging from charging a supervisor with sexual harassment to running for school board office to fighting for custody of children. And, in the wake of the sexual revolution, the line between "good" and "bad" girls is always shifting, keeping us unsteady, as it is meant to do.

"The Making of a Slut" by Naomi Wolf. Reprinted by permission of the author.

It will not be safe for us to live comfortably in our skins until we say: "You can no longer separate us out one from another. We are all 'bad' girls."

In any group of girls, someone has to be the slut.

In our group, Dinah became the slut. She found that role—or rather, it found her—and she did not deign to fight it. She put it on with dignity.

We were fourteen and a half; it was our eighth-grade year at our junior high. After school, before she became an outcast, I used to go over to Dinah's house in the Fillmore District almost every day.

She had the gift not only of inventing a more alluring world, but of extending it to others so they could see it too. When the two of us were alone, a glamour would descend on us. Dinah had a chewed-up collection of records of musicals, and for her these created an alternative world. Singing along with them, her pointed chin would lift upward as she sang, and her red-rimmed eyes would light up, and she would lose her tough scrapper quality. The headache-tight Lee jeans, the hair darkened with henna streaks, the pookah shell necklaces, the run-down hiking boots, would all disappear. She became Mary Martin in the South Seas or Auntie Mame loose on Manhattan.

But Dinah was the slut. She became the slut because of conditions so tangential that they could almost never have been, or could as easily have slipped the designation to someone else. She was poor; that is, poorer than the other white kids. And her body changed faster than many of the other girls'. Her breasts were large and high by seventh grade—but that visitation had come to other girls, too. It was how she decided to carry it that did her in.

She refused the good-girl slump, the binder held crosswise across her chest. She would not back down and rest her weight on her pelvis and ruin her line. Instead she flagrantly kept walking with her spine extended to her full height, her back slightly swayed. I understood what she was doing with her tailbone tucked under and her torso supple and erect like a figure on the prow of a ship, and her feet turned carefully out: she was being a star. She was thinking of the technique of stage movement that she was reading about in the books on drama, and trying always to imagine a fine filament connecting the top of her talented head to the heavens. She was walking always out to her public, graciously, for an encore. But there was no visual language in our world for a poor girl with big breasts walking tall except "slut."

By watching what happened to Dinah, we discovered that sex—for girls at least—was a game of musical chairs. It was very important to stay in the game, if always nervously moving; but finding yourself suddenly singled out was nothing short of fatal. And—just like that game—the rules that isolated one or another of us were arbitrary and capricious. One thing was certain: if you were targeted, no matter how randomly, whether you had moved not fast enough or too fast for the music, in some sure way your exclusion was your own fault.

Dinah was a spectacular dancer. On late afternoons, she could usually be found practicing steps alone in our school's shabby music room, head up, facing solemnly into the wall-length mirror. Dinah's kicks were higher and her splits deeper than those of any of the other girls over whom she towered in our class. She was more than disciplined with herself—she was almost brutal in the service of what she thought of, very levelly, as her art. There was a genre of teenage-girl novel in which a hardworking and usually orphaned ballet student pits her all to attain the great performance and accolades, and then a life of grace and ease. Dinah devoured these books.

It was no surprise that, when the call for cheerleader auditions went out, it provoked her competitive spirit. We were not the kind of girls to approach the cheerleader squad with straight faces. But the idea of a test—even more compellingly, a test of skill and charm—seduced us. Cheerleading was sexy, but for once it was a sexuality that was also absolutely safe for us.

The junior high school cheerleading squad would be chosen not by P.E. or drama teachers on the basis of physical skill, but rather, by a panel of regular subject teachers. These teachers thought of themselves as the conscience of the school. ("And," as one was overheard to say, "the cheerleaders represent the school.") They saw a heavily made-up girl, in her short red-leather jacket and midriff cropped T-shirt, leaning against a graffiti-stained wall every afternoon with the guys in the band, smoking; and they thought they knew all about Dinah.

For weeks, Dinah prepared. She believed in merit. In the try-out red plush outfit that she had sewn herself, she played the role of "wholesome cheerleader"—the only jarring note being the crease of metallic blue eye shadow that, against the dictates of *Seventeen* magazine, she insisted on applying daily. On the afternoon of the tryout, Dinah was tense. But her performance of the two cheers was, insofar as such a crude and bouncy set piece could be, a star turn. She held out her arms to the dark and silent auditorium seats, pom-poms lifted in an exuberant V, and then swooped them low.

The panel of teachers sat in the center of the pit, in the otherwise empty auditorium, their faces impassive.

Then the other girls and I tried out, sheepishly, in jeans. None of us were any better than pedestrian in contrast to Dinah. We went back outside to wait for the panel's decision.

A secretary posted a typewritten list outside the gym door. She avoided our eyes. All the new members of the team consisted of commonly acknowledged "popular" older girls. And me. In a mostly poor and working-class school, almost all of the chosen were daughters of the middle class. And—in a student population that was mostly Chinese, Japanese, Filipino, or African American—almost all were white. Dinah was not even an alternate.

I felt sick.

Dinah looked at the list on the door. She made her "Judy Garland chin-out struggling" face, then laughed at herself. "You," she said, "don't know what to say."

She shrugged her shoulders under her leather jacket. "It's that I hang out with the wrong group, that's all," she said. She looked past me to the hills above the playground, and assumed the ironic detachment she was so good at. "Well," she said crisply, lighting a Marlboro and then making one perfect French curl of smoke, "it can't be because they think I don't know how to dance."

We filed to the bus stop together in silence. We had been classified differently and we knew it. Our companionship was never exactly the same again.

The girl named head cheerleader, called "the cutest girl in ninth grade" and paragon of her church group, was no angel. But her parents were "nice" and her clothes were good. The popular girls whom the teachers approved of often conducted their sexual experiences after sneaking away from their parents' cabanas on the white-sand beaches of family vacations. Dinah went out with nineteen-year-old store clerk motorcycle rockers and lay around on foam mattresses in garages.

Dinah got called a slut because she was too poor and she was too proud of her body, and, by implication, she was too proud of her sexuality.

By the time we reached high school, Dinah had found a new gang. They were mostly guys, the rough kind of guys. Class considerations, which were like invisible, undeniable hands moving us over a school-sized chessboard, directed Dinah to a whole new group of girls. The whole school spread rumors that girls in that gang had mastered every technique in *The Sensuous Woman*.

Years later, another woman who as a girl was familiar with what was becoming Dinah's world, said that fellatio was the first genuine adult skill she ever mastered except driving, and that it made her feel just as powerful, just as valuable and free of her childhood helplessness. She spoke about the feeling among the girls in that subculture that sex was a performance for the benefit of boys.

Dinah's reputation worsened as we got older. But I also guess from having known her that during the same time in her life that her name became a fixture on the boys' bathroom walls, she was probably studying and trying to keep her family life together. According to the junior high and high school grapevine, when she heard about the graffiti in the bathrooms that talked about her blow jobs, she thought it was funny. At least, I heard she laughed. I believed it. She liked to shock the world that had repudiated her.

By our junior year in high school, her clothes tighter and her makeup heavier than ever, Dinah still seemed proud, and she still carried herself with that head-held-high, fuck-you regalness. I don't know for sure what she was thinking because I stopped " her—the result of that adolescent social dynamic, when class or race or gender pulls friends apart, that is so irrevocable. Class had declared her a slut by fourteen, while she was still technically a virgin, and kept her there, and kept me and my other wild little middle-class friends safe. As she passed us in the halls, her face grew more and more impassive with every year. That still haunts me.

From her story, and the stories of so many others, I knew that "keeping control of my desire was the only key to keeping myself and my emerging identity safe. So much depended on my taking the careful, balanced paces of a tightrope walker. Go—but DON'T JUMP!!! Go, but go slow, and keep watching. Yet part of me wanted above all else the experience of shutting my eyes and falling through the air.

I knew I was dangerous to myself the day that I let a boy walk me home from school and drew me into the overgrown alley that ran alongside the stone staircase up the hill to my house. He pushed the hair away from my forehead and then kissed my forehead, as if to make everything all right. He kissed down the side of my face to the corner of my mouth, too shy to look me in the eyes, but moving always closer to my lips. All I had to do was turn my face up toward him, and hold perfectly still. It was the easiest important thing I had ever done.

I knew that arching my neck just a little meant, "That's all right; go on." His hand lay against my clavicle and then against my chest above my collar. Finally, he slid just the tips of his fingers not even to my breast but to the skin between that lay just inside the line of my clothing. Through my closed eyes, the light went red. He withdrew his hand and watched my face. Even as the cold air rippled my shirt, his fingerprints were still burning.

He was watching to see if it was all right. It wasn't all right. I was capable of anything. I was capable of being Dinah.

Almost every society punishes its sluts in its own ways. It's just that right now, our own sometimes pretends it does not. The summer that I went back home to ask my friends about our girlhoods, there was a rash of sex industry films coming out of Hollywood. *Striptease* and *Showgirls* were following their predecessor, *Pretty Woman*. Teenage girls were reading about how Demi Moore worked out for hours each day to play a stripper; how she would go to the strip joints and hang with the dancers to "get it right."

As we drove through the hills above Marin, I asked a friend who had grown up with us what she thought about those films. Her opinion was better informed than most of ours was, for she had spent time as a stripper, and later as a professional mistress. She embodied the contradiction we live under: a college-educated, happily married, community-minded woman with curly black hair, a hip way of wearing her tailored clothes, a timid grin—indistinguishable from any of the rest of our tribe. But by the standards of the culture she had been a real whore, a true, dyed-in-the-wool, no-argument, verifiable slut. She had gone all the way. The bad girl, the good girl—the dimorphism was a fantasy. They were both here in the car; in her, in myself, in us all.

As she drove, the carefree mood of two women in their early thirties thinking about girlhood in an open car, feet on the dashboard and reggae on the radio, evaporated. "Here is all I have to say about how they are glamorizing those images for girls, who are just sucking it in," she said. Her words became slow and deliberate. "When men think a woman is a whore, it's open . . . season . . . on her. They can say anything to her they want, they can do anything they want, they can be absolutely as crass and vile and violent and cruel and uncaring as the darkest part of their personality wants to be. And it's okay. They don't have to afford the woman one ounce of respect for being a human being. She's not a human being. She's a thing.

"Since the sexual revolution, there's a license, and there's terror, and we're living under . . . both."

Then the words came out in a torrent. "I was shocked. I was shocked. I thought that because of the progress that women have made in our society men would have a clue that prostitutes are human beings and that they don't deserve to be treated so poorly, but they don't. It's almost as if now they see sex workers as the only women that they can be so aggressive and cruel to. They can't get away with it in their jobs anymore, they can't get away with it in their marriages, but with sex workers, it's okay. That's what they're paid for! They're paid to be sexually harassed, they're paid to be assaulted. Women outside the sex industry won't put up with it anymore."

I was quiet. I was thinking: if all women, even nice women, can do what only whores used to do, but you can no longer treat all women who do such things like whores—that is, if feminism is succeeding at breaking down some of the penalties that used to be directed at nonprofessional, sexually licentious women—then society will all the more rigidly professionalize and demarcate the bad girl for sale, to whom anything can be done. My friend was explaining that "real" prostitutes used to bear the burden of the fact that nice girls had a limited repertoire; now they bear the burden of the fact that nice girls have gotten wild.

The feeling of foreboding that had hung over the word "slut" in my sexually libertine girlhood became clearer. The culture had said: Take it off. Take it all off. The culture had also said, of the raped girl, of the hitchhiker, of the dead girl: She was in the wrong place at the wrong time, doing the wrong thing.

Suddenly, as the soft round hills sped by, I saw flash before my eyes a photograph from one of the social histories I had been reading. It was of the nearly intact, mummified remains, dating from the first century A.D., of a fourteen-year-old German girl. Her long, shapely legs and slender feet were intact, and her right arm still clutched the garrote that had been used to twist the rope around her neck. Her lips were still in an O of surprise or pain, and a twisted rag was still securely bound against her eyes. At fourteen, the girl had been blindfolded, strangled, and drowned, most likely as retribution for "adultery"—for what we would call a teenage love affair.

Given these origins, it is no wonder that even today fourteen-year-old girls who notice, let alone act upon, desire have the heart-racing sense that they are doing something obscurely, but surely, dangerous. It is also in part because of this inheritance that a contemporary woman wakes up after a night of being erotically "out of control" feeling sure, on some primal level, that something punitive is bound to happen to her—and that if it doesn't, it should.

Critical Eye

FOR DISCUSSION

a. Why are women held to a different sexual standard than men?

b. Are mothers now, in our modern-day society, more capable of speaking to their daughters about their own sexual experiences and desires?

c. Wolf argues that we make life very dangerous for the "bad girl." How is this true?

REAPPROACHING THE LITERATURE

Imagine a world where all women embrace the title of "slut." How would such a feat affect gender relations in America?

WRITING ASSIGNMENT

Can you argue that so-called "bad girls" are actually living Emerson's idea of being nonconformists?

Peter Marin

Helping and Hating the Homeless

When I was a child, I had a recurring vision of how I would end as an old man: alone, in a sparsely furnished second-story room I could picture quite precisely, in a walk-up on Fourth Avenue in New York, where the secondhand bookstores then were. It was not a picture which frightened me. I liked it. The idea of anonymity and solitude and marginality must have seemed to me, back then, for reasons I do not care to remember, both inviting and inevitable. Later, out of college, I took to the road, hitchhiking and traveling on freights, doing odd jobs here and there, crisscrossing the country. I liked that too: the anonymity and the absence of constraint and the rough community I sometimes found. I felt at home on the road, perhaps because I felt at home nowhere else, and periodically, for years, I would return to that world, always with a sense of relief and release.

I have been thinking a lot about that these days, now that transience and homelessness have made their way into the national consciousness, and especially since the town I live in, Santa Barbara, has become well known because of the recent successful campaign to do away with the meanest aspects of its "sleeping ordinances"—a set of foolish laws making it illegal for the homeless to sleep at night in public places. During that campaign I got to know many of the homeless men and women in Santa Barbara, who tend to gather, night and day, in a small park at the lower end of town, not far from the tracks and the harbor, under the rooflike, overarching branches of a gigantic fig tree, said to be the oldest on the continent. There one enters much the same world I thought, as a child, I would die in, and the one in which I traveled as a young man: a "marginal" world inhabited by all those unable to find a place in "our" world. Sometimes, standing on the tracks close to the park, you can sense in the wind, or in the smell of tar and ties, the presence and age of that marginal world: the way it stretches backward and inevitably forward in time, parallel to our own world, always present, always close, and yet separated from us—at least in the mind—by a gulf few of us are interested in crossing.

"Helping and Hating the Homeless" by Peter Marin, *Harper's Magazine,* January 1987. Copyright © 1987 by Harper's Magazine. All rights reserved. Reproduced from the January 1987 issued by special permission.

Late last summer, at a city council meeting here in Santa Barbara, I saw, close up, the consequences of that strange combination of proximity and distance. The council was meeting to vote on the repeal of the sleeping ordinances, though not out of any sudden sense of compassion or justice. Council members had been pressured into it by the threat of massive demonstrations—"The Selma of the Eighties" was the slogan one heard among the homeless. But this threat that frightened the council enraged the towncitizens. Hundreds of them turned out for the meeting. One by one they filed to the microphone to curse the council and castigate the homeless. Drinking, doping, loitering, panhandling, defecating, urinating, molesting, stealing—the litany went on and on, was repeated over and over, accompanied by fantasies of disaster: the barbarian hordes at the gates, civilization ended.

What astonished me about the meeting was not what was said; one could have predicted that. It was the power and depth of the emotion revealed: the mindlessness of the fear, the vengefulness of the fury. Also, almost none of what was said had anything to do with the homeless people I know—not the ones I once traveled with, not the ones in town. They, the actual homeless men and women, might not have existed at all.

If I write about Santa Barbara, it is not because I think the attitudes at work here are unique. They are not. You find them everywhere in America. In the last few months I have visited several cities around the country, and in each of them I have found the same thing: more and more people in the streets, more and more suffering. (There are at least 350,000 homeless people in the country, perhaps as many as 3 million.) And, in talking to the good citizens of these cities, I found, almost always, the same thing: confusion and ignorance, or simple indifference, but anger too, and fear.

What follows here is an attempt to explain at least some of that anger and fear, to clear up some of the confusion, to chip away at the indifference. It is not meant to be definitive; how could it be? The point is to try to illuminate some of the darker corners of homelessness, those we ordinarily ignore, and those in which the keys to much that is now going on may be hidden.

The trouble begins with the word "homeless." It has become such an abstraction, and is applied to so many different kinds of people, with so many different histories and problems, that it is almost meaningless.

Homelessness, in itself, is nothing more than a condition visited upon men and women (and, increasingly, children) as the final stage of a variety of problems about which the word "homelessness" tells us almost nothing. Or, to put it another way, it is a catch basin into which pour all of the people disenfranchised or marginalized or scared off by processes beyond their control, those which lie close to the heart of American life. Here are the groups packed into the single category of "the homeless":

- Veterans, mainly from the war in Vietnam. In many American cities, vets make up close to 50 percent of all homeless males.
- The mentally ill. In some parts of the country, roughly a quarter of the homeless would, a couple of decades ago, have been institutionalized.
- The physically disabled or chronically ill, who do not receive any benefits or whose benefits do not enable them to afford permanent shelter.
- The elderly on fixed incomes whose funds are no longer sufficient for their needs.
- Men, women, and whole families pauperized by the loss of a job.
- Single parents, usually women, without the resources or skills to establish new lives.
- Runaway children, many of whom have been abused.
- Alcoholics and those in trouble with drugs (whose troubles often begin with one of the other conditions listed here).
- Immigrants, both legal and illegal, who often are not counted among the homeless because they constitute a "problem" in their own right.
- Traditional tramps, hobos, and transients, who have taken to the road or the streets for a variety of reasons and who prefer to be there.

You can quickly learn two things about the homeless from this list. First, you can learn that many of the homeless, before they were homeless, were people more or less like ourselves: members of the working or middle class. And you can learn that the world of the homeless has its roots in various policies, events, and ways of life for which some of us are responsible and from which some of us actually prosper.

We decide, as a people, to go to war, we ask our children to kill and to die, and the result, years later, is grown men homeless on the street.

We change, with the best intentions, the laws pertaining to the mentally ill, and then, without intention, neglect to provide them with services; and the result, in our streets, drives some of us crazy with rage.

We cut taxes and prune budgets, we modernize industry and shift the balance of trade, and the result of all these actions and errors can be read, sleeping form by sleeping form, on our city streets.

The liberals cannot blame the conservatives. The conservatives cannot blame the liberals. Homelessness is the *sum total* of our dreams, policies, intentions, errors, omissions, cruelties, kindnesses, all of it recorded, in flesh, in the life of the streets.

You can also learn from this list one of the most important things there is to know about the homeless—that they can be roughly divided into two groups: those who have had homelessness forced upon them and want nothing more than to escape it; and those who have at least in part *chosen* it for themselves, and now accept, or in some cases, embrace it.

I understand how dangerous it is to introduce the idea of choice into a discussion of homelessness. It can all too easily be used to justify indifference or brutality toward the homeless, or to argue that they are only getting what they "deserve." And yet it seems to me that it is only by taking choice into account, in all of the intricacies of its various forms and expressions, that one can really understand certain kinds of homelessness.

The fact is, many of the homeless are not only hapless victims but voluntary exiles, "domestic refugees," people who have turned not against life itself but against *us*, our life, American life. Look for a moment at the vets. The price of returning to America was to forget what they had seen or learned in Vietnam, to "put it behind them." But some could not do that, and the stress of trying showed up as alcoholism, broken marriages, drug addiction, crime. And it showed up too as life on the street, which was for some vets a desperate choice made in the name of life—the best they could manage, it was a way of avoiding what might have occurred had they stayed where they were: suicide, or violence done to others.

We must learn to accept that there may indeed be people, and not only vets, who have seen so much of our world, or seen it so clearly, that to live in it becomes impossible. Here, for example, is the story of Alice, a homeless middle-aged woman in Los Angeles, where there are, perhaps, 50,000 homeless people. It was set down a few months ago by one of my students at the University of California, Santa Barbara, where I taught for a semester. I had encouraged them to go find the homeless and listen to their stories. And so, one day, when this student saw Alice foraging in a dumpster outside a McDonald's, he stopped and talked to her:

> She told me she had led a pretty normal life as she grew up and eventually went to college. From there she went on to Chicago to teach school. She was single and lived in a small apartment.
>
> One night, after she got off the train after school, a man began to follow her to her apartment building. When she got to her door she saw a knife and the man hovering behind her. She had no choice but to let him in. The man raped her.
>
> After that, things got steadily worse. She had a nervous breakdown. She went to a mental institution for three months, and when she went back to her apartment she found her belongings gone. The landlord had sold them to cover the rent she hadn't paid.

She had no place to go and no job because the school had terminated her employment. She slipped into depression. She lived with friends until she could muster enough money for a ticket to Los Angeles. She said she no longer wanted to burden her friends, and that if she had to live outside, at least Los Angeles was warmer than Chicago.

It is as if she began back then to take on the mentality of a street person. She resolved herself to homelessness. She's been out West since 1980, without a home or job. She seems happy, with her best friend being her cat. But the scars of memories still haunt her, and she is running from them, or should I say *him.*

This is, in essence, the same story one hears over and over again on the street. You begin with an ordinary life; then an event occurs—traumatic, catastrophic; smaller events follow, each one deepening the original wound; finally, homelessness becomes inevitable, or begins to *seem* inevitable to the person involved—the only way out of an intolerable situation. You are struck continually, hearing these stories, by something seemingly unique in American life, the absolute isolation involved. In what other culture would there be such an absence or failure of support from familial, social, or institutional sources? Even more disturbing is the fact that it is often our supposed sources of support—family, friends, government organizations—that have caused the problem in the first place.

Everything that happened to Alice—the rape, the loss of job and apartment, the breakdown—was part and parcel of a world gone radically wrong, a world, for Alice, no longer to be counted on, no longer worth living in. Her homelessness can be seen as flight, as failure of will or nerve, even, perhaps, as *disease.* But it can also be seen as a mute, furious refusal, a self-imposed exile far less appealing to the rest of us than ordinary life, but *better,* in Alice's terms.

We like to think, in America, that everything is redeemable, that everything broken can be magically made whole again, and that what has been "dirtied" can be cleansed. Recently I saw on television that one of the soaps had introduced the character of a homeless old woman. A woman in her thirties discovers that her long-lost mother has appeared in town, on the streets. After much searching the mother is located and identified and embraced; and then she is scrubbed and dressed in style, restored in a matter of days to her former upper-class habits and role.

A triumph—but one more likely to occur on television than in real life. Yes, many of those on the streets could be transformed, rehabilitated. But there are others whose lives have been irrevocably changed, damaged beyond repair, and who no longer want help, who no longer recognize the *need* for help, and whose experience in our world has made them want only to be left alone. How, for instance, would one restore Alice's life, or reshape it in a way that would satisfy *our* notion of what a life should be? What would it take to return her to the fold? How to erase the four years of homelessness, which have become as familiar to her, and as much a home, as her "normal" life once was? Whatever we think of the way in which she has resolved her difficulties, it constitutes a sad peace made with the world. Intruding ourselves upon it in the name of redemption is by no means as simple a task—or as justifiable a task—as one might think.

It is important to understand too that however disorderly and dirty and unmanageable the world of homeless men and women like Alice appears to us, it is not without its significance, and its rules and rituals. The homeless in our cities mark out for themselves particular neighborhoods, blocks, buildings, doorways. They impose on themselves often obsessively strict routines. They reduce their world to a small area, and thereby protect themselves from a world that might otherwise be too much to bear.

Daily the city eddies around the homeless. The crowds flowing past leave a few feet, a gap. We do not touch the homeless world. Perhaps we cannot touch it. It remains separate even as the city surrounds it.

The homeless, simply because they are homeless, are strangers, alien—and therefore a threat. Their presence, in itself, comes to constitute a kind of violence; it deprives us of our sense of safety. Let me use myself as an example. I know, and respect, many of those now homeless on the streets of Santa Barbara. Twenty years ago, some of them would have been my companions and friends. And yet, these days, if I walk through the park near my home and see strangers bedding down for the night, my first reaction, if not fear, is a sense of annoyance and intrusion, of worry and alarm. I think of my teenage daughter, who often walks through the park, and then of my house, a hundred yards away, and I am tempted—only tempted, but tempted, still—to call the "proper" authorities to have the strangers moved on. Out of sight, out of mind.

Notice: I do not bring them food. I do not offer them shelter or a shower in the morning. I do not even stop to talk. Instead, I think: my daughter, my house, my privacy. What moves me is not the threat of *danger*—nothing as animal as that. Instead there pops up inside of me, neatly in a row, a set of anxieties, ones you might arrange in a dollhouse living room and label: Family of bourgeois fears. The point is this: Our response to the homeless is fed by a complex set of cultural attitudes, habits of thought, and fantasies and fears so familiar to us, so common, that they have become a *second* nature and might as well be instinctive, for all the control we have over them. And it is by no means easy to untangle this snarl of responses. What does seem clear is that the homeless embody all that bourgeois culture has for centuries tried to eradicate and destroy.

If you look to the history of Europe you find that homelessness first appeared (or is first acknowledged) at the very same moment that bourgeois culture begins to appear. The same processes produced them both: the breakup of feudalism, the rise of commerce and cities, the combined triumphs of capitalism, industrialism, and individualism. The historian Fernand Braudel, in *The Wheels of Commerce,* describes, for instance, the armies of impoverished men and women who began to haunt Europe as far back as the eleventh century. And the makeup of these masses? Essentially the same then as it is now: the unfortunates, the throwaways, the misfits, the deviants.

> In the eighteenth century, all sorts and conditions were to be found in this human dross . . . widows, orphans, cripples . . . journeymen who had broken their contracts, out-of-work labourers, homeless priests with no living, old men, fire victims . . . war victims, deserters, discharged soldiers, would-be vendors of useless articles, vagrant preachers with or without licenses, "pregnant servant-girls and unmarried mothers driven from home," children sent out "to find bread or to maraud."

Then, as now, distinctions were made between the "homeless" and the supposedly "deserving" poor, those who knew their place and willingly sustained, with their labors, the emergent bourgeois world.

> The good paupers were accepted, lined up and registered on the official list; they had a right to public charity and were sometimes allowed to solicit it outside churches in prosperous districts, when the congregation came out, or in market places. . . .
>
> When it comes to beggars and vagrants, it is a very different story, and different pictures meet the eye: crowds, mobs, processions, sometimes mass emigrations, "along the country highways or the streets of the Towns and Villages," by beggars "whom hunger and nakedness has driven from home." . . . The towns dreaded these alarming visitors and drove them out as soon as they appeared on the horizon.

And just as the distinctions made about these masses were the same then as they are now, so too was the way society saw them. They seemed to bourgeois eyes (as they still do) the one segment of society that remained resistant to progress, unassimilable and incorrigible, inimical to all order.

It is in the nineteenth century, in the Victorian era, that you can find the beginnings of our modern strategies for dealing with the homeless: the notion that they should be controlled and perhaps eliminated through "help." With the Victorians we begin to see the entangling of self-protection with social obligation, the strategy of masking self-interest and the urge to control as *moral duty*. Michel Foucault has spelled this out in his books on madness and punishment: the zeal with which the overseers of early bourgeois culture tried to purge, improve, and purify all of urban civilization—whether through schools and prisons, or, quite literally, with public baths and massive new water and sewage systems. Order, ordure—this is, in essence, the tension at the heart of bourgeois culture, and it was the singular genius of the Victorians to make it the main component of their medical, aesthetic, *and* moral systems. It was not a sense of justice or even empathy which called for charity or new attitudes toward the poor; it was *hygiene*. The very same attitudes appear in nineteenth-century America. Charles Loring Brace, in an essay on homeless and vagrant children written in 1876, described the treatment of delinquents in this way: "Many of their vices drop from them like the old and verminous clothing they left behind. . . . The entire change of circumstances seems to cleanse them of bad habits." Here you have it all: *vices, verminous clothing, cleansing them of bad habits*—the triple association of poverty with vice with dirt, an equation in which each term comes to stand for all of them.

These attitudes are with us still; that is the point. In our own century the person who has written most revealingly about such things is George Orwell, who tried to analyze his own middle-class attitudes toward the poor. In 1933, in *Down and Out in Paris and London,* he wrote about tramps:

> In childhood we are taught that tramps are blackguards . . . a repulsive, rather dangerous creature, who would rather die than work or wash, and wants nothing but to beg, drink or rob hen-houses. The tramp monster is no truer to life than the sinister Chinaman of the magazines, but he is very hard to get rid of. The very word "tramp" evokes his image.

All of this is still true in America, though now it is not the word "tramp" but the word "homeless" that evokes the images we fear. It is the homeless who smell. Here, for instance, is part of a paper a student of mine wrote about her first visit to a Rescue Mission on skid row.

> The sermon began. The room was stuffy and smelly. The mixture of body odors and cooking was nauseating. I remember thinking: how can these people share this facility? They must be repulsed by each other. They had strange habits and dispositions. They were a group of dirty, dishonored, weird people to me.
>
> When it was over I ran to my car, went home, and took a shower. I felt extremely dirty. Through the day I would get flashes of that disgusting smell.

To put it as bluntly as I can, for many of us the homeless are *shit*. And our policies toward them, our spontaneous sense of disgust and horror, our wish to be rid of them—all of this has hidden in it, close to its heart, our feelings about excrement. Even Marx, that most bourgeois of revolutionaries, described the deviant *lumpen* in *The Eighteenth Brumaire of Louis Bonaparte* as "scum, offal, refuse of all classes." These days, in puritanical Marxist nations, they are called "parasites"—a word, perhaps not incidentally, one also associates with human waste.

What I am getting at here is the *nature* of the desire to help the homeless—what is hidden behind it and why it so often does harm. Every government program, almost every private project, is geared as much to the needs of those giving help as it is to the needs of the homeless. Go to any government agency, or, for that matter, to most private charities, and you will find yourself enmeshed, at once, in a bureaucracy so tangled and oppressive, or confronted with so much moral arrogance and contempt, that you will be driven back out into the streets for relief.

Santa Barbara, where I live, is as good an example as any. There are three main shelters in the city—all of them private. Between them they provide fewer than a hundred beds a night for the homeless. Two of the three shelters are religious in nature: the Rescue Mission and the Salvation Army. In the mission, as in most places in the country, there are elaborate and stringent rules. Beds go first to those who have not been there for two months, and you can stay for only two nights in any two-month period. No shelter is given to those who are not sober. Even if you go to the mission only for a meal, you are required to listen to sermons and participate in prayer, and you are regularly proselytized—sometimes overtly, sometimes subtly. There are obligatory, regimented showers. You go to bed precisely at ten: lights out, no reading, no talking. After the lights go out you will find fifteen men in a room with double-decker bunks. As the night progresses the room grows stuffier and hotter. Men toss, turn, cough, and moan. In the morning you are awakened precisely at five forty-five. Then breakfast. At seven-thirty you are back on the street.

The town's newest shelter was opened almost a year ago by a consortium of local churches. Families and those who are employed have first call on the beds—a policy which excludes the congenitally homeless. Alcohol is not simply forbidden *in* the shelter; those with a history of alcoholism must sign a "contract" pledging to remain sober and chemical-free. Finally, in a paroxysm of therapeutic bullying, the shelter has added a new wrinkle: If you stay more than two days you are required to fill out and then discuss with a social worker a complex form listing what you perceive as your personal failings, goals, and strategies—all of this for men and women who simply want a place to lie down out of the rain!

It is these attitudes, in various forms and permutations, that you find repeated endlessly in America. We are moved either to "redeem" the homeless or to punish them. Perhaps there is nothing consciously hostile about it. Perhaps it is simply that as the machinery of bureaucracy cranks itself up to deal with these problems, attitudes assert themselves automatically. But whatever the case, the fact remains that almost every one of our strategies for helping the homeless is simply an attempt to rearrange the world *cosmetically*, in terms of how it looks and smells to *us*. Compassion is little more than the passion for control.

The central question emerging from all this is, What does a society owe to its members in trouble, and *how* is that debt to be paid? It is a question which must be answered in two parts: first, in relation to the men and women who have been marginalized against their will, and then, in a slightly different way, in relation to those who have chosen (or accept or even prize) their marginality.

As for those who have been marginalized against their wills, I think the general answer is obvious: A society owes its members whatever it takes for them to regain their places in the social order. And when it comes to specific remedies, one need only read backward the various processes which have created homelessness and then figure out where help is likely to do the most good. But the real point here is not the specific remedies required—affordable housing, say—but the basis upon which they must be offered, the necessary underlying ethical notion we seem in this nation unable to grasp: that those who are the inevitable casualties of modern industrial capitalism and the free-market system are entitled, *by right,* and by the simple virtue of their participation in that system, to whatever help they need. They are entitled to help to find and hold their places in the society whose social contract they have, in effect, signed and observed.

Look at that for just a moment: the notion of a contract. The majority of homeless Americans have kept, insofar as they could, to the terms of that contract. In any shelter these days you can find men and women who have worked ten, twenty, forty years, and whose lives have nonetheless come to nothing. These are people who cannot afford a place in the world they helped create. And in return? Is it life on the street they have earned? Or the cruel charity we so grudgingly grant them?

But those marginalized against their will are only half the problem. There remains, still, the question of whether we owe anything to those who are voluntarily marginal. What about them: the street people, the rebels, and the recalcitrants, those who have torn up their social contracts or returned them unsigned?

I was in Las Vegas last fall, and I went out to the Rescue Mission at the lower end of town, on the edge of the black ghetto, where I first stayed years ago on my way west. It was twilight, still hot; in the vacant lot next-door to the mission 200 men were lining up for supper. A warm wind blew along the street lined with small houses and salvage yards, and in the distance I could see the desert's edge and the smudge of low hills in the fading light. There were elderly alcoholics in line, and derelicts, but mainly the men were the same sort I had seen here years ago: youngish, out of work, restless and talkative, the drifters and wanderers for whom the word "wanderlust" was invented.

At supper—long communal tables, thin gruel, stale sweet rolls, ice water—a huge black man in his twenties, fierce and muscular, sat across from me. "I'm from the Coast, man," he said. "Never been away from home before. Ain't sure I like it. Sure don't like *this* place. But I lost my job back home a couple of weeks ago and figured, why wait around for another. I thought I'd come out here, see me something of the world."

After supper, a squat Portuguese man in his mid-thirties, hunkered down against the mission wall, offered me a smoke and told me: "Been sleeping in my car, up the street, for a week. Had my own business back in Omaha. But I got bored, man. Sold everything, got a little dough, came out here. Thought I'd work construction. Let me tell you, this is one tough town."

In a world better than ours, I suppose, men (or women) like this might not exist. Conservatives seem to have no trouble imagining a society so well disciplined and moral that deviance of this kind would disappear. And leftists envision a world so just, so generous, that deviance would vanish along with inequity. But I suspect that there will always be something at work in some men and women to make them restless with the systems others devise for them, and to move them outward toward the edges of the world, where life is always riskier, less organized, and easier going.

Do we owe anything to these men and women, who reject our company and what we offer and yet nonetheless seem to demand *something* from us?

We owe them, I think, at least a place to exist, a way to exist. That may not be a *moral* obligation, in the sense that our obligation to the involuntarily marginal is clearly a moral one, but it is an obligation nevertheless, one you might call an existential obligation.

Of course, it may be that I think we owe these men something because I have liked men like them, and because I want their world to be there always, as a place to hide or rest. But there is more to it than that. I think we as a society need men like these. A society needs its margins as much as it needs art and literature. It needs holes and gaps, *breathing spaces,* let us say, into which men and women can escape and live, when necessary, in ways otherwise denied them. Margins guarantee to society a flexibility, an elasticity, and allow it to accommodate itself to the natures and needs of its members. When margins vanish, society becomes too rigid, too oppressive by far, and therefore inimical to life.

It is for such reasons that, in cultures like our own, marginal men and women take on a special significance. They are all we have left to remind us of the narrowness of the received truths we take for granted. "Beyond the pale," they somehow redefine the pale, or remind us, at least, that *something* is still out there, beyond the pale. They preserve, perhaps unconsciously, a dream that would otherwise cease to exist, the dream of having a place in the world, and of being *left alone.*

Quixotic? Infantile? Perhaps. But remember. . . . [w]hat we are talking about here is *freedom,* and with it, perhaps, an echo of the dream men brought, long ago, to wilderness America. I use the word "freedom" gingerly, in relation to lives like these: skewed, crippled, emptied of everything we associate with a full, or realized, freedom. But perhaps this is the condition into which freedom has fallen among us. Art has been "appreciated" out of existence; literature has become an extension of the university, replete with tenure and pensions; and as for politics, the ideologies which ring us round seem too silly or shrill by far to speak for life. What is left, then, is this mute and intransigent independence, this "waste" of life which refuses even interpretation, and which cannot be assimilated to any ideology, and which therefore can be put to no one's use. In its crippled innocence and the perfection of its superfluity it amounts, almost, to a rebellion against history, and that is no small thing.

Let me put it as simply as I can: What we see on the streets of our cities are two dramas, both of which cut to the troubled heart of the culture and demand from us a response we may not be able to make. There is the drama of those struggling to survive by regaining their place in the social order. And there is the drama of those struggling to survive outside of it.

The resolution of both struggles depends on a third drama occurring at the heart of the culture: the tension and contention between the magnanimity we owe to life and the darker tendings of the human psyche: our fear of strangeness, our hatred of deviance, our love of order and control. How we mediate by default or design between those contrary forces will determine not only the destinies of the homeless, but also something crucial about the nation, and perhaps—let me say it—about our own souls.

Critical Eye

FOR DISCUSSION

a. Do we wish to help the homeless, or do we want to vanquish them from our sight?

b. In what ways do we blame the homeless for their circumstances?

c. Why, in your opinion, do our current programs to assist the homeless seem to be failing?

d. Why does the United States, one of the wealthiest nations in the world, have a homeless problem?

REAPPROACHING THE LITERATURE

Considering that in America the largest group of poor and homeless people are women and children, reapply Marin's argument about our inner resentment of homeless people. Does his argument become even more shocking?

WRITING ASSIGNMENT

What, in your opinion, is the reason(s) for America's homeless problem?

CHAPTER

2

1 2 3 4 5

Death and Violence

A punishment to some, to some a gift, and to many a favor.
Lucius Annaeus Seneca

To answer brutality with brutality is to admit
one's moral and intellectual bankruptcy, and it
can only start a vicious cycle.
Mahatma Gandhi

Everything that lives dies. There is no escaping this reality. Birds, plants, fish, mammals—large and small—all, at some point, perish. Even though many variations of trees and reptiles may exist for what seems like forever, death is the only truly inevitable cycle for anything that breathes and grows. When it comes to people, Stewart Alsop's explanation seems right on: "A dying man needs to die, as a sleepy man needs to sleep, and there comes a time when it is wrong, as well as useless, to resist." If fortunate, death is about the end of days. If lucky, the race has been run and it is time to embrace the eternal rest. Whimsically speaking, the "internal clock will no longer reset," and "the end of the road is in sight." More succinctly put, we all hope and pray that when life is suspended and there is no more, it was "time."

Yet, as the world evolves and mankind pushes forward into this new millennium, there is an understood axiom that seems to be inescapable: earth's species will continue to reproduce, and human beings will, both indiscriminately and discriminately, try to kill them all. It does not matter if it grows out of the ground or swims in the ocean or soars through the sky or, even more tragically, looks just like themselves—humans have proven that nothing that breathes is sacred from their wrath. Since the dawn of time, man's reasons for violent behavior have ranged from

93

accidental to self-defense to calculated murder. Unfortunately, as time progresses, women have proven that they too are capable of committing aggressively heinous acts, sometimes at the expense of their children.

Understandably, violence as a mode of preservation is not uncommon. Many would argue that these types of acts are necessary for the very survival of our species. As a matter of fact, few would deny that the defense of one's family—one's way of life, for that matter—is a right of the living. Killing for food actually speaks to the essence of perpetuating the species. Yet, we live in a world where cruelties—not those deeds that speak to survival—have become the norm. Everyday, we are bombarded by brutal and often sadistic images: children's games are now based on mayhem; the news, our lens into everyday living, relays the horrendous acts that plague our world; and murder sells books and music more than the idea of love and harmony ever has. This embracement suggests that our social media have become so steeped in the world of violence that we have learned to expect that a destructive hand will one day knock upon our door.

As a result, too often the end comes too soon: the loss of a child; a tragic mishap that ends someone's life before being fully lived; the ominous hand of murder and unexplainable loss. No matter what the causes—be they accident, crime, war, or mental illness—what seems fascinating about death and violence is not only how we die, or who else is involved, but how family and friends—often passersby—are forced to adjust and bereave in the aftermath.

The chosen selections in this chapter can in no way answer the question, "why must we die?" Instead, they ponder how death and violence—so often joined at the hip—are received and accepted, even measured out, across gender, class, and ethnic boundaries.

Suzanne O'Malley

A Cry in the Dark: Andrea Yates

Her crime—drowning her five children in a bathtub—was unthinkable. But was it understandable? How did a clean-living, all-American woman like Andrea Yates snap? Suzanne O'Malley takes a hard look at a disturbing case that's riveted America.

Andrea Pia Yates is barely visible when I enter Judge Belinda Hill's packed Houston courtroom. Then her bright orange jumpsuit—with the words 'County Jail' stenciled across the back—grabs my eye as surely as her unthinkable crime captured the national consciousness. Last June, Yates drowned her five children one by one in the bathtub of her suburban Houston home.

The defense team has entered a plea of not guilty by reason of insanity. But Harris County District Attorney Charles Rosenthal Jr. believes that, after three months of antipsychotic medication and treatment in the jail's psychiatric unit, she is competent to stand trial. He is asking for the death penalty in a state that leads the nation in executions and a county that leads Texas in putting people on death row. The immediate business at this competency hearing, Assistant District Attorney Joe Owmby explains to the jury of 11 women and one man, is whether "Yates is rational today—not was she rational at the time of the crime."

Mention the name Andrea Yates and you'll start an avalanche of questions and opinions. Say she did go crazy: Maybe she drowns one child—but five? That takes conviction; it's not like someone who instantly regrets pulling a trigger. A 7-year-old is strong—how could she drown him? Did she drug him first? Didn't the husband notice his wife was psychotic? Where was her family? Her doctors? Child Protective Services? Where, some would like to know, was God?

After days of observing Andrea, talking to her family, and examining more than 2,000 pages of records from doctors, nurses, therapists and social workers, the answers become clearer. So does the fact that the murders of Noah, John, Paul, Luke and Mary Yates might have been prevented if even one thing had gone right.

"A Cry in the Dark" by Suzanne O'Malley. Copyright © 2002 by Suzanne O'Malley. Originally published in *O, The Oprah Magazine*. Reprinted by permission of the author.

The few who have heard Andrea's 90-minute taped confession call it chilling. Andrea, 37, first drowned 2-year-old Luke, followed by Paul, 3, and John, 5. She carried each child's body to the master bedroom, placed it on the bed, and covered it with a sheet. As she was drowning 6-month-old Mary, Noah, 7, confronted her. "What's wrong with Mary?" he asked and then, realizing what was happening, fled. Andrea chased Noah through the house, dragged him to the tub, and drowned him alongside his dead sister. There is no evidence that any of the children were drugged.

Next, Andrea telephoned the police, saying cryptically, "It's time."

Then she called her husband, Russell (Rusty) Yates, an $80,000-a-year computer expert for the Space Shuttle Vehicle Engineering Office of NASA. "You'd better come home," he recalls her telling him. "Is anyone hurt?" he asked, alarmed by her tone of voice. "Yes," she said. "The children. All of them."

Until her breakdown, Andrea had a seemingly spotless record as a daughter, sister, wife and mother. The youngest of five children and a high school valedictorian, Andrea Kennedy graduated from the University of Texas School of Nursing at Houston with a BSN degree. For eight years, she worked as a nurse at Houston's M.D. Anderson Cancer Center. She was studious and shy, and didn't date seriously until she was 23. One of her first experiences of depression followed a failed relationship when she was 24.

She met Rusty when they were neighbors in an apartment complex. Raised near Nashville, he played football and was active in the Fellowship of Christian Athletes at DuPont Senior High School. His classmates voted him Mr. DuPont—an ideal representative of their school. At Auburn University his gridiron career, like that of many high school athletes, ended. In and outside the courtroom, he is rarely without the thick-bound volume of his wife's medical records. He wears his wedding band.

After their first child, Noah, was born in 1994, Andrea became a stay-at-home mother and quickly had two more sons. She did not use birth control; she and Rusty agreed to accept as many children as God sent their way. When his job required a six-month stint in Florida, the family put most of their belongings in storage and accompanied him, living in a trailer home. Back in Houston, Rusty says, they'd forgotten why they ever needed half the things they'd stored. They moved into a customized Greyhound bus, described by Rusty as a 350-square-foot motor home.

With the birth of her fourth child, Luke, Andrea was—like many new mothers—breast-feeding every three hours and sleeping only a few hours a night. On June 16,1999, she called Rusty at work because she was extremely anxious. When he arrived home, Andrea was shaking and had difficulty speaking. "I need help," she said.

The next day Rusty took his wife and children to the home of Andrea's elderly parents, where he thought "she feels comfortable" and would have support, he later told a social worker. But that afternoon, while the family napped, Andrea took 40 trazodone tablets—a medication with a strong sedative quality—that had been prescribed for her father. That overdose could have killed her, but her mother found her in time to rush her to Houston's Ben Taub General Hospital's emergency room.

Yates was transferred to the psychiatric unit of Methodist Hospital, where James Flack, MD, diagnosed her with "major depressive disorder, single episode, severe." This marked the beginning of a spiral into full-blown psychosis that was never adequately treated.

Andrea was remorseful after trying to kill herself. "I have my family to live for," she told nurse Bridget Fenton, who recorded the conversation in her notes. She worried to another nurse that the trazodone would make it unsafe to continue breast-feeding. But she couldn't discuss her hopelessness. "She was only able to ask if she had done any permanent damage to her body," Flack reported.

June 18

Social worker Norma Tauriac described Andrea as "unwilling" or "not able to identify any recent life stressors." Rusty was "aware and accepting" of his wife's problems and was more comfortable calling her condition postpartum depression than major depression. Tauriac noted Rusty's concern that his wife was "struggling with the concept of salvation." Tauriac also found the Yates's living arrangements objectionable. "As a rule the patient and her husband and the four children live in a converted bus," she wrote in her notes. Tauriac called Texas's Child Protective Services abuse hotline on June 23 to report the family's "living arrangements and the fact that patients husband allows the 3½-year-old son to use a power drill."

Seven days after Tauriac's complaint, Dan Willbur, CPS Supervisor II, wrote to thank her for her concern. However, "because the situation does not appear to involve the occurrence and/or substantial risk of abuse or neglect . . . we plan no further inquiries," he said. The letter stated that her concerns had been forwarded to the Houston Police Department, because "they do appear to have jurisdiction in such matters." Tauriac jotted a note on the bottom of the CPS letter: "Important. Please place in the chart of Andrea Yates." The letter lay dormant in her file until the murders.

June 24

"Interviewed patient again this A.M.," Flack noted on. "I also spoke to the patient's husband at length. They are requesting that she be discharged to the family's care. They have agreed to watch her around the clock and are aware that she is at risk of harming herself again." But Flack later indicated that Yates was being "discharged because of insurance restrictions" after only seven days in the hospital. He also noted that she might be suffering from delusional guilt. Flack raised Andrea's dose of the antidepressant Zoloft to 150 milligrams a day (a fairly routine dosage), referred her to outpatient therapy with Eileen Starbranch, MD, and discharged her.

Three weeks later . . .

Andrea tried to slit her throat. Rusty found her in the bathroom and stopped her. This time she was admitted to Memorial Spring Shadows Glen hospital. She had been taking Zoloft inconsistently and had flushed the Zyprexa prescribed by Starbranch down the toilet when she realized the drug was an antipsychotic.

Asked what had happened, Yates was quoted by hospital psychologist James P. Thompson as saying "I had a fear I would hurt somebody. . . . I thought it better to end my own life and prevent it [from happening]." She described hallucinations: "There was a voice, then an image of the knife. I had a vision in my mind—get a knife, get a knife." She acknowledged obsessive thoughts "over our children and how they'll turn out." She grew nervous about "the kids, trying to train them up right, being so young. [It's a] big responsibility. . . . I don't want to fail." Asked to write a sentence spontaneously, she scribbled, "I love my husband and kids."

It was soon apparent that Andrea's disease was postpartum psychosis, a medical emergency that endangers both the mother's and the child's lives. It affects roughly one in 1,000 mothers and shouldn't be confused with postpartum depression, which affects about one in ten new mothers, or the common "baby blues," which gives up to 75 percent of new mothers mild emotional symptoms.

Psychiatrist Arturo Rios, MD, recommended electroshock therapy for Andrea, but both Yateses were against it. Instead Andrea began receiving an antipsychotic described in medical records as an "injectable cocktail including Haldol and Cogentin," in addition to the antidepressants Effexor and Wellbutrin. Slowly, she began responding.

Rusty visited his wife diligently in the psych ward. Nurses' reports describe him as "supportive and caring." Rusty brought flowers, complained when Andrea hadn't been bathed in three days, and worried over the effects of her medications. "Most of visit, patient was lying on sofa with husband sitting next to her stroking her head," one nurse wrote.

Three weeks into this second hospital stay, she was discharged to the Partial Hospitalization Program (PHP), in which she continued daily hospital care but slept at home. Home was now a three-bedroom house in Clear Lake, Texas.

"I bought the house when Andrea was sick the first time," Rusty said. "She never complained about the bus, I just thought the house might be better for her. I didn't even know if she liked the house until one day she told me, 'I'm glad you bought it.'" Rusty enthusiastically described how he built bunk beds for his sons in one of the bedrooms. Baby Mary would sleep with her parents. The third bedroom was used for storage.

On Andrea's first posthospital visit, Starbranch told her that even though she was feeling better she should "remain compliant with [her] medications." In the past Andrea often took half doses or skipped her medication altogether. Depending on drugs made her "feel like she's weak," she told her PHP therapy group. By the next visit, August 16, 1999, Starbranch reported in disbelief that Andrea "is talking of wanting off medications!" She "wants to get p.g. [pregnant] and have more kids. Wants to homeschool the children." On August 18 Starbranch wrote, "Apparently patient and husband plan to have as many babies as nature will allow! This will surely guarantee future psychotic depression."

"What was the deal with the Greyhound bus?" I asked Rusty of the vehicle that was still parked next to the Yates's house. He looked at me without humor, without anger, without comprehending why I might find a Greyhound bus an unusual place to live. The bus, however, provides a previously unreported link between the Yateses and an itinerant preacher named Michael Warnecki, who sold it—and perhaps a way of life—to the Yateses. He and his family travel the United States in a motor home, proselytizing on college campuses. Warnecki's wife, Rachel, was quoted in the Indiana Daily Student: "Seek Jesus not in the church or religion and not in Christianity and not in the system. The system cannot save you because it is based in Satan."

The Warneckis recommended seeking Jesus in the New Testament—at home. Rachel Warnecki homeschooled her six children so the family could remain together on the road. Andrea, who had corresponded with Rachel and Michael, pleaded with her mother and siblings to renounce

Roman Catholicism. She sent her family copies of a newsletter warning of the banishment to hell of all Catholics. The Yates family did not belong to the Church of Christ, where the children's funeral was held, as is widely assumed. They described themselves as nondenominational Christians.

Rusty conducted family Bible study classes for his wife and children roughly every three nights. By March 2000, Andrea was pregnant again.

Andrea was homeschooling Noah and caring for three toddlers. Rusty babysat one night a week. For a time Andrea continued monthly visits to Starbranch, whose notes of their December 1999 session quote Andrea as saying she is "doing great—baking cookies and getting ready for Xmas." Rusty accompanied Andrea to her January 12, 2000, appointment. Starbranch wrote that Andrea "admits she's off all meds since 11/99. Husband says he didn't like her doing this but [she] seems to be doing okay. [Patient] wants to be off meds unless symptomatic. Husband agrees." There are no records of further visits to Starbranch.

November 30, 2000

Andrea had been off medication for a year when she gave birth to Mary. Three months later Andrea's father, whom she had been nursing through Alzheimer's disease for seven years, died. Her psychosis returned with a vengeance. She held baby Mary in her arms nonstop, terrified to put her down. She stopped eating, drinking, and speaking. Her desperate husband brought her to nearby Devereux Hospital in League City, Texas, telling the admitting physician his wife "could not survive another night at home."

This time her attending psychiatrist, Mohammad A. Saeed, MD, and Patricia Corke, MD, an examining physician, quickly appealed to the probate court of Galveston County, Texas, to commit Andrea to Austin State Hospital. Both doctors checked committal form boxes indicating Andrea was a danger to herself and that she was unable to make a rational treatment choice. One box was left unchecked: "is likely to cause serious harm to others."

In the two-year span of her severe depression, neither her family, her friends, nor the many doctors, nurses, psychologists, and social workers who treated her indicated that Andrea could be a threat to her children's lives. The many Father's Day cards she'd art-directed, the costumes she'd sewn, the Valentine certificates for hugs and kisses she'd given her children, didn't add up to filicide. On the contrary there was an unshakable conviction in people who knew her, slightly or well, that Andrea must have lost her mind by the time she killed her children.

Rather than having Andrea committed to a state hospital, Rusty convinced her to voluntarily sign herself into Devereux. Had Andrea been placed in the state hospital, her stay would not have been limited to health plan maximums. After 12 days at Devereux, she was again discharged into her family's care.

As with her 1999 hospitalization, Andrea was back in a matter of weeks. "The patient was near catatonic. Sat in the chair and did not move at all," Saeed wrote. "At this time we decided to try the Haldol again at the husband's request."

May 22, 2001

(Almost four weeks before the murders.) After ten more days in the hospital and seven days of PHP, Andrea was discharged. Family members say that two weeks before the murders, Saeed took Andrea off Haldol. He testified at her grand jury hearing but has not commented to the press.

"What do you think about Mr. Emotional?" Andrea's brother Brian Kennedy, 45, asked me. He was referring—not kindly—to Rusty, "I couldn't sit there [in court] behind my wife or girlfriend or someone I loved and not touch them, not talk to them." He shook his head. "I remember looking into Andrea's eyes when I saw her two weeks before it happened. It was like looking into the mirror and seeing my own eyes," Brian paused. "I'm the black sheep of the family. When they talk about the brother with mental illness, that's me. I'm bipolar—the first to get arrested, the first to do drugs, you know, the troublemaker."

Another sibling suffers from depression, as did Andrea's father; the family medical history notes some alcohol problems. Brian told me his mother, Jutta Karin Kennedy, 72, lived through World War II in Germany and did not come out unscathed. She is a small, grandmotherly woman with thinning white hair who wears a white crucifix around her neck. Every day of the competency hearing, she sat in the row behind her daughter, using a small burgundy lower-back pillow for support. It's no wonder she looked shell-shocked: In six months' time she had lost her husband, five grandchildren, and a daughter.

By the time Andrea Yates killed her children, she apparently believed Satan was inside her and had irrevocably damaged her children. According to Steve Rubenzer, a Harris County forensic psychologist who interviewed her, she believed that after the drownings, the children would go to paradise. George W. Bush, who she believed was still governor of Texas, would see to her execution. Where she had failed to kill herself, the government would not.

Each of us sees in the Yates case our own issues—the death penalty, children's rights, women's rights, men's rights, rights of the mentally ill, religious rights, or just plain righteousness. What most people forget is that they have never been psychotic. Nothing in the normal—or even neurotic—mind lays the groundwork for organizing reasonable thought around such unreasonable acts.

Over the course of the unusually long—for a Texas competency hearing— 8½-hour deliberation, the jury panel unanimously voted her competent to stand trial. As the jurors, some visibly disturbed, exited the courtroom, Andrea patted her lawyer on the back, automatic, consoling, "What verdict are we hoping for?" she was overheard asking.

March 18, 2002

Andrea Pia Yates, 37, was formally sentenced to life in prison for drowning three of her five children. She will not be eligible for parole for 40 years.

Critical Eye

FOR DISCUSSION

a. The article attempts to determine who failed Andrea Yates. In your opinion, are people merely making excuses for a woman who committed a heinous act?

b. If Yates were a man, do you believe "he" would have been judged, treated, and sentenced the same as "she" was?

c. What is this article seeking to express about gender/motherhood in this country?

REAPPROACHING THE TEXT

Medical doctors have speculated that Andrea Yates was suffering from post-partum psychosis. Over the past thirty years, we have now become familiar with an array of illnesses and syndromes such as obsessive-compulsive disorder, attention deficit disorder, and post-traumatic stress disorder. Are we simply becoming a society that makes excuses for people's horrific or violent behavior, or for their inability to thrive in life? If we are indeed impacted by the events of our lives or the chemical misfirings of our bodies, are we really responsible for anything?

WRITING ASSIGNMENT

Given the fact that not all children are treated well by the parents who conceive them or give birth to them, should there be any governmental involvement in terms of regulating who gives birth and at what age and under what circumstances?

Toni Morrison

From
Paradise

The following excerpt takes place after a group of male townspeople from an all Black town, Ruby, decide to take action against women who live on the outskirts of their community. For these men, the standards of morality and "acceptable blackness" are being compromised because these women are beyond their control and seem to exude some form of influence over the townspeople. For these men, the only answer is the extermination of these five women who are of different ages, backgrounds, and races.

This selection opens the novel and begins after the men have invaded this "female" space—a renovated convent previously used as a missionary school designed to "Americanize" young Native American girls. The reader is privy to the internal monologues of each of the men after they have gunned down the five female inhabitants.

They shoot the white girl first. With the rest they can take their time. No need to hurry out here. They are seventeen miles from a town which has ninety miles between it and any other. Hiding places will be plentiful in the Convent, but there is time and the day has just begun.

They are nine, over twice the number of the women they are obliged to stampede or kill and they have the paraphernalia for either requirement: rope, a palm leaf cross, handcuffs, Mace and sunglasses, along with clean, handsome guns.

They have never been this deep in the Convent. Some of them have parked Chevrolets near its porch to pick up a string of peppers or have gone into the kitchen for a gallon of barbecue sauce; but only a few have seen the halls, the chapel, the schoolroom, the bedrooms. Now they all will. And at last they will see the cellar and expose its filth to the light that is soon to scour the Oklahoma sky. Meantime they are startled by the clothes they are wearing—suddenly aware of being ill-dressed. For at the dawn of a July day how could they have guessed the cold that is inside this place? Their T-shirts, work shirts and dashikis soak up cold like fever. Those who have worn work shoes are unnerved by the thunder of

From *Paradise* by Toni Morrison, copyright © 1997 by Toni Morrison. Used by permission of Alfred A. Knopf, a division of Random House, Inc.

their steps on marble floors; those in Pro-Keds by the silence. Then there is the grandeur. Only the two who are wearing ties seem to belong here and one by one each is reminded that before it was a Convent, this house was an embezzler's folly. A mansion where bisque and rose-tone marble floors segue into teak ones. Isinglass holds yesterday's light and patterns walls that were stripped and whitewashed fifty years ago. The ornate bathroom fixtures, which sickened the nuns, were replaced with good plain spigots, but the princely tubs and sinks, which could not be inexpensively removed, remain coolly corrupt. The embezzler's joy that could be demolished was, particularly in the dining room, which the nuns converted to a schoolroom, where stilled Arapaho girls once sat and learned to forget.

Now armed men search rooms where macramé baskets float next to Flemish candelabra; where Christ and His mother glow in niches trimmed in grapevines. The Sisters of the Sacred Cross chipped away all the nymphs, but curves of their marble hair still strangle grape leaves and tease the fruit. The chill intensifies as the men spread deeper into the mansion, taking their time, looking, listening, alert to the female malice that hides here and the yeast-and-butter smell of rising dough.

One of them, the youngest, looks back, forcing himself to see how the dream he is in might go. The shot woman, lying uncomfortably on marble, waves her fingers at him—or seems to. So his dream is doing okay, except for its color. He has never before dreamed in colors such as these: imperial black sporting a wild swipe of red, then thick, feverish yellow. Like the clothes of an easily had woman. The leading man pauses, raising his left hand to halt the silhouettes behind him. They stop, editing their breath, making friendly adjustments in the grip of rifles and handguns. The leading man turns and gestures the separations: you two over there to the kitchen; two more upstairs; two others into the chapel. He saves himself, his brother and the one who thinks he is dreaming for the cellar.

They part gracefully without words or haste. Earlier, when they blew open the Convent door, the nature of their mission made them giddy. But the target, after all, is detritus: throwaway people that sometimes blow back into the room after being swept out the door. So the venom is manageable now. Shooting the first woman (the white one) has clarified it like butter: the pure oil of hatred on top, its hardness stabilized below.

Outside, the mist is waist high. It will turn silver soon and make grass rainbows low enough for children's play before the sun burns it off, exposing acres of bluestem and maybe witch tracks as well.

The kitchen is bigger than the house in which either man was born. The ceiling barn-rafter high. More shelving than Ace's Grocery Store. The table is fourteen feet long if an inch, and it's easy to tell that the women they are hunting have been taken by surprise. At one end a full pitcher of milk stands near four bowls of shredded wheat. At the other end vegetable chopping has been interrupted: scallions piled like a handful of green confetti nestles brilliant disks of carrot, and the potatoes, peeled and whole, are bone white, wet and crisp. Stock simmers on the stove. It is restaurant size with eight burners and on a shelf beneath the great steel hood a dozen loaves of bread swell. A stool is overturned. There are no windows.

One man signals the other to open the pantry while he goes to the back door. It is closed but unlocked. Peering out he sees an old hen, her puffed and bloody hind parts cherished, he supposes, for delivering freaks— double, triple yolks in outsize and misshapen shells. Soft stuttering comes from the coop beyond; fryers padding confidently into the yard's mist disappear, reappear and disappear again, each flat eye indifferent to anything but breakfast. No footprints disturb the mud around the stone steps. This man closes the door and joins his partner at the pantry. Together they scan dusty mason jars and what is left of last year's canning: tomatoes, green beans, peaches. Slack, they think. August just around the corner and these women have not even sorted, let alone washed, the jars.

He turns the fire off under the stockpot. His mother bathed him in a pot no bigger than that. A luxury in the sod house where she was born. The house he lives in is big, comfortable, and this town is resplendent compared to his birthplace, which had gone from feet to belly in fifty years. From Haven, a dreamtown in Oklahoma Territory, to Haven, a ghosttown in Oklahoma State. Freedmen who stood tall in 1889 dropped to their knees in 1934 and were stomach-crawling by 1948. That is why they are here in this Convent. To make sure it never happens again. That nothing inside or out rots the one all-black town worth the pain. All the others he knew about or heard tell of knuckled to or merged with white towns; otherwise, like Haven, they had shriveled into tracery: foundation outlines marked by the way grass grew there, wallpaper turned negative behind missing windowpanes, schoolhouse floors moved aside by elder trees growing toward the bell housing. One thousand citizens in 1905 becoming five hundred by 1934. Then two hundred, then eighty as cotton collapsed or railroad companies laid their tracks elsewhere. Subsistence farming, once the only bounty a large family needed, became just scrap farming as each married son got his bit, which had to be broken up into more pieces for his children, until finally the owners of the bits and pieces who had not walked off in disgust welcomed any offer from a white speculator, so eager were they to get away and try someplace else. A big city this time, or a small townthat was already built.

But he and the others, veterans all, had a different idea. Loving what Haven had been—the idea of it and its reach—they carried that devotion, gentling and nursing it from Bataan to Guam, from Iwo Jima to Stuttgart, and they made up their minds to do it again. He touched the stove hood admiring its construction and power. It was the same length as the brick oven that once sat in the middle of his hometown. When they got back to the States, they took it apart, carrying the bricks, the hearthstone and its iron plate two hundred and forty miles west—far far from the old Creek Nation which once upon a time a witty government called "unassigned land." He remembers the ceremony they'd had when the Oven's iron lip was recemented into place and its worn letters polished for all to see. He himself had helped clean off sixty-two years of carbon and animal fat so the words shone as brightly as they did in 1890 when they were new. And if it hurt—pulling asunder what their grandfathers had put together—it was nothing compared to what they had endured and what they might become if they did not begin anew. As new fathers, who had fought the world, they could not (would not) be less than the Old Fathers who had outfoxed it; who had not let danger or natural evil keep them from cutting Haven out of mud and who knew enough to seal their triumph with that priority. An Oven. Round as a head, deep as desire. Living in or near their wagons, boiling meal in the open, cutting sod and mesquite for shelter, the Old Fathers did that first: put most of their strength into constructing the huge, flawlessly designed Oven that both nourished them and monumentalized what they had done. When it was finished—each pale brick perfectly pitched; the chimney wide, lofty; the pegs and grill secure; the draft pulling steadily from the tail hole; the fire door plumb—then the ironmonger did his work. From barrel staves and busted axles, from kettles and bent nails, he fashioned an iron plate five feet by two and set it at the base of the Oven's mouth. It is still not clear where the words came from. Something he heard, invented, or something whispered to him while he slept curled over his tools in a wagon bed. His name was Morgan and who knew if he invented or stole the half-dozen or so words he forged. Words that seemed at first to bless them; later to confound them; finally to announce that they had lost.

The man eyes the kitchen sink. He moves to the long table and lifts the pitcher of milk. He sniffs it first and then, the pistol in his right hand, he uses his left to raise the pitcher to his mouth, taking such long, mea sured swallows the milk is half gone by the time he smells the wintergreen.

On the floor above two men walk the hall and examine the four bedrooms, each with a name card taped on its door. The first name, written in lipstick, is Seneca. The next, Divine, is inked in capital letters. They exchange knowing looks when they learn that each woman sleeps not in a bed, like normal people, but in a hammock. Other than that, and except for a narrow desk or an end table, there is no additional furniture. No clothes in the closets, of course, since the women wore no-fit dirty dresses and nothing you could honestly call shoes. But there are strange things nailed or taped to the walls or propped in a corner. A 1968 calendar, large X's marking various dates (April 4, July 19): a letter written in blood so smeary its satanic message cannot be deciphered; an astrology chart; a fedora tilted on the plastic neck of a female torso, and, in a place that once housed Christians—well. Catholics anyway—not a cross of Jesus anywhere. But what alarms the two men most is the series of infant booties and shoes ribboned to a cord hanging from a crib in the last bedroom they enter. A teething ring, cracked and stiff, dangles among the tiny shoes. Signaling with his eyes, one man directs his partner to four more bedrooms on the opposite side of the hall. He himself moves closer to the bouquet of baby shoes. Looking for what? More evidence? He isn't sure. Blood? A little toe, maybe, left in a white calfskin shoe? He slides the safety on his gun and joins the search across the hall. -

These rooms are normal. Messy—the floor in one of them is covered with food-encrusted dishes, dirty cups, its bed invisible under a hill of clothes; another room sports two rocking chairs full of dolls; a third the debris and smell of a heavy drinker—but normal at least.

His saliva is bitter and although he knows this place is diseased, he is startled by the whip of pity flicking in his chest. What, he wonders, could do this to women? How can their plain brains think up such things: revolting sex, deceit and the sly torture of children? Out here in wide-open space tucked away in a mansion—no one to bother or insult them— they managed to call into question the value of almost every woman he knew. The winter coat money for which his father saved in secret for two harvests; the light in his mother's eyes when she stroked its seal collar. The surprise party he and his brothers threw for a sister's sixteenth birthday. Yet here, not twenty miles away from a quiet, orderly community, there were women like none he knew or ever heard tell of. In this place of all places. Unique and isolated, his was a town justifiably pleased with itself. It neither had nor needed a jail. No criminals had ever come from his town. And the one or two people who acted up, humiliated their families or threatened the town's view of itself were taken good care of. Certainly there wasn't a slack or sloven woman anywhere in town and the reasons, he thought, were clear. From the beginning its people were free and protected. A sleepless woman could always rise from her bed, wrap a shawl around her shoulders and sit on the steps in the moonlight. And if she felt like it she could walk out the yard and on down the road. No lamp and no fear. A hiss-crackle from the side of the road would never scare her because whatever it was that made the sound, it wasn't something creeping up on her. Nothing for ninety miles around thought she was prey. She could stroll as slowly as she liked, think of food preparations, war, of family things, or lift her eyes to stars and think of nothing at all. Lampless and without fear she could make her way. And if a light shone from a house up a ways and the cry of a colicky baby caught her attention, she might step over to the house and call out softly to the woman inside trying to soothe the baby. The two of them might take turns massaging the infant stomach, rocking, or trying to get a little soda water down. When the baby quieted they could sit together for a spell, gossiping, chuckling low so as not to wake anybody else.

The woman could decide to go back to her own house then, refreshed and ready to sleep, or she might keep her direction and walk further down the road, past other houses, past the three churches, past the feedlot. On out, beyond the limits of town, because nothing at the edge thought she was prey.

At each end of the hall is a bathroom. As each man enters one, neither is working his jaws because both believe they are prepared for anything. In one bathroom, the biggest, the taps are too small and dowdy for the wide sink. The bathtub rests on the backs of four mermaids—their tails split wide for the tub's security, their breasts arched for stability. The tile underfoot is bottle green. A Modess box is on the toilet tank and a bucket of soiled things stands nearby. There is no toilet paper. Only one mirror has not been covered with chalky paint and that one the man ignores. He does not want to see himself stalking females or their liquid. With relief he backs out and closes the door. With relief he lets his handgun point down.

Critical Eye

FOR DISCUSSION

a. What distinctions does the narrator make between what makes a woman good or bad?

b. It is clear that the men who enter the convent are in conflict with these women and mean to do them harm. Why does violence seem to be the "best" way to handle conflict rather than discussion?

REAPPROACHING THE TEXT

The women in the text are seen as "bad" women/girls. Feminist critic Naomi Wolf suggests that there is, in fact, no such thing as a "bad girl" and, moreover, we have created the bad girl persona in order to have someone to mistreat. Taking this idea into consideration, determine whether or not these women are indeed "bad" or are simply living outside of the stereotypical female archetype.

WRITING TOPIC

As human beings, we often deal harshly with those we feel are encroaching upon our territory or are not following our social/cultural mores. Why is this?

Guy de Maupassant

Mother Savage

I

It had been fifteen years since I had visited Virelogne. One autumn I
returned to do some hunting and stayed with my friend Serval, who had
finally rebuilt the château that the Prussians had destroyed.

I was madly in love with the area. It is one of those delightful corners
of the world that possess a sensual appeal for the eyes. This is almost a
physical kind of love. Those of us who are easily seduced by landscapes
retain fond memories of certain springs, certain woods, certain streams,
and certain hills which have become familiar to us and which can move
our hearts like happy events. Sometimes our daydreams return to a
wooded spot, or a riverbank, or an orchard bursting into blossom, seen
only once on a lovely day but held in our hearts like images of women
strolling the streets on a spring morning with fresh, clean faces, stirring
body and soul with unrequited desire, with the unforgettable sensation of
fleeting joy.

At Virelogne, I loved the whole countryside, dotted with little woods and
traversed by streams that course though the soil like veins carrying blood
to the earth. We fished for crawfish, for trout and eels. Such blessed
happiness! There were spots to swim, and we could flush snipe from the
tall weeds that grew along the banks of these narrow ribbons of water.

I walked along, lightly as a goat, watching my two dogs range in front of
me. Serval, a hundred meters to my right, beat through a field of high
grass. As I came around the bushes that mark the border of the Saudres
Forest, I saw a thatched cottage in ruins.

Suddenly I recalled that I had seen it before, the last time in 1869,
well kept up, covered with vines, and with a few chickens around the
front door. What can be sadder than a dead house with its skeleton still
standing, ruined and sinister?

"Mother Savage" by Guy de Maupassant, trans. by Lafcadio Hearn, edited and revised by R. S.
Gwynn from *Fiction: A Pocket Anthology, 4th ed.* by R. S. Gwynn. Copyright © 2005 by Pearson
Education. Reprinted by permission.

I also recalled that the good woman who lived there had asked me in, one day when I was bone-tired, for a glass of wine, and that Serval had later told me the family history. The father, an old poacher, had been shot by the police. The son, whom I had seen before, was a tall, wiry fellow who also had a reputation as a fierce killer of game. They were called the Savages.

Was this their name or nickname?

I called out to Serval. He walked over to me with his long, ambling stride.

I asked him:

"What's become of the people who lived here?"

And he told me this story.

II

When the war broke out, Mother Savage's son, who was then thirty-three years old, volunteered, leaving his mother all alone. However, no one felt sorry for the old woman because everybody knew that she had money.

So she lived by herself in her isolated cottage, far from the village at the edge of the forest. But she was not a bit afraid, being made of the same stuff as the men of the countryside—a hardy old woman, tall and gaunt, who seldom laughed and whom nobody dared to cross. The women of the countryside do not laugh much. That's the men's business! The souls of these women are melancholy and narrow, for their lives are dismal and rarely brightened by an hour of joy. The peasant husbands or sons enjoy a little noisy gaiety in taverns, but their wives or mothers remain serious, with perpetually severe expressions. The muscles of their faces have never learned the movements of laughter.

Mother Savage continued to live as she always had in her cottage, which was soon covered with snow. Once a week she used to come to the village to buy bread and meat, after which she would return home. As there was quite a bit of talk about wolves, she never went out without a gun slung on her shoulder, her son's rifle, a rusty weapon whose stock was quite worn from the hands that had rubbed against it; she made a strange sight, that tall old woman, a little stooped by age, walking with slow steps through the snow with the barrel of the gun sticking up behind the black scarf which covered her head and concealed the white hair that no one had ever seen.

One day the Prussians came. They were billeted with the people of the area, according to the wealth and resources of each family. The old woman had to take four of them because she was known to have money.

These were four big fellows with fair skin, blond beards, and blue eyes who had not grown thin in spite of all the wear and tear they had endured; they seemed to be good boys, even though they were in a conquered country. Finding themselves alone with the old woman, they took pains to show her all possible consideration and did everything they could to save her trouble or expense. You could see them every morning, all four of them, washing up at the well in their shirt sleeves, pouring great quantities of cold water over that fair, rosy Northern skin of theirs even on the days when it was snowing most heavily—while Mother Savage came and went, getting their soup ready. Later they could be seen cleaning up the kitchen, washing windows, chopping wood, peeling potatoes, washing linen—in short, doing all the chores like four good boys working for their own mother.

But the old woman was always thinking of her own son—her tall, gaunt boy with his hooked nose and brown eyes and thick mustache that seemed to cover his upper lip like a pelt of black fur. And every day she used to ask the four soldiers quartered in her home, "Do you know where that French regiment is, the 23rd of the line? My son is in it."

They would reply, "No, not know, not nothing." And sensing her pain and fear, they, who had mothers far away themselves, showed her a thousand little courtesies. She liked them well enough, too, those four enemies of hers; for country people do not as a rule feel patriotic hatred—those feelings are reserved for the upper classes. The humble folk—those who pay the most because they are poor and are always being weighed down with new burdens, those who are slaughtered wholesale, those who make up the real cannon fodder because there are so many of them, those who, to tell the truth, suffer most hideously from the miserable atrocities of war because they are the most vulnerable and the least powerful—such people do not understand war fever or the fine points of military honor or, even less, those so-called political necessities which exhaust two nations in six months, both victor and vanquished alike.

Speaking of Mother Savage's Germans, folks in the area would say, "Well, those four landed in a safe enough spot."

One morning while Mother Savage was at home alone, she caught sight of a man far off across the fields, hurrying towards her gate. He soon came near enough for her to recognize him: it was the rural postman. He handed her a sheet of folded paper, and she took her glasses, which she always wore when sewing, out of their case, and read:

> *Madam Savage,*
>   *This letter has a sad story to tell you. Your boy Victor was killed yesterday by a cannonball, which cut him practically in two. I was right there when it*

happened, for we stood next to each other in line and he was always talking to me about you so that I could let you know at once if he had any bad luck.

I took his watch out of his pocket to bring to you when the war is over.

Cordially,

Césaire Rivot, Private Second Class in the

Twenty-third Regiment of the Line

The letter was dated three weeks earlier.

She did not cry. She remained motionless, so overwhelmed, so stupefied by the blow that she did not immediately feel anything. She thought, "There's Victor, and now he's been killed." Then, little by little, tears slowly rose in her eyes, and sorrow invaded her heart. Thoughts came to her, one after the other—frightful, torturing ones. She would never kiss him again, her only child, her big, tall boy—never! The police had killed his father, and now the Prussians had killed the son . . . he had been cut in two by a cannonball. And it seemed to her she could see it all, the whole horrible thing: his head falling with his eyes wide open, his teeth still gnawing the corners of his thick mustache the way he used to do when he was angry.

What had they done afterward with his body? Couldn't they have brought her son back the same way they brought her husband back to her, with a bullet hole in the middle of his forehead?

But then she heard the sound of loud voices. It was the Prussians returning from the village. Quickly she hid the letter in her pocket and met them very calmly with her usual expression, for she had managed to wipe her eyes.

All four of them were laughing, quite delighted that they had been able to bring home a fine rabbit—doubtless stolen—and they made signs to the old woman that they were all going to have something really good to eat.

She set to work at once to prepare their dinner, but when the time came to kill the rabbit she did not have the heart to do it. Yet surely this wasn't the first rabbit she had ever been given to kill! One of the soldiers knocked it out by striking it behind the ears with his hand. Once it was dead she pulled the red body out of its skin, but the sight of the blood she was handling, which covered her fingers—the warm blood that she could feel cooling and coagulating—made her tremble from head to toe; all the while she kept seeing her tall son, cut in two and all red just like the body of the still quivering animal.

She sat down at the table with her Prussians, but she could not eat, not so much as a mouthful. They devoured the rabbit without paying any attention to her. Meanwhile she watched them from the corners of her eyes, not speaking—turning an idea over and over in her head, but with such an impassive face that none of them noticed anything unusual.

All of a sudden she said, "I don't even know your names, and we've been together for a whole month." They understood, with some difficulty, what she wanted and told her their names. But that was not enough; she made them write them down on a piece of paper along with the addresses of their families, and, placing her reading glasses on her big nose, she looked over the foreign writing; then she folded up the paper and put it into her pocket, next to the letter which had told her about the death of her son.

When the meal was over she said to them:

"Now I'm going to do something for you."

And she started carrying straw up into the loft where they slept.

They thought this was rather strange, but when she explained to them that it would keep them warmer they helped her. They stacked the bales all the way up to the thatched ceiling and made themselves a sort of large room with four walls of forage, warm and fragrant, where they could sleep peacefully.

At supper one of them became worried that Mother Savage still had not eaten anything. She told him that she had stomach cramps. Then she lit a good fire to warm herself, and the four Germans climbed up into their loft on the ladder they used every evening.

As soon as they had closed the trapdoor, the old woman took away the ladder, and, going outside without a sound, she began to collect straw and filled her kitchen with it. She walked barefoot through the snow—so softly that no one could hear her. From time to time she heard the loud and fitful snoring of the four sleeping soldiers.

When she decided that her preparations were complete, she thrust one of the bundles of straw into the fire, then flung the burning handful on top of the others and went outside to watch.

In several seconds a fierce glare lit the inside of the cottage; then the whole thing became a terrible furnace, a gigantic oven whose violent light blazed through the single narrow window and sent a bright ray reflecting over the snow.

Loud cries rang out from the upper part of the house. Then they were followed by a clamor of human screams full of agony and terror. Then, the trapdoor having been lifted, a storm of flame roared up into the loft, burnt through the roof of straw, rose up to the heavens like a vast bonfire, and the whole cottage went up in flames.

Nothing could now be heard but the crackling of the fire, the crumbling of the walls, the falling of the beams. The last fragments of the roof fell in, and the red-hot shell of the dwelling flung a huge shower of sparks skyward through clouds of thick smoke.

The snow-covered fields, lit up by the fire, shone like a sheet of silver tinged with crimson.

Far away, a bell began to ring.

Old Mother Savage stood at attention in front of the ruins of her home, armed with a gun, her dead son's rifle, to make sure that none of them could escape.

When she saw that it was all over, she threw the weapon into the fire. A single shot rang out.

People came running to the scene—the neighbors, the Prussian soldiers.

They found the old woman sitting on a tree stump, calm and satisfied.

A German officer, who spoke French like a son of France, asked her:

"Where are your soldiers?"

She stretched out her skinny arm towards the smoldering mass of ruins where the fire was dying down at last and answered in a strong voice:

"There! Inside!"

Everyone gathered around her. The Prussian asked:

"How did the fire start?"

She answered:

"I started it."

They could not believe her, and they thought that the disaster had driven her mad. Then, when everyone had moved closer to listen to her, she told the whole story from beginning to end—from the arrival of the letter down to the final screams of the burning men inside her house. She did not leave out a single detail of what she had felt and what she had done.

When she finished, she took two pieces of paper out of her pocket and, so she could tell one from the other by the last light of the fire, adjusted her glasses and announced, holding up one piece of paper, "This one is Victor's death." Holding up the other, she added, nodding her head towards the still-red ruins, "This one has their names on it so you can write home about them." She calmly handed the white sheet to the officer, who was now holding her by the shoulders, and she continued:

"You can write them how this all happened, and you can tell their parents that I was the one who did it—I, Victoire Simon, The Savage! Never forget it."

The officer screamed some orders in German. They seized her and pushed her up against the still-warm walls of her house. Then a dozen men lined up in front of her, twenty meters away. She never blinked an eye. She knew what was coming, and she waited.

An order rang out, followed by a loud volley. One shot echoed all by itself after the others.

The old woman did not fall. She sank straight down as though her legs had been cut away from under her.

The Prussian officer approached to look. She had been cut almost in two, and her stiffened fingers still clutched the letter, bathed in blood.

III

My friend Serval added, "In reprisal, the Germans destroyed the local château, which I owned."

For my own part, I thought about the mothers of those four poor boys who had burned inside, and of the terrible heroism of that other mother, shot dead against that wall.

And I picked up a little stone, which still bore the scorch marks of the fire.

—1884

Critical Eye

FOR DISCUSSION

a. Does any parent have the right to seek revenge against those who they perceive have caused harm to their child?

b. Does an act of revenge actually remedy a problem?

REAPPROACHING THE TEXT

Examine this story alongside the short story "War," written by Luigi Pirandello. Why is the mother in this case unable to reconcile her grief the way the parents in "War" are?

WRITING ASSIGNMENT

Our entire legal system exists not only to determine guilt or innocence, but also to punish those it deems guilty of a crime. How is it any different than the mother who acts as judge, jury, and executioner?

Irene Zabytko

Home Soil

I watch my son crack his knuckles, oblivious to the somber sounds of the Old Slavonic hymns the choir behind us is singing.

We are in the church where Bohdan, my son, was baptized nineteen years ago. It is Sunday. The pungent smell of frankincense permeates the darkened atmosphere of this cathedral. Soft sun rays illuminate the stained-glass windows. I sit near the one that shows Jesus on the cross looking down on some unidentifiable Apostles who are kneeling beneath His nailed feet. In the background, a tiny desperate Judas swings from a rope, the thirty pieces of silver thrown on the ground.

There is plenty of room in my pew, but my son chooses not to sit with me. I see him staring at the round carapace of a ceiling, stoic icons staring directly back at him. For the remainder of the Mass, he lightly drums his nervous fingers on top of the cover of *My Divine Friend,* the Americanized prayer book of the Ukrainian service. He took bongo lessons before he graduated high school, and learned the basic rolls from off a record, "Let's Swing with Bongos." I think it was supposed to make him popular with the girls at parties. I also think he joined the army because he wanted the virile image men in uniforms have that the bongos never delivered. When he returned from Nam, he mentioned after one of our many conversational silences that he lost the bongos, and the record is cracked, with the pieces buried somewhere deep inside the duffel bag he still hasn't unpacked.

Bohdan, my son, who calls himself Bob, has been back for three weeks. He looks so "American" in his green tailored uniform: his spit-shined vinyl dress shoes tap against the red-cushioned kneelers. It was his idea to go to church with me. He has not been anywhere since he came home. He won't even visit my garden.

Luba, my daughter, warned me he would be moody. She works for the Voice of America and saw him when he landed from Nam in San Francisco, "Just don't worry *tato,*"° she said to me on the telephone. "He's acting weird. Culture shock."

"Home Soil" by Irene Zabytko from *The Perimeter of Light* edited by Vivian Vie Balfour. Copyright © 1992 New Rivers Press. Reprinted by permission. All rights reserved.

tato: "Father" or "Dad."

"Explain what you mean."

"Just, you know, strange." For a disc jockey, and a bilingual one at that, she is so inarticulate. She plays American jazz and tapes concerts for broadcasts for her anonymous compatriots in Ukraine. That's what she was doing when she was in San Francisco, taping some jazz concert. Pure American music for the huddled gold-toothed youth who risk their *komsomol* privileges and maybe their lives listening to these clandestine broadcasts and to my daughter's sweet voice. She will never be able to visit our relatives back there because American security won't allow it, and she would lose her job. But that doesn't matter. After my wife died, I have not bothered to keep up with anyone there, and I don't care if they have forgotten all about me. It's just as well.

I noticed how much my son resembled my wife when I first saw him again at the airport. He was alone, near the baggage claim ramp. He was taller than ever, and his golden hair was bleached white from the jungle sun. He inherited his mother's high cheekbones, but he lost his baby fat, causing his cheeks to jut out from his lean face as sharp as the arrowheads he used to scavenge for when he was a kid.

We hugged briefly. I felt his medals pinch through my thin shirt "You look good, son," I lied. I avoided his eyes and concentrated on a pin shaped like an open parachute that he wore over his heart.

"Hi, *tato*," he murmured. We spoke briefly about his flight home from San Francisco, how he'd seen Luba. We stood apart, unlike the other soldiers with their families who were hugging and crying on each other's shoulders in a euphoric delirium.

He grabbed his duffle bag from the revolving ramp and I walked behind him to see if he limped or showed any signs of pain. He showed nothing.

"Want to drive?" I asked, handing him the keys to my new Plymouth.

"Nah," he said. He looked around at the cars crowding the parking lot, and I thought he seemed afraid. "I don't remember how the streets go anymore."

An usher in his best borscht-red polyester suit waits for me to drop some money into the basket. It is old Pan° Medved, toothless except for the prominent gold ones he flashes at me as he pokes me with his basket.

"*Nu*, give," he whispers hoarsely, but loud enough for a well-dressed woman with lacquered hair who sits in front of me to turn around and stare in mute accusation.

Pan: a term of respect for adult males, the equivalent of Mr.

I take out the gray and white snakeskin wallet Bohdan brought back for me, and transfer out a ten dollar bill. I want the woman to see it before it disappears into the basket. She smiles at me and nods.

Women always smile at me like that. Especially after they see my money and find out that I own a restaurant in the neighborhood. None of the Ukies° go there; they don't eat fries and burgers much. But the "jackees"—the Americans—do when they're sick of eating in the cafeteria at the plastics factory. My English is pretty good for a D.P., and no one has threatened to bomb my business because they accuse me of being a no-good bohunk commie. Not yet anyway.

But the women are always impressed. I usually end up with the emigrés—some of them Ukrainians. The Polish women are the greediest for gawdy trinkets and for a man to give them money so that they can return to their husbands and children in Warsaw. I like them the best anyway because they laugh more than the other women I see, and they know how to have a good time.

Bohdan knows nothing about my lecherous life. I told the women to stay clear after my son arrived. He is so lost with women. I think he was a virgin when he joined the army, but I'm sure he isn't now. I can't ask him.

After mass ends, I lose Bohdan in the tight clusters of people leaving their pews and genuflecting toward the iconostasis. He waits for me by the holy water font. It looks like a regular porcelain water fountain but without a spout. There is a sponge in the basin that is moistened with the holy water blessed by the priests here. Bohdan stands towering over the font, dabs his fingers into the sponge, but doesn't cross himself the way he was taught to do as a boy.

"What's the matter?" I ask in English. I hope he will talk to me if I speak to him in his language.

But Bohdan ignores me and watches an elderly woman gingerly entering the door of the confessional. "What she got to say? Why is she going in there?"

"Everyone has sins."

"Yeah, but who forgives?"

"God forgives," I say. I regret it because it makes me feel like a hypocrite whenever I parrot words I still find difficult to believe.

We walk together in the neighborhood; graffiti visible in the alley-ways despite the well-trimmed lawns with flowers and "bathtub" statues of the

---

Ukies: Ukrainian Americans.

Blessed Mary smiling benevolently at us as we pass by the small bungalows. I could afford to move out of here, out of Chicago and into some nearby cushy suburb, Skokie or something. But what for? Some smart Jewish lawyer or doctor would be my next door neighbor and find out that I'm a Ukie and complain to me about how his grandmother was raped by Petliura.° Iheard it before. Anyway, I like where I am. I bought a three-flat apartment building after my wife died and I live in one of the apartments rent-free. I can walk to my business, and see the past—old women in babushkas sweeping the sidewalks in front of their cherished gardens; men in Italian-made venetian-slat sandals and woolen socks rushing to a chess match at the Soyuiez, a local meeting place where the D.P.s sit for hours rehashing the war over beers and chess.

Bohdan walks like a soldier. Not exactly a march, but stiff gait that a good posture in a rigid uniform demands. He looks masculine, but tired and worn. Two pimples are sprouting above his lip where a faint moustache is starting.

"Want a cigarette?" I ask. Soldiers like to smoke. During the forties, I smoked that horrible cheap tobacco, *mahorka.* I watch my son puff heavily on the cigarette I've given him, with his eyes partially closed, delicately cupping his hands to protect it from the wind. In my life, I have seen so many soldiers in that exact pose; they all look the same. When their faces are contorted from sucking the cigarette, there is an unmistakable shadow of vulnerability and fear of living. That gesture and stance are more eloquent than the blood and guts war stories men spew over their beers.

Pan Medved, the battered gold-toothed relic in the church, has that look. Pan Holewski, one of my tenants, has it too. I would have known it even if he never openly displayed his old underground soldier's cap that sits on a bookshelf in the living room between small Ukrainian and American flags. I see it every time I collect the rent.

I wish Bohdan could tell me what happened to him in Vietnam. What did he do? What was done to him? Maybe now isn't the time to tell me. He may never tell me. I never told anyone either.

I was exactly his age when I became a soldier. At nineteen, I was a student at the university in L'vov, which the Poles occupied. I was going to be a poet, to study poetry and write it, but the war broke out, and my family could not live on the romantic epics I tried to publish, so I was paid very well by the Nazis to write propaganda pamphlets "Freedom for Ukrainians"

Petliura: Simeon Petliura (1879–1926), an anti-Bolshevik Ukrainian leader who was accused of responsibility for Jewish pogroms during World War I. When his forces were defeated by the Russians he went into exile in Paris where he was ultimately assassinated by a Jewish nationalist.

I wrote"Freedom for our people. Fight the Poles and Russians alongside our German brothers" and other such dreck. I even wrote light verse that glorified Hitler as the protector of the free Ukrainian nation that the Germans promised us. My writing was as naïve as my political ideas.

My new career began in a butcher shop, commandeered after the Polish owner was arrested and shot. I set my battered Underwood typewriter atop an oily wooden table where crescents of chicken feathers still clung between the cracks. Meat hooks that once held huge sides of pork hung naked in a back room, and creaked ominously like a deserted gallows whenever anyone slammed the frontdoor. Every shred of meat had been stolen by looters after the Germans came into the city. Even the little bell that shopkeepers kept at the entrance was taken. But I was very comfortable in my surroundings. I thought only about how I was to play a part in a historical destiny that my valiant words would help bring about. That delusion lasted only about a week or so until three burly Nazis came in. "*Schnell!*" they said to me, pushing me out of my chair and pointing to the windows where I saw crowds chaotically swarming about. Before I could question the soldiers, one of them shoved a gun into my hands and pushed me out into the streets. I felt so bewildered until the moment I pointed my rifle at a man who was about—I thought—to hit me with a club of some sort. Suddenly, I felt such an intense charge of power, more so than I had ever felt writing some of my best poems. I was no longer dealing with abstract words and ideas for a mythological cause; I was responsible for life and death.

I enjoyed that power, until it seeped into my veins and poisoned my soul. It was only an instant, a brief interlude, a matter of hours until that transformation occurred. I still replay that scene in my mind almost forty years after it happened, no matter what I am doing, or who I am with.

I think she was a village girl. Probably a Jew, because on that particular day, the Jews were the ones chosen to be rounded up and sent away in cattle cars. Her hair was golden red, short and wavy as was the style, and her neck was awash in freckles. It was a crowded station in the center of the town, not far from the butcher shop. There were Germans shouting and women crying and church bells ringing. I stood with that German regulation rifle I hardly knew how to handle, frozen because I was too lightheaded and excited. I too began to yell at people and held the rifle against my chest, and I was very much aware of how everyone responded to my authority.

Then, this girl appeared in my direct line of vision. Her back was straight, her shoulders tensed; she stopped in the middle of all the chaos. Simply stopped. I ran up and pushed her. I pushed her hard, she almost fell. I kept pushing her, feeling the thin material of her cheap wool jacket against my chapped eager hand; her thin muscles forced forward by my shoves. Once, twice, until she toppled into the open door of a train and fell toward a heap of other people moving deeper into the tiny confines of the stinking cattle car. She never turned around.

I should have shot her. I should have spared her from whatever she had to go through. I doubt she survived. I should have tried to find out what her name was, so I could track down her relatives and confess to them. At least in that way, they could have spat at me in justice and I would have finally received the absolution I will probably never find in this life.

• • •

I don't die. Instead, I go to the garden. It is Sunday evening. I am weeding the crop of beets and cabbages I planted in the watch in my backyard. The sun is lower, a breeze kicks up around me, but my forehead sweats. I breathe in the thick deep earth smells as the dirt crumbles and rotates against the blade of my hoe. I should destroy the honeysuckle vine that is slowly choking my plants, but the scent is so sweet, and its intoxicating perfume reminds me of a woman's gentleness.

I hoe for a while, but not for long, because out of the corner of my eye, I see Bohdan sitting on the grass tearing the firm green blades with his clenched hands. He is still wearing his uniform, all except the jacket, tie, and cap. He sits with his legs apart, his head down, ignoring the black flies that nip at his ears.

I wipe my face with a bright red bandana, which I brought with me to tie up the stalks of my drooping sunflowers. "Bohdan," I say to my son. "Why don't we go into the house and have a beer. I can finish this another time." I look at the orange sun. "It's humid and there's too many flies— means rain will be coming."

My son is quietly crying to himself.

"*Tato*, I didn't know anything," he cries out. "You know, I just wanted to jump out from planes with my parachute. I just wanted to fly . . ."

"I should have stopped you," I say more to myself than to him. Bohdan lets me stroke the thin spikes of his army regulation crew-cut which is soft and warm and I am afraid of how easily my hand can crush his skull.

I rock him in my arms the way I saw his mother embrace him when he was afraid to sleep alone.

There is not much more I can do right now except to hold him. I will hold him until he pulls away.

Critical Eye

FOR DISCUSSION

a. It is one thing to survive a life-or-death situation; it is quite another to hold the life and death of another human being in your hands. According to this story, which is worse? Is there really any difference at all?

b. How is it that experiencing something as overwhelming as war can cause someone to question his or her faith?

REAPPROACHING THE TEXT

In reading "What I Saw at the Abortion," we find that the doctor questions his former beliefs about abortion after being a witness to one. For him, he senses an ending of life. Is what the doctor feels anything like what Zabytoko's main character experiences knowing that he has sentenced a little girl to a concentration camp—to an almost certain death? And, is his inner turmoil even worse because he wishes he had shot her instead?

WRITING ASSIGNMENT

Once an adult child experiences a traumatic event that irrevocably changes his or her life, is there anything that a parent can do to make the child feel safe again?

Américo Paredes

The Hammon and the Beans

Once we lived in one of my grandfather's houses near Fort Jones.° It was just a block from the parade grounds, a big frame house painted a dirty yellow. My mother hated it, especially because of the pigeons that cooed all day about the eaves. They had fleas, she said. But it was a quiet neighborhood at least, too far from the center of town for automobiles and too near for musical, night-roaming drunks.

At this time Jonesville-on-the-Grande was not the thriving little city that it is today. We told off our days by the routine on the post. At six sharp the flag was raised on the parade grounds to the cackling of the bugles, and a field piece thundered out a salute. The sound of the shot bounced away through the morning mist until its echoes worked their way into every corner of town. Jonesville-on-the-Grande woke to the cannon's roar, as if to battle, and the day began.

At eight the whistle from the post laundry sent us children off to school. The whole town stopped for lunch with the noon whistle, and after lunch everybody went back to work when the post laundry said that it was one o'clock, except for those who could afford to be old-fashioned and took the siesta. The post was the town's clock, you might have said, or like some insistent elder person who was always there to tell you it was time.

At six the flag came down, and we went to watch through the high wire fence that divided the post from the town. Sometimes we joined in the ceremony, standing at salute until the sound of the cannon made us jump. That must have been when we had just studied about George Washington in school, or recited "The Song of Marion's Men"° about Marion the Fox

---

"The Hammon and the Beans" is reprinted with permission from the publisher of The Hammon and the Beans and Other Stories by Américo Paredes (Houston: Arte Público Press—University of Houston, © 1994).

Fort Jones: The setting of Fort Jones and Jonesville-on-the-Grande in Texas is fictional. The story takes place in the mid-1920s, one of the most turbulent periods of Mexican history and only a few years after the deaths of two of the greatest heroes of the Mexican revolution—Pancho Villa (1877–1923) and Emillano Zapata (ca. 1879–1919).

"*Song of Marion's Men*": a poem by William Cullen Bryant (1794–1878) about Colonel Francis Marion (ca. 1732–1795), who was a leader of irregular guerrilla forces in South Carolina during the Revolutionary War. Because of his hit-and-run tactics, involving his hiding in the swamps near the "broad Santee" river in South Carolina, Marion was nicknamed the "Swamp Fox."

and the British cavalry that chased him up and down the broad Santee. But at other times we stuck out our tongues and jeered at the soldiers. Perhaps the night before we had hung at the edges of a group of old men and listened to tales about Aniceto Pizaña and the "border troubles,"° as the local paper still called them when it referred to them gingerly in passing.

It was because of the border troubles, ten years or so before, that the soldiers had come back to old Fort Jones. But we did not hate them for that; we admired them even, at least sometimes. But when we were thinking about the border troubles instead of Marion the Fox we hooted them and the flag they were lowering, which for the moment was theirs alone, just as we would have jeered an opposing ball team, in a friendly sort of way. On these occasions even Chonita would join in the mockery, though she usually ran home at the stroke of six. But whether we taunted or saluted, the distant men in khaki uniforms went about their motions without noticing us at all.

The last word from the post came in the night when a distant bugle blew. At nine it was all right because all the lights were on. But sometimes I heard it at eleven when everything was dark and still, and it made me feel that I was all alone in the world. I would even doubt that I was me, and that put me in such a fright that I felt like yelling out just to make sure I was really there. But next morning the sun shone and life began all over again. With its whistles and cannon shots and bugles blowing. And so we lived, we and the post, side by side with the wire fence in between.

The wandering soldiers whom the bugle called home at night did not wander in our neighborhood, and none of us ever went into Fort Jones. None except Chonita. Every evening when the flag came down she would leave off playing and go down towards what was known as the "lower" gate of the post, the one that opened not on Main Street but against the poorest part of town. She went into the grounds and to the mess halls and pressed her nose against the screens and watched the soldiers eat. They sat at long tables calling to each other through food-stuffed mouths.

"Hey bud, pass the coffee!"

"Give me the ham!"

"Yeah, give me the beans!"

After the soldiers were through the cooks came out and scolded Chonita, and then they gave her packages with things to eat.

border troubles: The most serious border incidents occurred in 1916, when Pancho Villa was responsible for deaths of Americans on both sides of the border. He made repeated raids into New Mexico and Texas.

Chonita's mother did our washing, in gratefulness—as my mother put it—for the use of a vacant lot of my grandfather's which was a couple of blocks down the street. On the lot was an old one-room shack which had been a shed long ago, and this Chonita's father had patched up with flattened-out pieces of tin. He was a laborer. Ever since the end of the border troubles there had been a development boom in the Valley, and Chonita's father was getting his share of the good times. Clearing brush and building irrigation ditches he sometimes pulled down as much as six dollars a week. He drank a good deal of it up, it was true. But corn was just a few cents a bushel in those days. He was the bread-winner, you might say, while Chonita furnished the luxuries.

Chonita was a poet too. I had just moved into the neighborhood when a boy came up to me and said, "Come on! Let's go hear Chonita make a speech."

She was already on top of the alley fence when we got there, a scrawny little girl of about nine, her bare dirty feet clinging to the fence almost like hands. A dozen other kids were there below her, waiting. Some were boys I knew at school; five or six were her younger brothers and sisters.

"Speech! Speech!" they all cried. "Let Chonita make a speech! Talk in English, Chonita!"

They were grinning and nudging each other except for her brothers and sisters, who looked up at her with proud serious faces. She gazed out beyond us all with a grand, distant air and then she spoke.

"Give me the hammon and the beans!" she yelled. "Give me the hammon and the beans!"

She leaped off the fence and everybody cheered and told her how good it was and how she could talk English better than the teachers at the grammar school.

I thought it was a pretty poor joke. Every evening almost, they would make her get up on the fence and yell, "Give me the hammon and the beans!" And everybody would cheer and make her think she was talking English. As for me, I would wait there until she got it over with so we could play at something else. I wondered how long it would be before they got tired of it all. I never did find out because just about that time I got the chills and fever, and when I got up and around Chonita wasn't there anymore.

Many's the time I have seen her in my mind's eyes, in the picket lines demanding not bread, not cake, but the hammon and the beans. But it didn't work out that way.

One night Doctor Zapata came into our kitchen through the back door. He set his bag on the table and said to my father, who had opened the door for him, "Well, she is dead."

My father flinched. "What was it?" he asked.

The doctor had gone to the window and he stood with his back to us, looking out toward the light of Fort Jones. "Pneumonia, flu, malnutrition, worms, the evil eye," he said without turning around. "What the hell difference does it make?"

"I wish I had known how sick she was," my father said in a very mild tone. "Not that it's really my affair, but I wish I had."

The doctor snorted and shook his head.

My mother came in and I asked her who was dead. She told me. It made me feel strange but I did not cry. My mother put her arm around my shoulders. "She is in Heaven now," she said. "She is happy."

I shrugged her arm away and sat down in one of the kitchen chairs.

"They're like animals," the doctor was saying. He turned round suddenly and his eyes glistened in the light. "Do you know what that brute of a father was doing when I left? He was laughing! Drinking and laughing with his friends."

"There's no telling what the poor man feels," my mother said.

My father made a deprecatory gesture. "It wasn't his daughter anyway."

"No?" the doctor said. He sounded interested.

"This is the woman's second husband," my father explained. "First one died before the girl was born, shot and hanged from a mesquite limb. He was working too close to the tracks the day the Olmito train was derailed."

"You know what?" the doctor said. "In classical times they did things better. Take Troy, for instance. After they stormed the city they grabbed the babies by the heels and dashed them against the wall. That was more humane."

My father smiled. "You sound very radical. You sound just like your relative down there in Morelos."°

"No relative of mine," the doctor said. "I'm a conservative, the son of a conservative, and you know that I wouldn't be here except for that little detail."

Morelos: the home state of Zapata.

"Habit," my father said. "Pure habit, pure tradition. You're a radical at heart."

"It depends on how you define radicalism," the doctor answered. "People tend to use words too loosely. A dentist could be called a radical, I suppose. He pulls up things by the roots."

My father chuckled.

"Any bandit in Mexico nowadays can give himself a political label," the doctor went on, "and that makes him respectable. He's a leader of the people."

"Take Villa, now—" my father began.

"Villa was a different type of man," the doctor broke in.

"I don't see any difference."

The doctor came over to the table and sat down. "Now look at it this way," he began, his finger in front of my father's face. My father threw back his head and laughed.

"You'd better go to bed and rest," my mother told me. "You're not completely well, you know.

So I went to bed, but I didn't go to sleep, not right away. I lay there for a long time while behind my darkened eyelids Emiliano Zapata's cavalry charged down to the broad Santee, where there were grave men with hoary hairs.° I was still awake at eleven when the cold voice of the bugle went gliding in and out of the dark like something that couldn't find its way back to wherever it had been. I thought of Chonita in Heaven, and I saw her in her torn and dirty dress, with a pair of bright wings attached, flying round and round like a butterfly shouting, "Give me the hammon and the beans!"

Then I cried. And whether it was the bugle, or whether it was Chonita or what, to this day I do not know. But cry I did, and I felt much better after that.

---

grave men with hoary hairs: Cf. lines 49–52 of Bryant's "Song of Marion's Men":
> Grave men there are by broad Santee,
>   Grave men with hoary hairs;
> Their hearts are all with Marion,
>   For Marion are their prayers.

Critical Eye

FOR DISCUSSION

a. Why is the main character really grieving about the death of his friend?

b. How is this story about class?

REAPPROACHING THE TEXT

The citizens in the text are surrounded by images of war, yet they try to maintain a "normal" life. How is this similar to the way the characters in Cynthia Ozick's "The Shawl" try to maintain normalcy and dignity?

WRITING ASSIGNMENT

Why is death such a traumatic experience for those left behind?

Cynthia Ozick

The Shawl

Stella, cold, cold the coldness of hell. How they walked on the roads together, Rosa with Magda curled up between sore breasts, Magda wound up in the shawl. Sometimes Stella carried Magda. But she was jealous of Magda. A thin girl of fourteen, too small, with thin breasts of her own, Stella wanted to be wrapped in a shawl, hidden away, asleep, rocked by the march, a baby, a round infant in arms. Magda took Rosa's nipple, and Rosa never stopped walking, a walking cradle. There was not enough milk; sometimes Magda sucked air; then she screamed. Stella was ravenous. Her knees were tumors on sticks, her elbows chicken bones.

Rosa did not feel hunger; she felt light, not like someone walking but like someone in a faint, in trance, arrested in a fit, someone who is already a floating angel, alert and seeing everything, but in the air, not there, not touching the road. As if teetering on the tips of her fingernails. She looked into Magda's face through a gap in the shawl: a squirrel in a nest, safe, no one could reach her inside the little house of the shawl's windings. The face, very round, a pocket mirror of a face: but it was not Rosa's bleak complexion, dark like cholera, it was another kind of face altogether, eyes blue as air, smooth feathers of hair nearly as yellow as the Star sewn into Rosa's coat. You could think she was one of *their* babies.

Rosa, floating, dreamed of giving Magda away in one of the villages. She could leave the line for a minute and push Magda into the hands of any woman on the side of the road. But if she moved out of line they might shoot. And even if she fled the line for half a second and pushed the shawl-bundle at a stranger, would the woman take it? She might be surprised, or afraid; she might drop the shawl, and Magda would fall out and strike her head and die. The little round head. Such a good child, she gave up screaming, and sucked now only for the taste of the drying nipple itself. The neat grip of the tiny gums. One mite of a tooth tip sticking up in the bottom gum, how shining, an elfin tombstone of white marble gleaming there. Without complaining, Magda relinquished Rosa's teats, first the left, then the right; both were cracked, not a sniff of milk. The duct crevice extinct, a dead volcano, blind eye, chill hole, so Magda took

"The Shawl" from *The Shawl* by Cynthia Ozick, copyright © 1980, 1983 by Cynthia Ozick. Used by permission of Alfred A. Knopf, a division of Random House, Inc.

the corner of the shawl and milked it instead. She sucked and sucked, flooding the threads with wetness. The shawl's good flavor, milk of linen.

It was a magic shawl, it could nourish an infant for three days and three nights. Magda did not die, she stayed alive, although very quiet. A peculiar smell, of cinnamon and almonds, lifted out of her mouth. She held her eyes open every moment, forgetting how to blink or nap, and Rosa and sometimes Stella studied their blueness. On the road they raised one burden of a leg after another and studied Magda's face. "Aryan," Stella said, in a voice grown as thin as a string; and Rosa thought how Stella gazed at Magda like a young cannibal. And the time that Stella said "Aryan," it sounded to Rosa as if Stella had really said "Let us devour her."

But Magda lived to walk. She lived that long, but she did not walk very well, partly because she was only fifteen months old, and partly because the spindles of her legs could not hold up her fat belly. It was fat with air, full and round. Rosa gave almost all her food to Magda, Stella gave nothing; Stella was ravenous, a growing child herself, but not growing much. Stella did not menstruate. Rosa did not menstruate. Rosa was ravenous, but also not; she learned from Magda how to drink the taste of a finger in one's mouth. They were in a place without pity, all pity was annihilated in Rosa, she looked at Stella's bones without pity. She was sure that Stella was waiting for Magda to die so she could put her teeth into the little thighs.

Rosa knew Magda was going to die very soon; she should have been dead already, but she had been buried away deep inside the magic shawl, mistaken there for the shivering mound of Rosa's breasts; Rosa clung to the shawl as if it covered only herself. No one took it away from her. Magda was mute. She never cried. Rosa hid her in the barracks, under the shawl, but she knew that one day someone would inform; or one day someone, not even Stella, would steal Magda to eat her. When Magda began to walk Rosa knew that Magda was going to die very soon, something would happen. She was afraid to fall asleep; she slept with the weight of her thigh on Magda's body; she was afraid she would smother Magda under her thigh. The weight of Rosa was becoming less and less; Rosa and Stella were slowly turning into air.

Magda was quiet, but her eyes were horribly alive, like blue tigers. She watched. Sometimes she laughed—it seemed a laugh, but how could it be? Magda had never seen anyone laugh. Still, Magda laughed at her shawl when the wind blew its corners, the bad wind with pieces of black in it, that made Stella's and Rosa's eyes tear. Magda's eyes were always clear and tearless. She watched like a tiger. She guarded her shawl. No one could touch it; only Rosa could touch it. Stella was not allowed. The shawl was Magda's own baby, her pet, her little sister. She tangled herself up in it and sucked on one of the corners when she wanted to be very still.

Then Stella took the shawl away and made Magda die.

Afterward Stella said: "I was cold."

And afterward she was always cold, always. The cold went into her heart: Rosa saw that Stella's heart was cold. Magda flopped onward with her little pencil legs scribbling this way and that, in search of the shawl; the pencils faltered at the barracks opening, where the light began. Rosa saw and pursued. But already Magda was in the square outside the barracks, in the jolly light. It was the roll-call arena. Every morning Rosa had to conceal Magda under the shawl against a wall of the barracks and go out and stand in the arena with Stella and hundreds of others, sometimes for hours, and Magda, deserted, was quiet under the shawl, sucking on her corner. Every day Magda was silent, and so she did not die. Rosa saw that today Magda was going to die, and at the same time a fearful joy ran into Rosa's two palms, her fingers were on fire, she was astonished, febrile: Magda, in the sunlight, swaying on her pencil legs, was howling. Ever since the drying up of Rosa's nipples, ever since Magda's last scream on the road, Magda had been devoid of any syllable; Magda was a mute. Rosa believed that something had gone wrong with her vocal cords, with her windpipe, with the cave of her larynx; Magda was defective, without a voice; perhaps she was deaf; there might be something amiss with her intelligence; Magda was dumb. Even the laugh that came when the ash-stippled wind made a clown out of Magda's shawl was only the air-blown showing of her teeth. Even when the lice, head lice and body lice, crazed her so that she became as wild as one of the big rats that plundered the barracks at daybreak looking for carrion, she rubbed and scratched and kicked and bit and rolled without a whimper. But now Magda's mouth was spilling a long viscous rope of clamor.

"Maaaa—"

It was the first noise Magda had ever sent out from her throat since the drying up of Rosa's nipples.

"Maaaa . . . aaa!"

Again! Magda was wavering in the perilous sunlight of the arena, scrabbling on such pitiful little bent shins. Rosa saw. She saw that Magda was grieving for the loss of her shawl, she saw that Magda was going to die. A tide of commands hammered in Rosa's nipples: Fetch, get, bring!

But she did not know which to go after first, Magda or the shawl. If she jumped out into the arena to snatch Magda up, the howling would not stop, because Magda would still not have the shawl; but if she ran back into the barracks to find the shawl, and if she found it, and if she came after Magda holding it and shaking it, then she would get Magda back, Magda would put the shawl in her mouth and turn dumb again.

Rosa entered the dark. It was easy to discover the shawl. Stella was heaped under it, asleep in her thin bones. Rosa tore the shawl free and flew—she could fly, she was only air—into the arena. The sunheat murmured of another life, of butterflies in summer. The light was placid, mellow. On the other side of the steel fence, far away, there were green meadows speckled with dandelions and deep-colored violets; beyond them, even farther, innocent tiger lilies, tall, lifting their orange bonnets. In the barracks they spoke of "flowers," of "rain": excrement, thick turd-braids, and the slow stinking maroon waterfall that slunk down from the upper bunks, the stink mixed with a bitter fatty floating smoke that greased Rosa's skin. She stood for an instant at the margin of the arena. Sometimes the electricity inside the fence would seem to hum; even Stella said it was only an imagining, but Rosa heard real sounds in the wire: grainy sad voices. The farther she was from the fence, the more clearly the voices crowded at her. The lamenting voices strummed so convincingly, so passionately, it was impossible to suspect them of being phantoms. The voices told her to hold up the shawl, high; the voices told her to shake it, to whip with it, to unfurl it like a flag. Rosa lifted, shook, whipped, unfurled. Far off, very far, Magda leaned across her air-fed belly, reaching out with the rods of her arms. She was high up, elevated, riding someone's shoulder. But the shoulder that carried Magda was not coming toward Rosa and the shawl, it was drifting away, the speck of Magda was moving more and more into the smoky distance. Above the shoulder a helmet glinted. The light tapped the helmet and sparkled it into a goblet. Below the helmet a black body like a domino and a pair of black boots hurled themselves in the direction of the electrified fence. The electric voices began to chatter wildly. "Maa-maa, maaamaaa," they all hummed together. How far Magda was from Rosa now, across the whole square, past a dozen barracks, all the way on the other side! She was no bigger than a moth.

All at once Magda was swimming through the air. The whole of Magda traveled through loftiness. She looked like a butterfly touching a silver vine. And the moment Magda's feathered round head and her pencil legs and balloonish belly and zigzag arms splashed against the fence, the steel voices went mad in their growling, urging Rosa to run and run to the spot where Magda had fallen from her flight against the electrified fence; but of course Rosa did not obey them. She only stood, because if she ran they would shoot, and if she tried to pick up the sticks of Magda's body they would shoot, and if she let the wolf's screech ascending now through the ladder of her skeleton break out, they would shoot; so she took Magda's shawl and filled her own mouth with it, stuffed it in and stuffed it in, until she was swallowing up the wolf's screech and tasting the cinnamon and almond depth of Magda's saliva; and Rosa drank Magda's shawl until it dried.

Critical Eye

FOR DISCUSSION

a. In what ways does Ozick's story discuss how the horrors of trauma affect the mind?

b. Many Jews survived the atrocity of the Holocaust, and they remember with vivid clarity horrors that occurred around them. What are we learning from their remembrances?

REAPPROACHING THE TEXT

Examine the mother in this story alongside the article about Andrea Yates. Was one mother able to see past the madness around her while the other was not?

WRITING ASSIGNMENT

The mother considers two costly choices as a means of saving/ending Magda's life. Can the choices be excused because of the circumstances?

Aesop

A Lion and Other Animals Go Hunting

A lion, an ass, a jackal, and a wolf went hunting one day, and every one was to share and share alike in what they took. They plucked down a stag, and cut him up into four parts, but as they were beginning to divide shares, the lion said, "Hands off. *This* quarter is mine, by privilege of my rank, as King of Beasts. *This* quarter is mine because I frightened the stag with my roar. *This* quarter is mine because I delivered the first blow. As for *this* quarter, well, take it who dares." So the mouths of the allies were shut, and they went away, quiet as fishes.

Moral: There is no partnership with those who have the power.

Critical Eye

FOR DISCUSSION

a. Does the lion's final statement speak to the historical posturing of the bully?

b. Provide current or historical evidence that presents a nation or governing body as a bully.

c. Thinking in terms of gender, race, and politics, who is generally seen as the bully?

d. Does historical evidence exist in which the "other," or those presumed to be powerless, assumed power and, subsequently, took on the persona of the bully?

REAPPROACHING THE LITERATURE

Look at the relationships between the animals in terms of political domination. How will the lion's behavior affect those deemed lesser? Be sure to juxtapose the story with issues of domination from our larger global society.

WRITING ASSIGNMENT

Using Aseop's tale as a platform, argue that the notion of the bully is a myth and that those in power are entitled to lead and set the gender, social, political, and cultural standards for those deemed weaker.

1 2 **3** 4 5

Racial Matters

> George Bush does not care about Black people!
> *Kanye West*

> If I can send the flower of the German nation into the hell of war without the smallest pity for the shedding of precious German blood, then surely I have the right to remove millions of an inferior race that breeds like vermin.
> *Adolf Hitler*

Humans are essentially comprised of ethnic, cultural, and regional groupings that we generally oversimplify by lumping into what we call "races" of people. Actually, Homo sapiens are all of one race—the human race. Yet, we still continue—based on skin color and language, cultural and religious affiliations, social mandates and values—to separate ourselves to the extent of judgment and, too often, violent segregation. These problems with those who are "other" in our worlds frequently result in blaming and, more tragically, self-incrimination. As a result, these so-called racial conflicts continue to flare up and burn out of control. But, when examined from a position of personal intuitiveness, these moments of narrow-mindedness seem to be, moreso, issues of how we see ourselves—those flawed reflections we cast in the mirror.

Perceived differences have represented the largest gap among humankind. Historically, the world has demonstrated little tolerance for difference, making so-called matters of race the most debated issue since the evolution of our species. That said, how do we move forward in a world that, currently, seems as ethnically intolerant as at any point in history? Moreover, how do we learn to embrace ourselves and our neighbors when the diverse images of our reflective lives continue to be attacked and subjugated to the point of self-hatred and confusion?

What seems most perplexing about the issue of race is that, in fact, there is an issue of "race." Somehow, we do not look at our fellow humans and see our own humanity. Perhaps what we must do is not examine the areas where racism is a threat or problem, but, instead, excise the very roots of difference, in order to define, combat, and eliminate one of, if not the, largest quandary to ever impact our world. The following selections allow readers to consider who they are in relation to the skin color that defines them and further question how and why these notions of race and racial matters color their views of the world.

James Alan McPherson

Umbilicus

In the late fall of the first year, when I was growing secure in my solitude, a friend, an Englishman, came to this house and offered what he believed was an act of compassion: "Now look here," he told me, "you are becoming a recluse. Why don't you go out once in a while? At least go out into your own backyard and see how delightful the fall is. I'm told that way north of here, along the Minnesota border, it is even more beautiful. Why don't you at least take a drive up there before winter comes?" His was a call back to the more complex rituals of life. After some serious reflection, I accepted it as such. I had always wanted to see the northeastern part of the state, the sources of the Mississippi. And so, on a Saturday morning, a golden and blue fall day, I pulled away from the security of this house. I drove northeasterly on county roads. I drove very slowly and very carefully from one rural town to the next. I saw the light brown beauty of harvested fields, when soybeans and corn and wheat had given up their energy to entropy, to the enigma of renewal, for the risk of winter and the promise of the spring. I saw that life, my own life, too, *all life,* lay under the promise of an agreement with something outside, and far, far beyond, the little roles we play on the surface of things. I am saying that the slow drive along the backroads reawakened my spirits. I began to reconsider the essential importance of risk to the enterprise of life. I mustered sufficient courage to stop several times along the road, once for lunch, and again for gasoline and oil. I drove as far north as I thought was necessary, and then I turned around and drove back toward home. But in the late afternoon, on the far side of Cedar Rapids, the engine of my car began to smoke and burn. By the time I had parked on the narrow road bank, the engine was on fire. It was here that the old sickness began to reclaim its place in my emotions. I began to feel that the burning engine was God's punishment for my abandoning the simple rituals that had become my life. I felt that, because I had left the refuge of my house, I had *earned* this fate. I abandoned the car. I steeled myself to walk back home, or at least to walk as far as the outskirts of Cedar Rapids, many miles down that county road, as a form of self-punishment. I focused my mind on my house, my bed, my table, and I began walking toward these three things, and *only* these three things.

"Umbilicus" by James Alan McPherson. Reprinted by permission of the author.

But several miles along that road, approaching dusk, a truck with two men in it stopped just ahead of me. The two men, both white, sat in the truck and waited for me to approach it. "We saw your car smoking back there, brother," the man in the passenger seat said to me, "Can we give you a ride?" The two of them seemed to be laborers, or at least farmers. The gun rack stretched across the rear window took my memories back to the terror of that long road I had traveled to this place. There was the truck, the gun rack, the white faces, the road. But they did not have the oily Southern accent. I accepted their offer, and the passenger moved over and allowed me to take his seat. Now the three of us were squeezed together on the high seat. They gave me a beer, from the remains of a case of beer on the floor, and we drove toward Cedar Rapids. "A lot of our friends don't like the colored," the driver, who seemed the older of the two, announced to me. "But, hell, me and my brother here, we got colored neighbors. We go over to their houses sometimes for parties. They ain't exactly like us, but we like them all the same." We toasted with our beer and talked of the need for more brotherhood in the world, and of the house parties given by their black neighbors in Cedar Rapids. But at the first service station we reached, just on the outskirts of Cedar Rapids, we were informed that no tow truck was available. The attendant advised us to continue on into Cedar Rapids, toward a station where a tow truck could be available.

Now the older of the two men, in the proximity of safety and social gradation seeming to look more and more "poor white," used this opportunity to offer a radical plan. "Now look," he told me. "I already told you that we *like* the colored. We go over to their house parties in Cedar. You know that some colored are our neighbors. Now here's what I'm gonna do. There's a rope on the back of this truck. We can drive on back and tie that rope to the front bumper of your car. Then we'll just tow her on in to Cedar. You can pay us what you were gonna pay the tow truck, plus we'll do it for less money.

The cool fall evening was closing in. I hesitated, but the desperation of the situation caused me to risk some trust. I accepted their offer. With the bargain struck, with the night closing around us, we drove back to the dead car. We drank more beer in celebration of brotherhood, and we even made some jokes. At the car, after the ropes had been tied to link my own wreck to the back end of their truck, the connection, the *umbilicus*, was tightened until my car could be raised so that only its back wheels were grounded. The two brothers cautioned me to take my former place behind the wheel and manage my car as best I could while they drove the truck. I was handed another beer, for toasting our newly struck brotherhood, while we steered in unison toward the distant lights of Cedar Rapids. And so we started out, slowly and jerkily at first, but then with more and more speed.

Legend has it that all the "I" states are flat. This is not so. There are reasons why the Mississippi River begins in Minnesota, and why its tributaries contribute every drop of water in its meandering and then rapid flow down to the Gulf of Mexico. There are hills in this landscape, and hillocks and dales and rills. The expression *from here to there*, with its promise of fixed purpose, is found in the engineering of straight roadways. But, in contradiction to this illusion of purposeful will, nature itself still has something else to say. Nature will not cede an inch, without struggle, to *any* expression of fixed purpose. Something mysterious in nature, or in the restless growing edge of life itself, imposes a counterintention on all illusion of control. The Great River overflows its banks, flows and ebbs, crests and slackens, rushes and lingers, dies, and then is mighty and waterful again, according to its *own* instincts. So also the straightest of roads are forced to acknowledge the rhythms of the lands that lap under them. Such rhythms are gentle under the four wheels of a tractioned car. But under only two wheels, these same rhythms are foreboding. They speak waywardly of the tenuous nature of life. And in the fall, after harvest time, the uniform brownness of the field, or perhaps it is the withdrawal of the subtle shades of green, keeps one close to the recognition that *death* is the very next season after *life*. You must also add to this the horror of the peculiar angle of a windshield looking *up* into the dark, evening sky, closing down on the emptiness all around the roadbed and over the top of a truck ahead that you cannot really see. And add also the swaying of the elevated car, first leftward, toward possibly oncoming traffic you cannot see, then rightward, toward sharp and narrow embankments, black-dirted and brown-coated and deathly deep. Imagine also the unsteady stretching of the ropes, the *umbilicus,* connecting the two vehicles. It stretches close to breaking when the truck moves uphill; it relaxes, and the weight of the towed car pushes forward freely and crazily, when the towing truck goes down a dale. Such a haphazardly improvised *umbilical cord* cares nothing for *verbal* affirmations of brotherhood. It encourages very bad manners. It permits the front of the towed car to bump the back of the towing truck, and when the towed car brakes—because its driver tries to steady it when it bumps the rear of the truck ahead, and releases the brake when the rope becomes too tight—both car and towing truck begin to sway dangerously. And add more to it. Add to it the fading illusion of rescue, and the more sharply focused recognition that these are two *white men*, blood brothers, both drunk on beer, who are pulling off the rescue. Add also to it the fact that you have had two beers yourself, and that there is a third beer, open but untouched, on the seat beside you. An additional inducement for fear is that, while these two white men say that they like the colored, and while the three of you have raised two toasts to *abstract* brotherhood, the world you live in, especially now, does not perceive things in this same idealized light.

Now, in the entire history of this country there has developed absolutely no substantial body of evidence to support either the authenticity, the genuineness, or the practicality of such a web of self-extension, such an *umbilicus,* extending from either extreme of this great psychological divide. There has been no *real* trust between black and white, especially in such life-risking circumstances. With each sway of the car, within every pull and slack of the rope, the improvised *umbilical* cord—up dale and down dale, inching and then swaying toward the evening lights of Cedar Rapids, the old life lessons came back. *There has never been a life-affirming umbilicus between black and white.* And if this is true, then something else must follow. If the rope should break and the car should crash, no one will really care or even attempt to understand just how this failed and how this sloppily improvised community of purpose had first come into existence. On the evening news, if even there, it will be dismissed as just another roadkill. *I will never be able to reclaim my bed, my table, or the simple, little, self-protective rituals—sleeping and eating and reading and being reclusive—that I had created to protect what remained of my life.*

I braked my car and both vehicles, my car and their truck, went off the road.

But the rope, the *umbilicus, held,* while both the car and truck swerved into the ditch at the edge of the roadside.

The two vehicles, the three of us, went into the ditch together. There was no moon over the brown harvested fields that evening. There was no magnetic field, no spiritual center. There was only the spilled can of beer, and its acrid scent mingled with the smell of burning oil, inside my car. Death was announcing itself all around.

I had no trust left in me.

But the three of us were unhurt. The two brothers, after inspecting their truck, dismissed the incident as no more than a joke played on the three of us by the rhythm of the road. "Now we told you we like the colored," the older brother announced. "See, the rope is still tight. We can just push our truck out of the ditch and then hook you up again to it. We'll still drive you on in to Cedar."

I paid the brothers much more than I had promised them, and I began walking down the road toward the lights of Cedar Rapids, toward my bed, my window looking out on my backyard, my table, and toward the simple rituals I had worked out for my life. These things still resided on the far side of Cedar Rapids. I walked away from the urgings of my brothers that we could very easily rescue both truck and car from the ditch, that we had only a few more miles to go before hitting Cedar, that they had always been good neighbors to the colored who lived next door. I kept walking away from them. In my own reduced frame of reference, my two rescuers, my brothers, had become two drunk white men, who, through uncaring, had put my life at risk. I walked away, while behind me they pleaded for the unimportance of money and for the practicality of their plan.

I left it to them to cut the rope, the *umbilicus,* connecting my dead car to their truck.

Critical Eye

FOR DISCUSSION

a. Is the author merely caught up in his own racist preconceptions, or does he really have true concerns about the issues of racism that exist between Blacks and Whites?

b. Are the White gentlemen wrong in their approach with the author, or are they just being themselves? And, if so, is there anything wrong with that?

REAPPROACHING THE TEXT

Putting the author's racial reservations aside, is he a part of the problem? Are his own issues about race helping to contribute to the racial divide?

WRITING ASSIGNMENT

Taking into consideration your cares, concerns, and knowledge of race in America, why do you believe American has a "race problem?"

Wooden Leg

Young Men, Go Out
and Fight Them

*The gold rush of 1874, which lured thousands of white prospectors into
the Black Hills of South Dakota, was a crucial factor in provoking a
major confrontation between the United States and the Plains Indians.
To the powerful Sioux nation these mountains were sacred terrain, and
also properly protected by the Fort Laramie Treaty of 1868, signed by
the Sioux and the United States government. It was Lieutenant Colonel
George Armstrong Custer who originally violated that treaty. In July 1874,
ostensibly to locate a site for a new fort, but covertly to hunt for mineral
resources, Custer led the expedition into the Black Hills and reported that
there was gold "from the grassroots down."*

*So it was poetic justice that in late June 1876 Custer's small command
should blunder into the largest gathering of Plains Indian fighters ever
assembled—an estimated twelve to fifteen thousand Indians, with at least four
thousand fighting men, drawn from the Teton, Santee and Yankton Sioux,
Assiniboine, Cheyenne, Arapaho, and Gros Ventre, camped together along
three miles of the bank of the Little Big Horn River in central Montana. Under
the leadership of the Sioux war chiefs Sitting Bull and Crazy Horse and the
Cheyenne headman Two Moons, the natives comprised die-hard hostiles and
recent reservation runaways come together momentarily as a united front.*

*Here is one warrior's memory of the tumultuous day of "many soldiers
falling into camp," the battle of the Little Big Horn. Wooden Leg, the
narrator, was about eighteen years old when Custer disastrously divided his
Seventh Cavalry forces, ignored warnings from his Crow scouts, and was cut
down along with all 225 of his officers and men. The battle was a freakish
victory for the Indians, stunning the victors along with the vanquished.
The tribes did not have sufficient unity or ammunition to follow it up with
a broader offensive. Their forces quickly scattered, with Sitting Bull and his
followers hiding out in Canada until 1881.*

In my sleep I dreamed that a great crowd of people were making lots of
noise. Something in the noise startled me. I found myself wide awake,
sitting up and listening. My brother too awakened, and we both jumped

"Young Men, Go Out and Fight Them" from *Wooden Leg: A Warrior Who Fought Custer.* Interpreted
by Thomas B. Marquis. Published by the University of Nebraska Press.

to our feet. A great commotion was going on among the camps. We heard shooting. We hurried out from the trees so we might see as well as hear.

The shooting was somewhere at the upper part of the camp circles. It looked as if all of the Indians there were running away toward the hills to the westward or down toward the village. Women were screaming and men were letting out war cries. Through it all we could hear old men calling: "Soldiers are here! Young men, go out and fight them."

We ran to our camp and to our home lodge. Everybody there was excited. Women were hurriedly making up little packs for flight. Some were going off northward or across the river without any packs. Children were hunting for their mothers. Mothers were anxiously trying to find their children. I got my lariat and my six-shooter. I hastened on down toward where had been our horse herd. . . .

My father had caught my favorite horse from the herd brought in by the boys and Bald Eagle. I quickly emptied out my war bag and set myself at getting ready to go into battle. I jerked off my ordinary clothing. I jerked on a pair of new breeches that had been given to me by an Uncpapa Sioux. I had a good cloth shirt, and I put it on. My old moccasins were kicked off and a pair of beaded moccasins substituted for them.

My father strapped a blanket upon my horse and arranged the rawhide lariat into a bridle. He stood holding my mount. "Hurry," he urged me.

The air was so full of dust I could not see where to go. But it was not, needful that I see that far. I kept my horse headed in the direction of movement by the crowd of Indians on horseback. I was led out around and far beyond the Uncpapa camp circle. Many hundreds of Indians on horseback were dashing to and fro in front of a body of soldiers. The soldiers were on the level valley ground and were shooting with rifles. Not many bullets were being sent back at them, but thousands of arrows were falling among them. I went on with a throng of Sioux until we got beyond and behind the white men. By this time, though, they had mounted their horses and were hiding themselves in the timber. . . .

Suddenly the hidden soldiers came tearing out on horseback, from the woods. I was around on that side where they came out. I whirled my horse and lashed it into a dash to escape from them. All others of my companions did the same. But soon we discovered they were not following us. They were running away from us. They were going as fast as their tired horses could carry them across an open valley space and toward the river. We stopped, looked a moment, and then we whipped our ponies into swift pursuit. A great throng of Sioux also were coming after them. A distant position put them among the leaders in the chase. The soldier horses moved slowly, as if they were very tired. Ours were lively. We gained rapidly on them.

I fired four shots with my six-shooter. I do not know whether or not any of my bullets did harm. I saw a Sioux put an arrow into the back of a soldier's head. Another arrow went into his shoulder. He tumbled from his horse to the ground. Others fell dead either from arrows or from stabbings or jabbings or from blows by the stone war clubs of the Sioux. Horses limped or staggered or sprawled out dead or dying.

Our war cries and war songs were mingled with many jeering calls, such as: "You are only boys. You ought not to be fighting. We whipped you on the Rosebud. You should have brought more Crows or Shoshones with you to do your fighting."

Little Bird and I were after one certain soldier. Little Bird was wearing a trailing warbonnet. He was at the right and I was at the left of the fleeing man. We were lashing him and his horse with our pony whips. It seemed not brave to shoot him. Besides, I did not want to waste my bullets. He pointed back his revolver, though, and sent a bullet into Little Bird's thigh. Immediately I whacked the white man fighter on his head with the heavy elk-horn handle of my pony whip. The blow dazed him. I seized the rifle strapped on his back. I wrenched it and dragged the looping strap over his head. As I was getting possession of this weapon, he fell to the ground. I did not harm him further. I do not know what became of him. The jam of oncoming Indians swept me on. . . .

I returned to the west side of the river. Lots of Indians were hunting around there for dead soldiers or for wounded ones to kill. I joined in this search. I got some tobacco from the pockets of one dead man. I got also a belt having in it a few cartridges. All of the weapons and clothing and all other possessions were being taken from the bodies. The warriors were doing this. No old people nor women were there. They all had run away to the hill benches to the westward.

I went to a dead horse, to see what might be found there. Leather bags were on them, behind the saddles. I rummaged into one of these bags. I found there two pasteboard boxes. I broke open one of them. "Oh, cartridges!"

There were twenty of them in each box, forty in all. Thirty of them were used to fill up the vacant places in my belt. The remaining ten I wrapped into a piece of cloth and dropped them down into my own little kit bag. Now I need not be so careful in expending ammunition. Now I felt very brave. . . .

The shots quit coming from the soldiers. Warriors who had crept close to them began to call out that all of the white men were dead. All of the Indians then jumped up and rushed forward. All of the boys and old men on their horses came tearing into the crowd. The air was full of dust and smoke. Everybody was greatly excited. It looked like thousands of dogs might look if all of them were mixed together in a fight. All of the Indians were saying these soldiers also went crazy and killed themselves. I do not know. I could not see them. But I believe they did so. . . .

I took one scalp. As I went walking and leading my horse among the dead, I observed one face that interested me. The dead man had a long beard growing from both sides of his face and extending several inches below the chin. He had also a full mustache. All of the beard hair was of a light, yellow color, as I now recall it. Most of the soldiers had beards growing, in different lengths, but this was the longest one I saw among them. I think the dead man may have been thirty or more years old. "Here is a new kind of scalp," I said to a companion. I skinned one side of the face and half of the chin, so as to keep the long beard yet on the part removed. I got an arrow shaft and tied the strange scalp to the end of it. . . .

I waved my scalp as I rode among our people. The first person I met who took special interest in me was my mother's mother. She was living in a little willow dome lodge of her own. "What is that?" she asked me when I flourished the scalp stick toward her. I told her. "I give it to you," I said, and I held it out to her. She screamed and shrank away. "Take it," I urged. "It will be good medicine for you." Then I went on to tell her about my having killed the Crow or Shoshone at the first right up the river, about my getting the two guns, about my knocking in the head two soldiers in the river, about what I had done in the next fight on the hill where all of the soldiers had been killed. We talked about my soldier clothing. She said I looked good dressed that way. I had thought so too, but neither the coat nor the breeches fit me well. The arms and legs were too short for me. Finally she decided she would take the scalp. She went then into her own little lodge. . . .

There was no dancing nor celebrating of any kind in any of the camps that night. Too many people were in mourning, among all of the Sioux as well as among the Cheyennes. Too many Cheyenne and Sioux women had gashed their arms and legs, in token of their grief. The people generally were praying, not cheering. There was much noise and confusion, but this was from other causes. Young men were going out to fight the first soldiers now hiding themselves on the hill across the river from where had been the first fighting during the morning. . . .

I did not go back that afternoon nor that night to help in fighting the first soldiers. Late in the night, though, I went as a scout. Five young men of the Cheyennes were appointed to guard our camp while other people slept. These were Big Nose, Yellow Horse, Little Shield, Horse Road and Wooden Leg. One or other of us was out somewhere looking over the country all the time. Two of us went once over to the place where the soldiers were hidden. We got upon hill points higher than they were. We could look down among them. We could have shot among them, but we did not do this. We just saw that they yet were there.

Five other young men took our duties in the last part of the night. I was glad to be relieved. I did not go to my family group for rest. I let loose my horse and dropped myself down upon a thick pad of grassy sod.

WOODEN LEG, *Northern Cheyenne*

Critical Eye

FOR DISCUSSION

a. Why does war seem to be such a necessary component of every society?

b. Why was the resistance to the colonists of such grave importance to the tribal peoples, even though their battles, in many cases, were futile?

REAPPROACHING THE TEXT

Some people say that the conquering of "weaker" peoples is a part of human nature. Keeping this in mind, discuss the rights of the settlers to the native lands.

WRITING ASSIGNMENT

Many ethnic groups in the United States, such as the Irish and Blacks, have undergone some form of harsh treatment at the hands of those perceived to be stronger or more superior. Have we resolved our differences or, racially speaking, are we worse off than at any time in American history?

Anna Lisa Raya

It's Hard Enough Being Me

When I entered college, I *discovered* I was Latina. Until then, I had never questioned who I was or where I was from: My father is a second-generation Mexican-American, born and raised in Los Angeles, and my mother was born in Puerto Rico and raised in Compton, Calif. My home is El Sereno, a predominantly Mexican neighborhood in L.A. Every close friend I have back home is Mexican. So I was always just Mexican. Though sometimes I was just Puerto Rican—like when we would visit Mamo (my grandma) or hang out with my Aunt Titi.

Upon arriving in New York as a first-year student, 3000 miles from home, I not only experienced extreme culture shock, but for the first time I had to define myself according to the broad term "Latina." Although culture shock and identity crisis are common for the newly minted collegian who goes away to school, my experience as a newly minted Latina was, and still is, even more complicating. In El Sereno, I felt like I was part of a majority, whereas at the College I am a minority.

I've discovered that many Latinos like myself have undergone similar experiences. We face discrimination for being a minority in this country while also facing criticism for being "whitewashed" or "sellouts" in the countries of our heritage. But as an ethnic group in college, we are forced to define ourselves according to some vague, generalized Latino experience. This requires us to know our history, our language, our music, and our religion. I can't even be a content "Puerto Mexican" because I have to be a politically-and-socially-aware-Latina-with-a-chip-on-my-shoulder-because-of-how-repressed-I-am-in-this-country.

I am none of the above. I am the quintessential imperfect Latina. I can't dance salsa to save my life, I learned about Montezuma and the Aztecs in sixth grade, and I haven't prayed to the *Virgen de Guadalupe* in years.

Apparently I don't even look Latina. I can't count how many times people have just assumed that I'm white or asked me if I'm Asian. True, my friends back home call me *güera* ("whitey") because I have green eyes and pale skin, but that was as bad as it got. I never thought I would wish my

"It's Hard Enough Being Me" by Anna Lisa Raya from *Columbia College Today*, Winter/Spring 1994. Reprinted with permission from Columbia College Today, © 1994.

skin were a darker shade or my hair a curlier texture, but since I've been in college, I have—many times.

Another thing: my Spanish is terrible. Every time I call home, I berate my mama for not teaching me Spanish when I was a child. In fact, not knowing how to speak the language of my home countries is the biggest problem that I have encountered, as have many Latinos. In Mexico there is a term, *pocha,* which is used by native Mexicans to ridicule Mexican-Americans. It expresses a deep-rooted antagonism and dislike for those of us who were raised on the other side of the border. Our failed attempts to speak pure, Mexican Spanish are largely responsible for the dislike. Other Latin American natives have this same attitude. No matter how well a Latino speaks Spanish, it can never be good enough.

Yet Latinos can't even speak Spanish in the U.S. without running the risk of being called "spic" or "wetback." That is precisely why my mother refused to teach me Spanish when I was a child. The fact that she spoke Spanish was constantly used against her: It prevented her from getting good jobs, and it would have placed me in bilingual education—a construct of the Los Angeles public school system that has proved to be more of a hindrance to intellectual development than a help.

To be fully Latina in college, however, I *must* know Spanish. I must satisfy the equation: Latina [equals] Spanish-speaking.

So I'm stuck in this black hole of an identity crisis, and college isn't making my life any easier, as I thought it would. In high school, I was being prepared for an adulthood in which I would be an individual, in which I wouldn't have to wear a Catholic school uniform anymore. But though I led an anonymous adolescence, I knew who I was. I knew I was different from white, black, or Asian people. I knew there was a language other than English that I could call my own if I only knew how to speak it better. I knew there were historical reasons why I was in this country, distinct reasons that make my existence here easier or more difficult than other people's existence. Ultimately, I was content.

Now I feel pushed into a corner, always defining, defending, and proving myself to classmates, professors, or employers. Trying to understand who and why I am, while understanding Plato or Homer, is a lot to ask of myself.

A month ago, I heard three Nuyorican (Puerto Ricans born and raised in New York) writers discuss how New Your City has influenced their writing. One problem I have faced as a young writer is finding a voice that is true to my community. I was surprised and reassured to discover that as Latinos, these writers had faced similar pressures and conflicts as myself; some weren't even taught Spanish in childhood. I will never forget the advice that one of them gave me that evening: She said that I need to be true to myself. "Because people will always complain about what you are doing—you're a 'gringa' or a 'spic' no matter what," she explained. "So you might as well do things for yourself and not for them."

I don't know why it has taken 20 years to hear this advice, but I'm going to give it a try. *Soy yo* and no one else. *Punto.*[1]

(1994)

---

[1] *Soy yo . . . Punto* I'm me . . . Period. (Editors' note.)

Critical Eye

FOR DISCUSSION

a. Do you believe that most children of immigrants who live in America suffer from the same issues as the author?

b. How plausible do you think it would be to have all immigrants rid themselves of monikers such as *Chinese American* and *Hispanic American* and to simply be Americans in the interest of racial harmony?

REAPPROACHING THE TEXT

What could the college experience have done to make the author's transition better or alleviate her racial tensions?

WRITING ASSIGNMENT

Why are we all so obsessed with racial identity in America?

Maxine Hong Kingston

The Misery of Silence[1]

When I went to kindergarten and had to speak English for the first time, I became silent. A dumbness—a shame—still cracks my voice in two, even when I want to say "hello" casually, or ask an easy question in front of the check-out counter, or ask directions of a bus driver. I stand frozen, or I hold up the line with the complete, grammatical sentence that comes squeaking out at impossible length. "What did you say?" says the cab driver, or "Speak up," so I have to perform again, only weaker the second time. A telephone call makes my throat bleed and takes up that day's courage. It spoils my day with self-disgust when I hear my broken voice come skittering out into the open. It makes people wince to hear it. I'm getting better, though. Recently I asked the postman for special-issue stamps; I've waited since childhood for postmen to give me some of their own accord. I am making progress, a little every day.

My silence was thickest—total—during the three years that I covered my school paintings with black paint. I painted layers of black over houses and flowers and suns, and when I drew on the blackboard, I put a layer of chalk on top. I was making a stage curtain, and it was the moment before the curtain parted or rose. The teachers called my parents to school, and I saw they had been saving my pictures, curling and cracking, all alike and black. The teachers pointed to the pictures and looked serious, talked seriously too, but my parents did not understand English. ("The parents and teachers of criminals were executed," said my father.) My parents took the pictures home. I spread them out (so black and full of possibilities) and pretended the curtains were swinging open, flying up, one after another, sunlight underneath, mighty operas.

During the first silent year I spoke to no one at school, did not ask before going to the lavatory, and flunked kindergarten. My sister also said nothing for three years, silent in the playground and silent at lunch. There were other quiet Chinese girls not of our family, but most of them got over it sooner than we did. I enjoyed the silence. At first it did not occur to me I was supposed to talk or to pass kindergarten. I talked at home and to one or two of the

[1]Editor's title.

From *The Woman Warrior* by Maxine Hong Kingston, copyright © 1975, 1976 by Maxine Hong Kingston. Used by permission of Alfred A. Knopf, a division of Random House, Inc.

Chinese kids in class. I made motions and even made some jokes. I drank out of a toy saucer when the water spilled out of the cup, and everybody laughed, pointing at me, so I did it some more. I didn't know that Americans don't drink out of saucers.

I liked the Negro students (Black Ghosts) best because they laughed the loudest and talked to me as if I were a daring talker too. One of the Negro girls had her mother coil braids over her ears Shanghai-style like mine; we were Shanghai twins except that she was covered with black like my paintings. Two Negro kids enrolled in Chinese school, and the teachers gave them Chinese names. Some Negro kids walked me to school and home, protecting me from the Japanese kids, who hit me and chased me and stuck gum in my ears. The Japanese kids were noisy and tough. They appeared one day in kindergarten, released from concentration camp, which was a tic-tac-toe mark, like barbed wire, on the map.

It was when I found out I had to talk that school become a misery, that the silence became a misery. I did not speak and felt bad each time that I did not speak. I read aloud in first grade, though, and heard the barest whisper with little squeaks come out of my throat. "Louder," said the teacher, who scared the voice away again. The other Chinese girls did not talk either, so I knew the silence had to do with being a Chinese girl.

Reading out loud was easier than speaking because we did not have to make up what to say, but I stopped often, and the teacher would think I'd gone quiet again. I could not understand "I." The Chinese "I" has seven strokes, intricacies. How could the American "I," assuredly wearing a hat like the Chinese, have only three strokes, the middle so straight? Was it out of politeness that this writer left off the strokes the way a Chinese has to write her own name small and crooked? No, it was not politeness; "I" is a capital and "you" is lower-case. I stared at that middle line and waited so long for its black center to resolve into tight strokes and dots that I forgot to pronounce it. The other troublesome word was "here," no strong consonant to hang on to, and so flat, when "here" is two mountainous ideographs. The teacher, who had already told me every day how to read "I" and "here," put me in the low corner under the stairs again, where the noisy boys usually sat.

When my second grade class did a play, the whole class went to the auditorium except the Chinese girls. The teacher, lovely and Hawaiian, should have understood about us, but instead left us behind in the classroom. Our voices were too soft or nonexistent, and our parents never signed the permission slips anyway. They never signed anything unnecessary. We opened the door a crack and peeked out, but closed it again quickly. One of us (not me) won every spelling bee, though.

I remember telling the Hawaiian teacher, "We Chinese can't sing 'land where our fathers died.'" She argued with me about politics, while I meant because of curses. But how can I have that memory when I couldn't talk? My mother says that we, like the ghosts, have no memories.

After American school, we picked up our cigar boxes, in which we had arranged books, brushes, and an inkbox neatly, and went to Chinese school, from 5:00 to 7:30 P.M. There we chanted together, voices rising and falling, loud and soft, some boys shouting, everybody reading together, reciting together and not alone with one voice. When we had a memorization test, the teacher let each of us come to his desk and say the lesson to him privately, while the rest of the class practiced copying or tracing. Most of the teachers were men. The boys who were so well behaved in the American school played tricks on them and talked back to them. The girls were not mute. They screamed and yelled during recess, when there were no rules; they had fistfights. Nobody was afraid of children hurting themselves or of children hurting school property. The glass doors to the red and green balconies with the gold joy symbols were left wide open so that we could run out and climb the fire escapes. We played capture-the-flag in the auditorium, where Sun Yat-sen and Chiang Kai-shek's pictures hung at the back of the stage, the Chinese flag on their left and the American flag on their right. We climbed the teak ceremonial chairs and made flying leaps off the stage. One flag headquarters was behind the glass door and the other on stage right. Our feet drummed on the hollow stage. During recess the teachers locked themselves up in their office with the shelves of books, copybooks, inks from China. They drank tea and warmed their hands at a stove. There was no play supervision. At recess we had the school to ourselves, and also we could roam as far as we could go—downtown, Chinatown stores, home—as long as we returned before the bell rang.

At exactly 7:30 the teacher again picked up the brass bell that sat on his desk and swung it over our heads, while we charged down the stairs, our cheering magnified in the stairwell. Nobody had to line up.

Not all of the children who were silent at American school found voice at Chinese school. One new teacher said each of us had to get up and recite in front of the class, who was to listen. My sister and I had memorized the lesson perfectly. We said it to each other at home, one chanting, one listening. The teacher called on my sister to recite first. It was the first time a teacher had called on the second-born to go first. My sister was scared. She glanced at me and looked away; I looked down at my desk. I hoped that she could do it because if she could, then I would have to. She opened her mouth and a voice came out that wasn't a whisper, but it wasn't a proper voice either. I hoped that she would not cry, fear breaking up her voice like twigs underfoot. She sounded as if she were trying to sing through weeping and strangling. She did not pause or stop to end the embarrassment. She kept going until she said the last word, and then she sat down. When it was my turn, the same voice came out, a crippled animal running on broken legs. You could hear splinters in my voice, bones rubbing jagged against one another. I was loud, though. I was glad I didn't whisper.

How strange that the emigrant villagers are shouters, hollering face to face. My father asks, "Why is it I can hear Chinese from blocks away? Is it that I understand the language? Or is it they talk loud?" They turn the radio up full blast to hear the operas, which do not seem to hurt their ears. And they yell over the singers that wail over the drums, everybody talking at once, big arm gestures, spit flying. You can see the disgust on American faces looking at women like that. It isn't just the loudness. It is the way Chinese sounds, ching-chong ugly, to American ears, not beautiful like Japanese sayonara words with the consonants and vowels as regular as Italian. We make guttural peasant noise and have Ton Duc Thang names you can't remember. And the Chinese can't hear Americans at all; the language is too soft and western music unhearable. I've watched a Chinese audience laugh, visit, talk-story, and holler during a piano recital, as if the musician could not hear them. A Chinese-American, somebodyson, was playing Chopin, which has no punctuation, no cymbals, no gongs. Chinese piano music is five black keys. Normal Chinese women's voices are strong and bossy. We American-Chinese girls had to whisper to make ourselves American-feminine. Apparently we whispered even more softly than the Americans. Once a year the teachers referred my sister and me to speech therapy, but our voices would straighten out, unpredictably normal, for the therapists. Some of us gave up, shook our heads, and said nothing, not one word. Some of us could not even shake our heads. At times shaking my head no is more self-assertion than I can manage. Most of us eventually found some voice, however faltering. We invented an American-feminine speaking personality.

Critical Eye

FOR DISCUSSION

a. Do you believe the issues presented in the text are experienced by most non-native speakers?

b. How is it that, for the most part, Asian Americans are viewed as the "model minority" in terms of professions and academics while Hong Kingston's experience seems so horrific?

REAPPROACHING THE TEXT

How does this story and the essay "The Human Cost of an Illiterate Society" speak to each other?

WRITING ASSIGNMENT

Is what happened to Hong Kingston an example of racism?

Tahira Naqvi

Brave We Are

"Mom, Ammi," he asks, the little boy Kasim who is my son, who has near-black eyes and whose buck teeth give him a Bugs Bunny look when his mouth is open, as it is now, in query. "What does hybrid mean?"

"Hybrid?" I'm watching the water in the pot very closely; the tiny bubbles quivering restlessly on its surface indicate it's about to come to boil. Poised over the pot, clutching a batch of straw-colored Prince spaghetti, is my hand, suspended, warm from the steam and waiting for the moment when the bubbles will suddenly and turbulently come to life.

I'm not fussy about brands, especially where spaghetti is concerned (it's all pasta, after all), but I wish there was one which would fit snugly at the outset into my largest pot. As things stand now, the strands bend uncomfortably, contort, embroiling themselves in something of a struggle within the confines of the pot once they've been dropped into the boiling water. Someday of course, I will have a pot large enough to accommodate all possible lengths and varieties.

"Yeah, hybrid. Do you know what it means?"

The note of restive insistence in his voice compels me to tear my gaze away from the water. Kasim's face looks darker now than when he left for school this morning. Perhaps running up the steep driveway with the March wind lashing against his lean nine-year-old frame has forced the blood to rush to his face. Flushed, his face reminds me he's still only a child, 'only ten, just a baby,' as my mother often says when I sometimes take him to task in her presence, arguing with him as if he were a man behaving like a child.

A new spelling word? Such a difficult word for a fourth-grader. "Are you studying plants?"

"No, but can you tell me what it means?" Impatient, so impatient, so like the water that's hissing and tumbling in the pot, demanding immediate attention. He slides against the kitchen counter and hums, his fingers beating an indecipherable rhythm on the Formica, his eyes raised above mine, below mine, behind me, to the window outside which white,

"Brave We Are" from *Dying in a Strange Country* (Tsar, 2001), reprinted by permission of Tsar Publications.

lavender and gray have mingled to become a muddied brown. Just as he reaches for the cookie jar I quickly throw in the spaghetti.

"Well, that's a hard word. Let me see." Helplessly I watch as he breaks off a Stella Doro biscuit in his mouth and crumbs disperse in a steady fall-out, over the counter, on the kitchen tile, some getting caught in his blue-and-green striped sweater, like flies in a spider's web. "It's a sort of mixture, a combination of different sorts of things," I say wisely, with the absolute knowledge that 'things' is susceptible to misinterpretation. I rack my brain for a good example. If I don't hurry up with one he's going to move away with the notion that his mother doesn't know what hybrid means.

"You mean if you mix orange juice with lemonade it's going to become hybrid juice?" The idea has proved ticklish, he smiles, crumbs from the Stella Doro dangling on the sides of his face; they obviously don't bother him as much as they bother me. I lean forward and rub a hand around his mouth just as he lunges toward the cookie jar again. He squirms and recoils at the touch of my ministering hand. Another biscuit is retrieved. I turn down the heat under the spaghetti to medium and start chopping onions.

Today I'm making spaghetti the way my mother makes it in Lahore, like pulao, the way I used to make it after I got married and was just learning to cook for a husband who had selective tastes in food. That was about the only thing I could make then so I worked hard to embellish and innovate. There, we call it noodles, although it's unmistakably spaghetti, with no tomato sauce or meatballs in or anywhere near it, no cheese either, and no one has heard of mozzarella or romano. The idea of cheese with our recipe would surprise the people in Lahore; even the ones with the most adventurous palates will cringe.

"Well, that too." And why not? My eyes smart from the sharpness of the onions, tears fill my eyes and spill over my cheeks. I turn away from the chopping board. "The word is used when you breed two different kinds of plants or animals, it's called cross-breeding." I snaffle. This gets harder. I know his knowledge of breeding is limited and 'cross' isn't going to help at all.

"What's cross-what you may call it?"

An example. One that will put the seal on hybrid forever. So he can boast his mother knows everything.

I wipe my watering eyes with a paper napkin and turn to the onions again. These, chopped thinly, are for the ground beef which will be cooked with small green peas, cubed potatoes and cut-leaf spinach and will be spiced with coriander, garlic, cumin, a touch of turmeric and half-inch long bristly strands of fresh ginger root. I'll throw the beef into the spaghetti when it's done and my husband and I alone will eat what I make. My children like spaghetti the way it should be, the way it is in America.

Moisture runs down my cheeks and my eyes smart. I place the knife down on the chopping board, tear out another sheet from the roll of Bounty towels on my right and rub my eyes and nose with it, my attention driven to the stark, brown limbs of trees outside as I wipe my face. The kitchen window that I now face as I do innumerable times during the day, faithfully reflects the movements of time and seasons of the small town in Connecticut where we live, compelling the spirit to buoyancy or, when the tones on its canvas are achromatous and dark, to melancholy, to sadness. Today, the sun is visible again and the white of the snow is distinguishable from the lavender of the bare, thin, stalky birches, unhealthy because we haven't tended them well. Sharply the sun cuts shadows on the clean, uncluttered snow.

Why does snow in February always remind me of February in Lahore? Incongruent, disparate, the seasons have so little in common. March is spring, grass so thick your foot settles into it, roses that bloom firm, their curves fleshy, the colors like undisturbed paint on an artist's palette, the air timberous, weaving in and out of swishing tree branches with *the sar, sar, sar* of a string instrument. Why do I turn to Eileen, my cleaning lady, and say, "Eileen, do you know it's spring in Lahore?" She looks up from the pot she's scrubbing in the kitchen sink with a good-humored smile. "No kidding? Really?" she asks, as if she didn't already know, as if she hadn't already heard it from me before.

An example, yes. "Now take an apple. A farmer can cross-breed a Macintosh apple with a Golden Yellow and get something which is a little bit like both. That will be a hybrid apple." I look closely at the boy's face for some signs of comprehension.

"You mean the apple's going to have a new name, like Macintosh Yellow?" he asks, his forehead creased thoughtfully.

"Yes." Relieved, I return to the onions, making a mental note to check the spaghetti soon, which, languorously swelled now, will have to be taken off from the stove and drained.

"But what about animals? You said there's *cross what you may call it* in animals too." He sprawls against the counter, up and down, right and left, like a gymnast.

"Yes there is. A cow from one family may be bred with a steer from another family and they'll end up with a calf that's a bit like the two of them." I wash my hands and he skips on the floor, dance-like steps, his arms raised.

"But man's an animal too, teacher says. Do people also cross . . . *umm* . . . breed?"

He's humming again. I know the tune now; "*Suzie Q/ Suzie Q/ I love you/O Suzie Q!*" It's from a song on his older brother Haider's tape, a catchy tune, sort of stays with you and you can't stop humming it. Both Haider and my younger son, Asghar, were amused when I showed an interest in the song. What do I know about music, their kind of music? Once, nearly two years ago, I tried to bribe Haider to memorize a ghazal by the poet Ghalib. The greatest Urdu poet of the subcontinent, I said passionately, the most complex. Egged on by the fifty dollars I was offering, he mastered the first verse by listening to a tape of ghazals sung by Mehdi Hasan.

> *Yeh naa thi hamari qismet ke visal-e-yaar ho*
> *Agar aurjeete rehte yehi intizar hota*

> It was not fated that I should meet my beloved,
> Life will merely prolong the waiting

Then, unable to sustain his interest, despite the now thirty-dollar a verse rate, Haider abandoned the project.

"The words are too hard," he complained when I protested, somewhat angrily. "The music's easy, but I can't keep up with the lyrics."

And I would have given him the money too. Actually I had decided to give him all of it after he had moved on to the second verse.

"Does that mean Mary is also hybrid?" Kasim's voice crashes into my thoughts of Suzie Q with a loud boom.

I lower the heat under the spaghetti—so what if it's a bit overdone. The yellow-white strands jump at each other in frantic embraces, hurried, as if there's no time to be lost.

"Mary? What are you talking about?" I know exactly what he's talking about. His vagueness passes through the sieve in my head and comes out as clarity. I fill in any blanks, uncannily, never ceasing to be surprised at the way this peculiar magic works.

"You know, Mary Khan, Dr. Khan's daughter? She's in my class Mom, you know her."

Yes, I know Mary well. Her full name is Marium. Her father, Amjad Khan and my husband, Ali, were together in the same medical school in Lahore, they graduated the same year, they completed residencies together at the same hospital in New York, where Amjad met and married Helen, a nurse. Helen is English. She's a few years older than I, very tall, almost a half-inch taller than Amjad, and has sleek, golden hair. We're good friends, Helen and I, and at least once a week we meet for lunch at a restaurant, an activity we decided to call 'sampling restaurants for later.' Over salmon lasagna or papadi chat and dosa or tandoori chicken she'll tell me how difficult Amjad is when it comes to their children, how upset he is that their son has taken it upon himself to date without his father's consent or approval. I'll shake my head and try to explain that Amjad might have dated *her*, but like a good Muslim father, he can't accept that his son can have girlfriends. "Wait till Mary is older," I say with my hand on Helen's arm, "the Muslim father in him will drop all his masks." Together we do what most women do quite unabashedly: spend a great deal of time talking about husbands.

When Mary was born Amjad said, "We're going to call her Marium, it's a name everyone knows." Familiar and convenient is what he meant, since it's tri-religious. That doesn't sound right, but if we can say bisexual, surely we can say tri-religious too. Why not? After all Islam, Christianity and Judaism all profess a claim to this name. However, before the child was quite one 'Marium' was shortened permanently to Mary.

Kasim is at the breakfast table now, some of his earlier energy dissipated. A small piece of biscuit lies forlornly before him on the table and he fusses with it slowly, obviously unwilling to pop the last bit in his mouth, content just to play with it.

"You know, her mother's English and her father's Pakistani like Dad, and she's got blue eyes and black hair."

"Yes, she does have lovely blue eyes and they look so pretty with her dark hair." I grapple with something to blunt the sharpness of his next question which I anticipate and I know I cannot repel.

"Well, then she's hybrid too, isn't she?" He's looking straight at me. His eyes are bright with the defiance of someone who knows he's scored a point.

Brave we are, we who answer questions that spill forth artlessly from the mouths of nine-year-old purists, questions that can neither be waved nor dismissed with flippant ambiguity. Vigilant and alert, we must be ready with our answers.

"Technically speaking she is, I mean, wait, you can say she is." I lift a hand and stop him before he says more. "But we don't use the word for people." The firmness in my voice sounds forced. "Don't say anything to her, okay?"

"Why? Is it a swear?"

"No!" I hasten with denial. "Of course not. It's just a word we don't use for people, that's all. Understand?"

"But what do you call them then?" He persists. "Mary's like the apple, isn't she? Isn't she? Her name's Mary Khan, isn't it?"

"Yes, Kas, it is. But there's nothing wrong with that name, a name's a name." Kasim looks contemplative. I know he's saying to himself, *Mom doesn't really know, but Mary's a hybrid, she's got blue eyes and black hair.*

"She's a person Kasim, not an apple. Anyway, you didn't tell me where you heard that word. Is it on your spelling list for this week?"

"No, Mrs. Davis was reading us something about plants in the *Weekly Reader.* It's not homework." He shrugs, abandons the Stella Doro and humming, leaves the kitchen.

"Get to homework now," I call after him, wondering if there's an equivalent of 'hybrid' in Urdu, a whole word, not one or two strung together in a phrase to mean the same thing. Offhand I can't think of one.

Without meaning to I throw some oregano into the boiling spaghetti. I shouldn't have done that. How's oregano going to taste in the company of coriander and cumin? Well, no matter, it's too late anyway.

After I've drained the spaghetti I will take some out for the meat mixture, saving the rest for my children. Then I'll add to our portion, my husband's and mine, the beef and vegetable mixture and turn everything over ever so gently, making sure that the spaghetti isn't squelched. The strands must remain smooth, elusive, separate.

Critical Eye

FOR DISCUSSION

a. Can you make the argument that issues of race are very difficult for parents to discuss with their children?

b. Is it necessary for a child from a mixed background to choose a race?

c. In your opinion, why is the mother uncomfortable?

d. What do you think about the mother's responses to her child's questions about the notion of a "hybrid?"

e. Compare the mother in "Brave We Are" to the mother in Nella Larsen's *Passing*. In what ways are their views on race similar?

REAPPROACHING THE LITERATURE

Consider how the story would change if the mother were to simply tell her child that race should never be an issue when determining one's worth.

WRITING ASSIGNMENT

Imagine a world where everyone has a mixed background. Would we then finally be rid of racial intolerance?

Vine Deloria

The Red and the Black

from *Custer Died for Your Sins*

Civil Rights has been the most important and least understood movement of our generation. To some it has seemed to be a simple matter of fulfilling rights outlined by the Constitutional amendments after the Civil War. To others, particularly church people, Civil Rights has appeared to be a fulfillment of the brotherhood of man and the determination of humanity's relationship to God. To those opposing the movement, Civil Rights has been a foreign conspiracy which has threatened the fabric of our society.

For many years the movement to give the black people rights equal to those of their white neighbors was called Race Relations. The preoccupation with race obscured the real issues that were developing and meant that programs devised to explore the area of race always had a black orientation.

To the Indian people it has seemed quite unfair that churches and government agencies concentrated their efforts primarily on the blacks. By defining the problem as one of race and making race refer solely to black, Indians were systematically excluded from consideration. National church groups have particularly used race as a means of exploring minority-group relations. Whatever programs or policies outlined from national churches to their affiliates and parishes were generally black-oriented programs which had been adapted to include Indians.

There was probably a historical basis for this type of thinking. In many states in the last century, Indians were classified as white by laws passed to exclude blacks. So there was a connotation that Indians might in some way be like whites. But in other areas, particularly marriage laws, Indians were classified as blacks and this connotation really determined the role into which the white man forced the red man. Consequently, as far as most Race Relations were concerned, Indians were classified as non-whites.

There has been no way to positively determine in which category Indians belong when it comes to federal agencies. The Bureau of Indian Affairs

"The Red and the Black." Reprinted with the permission of Scribner, an imprint of Simon & Schuster Adult Publishing Group, from Custer Died for Your Sins: An Indian Manifesto by Vine Deloria, Jr. Copyright © 1969 by Vine Deloria, Jr.; copyright renewed © 1997 by Vine Deloria, Jr.

consistently defined Indians as good guys who have too much dignity to demonstrate, hoping to keep the Indian people separate from the ongoing Civil Rights movement. Other agencies generally adopted a semi-black orientation. Sometimes Indians were treated as if they were blacks and other times not.

The Civil Rights Commission and the Community Relations Service always gave only lip service to Indians until it was necessary for them to write an annual report. At that time they always sought out some means of including Indians as a group with which they had worked the previous fiscal year. That was the extent of Indian relationship with the agency: a paragraph in the annual report and a promise to do something next year.

Older Indians, as a rule, have been content to play the passive role outlined for them by the bureau. They have wanted to avoid the rejection and bad publicity given activists.

The Indian people have generally avoided confrontations between the different minority groups and confrontations with the American public at large. They have felt that any publicity would inevitably have bad results and since the press seemed dedicated to the perpetuation of sensationalism rather than straight reporting of the facts, great care has been taken to avoid the spotlight. Because of this attitude, Indian people have not become well known in the field of inter-group and race relations. Consequently they have suffered from the attitudes of people who have only a superficial knowledge of minority groups and have attached a certain stigma to them.

The most common attitude Indians have faced has been the unthoughtful Johnny-come-lately liberal who equates certain goals with a dark skin. This type of individual generally defines the goals of all groups by the way he understands what he wants for the blacks. Foremost in this category have been younger social workers and clergymen entering the field directly out of college or seminary. For the most part they have been book-fed and lack experience in life. They depend primarily upon labels and categories of academic import rather than on any direct experience. Too often they have achieved positions of prominence as programs have been expanded to meet needs of people. In exercising their discretionary powers administratively, they have run roughshod over Indian people. They have not wanted to show their ignorance about Indians. Instead, they prefer to place all people with darker skin in the same category of basic goals, then develop their programs to fit these preconceived ideas.

Since the most numerous group has been the blacks, programs designed for blacks were thought adequate for all needs of all groups. When one asks a liberal about minority groups, he unconsciously seems to categorize them all together for purposes of problem solving. Hence, dark-skinned and minority group as categorical concepts have brought about the same basic results—the Indian is defined as a subcategory of black.

Cultural differences have only seemed to emphasize the white liberal's point of view in lumping the different communities together. When Indians have pointed out real differences that do exist, liberals have tended to dismiss the differences as only minor aberrations which distinguish different racial groups.

At one conference on education of minority groups, I once mentioned the existence of some three hundred Indian languages which made bicultural and bilingual education a necessity. I was immediately challenged by several white educators who attempted to prove that blacks also have a language problem. I was never able to make the difference real to them. For the conference people the point had again been established that minority groups all had the same basic problems.

Recently, blacks and some Indians have defined racial problems as having one focal point—the White Man. This concept is a vast oversimplification of the real problem, as it centers on a racial theme rather than on specific facts. And it is simply the reversal of the old prejudicial attitude of the white who continues to define minority groups as problems of his—that is, Indian problem, Negro problem, and so on.

Rather than race or minority grouping, non-whites have often been defined according to their function within the American society. Negroes, as we have said, were considered draft animals, Indians wild animals. So too, Orientals were considered domestic animals and Mexicans humorous lazy animals. The white world has responded to the non-white groups in a number of ways, but primarily according to the manner in which it believed the non-whites could be rescued from their situation.

Thus Orientals were left alone once whites were convinced that they preferred to remain together and presented no basic threat to white social mores. Mexicans were similarly discarded and neglected when whites felt that they preferred to remain by themselves. In both cases there was no direct confrontation between whites and the two groups because there was no way that a significant number of them could be exploited. They owned little; they provided little which the white world coveted.

With the black and the Indian, however, tensions increased over the years. Both groups had been defined as animals with which the white had to have some relation and around whom some attitude must be formed. Blacks were ex-draft animals who somehow were required to become non-black. Indeed, respectability was possible for a black only by emphasizing characteristics and features that were non-black. Indians were the ex-wild animals who had provided the constant danger for the civilizing tendencies of the invading white. They always presented a foreign aspect to whites unfamiliar with the western hemisphere.

The white man adopted two basic approaches in handling blacks and Indians. He systematically excluded blacks from all programs, policies, social events, and economic schemes. He could not allow blacks to rise from their position because it would mean that the evolutionary scheme had superseded the Christian scheme and that man had perhaps truly descended from the ape.

With the Indian the process was simply reversed. The white man had been forced to deal with the Indian in treaties and agreements. It was difficult, therefore, to completely overlook the historical antecedents such as Thanksgiving, the plight of the early Pilgrims, and the desperate straits from which various Indian tribes had often rescued the whites. Indians were therefore subjected to the most intense pressure to become white. Laws passed by Congress had but one goal—the Anglo-Saxonization of the Indian. The antelope had to become a white man.

Between these two basic attitudes, the apelike draft animal and the wild free-running antelope, the white man was impaled on the horns of a dilemma he had created within himself.

It is well to keep these distinctions clearly in mind when talking about Indians and blacks. When the liberals equate the two they are overlooking obvious historical facts. Never did the white man systematically exclude Indians from his schools and meeting places. Nor did the white man ever kidnap black children from their homes and take them off to a government boarding school to be educated as whites. The white man signed no treaties with the black. Nor did he pass any amendments to the Constitution to guarantee the treaties of the Indian.

The basic problem which has existed between the various racial groups has not been one of race but of culture and legal status. The white man systematically destroyed Indian culture where it existed, but separated blacks from his midst so that they were forced to attempt the creation of their own culture.

The white man forbade the black to enter his own social and economic system and at the same time force-fed the Indian what he was denying the black. Yet the white man demanded that the black conform to white standards and insisted that the Indian don feathers and beads periodically to perform for him.

The white man presented the *problem* of each group in contradictory ways so that neither black nor Indian could understand exactly where the problem existed or how to solve it. The Indian was always told that his problem was one of conflicting cultures. Yet, when solutions were offered by the white man, they turned out to be a reordering of the legal relationship between red and white. There was never a time when the white man said he was trying to help the Indian get into the mainstream of American life that he did not also demand that the Indian give up land, water, minerals, timber, and other resources which would enrich the white men.

The black also suffered from the same basic lie. Time after time legislation was introduced which purported to give the black equal rights with the white but which ultimately restricted his life and opportunities, even his acceptance by white people. The initial Civil Rights Act following the thirteenth, fourteenth, and fifteenth amendments was assumed to give the blacks equal rights with "white citizens." In fact, it was so twisted that it took nearly a century to bring about additional legislation to confirm black rights.

In June of 1968 the Supreme Court finally interpreted an ancient statute in favor of blacks in the matter of purchasing a house. Had the right existed for nearly a century without anyone knowing it? Of course not, the white had simply been unwilling to give in to the black. Can one blame the black athletes at the recent Olympic Games for their rebellion against the role cast for them by white society? Should they be considered as specially trained athletic animals suitable only for hauling away tons of gold medals for the United States every four years while equality remains as distant as it ever was?

It is time for both black and red to understand the ways of the white man. The white is after Indian lands and resources. He always has been and always will be. For Indians to continue to think of their basic conflict with the white man as cultural is the height of folly. The problem is and always has been the adjustment of the legal relationship between the Indian tribes and the federal government, between the true owners of the land and the usurpers.

The black must understand that whites are determined to keep him out of their society. No matter how many Civil Rights laws are passed or how many are on the drawing board, the basic thrust is to keep the black out of society and harmless. The problem, therefore, is not one of legal status, it is one of culture and social and economic mobility. It is foolish for a black to depend upon a law to make acceptance of him by the white possible. Nor should he react to the rejection. His problem is social, and economic, and cultural, not one of adjusting the legal relationship between the two groups.

When the black seeks to change his role by adjusting the laws of the nation, he merely raises the hope that progress is being made. But for the majority of blacks progress is not being made. Simply because a middle-class black can eat at the Holiday Inn is not a gain. People who can afford the best generally get it. A socio-economic, rather than legal adjustment must consequently be the goal.

But the understanding of the racial question does not ultimately involve understanding by either blacks or Indians. It involves the white man himself. He must examine his past. He must face the problems he has created within himself and within others. The white man must no longer project his fears and insecurities onto other groups, races, and countries. Before the white man can relate to others he must forego the pleasure of defining them. The white man must learn to stop viewing history as a plot against himself.

It was more than religious intolerance that drove the early colonists across the ocean. More than a thousand years before Columbus, the barbaric tribes destroyed the Roman Empire. With utter lack of grace, they ignorantly obliterated classical civilization, Christianity swept across the conquerors like the white man later swept across North America, destroying native religions and leaving paralyzed groups of disoriented individuals in its wake. Then the combination of Christian theology, superstition, and forms of the old Roman civil government began to control the tamed barbaric tribes. Gone were the religious rites of the white tribesmen. Only the Gothic arches in the great cathedrals, symbolizing the oaks under which their ancestors worshiped, remained to remind them of the glories that had been.

Not only did the European tribes lose their religion, they were subjected to a new form of economics which totally destroyed them: feudalism. The freedom that had formerly been theirs became only the freedom to toil on the massive estates. Even their efforts to maintain their ancient ways fell to the requirements of the feudal state as power centered in a few royal houses.

Feudalism saw man as a function of land and not as something in himself. The European tribes, unable to withstand the chaos of medieval social and political forces, were eliminated as power consolidated in a few hands. Far easier than the Indian tribes of this continent, the Europeans gave up the ghost and accepted their fate without questioning it. And they remained in subjection for nearly a millennium.

The religious monolith which Christianity had deviously constructed over the Indo-European peasants eventually showed cracks in its foundations. The revolution in religious thought triggered by Martin Luther's challenge to Papal authority was merely an afterthought. It did no more than acknowledge that the gates had been opened a long time and that it was perfectly natural to walk through them into the new era.

In the sixteenth century Europe opened up the can of worms which had been carefully laid to rest a millenium earlier. The Reformation again brought up the question of the place of Western man in God's scheme of events. Because there was no way the individual could relate to the past, he was told to relate to the other world, leaving this world free for nationalistic exploitation—the real forger of identity.

Because tribes and groups had been unable to survive, the common denominator, the individual, became the focal point of the revolt. Instead of socially oriented individuals, the Reformation produced self-centered individuals. Social and economic Darwinism, the survival of the fittest at any cost, replaced the insipid brotherhood of Christianity not because Christianity's basic thrust was invalid, but because it had been corrupted for so long that it was no longer recognizable.

The centuries following the Reformation were marked with incredible turmoil. But the turmoil was not so much over religious issues as it was over interpretation of religious doctrines. Correctness of belief was preferred over truth itself. Man charged back into the historical mists to devise systems of thought which would connect him with the greats of the past. Fear of the unfamiliar became standard operating procedure.

Today Europe is still feeling the effects of the submersion of its original tribes following the demise of the Roman Empire. Western man smashes that which he does not understand because he never had the opportunity to evolve his own culture. Instead ancient cultures were thrust upon him while he was yet unprepared for them.

There lingers still the unsolved question of the primacy of the Roman Empire as contrasted with the simpler more relaxed life of the Goths, Celts, Franks, and Vikings.

Where feudalism conceived man as a function of land, the early colonists reversed the situation in their efforts to create "new" versions of their motherlands. Early settlers made land a function of man, and with a plentitude of land, democracy appeared to be the inevitable desire of God. It was relatively simple, once they had made this juxtaposition, to define Indians, blacks, and other groups in relation to land.

The first organizing efforts of the new immigrants were directed toward the process of transplanting European social and political systems in the new arms they settled. Thus New England, New France, New Spain, New Sweden, New Haven, New London, New York, New Jersey, Troy, Ithaca, and other names expressed their desire to relive the life they had known on the other side of the Atlantic—but to relive it on their own terms. No one seriously wanted to return to the status of peasant, but people certainly entertained the idea of indigenous royalty. If your ancestor got off the boat, you were one step up the ladder of respectability. Many Indians, of course, believe it would have been better if Plymouth Rock had landed on the Pilgrims than the Pilgrims on Plymouth Rock.

The early colonists did not flee religious persecution so much as they wished to perpetuate religious persecution under circumstances more favorable to them. They wanted to be the persecutors. The rigorous theocracies which quickly originated in New England certainly belie the myth that the first settlers wanted only religious freedom. Nothing was more destructive of man than the early settlements on this continent.

It would have been far better for the development of this continent had the first settlers had no illusions as to their motives. We have seen nearly five centuries of white settlement on this continent, yet the problems brought over from Europe remain unsolved and grow in basic intensity daily. And violence as an answer to the problem of identity has only covered discussion of the problem.

In transplanting Europe to these peaceful shores, the colonists violated the most basic principle of man's history: certain lands are given to certain peoples. It is these peoples only who can flourish, thrive, and survive on the land. Intruders may hold sway for centuries but they will eventually be pushed from the land or the land itself will destroy them. The Holy Land, having been periodically conquered and beaten into submission by a multitude of invaders, today remains the land which God gave to Abraham and his descendants. So will America return to the red man.

The message of the Old Testament, the Hebrew-Jewish conception of the Homeland, has been completely overlooked. Culture, if any exists, is a function of the homeland, not a function of the economic system that appears to hold temporary sway over a region.

Thus the fundamental error of believing a transplant possible practically canceled any chances for significant evolution of a homogeneous people. Even more so, it canceled the potentiality of making the new settlements the land of the free and the home of the brave—not when it was already the home of the Indian brave.

There never really was a transplant. There was only a three-hundred-year orgy of exploitation. The most feverish activity in America has been land speculation. Nearly all transactions between Indian and white have been land transactions. With Emancipation, the first program offered the black was one hundred dollars, forty acres, and a mule! But when it appeared the black might be able to create something on the land, that was immediately taken away from him.

Land has been the basis on which racial relations have been defined ever since the first settlers got off the boat. Minority groups, denominated as such, have always been victims of economic forces rather than beneficiaries of the lofty ideals proclaimed in the Constitution and elsewhere. One hundred years of persecution after Emancipation, the Civil Rights laws of the 1950's and 1960's were all passed by use of the Interstate Commerce Clause of the Constitution. Humanity, at least on this continent, has been subject to the whims of the marketplace.

When we begin to talk of Civil Rights, therefore, it greatly confuses the issue and lessens our chances of understanding the forces involved in the rights of human beings. Rather, we should begin talking about actual economic problems; and in realistic terms we are talking about land.

No movement can sustain itself, no people can continue, no government can function, and no religion can become a reality except it be bound to a land area of its own. The Jews have managed to sustain themselves in the Diaspora for over two thousand years, but in the expectation of their homeland's restoration. So-called *power* movements are primarily the urge of peoples to find their homeland and to channel their psychic energies through their land into social and economic reality. Without land and a homeland no movement can survive. And any movement attempting to build without clarifying its goals usually ends in violence, the energy from which could have been channeled toward sinking the necessary roots for the movement's existence.

Civil Rights is a function of man's desire for self-respect, not of his desire for equality. The dilemma is not one of tolerance or intolerance but one of respect or contempt. The tragedy of the early days of the Civil Rights movement is that many people, black, white, red, and yellow, were sold a bill of goods which said that *equality* was the eventual goal of the movement. But no one had considered the implications of so simple a slogan. Equality became sameness. Nobody noticed it, but everyone was trained to expect it. When equality did not come, black power did come and everybody began to climb the walls in despair.

In 1963, when the Civil Rights drive was at its peak, many of us who occupied positions of influence in Indian Affairs were severely chastised by the more militant churchmen for not having participated in the March on Washington. One churchman told me rather harshly that unless Indians *got with it* there would be no place for us in America's future. Equality, he assured me, was going to be given to us whether we want it or not.

We knew, of course, that he had equality confused with sameness, but there was no way to make him understand. In the minds of most people in 1963, legal equality and cultural conformity were identical.

We refused to participate in the Washington March. In our hearts and minds we could not believe that blacks wanted to be the same as whites. And we knew that even if they did want that, the whites would never allow it to happen. As far as we could determine, white culture, if it existed, depended primarily upon the exploitation of land, people, and life itself. It relied upon novelties and fads to provide an appearance of change but it was basically an economic Darwinism that destroyed rather than created.

It was therefore no surprise to us when Stokely Carmichael began his black power escapade. We only wondered why it had taken so long to articulate and why blacks had not been able to understand their situation better at the beginning.

A year earlier, during the Selma March, Abernathy introduced Martin Luther King with a stirring speech. He reminded his audience that "God never leaves His people without a leader." When we heard those words we knew where the Civil Rights movement was heading. It was then merely a question of waiting until the blacks began to explore *peoplehood,* toy with that idea for awhile, and then consider tribalism and nationalism.

Peoplehood is impossible without cultural independence, which in turn is impossible without a land base. Civil Rights as a movement for legal equality ended when the blacks dug beneath the equality fictions which white liberals had used to justify their great crusade. Black power, as a communications phenomenon, was a godsend to other groups. It clarified the intellectual concepts which had kept Indians and Mexicans confused and allowed the concept of self-determination suddenly to become valid.

In 1954, when the tribes were faced with the threat of termination as outlined in House Concurrent Resolution 108, the National Congress of American Indians had developed a Point Four Program aimed at creating self-determinative Indian communities. This program was ignored by Congress, bitterly opposed by the national church bodies and government agencies, undercut by white interest groups, and derided by the Uncle Tomahawks who had found security in being the household pets of the white establishment.

So, for many people, particularly those Indian people who had supported self-determination a decade earlier, Stokely Carmichael was the first black who said anything significant. Indian leadership quickly took the initiative, certain that with pressures developing from many points the goal of Indian development on the basis of tribal integrity could be realized. Using political leverage, the NCAI painstakingly began to apply itself to force change within the Bureau of Indian Affairs.

In April of 1966, following the forced resignation of Philleo Nash as Commissioner of Indian Affairs, Stewart Udall, Secretary of the Interior, held a conference to determine what "they" could do for "their" Indians. The tribes balked at the idea of bureaucrats planning the future of Indian people without so much as a polite bow in their direction. So sixty-two tribes arrived Santa Fe for their own meeting and forced Interior to realize that the days of casually making Indian policy at two-day conferences was officially over. It took, unfortunately, another two years for Udall to get the message that the Indian people meant business.

All through 1966 and 1967 Interior tried one scheme after another in an effort to sell an incredibly bad piece of legislation, the Omnibus Bill, to the tribes. In May of 1966 an embryo bill was conceived within Interior, which purported to solve all existing Indian problems. September of that year saw the Commissioner of Indian Affairs embark on a tour of the West to gather tribal suggestions "in case the Interior Department wanted to suggest some legislation"—coincidentally the bill of May, 1966.

In July of 1966, however, the National Congress of American Indians obtained a copy of the Interior bill. By September all of the tribes had versions of the proposed legislation—the same legislation which Interior claimed wouldn't even be on the drawing boards until after the regional meetings to gather tribal opinions on legislative needs.

Commissioner Bennett's task of presenting a facade of consultation while Udall rammed the bill down the Indians' throats later that year dissolved in smoke as irate tribal chairmen shot down the proposal before it left the launching pad.

As success followed success, Indians began to talk playfully of *red power* in terms similar to what SNCC was saying. The bureaucrats became confused as to which path the tribes would take next. After all, a two-year skirmish with the Secretary of the Interior and achievement of a standoff is enough to whet one's appetite for combat.

As 1968 opened, national Indian Affairs appeared to be heading faster and faster toward real involvement with other minority groups. In January, twenty-six urban centers met at Seattle, Washington, to begin to plan for participation of urban Indians in national Indian affairs. Seattle was the high point of the red power movement. But Indians quickly veered away from "power" as a movement. We knew we had a certain amount of power developing. There was no need to advocate it. The task was now to use it.

Too, black power, as many Indian people began to understand it, was not so much an affirmation of black people as it was an anti-white reaction. Blacks, many Indian people felt, had fallen into the legal-cultural trap. They obviously had power in many respects. In some instances, publicity for example, blacks had much more power than anyone dreamed possible. Indians began to question why blacks did not use their impetus in decisive ways within the current administration, which was then sympathetic to the different minority groups.

As spring came Martin Luther King had begun to organize the Poor People's Campaign. The thesis of the movement, as many of us understood it, was to be built around the existing poverty among the minority groups.

Indians had understood when Carmichael talked about racial and national integrity and the need for fine distinctions to be made between white and black. But when King began to indiscriminately lump together as one all minority communities on the basis of their economic status, Indians became extremely suspicious. The real issue for Indians—tribal existence within the homeland reservation—appeared to have been completely ignored. So where Indians could possibly have come into the continuing social movement of the 1960's, the Poor People's Campaign was too radical a departure from Indian thinking for the tribes to bridge.

Some Indians, under the name of Coalition of Indian Citizens, did attend the Washington encampment, but they remained by themselves, away from Resurrection City. By and large they did not have the support of the Indian community and were largely the creation of some national churches who wished to get Indians involved in the Poor People's Campaign. With church funding, these individuals wandered around Washington vainly trying to bring about a "confrontation" with Interior officials. They were sitting ducks for the pros of Interior, however, and the effects of their visits were negligible.

The remainder of 1968 was a traumatic experience for Indian tribes. Ideology shifted rapidly from topic to topic and dared not solidify itself in any one place for fear of rejection. National leaders trod softly when discussing issues. No one seemed to know which direction the country would take. Return to the old integration movement seemed out of the question. Continuing to push power movements against the whole of society seemed just as senseless.

Cautiously the subject of capital began to come into discussions. Too many Indian people realized the gulf that existed between the various groups in American society. A tremendous undefined need for consolidation, capitalization, and withdrawal took hold of Indian Affairs. Many tribal chairmen began to withdraw from conferences and others began to hedge their bets by remaining close to the reservation.

Tribal leaders became concerned about ongoing economic development which would be aimed at eventual economic independence for their tribes, rather than accepting every grant they could squeeze out of government agencies.

The National Congress of American Indians refused to join the Poor People's March because the goals were too generalized. Instead the NCAI began a systematic national program aimed at upgrading tribal financial independence.

In 1968 Indian leadership finally accepted the thesis that they would have to match dollar for dollar in income and program to fight the great clash between white and non-white that was coming in the months ahead. And Indian leaders began to realize that they had a fair chance of winning.

Many tribes began to shift their funds from the U.S. Treasury into the stock market. Mutual funds and stocks and bonds became the primary interest of the tribal councils. Those tribes with funds available put them into high-paying investment programs. Other tribes ordered a general cutback on overhead to give them additional funds for programming and investment.

In the move toward capitalization the tribes followed the basic ideas outlined years before by Clyde Warrior and others when the National Indian Youth Council first began to concentrate on building viable Indian communities. But it was too late for the National Indian Youth Council to take advantage of their success. Warrior died in July of 1968, some say of alcohol, most say of a broken heart.

Warrior had already been a rebel in 1964 when the majority of the tribes had lined up to support the Johnson-Humphrey ticket in the general election. Clyde supported Goldwater. His basic thesis in supporting Goldwater was that emotional reliance on a Civil Rights bill to solve the black's particular cultural question was the way to inter-group disaster. Warrior had been right.

What the different racial and minority groups had needed was not a new legal device for obliterating differences but mutual respect with economic and political independence. By not encouraging any change in the status quo, Goldwater had offered the chance for consolidation of gains at a time when the Indian people had great need to consolidate. Now consolidation was a move that may have started too late.

When a person understands the basic position developed by Warrior in 1964, one comes to realize the horror with which the Indian people contemplated their situation in 1968.

All the white man could offer, all that Johnson offered, was a minor adjustment in the massive legal machinery that had been created over a period of three hundred years. Rights of minority groups and reactions of the white majority depended solely on which parts of the machinery were being adjusted.

For many Indians the white had no culture other than one of continual exploitation. How then, they wondered, could an adjustment in methods of exploitation which had prevented formation of a culture solve their cultural problem? Thoughtful Indians, young and old, began to withdraw as they saw America building up toward a period of violent conflict. The basic problems which the colonists had brought over from Europe had not been solved and many felt there was a great danger that they would be solved violently in the future.

Culture, as Indian people understood it, was basically a lifestyle by which a people acted. It was self-expression, but not a conscious self-expression. Rather, it was an expression of the essence of a people.

All the white man had succeeded in creating in his time on this continent had been a violent conglomerate of individuals, not a people. Being a people is more a state of mind than it is a definable quality. Indians had it and now they began to give much consideration to strengthening that state of mind before racial conflict engulfed them.

When one is an integral part of the Indian world view, his values are oriented according to the social values inherent in the culture itself. Social relations become not merely patterns of behavior but customs which dominate behavior so that the culture becomes self-perpetuating. Once the cultural values take hold, crises do not cause disorientation. Thus the Indian enters a state of mind and behavior in which many things of secondary concern to him would ordinarily cause a non-Indian great emotional turmoil. Once a person is a vital part of the Indian frame of mind, it is impossible to leave. Like an old cavalry or circus horse, the call to action invoked by some distant echo produces certain action which everyone accepts as Indian. Since definition, any definition, is canceled by experience, Indian people have tended to equate behavior patterns with culture. Racial conflicts have not tended to be as important as have actual events.

There is, therefore, basically no way in which the ideology of the Civil Rights movement could reach Indian communities in a communicative sense. Outside of black power nothing that the Civil Rights people could have said would have indicated their meaning or opened lines of interaction by which the Indian people would have understood what the movement was all about.

The sight of blacks carrying TV sets through riot-torn streets completely turned off those Indian people who were trying to understand Civil Rights. America, rioters seemed to be saying, is a color TV and this is what we want from her.

Where we were hopeful of eventual peace, friendship, and cooperation between the various groups, many of us felt betrayed and confused. For years we had fought the fight for cultural survival only to find the situation reversed on us when we thought we were beginning to understand it.

It was incomprehensible to us that a people would rebel against a system that they felt was irrelevant and unresponsive to their needs. Blacks seemed to be saying that white society was bad, but they wanted it anyway.

Consequently, when a number of young Indians joined the Poor People's Campaign, they seemed to be betraying the Indian fight for survival. Feelings ran extremely high during the Poor People's March, particularly when Indian people were shown on television conducting demonstrations for fishing rights and food. Too many Indian people confused the means used with the ends to be achieved. Ideologically, Indian participation in the Poor People's March seemed to be a surrender to white society because the basic thrust of the campaign was to endorse middle-class values through pointing out their absence in the life of the poor.

Resistance to Civil Rights ideas by tribal leaders has proved a catalyst to some Indian participants in the Poor People's Campaign. Discussions with some of these Indians have convinced tribal leaders that dangerous times lie ahead for reservation people. The new militants appear ready to destroy the legal status of the tribes in order to introduce change. This attitude frightens tribal councils immensely and their fright convinces the new militants that their way is right. There appears to be very little leeway for compromise between the two groups.

Frightened tribal councils are beginning to create an atmosphere within which issues can be brought forward for solution, however. One good tangible result of Indian participation in the Poor People's Campaign is that Indian people all over have begun to question the nature of their situation. They are asking what their specific rights and benefits are and what the Poor People's March could possibly do to improve their situation.

In the defensive gesture of counting their blessings to show that the new militants should not have participated in the campaign, Indians have spent much time suffering new insights and attempting to digest what they have learned.

To many young Indians it has come through quite clearly that the problem of the Indian people is legal and not cultural, although the problem between Indians and other groups insofar as they inter-relate is cultural. That is to say, the white always presents opportunities for cultural enrichment when he is trying to steal Indian land. When the white sincerely wants to develop capital resources of the Indian people he invariably strengthens Indian cultural traits.

One has only to hear speeches by leading Democratic Senators who want to *help Indians,* to realize that there is a quiet move against the Indian land base. On the other hand, when attempts are made to develop Indian resources these thoughts are interpreted by Indian people as an affirmation of their way of life.

When we talk about basic solutions to the problems of each group, we talk about a startling reversal of concepts. Indian tribes need the basic gift of the white to the Negro—readjustment of tribal rights to protect person and property from exploitation by the federal government and private persons. Treaties need to be reaffirmed as the law of the land. Guarantees of free and undisturbed use of the reservation lands need to be enforced. Congressional pressure to destroy the Indian tribes and communities needs to be lifted.

On the other hand, the federal government needs to be the main supporter of the black quest for cultural development. The black does not need more legal rights so much as he needs the freedom to develop himself through experimentation. Prejudicial practices in law enforcement continually impinge upon the black communities, with cessions of police power and law to the local communities. During the riots after the assassination of Martin Luther King, those cities where militant black nationalists were strongest were the quietest because the young blacks kept order in spite of the white police.

White culture destroys other cultures because of its abstractness. As a destroyer of culture it is not a culture but a cancer. In order to keep the country from complete divisiveness, separatism must be accepted as a means to achieve equality of personality both for groups and individuals. Separatism can be the means by which blacks gain time for reflection, meditation, and eventual understanding of themselves as a people.

The black needs time to develop his roots, to create his sacred places, to understand the mystery of himself and his history, to understand his own purpose. These things the Indian has and is able to maintain through his tribal life. The Indian now needs to create techniques to provide the economic strength needed to guarantee the survival of what he has.

In a real way, white culture, if there is such, is already doomed to its own destruction. Continual emphasis on racial rather than cultural problems will not only bring down white society but may also endanger ancient Indian society and newly emerging black and Mexican social movements.

The white man has the marvelous ability to conceptualize. He has also the marvelous inability to distinguish between sacred and profane. He therefore arbitrarily conceptualizes all things and understands none of them. His science creates gimmicks for his use. Little effort is made to relate the gimmicks to the nature of life or to see them in a historical context.

The white man is problem-solving. His conceptualizations merge into science and then emerge in his social life as problems, the solutions of which are the adjustments of his social machine. Slavery, prohibition, Civil Rights, and social services are all important adjustments of the white man's social machine. No solution he has reached has proven adequate. Indeed, it has often proven demonic.

White solutions fail because *white* itself is an abstraction of an attitude of mind, not a racial or group reality. The white as we know him in America is an amalgam of European immigrants, not a racial phenomenon. But the temptation has always been present to define groups according to their most superficial aspect. Hence we have white, black, red, and the Yellow Peril. And we are taught to speak of the *Negro problem,* the *Indian problem,* and so forth.

White has been abstracted into a magical nebulous mythology that dominates all inhabitants of our country in their attitudes toward one another. We are, consequently, all prisoners of that mythology so far as we rebel against it. It is our misfortune that our economic system reflects uncritical acceptance of the mythology and that economic movements tend to reinforce the myth.

There is basically nothing real about our economic system. It is neither good nor bad, but neutral. Only when we place connotations on it and use it to manipulate people does it become a thing in itself.

Our welfare system demonstrates better than anything else the means to which uncritical *white* economics can be used. We have all types of welfare programs: old age, disability, aid to dependent children, orphanages, and unemployment. There is continual controversy in the halls of Congress, state legislatures, and city halls over the welfare programs.

Conservatives insist that those receiving welfare are lazy and are getting a free ride at the expense of hard-working citizens. Liberals insist that all citizens have a basic right to life and that it is the government's responsibility to provide for those unable to provide for themselves.

What are we really saying?

Welfare is based upon the norm set up by the Puritans long ago. A man is defined as a white, Anglo-Saxon Protestant, healthy, ambitious, earnest, and honest, a man whom the Lord smiles upon by increasing the fruits of his labor. Welfare is designed to compensate people insofar as they deviate from that norm. Insofar as a woman has an illegitimate child, she receives compensation. Insofar as a man is disabled, he receives compensation. Insofar as a person is too old to work, he receives compensation.

Welfare buys that portion of a person which does not match the stereotype of the real man. Welfare payments are never sufficient, never adequate. This is because each person bears some relation to the norm and in proportion to their resemblance, they receive less.

When this attitude is applied to groups, it is best seen in the political parties. The Republicans represent the best of the white economics. The Democrats represent all of the deviations.

The Republican Party has ostensibly stood for less government as a political philosophical position. But when you listen carefully to the Republicans you do not really hear less government, you hear a strange religion of early Puritan mythology. The Republican Party is in reality the truest expression of America's religion of progress and white respectability. It stands for the white superman who never existed. The peddler's grandson who conquered the unknown by inheriting a department store—such is the basic American religion unmasked. The measure of America's willingness to examine the basis of its existence is to be counted in the number of registered voters who claim to be Republicans.

The measure of truth in the above assertion is the Republican willingness to lose elections rather than depart from cherished doctrines and myths. Only a religion can attract and hold such loyalty.

The other party is something else. Popular conceptions gloss over reality and continue the Rooseveltian myth that the Democrats are the party of the people. The old Roosevelt coalition of labor, minority and ethnic groups, and farmers fails to acknowledge one unpublicized member—the special interests.

More than the Republicans, the Democrats are the party of the special interests. Who else defends the oil-depletion allowance more than the Democrats? Who else creates farm subsidies, tariffs, foreign aid, large development projects? Who else piles special programs on top of special programs? Could the Republicans create the poor as a class in themselves? For, the Republicans know no poor because it is not within their religious comprehension. Nixon's election was the last gasp of this quasi-religious nineteenth-century, Horatio Alger, WASP ethic.

Until 1968 the Democrats won election after election by gathering the rejected into an amalgam of special interests for the sole purpose of splitting the pie which they would then attempt to create. The pie never exists; it is continually being created by the adjustment of the governmental machinery to include additional special interests, while eligible parties participate in the American religion carefully being nurtured by the Republicans in their isolation.

Recent elections tend to show the reality of this analysis. Eisenhower proved that a President was not necessary for the true American religion to progress. Kennedy proved that if enough special interests are combined, even Americans will desert the long-term goals of progress for the immediacy of splitting the pie which was to be created. The New Frontier promised a new chance to be cut in on the action, a short cut into Republican heaven for those groups who had deviated from the norm either by birth, place of origin, or failure to deal themselves in at some previous point in history.

Johnson simply dealt more cards to more people than had ever been dealt before. And his opponent was out preaching salvation by works alone. No wonder there was a religious revolt! The election of 1964 was comparable to the Protestant Reformation, for never had the choices been so clear between faith and works.

Politically, most minority groups have shifted to the Democrats and remained loyal through thick and thin. Margins compiled by blacks, Indians, and Mexicans for Democratic candidates have been incredible. In 1964 it took a strong Indian to support Goldwater in spite of his publicized heroic flights to the Navajo and his superb collection of Hopi Kachina dolls.

The Kennedys increased the normal margins which minority groups gave to the Democrats because of their apparent interest in minority groups. Few members of the Indian community realize or will admit how little the Kennedys really did for Indians. Although the mythology of the Kennedys has made them appear as the only saviors of minority communities, the legislative record compiled by both Jack and Robert Kennedy shows another story.

Jack Kennedy broke the Pickering Treaty and had accomplished little besides the usual Interior Task Force study of Indians before his death. Robert Kennedy did little for Indians legislatively or administratively. He drew some fire and spotlighted some of the problems, but in doing so he practically pre-empted any chance of action because of his many political enemies and their outright rejection of causes he advocated.

Robert Kennedy did prove that race was not the real thing bothering this country and that the turmoil over Civil Rights was misunderstood. He presented himself as a person who could move from world to world and never be a stranger anywhere. His genius was that he personified the best traits of his Irish heritage and made an attempt to define *white* in a different way.

Other people were frightened at Kennedy's obvious attempt to re-create the days of the New Frontier. White mythology sees the kingship as demonic, as against the American religion of ostensible equality.

Indian people loved the idea of Robert Kennedy replacing Jack. For them it was an affirmation of the great war chief from the great family leading his people in his brother's place. Robert Kennedy became as great a hero as the most famous Indian war chiefs precisely because of his ruthlessness. Indians saw him as a warrior, the white Crazy Horse. He somehow validated obscure undefined feelings of Indian people which they had been unwilling to admit to themselves. Spiritually, he was an Indian!

Robert Kennedy's death has completely changed the nature of the Civil Rights movement and has altered the outlook of the American Indian toward American society.

Winds of caution have set in and sails are being trimmed. There appears to be no means by which the cultural crisis can be understood by those outside the group. Indian people are becoming more and more reluctant to consider alternatives. They are becoming distrustful of people who talk equality because they do not see how equality can be achieved without cultural separateness. To the degree that other groups demand material ransoms for peace and order, Indian people are fearful of the ultimate goals of the different movements.

There is no basic antagonism between black and red, or even between red and white. Conflicts are created when Indians feel they are being defined out of existence by the other groups. Historically, each group has its own road to travel. All roads lead to personal and group affirmation. But the obstacles faced by each group are different and call for different solutions and techniques.

While it is wrong and harmful to define all dark-skinned people by certain criteria, it is also wrong to pretend that they have nothing in common. It is what Indians, blacks, and Mexicans have in common and where their differences lie which should be carefully studied.

Time and again blacks have told me how lucky they were not to have been placed on reservations after the Civil War. I don't think they were lucky at all. I think it was absolute disaster that blacks were not given reservations.

Indian tribes have been able to deal directly with the federal government because they had a recognized status within the Constitutional scheme. Leadership falls into legal patterns on each reservation through the elective process. A tribal chairman is recognized by federal agencies, Congressional committees, and private agencies as the representative of the group. Quarrels over programs, rivalry between leaders, defense of rights, and expressions of the mood of the people are all channeled through the official governing body. Indian people have the opportunity to deal officially with the rest of the world as a corporate body.

The blacks, on the other hand, are not defined with their own community. Leadership too often depends upon newspaper coverage. Black communities do not receive the deference tribes receive, because they are agencies in the private arena and not quasi-governmental. Law and order is something imposed brutally from without, not a housekeeping function of the group.

Above all, Indian people have the possibility of total withdrawal from American society because of their special legal status. They can, when necessary, return to a recognized homeland where time is static and the world becomes a psychic unity again.

To survive, blacks must have a homeland where they can withdraw, drop the facade of integration, and be themselves. Whites are inevitably torn because they have no roots, they do not understand the past, and they have already mortgaged their future. Unless they can renew their psychic selves and achieve a sense of historical participation as a people they will be unable to survive.

Already the cracks are showing. The berserk sniper characterizes the dilemma of the white man. Government by selective assassination is already well established as the true elective process.

All groups must come to understand themselves as their situation defines them and not as other groups see them. By accepting ourselves and defining the values within which we can be most comfortable we can find peace. In essence, we must all create social isolates which have economic bases that support creative and innovative efforts to customize values we need.

Myths must be re-examined and clarified. Where they are detrimental, sharp and necessary distinctions must be made. The fear of the unknown must be eliminated. The white mythologizes the racial minorities because of his lack of knowledge of them. These myths then create barriers for communication between the various segments of society.

What the white cannot understand he destroys lest it prove harmful. What the Indian cannot understand he withdraws from. But the black tries everything and fears nothing. He is therefore at liberty to build or destroy both what he knows and what he does not know or understand.

The red and the black must not be fooled either by themselves, by each other, or by the white man. The black has moved in a circle from *Plessy v. Ferguson,* where Separate but Equal was affirmed, to *Brown v. the Board of Education,* where it was denied by the Supreme Court, to Birmingham, Washington, Selma, and the tragedies of Memphis and Los Angeles. Now, Separate but Equal has become a battle cry of the black activists.

It makes a great deal of difference who carries this cry into battle. Is it the cry of a dying amalgam of European immigrants who are plagued by the European past? Or is it the lusty cry of a new culture impatient to be born?

The American Indian meditates on these things and waits for their solution. People fool themselves when they visualize a great coalition of the minority groups to pressure Congress for additional programs and rights. Indians will not work within an ideological basis which is foreign to them. Any cooperative movement must come to terms with tribalism in the Indian context before it will gain Indian support.

The future, therefore, as between the red, white, and black, will depend primarily upon whether white and black begin to understand Indian nationalism. Once having left the wild animal status, Indians will not revert to their old position on the totem pole. Hopefully black militancy will return to nationalistic philosophies which relate to the ongoing conception of the tribe as a nation extending in time and occupying space. If such is possible within the black community, it may be possible to bring the problems of minority groups into a more realistic focus and possible solution in the years ahead.

Critical Eye

FOR DISCUSSION

a. Do you agree with Deloria's ideas about civil rights separatism as it relates to Native Americans and Blacks?

b. According to Deloria, our country tends to lump all non-White, so-called minorities together. Is this true? Why?

c. Examine Deloria's argument against the current plight of Native Americans along the lines of political power and poverty. Has anything changed, or are Indians still dealing with the issues Deloria speaks to in his essay?

REAPPROACHING THE TEXT

Imagine that Deloria's argument was made by another racial group. Would the positions being made be as valid, or has the American Indian laid complete claim to these positions because of America's history with indigenous peoples?

WRITING ASSIGNMENT

How do you believe America regards its Native American population? Do you believe the country is responsible for honoring the hundreds of treaties that have been broken since colonialization?

Gloria Miklowitz

From
The War Between the Classes

From the moment I joined Adam the next day I felt uneasy and deceitful. It was as if Papa were standing just behind me, watching. Of course that was ridiculous; he was at work thinking of other things, yet I couldn't shake the sense that I was doing wrong. Papa had intended I not see Adam *at all,* and that meant anyplace, not at school or after. And here we were talking, pretending Papa wouldn't mind.

"I'm beginning to feel as if I'm Romeo and you're Juliet," Adam joked as we stood apart from the other students for the few minutes before the bell rang. "My mother's not too crazy about us, either."

"How do you know? Did she say something?"

Adam squeezed my shoulders reassuringly. "Now, don't start worrying. You have to know my mother. She's just funny about some things. Won't come right out and say what she thinks, but comes at it through the back door. 'Have you seen that Conley girl lately, dear? Such a lovely young woman.' That's Mom." Adam made a face. "Eileen Conley's a spoiled brat, about as nice as a spider. When I told Mom that, you can guess she wasn't too pleased."

"I suppose we'll survive," I said. "Papa said one week, so maybe it won't be too awful. Except . . ."

"Except what?"

"What if we choose different colors in Mr. Otero's class?" I looked aside as the first period bell rang. "Will it mean we're not supposed to talk to each other?"

"Don't even *think* such a terrible thing!" Adam took my arm and we began pushing through the crowd into the building. "Listen, Amy. Nobody can keep us apart. Not your father, my mother, Otero, or his entire so-called

From *The War Between the Classes* by Gloria D. Miklowitz, copyright © 1985 by Gloria D. Miklowitz. Used by permission of Dell Publishing, a division of Random House, Inc.

police force. Nobody." He stepped aside to let me pass. "It's entirely up to us and how *we* feel about each other, right?"

"Right," I echoed, wanting to believe him, but my stomach churned with uncertainty. It had seemed a fun idea, taking Otero's social studies elective together because of his "Color Game." I'd heard about the game from others who'd taken the class before, heard enough to think it might be more than just interesting. It might be important to Adam and me in some way, might prove if our relationship really had a future. I hadn't considered when I teased Adam into signing up with me that the game might also separate us for the next umpteen weeks. Would our feelings for each other survive?

Trying to ignore those fears, I climbed the stairs to the second-floor class with Adam three periods later. As we hurried down the hall I saw the cluster of kids waiting outside the social studies room because Otero was late. There were the usual groupings—black kids off to one side, a small circle of Latino kids, and nearest the room the white kids, with Justin in their midst, getting laughs. Several students were hanging around who weren't in the class; the G4 police force, I wondered?

Otero catapulted from a room across the hall, shaking out a clump of keys. He unlocked the classroom door and everyone started pouring in. I took my usual seat with Adam beside me, near the front of the room. "Do you suppose where you sit means anything?" I asked, settling my books under the chair. "Just look. You and I always sit where we can look Otero straight in the eye. Justin always sits right near the door so he can bolt as soon as the bell rings."

"Yeah," Adam said. "And Paul Thomas always sits where Otero can't see him, kind of slouched down. So, what's it mean? For that matter, does the fact that Otero scurries around like a squirrel whenever we see him mean anything?"

I liked Mr. Otero. Most kids did. It was because he seemed so really excited about what he taught. And from what I heard, he cared about the students, because you'd often find him staying late to talk. He was kind of funny, too. I liked how he joked about his baldness, saying what didn't grow on top grew twice as thick at his chin. And he sure had a knack of keeping my interest in class; fifty minutes went by like ten.

"Today," he said, coming around to the front of his desk, "we're going to begin a great social experiment. For the next four weeks we'll be playing what I call the Color Game. In just four weeks we're going to change the world." Otero began writing on the board as he spoke, turning from time to time back to the class. "Imagine you're on a new planet where colors represent special status," he said. "Blue is the highest color. Blues are superior beings. Think of purity, of blue bloods, those with money, respect, and prestige. Blue children attend private schools and go to the best colleges. Their parents travel without worrying about cost; they live the good life in beautiful homes with maids and gardeners. And they intend to keep it that way." Otero stood aside so the class could read what he'd written on the board. I copied it into my notebook: Blue = upper class.

"Now, below the Blues are the Dark Greens. Like the upper middle class on earth. Dark Green people are often workaholics. They figure if they try a little harder they'll make it to the Blues. Dark Green children almost always finish college. They're expected by their parents to go into the family business or become important in their professions. They're aware of the colors below them, the Light Greens and Oranges. But they're too busy trying to keep what they have and do even better to consider lending these less fortunate colors a hand."

What is my family? I wondered uneasily. *Dark Green? No, not quite. Aspiring to be.* Adam, of course was a Blue.

"Now, below the Dark Greens you'll find the Light Greens. They are the most numerous in society—the blue-collar workers, the lower middle class. Light Greens don't have it easy. If they have a job and a decent place to live where crime isn't too terrible, they're grateful. Their kids may go to junior college; few graduate. Light Greens aspire to become Dark Greens, but many are happy just to keep their heads above water."

Otero chuckled with a kind of delighted satisfaction. "Finally we come to the Oranges. Now, there's a sad group. They're often out of work, on welfare, in trouble with the law, and no matter how hard they work, if indeed they can get jobs, they can barely make ends meet. Since welfare breeds welfare, you find second- and third-generation Oranges with big families and often no father figure around.

"Oranges would like a bigger piece . . . in fact any piece . . . of the planet's apple pie, but the way society operates, they may never get it." He paused, then said, "Of course these are all the stereotypes of our class system."

Even though I'd written it down, I wasn't sure all the colors were sorted out in my head yet. Pretty soon Otero would have us selecting a color. What did I want to be? Certainly not an Orange or Light Green. No.

Who'd want to have to struggle so hard to get along? It would be fine to be a Dark Green or Blue. They had respect and money to live well. That's what I wanted.

"I hope you've got all the colors straight," Otero said, "because now I'm going to explain the rules of etiquette on this unique planet." He toyed with a stick of chalk, then said, "We have a system of bowing in our new society. Oranges must always show their inferiority by bowing when they meet their superiors, all colors above them. Light Greens must bow to the Dark Greens and Blues. Dark Greens bow to the Blues. But the Blues, bless them, don't bow to anyone. Why should they? They're top dogs." He thought for a moment. "We have sex discrimination in our society, also, but we'll discuss that next time we meet. I wouldn't want to confuse you with too much at once. Especially you *Oranges.*"

I laughed, along with everyone else. It was easy laughing when you weren't the one looked down on, and I had no thought that I could possibly become an Orange.

"Any questions so far?"

I raised my hand, "What if you aren't the same color as a friend? Besides bowing, is there anything else you have to do?"

Otero glanced at Adam, and I blushed, sure he knew why I asked the question. "Inferior colors may *not* speak with or socialize with superior colors. A superior color may address an inferior one, but not vice versa. Understood?"

I reached an icy hand across the aisle to join with Adam's warm one and gave him a worried look.

"What's the penalty for disobedience?" Adam asked.

"You can be fined, harassed, given lower status, any of a number of things."

"That's okay." Adam grinned that warm, confident smile I loved so much. "We just won't let anyone know."

Otero grinned right back. "I wouldn't count on that, Tarcher. We've got a spy network you wouldn't believe. Anyone who ever took part in the Color Game before—maybe three hundred students—will be watching you. And then, of course, there's the police force you'll meet in a moment, the G4's. In addition, you're encouraged to report on each other if you see any rules broken. You get extra points for squeal—er, uh . . . reporting, and the more points you earn, the better chance to move up in society."

"Ah, come on, Mr. Otero," Adam said. "We don't go around squealing on each other in real life. Besides, we don't really have class differences. Look around. We're all friends here. I don't care how much money anybody's got, and I don't give a hoot what color anyone is."

"Really? Tell me, Tarcher. When was the last time you had a black friend home to dinner, or a Latino? How many minority students sit at the same lunch table with you and your white friends?"

Adam's face turned a bright shade of pink. "I have soccer friends to the house. . . ." he protested, but I knew Otero had made a point.

"For that matter," the teacher continued, his attention back to the class, "how many of you *black* students have Latino or white friends? *Friends,* not acquaintances? And how many of you Latinos have black friends?" Only a few hands went up. "I thought so. Well, that's what this class is all about. We're going to expose the prejudices many of us have and maybe build some bridges between us." He pulled at his beard and said, "Okay! Now to sum up before you meet the G4's. Good behavior counts. The students who earn the most game points get credits toward a higher grade. Call it a prize. So, if you want a good grade in this class, play the game to win." He stepped back behind the desk. "Okay, G4's. Explain about the armbands and journals before we choose colors."

"Journals?"

"Right." Otero reached behind him for a small spiral notebook, which he held up to the class. "You'll need something like this to keep a daily record of your feelings and experiences during the Color Game. If you don't keep it up to date, or don't have it with you wherever you are, you can get in trouble from a G4."

"Everywhere? I'm on the track team. Got no pockets in my shorts."

"Everywhere," Otero repeated. "Tie it to your back, if you have to!"

Five students came to the front of the room. Otero said they'd all played the Color Game before and had volunteered to be G4's, the police force. "You can't put much over on them because they've been exactly where you are now," he explained. "They know just what you're thinking and feeling and what ways you may try to sabotage the game. But they're also here as counselors. When things get too heavy and you need someone to sort things out with, they're here to help."

Police force. It sounded so formidable, but they stood there watching us and smiling.

Mary, one of the girl G4's, stepped forward. She wore a karate uniform that made her look sort of intimidating and official. She introduced each of the G4's by name and then said, "We can challenge you any time of day or night. Anyplace. Asking to see your armbands and journals. We keep records on everyone, putting down what we observe and what others tell us about civil disobedience, uppityness to the higher classes, and so on."

"What's the penalty for assaulting a G4?" Juan called out, making everyone laugh.

"Death."

I giggled, beginning to relax. Nobody seemed to take the game very seriously. A few more questions were answered, then one of the G4's took a box and plastic bag from Otero.

"Now, this is how we go about choosing colors," Mary said. "In this bag we have a lot of disks, blue ones, darkgreen ones, light greens, and oranges." She held up the plastic bag and handed the box to another G4. "Since there are many more poor people than rich, there are more light greens and oranges than other colors.

"What you'll do is reach into the plastic bag, pick a disk, and show it to me. Jennifer will hand you an armband of the color you chose, and Brian will make a record of your color in our record book." She shook the disk bag vigorously. "Okay, who wants to go first?"

As students began reaching into the bag for their disks I turned to Adam. "What color would you like to be?"

"Light Green, I think. Then I'd get to see how the other half lives without having to be in abject poverty. How about you?"

"I'd like that, too." I didn't want to admit my real preference. After all, any color would be fine as long as Adam chose it, too.

In moments Mary was in front of me holding the bag out. "Oh, I don't like this!" I cried, backing off. "You go first, Adam."

"Pick!" Mary ordered. "You're holding us up."

Her harsh tone startled me. I closed my eyes and reached into the bag, feeling around among the cold disks for the right one. If I concentrated hard enough, maybe I could influence my choice so I'd pick a light green. At last I grasped a disk and slowly withdrew it. "I can't even look! What is it?"

"Blue!" Adam announced, disappointed. "You're a Blue."

"Here's your band," Jennifer said. She helped me put it on. "Always wear it on your right arm so we can see it, and give your name and color to G4 Brian."

Secretly pleased, I tightened the Velcro, then held my arm out for Adam to see. "Now you! And please pick a blue!"

"I've got one chance in four, so who knows?" Adam plunged his hand into the bag, dug around a while, then brought out a disk.

"Orange!" I cried as he opened his fist. "Oh, Adam, no!"

Adam's forehead wrinkled in uncertainty, but he took it all in good cheer. "So, I'm an Orange. Bottom of the barrel. This should be interesting." He held out his arm for the color band. Jennifer contemptuously threw his band on the floor and turned away.

The G4's moved on, holding out the disk bag, handing, out color bands and recording each student's choice, but all of a sudden Adam and I didn't have anything to say to each other. Just wearing the blue band and knowing what it stood for made me feel different, kind of important somehow. I don't know how or why, but with the orange band on Adam, he seemed quieter, less self-assured.

Otero's voice boomed out over the commotion.

"When you've got your bands, change seats. Blues get the superior seats up front. Dark Greens behind them, Light Greens behind them, and Oranges in the back. Tomorrow there'll be some further seat changes according to sex, but we haven't time to explain that now, so just seat yourselves by color."

Adam picked up his books and prepared to take a seat in the back. I put a hand on his.

"Gotta play the game right, honey. But don't worry. Maybe we can change to the same color later. You be bad and get demoted, and I'll be good and get promoted. Never know. So long. See you after class."

I watched him weave through the disorder of students moving to different seats until he found a place in the back of the room with the Oranges. He waved to me, then turned to a girl beside him.

Paul Thomas settled in the seat Adam had left, a wide grin on his dark face. Once I'd joined him at a cafeteria table, not knowing only blacks sat there. I'd felt as welcome as a good bout of flu and never made that mistake again.

"Hi, Amy," he greeted. "Man, this game's gonna be fun. I'm gonna love lording it over those poor Orange brothers; they always got it so good."

"Oh, come on, Paul," I chided. "You're not going to take advantage of anyone just because you're a Blue?"

"Wanna bet?" He laughed with villainous glee. "Just watch. Hey, girl!" he called out to Carol, who was a Dark Green. "You didn't bow proper, G4! You see that?"

Had the game been rigged? So many of the minority students seemed to have chosen the dark colors, the upper classes, while most of the white students including Justin and Adam were either Light Green or Orange. Before I could prove my suspicion, Otero began explaining about the game money, which equaled the points. Blues would get more, and so on down the line, with Oranges getting the least.

"Hey, no fair!" Juan called out.

"Who said life is fair? G4, mark that Light Green's name down. If he complains again, we'll fine him." Otero paused as the bell rang to end the period. "G4's will pass out the money. Stay in your seats until you get yours," He held up a hand as several students rose to leave. "You may as well start playing the game right now! None of you will leave before your superior colors do. Blues first, Oranges last. See you tomorrow."

Adam bolted from his seat, ignoring Otero's instructions just as Brian handed me a wad of play money.

"Just a minute, you dumb Orange!" he cried. "What are you doing bothering this Blue? Get back to your seat and don't dare enter blue territory again or you'll be sorry!"

Adam hesitated, then grinned, clicking his heels together. "*Jawohl mein Kommandant!*"

"Bow before you leave, Orange! Bow to the female Blue!"

"You're kidding!"

"Record keeper . . . get this Orange's name."

"Adam, please. Don't get into trouble. Remember what you said about moving up," I pleaded.

Adam bowed, his face a deep shade of pink. I hated being bowed to, especially by him, and looked away.

"Blue!" Mary called out. "In the future you report it when an inferior addresses you without permission! Understand? Now, lead the other Blues out, please."

I began to tremble, unused to such harsh criticism made so publicly.

"Come on, girl," Paul said, nudging me. "Let's go! Those lowly Oranges aren't worth a bag o' beans." He lapsed into black jive. "They's nothin' but lowdown lazy bums who won't work for a living an' just waste the big taxes us rich folk pay!"

I gathered up my books, eyes on Adam, who had returned to his seat. With an uneasy pain in my stomach I led the Blues . . . all six of us, all minorities . . . out the door.

Critical Eye

FOR DISCUSSION

a. America has been established as the world's "melting pot." That
   understood, how dangerous is the "color game"?

b. Currently, in the 21st century, are we still concerned with the so-called
   mongrelization of the races?

REAPPROACHING THE LITERATURE

Looking at Miklowitz's story, does her argument imply that race is more
damaging than culture?

WRITING ASSIGNMENT

Despite Miklowitz's characters seeking to embrace one another as
individuals, statistics tell us that the races tend to segregate from
other cultures when they are free to do so. In short, people feel more
comfortable with their "own kind." With this in mind, make the argument
as to why America must continue to push towards multiculturalism and
desegregation.

Abraham Lincoln

House Divided Speech

Springfield, Illinois
June 16, 1858

Mr. President and Gentlemen of the Convention.

If we could first know *where* we are, and *whither* we are tending, we could then better judge *what* to do, and *how* to do it. We are now far into the *fifth* year, since a policy was initiated, with the *avowed* object, and *confident* promise, of putting an end to slavery agitation. Under the operation of that policy, that agitation has not only, *not ceased*, but has *constantly augmented*. In *my* opinion, it *will* not cease, until a *crisis* shall have been reached, and passed. "A house divided against itself cannot stand." I believe this government cannot endure, permanently half *slave* and half *free*. I do not expect the Union to be *dissolved*—I do not expect the house to *fall*—but I *do* expect it will cease to be divided. It will become *all* one thing or *all* the other. Either the *opponents* of slavery, will arrest the further spread of it, and place it where the public mind shall rest in the belief that it is in the course of ultimate extinction; or its *advocates* will push it forward, till it shall become alike lawful in *all* the States, *old* as well as *new*—*North* as well as *South*.

Have we no *tendency* to the latter condition?

Let any one who doubts, carefully contemplate that now almost complete legal combination—piece of *machinery* so to speak—compounded of the Nebraska doctrine, and the Dred Scott decision. Let him consider not only *what* work the machinery is adapted to do, and *how well* adapted; but also, let him study the *history* of its construction, and trace, if he can, or rather *fail*, if he can, to trace the evidence of design and concert of action, among its chief architects, from the beginning.

The new year of 1854 found slavery excluded from more than half the States by State Constitutions, and from most of the national territory by congressional prohibition. Four days later, commenced the struggle,

House Divided Speech by Abraham Lincoln.

which ended in repealing that congressional prohibition. This opened all the national territory to slavery, and was the first point gained.

This necessity had not been overlooked; but had been provided for, as well as might be, in the notable argument of *"squatter sovereignty,"* otherwise called *"sacred right of self government,"* which latter phrase, though expressive of the only rightful basis of any government, was so perverted in this attempted use of it as to amount to just this: That if any *one* man, choose to enslave *another,* no *third* man shall be allowed to object. That argument was incorporated into the Nebraska bill itself, in the language which follows:

> *It being the true intent and meaning of this act not to legislate slavery into any Territory or state, not to exclude it therefrom; but to leave the people thereof perfectly free to form and regulate their domestic institutions in their own way, subject only to the Constitution of the United States."*

Then opened the roar of loose declamation in favor of "Squatter Sovereignty," and "Sacred right of self-government." "But," said opposition members, "let us be more *specific*—let us *amend* the bill so as to expressly declare that the people of the territory may exclude slavery." "Not we," said the friends of the measure; and down they voted the amendment.

While the Nebraska Bill was passing through congress, a *law case* involving the question of a negroe's freedom, by reason of his owner having voluntarily taken him first into a free state and then a territory covered by the congressional prohibition, and held him as a slave, for a long time in each, was passing through the U.S. Circuit Court for the District of Missouri; and both Nebraska bill and law suit were brought to a decision in the same month of May, 1854. The negroe's name was "Dred Scott," which name now designates the decision finally made in the case. *Before* the *then* next Presidential election, the law case came *to,* and was argued *in,* the Supreme Court of the United States; but the *decision* of it was deferred until *after* the election. Still, *before* the election, Senator Trumbull, on the floor of the Senate, requests the leading advocate of the Nebraska bill to state *his opinion* whether the people of a territory can constitutionally exclude slavery from their limits; and the latter answers: "That is a question for the Supreme Court."

The election came. Mr. Buchanan was elected, and the *indorsement,* such as it was, secured. That was the *second* point gained. The indorsement, however, fell short of a clear popular majority by nearly four hundred thousand votes, and so, perhaps, was not overwhelmingly reliable and satisfactory. The *outgoing* President, in his last annual message, as impressively as possible, *echoed back* upon the people the weight and *authority* of the indorsement. The Supreme Court met again; *did not* announce their decision, but ordered a re-argument.

The Presidential inauguration came, and still no decision of the court; but the *incoming* President, in his inaugural address, fervently exhorted the people to abide by the forthcoming decision, *whatever might be.* Then, in a few days, came the decision.

The reputed author of the Nebraska Bill finds an early occasion to make a speech at this capital indorsing the Dred Scott Decision, and vehemently denouncing all opposition to it. The new President, too, seizes the early occasion of the Silliman letter to *indorse* and strongly *construe* that decision, and to express his *astonishment* that any different view had ever been entertained!

At length a squabble springs up between the President and the author of the Nebraska Bill, on the *mere* question of *fact,* whether the Lecompton constitution was or was not, in any just sense, made by the people of Kansas; and in that squabble the latter declares that all he wants is a fair vote for the people, and that he *cares* not whether slavery be voted *down* or voted *up.* I do not understand his declaration that he cares not whether slavery be voted down or voted up, to be intended by him other than as an *apt definition* of the *policy* he would impress upon the public mind—the *principle* for which he declares he has suffered much, and is ready to suffer to the end. And well may he cling to that principle. If he has any parental feeling, well may he cling to it. That principle, is the only *shred* left of his original Nebraska doctrine.

Under the Dred Scott decision, "squatter sovereignty" squatted out of existence, tumbled down like temporary scaffolding—like the mould at the foundry served through one blast and fell back into loose sand— helped to carry an election, and then was kicked to the winds. His late *joint* struggle with the Republicans, against the Lecompton Constitution, involves nothing of the original Nebraska doctrine. That struggle was made on a point, the right of a people to make their own constitution, upon which he and the Republicans have never differed.

The several points of the Dred Scott decision, in connection with Senator Douglas's "care-not" policy, constitute the piece of machinery, in its present state of advancement. This was the third point gained. The working points of that machinery are:

First, that no negro slave, imported as such from Africa, and no descendant of such slave, can ever be a citizen of any State, in the sense of that term as used in the Constitution of the United States. This point is made in order to deprive the negro, in every possible event, of the benefit of that provision of the United States Constitution, which declares that: "The citizens of each State shall be entitled to all privileges and immunities of citizens in the several States."

Second, that "subject to the Constitution of the United States," neither Congress nor a Territorial legislature can exclude slavery from any United States Territory. This point is made in order that individual men may fill up the Territories with slaves, without danger of losing them as property, and thus to enhance the chances of permanency to the institution through all the future. Third, that whether holding a negro in actual slavery in a free State makes him free, as against the holder, the United States courts will not decide, but will leave to be decided by the courts of any slave State the negro may be forced into by the master. This point is made, not to be pressed immediately; but, if acquiesced in for a while, and apparently indorsed by the people at an election, then to sustain the logical conclusion that what Dred Scott's master might lawfully do with Dred Scott, in the free State of Illinois, every other master may lawfully do with any other one, or one thousand slaves, in Illinois, or in any other free State.

Auxiliary to all this, and working hand in hand with it, the Nebraska doctrine, or what is left of it, is to educate and mold public opinion, at least Northern public opinion, not to care whether slavery is voted down or voted up. This shows exactly where we now are; and partially, also, whither we are tending.

It will throw additional light on the latter, to go back, and run the mind over the string of historical facts already stated. Several things will now appear less dark and mysterious than they did when they were transpiring. The people were to be left "perfectly free," subject only to the Constitution. What the Constitution had to do with it, outsiders could not then see. Plainly enough now, it was an exactly fitted niche, for the Dred Scott decision to afterward come in, and declare the perfect free freedom of the people to be just no freedom at all. Why was the amendment, expressly declaring the right of the people, voted down? Plainly enough now: the adoption of it would have spoiled the niche for the Dred Scott decision. Why was the court decision held up? Why even a Senator's individual opinion withheld, till after the presidential election? Plainly enough now—the speaking out then would have damaged the perfectly free argument upon which the election was to be carried. Why the outgoing President's felicitation on the indorsement? Why the delay of a re-argument? Why the incoming President's advance exhortation in favor of the decision? These things look like the cautious patting and petting of a spirited horse, preparatory to mounting him, when it is dreaded that he may give the rider a fall. And why the hasty after-indorsement of the decision by the President and others?

We cannot absolutely know that all these exact adaptations are the result of preconcert. But when we see a lot of framed timbers, different portions of which we know have been gotten out at different times and places, and by different workmen—Stephen, Franklin, Roger, and James, for instance—and when we see these timbers joined together, and see they exactly matte the frame of a house or a mill, all the tenons and mortices exactly fitting, and all the lengths and proportions of the different l pieces exactly adapted to their respective places, and not a piece. Too many or too few, not omitting even scaffolding—or, if a single piece be lacking, we see the place in the frame exactly fitted and prepared yet to bring such piece in—in such a case we find it impossible not to believe that Stephen and Franklin and Roger and James all understood one another from the beginning and all worked upon a common plan or draft drawn up before the first blow was struck.

Critical Eye

FOR DISCUSSION

a. Putting the racial component aside, why was it important as a leader for Mr. Lincoln to take up such a position on slavery and its place in American society?

b. Would you argue that his stance weakened or strengthened his position as President? Keep in mind that a huge section of the country stood in direct opposition to his ideas.

REAPPROACHING THE LITERATURE

Why is it important for a leader of a nation to support and defend the oppressed and impoverished segments of their country? What is gained in doing so? What then is the signal to the rest of the society, and do they in turn become disenfranchised in favor of the oppressed and poor? In short, can there be a balance?

WRITING ASSIGNMENT

Why, in your opinion, have racial matters always centered around Blacks and Whites? As you see it, are we still dealing with the ideas that Mr. Lincoln addresses in his speech? Are we still hurting as a nation because of the evil of African slavery?

1 2 3 **4** 5

Class and the Culture of Power

> It is a very grave matter to be forced to imitate a people for whom you know—
> which is the price of your performance and survival—you do not exist. It is hard
> to imitate a people whose existence appears, mainly, to be made tolerable by their
> bottomless gratitude that they are not, thank heaven, you.
>
> *James Baldwin*

To socially classify a group of people is an idea as old as the development
of civilization itself. Since the dawn of human beings, mankind has always
compared itself to those forms of nature it could most readily relate
with—ultimately deeming itself the dominant species. The obvious luxury
of this positioning—of recognizing the species of humankind as being
number one—is that those who are beneath humans on the measuring
stick are often privy to the whims of humans as king of the world.

With this understanding, the differentiating of humanity was inevitable.
Undeniably, differentiating the "haves" and the "have-nots" has been
the main platform for establishing social difference—of distinguishing
a society's vision of what we have come to call "Class." When it comes to
Class, individuals function in society based upon the stratification that
accords their grouping status.

Scientists would argue that this separation is no different than the
established hierarchy that other species employ. Yet, around the globe,
sociologists, philosophers, and politicians alike have attempted to discern
what exactly makes and who actually fits into particular groupings. Some
suggest that it is mainly a matter of race. Others claim that gender is the
dominant factor. And, many claim that Class is most notably an economic
consideration. Yet, confusion and disharmony arise because the reality is
that language, neighborhood, occupation, and education—even looks—

often become determining factors of how we are judged by society and how we, in turn, will judge others.

Unlike the strong and domineering creatures that rule the jungle or the sea, humankind's grouping and separating is far more perplexing. The interesting thing about who fits and who does not—what determines Class and what should not be a consideration—is that even though finding a set definition of social Class is, at best, as obscure as it is convoluted, all agree that social differentiation is undeniable and inescapable. The following selections seek to explore these complexities and considerations surrounding Class.

Mark Twain

The Lowest Animal

I have been studying the traits and dispositions of the "lower animals" (so-called), and contrasting them with the traits and dispositions of man. I find the result humiliating to me. For it obliges me to renounce my allegiance to the Darwinian theory of the Ascent of Man from the Lower Animals; since it now seems plain to me that that theory ought to be vacated in favor of a new and truer one, this new and truer one to be named the Descent of Man from the Higher Animals.

In proceeding toward this unpleasant conclusion I have not guessed or speculated or conjectured, but have used what is commonly called the scientific method. That is to say, I have subjected every postulate that presented itself to the crucial test of actual experiment, and have adopted it or rejected it according to the result. Thus I verified and established each step of my course in its turn before advancing to the next. These experiments were made in the London Zoological Gardens, and covered many months of painstaking and fatiguing work.

Before particularizing any of the experiments, I wish to state one or two things which seem to more properly belong in this place than further along. This in the interest of clearness. The massed experiments established to my satisfaction certain generalizations, to wit:

1. That the human race is of one distinct species. It exhibits slight variations—in color, stature, mental caliber, and so on—due to climate, environment, and so forth: but it is a species by itself, and not to be confounded with any other.
2. That the quadrupeds are a distinct family, also. This family exhibits variations—in color, size, food preferences and so on; but it is a family by itself.
3. That the other families—the birds, the fishes, the insects, the reptiles, etc.—are more or less distinct, also. They are in the procession. They are links in the chain which stretches down from the higher animals to man at the bottom.

Some of my experiments were quite curious. In the course of my reading I had come across a case where, many years ago, some hunters on our Great Plains organized a buffalo hunt for the entertainment of an English earl—that, and to provide some fresh meat for his larder. They had charming sport. They killed seventy-two of those great animals: and ate part of one of them and left the seventy-one to rot. In order to determine the difference between an anaconda and an earl—if any—I caused seven young calves to be turned into the anaconda's cage. The grateful reptile immediately crushed one of them and swallowed it. Then lay back satisfied. It showed no further interest in the calves, and no disposition to harm them. I tried this experiment with other anacondas: always with the same result. The fact stood proven that the difference between an earl and an anaconda is that the earl is cruel and the anaconda isn't; and that the earl wantonly destroys what he has no use for, but the anaconda doesn't. This seemed to suggest that the anaconda was not descended from the earl. It also seemed to suggest that the earl was descended from the anaconda, and had lost a good deal in the transition.

I was aware that many men who have accumulated more millions of money than they can ever use have shown a rabid hunger for more, and have not scrupled to cheat the ignorant and the helpless out of their poor servings in order to partially appease that appetite. I furnished a hundred different kinds of wild and tame animals the opportunity to accumulate vast stores of food, but none of them would do it. The squirrels and bees and certain birds made accumulations, but stopped when they had gathered a winter's supply, and could not be persuaded to add to it either honestly or by chicane. In order to bolster up a tottering reputation the ant pretended to store up supplies, but I was not deceived. I know the ant. These experiments convinced me that there is this difference between man and the higher animals: he is avaricious and miserly, they are not.

In the course of my experiments I convinced myself that among the animals man is the only one that harbors insults and injuries, broods over them, waits till a chance offers, then takes revenge. The passion of revenge is unknown to the higher animals.

Roosters keep harems, but it is by consent of their concubines: therefore no wrong is done. Men keep harems, but it is by brute force, privileged by atrocious laws which the other sex is allowed no hand in making. In this matter man occupies a far lower place than the rooster.

Cats are loose in their morals, but not consciously so. Man, in his descent from the cat, has brought the cat's looseness with him but has left the unconsciousness behind—the saving grace which excuses the cat. The cat is innocent, man is not.

Indecency, vulgarity, obscenity—these are strictly confined to man: he invented them. Among the higher animals there is no trace of them. They hide nothing; they are not ashamed. Man, with his soiled mind, covers himself. He will not even enter a drawing room with his breast and back naked, so alive are he and his mates to indecent suggestion. Man is "The Animal that Laughs." But so does the monkey, as Mr. Darwin pointed out; and so does the Australian bird that is called the laughing jackass. No—Man is the Animal that Blushes. He is the only one that does it—or has occasion to.

At the head of this article we see how "three monks were burnt to death" a few days ago, and a prior "put to death with atrocious cruelty." Do we inquire into the details? No; or we should find out that the prior was subjected to unprintable mutilations. Man—when he is a North American Indian— gouges out his prisoner's eyes; when he is King John, with a nephew to render untroublesome, he uses a red-hot iron; when he is a religious zealot dealing with heretics in the Middle Ages, he skins his captive alive and scatters salt on his back; in the first Richard's time he shuts up a multitude of Jew families in a tower and sets fire to it; in Columbus's time he captures a family of Spanish Jews and—but *that* is not printable; in our day in England a man is fined ten shillings for beating his mother nearly to death with a chair, and another man is fined forty shillings for having four pheasant eggs in his possession without being able to satisfactorily explain how he got them. Of all the animals, man is the only one that is cruel. He is the only one that inflicts pain for the pleasure of doing it. It is a trait that is not known to the higher animals. The cat plays with the frightened mouse; but she has this excuse, that she does not know that the mouse is suffering. The cat is moderate—unhumanly moderate: she only scares the mouse, she does not hurl it; she doesn't dig out its eyes, or tear off its skin, or drive splinters under its nails—man-fashion; when she is done playing with it she makes a sudden meal of it and puts it out of its trouble. Man is the Cruel Animal. He is alone in that distinction.

The higher animals engage in individual fights, but never in organized masses. Man is the only animal that deals in that atrocity of atrocities. War. He is the only one that gathers his brethren about him and goes forth in cold blood and with calm pulse to exterminate his kind. He is the only animal that for sordid wages will march out, as the Hessians[1] did in our Revolution, and as the boyish Prince Napoleon did in the Zulu war, and help to slaughter strangers of his own species who have done him no harm and with whom he has no quarrel.

Man is the only animal that robs his helpless fellow of his country—takes possession of it and drives him out of it or destroys him. Man has done this in all the ages. There is not an acre of ground on the globe that is in possession

---

[1]Hessians: the German auxillary soldiers brought over by the British to fight the Americans during the Revolutionary War.

of its rightful owner, or that has not been taken away from owner after owner, cycle after cycle, by force and bloodshed.

Man is the only Slave. And he is the only animal who enslaves. He has always been a slave in one form or another, and has always held other slaves in bondage under him in one way or another. In our day he is always some man's slave for wages, and does that man's work; and this slave has other slaves under him for minor wages, and they do *his* work. The higher animals are the only ones who exclusively do their own work and provide their own living.

Man is the only Patriot. He sets himself apart in his own country, under his own flag, and sneers at the other nations, and keeps multitudinous uniformed assassins on hand at heavy expense to grab slices of other people's countries, and keep *them* from grabbing slices of *his*. And in the intervals between campaigns he washes the blood off his hands and works for "the universal brotherhood of man"—with his mouth.

Man is the Religious Animal. He is the only Religious Animal. He is the only animal that has the True Religion—several of them. He is the only animal that loves his neighbor as himself, and cuts his throat if his theology isn't straight. He has made a graveyard of the globe in trying his honest best to smooth his brother's path to happiness and heaven. He was at it in the time of the Caesars, he was at it in Mahomet's time, he was at it in the time of the Inquisition, he was at it in France a couple of centuries, he was at it in England in Mary's day, he has been at it ever since he first saw the light, he is at it today in Crete—as per the telegrams quoted above—he will be at it somewhere else tomorrow. The higher animals have no religion. And we are told that they are going to be left out, in the Hereafter. I wonder why? It seems questionable taste.

Man is the Reasoning Animal. Such is the claim. I think it is open to dispute. Indeed, my experiments have proven to me that he is the Unreasoning Animal. Note his history, as sketched above. It seems plain to me that whatever he is he is *not* a reasoning animal. His record is the fantastic record of a maniac. I consider that the strongest count against his intelligence is the fact that with that record back of him he blandly sets himself up as the head animal of the lot: whereas by his own standards he is the bottom one.

In truth, man is incurably foolish. Simple things which the other animals easily learn, he is incapable of learning. Among my experiments was this. In an hour I taught a cat and a dog to be friends. I put them in a cage. In another hour I taught them to be friends with a rabbit. In the course of two days I was able to add a fox, a goose, a squirrel and some doves. Finally a monkey. They lived together in peace; even affectionately.

Next, in another cage I confined an Irish Catholic from Tipperary, and as soon as he seemed tame I added a Scotch Presbyterian from Aberdeen. Next a Turk from Constantinople; a Greek Christian from Crete; an Armenian; a Methodist from the wilds of Arkansas; a Buddhist from China; a Brahman from Benares. Finally, a Salvation Army Colonel from Wapping. Then I stayed away two whole days. When I came back to note result, the cage of Higher Animals was all right, but in the other there was but a chaos of gory odds and ends of turbans and fezzes and plaids and bones and flesh—not a specimen left alive. These Reasoning Animals had disagreed on a theological detail and carried the matter to a Higher Court.

One is obliged to concede that in true loftiness of character, Man cannot claim to approach even the meanest of the Higher Animals. It is plain that he is constitutionally incapable of approaching that altitude; that he is constitutionally afflicted with a Defect which must make such approach forever impossible, for it is manifest that this defect is permanent in him, indestructible, ineradicable.

I find this Defect to be *the Moral Sense*. He is the only animal that has it. It is the secret of his degradation. It is the quality *which enables him to do wrong*. It has no other office. It is incapable of performing any other function. It could never have been intended to perform any other. Without it, man could do no wrong. He would rise at once to the level of the Higher Animals.

Since the Moral Sense has but the one office, the one capacity—to enable man to do wrong—it is plainly without value to him. It is as valueless to him as is disease. In fact, it manifestly is a disease. *Rabies* is bad, but it is not so bad as this disease. Rabies enables a man to do a thing which he could not do when in a healthy state: kill his neighbor with a poisonous bite. No one is the better man for having rabies. The Moral Sense enables a man to do wrong. It enables him to do wrong in a thousand ways. Rabies is an innocent disease, compared to the Moral Sense. No one, then, can be the better man for having the Moral Sense. What, now, do we find the Primal Curse to have been? Plainly what it was in the beginning: the infliction upon man of the Moral Sense; the ability to distinguish good from evil; and with it, necessarily, the ability to *do* evil; for there can be no evil act without the presence of consciousness of it in the doer of it.

And so I find that we have descended and degenerated, from some far ancestor—some microscopic atom wandering at its pleasure between the mighty horizons of a drop of water perchance—insect by insect, animal by animal, reptile by reptile, down the long highway of smirchless innocence, till we have reached the bottom stage of development—namable as the Human Being. Below us—nothing. Nothing but the Frenchman.

Critical Eye

FOR DISCUSSION

a. What commentary is Twain making about mankind?

b. Is he making a distinction between men and women?

c. Throughout history, what has man done to prove the validity of Twain's essay?

d. Read Emerson's *Nature* (download) and examine how it addresses Twain's positions.

REAPPROACHING THE LITERATURE

Apply Twain's perspective to how man continues to treat endangered species.

WRITING ASSIGNMENT

Early American colonists believed in the notion of Manifest Destiny, which stressed the notion of the settlers being ordained by God to cultivate America and tame its inhabitants. The book of Genesis in the Old Testament stresses the right of Adam to have dominion over the Earth and the animals therein. In what way does this biblical assessment subvert Twain's argument?

Frederick Douglass

What to the Slave Is the 4th of July?

From Independence Day Speech at Rochester, 1852

Fellow citizens, pardon me, allow me to ask, why am I called upon to speak here today? What have I, or those I represent, to do with your national independence? Are the great principles of political freedom and of natural justice, embodied in that Declaration of Independence, extended to us? and am I, therefore, called upon to bring our humble offering to the national altar, and to confess the benefits and express devout gratitude for the blessings resulting from your independence to us?

Would to God, both for your sakes and ours, that an affirmative answer could be truthfully returned to these questions! Then would my task be light, and my burden easy and delightful. For who is there so cold that a nation's sympathy could not warm him? Who so obdurate and dead to the claims of gratitude that would not thankfully acknowledge such priceless benefits? Who so stolid and selfish that would not give his voice to swell the hallelujahs of a nation's jubilee, when the chains of servitude had been torn from his limbs? I am not that man. In a case like that the dumb might eloquently speak and the "lame man leap as an hart."

But such is not the state of the case. I say it with a sad sense of the disparity between us. I am not included within the pale of this glorious anniversary! Your high independence only reveals the immeasurable distance between us. The blessings in which you, this day, rejoice are not enjoyed in common. The rich inheritance of justice, liberty, prosperity, and independence bequeathed by your fathers is shared by you, not by me. The sunlight that brought light and healing to you has brought stripes and death to me. This Fourth of July is yours, not mine. You may rejoice, I must mourn. To drag a man in fetters into the grand illuminated temple of liberty, and call upon him to join you in joyous anthems, were inhuman mockery and sacrilegious irony. Do you mean, citizens, to mock me by asking me to speak today? If so, there is a parallel to your conduct. And let me warn that it is dangerous to copy the example of a nation whose crimes, towering up to heaven, were thrown down by the breath of the

Almighty, burying that nation in irrevocable ruin! I can today take up the plaintive lament of a peeled and woe-smitten people.

"By the rivers of Babylon, there we sat down. Yea! We wept when we remembered Zion. We hanged our harps upon the willows in the midst thereof. For there, they that carried us away captive, required of us a song; and they who wasted us required of us mirth, saying, Sing us one of the songs of Zion. How can we sing the Lord's song in a strange land? If I forget thee, O Jerusalem, let my right hand forget her cunning. If do not remember thee, let my tongue cleave to the roof of my mouth."

Fellow citizens, above your national, tumultuous joy, I hear the mournful wail of millions! Whose chains, heavy and grievous yesterday, are, today, rendered more intolerable by the jubilee shouts that reach them. If I do forget, if I do not faithfully remember those bleeding children of sorry this day, "may my right hand cleave to the roof of my mouth"! To forget them, to pass lightly over their wrongs, and to chime in with the popular theme would be treason most scandalous and shocking, and would make me a reproach before God and the world. My subject, then, fellow citizens, is American slavery. I shall see this day and its popular characteristics from the slave's point of view. Standing there identified with the American bondman, making his wrongs mine. I do not hesitate to declare with all my soul that the character and conduct of this nation never looked blacker to me than on this Fourth of July! Whether we turn to the declarations of the past or to the professions of the present, the conduct of the nation seems equally hideous and revolting. America is false to the past, false to the present, and solemnly binds herself to be false to the future. Standing with God and the crushed and bleeding slave on this occasion, I will, in the name of humanity which is outraged, in the name of liberty which is fettered, in the name of the Constitution and the Bible which are disregarded and trampled upon, dare to call in question and to denounce, with all the emphasis I can command, everything that serves to perpetuate slavery-the great sin and shame of America! "I will not equivocate, I will not excuse"; I will use the severest language I can command; and yet not one word shall escape me that any man, whose judgment is not blinded by prejudice, shall not confess to be right and just....

For the present, it is enough to affirm the equal manhood of the Negro race. Is it not as astonishing that, while we are plowing, planting, and reaping, using all kinds of mechanical tools, erecting houses, constructing bridges, building ships, working in metals of brass, iron, copper, and secretaries, having among us lawyers doctors, ministers, poets, authors, editors, orators, and teachers; and that, while we are engaged in all manner of enterprises common to other men, digging gold in California, capturing the whale in the Pacific, feeding sheep and cattle on the hillside, living, moving, acting, thinking, planning, living in families as husbands, wives, and children, and above all, confessing and worshiping the Christian's God, and looking hopefully for life and immortality beyond the grave, we are called upon to prove that we are men!...

What, am I to argue that it is wrong to make men brutes, to rob them of their liberty, to work them without wages, to keep them ignorant of their relations to their fellow men, to beat them with sticks, to flay their flesh with the lash, to load their limbs with irons, to hunt them with dogs, to sell them at auction, to sunder their families, to knock out their teeth, to burn their flesh, to starve them into obedience and submission to their masters? Must I argue that a system thus marked with blood, and stained with pollution, is wrong? No! I will not. I have better employment for my time and strength than such arguments would imply....

What, to the American slave, is your Fourth of July? I answer: a day that reveals to him, more than all other days in the year, the gross injustice and cruelty to which he is the constant victim. To him, your celebration is a sham; your boasted liberty, an unholy license; your national greatness, swelling vanity; your sounds of rejoicing are empty and heartless; your denunciation of tyrants, brass-fronted impudence; your shouts of liberty and equality, hollow mockery; your prayers and hymns, your sermons and thanksgivings, with all your religious parade and solemnity, are, to Him, mere bombast, fraud, deception, impiety, and hypocrisy-a thin veil to cover up crimes which would disgrace a nation of savages. There is not a nation of savages. There is not a nation on the earth guilty of practices more shocking and bloody than are the people of the United States at this very hour.

Go where you may, search where you will, roam through all the monarchies and despotisms- of the Old World, travel through South America, search out every abuse, and when you have found the last, lay your facts by the side of the everyday practices of this nation, and you will say with me that, for revolting barbarity and shameless hypocrisy, America reigns without a rival.

Critical Eye

FOR DISCUSSION

a. Can Douglass' speech be interpreted as a patriotic speech? Consider this point, keeping in mind that seeking to become involved with the betterment of one's country can be construed as the ultimate example of love of one's country.

b. Would you argue that Blacks are still disenfranchised from obtaining their portion of the American Dream?

c. Why do different cultural groups seem to have diverging and, at times, negative view points about inclusion and patriotism?

REAPPROACHING THE LITERATURE

Examine the argument set forth by Douglass alongside of Barack Obama's "A More Perfect Union" (download) speech. How are these two documents similar? In essence, in what way(s) are these men examining the same highly charged race matters between Blacks and Whites? Does the Obama speech signal the strides that have been made along the lines of racial harmony, or is he arguing that not nearly enough has changed for either side?

WRITING ASSIGNMENT

Examine the myriad of so-called "racial minority groups" within America, determine whether or not they can all make the charge that somehow "true" inclusion has evaded them.

Jacob Neusner

Grading Your Professors

Since professors stand at the center of the student's encounter with college learning, students ought to ask what marks a good professor, what indicates a bad one. The one who sets high standards and persists in demanding that students try to meet them provides the right experiences. The professor who gives praise cheaply or who pretends to a relationship that does not and cannot exist teaches the wrong lessons. True, the demanding and the critical teacher does not trade in the currency students possess, which is their power to praise or reject teachers. The demanding professor knows that students will stumble. But the ones who pick themselves up and try again—whether in politics or music or art or sports—have learned a lesson that will save them for a lifetime: A single failure is not the measure of any person, and success comes hard. A banal truth, but a truth all the same.

The only teacher who taught me something beyond information, who gave me something to guide my life, was the only teacher who read my work carefully and criticized it in detail. To that point everyone had given me A's. After that I learned to criticize myself and not to believe the A's. The teacher who read my writing and corrected not so much the phrasing as the mode of thought—line by line, paragraph by paragraph, beginning to end—and who composed paragraphs as models for what I should be saying is the sole true teacher I ever had. But I did not need more than one, and neither do you.

I do not mean to suggest that for each one of us there is one perfect teacher who changes our lives and is the only teacher we need. We must learn from many teachers as we grow up and grow old; and we must learn to recognize the good ones. The impressive teacher of one's youth may want to continue to dominate—as teachers do—and may not want to let go. The great teacher is the one who wants to become obsolete in the life of the student. The good teacher is the one who teaches lessons and moves on, celebrating the student's growth. The Talmud relates the story of a disciple in an academy who won an argument over the position held by God in the academy on high. The question is asked, "What happened in heaven that day?" The answer: "God clapped hands in joy, saying, 'My

From "Grading Your Professors" in *How to Grade Your Professors* by Jacob Neusner. Reprinted by permission of the author.

children have vanquished me, my children have vanquished me.'" That is a model for the teacher—to enjoy losing an argument to a student, to recognize his or her contribution, to let the student surpass the teacher.

In the encounter with the teacher who takes you seriously, you learn to take yourself seriously. In the eyes of the one who sees what you can accomplish, you gain a vision of yourself as more than you thought you were. The ideal professor is the one who inspires to dream of what you can be, to try for more than you ever have accomplished before. Everyone who succeeds in life can point to such a teacher, whether in the classroom or on the sports field. It may be a parent, a coach, employer, grade school or high school or art or music teacher. It is always the one who cared enough to criticize, and stayed around to praise.

But what about college professors? To define an ideal for their work, let me offer guidelines on how to treat professors the way we treat students: to give grades.

Professors grade students' work. The conscientious ones spend time reading and thinking about student papers, inscribing their comments and even discussing with students the strengths and weaknesses of their work. But no professor spends as much time on grading students' work as students spend on grading their professors as teachers and as people. For from the beginning of a course ("Shall I register?") through the middle ("It's boring . . . shall I stick it out?") to the very end ("This was a waste of time"), the students invest time and intellectual energy in deciding what they think, both about how the subject is studied and about the person who presents it. Since effective teaching requires capturing the students' imagination, and since sharp edges and colorful ways excite imagination, the professor who is a "character" is apt, whether liked or disliked, to make a profound impression and perhaps also to leave a mark on the students' minds. The drab professors, not gossiped about and not remembered except for what they taught, may find that even what they taught is forgotten. People in advertising and public relations, politics and merchandising, know that. A generation raised on television expects to be manipulated and entertained.

Yet the emphasis on striking characteristics is irrelevant. Many students have no more sophistication in evaluating professors than they do in evaluating deodorants. This should not be surprising, since they approach them both in the same manner. The one who is "new, different, improved" whether a professor or a bar of soap, wins attention. In this context people have no way of determining good from bad. I once asked an airline pilot, "What is the difference between a good landing and a bad one?" He replied, "A good landing is any landing you can pick yourself up and walk away from." To this pilot, the landing is judged solely by its ultimate goal—safely delivering the plane's passengers. Can we tell when a teacher has safely delivered the student for the next stage of the journey? Can we define the differences between a good teacher and a bad one?

Students have their own definitions of *good* and *bad,* and professors generally have a notion of the meaning of students' grades. Let us consider how students evaluate their teachers, examining in turn the A, B, and C professors. We will begin at the bottom of one scale and work our way up. Let us at the same time consider what kind of student seeks which grade.

Grade C Professors

The first type is the C professor. This is the professor who registers minimum expectations and adheres to the warm-body theory of grading. If a warm body fills a seat and exhibits vital signs, such as breathing at regular intervals, occasionally reading, and turning in some legible writing on paper, then cosmic justice demands, and the professor must supply, the grade of C or *Satisfactory.* The effort needed to achieve F or *No Credit* is considerably greater. One must do no reading, attend few class sessions, and appear to the world to be something very like a corpse.

The professor who, by the present criteria, earns a C respects the students' rights and gives them their money's worth. He or she sells them a used car, so to speak, that they at least can drive off the lot. At the very least the professor does the following:

1. Attends all class sessions, reaches class on time, and ends class at the scheduled hour.

2. Prepares a syllabus for the course and either follows it or revises it, so that students always know what topic is under (even totally confused) discussion.

3. Announces and observes scheduled office hours, so that students have access to the professor without groveling or special pleading, heroic efforts at bird-dogging, or mounting week-long treasure hunts.

4. Makes certain that books assigned for a course are on reserve in the library and sees to it that the bookstore has ample time in which to order enough copies of the textbooks and ancillary reading for a course.

5. Comes to class with a clear educational plan, a well-prepared presentation, a concrete and specific intellectual agenda.

6. Reads examinations with the care invested in them (certainly no more, but also no less) and supplies intelligible grades and at least minimal comments; or keeps office hours for the discussion of the substance of the examination (but not the grade); and supplies course performance reports—all these as duty, not acts of grace.

These things constitute student rights. No student has to thank a professor for doing what he or she is paid to do, and these six items, at a minimum, are the prerequisites of professional behavior. They are matters of form, to be sure, but the grade C is deemed by (some) students to be a matter of good form alone; the warm-body theory of this grade applies to professors and students alike.

"Tell me my duty and I shall do it" are the words of the minimally prepared. Just as students of mediocre quality want to know the requirements and assume that if they meet them, they have fulfilled their whole obligation to the subject, so mediocre professors do what they are supposed to do. The subject is in hand; there are no problems. The C professor need not be entirely bored with the subject, but he or she is not apt to be deeply engaged by it.

Grade C professors may be entertaining, warm, and loving. Indeed, many of them must succeed on the basis of personality, because all they have to offer is the studied technology of attractive personalities. They may achieve huge followings among the students, keep students at the edge of their seats with jokes and banter, badger students to retain their interest, but in the end what they have sold, conveyed, or imparted to the students' minds is themselves, not their mode of thinking or analyzing. Why? Because C professors do not think much; they rely on the analysis of others.

Above all, the grade C professor has made no effort to take over and reshape the subject. This person is satisfied with the mere repetition, accurate and competent repetition to be sure, of what others have discovered and declared to be true. If this sort of professor sparks any vitality and interest in students, then he or she will remind students of their better high school teachers, the people who, at the very least, knew what they were talking about and wanted the students to know. At the end of a course, students should ask themselves, Have I learned facts, or have I grasped how the subject works, its inner dynamic, its logic and structure? If at the end students know merely one fact after another, students should be grateful—at least they have learned that much—but award the professor a polite C. For the professor has done little more than what is necessary.

Grade B Professors

A course constitutes a large and detailed statement on the nature of a small part of a larger subject, a practical judgment upon a particular field of study and how it is to be organized and interpreted. The grade of B is accorded to the student who has mastered the basic and fundamental modes of thought about, and facts contained within, the subject of a course.

The grade B professor is one who can present coherently the larger theory and logic of the subject, who will do more than is required to convey his or her ideas to the students, and who will sincerely hope he or she is inspiring the minds of the students. B professors, as they continue to grow as scholars, are not very different from A professors; they might be described as teachers striving to become A professors. But they are definitely very different from C professors. Let us, then, move on to consider A professors, keeping in mind that B professors will probably become A professors.

Grade A Professors

Grade A professors are the scholar-teachers, a university's prized treasures among a faculty full of intangible riches. America has many faculties of excellence, groups of men and women who with exceptional intelligence take over a subject and make it their own, reshape it and hand it on, wholly changed but essentially unimpaired in tradition, to another generation.

The grade of A goes to student work that attends in some interesting way and with utmost seriousness to the center and whole of the subject of the course. Notice, I did not say that an A goes to the student who says something new and original. That is too much to hope, especially in studying a subject that for hundreds or thousands of years has appeared to the best minds as an intricate and difficult problem.

The grade A professors may have odd ideas about their subjects, but they are asking old-new questions, seeking fresh insight, trying to enter into the way in which the subject works, to uncover its logic and inner structure. What makes an effective high school teacher is confidence, even glibness. What makes an effective university teacher is doubt and dismay. The scholarly mind is marked by self-criticism and thirsty search; it is guided by an awareness of its own limitations and those of knowledge. The scholar-teacher, of whatever subject or discipline, teaches one thing: Knowledge is not sure but uncertain, scholarship is search, and to teach is to impart the lessons of doubt. What is taught is what we do not know.

On whom do you bestow a grade A? It is given to the professor who, stumbling and falling, yet again rising up and walking on, seeks both knowledge and the meaning of knowledge. It is to the one who always asks, *Why* am I telling you these things? Why should you know them? It is to the professor who demands ultimate seriousness for his or her subject because the subject must be known, who not only teaches but professes, stands for, represents, the thing taught. The grade A professor lives for the subject, needs to tell you about it, wants to share it. The Nobel Prize scientist who so loved biology that she gave her life to it even without encouragement and recognition for a half a century of work, the literary critic who thinks getting inside a poem is entering Paradise, the historian who assumes the human issues of the thirteenth century live today—these exemplify the ones who are ultimately serious about a subject.

One who has made this commitment to a field of scholarship can be readily identified. This is the one full of concern, the one who commits upon the facts the act of advocacy, who deems compelling what others find merely interesting. The scholar-teacher is such because he or she conveys the self-evident, the obvious fact that facts bear meaning, constituting a whole that transcends the sum of the parts. True, to the world this sense of ultimate engagement with what is merely interesting or useful information marks the professor as demented, as are all those who march to a different drummer. What I mean to say is simple. Anybody who cares so much about what to the rest of the world is so little must be a bit daft. Why should such things matter so much—why, above all, things of the mind or the soul or the heart, things of nature and mathematics, things of structure and weight and stress, things of technology and science, society and mind? Professors often remember lonely childhoods (for my part, I don't). As adults, too, professors have to spend long hours by themselves in their offices, reading books, or in their laboratories or at their computers, or just thinking all by themselves. That is not ordinary and commonplace behavior. This is what it means to march to a different drummer. A student earns an A when he or she has mastered the larger theory of the course, entered into its logic and meaning, discovered a different way of seeing. Like a professor, the student who through accurate facts and careful, critical thought seeks meaning, the core and center of the subject, earns the grade A.

Yet matters cannot be left here, I do not mean to promote advocacy for its own sake. Students have rights too, and one of these is the right to be left alone, to grow and mature in their own distinctive ways. They have the right to seek their way, just as we professors find ours. The imperial intellect, the one that cannot allow autonomy, is a missionary, not a teacher. Many compare the imperial teacher with the A professor, but if you look closely at their different ways of teaching, you will see that this is an error. The teacher leads, says, "Follow me," without looking backward. The missionary pushes, imposes self upon another autonomous self. This is the opposite of teaching, and bears no relevance to learning or to scholarship. The teacher persuades; the missionary preaches. The teacher argues; the missionary shouts others to silence. The teacher wants the student to discover; the missionary decides what the student must discover. The teacher enters class with fear and trembling, not knowing where the discussion will lead. The missionary knows at the start of a class exactly what the students must cover by the end of the class.

Grade A professors teach, never indoctrinate. They educate rather than train. There is a fine line to be drawn, an invisible boundary, between great teaching and self-aggrandizing indoctrination.

Knowledge and even understanding do not bring salvation and therefore do not have to be, and should not be, forced upon another. And this brings me back to the earlier emphasis upon scholarship as the recognition of ignorance, the awareness not of what we know but of how we know and of what we do not know. The true scholar, who also is the true teacher, is drawn by self-criticism, compelled by doubting, skeptical curiosity, knows the limits of knowing. He or she cannot be confused with the imperial, the arrogant, and the proselytizing. By definition, we stand for humility before the unknown.

A good professor wants to answer the question, Why am I telling you these things? A good student wants to answer the question, Why am I taking these courses? What do I hope to get out of them? Why are they important to me? I have not put before you any unattainable ideals in these questions. Some of us realize them every day, and nearly all of us realize them on some days. Just as students' transcripts rarely present only A's or *No Credits,* so professors rarely succeed all of the time. No one bears the indelible grade of A.

Critical Eye

FOR DISCUSSION

a. Currently, most colleges allow students to rate their professors' performance at the end of each semester. In your opinion, do these types of evaluations work?

b. If a professor constantly receives bad evaluations from students, should the professor be terminated?

c. If we use student evaluations as a true indicator of a professor's teaching prowess, how can we distinguish a poor professor from a group effort to destroy a professor's career?

REAPPROACHING THE LITERATURE

After several years of undergraduate and graduate study, can you understand why professors might feel that being judged by their students is insulting?

WRITING ASSIGNMENT

Make the argument that both professors and students gain when there is an evaluative process that measures their performance.

Ngũgĩ Wa Thiong'o

Decolonising the Mind

I was born into a large peasant family: father, four wives and about twenty-eight children. I also belonged, as we all did in those days, to a wider extended family and to the community as a whole.

We spoke Gĩkũyũ as we worked in the fields. We spoke Gĩkũyũ in and outside the home. I can vividly recall those evenings of story-telling around the fireside. It was mostly the grown-ups telling the children but everybody was interested and involved. We children would re-tell the stories the following day to other children who worked in the fields picking the pyrethrum flowers, tea-leaves or coffee beans of our European and African landlords.

The stories, with mostly animals as the main characters, were all told in Gĩkũyũ. Hare, being small, weak but full of innovative wit and cunning, was our hero. We identified with him as he struggled against the brutes of prey like lion, leopard, hyena. His victories were our victories and we learnt that the apparently weak can outwit the strong. We followed the animals in their struggle against hostile nature—drought, rain, sun, wind—a confrontation often forcing them to search for forms of co-operation. But we were also interested in their struggles amongst themselves, and particularly between the beasts and the victims of prey. These twin struggles, against nature and other animals, reflected real-life struggles in the human world.

Not that we neglected stories with human beings as the main characters. There were two types of characters in such human-centered narratives: the species of truly human beings with qualities of courage, kindness, mercy, hatred of evil, concern for others; and a man-eat-man two-mouthed species with qualities of greed, selfishness, individualism and hatred of what was good for the larger co-operative community. Co-operation as the ultimate good in a community was a constant theme. It could unite human beings with animals against ogres and beasts of prey, as in the story of how dove, after being fed with castor-oil seeds, was sent to fetch a smith working far away from home and whose pregnant wife was being threatened by these man-eating two-mouthed ogres.

Reprinted with permission from *Decolonising the Mind* by Ngũgĩ Wa Thoing'o. Copyright © 1986 by Ngũgĩ Wa Thoing'o. Published by Heinemann, a division of Reed Elsevier, Inc. Portsmouth, NH. All rights reserved.

There were good and bad story-tellers. A good one could tell the same story over and over again, and it would always be fresh to us, the listeners. He or she could tell a story told by someone else and make it more alive and dramatic. The differences really were in the use of words and images and the inflexion of voices to effect different tones.

We therefore learnt to value words for their meaning and nuances. Language was not a mere string of words. It had a suggestive power well beyond the immediate and lexical meaning. Our appreciation of the suggestive magical power of language was reinforced by the games we played with words through riddles, proverbs, transpositions of syllables, or through nonsensical but musically arranged words.[1] So we learnt the music of our language on top of the content. The language, through images and symbols, gave us a view of the world, but it had a beauty of its own. The home and the field were then our pre-primary school but what is important, for this discussion, is that the language of our evening teach-ins, and the language of our immediate and wider community, and the language of our work in the fields were one.

And then I went to school, a colonial school, and this harmony was broken. The language of my education was no longer the language of my culture. I first went to Kamaandura, missionary run, and then to another called Maanguuū run by nationalists grouped around the Gīkūyū Independent and Karinga Schools Association. Our language of education was still Gīkūyū. The very first time I was ever given an ovation for my writing was over a composition in Gīkūyū. So for my first four years there was still harmony between the language of my formal education and that of the Limuru peasant community.

It was after the declaration of a state of emergency over Kenya in 1952 that all the schools run by patriotic nationalists were taken over by the colonial regime and were placed under District Education Boards chaired by Englishmen. English became the language of my formal education. In Kenya, English became more than a language: It was *the* language, and all the others had to bow before it in deference.

Thus one of the most humiliating experiences was to be caught speaking Gīkūyū in the vicinity of the school. The culprit was given corporal punishment—three to five strokes of the cane on bare buttocks—or was made to carry a metal plate around the neck with inscriptions such as

[1] Example from a tongue twister: 'Kaana ka Nikoora koona koora koora: na ko koora koona kaana ka Nikoora koora koora.' I'm indebted to Wangul wa Gora for this example. "Nichola's child saw a baby frog and ran away: and when the baby frog saw Nichola's child it also ran away." A Gīkūyū speaking child has to get the correct tone and length of vowel and pauses to get it right. Otherwise it becomes a jumble of k's and r's and na's [author's note].

i am stupid or I AM A DONKEY. Sometimes the culprits were fined money they could hardly afford. And how did the teachers catch the culprits? A button was initially given to one pupil who was supposed to hand it over to whoever was caught speaking his mother tongue. Whoever had the button at the end of the day would sing who had given it to him and the ensuing process would bring out all the culprits of the day. Thus children were turned into witch-hunters and in the process were being taught the lucrative value of being a traitor to one's immediate community.

The attitude to English was the exact opposite: any achievement in spoken or written English was highly rewarded: prizes, prestige, applause: the ticket to higher realms. English became the measure of intelligence and ability in the arts, the sciences, and all the other branches of learning. English became *the* main determinant of a child's progress up the ladder of formal education.

As you may know, the colonial system of education in addition to its apartheid racial demarcation had the structure of a pyramid: a broad primary base, a narrowing secondary middle, and an even narrower university apex. Selections from primary into secondary were through an examination, in my time called Kenya African Preliminary Examination, in which one had to pass six subjects ranging from Math to Nature Study and Kiswahili. All the papers were written in English. Nobody could pass the exam who failed the English language paper no matter how brilliantly he had done in the other subjects. I remember one boy in my class of 1954 who had distinctions in all subjects except English, which he had failed. He was made to fail the entire exam. He went on to become a turn boy in a bus company. I who had only passed but a credit in English got a place at the Alliance High School, one of the most elitist institutions for Africans in colonial Kenya. The requirements for a place at the University, Makerere University College, were broadly the same: nobody could go on to wear the undergraduate red gown, no matter how brilliantly they had performed in all the other subjects unless they had a credit—not even a simple pass!—in English. Thus the most coveted place in the pyramid and in the system was only available to the holder of an English language credit card. English was the official vehicle and the magic formula to colonial elitedom.

Literary education was now determined by the dominant language while also reinforcing that dominance. Orature (oral literature) in Kenyan languages stopped. In primary school I now read simplified Dickens and Stevenson alongside Rider Haggard. Jim Hawkins, Oliver Twist, Tom Brown—not Hare, Leopard and Lion—were now my daily companions in the world of imagination. In secondary school, Scott and G.B. Shaw vied with more Rider Haggard, John Buchan, Alan Paton, Captain W.K. Johns. At Makerere I read English: from Chaucer to T.S. Eliot with a touch of Graham Greene.

Thus language and literature were taking us further and further from ourselves to other selves, from our world to other worlds.

What was the colonial system doing to us Kenyan children? What were the consequences of, on the one hand, this systematic suppression of our languages and the literature they carried, and on the other the elevation of English and the literature it carried? To answer those questions, let me first examine the relationship of language to human experience, human culture, and the human perception of reality.

Language, any language, has a dual character: it is both a means of communication and a carrier of culture. Take English. It is spoken in Britain and in Sweden and Denmark. But for Swedish and Danish people English is only a means of communication with non-Scandinavians. It is not a carrier of their culture. For the British, and particularly the English, it is additionally, and inseparably from its use as a tool of communication, a carrier of their culture and history. Or take Swahili in East and Central Africa. It is widely used as a means of communication across many nationalities. But it is not the carrier of a culture and history of many of those nationalities. However in parts of Kenya and Tanzania, and particularly in Zanzibar, Swahili is inseparably both a means of communication and a carrier of the culture of those people to whom it is a mother-tongue.

Culture transmits or imparts those images of the world and reality through the spoken and the written language, that is through a specific language. In other words, the capacity to speak, the capacity to order sounds in a manner that makes for mutual comprehension between human beings is universal. This is the universality of language, a quality specific to human beings. It corresponds to the universality of the struggle against nature and that between human beings. But the particularity of the sounds, the words, the word order into phrases and sentences, and the specific manner, or laws, of their ordering is what distinguishes one language from another. Thus a specific culture is not transmitted through language in its universality but in its particularity as the language of a specific community with a specific history. Written literature and orature are the main means by which a particular language transmits the images of the world contained in the culture it carries.

Language as communication and as culture are then products of each other. Communication creates culture: culture is a means of communication. Language carries culture, and culture carries, particularly through orature and literature, the entire body of values by which we come to perceive ourselves and our place in the world. How people perceive themselves affects how they look at their culture, at their politics and at the social production of wealth, at their entire relationship to nature and to other beings. Language is thus inseparable from ourselves as a community of human beings with a specific form and character, a specific history, a specific relationship to the world.

So what was the colonialist imposition of a foreign language doing to us children?

The real aim of colonialism was to control the people's wealth: what they produced, how they produced it, and how it was distributed; to control, in other words, the entire realm of the language of real life. Colonialism imposed its control of the social production of wealth through military conquest and subsequent political dictatorship. But its most important area of domination was the mental universe of the colonised, the control, through culture, of how people perceived themselves and their relationship to the world. Economic and political control can never be complete or effective without mental control. To control a people's culture is to control their tools of self-definition in relationship to others.

For colonialism this involved two aspects of the same process: the destruction or the deliberate undervaluing of a people's culture, their art, dances, religions, history, geography, education, orature and literature, and the conscious elevation of the language of the coloniser. The domination of a people's language by the languages of the colonising nations was crucial to the domination of the mental universe of the colonised.

Take language as communication. Imposing a foreign language, and suppressing the native languages as spoken and written, were already breaking the harmony previously existing between the African child and the three aspects of language. Since the new language as a means of communication was a product of and was reflecting the 'real language of life' elsewhere, it could never as spoken or written properly reflect or imitate the real life of that community. This may in part explain why technology always appears to us as slightly external, their product and not ours. The word 'missile' used to hold an alien far-away sound until I recently learnt its equivalent in Gĩkũyũ, ngurukuhĩ, and it made me apprehend it differently. Learning, for a colonial child, became a cerebral activity and not an emotionally felt experience.

But since the new, imposed languages could never completely break the native languages as spoken, their most effective area of domination was the third aspect of language as communication, the written. The language of an African child's formal education was foreign. The language of the books he read was foreign. The language of his conceptualisation was foreign. Thought, in him, took the visible form of a foreign language. So the written language of a child's upbringing in the school (even his spoken language within the school compound) became divorced from his spoken language at home. There was often not the slightest relationship between the child's written world, which was also the language of his schooling, and the world of his immediate environment in the family and the community. For a colonial child, the harmony existing between the three aspects of language as communication was irrevocably broken. This resulted in the disassociation of the sensibility of that child from his natural and social environment, what we might call colonial alienation. The alienation became reinforced in the teaching of history, geography, music, where bourgeois Europe was always the centre of the universe.

This disassociation, divorce, or alienation from the immediate environment becomes clearer when you look at colonial language as a carrier of culture.

Since culture is a product of the history of a people which it in turn reflects, the child was now being exposed exclusively to a culture that was a product of a world external to himself. He was being made to stand outside himself to look at himself. *Catching Them Young* is the title of a book on racism, class, sex, and politics in children's literature by Bob Dixon. 'Catching them young' as an aim was even more true of a colonial child. The images of this world and his place in it implanted in a child take years to eradicate, if they ever can be.

Since culture does not just reflect the world in images but actually, through those very images, conditions a child to see that world in a certain way, the colonial child was made to see the world and where he stands in it as seen and defined by or reflected in the culture of the language of imposition.

And since those images are mostly passed on through orature and literature it meant the child would now only see the world as seen in the literature of his language of adoption. From the point of view of alienation, that is of seeing oneself from outside oneself as if one was another self, it does not matter that the imported literature carried the great humanist tradition of the best in Shakespeare, Goethe, Balzac, Tolstoy, Gorky, Brecht, Sholokhov, Dickens. The location of this great mirror of imagination was necessarily Europe and its history and culture and the rest of the universe was seen from that centre.

But obviously it was worse when the colonial child was exposed to images of his world as mirrored in the written languages of his coloniser. Where his own native languages were associated in his impressionable mind with low status, humiliation, corporal punishment, slow-footed intelligence and ability or downright stupidity, non-intelligibility and barbarism, this was reinforced by the world he met in the works of such geniuses of racism as a Rider Haggard or a Nicholas Monsarrat; not to mention the pronouncement of some of the giants of western intellectual and political establishment, such as Hume ('. . . the negro is naturally inferior to the whites . . .'),[2] Thomas Jefferson ('. . . the blacks . . . are inferior to the whites on the endowments of both body and mind . . .'),[3] or Hegel with his Africa comparable to a land of childhood still enveloped in the dark mantle of the night as far as the development of self-conscious history was concerned. Hegel's statement that there was nothing harmonious with humanity to be found in the African character is representative of the racist images of Africans and Africa such a colonial child was bound to encounter in the literature of the colonial languages.[4] The results could be disastrous.

In her paper read to the conference on the teaching of African literature in schools held in Nairobi in 1973, entitled 'Written Literature and Black Images'[5] the Kenyan writer and scholar Professor Mīcere Mūgo related how a reading of the description of Gagool as an old African woman in Rider Haggard's *King Solomon's Mines* had for a long time made her feel mortal terror whenever she encountered old African women. In his autobiography *This Life* Sydney Poitier describes how, as a result of the literature he had read, he had come to associate Africa with snakes. So on arrival in Africa and being put up in a modern hotel in a modern city, he could not sleep because he kept on looking for snakes everywhere, even under the bed. These two have been able to pinpoint the origins of their fears. But for most others the negative image becomes internalised and it affects their cultural and even political choices in ordinary living.

---

[2]Quoted in Eric Williams, *A History of the People of Trinidad and Tobago,* London 1964, p. 32 [Author's note].

[3]Eric Williams, ibid. p. 31 [Author's note].

[4]In references to Africa in the introduction to his lectures in *The Philosophy of History,* Hegel gives historical, philosophical, rational expression and legitimacy to every conceivable European racist myth about Africa. Africa is even denied her own geography where it does not correspond to the myth. Thus Egypt is not part of Africa; and North Africa is part of Europe. Africa proper is the especial home of ravenous beasts, snakes of all kinds. The African is not part of humanity. Only slavery to Europe can raise him, possibly, to the lower ranks of humanity. Slavery is good for the African. 'Slavery is in and for itself *injustice,* for the essence of humanity is *freedom;* but for this man must be matured. The gradual abolition of slavery is therefore wiser and more equitable than its sudden removal.' (Hegel, *The Philosophy of History,* Dover edition. New York: 1956, pp. 91–9.) Hegel clearly reveals himself as the nineteenth-century Hitler of the intellect [Author's note].

[5]The paper is now in Akivaga and Gachukiah's *The Teaching of African Literature in Schools,* published by Kenya Literature Bureau [Author's note].

Critical Eye

FOR DISCUSSION

a. Looking at the British domination of Kenya, note how important language and education are to the domination of a people.

b. Looking at the oppression of Kenyans, does Thiong'o's essay suggest that the British are attempting to civilize the ignorant or dismantle their culture?

REAPPROACHING THE LITERATURE

Given that Puerto Rico is a principality of the United States, can you find any similarities between the way the United States handles Puerto Rico and its own citizens?

WRITING ASSIGNMENT

As Kenya is a principality, would you suggest that the colonizer has the right to rule the land and citizens of its owned property as it sees fit, or must the citizens make efforts to govern themselves?

Piper Fogg

Don't Stand So Close to Me

When does a popular professor's
friendliness become inappropriate?

At the university of Virginia, where faculty members are known to hole up with their research, students praised James R. Sofka as a welcome anomaly.

The young assistant professor met with students whether he had office hours or not. On warm afternoons he could be found on the university's famed lawn playing chess with undergraduates. As a faculty adviser to a debate society and a campus sorority, he could be counted on to attend students' plays and concerts, or meet up later for a drink. His fall course on international law filled up quickly. Since he became a full-time professor at Virginia in 1998, his dynamic lectures on 18th-century international relations and early American foreign policy have dazzled students.

But after hours, some of his former students allege, Mr. Sofka put his hands where they did not belong. In a January 14 letter, a university dean informed the politics professor that because of repeated complaints of "inappropriate behavior" with female students, he was being removed immediately from his position as dean of an undergraduate honors program. His contract, which is set to expire in 2007, would not be renewed, he was told.

In the letter, the dean ordered the professor to refrain from having drinks with students off campus, and from "touching and hugging" them. But it did not give names or details about any of the complaints.

Mr. Sofka maintains that he has no reason to feel ashamed of his interactions with students. He calls the dean's allegations an attack on his character. The professor, who is not on the tenure track, complains that he has never had a formal opportunity to defend himself. He has appealed to the provost and president.

"Don't Stand So Close to Me" by Piper Fogg, *The Chronicle of Higher Education*, April 29, 2005. Copyright 2005, The Chronicle of Higher Education. Reprinted with permission.

Regardless of the outcome, Mr. Sofka's case illustrates the risks of being a chummy professor. When does fraternizing become unseemly? Is it OK to have drinks with students, or give one a hug after a big accomplishment? What about taking out a student of the opposite sex off campus? What about inviting a student home when one's spouse is away?

Ultimately, it seems that what made Mr. Sofka so popular—his desire to be close to students—became his downfall.

Big Man on Campus

The square-jawed professor with close-cropped hair looks younger than his 37 years. Mr. Sofka, who received his Ph.D. from Virginia in 1995, is married; his wife, Amy Sofka, works on a child-literacy program in the education school at Virginia. Often dressed in a conservative blazer and preppy tie, Mr. Sofka might be confused for a stock trader. Florian P. Aigrain, a sophomore, says that Mr. Sofka even has the personality of someone who works on Wall Street. "He's not your typical professor who's artsy-fartsy," says Mr. Aigrain. Mr. Sofka is dynamic, opinionated, and aggressive, the sophomore says, but not in a negative way. When Mr. Aigrain was applying to colleges, meeting Mr. Sofka helped persuade him to attend Virginia.

"He was young, he was smart, and involved with student life," says Adele Bruce Shartzer, who graduated in 2003. "And he's not unattractive. For every girl who's had a crush on a professor . . . ," she says, her voice trailing off. Ms. Shartzer goes on to explain that it is easier to have a relationship with a professor who is more on "your wavelength, closer to college than to retirement."

Mr. Sofka relished his reputation. "I'm a popular and well-known professor," he explains in an interview. He says he has drinks and lunches with students, and if he has an extra ticket to a concert, he occasionally invites an undergraduate.

Sarah C. Greer, a sophomore, was assigned Mr. Sofka as her faculty adviser in the Echols Scholars Program, the honors program for undergraduates that Mr. Sofka had directed since 2002. Ms. Greer says he encouraged her to apply to an even more elite honors program that accepts only a few politics majors each year. "A lot of these advisers are like, let's shovel these students through the door . . . I have better things to do," she says. Mr. Sofka, in contrast, "really believes in his students."

In an open letter to others at the university, the professor defended his interactions with students, calling them "the source of great joy to me and the genesis of many lasting friendships. Indeed, my cherished times of . . . taking an interest in the lives of my students have been publicly documented and praised."

The professor acknowledged that while some may see any close relationship between students and faculty members as "the appearance of a conflict of interest," he sees it as "the vital humanism of academic life."

But Edward L. Ayers, dean of arts and sciences, apparently did not see it that way. In his January letter to Mr. Sofka, Dean Ayers said he had warned the professor back in 2003 about his interactions with students. "Specifically," he wrote, "I directed you to cease inappropriate behavior with female Echols Scholars." The dean said he was removing Mr. Sofka because of complaints that the behavior "has not abated." Mr. Ayers reassigned him to teaching full time in the politics department.

The news came as a shock to Mr. Sofka. "Nobody really has ever seen a letter like that," he says.

But what about the 2003 complaints? According to Mr. Sofka, a female student with whom he attended a concert that spring was spreading rumors about him. He heard that she was telling people that his leg had brushed up against hers and that he had propositioned her. He says the student had received a D on the final exam in his course and protested to a teaching assistant.

Mr. Sofka says he encouraged the student to file a complaint with the university's equal-opportunity office, which investigates sexual-harassment claims. He wanted to clear his name. She filed a complaint, he says, it was resolved, and the grade stood. He says the recommendation that resulted from the investigation of her complaint "was as bland as they come." Mr. Ayers did call him in to tell him to be careful, Mr. Sofka says.

But he maintains that it was a broad, collegial talk. And he has not faced any complaints since, he says.

The Lecherous Professor?

Students at Virginia say rumors have persisted for years that Mr. Sofka was not always professional with his female students. Some dismissed it as campus gossip. But three women who talked to *The Chronicle* say that their experiences with the professor suggest otherwise. The women, who are all graduates, agreed to speak about the incidents only if their names were not used.

One graduate says that Mr. Sofka, who was her adviser, constantly asked her out to dinner and drinks alone. She says he even asked her to have a

Scotch with him when his wife was out of town—an invitation she found "creepy." At events where she knew Mr. Sofka would show up, she began timing her entrance to avoid him. She considered leaving the university because she was so uncomfortable, but decided to stay.

Another graduate, from the class of 2003, says she was initially impressed with Mr. Sofka, also her faculty adviser. "He had seemed so wonderful and friendly and nonintimidating," she says. Early in her undergraduate years, she says, he invited her over to his apartment. She went, thinking it was to discuss her major.

"It felt not right," she says. Even though she was under age and had driven to his home, she says, Mr. Sofka offered her Scotch. According to her account, they began the meeting sitting opposite each other, but the professor later moved next to her on the couch. "He'd talk and pat my leg," she says. She was uncomfortable, so she told him she had to go, left, then called a friend. "I was very shaken up," she says.

But she didn't file a complaint or tell an administrator. "I didn't want my time at the university to be tainted," she says. Instead, she stopped going to his office. The only time she would was to get her course-registration forms signed.

A third woman says she was "thrilled" when Mr. Sofka first paid attention to her as an undergraduate. She describes herself then as a dorky, high-strung student who loved attention from faculty members. Mr. Sofka, who made his home number available to his students, seemed to invite relationships with undergraduates. In his office, she says, he had a bulletin board where he tacked up notes from some of his students. "That was really attractive—to be one of his favorites," she says.

One night, with her graduation date drawing near, she says, they were out at a bar drinking. While he was walking her home, she says, Mr. Sofka put his arms around her. "He really wrapped his arms around my waist, like body to body," she says. "I pushed him away." She went inside and says she never saw him again. She didn't tell anyone, not even her friends. She thought people would think she had encouraged him.

"I really thought I was going to get blamed for it," she says. "I didn't want people to think I was flirting with the professor."

The Aftermath

Mr. Sofka, when told about the women's descriptions of his behavior, says he has no idea who they are. "Without names, I can't say anything," he says. Through his lawyer, he "denies that he ever made any inappropriate romantic advances towards any student."

Mr. Sofka has not been allowed a hearing to respond to the recent complaints mentioned in the dean's January letter. The equal-opportunity office does not investigate anonymous complaints. And a university spokeswoman says that because Mr. Sofka has no expectation of continued employment, the university does not need to hold an appeals hearing regarding its decision to terminate his contract. Mr. Sofka says he has been denied due process and has hired a lawyer.

Student Support

When the news of the popular professor's troubles first broke, some students rallied around him. "We were just appalled at how it was dealt with," says Ms. Greer. She sent a letter to Dean Ayers, saying she was disappointed with the outcome. She was especially concerned that the Echols Scholars Program lost "its passionate leader," she says.

Mr. Aigrain agrees, noting that the administration did not handle the situation "as properly" as it could have.

But a groundswell of support for the politics professor never materialized. Faculty members have been loath to openly discuss Mr. Sofka's plight. Marcia D. Childress, chairwoman of the Faculty Senate and a professor in the medical school, says she hasn't heard from professors who are upset about the issues surrounding Mr. Sofka. But one professor, who declined to be named says a chill has gone through the faculty.

Mr. Sofka "was given no real warning about this," says the faculty member. "Most professors realize this could have been them." The professor also suggests that top officials are "enormously unhappy with the dean for having created this mess."

Mr. Ayers did not respond to telephone messages, and his assistant referred calls to the university's public-relations office. Carol Wood, a spokeswoman, declined to discuss the case in detail, calling it a "personnel matter." But she says that Mr. Ayers continues to have the full support of both the president and the provost.

A better approach, says the professor who requested anonymity, would have been to quietly put Mr. Sofka on administrative leave while investigating the allegations. "If this guy is such a threat," adds the professor, "then please explain to me why he's been put in front of hundreds and hundreds of students in political studies? . . . It has people mystified."

Billie Wright Dziech, a professor of language arts at the University of Cincinnati who has written several books about sexual harrassment, says she doesn't know much about the details of Mr. Sofka's case, but says it is clear from the letter that the professor had been warned. Ms. Dziech suggests that faculty members, in general, should maintain certain boundaries when dealing with students. She suggests not going places with them alone and not drinking too much—or at all—with them. "You can be sympathetic without ever touching them or drinking with them," she says. But following a set of rules is not as important as learning to take cues from students' body language and facial expressions, she adds. "If you're really a good teacher . . . you know when you've offended someone."

The Safest Approach

"You can still be a mentor without engaging in touching, hugging, or drinking," says Michael W. Hawkins, an adjunct professor at Xavier University in Ohio and a lawyer who has represented colleges in sexual-harassment cases.

The most conservative approach is often the safest, agrees Ms. Dziech, because people have different concepts of personal boundaries. She says, "You don't have to French kiss someone or rape someone to offend them."

Ms. Dziech says buddy-buddy professors who make passes at students often fit the same mold: They have very good student evaluations and are considered entertaining in and out of class. "It's all about making people like you so you can get an inroad," she says. "It's like a teenage thing: I want the people to like me." A professor who takes advantage of his or her popularity puts students in a bind, she says. Students often feel they have to drop a course, change majors or switch advisers to get away.

Even if a faculty member is not guilty of acting inappropriately, being known as the professor who's always hanging out at the student bar can damage one's reputation, let alone career. At Virginia, Mr. Sofka has become the butt of student jokes. The April Fool's Day edition of the student newspaper featured a doctored photo of Mr. Sofka in a tuxedo with three scantily-clad blondes. The article joked that he has been named head of the women-and-gender-studies department and suggested a new course, "Studying A Broad: Sexism in Foreign Countries." Priority registration, it said, had been given to sorority members and the women's volleyball team.

And yet just ten days later, his two real fall courses filled up within 24 hours. More than 130 students are already on the waiting lists.

Critical Eye

FOR DISCUSSION

a. Have we become so hypersensitive about sexual harassment in this society that educators cannot show genuine interest/concern for their students?

b. Given what you know about sexual harassment, has this professor done anything wrong?

c. What responsibility, if any, does the accusing student have in this incident?

d. As a result of the accusation, is what the administration did a violation of the professor's rights?

REAPPROACHING THE TEXT

The Anita Hill/Clarence Thomas case brought the issue of sexual harassment into the forefront of American society. Are these cases in any way the same?

WRITING ASSIGNMENT

Discuss how real the problem of sexual harassment is in our everyday lives. Have we gone too far in labeling people as offenders?

Angela Nissel

From
The Broke Diaries

OCTOBER 7

Dear Broke Diary:

Knowledge should be free.

And today, at the University of Pennsylvania, it was.

Only with the truly broke can a beautifully planned day of study turn into a burglary.

I love having the same classes as my friends. Usually, when we combine our purchasing power, we can afford all of the books for the class. One set that we all share, of course.

But not this anthropology class me and Janelle, my closest brokest friend, are enrolled in. This class has three required books *and* a bulkpack (a bound collection of essays from multiple authors). What the hell was this professor thinking?

I wish they bootlegged books like they bootleg albums. Where's the man with the briefcase full of stolen books?

Eff a fake Gucci watch. Start hawking photocopies of textbooks. You'll be a tax-free millionaire in no time.

No, know what I want? Thugs who just rough up professors who assign too many books. Especially professors who assign books they themselves authored. The book thugs wouldn't hurt 'em, just, like, corner them in a lab late one night and scare them into shame.

> Thug [knocking petri dish to the floor]: Yeah, I knocked over your little dish! You wanna do something about it?! Huh, do you??!
> Professor [cowering in corner]: Please, sir!!! Leave me be!! Is it money you're after? I don't have any money in here! Just fetal pigs!
> Thug: Sure, you don't have any money! We know you're getting kickbacks from the publishing companies for assigning these

"October 7," from *The Broke Diaries* by Angela Nissel, copyright © 2001 by Angela Nissel. Used by permission of Villard Books, a division of Random House, Inc.

overpriced books!! And how are you going to assign a book you wrote your damn self?!! Why, I should—

    Professor: Please, take all the drugs you want! In fact, I'll make you some drugs! Please, go!

    Thug [punches hole in Periodic Table of Elements Chart]: I'll be back.

Oops. I didn't mean to start writing a screenplay. Sorry. Just get a little emotional sometimes. Got all this aggression up in me 'cause, man, I wanna learn, too!

Anyway. Me and 'Nelie did split the cost of the anthro bulkpack but, man, we were jonesing for that textbook. Not having that textbook has put us mad behind.

Yesterday, we made a plan to bridge that broke learning gap. Janelle is convinced Joel, the teaching assistant, gives her special looks during class. (Yes, she said "special looks." How funny, right?!! What the hell is a "special look"?) So she suggested we go to his office hours and double-team him: I'd kiss up and she'd flirt.

Anyway, I was down for the plan, but the only special look I want from Joel is the look he gives my midterms and final when he smacks an A on both of 'em.

Today was supposed to be the first day on the quest to have Joel smack my A.

Janelle and I met up in front of Van Pelt Library and walked over to the university museum. Just two normal, innocent college girls walking to class. We could have made the "Guide for Prospective Parents" video. Janelle even had a bow in her hair. Ah, it was perfect.

We were still pure and innocent as we walked up the museum stairs, down the left-end hall, and into Joel's office. He wasn't there, so we just plopped down on the beat-up office love seat and started chatting.

That's when we saw it. Perched on top of a stack of papers on his desk.

Yes, it was . . . The Textbook.

Okay, actually, 'Nelle saw it first. We were talking, and all of a sudden her eyes got wide like saucers. Her voice dropped to an urgent whisper. "Oh shit, Ang! Look! Look! On the desk!"

Mmmm, yes. That book looked beautiful in all of its unbroken-spined glory. Shiny, happy book. With the words "Educator's Edition" emblazoned in gold across the front. Polished gold, not dull gold like the cafeteria workers' teeth.

I wanted to pick it up, to touch it, to write down some of the sacred "Educator's Edition" notes I knew were contained therein.

I wanted to look in it so badly, but that's rude, right? You can't touch someone's stuff while they aren't there. Oh, but it was calling me. . . . It was so shiny, so new . . . so—

WOW.

Janelle's a bad sis.

I was scared to touch the book, but in some wild fit of broke bibliomania, her ass done picked it up and ran out the door with it.

Damn!

Ladies and gentlemen, the book has left the building!

I was thinking, Oh my God! Do I sit here? Do I follow her?

One of those lectures my mom gave me when I was little came into my head. How if my friends stole Now and Laters from the corner store and I was with them, I'd go to jail, too.

I can see us now, getting kicked out of college for this. Liberal politicians would use our dilemma as evidence of how unequal educational opportunities are: "They got kicked out of school for wanting to learn!"

And can you imagine me telling my mom what I got kicked out of school for?

Oh my God, what do I do?

Then reality kicked in.

Um, do I want to be the only one sitting here when Joel comes back and sees his book is missing?

I gotta have my girl's back. And I have to pass this class.

Viva la Stolen Textbook!

And an Educator's Edition, at that. Damn, I am so proud of Janelle. That's my girl!

Now that I'm home, and I realize we're probably not going to get caught, I'm a little jealous she has the textbook.

I'm going to go to the other T.A.'s office hours tomorrow. Bet he got an Educator's Edition book, too. I'll be damned if Janelle gets better grades and special looks.

Misdemeanor,

Ang

Critical Eye

FOR DISCUSSION

a. Nissel's text takes a comedic look at the "academic poverty" many college students face once they become undergraduates. Why, in your opinion, are so many young college students in debt?

b. Are Angie and Janelle justified in their actions?

c. Does the overpricing of college make it almost impossible for students who wish to learn to do so?

REAPPROACHING THE LITERATURE

Almost haphazardly, Angela glosses over the fact that the teaching assistant may have a crush on her best friend. Clearly, they both intend on taking advantage of the situation. What is wrong, if anything, about their willingness to use sex as a means of getting what they want?

WRITING ASSIGNMENT

In what way is this piece an indictment of the university system?

Eliza Haywood

Fantomina: Or, Love in a Maze

Being a Secret History of an Amour
Between Two Persons of Condition

> In love the victors from vanquished fly.
> They fly that wound, and they pursue that die.
> *Waller*

A young lady of distinguished birth, wit, and spirit, happened to be
in a box one night at the playhouse; where though there were a great
number of celebrated toasts, she perceived several gentlemen extremely
pleasing themselves with entertaining a woman who sat in a corner of
the pit, and, by her air and manner of receiving them, might easily be
known to be one of those who come there for no other purpose, than to
create acquaintance with as many as seem desirous of it. She could not
help testifying her contempt of men, who, regardless either of the play,
or circle, threw away their time in such a manner, to some ladies that
sat by her: but they, either less surprised by being more accustomed to
such sights than she who had been bred for the most part in the country,
or not of a disposition to consider anything very deeply, took but little
notice of it. She still thought of it, however, and the longer she reflected
on it, the greater was her wonder, that men, some of whom she knew
were accounted to have wit, should have tastes so very depraved.—This
excited a curiosity in her to know in what manner these creatures were
addressed:—she was young, a stranger to the world, and consequently
to the dangers of it; and having nobody in town, at that time, to whom
she was obliged to be accountable for her actions, did in everything as
her inclinations or humors rendered most agreeable to her: therefore
thought it not in the least a fault to put in practice a little whim which
came immediately into her head, to dress herself as near as she could in
the fashion of those women who make sale of their favors, and set herself
in the way of being accosted as such a one, having at that time no other
aim, than the gratification of an innocent curiosity.—She no sooner
designed this frolic, than she put it in execution; and muffling her hoods
over her face, went the next night into the gallery-box, and practicing as

much as she had observed at that distance, the behavior of that woman, was not long before she found her disguise had answered the ends she wore it for:—a crowd of purchasers of all degrees and capacities were in a moment gathered about her, each endeavoring to outbid the other, in offering her a price for her embraces.—She listened to 'em all, and was not a little diverted in her mind at the disappointment she should give to so many, each of which thought himself secure of gaining her.—She was told by 'em all, that she was the most lovely woman in the world; and some cried, *God, she is mighty like my fine Lady Such-a-one,*—naming her own name. She was naturally vain, and received no small pleasure in hearing herself praised, though in the person of another, and a supposed prostitute; but she dispatched as soon as she could all that had hitherto attacked her, when she saw the accomplished *Beauplasir'* was making his way through the crowd as fast as he was able, to reach the bench she sat on. She had often seen him in the drawing-room, had talked with him; but then her quality and reputed virtue kept him from using her with that freedom she now expected he would do, and had discovered something in him, which had made her often think she should not be displeased, if he would abate some part of his reserve.—Now was the time to have her wishes answered:—he looked in her face, and fancied, as many others had done, that she very much resembled that lady whom she really was; but the vast disparity there appeared between their characters prevented him from entertaining even the most distant thought that they could be the same.—He addressed her at first with the usual salutations of her pretended profession, as, *Are you engaged, Madam?—Will you permit me to wait on you home after the play?—By Heaven, you are a fine girl!—How long have you used this house?* and such like questions; but perceiving she had a turn of wit, and a genteel manner in her raillery, beyond what is frequently to be found among those wretches, who are for the most part gentlewomen but by neccessity, few of 'em having had an education suitable to what they affect to appear, he changed the form of his conversation, and showed her it was not because he understood better that he had made use of expressions so little polite.—In time, they were infinitely charmed with each other: he was transported to find so much beauty and wit in a woman, who he doubted not but on very easy terms he might enjoy; and she found a vast deal of pleasure in conversing with him in this free and unrestrained manner. They passed their time all the play with an equal satisfaction; but when it was over, she found herself involved in a difficulty, which before never entered into her head, but which she knew not well how to get over.—The passion he professed for her, was not of that humble nature which can be content with distant adorations:—he resolved not to part from her without the gratifications of those desires she had inspired; and presuming on the liberties which her supposed function allowed of, told her she must either go with him to some convenient house of his procuring, or permit him to wait on her to her own lodgings.—Never had she been in such a *dilemma:* three or four times did she open her mouth to confess her real quality; but the influence of her ill stars prevented it, by putting an excuse into her head, which did the business as well, and at the same time did not take from her the power of seeing and entertaining him a second time with the same freedom she had done this.—She told him, she was under obligations to a man who maintained her, and whom she durst not disappoint, having promised to meet him that night at a house hard by.—This story so like what those ladies sometimes tell was not at all suspected by *Beauplaisir;* and assuring her he would be far from doing her a prejudice, desired that in return for the pain he should suffer in being deprived of her company that night, that she would order her affairs, so as not to render him unhappy the next. She gave a solemn promise to be in the same box on the morrow evening; and they took leave of each other; he to the tavern to drown the remembrance of his disappointment; she in a hackney-chair hurried home to indulge contemplation on the frolic she had taken, designing nothing less on her first reflections than to keep the promise she had made him, and hugging herself with joy, that she had the good luck to come off undiscovered.

But these cogitations were but of a short continuance; they vanished with the hurry of her spirits, and were succeeded by others vastly different and ruminous:—all the charms of *Beauplaisir* came fresh into her mind; she languished, she almost died for another opportunity of conversing with him; and not all the admonitions of her discretion were effectual to oblige her to deny laying hold of that which offered itself the next night.—She depended on the strength of her virtue, to bear her fate through trials more dangerous than she apprehended this to be, and never having been addressed by him as Lady—was resolved to receive his devoirs as a town-mistress, imagining a world of satisfaction to herself in engaging him in the character of such a one, observing the surprise he would be in to find himself refused by a woman, who he supposed granted her favors without exception.—Strange and unaccountable were the whimsies she was possessed of—wild and incoherent her desires—unfixed and undetermined her resolutions, but in that of seeing *Beauplaisir* in the manner she had lately done. As for her proceedings with him, or how a second time to escape him, without discovering who she was, she could neither assure herself, nor whether or not in the last extremity she would do so.—Bent, however, on meeting him, whatever should be the consequence, she went out some hours before the time of going to the playhouse, and took lodgings in a house not very far from it, intending, that if he should insist on passing some part of the night with her, to carry him there, thinking she might with more security to her honor entertain him at a place where she was mistress, than at any of his own choosing.

The appointed hour being arrived, she had the satisfaction to find his love in his assiduity: he was there before her; and nothing could be more tender than the manner in which he accosted her: but from the first moment she came in, to that of the play being done, he continued to assure her no consideration should prevail with him to part from her again, as she had done the night before; and she rejoiced to think she had taken that precaution of providing herself with a lodging, to which she thought she might invite him, without running any risk, either of her virtue or reputation.—Having told him she would admit of his accompanying her home, he seemed perfectly satisfied; and leading her to the place, which was not above twenty houses distant, would have ordered a collation to be brought after them. But she would not permit it, telling him she was not one of those who suffered themselves to be treated at their own lodgings; and as soon she was come in, sent a servant, belonging to the house, to provide a very handsome supper, and wine and everything was served to table in a manner which showed the director neither wanted money, nor was ignorant how it should be laid out.

This proceeding, though it did not take from him the opinion that she was what she appeared to be, yet it gave him thoughts of her, which he had not before.—He believed her a *mistress,* but believed her to be one of a superior rank, and began to imagine the possession of her would be much more expensive than at first he had expected: but not being of a humor to grudge anything for his pleasures, he gave himself no farther trouble than what were occasioned by fears of not having money enough to reach her price, about him.

Supper being over, which was intermixed with a vast deal of amorous conversation, he began to explain himself more than he had done; and both by his words and behavior let her know he would not be denied that happiness the freedoms she allowed had made him hope.—It was in vain; she would have retracted the encouragement she had given:—in vain she endeavored to delay, till the next meeting, the fulfilling of his wishes:— she had now gone too far to retreat:—*he* was bold;—he was resolute: *she* fearful—confused, altogether unprepared to resist in such encounters, and rendered more so, by the extreme liking she had to him.—Shocked, however, at the apprehension of really losing her honor, she struggled all she could, and was just going to reveal the whole secret of her name and quality, when the thoughts of the liberty he had taken with her, and those he still continued to prosecute, prevented her, with representing the danger of being exposed, and the whole affair made a theme for public ridicule.—Thus much, indeed, she told him, that she was a virgin, and had assumed this manner of behavior only to engage him. But that he little regarded, or if he had, would have been far from obliging him to desist;—nay, in the present burning eagerness of desire, 'tis probable, that had he been acquainted both with who and what she really was, the knowledge of her birth would not have influenced him with respect sufficient to have curbed the wild exuberance of his luxurious wishes, or made him in that longing—that impatient moment, change the form of his address. In fine, she was undone; and he gained a victory, so highly rapturous, that had he known over whom, scarce could he have triumphed more. Her tears, however, and the distraction she appeared in, after the ruinous ecstasy was past, as it heightened his wonder, so it abated his satisfaction:—he could not imagine for what reason a woman, who, if she intended not to be a *mistress,* had counterfeited the part of one, and taken so much pains to engage him, should lament a consequence which she could not but expect, and till the last test, seemed inclinable to grant; and was both surprised and troubled at the mystery.—He omitted nothing that he thought might make her easy; and still retaining an opinion that the hope of interest had been the chief motive which had led her to act in the manner she had done, and believing that she might know so little of him, as to suppose, now she had nothing left to give, he might not make that recompense she expected for her favors: to put her out of that pain, he pulled out of his pocket a purse of gold, entreating her to accept of that as an earnest of what he intended to do for her; assuring her, with ten thousand protestations, that he would spare nothing, which his whole estate could purchase, to procure her content and happiness. This treatment made her quite forget the part she had assumed, and throwing it from her with an air of disdain, Is this a reward *(said she)* for condescensions, such as I have yielded to?—Can all the wealth you are possessed of make a reparation for my loss of honor?—Oh! no, I am undone beyond the power of heaven itself to help me!—She uttered many more such exclamations; which the amazed *Beauplaisir* heard without being able to reply to, till by degrees sinking from that rage of temper, her eyes resumed their softening glances, and guessing at the consternation he was in, No, my dear *Beauplaisir, (added she)* your love alone can compensate for the shame you have involved me in; be you sincere and constant, and I hereafter shall, perhaps, be satisfied with my fate, and forgive myself the folly that betrayed me to you.

Beauplaisir thought he could not have a better opportunity than these words gave him of inquiring who she was, and wherefore she had feigned herself to be of a profession which he was now convinced she was not;

and after he had made her a thousand vows of an affection, as inviolable and ardent as she could wish to find in him, entreated she would inform him by what means his happiness had been brought about, and also to whom he was indebted for the bliss he had enjoyed.—Some remains of yet unextinguished modesty, and sense of shame, made her blush exceedingly at this demand; but recollecting herself in a little time, she told him so much of the truth, as to what related to the frolic she had taken of satisfying her curiosity in what manner *mistresses,* of the sort she appeared to be were treated by those who addressed them; but forbore discovering her true name and quality, for the reasons she had done before, resolving, if he boasted of this affair, he should not have it in his power to touch her character: she therefore said she was the daughter of a country gentleman, who was come to town to buy clothes, and that she was called *Fantomina.* He had no reason to distrust the truth of this story, and was therefore satisfied with it; but did not doubt by the beginning of her conduct, but that in the end she would be in reality, the thing she so artfully had counterfeited; and had good nature enough to pity the misfortunes he imagined would be her lot: but to tell her so, or offer his advice in that point, was not his business, at least, as yet.

They parted not till towards morning; and she obliged him to a willing vow of visiting her the next day at three in the afternoon. It was too late for her to go home that night, therefore contented herself with lying there. In the morning she sent for the woman of the house to come up to her; and easily perceiving, by her manner, that she was a woman who might be influenced by gifts, made her a present of a couple of broad pieces, and desired her, that if the gentleman, who had been there the night before, should ask any questions concerning her, that he should be told, she was lately come out of the country, had lodged there about a fortnight, and that her name was *Fantomina.* I shall *(also added she)* lie but seldom here; not indeed, ever come but in those times when I expect to meet him: I would, therefore, have you order it so, that he may think I am but just gone out, if he should happen by any accident to call when I am not here; for I would not, for the world, have him imagine I do not constantly lodge here. The landlady assured her she would do everything as she desired, and gave her to understand she wanted not the gift of secrecy.

Everything being ordered at this home for the security of her reputation, she repaired to the other, where she easily excused to an unsuspecting aunt, with whom she boarded, her having been abroad all night, saying, she went with a gentleman and his lady in a barge, to a little country seat of theirs up the river, all of them designing to return the same evening; but that one of the bargemen happening to be taken ill on the sudden, and no other waterman to be got that night, they were obliged to tarry till morning. Thus did this lady's wit and vivacity assist her in all, but where it was most needed.—She had discernment to foresee, and avoid all those ills which might attend the loss of her *reputation,* but was wholly blind to those of the ruin of her *virtue;* and having managed her affairs so as to secure the *one,* grew perfectly easy with the remembrance she had forfeited the *other.*—The more she reflected on the merits of *Beauplaisir,* the more she excused herself for what she had done; and the prospect of that continued bliss she expected to share with him took from her all remorse for having engaged in an affair which promised her so much satisfaction, and in which she found not the least danger of misfortune.— If he is really *(said she, to herself)* the faithful, the constant lover he has sworn to be, how charming will be our armor?—And if he should be false, grow satiated, like other men, I shall but, at the worst, have the private vexation of knowing I have lost him;—the intrigue being a secret, my disgrace will be so too:—I shall hear no whispers as I pass—She is forsaken:—the odious word *forsaken* will never wound my ears; nor will my wrongs excite either the mirth or pity of the talking world:—it would not be even in the power of my undoer himself to triumph over me; and while he laughs at, and perhaps despises the fond, the yielding *Fantomina,* he will revere and esteem the virtuous, the reserved lady.—In this manner did she applaud her own conduct, and exult with the imagination that she had more prudence than all her sex beside. And it must be confessed, indeed, that she preserved an economy in the management of this intrigue beyond what almost any woman but herself ever did: in the first place, by making no person in the world a confident in it; and in the next, in concealing from *Beauplaisir* himself the knowledge who she was; for though she met him three of four days in a week, at that lodging she had taken for that purpose, yet as much as he employed her time and thoughts, she was never missed from any assembly she had been accustomed to frequent.—The business of her love has engrossed her till six in the evening, and before seven she has been dressed in a different habit, and in another place.—Slippers, and a night-gown loosely flowing, has been the grab in which he has left the languishing *Fantomina;*—laced and adorned with all the blaze of jewels has he, in less than an hour after, beheld at the royal chapel, the palace gardens, drawing-room, opera, or play, the haughty awe-inspiring lady—a thousand times has he stood amazed at the prodigious likeness between his little mistress and this court beauty; but was still as far from imagining they were the same as he was the first hour he had accosted her in the playhouse, though it is not impossible but that her resemblance to this celebrated lady might keep his inclination alive something longer than otherwise they would have been; and that it was to the thoughts of this (as he supposed) unenjoyed charmer she owed in great measure the vigor of his latter caresses.

But he varied not so much from his sex as to be able to prolong desire to any great length after possession: the rifled charms of *Fantomina* soon lost their potency, and grew tasteless and insipid; and when the season of the year inviting the company to the *Bath*, she offered to accompany him, he made an excuse to go without her. She easily perceived his coldness, and the reason why he pretended her going would be inconvenient, and endured as much from the discovery as any of her sex could do: she dissembled it, however, before him, and took her leave of him with the show of no other concern than his absence occasioned: but this she did to take from him all suspicion of her following him, as she intended, and had already laid a scheme for.—From her first finding out that he designed to leave her behind, she plainly saw it was for no other reason, than that being tired of her conversation, he was willing to be at liberty to pursue new conquests; and wisely considering that complaints, tears, swoonings, and all the extravagancies which women make use of in such cases, have little prevalence over a heart inclined to rove, and only serve to render those who practice them more contemptible, by robbing them of that beauty which alone can bring back the fugitive lover, she resolved to take another course; and remembering the height of transport she enjoyed when the agreeable *Beauplaisir* kneeled at her feet, imploring her first favors, she longed to prove the same again. Not but a woman of her beauty and accomplishments might have beheld a thousand in that condition *Beauplaisir* had been; but with her sex's modesty, she had not also thrown off another virtue equally valuable, though generally unfortunate, *constancy:* she loved *Beauplaisir;* it was only he whose solicitations could give her pleasure; and had she seen the whole species despairing, dying for her sake, it might, perhaps, have been a satisfaction to her pride, but none to her more tender inclination.—Her design was once more to engage him, to hear him sigh, to see him languish, to feel the strenuous pressures of his eager arms, to be compelled, to be sweetly forced to what she wished with equal ardor, was what she wanted, and what she had formed a stratagem to obtain, in which she promised herself success.

She no sooner heard he had left the town, than making a pretense to her aunt, that she was going to visit a relation in the country, went towards *Bath,* attended but by two servants, who she found reasons to quarrel with on the road and discharged: clothing herself in a habit she had brought with her, she forsook the coach, and went into a wagon, in which equipage she arrived at *Bath*. The dress she was in was a round-eared cap, a short red petticoat, and a little jacket of gray stuff; all the rest of her accoutrements were answerable to these, and joined with a broad country dialect, a rude unpolished air, which she, having been bred in these parts, knew very well how to imitate, with her hair and eye-brows blacked, made it impossible for her to be known, or taken for any other than what she seemed. Thus disguised did she offer herself to service in the house where *Beauplaisir* lodged, having made it her business to find out immediately where he was. Not withstanding this metamorphosis she was still extremely pretty; and the mistress of the house happening at that time to want a maid was very glad of the opportunity of taking her. She was presently received into the family; and had a post in it (such as she would have chose, had she been left at her liberty), that of making the gentlemen's beds, getting them their breakfasts, and waiting on them in their chambers. Fortune in this exploit was extremely on her side; there were no others of the male-sex in the house than an old gentleman, who had lost the use of his limbs with the rheumatism, and had come thither for the benefit of the waters, and her beloved *Beauplaisir;* so that she was in no apprehensions of any amorous violence, but where she wished to find it. Nor were her designs disappointed: He was fired with the first sight of her; and though he did not presently take any farther notice of her, than giving her two or three hearty kisses, yet she, who now understood that language but too well, easily saw they were the preclude to more substantial joys.—Coming the next morning to bring his chocolate, as he had ordered, he catched her by the pretty leg, which the shortness of her petticoat did not in the least oppose; then pulling her gently to him, asked her, how long she had been at service?—How many sweethearts she had? If she had ever been in love? and many other such questions, befitting one of the degree she appeared to be: all which she answered with such seeming innocence, as more enflamed the amorous heart of him who talked to her. He compelled her to sit in his lap; and gazing on her blushing beauties, which, if possible, received addition from her plain and rural dress, he soon lost the power of containing himself.—His wild desires burst out in all his words and actions: he called her little angel, cherubim, swore he must enjoy her, though death were to be the consequence, devoured her lips, her breasts with greedy kisses, held to his burning bosom her half-yielding, half-reluctant body, nor suffered her to get loose, till he had ravaged all, and glutted each rapacious sense with the sweet beauties of the pretty *Celia,* for that was the name she bore in this second expedition.—Generous as liberality itself to all who gave him joy this way, he gave her a handsome sum of gold, which she darst not now refuse, for fear of creating some mistrust, and losing the heart she so lately had regained; therefore taking it with an humble courtesy, and a well counterfeited show of surprise and joy, cried, O law, Sir! what must I do for all this? He laughed at her simplicity, and kissing her again, thought less fervently than he had done before, bad her not be out of the way when he came home at night. She promised she would not, and very obediently kept her word.

His stay at *Bath* exceeded not a month; but in that time his supposed country lass had persecuted him so much with her fondness, that in spite of the eagerness with which he first enjoyed her, he was at last grown more weary of her, than he had been of *Fantomina;* which she perceiving, would not be troublesome, but quitting her service, remained privately in the town till she heard he was on his return; and in that time provided herself of another disguise to carry on a third plot, which her inventing brain had furnished her with, once more to renew his twice-decayed ardors. The dress she had ordered to be made, was such as widows wear in their first mourning, which, together with the most afflicted and penitential countenance that ever was seen, was no small alteration to her who used to seem all gaiety.—To add to this, her hair, which she was accustomed to wear very loose, both when *Fantomina* and *Celia,* was now tied back so straight, and her pincers coming so very forward, that there was none of it to be seen. In fine, her habit and her air were so much changed, that she was not more difficult to be known in the rude country *girl,* than she was now in the sorrowful *widow.*

She knew that *Beauplaisir* came alone in his chariot to the *Bath,* and in the time of her being servant in the house where he lodged, heard nothing of any body that was to accompany him to *London,* and hoped he would return in the same manner he had gone: She therefore hired horses and a man to attend her to an inn about ten miles on this side of *Bath,* where having discharged them, she waited till the chariot should come by; which when it did, and she saw that he was alone in it, she called to him that drove it to stop a moment, and going to the door saluted the master with these words:

The distressed and wretched, Sir *(said she),* never fail to excite compassion in a generous mind; and I hope I am not deceived in my opinion that yours is such:—You have the appearance of a gentleman, and cannot, when you hear my story, refuse that assistance which is in your power to give to an unhappy woman, who without it, may be rendered the most miserable of all created beings.

It would not be very easy to represent the surprise, so odd an address created in the mind of him to whom it was made.—She had not the appearance of one who wanted charity; and what other favor she required he could not conceive: but telling her she might command any thing in his power gave her encouragement to declare herself in this manner: You may judge *(resumed she),* by the melancholy garb I am in, that I have lately lost all that ought to be valuable to womankind; but it is impossible for you to guess the greatness of my misfortune, unless you had known my husband, who was master of every perfection to endear him to a wife's affections.—But, notwithstanding, I look on myself as the most unhappy of my sex in out-living him, I must so far obey the dictates of my discretion, as to take care of the little fortune he left behind him, which being in the hands of a brother of his in *London,* will be all carried off to *Holland,* where he is going to settle; if I reach not the town before he leaves it, I am undone for ever.—To which end I left *Bristol,* the place where we lived, hoping to get a place in the stage at *Bath,* but they were all taken up before I came; and being, by a hurt I got in a fall, rendered incapable of traveling any long journey on horseback, I have no way to go to *London,* and must be inevitably ruined in the loss of all I have on earth, without you have good nature enough to admit me to take part of your chariot.

Here the feigned widow ended her sorrowful tale, which had been several times interrupted by a parenthesis of sighs and groans; and *Beauplaisir,* with a complaisant and tender air, assured her of his readiness to serve her in things of much greater consequence than what she desired of him; and told her it would be an impossibility of denying a place in his chariot to a lady who he could not behold without yielding one in his heart. She answered the compliments he made her but with tears, which seemed to stream in such abundance from her eyes, that she could not keep her handkerchief from her face one moment. Being come into the chariot, *Beauplaisir* said a thousand handsome things to persuade her from giving way to so violent a grief; which, he told her, would not only be destructive to her beauty, but likewise her health. But all his endeavors for consolement appeared ineffectual, and he began to think he should have but a dull journey, in the company of one who seemed so obstinately devoted to the memory of her dead husband, that there was no getting a word from her on any other theme:—but bethinking himself of the celebrated story of the *Ephesian* matron, it came into his head to make trial, she who seemed equally susceptible of *sorrow,* might not also be so too of *love:* and having began a discourse on almost every other topic, and finding her still incapable of answering, resolved to put it to the proof, if this would have no more effect to rouse her sleeping spirits:—with a gay air, therefore, though accompanied with the greatest modesty and respect, he turned the conversation, as though without design, on that joy-giving passion, and soon discovered that was indeed the subject she was best pleased to be entertained with; for on his giving her a hint to begin upon, never any tongue run more voluble than hers, on the prodigious power it had to influence the souls of those possessed of it, to actions even the most distant from their intentions, principles, or humors.—From that she passed to a description of the happiness of mutual affection;— the unspeakable ecstasy of those who meet with equal ardency; and represented it in colors so lively, and disclosed by the gestures with which her words were accompanied, and the accent of her voice so true a feeling of what she said, that *Beauplaisir,* without being as stupid, as he was really the contrary, could not avoid perceiving there were seeds of fire, not yet extinguished, in this fair widow's soul, which wanted but the kindling breath of tender sighs to light into a blaze.—He now thought himself as fortunate, as some moments before he had the reverse; and doubted not, but, that before they parted, he should find a way to dry the tears of this lovely mourner, to the satisfaction of them both. He did not, however, offer, as he had done to *Fantomina* and *Celia,* to urge his passion directly to her, but by a thousand little softening artifices, which he well knew how to use, gave her leave to guess he was enamored. When they came to the inn where they were to lie, he declared himself somewhat more freely, and perceiving she did not resent it past forgiveness, grew more encroaching still:—he now took the liberty of kissing away her tears, and catching the sighs as they issued from her lips; telling her if grief was infectious, he was resolved to have his share; protesting he would gladly exchange passions with her, and be content to bear her load of *sorrow,* if she would as willingly ease the burden of his *love.*—She said little in answer to the strenuous pressures with which at last he ventured to enfold her, but not thinking it decent, for the character she had assumed, to yield so suddenly, and unable to deny both his and her own inclinations, she counterfeited a fainting, and fell motionless upon his breast.—He had no great notion that she was in a real fit, and the room they supped in happening to have a bed in it, he took her in his arms and laid her on it, believing, that whatever her distemper was, that was the most proper place to convey her to.—He laid himself down by her, and endeavored to bring her to herself; and she was too grateful to her kind physician at her returning sense, to remove from the posture he had put her in, without his leave.

It may, perhaps, seem strange that *Beauplaisir* should in such near intimacies continue still deceived: I know there are men who will swear it is an impossibility, and that no disguise could hinder them from knowing a woman they had once enjoyed. In answer to these scruples, I can only say, that besides the alteration which the change of dress made in her, she was so admirably skilled in the art of feigning, that she had the power of putting on almost what face she pleased, and knew so exactly how to form her behavior to the character she represented, that all the comedians at both playhouses are infinitely short of her performances: she could vary her very glances, tune her voice to accents the most different imaginable from those in which she spoke when she appeared herself. These aids from nature, joined to the wiles of art, and the distance between the places where the imagined Fantomina and Celia were, might very well prevent his having any thought that they were the same, or that the fair *widow* was either of them: it never so much as entered his head, and though he did fancy he observed in the face of the latter, features which were not altogether unknown to him, yet he could not recollect when or where he had known them;—and being told by her, that from her birth, she had never removed from *Bristol,* a place where he never was, he rejected the belief of having seen her, and supposed his mind had been deluded by an idea of some other, whom she might have a resemblance of.

They passed the time of their journey in as much happiness as the most luxurious gratification of wild desires could make them; and when they came to the end of it, parted not without a mutual promise of seeing each other often.—He told her to what place she should direct a letter to him; and she assured him she would send to let him know where to come to her, as soon as she was fixed in lodgings.

She kept her promise; and charmed with the continuance of his eager fondness, went not home, but into private lodgings, whence she wrote to him to visit her the first opportunity, and inquire for the Widow *Bloomer.*— She had no sooner dispatched this billet, than she repaired to the house where she had lodged as *Fantomina,* charging the people if *Beauplaisir* should come there, not to let him know she had been out of town. From thence she wrote to him, in a different hand, a long letter of complaint, that he had been so cruel in not sending one letter to her all the time he had been absent, entreated to see him, and concluded with subscribing herself his unalterably affectionate *Fantomina.* She received in one day answers to both these. The first contained these lines:

To the Charming Mrs. Bloomer,
It would be impossible, my Angel! for me to express the thousandth part of that infinity of transport, the sight of your dear letter gave me.—Never was woman formed to charm like you: never did any look like you,—write like you,—bless like you;—nor did ever man adore as I do.—Since yesterday we parted, I have seemed a body without a soul; and had you not by this inspiring billet, gave me new life, I know not what by tomorrow I should have been.—I will be with you this evening about five:—O, 'tis an age till then!—But the cursed formalities of duty oblige me to dine with my lord—who never rises from table till that hour;—therefore adieu till then sweet lovely mistress of the soul and all the faculties of

Your most faithful,
Beauplaisir.

The other was in this manner:

To the Lovely Fantomina,

If you were half so sensible as you ought of your own power of charming, you would be assured, that to be unfaithful or unkind to you, would be among the things that are in their very natures impossibilities.—It was my misfortune, not my fault, that you were not persecuted every past with a declaration of my unchanging passion; but I had unluckily forgot the name of the woman at whose house you are, and knew not how to form a direction that it might come safe to your hands.—And, indeed, the reflection how you might misconstrue my silence, brought me to town some weeks sooner than I intended—If you knew how I have languished to renew those blessings I am permitted to enjoy in your society, you would rather pity than condemn

Your ever faithful,
Beauplaisir.

P.S. *I fear I cannot see you till tomorrow; some business has unluckily fallen out that will engross my hours till then.—Once more, my dear,* Adieu.

Traitor! *(cried she)* as soon as she had read them, 'tis thus our silly, fond, believing sex are served when they put faith in man: so had I been deceived and cheated, had I like the rest believed, and sat down mourning in absence, and vainly waiting recovered tendernesses.do some women *(continued she)* make their life a hell, burning in fruitless expectations, and dreaming out their days in hopes and fears, then wake at last to all the horror of despair?—But I have outwitted even the most subtle of the deceiving kind, and while he thinks to fool me, is himself the only beguiled person.

She made herself, most certainly, extremely happy in the reflection on the success of her stratagems; and while the knowledge of his inconstancy and levity of nature kept her from having that real tenderness for him she would else have had, she found the means of gratifying the inclination she had for his agreeable person, in as full a manner as she could wish. She had all the sweets of love, but as yet had tasted none of the gall, and was in a state of contentment, which might be envied by the more delicate.

When the expected hour arrived, she found that her lover had lost no part of the fervency with which he had parted from her; but when the next day she received him as *Fantomina,* she perceived a prodigious difference; which led her again into reflections on the unaccountableness of men's fancies, who still prefer the last conquest, only because it is the last.—Here was an evident proof of it; for there could not be a difference in merit, because they were the same person; but the Widow *Bloomer* was a more new acquaintance than *Fantomina,* and therefore esteemed more valuable. This, indeed, must be said of *Beauplaisir,* that he had a greater share of good nature than most of his sex, who, for the most part, when they are weary of an intrigue, break it entirely off, without any regard to the despair of the abandoned nymph. Though he retained no more than a bare pity and complaisance for *Fantomina*, yet believing she loved him to an excess, would not entirely forsake her, though the continuance of his visits was now become rather a penance than a pleasure.

The Widow *Bloomer* triumphed some time longer over the heart of this inconstant, but at length her sway was at an end, and she sunk in this character, to the same degree of tastelessness, as she had done before in that of *Fantomina* and *Celia*.—She presently perceived it, but bore it as she had always done; it being but what she expected, she had prepared herself for it, and had another project in *embrio*, which she soon ripened into action. She did not, indeed, complete it altogether so suddenly as she had done the others, by reason there must be persons employed in it; and the aversion she had to any *confidents* in her affairs, and the caution with which she had hitherto acted, and which she was still determined to continue, made it very difficult for her to find a way without breaking through that resolution to compass what she wished.—She got over the difficulty at last, however, by proceeding in a manner, if possible, more extraordinary than all her former behavior:—muffling herself up in her hood one day, she went into the park about the hour when there are a great many necessitous gentlemen, who think themselves above doing what they call little things for a maintenance, walking in the *Mall*, to take a *Camelion* Treat, and fill their stomachs with air instead of meat. Two of those, who by their physiognomy she thought most proper for her purpose, she beckoned to come to her; and taking them into a walk more remote from company, began to communicate the business she had with them in these words: I am sensible, gentlemen *(said she)*, that, through the blindness of fortune, and partiality of the world, merit frequently goes unrewarded, and that those of the best pretentions meet with the least encouragement:—I ask your pardon *(continued she)*, perceiving they seemed surprised, if I am mistaken in the notion, that you two may, perhaps, be of the number of those who have reason to complain of the injustice of fate; but if you are such as I take you for, I have a proposal to make you, which may be of some little advantage to you. Neither of them made any immediate answer, but appeared buried in consideration for some moments. At length, We should, doubtless, madam *(said one of them)*, willingly come into any measures to oblige you, provided they are such as may bring us into no danger, either as to our persons or reputations. That which I require of you *(resumed she)*, has nothing in it criminal: All that I desire is *secrecy* in what you are entrusted, and to disguise yourselves in such a manner as you cannot be known, if hereafter seen by the person on whom you are to impose.—In fine, the business is only an innocent frolic, but if blazed abroad, might be taken for too great a freedom in me:—Therefore, if you resolve to assist me, here are five pieces to drink my health, and assure you, that I have not discoursed you on an affair, I design not to proceed in; and when it is accomplished fifty more lie ready for your acceptance. These words, and, above all, the money, which was a sum which, 'tis probable, they had not seen of a long time, made them immediately assent to all she desired, and press for the beginning of their employment; but things were not yet ripe for execution; and she told them, that the next day they should be let into the secret, charging them to meet her in the same place at an hour she appointed. 'Tis hard to say, which of these parties went away best pleased; *they,* that fortune had sent them so unexpected a windfall; or *she,* that she had found persons, who appeared so well qualified to serve her.

Indefatigable in the pursuit of whatsoever her humor was bent upon, she had no sooner left her new-engaged emissaries, than she went in search of a house for the completing of her project.—She pitched on one very large, and magnificently furnished, which she hired by the week, giving them the money beforehand, to prevent any inquiries. The next day she repaired to the park, where she met the punctual 'squires of low degree; and ordering them to follow her to the house she had taken, told them they must condescend to appear like servants, and gave each of them a very rich livery. Then writing a letter to *Beauplaisir,* in a character vastly different from either of those she had made use of, as *Fantomina,* or the fair Widow *Bloomer,* ordered one of them to deliver it into his own hands, to bring back an answer, and to be careful that he sifted out nothing of the truth.—I do not fear *(said she),* that you should discover to him who I am, because that is a secret, of which you yourselves are ignorant; but I would have you be so careful in your replies, that he may not think the concealment springs from any other reasons than your great integrity to your trust.—Seem therefore to know my whole affairs; and let your refusing to make him partaker in the secret, appear to be only the effect of your zeal for my interest and reputation. Promises of entire fidelity on the one side, and reward on the other, being past, the messenger made what haste he could to the house of *Beauplaisir;* and being there told where he might find him, performed exactly the injunction that had been given him. But never astonishment exceeding that which *Beauplaisir* felt at the reading this billet, in which he found these lines:

To the All-conquering Beauplaisir.

I imagine not that 'tis a new thing to you, to be told, you are the greatest charm in nature to our sex: I shall therefore, not to fill up my letter with any impertinent praises on your wit or person, only tell you, that I am infinite in love with both, and if you have a heart not too deeply engaged, should think myself the happiest of my sex in being capable of inspiring it with some tenderness.—There is but one thing in my power to refuse you, which is the knowledge of my name, which believing the sight of my face will render no secret, you must not take it ill that I conceal from you.—The bearer of this is a person I can trust; send by him your answer; but endeavor not to dive into the meaning of this mystery, which will be impossible for you to unravel, and at the time very much disoblige me:—But that you may be in no apprehensions of being imposed on by a woman unworthy of your regard. I will venture to assure you, the first and greatest men in the kingdom would think themselves blessed to have that influence over me you have, though unknown to yourself acquired.—But I need not go about to raise your curiosity, by giving you any idea of what my person is; if you think fit to be satisfied, resolved to visit me tomorrow about three in the afternoon; and though my face is hid, you shall not want sufficient demonstration, that she who takes these unusual measures to commence a friendship with you, is neither old, nor deformed. Till then I am.

Yours,
Incognita.

He had scarce come to the conclusion, before he asked the person who brought it, from what place he came;—the name of the lady he served;—if she were a wife, or widow, and several other questions directly opposite to the directions of the letter; but silence would have availed him as much as did all those testimonies of curiosity: no *Italian Bravo,* employed in a business of the like nature, performed his office with more artifice; and the impatient inquirer him? He was still in the same darkness as before; for she had taken care to blind the windows in such a manner, that not the least chink was left to let in day.—He complained of her behavior in terms that she would not have been able to resist yielding to, if she had not been certain it would have been the ruin of her passion:—she, therefore, answered him only as she had done before; and getting out of the bed from him, flew out of the room with too much swiftness for him to have overtaken her, if he had attempted it. The moment she left him, the two attendants entered the chamber, and plucking down the implements which had screened him from the knowledge of that which he so much desired to find out, restored his eyes once more to day:— they attended to assist him in dressing, brought him tea, and by their obsequiousness, let him see there was but one thing which the mistress of them would not gladly oblige him in.—He was so much out of humor, however, at the disappointment of his curiosity, that he resolved never to make a second visit.—Finding her in an outer room, he made no scruple of expressing the sense he had of the little trust she reposed in him, and at last plainly told her, he could not submit to receive obligations from a lady, who thought him uncapable of keeping a secret, which she made no difficulty of letting her servants into.—He resented—he once more entreated—he said all that man could do, to prevail on her to unfold the mystery; but all his adjurations were fruitless; and he went out of the house determined never to re-enter it, till she should pay the price of his company with the discovery of her face and circumstances.—She suffered him to go with this resolution, and doubted not but he would recede from it, when he reflected on the happy moments they had passed together; but if he did not, she comforted herself with the design of forming some other stratagem, with which to impose on him a fourth time.

She kept the house, and her gentlemen-equipage for about a fortnight, in which time she continued to write to him as *Fantomina* and the Widow *Bloomer,* and received the visits he sometimes made to each; but his behavior to both was grown so cold, that she began to grow as weary of receiving his now insipid caresses as he was of offering them: she was beginning to think in what manner she should drop these two characters, when the sudden arrival of her mother, who had been some time in a foreign country, obliged her to put an immediate stop to the course of her whimsical adventures.—That lady, who was severely virtuous, did not approve of many things she had been told of the conduct of her daughter; and though it was not in the power of any person in the world to inform her of the truth of what she had been guilty of, yet she heard enough to make her keep her afterwards in a restraint, little agreeable to her humor, and the liberties to which she had been accustomed.

But this confinement was not the greatest part of the trouble of this now afflicted lady: she found the consequences of her amorous follies would be, without almost a miracle, impossible to be concealed:—she was with child; and though she would easily have found means to have screened even this from the knowledge of the world, had she been at liberty to have acted with the same unquestionable authority over herself, as she did before the coming of her mother, yet now all her invention was at a loss for a stratagem to impose on a woman of her penetration:—by eating little, lacing prodigious straight, and the advantage of a great hoop-petticoat, however, her bigness was not taken notice of, and, perhaps, she would not have been suspected till the time of her going into the country, where her mother designed to send her, and from whence she intended to make her escape to some place where she might be delivered with secrecy, if the time of it had not happened much sooner than she expected.—A ball being at court, the good old lady was willing she should partake of the diversion of it as a farewell to the town.—It was there she was seized with those pangs, which none in her condition are exempt from:—she could not conceal the sudden rack which all at once invaded her; or had her tongue been mute, her wildly rolling eyes, the distortion of her features, and the convulsions which shook her whole frame, in spite of her, would have revealed she labored under some terrible shock of nature.—Everybody was surprised, everybody was concerned, but few guessed at the occasion.—Her mother grieved beyond expression, doubted not but she was struck with the hand of death; and ordered her to be carried home in a chair, which herself followed in another.—A physician was immediately sent for: but he presently perceiving what was her distemper, called the old lady aside, and told her, it was not a doctor of his sex, but one of her own, her daughter stood in need of.—Never was astonishment and horror greater than that which seized the soul of this afflicted parent at these words: she could not for a time believe the truth of what she heard; but he insisting on it, and conjuring her to send for a midwife, she was at length convinced of it.—All the pity and tenderness she had been for some moment before possessed of now vanished, and were succeeded by an adequate shame and indignation:—she flew to the bed where her daughter was lying, and telling her what she had been informed of, and which she was now far from doubting, commanded her to reveal the name of the person whose insinuations had drawn her to this dishonor.—It was a great while before she could be brought to confess anything, and much longer before she could be prevailed on to name the man whom she so fatally had loved; but the rack of nature growing more fierce, and the enraged old lady protesting no help should be afforded her while she persisted in her obstinacy, she with great difficulty and hesitation in her speech, at last pronounced the name of *Beauplaisir*. She had no sooner satisfied her weeping mother, than that sorrowful lady sent messengers at the same time, for a midwife, and for that gentleman who had occasioned the other's being wanted.—He happened by accident to be at home, and immediately obeyed the summons, though prodigiously surprised what business a lady so much a stranger to him could have to impart.—But how much greater was his amazement, when taking him into her closet, she there acquainted him with her daughter's misfortune, of the discovery she had made, and how far he was concerned in it?—All the idea one can form of wild astonishment, was mean to what he felt:—he assured her, that the young lady her daughter was a person whom he had never, more than at a distance, admired:—that he had indeed, spoke to her in public company, but that he never had a thought which tended to her dishonor.—His denials, if possible, added to the indignation she was before enflamed with:—she had no longer patience; and carrying him into the chamber, where she was just delivered of a fine girl, cried out I will not be imposed on: the truth by one of you shall be revealed.— *Beauplaisir* being brought to the bedside, was beginning to address himself to the lady in it, to beg she would clear the mistake her mother was involved in: when she, covering herself with cloths, and ready to die a second time with the inward agitations of her soul, shrieked out, Oh, I am undone!—I cannot live, and bear this shame!—But the old lady believing that now or never was the time to dive into the bottom of this mystery, forcing her to rear her head, told her, she should not hope to escape the scrutiny of a parent she had dishonored in such a manner, and pointing to *Beauplaisir,* Is this the gentleman *(said she),* to whom you owe your ruin? or have you deceived me by a fictitious tale? Oh! no *(resumed the trembling creature),* he is, indeed, the innocent cause of my undoing:—Promise me your pardon *(continued she),* and I will relate the means. Here she ceased, expecting what she would reply, which, on hearing *Beauplaisir* cry out, What mean you, madam? I your undoing, who never harbored the least design on you in my life, she did in these words. Though the injury you have done your family *(said she),* is of a nature which cannot justly hope forgiveness, yet be assured, I shall much sooner excuse you when satisfied of the truth, than while I am kept in a suspense, if possible, as vexatious as the crime itself is to me. Encouraged by this she related the whole truth. And 'tis difficult to determine, if *Beauplaisir,* or the lady, were most surprised at what they heard; he, that he should have been blinded so often by her artifices; or she, that so young a creature should have the skill to make use of them. Both sat for some time in a profound reverie; till at length she broke it first in these words: Pardon, sir *(said she),* the trouble I have given you: I must confess it was with a design to oblige you to repair the supposed injury you had done this unfortunate girl, by marrying her, but now I know not what to say:—The blame is wholly hers, and I have nothing to request further of you, than that you will not divulge the distracted folly she has been guilty of.—He answered her in terms perfectly polite; but made no offer of that which, perhaps, she expected, though could not, now informed of her daughter's proceedings, demand. He assured her, however, that if she would commit the newborn lady to his care, he would discharge it faithfully. But neither of them would consent to that; and he took his leave, full of cogitations, more confused than ever he had known in his whole life. He continued to visit there, to inquire after her health every day; but the old lady perceiving there was nothing likely to ensue from these civilities, but, perhaps, a renewing of the crime, she entreated him to refrain; and as soon as her daughter was in a condition, sent her to a monastery in *France,* the abbess of which had been her particular friend. And thus ended an intrigue, which, considering the time it lasted, was as full of variety as any, perhaps, that many ages has produced.

1724

Critical Eye

FOR DISCUSSION

a. How practical is the experiment the main character engages in?

b. One of the implications of what the main character does is that she feels men are simplistic and can be fooled easily. How offensive or realistic are these claims?

c. Consider this piece alongside Wolf's "The Making of a Slut." Is Fantomina a "bad girl," or is she ahead of her time?

REAPPROACHING THE TEXT

From a male standpoint, could this text be viewed as sexist toward men?

WRITING ASSIGNMENT

How much of the main character's dilemma stems from the "dream" that women are sold about love and finding a "Prince Charming"?

Jhumpa Lahiri

Interpreter of Maladies

At the tea stall Mr. and Mrs. Das bickered about who should take Tina to the toilet. Eventually Mrs. Das relented when Mr. Das pointed out that he had given the girl her bath the night before. In the rearview mirror Mr. Kapasi watched as Mrs. Das emerged slowly from his bulky white Ambassador, dragging her shaved, largely bare legs across the back seat. She did not hold the little girl's hand as they walked to the rest room.

They were on their way to see the Sun Temple at Konarak. It was a dry, bright Saturday, the mid-July heat tempered by a steady ocean breeze, ideal weather for sightseeing. Ordinarily Mr. Kapasi would not have stopped so soon along the way, but less than five minutes after he'd picked up the family that morning in front of Hotel Sandy Villa, the little girl had complained. The first thing Mr. Kapasi had noticed when he saw Mr. and Mrs. Das, standing with their children under the portico of the hotel, was that they were very young, perhaps not even thirty. In addition to Tina they had two boys, Ronny and Bobby, who appeared very close in age and had teeth covered in a network of flashing silver wires. The family looked Indian but dressed as foreigners did, the children in stiff, brightly colored clothing and caps with translucent visors. Mr. Kapasi was accustomed to foreign tourists; he was assigned to them regularly because he could speak English. Yesterday he had driven an elderly couple from Scotland, both with spotted faces and fluffy white hair so thin it exposed their sunburnt scalps. In comparison, the tanned, youthful faces of Mr. and Mrs. Das were all the more striking. When he'd introduced himself, Mr. Kapasi had pressed his palms together in greeting, but Mr. Das squeezed hands like an American so that Mr. Kapasi felt it in his elbow. Mrs. Das, for her part, had flexed one side of her mouth, smiling dutifully at Mr. Kapasi, without displaying any interest in him.

As they waited at the tea stall, Ronny, who looked like the older of the two boys, clambered suddenly out of the back seat, intrigued by a goat tied to a stake in the ground.

"Don't touch it," Mr. Das said. He glanced up from his paperback tour book, which said "INDIA" in yellow letters and looked as if it had been

"Interpreter of Maladies," from *Interpreter of Maladies* by Jhumpa Lahiri. Copyright © 1999 by Jhumpa Lahiri. Reprinted by permission of Houghton Mifflin Company. All rights reserved.

published abroad. His voice, somehow tentative and a little shrill, sounded as though it had not yet settled into maturity.

"I want to give it a piece of gum," the boy called back as he trotted ahead.

Mr. Das stepped out of the car and stretched his legs by squatting briefly to the ground. A clean-shaven man, he looked exactly like a magnified version of Ronny. He had a sapphire blue visor, and was dressed in shorts, sneakers, and a T-shirt. The camera slung around his neck, with an impressive telephoto lens and numerous buttons and markings, was the only complicated thing he wore. He frowned, watching as Ronny rushed toward the goat, but appeared to have no intention of intervening. "Bobby, make sure that your brother doesn't do anything stupid."

"I don't feel like it," Bobby said, not moving. He was sitting in the front seat beside Mr. Kapasi, studying a picture of the elephant god taped to the glove compartment.

"No need to worry," Mr. Kapasi said. "They are quite tame." Mr. Kapasi was forty-six years old, with receding hair that had gone completely silver, but his butterscotch complexion and his unlined brow, which he treated in spare moments to dabs of lotus-oil balm, made it easy to imagine what he must have looked like at an earlier age. He wore gray trousers and a matching jacket-style shirt, tapered at the waist, with short sleeves and a large pointed collar, made of a thin but durable synthetic material. He had specified both the cut and the fabric to his tailor—it was his preferred uniform for giving tours because it did not get crushed during his long hours behind the wheel. Through the windshield he watched as Ronny circled around the goat, touched it quickly on its side, then trotted back to the car.

"You left India as a child?" Mr. Kapasi asked when Mr. Das had settled once again into the passenger seat.

"Oh, Mina and I were both born in America," Mr. Das announced with an air of sudden confidence. "Born and raised. Our parents live here now, in Assansol.° They retired. We visit them every couple years." He turned to watch as the little girl ran toward the car, the wide purple bows of her sundress flopping on her narrow brown shoulders. She was holding to her chest a doll with yellow hair that looked as it it had been chopped, as a punitive measure, with pair of dull scissors. "This is Tina's first trip to India, isn't it, Tina?"

"I don't have to go to the bathroom anymore," Tina announced.

Assansol, a city in the state of West Bengal in northeastern India.

"Where's Mina?" Mr. Das asked.

Mr. Kapasi found it strange that Mr. Das should refer to his wife by her first name when speaking to the little girl. Tina pointed to where Mrs. Das was purchasing something from one of the shirtless men who worked at the tea stall. Mr. Kapasi heard one of the shirtless men sing a phrase from a popular Hindi love song as Mrs. Das walked back to the car, but she did not appear to understand the words of the song, for she did not express irritation, or embarrassment, or react in any other way to the man's declarations.

He observed her. She wore a red-and-white-checkered skirt that stopped above her knees, slip-on shoes with a square wooden heel, and a close-fitting blouse styled like a man's undershirt. The blouse was decorated at chest-level with a calico appliqué in the shape of a strawberry. She was a short woman, with small hands like paws, her frosty pink fingernails painted to match her lips, and was slightly plump in her figure. Her hair, shorn only a little longer than her husband's, was parted far to one side. She was wearing large dark brown sunglasses with a pinkish tint to them, and carried a big straw bag, almost as big as her torso, shaped like a bowl, with a water bottle poking out of it. She walked slowly, carrying some puffed rice tossed with peanuts and chili peppers in a large packet made from newspapers. Mr. Kapasi turned to Mr. Das.

"Where in America do you live?"

"New Brunswick, New Jersey."

"Next to New York?"

"Exactly. I teach middle school there."

"What subject?"

"Science. In fact, every year I take my students on a trip to the Museum of Natural History in New York City. In a way we have a lot in common, you could say, you and I. How long have you been a tour guide, Mr. Kapasi?"

"Five years."

Mrs. Das reached the car. "How long's the trip?" she asked, shutting the door,

"About two and a half hours," Mr. Kapasi replied.

At this Mrs. Das gave an impatient sigh, as if she had been traveling her whole life without pause. She fanned herself with a folded Bombay film magazine written in English.

"I thought that the Sun Temple is only eighteen miles north of Puri," Mr. Das said, tapping on the tour book.

"The roads to Konarak are poor. Actually it is a distance of fifty-two miles," Mr. Kapasi explained.

Mr. Das nodded, readjusting the camera strap where it had begun to chafe the back of his neck.

Before starting the ignition. Mr. Kapasi reached back to make sure the cranklike locks on the inside of each of the back doors were secured. As soon as the car began to move the little girl began to play with the lock on her side, clicking it with some effort forward and backward, but Mrs. Das said nothing to stop her. She sat a bit slouched at one end of the back seat, not offering her puffed rice to anyone. Ronny and Tina sat on either side of her, both snapping bright green gum.

"Look," Bobby said as the car began to gather speed. He pointed with his finger to the tall trees that lined the road. "Look."

"Monkeys!" Ronny shrieked. "Wow!"

They were seated in groups along the branches, with shining black faces, silver bodies, horizontal eyebrows, and crested heads. Their long gray tails dangled like a series of ropes among the leaves. A few scratched themselves with black leathery hands, or swung their feet, staring as the car passed.

"We call them the hanuman," Mr. Kapasi said. "They are quite common in the area."

As soon as he spoke, one of the monkeys leaped into the middle of the road, causing Mr. Kapasi to brake suddenly. Another bounced onto the hood of the car, then sprang away. Mr. Kapasi beeped his horn. The children began to get excited, sucking in their breath and covering their faces partly with their hands. They had never seen monkeys outside of a zoo, Mr. Das explained. He asked Mr. Kapasi to stop the car so that he could take a picture.

While Mr. Das adjusted his telephoto lens, Mrs. Das reached into her straw bag and pulled out a bottle of colorless nail polish, which she proceeded to stroke on the tip of her index finger.

The little girl stuck out a hand. "Mine too. Mommy, do mine too."

"Leave me alone," Mrs. Das said, blowing on her nail and turning her body slightly. "You're making me mess up."

The little girl occupied herself by buttoning and unbuttoning a pinafore on the doll's plastic body.

"All set," Mr. Das said, replacing the lens cap.

The car rattled considerably as it raced along the dusty road, causing them all to pop up from their seats every now and then, but Mrs. Das continued to polish her nails. Mr. Kapasi eased up on the accelerator, hoping to produce a smoother ride. When he reached for the gearshift the boy in front accommodated him by swinging his hairless knees out of the way. Mr. Kapasi noted that this boy was slightly paler than than other children. "Daddy, why is the driver sitting on the wrong side in this car, too?" the boy asked.

"They all do that here, dummy," Ronny said.

"Don't call your brother a dummy," Mr. Das said. He turned to Mr. Kapasi. "In America, you know . . . it confuses them."

"Oh yes, I am well aware," Mr. Kapasi said. As delicately as he could, he shifted gears again, accelerating as they approached a hill in the road. "I see it on *Dallas*,° the steering wheels are on the left-hand side."

"What's *Dallas?*" Tina asked, hanging her now naked doll on the seat behind Mr. Kapasi.

"It went off the air," Mr. Das explained. "It's a television show."

They were all like siblings, Mr. Kapasi thought as they passed a row of date trees. Mr. and Mrs. Das behaved like an older brother and sister, not parents. It seemed that they were in charge of the children only for the day; it was hard to believe they were regularly responsible for anything other than themselves. Mr. Das tapped on his lens cap, and his tour book, dragging his thumbnail occasionally across the pages so that they made a scraping sound. Mrs. Das continued to polish her nails. She had still not removed her sunglasses. Every now and then Tina renewed her plea that she wanted her nails done, too, and so at one point Mrs. Das flicked a drop of polish on the little girl's finger before depositing the bottle back inside her straw bag.

"Isn't this an air-conditioned car?" she asked, still blowing on her hand. The window on Tina's side was broken and could not be rolled down.

"Quit complaining," Mr. Das said. "It isn't so hot."

Dallas: extremely popular 1980s television drama centered on the professional and romantic affairs of unscrupulous oil baron J. R. Ewing and his family.

"I told you to get a car with air-conditioning," Mrs. Das continued. "Why do you do this, Raj, just to save a few stupid rupees. What are you saving us, fifty cents?"

Their accents sounded just like the ones Mr. Kapasi heard on American television programs, though not like the ones on *Dallas*.

"Doesn't it get tiresome, Mr. Kapasi, showing people the same thing every day?" Mr. Das asked, rolling down his own window all the way. "Hey, do you mind stopping the car? I just want to get a shot of this guy."

Mr. Kapasi pulled over to the side of the road as Mr. Das took a picture of a barefoot man, his head wrapped in a dirty turban, seated on top of a cart of grain sacks pulled by a pair of bullocks.° Both the man and the bullocks were emaciated. In the back seat Mrs. Das gazed out another window, at the sky, where nearly transparent clouds passed quickly in front of one another.

"I look forward to it, actually," Mr. Kapasi said as they continued on their way. "The Sun Temple is one of my favorite places. In that way it is a reward for me. I give tours on Fridays and Saturdays only. I have another job during the week."

"Oh? Where?" Mr. Das asked.

"I work in a doctor's office."

"You're a doctor?"

"I am not a doctor. I work with one. As an interpreter."

"What does a doctor need an interpreter for?"

"He has a number of Gujarati patients. My father was Gujarati, but many people do not speak Gujarati in this area, including the doctor. And so the doctor asked me to work in his office, interpreting what the patients say."

"Interesting. I've never heard of anything like that," Mr. Das said.

Mr. Kapasi shrugged. "It is a job like any other."

"But so romantic," Mrs. Das said dreamily, breaking her extended silence. She lifted her pinkish brown sunglasses and arranged them on top of her head like a tiara. For the first time, her eyes met Mr. Kapasi's in the rearview mirror: pale, a bit small, their gaze fixed but drowsy.

Mr. Das craned to look at her. "What's so romantic about it?"

"I don't know. Something." She shrugged, knitting her brows together for an instant. "Would you like a piece of gum, Mr. Kapasi?" she asked

bullocks: young or castrated bulls; steer.

brightly. She reached into her straw bag and handed him a small square wrapped in green-and-striped paper. As soon as Mr. Kapasi put the gum in his mouth a thick sweet liquid burst onto his tongue.

"Tell us more about your job, Mr. Kapasi," Mrs. Das said.

"What would you like to know, madame?"

"I don't know," she shrugged, munching on some puffed rice and licking the mustard oil from the corners of her mouth. "Tell us a typical situation." She settled back in her seat, her head tilted in a patch of sun, and closed her eyes. "I want to picture what happens."

"Very well. The other day a man came in with a pain in his throat."

"Did he smoke cigarettes?"

"No. It was very curious. He complained that he felt as if there were long pieces of straw stuck in his throat. When I told the doctor he was able to prescribe the proper medication."

"That's so neat."

"Yes," Mr. Kapasi agreed after some hesitation.

"So these patients are totally dependent on you," Mrs. Das said. She spoke slowly, as if she were thinking aloud. "In a way, more dependent on you than the doctor."

"How do you mean? How could it be?"

"Well, for example, you could tell the doctor that the pain felt like a burning, not straw. The patient would never know what you had told the doctor, and the doctor wouldn't know that you had told the wrong thing. It's a big responsibility."

"Yes, a big responsibility you have there, Mr. Kapasi," Mr. Das agreed.

Mr. Kapasi had never thought of his job in such complimentary terms. To him it was a thankless occupation. He found nothing noble in interpreting people's maladies, assiduously translating the symptoms of so many swollen bones, countless cramps of bellies and bowels, spots on people's palms that changed color, shape, or size. The doctor, nearly half his age, had an affinity for bell-bottom trousers and made humorless jokes about the Congress party.° Together they worked in a stale little infirmary where Mr. Kapasi's smartly tailored clothes clung to him in the heat, in spite of the blackened blades of a ceiling fan churning over their heads.

---

the Congress party: India's governing party for five decades after independence in 1947, widely perceived as corrupt.

The job was a sign of his failings. In his youth he'd been a devoted scholar of foreign languages, the owner of an impressive collection of dictionaries. He had dreamed of being an interpreter for diplomats and dignitaries, resolving conflicts between people and nations, settling disputes of which he alone could understand both sides. He was a self-educated man. In a series of notebooks, in the evenings before his parents settled his marriage, he has listed the common etymologies of words, and at one point in his life he was confident that he could converse, if given the opportunity, in English, French, Russian, Portuguese, and Italian, not to mention Hindi, Bengali, Orissi, and Gujarati. Now only a handful of European phrases remained in his memory, scattered words for things like saucers and chairs. English was the only non-Indian language he spoke fluently anymore. Mr. Kapasi knew it was not a remarkable talent. Sometimes he feared that his children knew better English than he did, just from watching television. Still, it came in handy for the tours.

He had taken the job as an interpreter after his first son, at the age of seven, contracted typhoid—that was how he had first made the acquaintance of the doctor. At the time Mr. Kapasi had been teaching English in a grammar school, and he bartered his skills as an interpreter to pay the increasingly exorbitant medical bills. In the end the boy had died one evening in his mother's arms, his limbs burning with fever, but then there was the funeral to pay for, and the other children who were born soon enough, and the newer, bigger house, and the good schools and tutors, and the fine shoes and the television, and the countless other ways he tried to console his wife and to keep her from crying in her sleep, and so when the doctor offered to pay him twice as much as he earned at the grammar school, he accepted. Mr. Kapasi knew that his wife had little regard for his career as an interpreter. He knew it reminded her of the son she'd lost, and that she resented the other lives he helped, in his own small way, to save. If ever she referred to his position, she used the phrase "doctor's assistant," as if the process of interpretation were equal to taking someone's temperature, or changing a bedpan. She never asked him about the patients who came to the doctor's office, or said that his job was a big responsibility.

For this reason it flattered Mr. Kapasi that Mrs. Das was so intrigued by his job. Unlike his wife, she had reminded him of its intellectual challenges. She had also used the word "romantic." She did not behave in a romantic way toward her husband, and yet she had used the word to describe him. He wondered if Mr. and Mrs. Das were a bad match, just as he and his wife were. Perhaps they, too, had little in common apart from three children and a decade of their lives. The signs he recognized from his own marriage were there—the bickering, the indifference, the protracted silences. Her sudden interest in him, an interest she did not express in either her husband or her children, was mildly intoxicating. When Mr. Kapasi thought once again about how she had said "romantic," the feeling of intoxication grew.

He began to check his reflection in the rearview mirror as he drove, feeling grateful that he had chosen the gray suit that morning and not the brown one, which tended to sag a little in the knees. From time to time he glanced through the mirror at Mrs. Das. In addition to glancing at her face he glanced at the strawberry between her breasts, and the golden brown hollow in her throat. He decided to tell Mrs. Das about another patient, and another: the young woman who had complained of a sensation of raindrops in her spine, the gentleman whose birthmark had begun to sprout hairs. Mrs. Das listened attentively, stroking her hair with a small plastic brush that resembled an oval bed of nails, asking more questions, for yet another example. The children were quiet, intent on spotting more monkeys in the trees, and Mr. Das was absorbed by his tour book, so it seemed like a private conversation between Mr. Kapasi and Mrs. Das. In this manner the next half hour passed, and when they stopped for lunch at a roadside restaurant that sold fritters and omelette sandwiches, usually something Mr. Kapasi looked forward to on his tours so that he could sit in peace and enjoy some hot tea, he was disappointed. As the Das family settled together under a magenta umbrella fringed with white and orange tassels, and placed their orders with one of the waiters who marched about in tricornered caps, Mr. Kapasi reluctantly headed toward a neighboring table.

"Mr. Kapasi, wait. There's room here," Mrs. Das called out. She gathered Tina onto her lap, insisting that he accompany them. And so, together, they had bottled mango juice and sandwiches and plates of onions and potatoes deep-fried in graham-flour batter. After finishing two omelette sandwiches Mr. Das took more pictures of the group as they ate.

"How much longer?" he asked Mr. Kapasi as he paused to load a new roll of film in the camera.

"About half an hour more."

By now the children had gotten up from the table to look at more monkeys perched in a nearby tree, so there was a considerable space between Mrs. Das and Mr. Kapasi. Mr. Das placed the camera to his face and squeezed one eye shut, his tongue exposed at one corner of his mouth. "This looks funny. Mina, you need to lean in closer to Mr. Kapasi."

She did. He could smell a scent on her skin, like a mixture of whiskey and rosewater. He worried suddenly that she could smell his perspiration, which he knew had collected beneath the synthetic material of his shirt.

He polished off his mango juice in one gulp and smoothed his silver hair with his hands. A bit of the juice dripped onto his chin. He wondered if Mrs. Das had noticed.

She had not. "What's your address, Mr. Kapasi?" she inquired, fishing for something inside her straw bag.

"You would like my address?"

"So we can send you copies," she said. "Of the pictures." She handed him a scrap of paper which she had hastily ripped from a page of her film magazine. The blank portion was limited, for the narrow strip was crowded by lines of text and a tiny picture of a hero and heroine embracing under a eucalyptus tree.

The paper curled as Mr. Kapasi wrote his address in clear, careful letters. She would write to him, asking about his days interpreting at the doctor's office, and he would respond eloquently, choosing only the most entertaining anecdotes, ones that would make her laugh out loud as she read them in her house in New Jersey. In time she would reveal the disappointment of her marriage, and he his. In this way their friendship would grow, and flourish. He would possess a picture of the two of them, eating fried onions under a magenta umbrella, which he would keep, he decided, safely tucked between the pages of his Russian grammar. As his mind raced, Mr. Kapasi experienced a mild and pleasant shock. It was similar to a feeling he used to experience long ago when, after months of translating with the aid of a dictionary, he would finally read a passage from a French novel, or an Italian sonnet, and understand the words, one after another, unencumbered by his own efforts. In those moments Mr. Kapasi used to believe that all was right with the world, that all struggles were rewarded, that all of life's mistakes made sense in the end. The promise that he would hear from Mrs. Das now filled him with the same belief.

When he finished writing his address Mr. Kapasi handed her the paper, but as soon as he did so he worried that he had either misspelled his name, or accidentally reversed the numbers of his postal code. He dreaded the possibility of a lost letter, the photograph never reaching him, hovering somewhere in Orissa,° close but ultimately unattainable. He thought of asking for the slip of paper again, just to make sure he had written his address accurately, but Mrs. Das had already dropped it into the jumble of her bag.

They reached Konarak at two-thirty. The temple, made of sandstone, was a massive pyramid-like structure in the shape of a chariot. It was dedicated

Orissa: a state on the southwest border of West Bengal.

to the great master of life, the sun, which struck three sides of the edifice as it made its journey each day across the sky. Twenty-four giant wheels were carved on the north and south sides of the plinth. The whole thing was drawn by a team of seven horses, speeding as if through the heavens. As they approached, Mr. Kapasi explained that the temple had been built between A.D. 1243 and 1255, with the efforts of twelve hundred artisans, by the great ruler of the Ganga dynasty, King Narasimhadeva the First, to commemorate his victory against the Muslin army.

"It says the temple occupies about a hundred and seventy acres of land," Mr. Das said, reading from his book.

"It's like a desert," Ronny said, his eyes wandering across the sand that stretched on all sides beyond the temple.

"The Chandrabhaga River once flowed one mile north of here. It is dry now," Mr. Kapasi said, turning off the engine.

They got out and walked toward the temple, posing first for pictures by the pair of lions that flanked the steps. Mr. Kapasi led them next to one of the wheels of the chariot, higher than any human being, nine feet in diameter.

"'The wheels are supposed to symbolize the wheel of life,'" Mr. Das read. "'They depict the cycle of creation, preservation, and achievement of realization.' Cool." He turned the page of his book. "'Each wheel is divided into eight thick and thin spokes, dividing the day into eight equal parts. The rims are carved with designs of birds and animals, whereas the medallions in the spokes are carved with women in luxurious poses, largely erotic in nature.'"

What he referred to were the countless friezes of entwined naked bodies, making love in various positions, women clinging to the necks of men, their knees wrapped eternally around their lovers' thighs. In addition to these were assorted scenes from daily life, of hunting and trading, of deer being killed with bows and arrows and marching warriors holding swords in their hands.

It was no longer possible to enter the temple, for it had filled with rubble years ago, but they admired the exterior, as did all the tourists Mr. Kapasi brought there, slowly strolling along each of its sides. Mr. Das trailed behind, taking pictures. The children ran ahead, pointing to figures of naked people, intrigued in particular by the Nagamithunas, the half-human, half-serpentine couples who were said, Mr. Kapasi told them, to live in the deepest waters of the sea. Mr. Kapasi was pleased that they liked the temple, pleased especially that it appealed to Mrs. Das. She stopped every three or four paces, staring silently at the carved lovers, and the processions of elephants, and the topless female musicians beating on two-sided drums.

Though Mr. Kapasi had been to the temple countless times, it occurred to him, as he, too, gazed at the topless women, that he had never seen his own wife fully naked. Even when they had made love she kept the panels of her blouse hooked together, the string of her petticoat knotted around her waist. He had never admired the backs of his wife's legs the way he now admired those of Mrs. Das, walking as if for his benefit alone. He had, of course, seen plenty of bare limbs before, belonging to the American and European ladies who took his tours. But Mrs. Das was different, Unlike the other women, who had an interest only in the temple, and kept their noses buried in a guidebook, or their eyes behind the lens of a camera, Mrs. Das had taken an interest in him.

Mr. Kapasi was anxious to be alone with her, to continue their private conversation, yet he felt nervous to walk at her side. She was lost behind her sunglasses, ignoring her husband's requests that she pose for another picture, walking past her children as if they were strangers. Worried that he might disturb her, Mr. Kapasi walked ahead, to admire, as he always did, the three life-sized bronze avatars of Surya, the sun god, each emerging from its own niche on the temple facade to greet the sun at dawn, noon, and evening. They wore elaborate headdresses, their languid, elongated eyes closed, their bare chests draped with carved chains and amulets. Hibiscus petals, offerings from previous visitors, were strewn at their gray-green feet. The last statue, on the northern wall of the temple, was Mr. Kapasi's favorite. This Surya had a tired expression, weary after a hard day of work, sitting astride a horse with folded legs. Even his horse's eyes were drowsy. Around his body were smaller sculptures of women in pairs, their hips thrust to one side.

"Who's that?" Mrs. Das asked. He was startled to see that she was standing beside him.

"He is the Astachala-Surya," Mr. Kapasi said. "The setting sun."

"So in a couple of hours the sun will set right here?" She slipped a foot out of one of her square-heeled shoes, rubbed her toes on the back of her other leg.

"That is correct."

She raised her sunglasses for a moment, then put them back on again. "Neat."

Mr. Kapasi was not certain exactly what the word suggested, but he had a feeling it was a favorable response. He hoped that Mrs. Das had understood Surya's beauty, his power. Perhaps they would discuss it further in their letters. He would explain things to her, things about India, and she would explain things to him about America. In its own way this correspondence would fulfill his dream, of serving as an interpreter between nations. He looked at her straw bag, delighted that his address lay nestled among its contents. When he pictured her so many thousands of miles away he plummeted, so much so that he had an overwhelming urge to wrap his arms around her, to freeze with her, even for an instant, in an embrace witnessed by his favorite Surya. But Mrs. Das had already started walking.

"When do you return to America?" he asked, trying to sound placid.

"In ten days."

He calculated: A week to settle in, a week to develop the pictures, a few days to compose her letter, two weeks to get to India by air. According to his schedule, allowing room for delays, he would hear from Mrs. Das in approximately six weeks' time.

The family was silent as Mr. Kapasi drove them back, a little past four-thirty, to Hotel Sandy Villa. The children had bought miniature granite versions of the chariot's wheels at a souvenir stand, and they turned them round in their hands. Mr. Das continued to read his book. Mrs. Das untangled Tina's hair with her brush and divided it into two little ponytails.

Mr. Kapasi was beginning to dread the thought of dropping them off. He was not prepared to begin his six-week wait to her from Mrs. Das. As he stole glances at her in the rearview mirror, wrapping elastic bands around Tina's hair, he wondered how he might make the tour last a little longer. Ordinarily he sped back to Puri using a shortcut, eager to return home, scrub his feet and hands with sandalwood soap, and enjoy the evening newspaper and a cup of tea that his wife would serve him in silence. The though of that silence, something to which he'd long been resigned, now oppressed him. It was then that he suggested visiting the hills and Udayagiri and Khandagiri, where a number of monastic dwellings were hewn out of the ground, facing one another across a defile. It was some miles away, but well worth seeing, Mr. Kapasi told them.

"Oh yeah, there's something mentioned about it in this book," Mr. Das said. "Built by a Jain° king or something."

"Shall we go then?" Mr. Kapasi asked. He paused at a turn in the road. "It's to the left."

Jain: an adherent of Jainism, a dualistic, ascetic religion founded in the sixth century B.C. in revolt against the Hindu caste system.

Mr. Das turned to look at Mrs. Das. Both of them shrugged.

"Left, left," the children chanted.

Mr. Kapasi turned the wheel, almost delirious with relief. He did not know what he would do or say to Mrs. Das once they arrived at the hills. Perhaps he would tell her what a pleasing smile she had. Perhaps he would compliment her strawberry shirt, which he found irresistibly becoming. Perhaps, when Mr. Das was busy taking a picture, he would take her hand.

He did not have to worry. When they got to the hills, divided by a steep path thick with trees, Mrs. Das refused to get out of the car. All along the path, dozens of monkeys were seated on stones, as well as on the branches of the trees. Their hind legs were stretched out in front and raised to shoulder level, their arms resting on their knees.

"My legs are tired," she said, sinking low in her seat. "I'll stay here."

"Why did you have to wear those stupid shoes?" Mr. Das said. "You won't be in the pictures."

"Pretend I'm there."

"But we could use one of these pictures for our Christmas card this year. We didn't get one of all five of us at the Sun Temple. Mr. Kapasi could take it."

"I'm not coming. Anyway, those monkeys give me the creeps."

"But they're harmless," Mr. Das said. He turned to Mr. Kapasi. "Aren't they?"

"They are more hungry than dangerous," Mr. Kapasi said. "Do not provoke them with food, and they will not bother you."

Mr. Das headed up the defile with the children, the boys at his side, the little girl on his shoulders. Mr. Kapasi watched as they crossed paths with a Japanese man and woman, the only other tourists there, who paused for a final photograph, then stepped into a nearby car and drove away. As the car disappeared out of view some of the monkeys called out, emitting soft whooping sounds, and then walked on their flat black hands and feet up the path. At one point a group of them formed a little ring around Mr. Das and the children. Tina screamed in delight. Ronny ran in circles around his father. Bobby bent down and picked up a fat stick on the ground. When he extended it, one of the monkeys approached him and snatched it, then briefly beat the ground.

"I'll join them," Mr. Kapasi said, unlocking the door on his side. "There is much to explain about the caves."

"No. Stay a minute," Mrs. Das said. She got out of the back seat and slipped in beside Mr. Kapasi. "Raj has his dumb book anyway." Together, through the windshield, Mrs. Das and Mr. Kapasi watched as Bobby and the monkey passed the stick back and forth between them.

"A brave little boy," Mr. Kapasi commented.

"It's not so surprising," Mrs. Das said.

"No?"

"He's not his."

"I beg your pardon?"

"Raj's. He's not Raj's son."

Mr. Kapasi felt a prickle on his skin. He reached into his shirt pocket for the small tin of lotus-oil balm he carried with him at all times, and applied it to three spots on his forehead. He knew that Mrs. Das was watching him, but he did not turn to face her. Instead he watched as the figures of Mr. Das and the children grew smaller, climbing up the steep path, pausing every now and then for a picture, surrounded by a growing number of monkeys.

"Are you surprised?" The way she put it made him choose his words with care.

"It's not the type of thing one assumes," Mr. Kapasi replied slowly. He put the tin of lotus-oil balm back in his pocket.

"No, of course not. And no one knows, of course. No one at all. I've kept it a secret for eight whole years." She looked at Mr. Kapasi, tilting her chin as if to gain a fresh perspective. "But now I've told you."

Mr. Kapasi nodded. He felt suddenly parched, and his forehead was warm and slightly numb from the balm. He considered asking Mrs. Das for a sip of water, then decided against it.

"We met when we were very young," she said. She reached into her straw bag in search of something, then pulled out a packet of puffed rice. "Want some?"

"No, thank you."

She put a fistful in her mouth, sank into the seat a little, and looked away from Mr. Kapasi, out the window on her side of the car. "We married when we were still in college. We were in high school when he proposed. We went to the same college, of course. Back then we couldn't stand the thought of being separated, not for a day, not for a minute. Our parents were best friends who lived in the same town. My entire life I saw him every weekend, either at our house or theirs. We were sent upstairs to play together while our parents joked about our marriage. Imagine! They never caught us at anything, though in a way I think it was all more or less a setup. The things we did those Friday and Saturday nights, while our parents sat downstairs drinking tea . . . I could tell you stories, Mr. Kapasi."

As a result of spending all her time in college with Raj, she continued, she did not make many close friends. There was no one to confide in about him at the end of a difficult day, or to share a passing thought or a worry. Her parents now lived on the other side of the world, but she had never been very close to them, anyway. After marrying so young she was overwhelmed by it all, having a child so quickly, and nursing, and warming up bottles of milk and testing their temperature against her wrist while Raj was at work, dressed in sweaters and corduroy pants, teaching his students about rocks and dinosaurs. Raj never looked cross or harried, or plump as she had become after the first baby.

Always tired, she declined invitations from her one or two college girlfriends, to have lunch or shop in Manhattan. Eventually the friends stopped calling her, so that she was left at home all day with the baby, surrounded by toys that made her trip when she walked or wince when she sat, always cross and tired. Only occasionally did they go out after Ronny was born, and even more rarely did they entertain. Raj didn't mind; he looked forward to coming home from teaching and watching television and bouncing Ronny on his knee. She had been outraged when Raj told her that a Punjabi° friend, someone whom she had once met but did not remember, would be staying with them for a week for some job interviews in the New Brunswick area.

Bobby was conceived in the afternoon, on a sofa littered with rubber teething toys, after the friend learned that a London pharmaceutical company had hired him, while Ronny cried to be freed from his playpen. She made no protest when the friend touched the small of her back as she was about to make a pot of coffee, then pulled her against his crisp navy suit. He made love to her swiftly, in silence, with an expertise she had never known, without the meaningful expressions and smiles Raj always insisted on afterward. The next day Raj drove the friend to JFK. He was married now, to a Punjabi girl, and they lived in London still, and every year they exchanged Christmas cards with Raj and Mina, each couple tucking photos of their families into the envelopes. He did not know that he was Bobby's father. He never would.

Punjabi: a native of Punjab, a state in northwest India.

"I beg your pardon, Mrs. Das, but why have you told me this information?" Mr. Kapasi asked when she had finally finished speaking, and had turned to face him once again.

"For God's sake, stop calling me Mrs. Das. I'm twenty-eight. You probably have children my age."

"Not quite." It disturbed Mr. Kapasi to learn that she thought of him as a parent. The feeling he had had toward her, that had made him check his reflection in the rearview mirror as they drove, evaporated a little.

"I told you because of your talents." She put the packet of puffed rice back into her bag without folding over the top.

"I don't understand," Mr. Kapasi said.

"Don't you see? For eight years I haven't been able to express this to anybody, not friends, certainly not to Raj. He doesn't even suspect it. He thinks I'm still in love with him. Well, don't you have anything to say?"

"About what?"

"About what I've just told you. About my secret, and about how terrible it makes me feel. I feel terrible looking at my children, and at Raj, always terrible. I have terrible urges, Mr. Kapasi, to throw things away. One day I had the urge to throw everything I own out the window, the television, the children, everything. Don't you think it's unhealthy?"

He was silent.

"Mr. Kapasi, don't you have anything to say? I thought that was your job."

"My job is to give tours, Mrs. Das."

"Not that. Your other job. As an interpreter."

"But we do not face a language barrier. What need is there for an interpreter?"

"That's not what I mean. I would never have told you otherwise. Don't you realize what it means for me to tell you?"

"What does it mean?"

"It means that I'm tired of feeling so terrible all the time. Eight years, Mr. Kapasi, I've been in pain eight years. I was hoping you could help me feel better, say the right thing. Suggest some kind of remedy."

He looked at her, in her red plaid skirt and strawberry T-shirt, a woman not yet thirty, who loved neither her husband nor her children, who had already fallen out of love with life. Her confession depressed him, depressed him all the more when he thought of Mr. Das at the top of the path, Tina clinging to his shoulders, taking pictures of ancient monastic cells cut into the hills to show his students in America, unsuspecting and unaware that one of his sons was not his own. Mr. Kapasi felt insulted that Mrs. Das should ask him to interpret her common, trivial little secret. She did not resemble the patients in the doctor's office, those who came glassy-eyed and desperate, unable to sleep or breathe or urinate with ease, unable, above all, to give words to their pains. Still, Mr. Kapasi believed it was his duty to assist Mrs. Das. Perhaps he ought to tell her to confess the truth to Mr. Das. He would explain that honesty was the best policy. Honesty, surely, would help her feel better, as she'd put it. Perhaps he would offer to preside over the discussion, as a mediator. He decided to begin with the most obvious question, to get to the heart of the matter, and so he asked, "Is it really pain you feel, Mrs. Das, or is it guilt?"

She turned to him and glared, mustard oil thick on her frosty pink lips. She opened her mouth to say something, but as she glared at Mr. Kapasi some certain knowledge seemed to pass before her eyes, and she stopped. It crushed him; he knew at that moment that he was not even important enough to be properly insulted. She opened the car door and began walking up the path, wobbling a little on her square wooden heels, reaching into her straw bag to eat handfuls of puffed rice. It fell through her fingers, leaving a zigzagging trail, causing a monkey to leap down from a tree and devour the little white grains. In search of more, the monkey began to follow Mrs. Das. Others joined him, so that she was soon being followed by about half a dozen of them, their velvety tails dragging behind.

Mr. Kapasi stepped out of the car. He wanted to holler, to alert her in some way, but he worried that if she knew they were behind her, she would grow nervous. Perhaps she would lose her balance. Perhaps they would pull at her bag or her hair. He began to jog up the path, taking a fallen branch in his hand to scare away the monkeys. Mrs. Das continued walking, oblivious, trailing grains of puffed rice. Near the top of the incline, before a group of cells fronted by a row of squat stone pillars, Mr. Das was kneeling on the ground focusing the lens of his camera. The children stood under the arcade, now hiding, now emerging from view.

"Wait for me," Mrs. Das called out. "I'm coming."

Tina jumped up and down. "Here comes Mommy!"

"Great," Mr. Das said without looking up. "Just in time. We'll get Mr. Kapasi to take a picture of the five of us."

Mr. Kapasi quickened his pace, waving his branch so that the monkeys scampered away, distracted, in another direction.

"Where's Bobby?" Mrs. Das asked when she stopped.

Mr. Das looked up from the camera. "I don't know. Ronny, where's Bobby?"

Ronny shrugged, "I thought he was right here."

"Where is he?" Mrs. Das repeated sharply. "What's wrong with all of you?"

They began calling his name, wandering up and down the path a bit. Because they were calling, they did not initially hear the boy's screams. When they found him, a little farther down the path under a tree, he was surrounded by a group of monkeys, over a dozen of them, pulling at his T-shirt with their long black fingers. The puffed rice Mrs. Das had spilled was scattered at his feet, raked over by the monkeys' hands. The boy was silent, his body frozen, swift tears running down his startled face. His bare legs were dusty and red with welts from where one of the monkeys struck him repeatedly with the stick he had given to it earlier.

"Daddy, the monkey's hurting Bobby," Tina said.

Mr. Das wiped his palms on the front of his shorts. In his nervousness he accidentally pressed the shutter on his camera; the whirring noise of the advancing film excited the monkeys, and the one with the stick began to beat Bobby more intently. "What are we supposed to do? What if they start attacking?"

"Mr. Kapasi," Mrs. Das shrieked, noticing him standing to one side. "Do something, for God's sake, do something!"

Mr. Kapasi took his branch and shooed them away, hissing at the ones that remained, stomping his feet to scare them. The animals retreated slowly, with a measured gait, obedient but unintimidated. Mr. Kapasi gathered Bobby in his arms and brought him back to where his parents and siblings were standing. As he carried him he was tempted to whisper a secret into the boy's ear. But Bobby was stunned, and shivering with fright, his legs bleeding slightly where the stick had broken the skin. When Mr. Kapasi delivered him to his parents, Mrs. Das brushed some dirt off the boy's T-shirt and put the visor on him the right way. Mrs. Das reached into her straw bag to find a bandage which she taped over the cut on his knee. Ronny offered his brother a fresh piece of gum. "He's fine. Just a little scared, right, Bobby?" Mr. Das said, patting the top of his head.

"God, let's get out of here," Mrs. Das said. She folded her arms across the strawberry on her chest. "This place gives me the creeps."

"Yeah. Back to the hotel, definitely," Mr. Das agreed.

"Poor Bobby," Mrs. Das said. "Come here a second. Let Mommy fix your hair." Again she reached into her straw bag, this time for her hairbrush, and began to run it around the edges of the translucent visor. When she whipped out the hairbrush, the slip of paper with Mr. Kapasi's address on it fluttered away in the wind. No one but Mr. Kapasi noticed. He watched as it rose, carried higher and higher by the breeze, into the trees where the monkeys now sat, solemnly observing the scene below. Mr. Kapasi observed it too, knowing that this was the picture of the Das family he would preserve forever in his mind.

Critical Eye

FOR DISCUSSION

a. How is it that all of the individuals in the story share the same ethnic identity but are so drastically different? What has informed their adult lives?

b. Discuss the metaphorical meaning of the phrase "interpreter of the maladies."

c. How is this story about the life of an unfulfilled woman?

REAPPROACHING THE TEXT

Examine the main character in the film *Fight Club* and the woman from Lahiri's text. What do these two have in common, and how do both explore the notion of the need for confession?

WRITING ASSIGNMENT

Is this story an allusion to how adults often feel that their lives have been wasted?

Charles Chestnut

An Evening Visit

From "The House Behind the Cedars"

TOWARD evening of the same day, Warwick took his way down Front Street in the gathering dusk. By the time night had spread its mantle over the earth, he had reached the gate by which he had seen the girl of his morning walk enter the cedar-bordered garden. He stopped at the gate and glanced toward the house, which seemed dark and silent and deserted.

"It's more than likely," he thought, "that they are in the kitchen. I reckon I'd better try the back door."

But as he drew cautiously near the corner, he saw a man's figure outlined in the yellow light streaming from the open door of a small house between Front Street and the cooper shop. Wishing, for reasons of his own, to avoid observation, Warwick did not turn the corner, but walked on down Front Street until he reached a point from which he could see, at a long angle, a ray of light proceeding from the kitchen window of the house behind the cedars.

"They are there," he muttered with a sigh of relief, for he had feared they might be away. "I suspect I'll have to go to the front door, after all. No one can see me through the trees."

He retraced his steps to the front gate, which he essayed to open. There was apparently some defect in the latch, for it refused to work. Warwick remembered the trick, and with a slight sense of amusement, pushed his foot under the gate and gave it a hitch to the left, after which it opened readily enough. He walked softly up the sanded path, tiptoed up the steps and across the piazza, and rapped at the front door, not too loudly, lest this too might attract the attention of the man across the street. There was no response to his rap. He put his ear to the door and heard voices within, and the muffled sound of footsteps. After a moment he rapped again, a little louder than before.

There was an instant cessation of the sounds within. He rapped a third time, to satisfy any lingering doubt in the minds of those who he felt sure were listening in some trepidation. A moment later a ray of light streamed through the keyhole.

"Who's there?" a woman's voice inquired somewhat sharply.

From *The House Behind the Cedars* by Charles Chestnut, Houghton Mifflin 1990.

"A gentleman," answered Warwick, not holding it yet time to reveal himself. "Does Mis' Molly Walden live here?"

"Yes," was the guarded answer. "I'm Mis' Walden. What's yo'r business?"

"I have a message to you from your son John."

A key clicked in the lock. The door opened, and the elder of the two women Warwick had seen upon the piazza stood in the doorway, peering curiously and with signs of great excitement into the face of the stranger.

"You've got a message from my son, you say?" she asked with tremulous agitation. "Is he sick, or in trouble?"

"No. He's well and doing well, and sends his love to you, and hopes you've not forgotten him."

"Fergot him? No, God knows I ain't fergot him! But come in, sir, an' tell me somethin' mo' about him."

Warwick went in, and as the woman closed the door after him, he threw a glance round the room. On the wall, over the mantelpiece, hung a steel engraving of General Jackson at the battle of New Orleans, and, on the opposite wall, a framed fashion-plate from "Godey's Lady's Book." In the middle of the room an octagonal centre-table with a single leg, terminating in three sprawling feet, held a collection of curiously shaped sea-shells. There was a great haircloth sofa, somewhat the worse for wear, and a well-filled bookcase. The screen standing before the fireplace was covered with Confederate bank-notes of various denominations and designs, in which the heads of Jefferson Davis and other Confederate leaders were conspicuous.

> "Imperious Cæsar, dead, and turned to clay,
> Might stop a hole to keep the wind away,"

murmured the young man, as his eye fell upon this specimen of decorative art.

The woman showed her visitor to a seat. She then sat down facing him and looked at him closely. "When did you last see my son?" she asked.

"I've never met your son," he replied.

Her face fell. "Then the message comes through you from somebody else?"

"No, directly from your son."

She scanned his face with a puzzled look. This bearded young gentleman, who spoke so politely and was dressed so well, surely—no, it could not be! and yet—

Warwick was smiling at her through a mist of tears. An electric spark of sympathy flashed between them. They rose as if moved by one impulse, and were clasped in each other's arms.

"John, my John! It *is* John!"

"Mother—my dear old mother!"

"I didn't think," she sobbed, "that I'd ever see you again."

He smoothed her hair and kissed her. "And are you glad to see me, mother?"

"Am I glad to see you? It's like the dead comin' to life. I thought I'd lost you forever, John, my son, my darlin' boy!" she answered, hugging him strenuously.

"I couldn't live without seeing you, mother," he said. He meant it, too, or thought he did, although he had not seen her for ten years.

"You've grown so tall, John, and are such a fine gentleman! And you *are* a gentleman now, John, ain't you—sure enough? Nobody knows the old story?"

"Well, mother, I've taken a man's chance in life, and have tried to make the most of it; and I haven't felt under any obligation to spoil it by raking up old stories that are best forgotten. There are the dear old books: have they been read since I went away?"

"No, honey, there's be'n nobody to read 'em, excep' Rena, an' she don't take to books quite like you did. But I've kep' 'em dusted clean, an' kep' the moths an' the bugs out; for I hoped you'd come back some day, an' knowed you'd like to find 'em all in their places, jus' like you left 'em."

"That's mighty nice of you, mother. You could have done no more if you had loved them for themselves. But where is Rena? I saw her on the street to-day, but she didn't know me from Adam; nor did I guess it was she until she opened the gate and came into the yard."

"I've be'n so glad to see you that I'd fergot about her," answered the mother. "Rena, oh, Rena!"

The girl was not far away; she had been standing in the next room, listening intently to every word of the conversation, and only kept from coming in by a certain constraint that made a brother whom she had not met for so many years seem almost as much a stranger as if he had not been connected with her by any tie.

"Yes, mamma," she answered, coming forward.

"Rena, child, here's yo'r brother John, who's come back to see us. Tell 'im howdy."

As she came forward, Warwick rose, put his arm around her waist, drew her toward him, and kissed her affectionately, to her evident embarrassment. She was a tall girl, but he towered above her in quite a protecting fashion; and she thought with a thrill how fine it would be to have such a brother as this in the town all the time. How proud she would be, if she could but walk up the street with such a brother by her side! She could then hold up her head before all the world, oblivious to the glance of pity or contempt. She felt a very pronounced respect for this tall gentleman who held her blushing face between his hands and looked steadily into her eyes.

"You're the little sister I used to read stories to, and whom I promised to come and see some day. Do you remember how you cried when I went away?"

"It seems but yesterday," she answered. "I've still got the dime you gave me."

He kissed her again, and then drew her down beside him on the sofa, where he sat enthroned between the two loving and excited women. No king could have received more sincere or delighted homage. He was a man, come into a household of women,—a man of whom they were proud, and to whom they looked up with fond reverence. For he was not only a son,—a brother—but he represented to them the world from which circumstances had shut them out, and to which distance lent even more than its usual enchantment; and they felt nearer to this far-off world because of the glory which Warwick reflected from it.

"You're a very pretty girl," said Warwick, regarding his sister thoughtfully. "I followed you down Front Street this morning, and scarcely took my eyes off you all the way; and yet I didn't know you, and scarcely saw your face. You improve on acquaintance; to-night, I find you handsomer still."

"Now, John," said his mother, expostulating mildly, "you'll spile her, if you don't min'."

The girl was beaming with gratified vanity. What woman would not find such praise sweet from almost any source, and how much more so from this great man, who, from his exalted station in the world, must surely know the things whereof he spoke! She believed every word of it; she knew it very well indeed, but wished to hear it repeated and itemized and emphasized.

"No, he won't, mamma," she asserted, "for he's flattering me. He talks as if I was some rich young lady, who lives on the Hill,"—the Hill was the aristocratic portion of the town,—"instead of a poor"—

"Instead of a poor young girl, who has the hill to climb," replied her brother, smoothing her hair with his hand. Her hair was long and smooth and glossy, with a wave like the ripple of a summer breeze upon the surface of still water. It was the girl's great pride, and had been sedulously cared for. "What lovely hair! It has just the wave that yours lacks, mother."

"Yes," was the regretful reply, "I've never be'n able to git that wave out. But her hair's be'n took good care of, an' there ain't nary gal in town that's got any finer."

"Don't worry about the wave, mother. It's just the fashionable ripple, and becomes her immensely. I think my little Albert favors his Aunt Rena somewhat."

"Your little Albert!" they cried. "You've got a child?"

"Oh, yes," he replied calmly, "a very fine baby boy."

They began to purr in proud contentment at this information, and made minute inquiries about the age and weight and eyes and nose and other important details of this precious infant. They inquired more coldly about the child's mother, of whom they spoke with greater warmth when they learned that she was dead. They hung breathless on Warwick's words as he related briefly the story of his life since he had left, years before, the house behind the cedars—how with a stout heart and an abounding hope he had gone out into a seemingly hostile world, and made fortune stand and deliver. His story had for the women the charm of an escape from captivity, with all the thrill of a pirate's tale. With the whole world before him, he had remained in the South, the land of his fathers, where, he conceived, he had an inalienable birthright. By some good chance he had escaped military service in the Confederate army, and, in default of older and more experienced men, had undertaken, during the rebellion, the management of a large estate, which had been left in the hands of women and slaves. He had filled the place so acceptably, and employed his leisure to such advantage, that at the close of the war he found himself—he was modest enough to think, too, in default of a better man—the husband of the orphan daughter of the gentleman who had owned the plantation, and who had lost his life upon the battlefield. Warwick's wife was of good family, and in a more settled condition of society it would not have been easy for a young man of no visible antecedents to win her hand. A year or two later, he had taken the oath of allegiance, and had been admitted to the South Carolina bar. Rich in his wife's right, he had been able to practice his profession upon a high plane, without the worry of sordid cares, and with marked success for one of his age.

"I suppose," he concluded, "that I have got along at the bar, as elsewhere, owing to the lack of better men. Many of the good lawyers were killed in the war, and most of the remainder were disqualified; while I had the advantage of being alive, and of never having been in arms against the government. People had to have lawyers, and they gave me their business in preference to the carpet-baggers. Fortune, you know, favors the available man."

His mother drank in with parted lips and glistening eyes the story of his adventures and the record of his successes. As Rena listened, the narrow walls that hemmed her in seemed to draw closer and closer, as though they must crush her. Her brother watched her keenly. He had been talking not only to inform the women, but with a deeper purpose, conceived since his morning walk, and deepened as he had followed, during his narrative, the changing expression of Rena's face and noted her intense interest in his story, her pride in his successes, and the occasional wistful look that indexed her self-pity so completely.

"An' I s'pose you're happy, John?" asked his mother.

"Well, mother, happiness is a relative term, and depends, I imagine, upon how nearly we think we get what we think we want. I have had my chance and haven't thrown it away, and I suppose I ought to be happy. But then, I have lost my wife, whom I loved very dearly, and who loved me just as much, and I'm troubled about my child."

"Why?" they demanded. "Is there anything the matter with him?"

"No, not exactly. He's well enough, as babies go, and has a good enough nurse, as nurses go. But the nurse is ignorant, and not always careful. A child needs some woman of its own blood to love it and look after it intelligently."

Mis' Molly's eyes were filled with tearful yearning. She would have given all the world to warm her son's child upon her bosom; but she knew this could not be.

"Did your wife leave any kin?" she asked with an effort.

"No near kin; she was an only child."

"You'll be gettin' married again," suggested his mother.

"No," he replied; "I think not."

Warwick was still reading his sister's face, and saw the spark of hope that gleamed in her expressive eye.

"If I had some relation of my own that I could take into the house with me," he said reflectively, "the child might be healthier and happier, and I should be much more at ease about him."

The mother looked from son to daughter with a dawning apprehension and a sudden pallor. When she saw the yearning in Rena's eyes, she threw herself at her son's feet.

"Oh, John," she cried despairingly, "don't take her away from me! Don't take her, John, darlin', for it'd break my heart to lose her!"

Rena's arms were round her mother's neck, and Rena's voice was sounding in her ears. "There, there, mamma! Never mind! I won't leave you, mamma—dear old mamma! Your Rena'll stay with you always, and never, never leave you."

John smoothed his mother's hair with a comforting touch, patted her withered cheek soothingly, lifted her tenderly to her place by his side, and put his arm about her.

"You love your children, mother?"

"They're all I've got," she sobbed, "an' they cos' me all I had. When the las' one's gone, I'll want to go too, for I'll be all alone in the world. Don't take Rena, John; for if you do, I'll never see her again, an' I can't bear to think of it. How would you like to lose yo'r one child?"

"Well, well, mother, we'll say no more about it. And now tell me all about yourself, and about the neighbors, and how you got through the war, and who's dead and who's married—and everything."

The change of subject restored in some degree Mis' Molly's equanimity, and with returning calmness came a sense of other responsibilities.

"Good gracious, Rena!" she exclaimed. "John's be'n in the house an hour, and ain't had nothin' to eat yet! Go in the kitchen an' spread a clean tablecloth, an' git out that 'tater pone, an' a pitcher o' that las' kag o' persimmon beer, an' let John take a bite an' a sip."

Warwick smiled at the mention of these homely dainties. "I thought of your sweet-potato pone at the hotel to-day, when I was at dinner, and wondered if you'd have some in the house. There was never any like yours; and I've forgotten the taste of persimmon beer entirely."

Rena left the room to carry out her hospitable commission. Warwick, taking advantage of her absence, returned after a while to the former subject.

"Of course, mother," he said calmly, "I wouldn't think of taking Rena away against your wishes. A mother's claim upon her child is a high and holy one. Of course she will have no chance here, where our story is known. The war has wrought great changes, has put the bottom rail on top, and all that—but it hasn't wiped *that* out. Nothing but death can remove that stain, if it does not follow us even beyond the grave. Here she must forever be—nobody! With me she might have got out into the world; with her beauty she might have made a good marriage; and, if I mistake not, she has sense as well as beauty."

"Yes," sighed the mother, "she's got good sense. She ain't as quick as you was, an' don't read as many books, but she's keerful an' painstakin', an' always tries to do what's right. She's be'n thinkin' about goin' away somewhere an' tryin' to git a school to teach, er somethin', sence the Yankees have started 'em everywhere for po' white folks an' niggers too. But I don't like fer her to go too fur."

"With such beauty and brains," continued Warwick, "she could leave this town and make a place for herself. The place is already made. She has only to step into my carriage—after perhaps a little preparation— and ride up the hill which I have had to climb so painfully. It would be a great pleasure to me to see her at the top.

But of course it is impossible—a mere idle dream. *Your* claim comes first; her duty chains her here."

"It would be so lonely without her," murmured the mother weakly, "an' I love her so—my las' one!"

"No doubt—no doubt," returned Warwick, with a sympathetic sigh; "of course you love her. It's not to be thought of for a moment. It's a pity that she couldn't have a chance here—but how could she! I had thought she might marry a gentleman, but I dare say she'll do as well as the rest of her friends—as well as Mary B., for instance, who married—Homer Pettifoot, did you say? Or maybe Billy Oxendine might do for her. As long as she has never known any better, she'll probably be as well satisfied as though she married a rich man, and lived in a fine house, and kept a carriage and servants, and moved with the best in the land."

The tortured mother could endure no more. The one thing she desired above all others was her daughter's happiness. Her own life had not been governed by the highest standards, but about her love for her beautiful daughter there was no taint of selfishness. The life her son had described had been to her always the ideal but unattainable life. Circumstances, some beyond her control, and others for which she was herself in a measure responsible, had put it forever and inconceivably beyond her reach. It had been conquered by her son. It beckoned to her daughter. The comparison of this free and noble life with the sordid existence of those around her broke down the last barrier of opposition.

"O Lord!" she moaned, "what shall I do with out her? It'll be lonely, John—so lonely!"

"You'll have your home, mother," said Warwick tenderly, accepting the implied surrender. "You'll have your friends and relatives, and the knowledge that your children are happy. I'll let you hear from us often, and no doubt you can see Rena now and then. But you must let her go, mother,— it would be a sin against her to refuse."

"She may go," replied the mother brokenly. "I'll not stand in her way —I've got sins enough to answer for already."

Warwick watched her pityingly. He had stirred her feelings to unwonted depths, and his sympathy went out to her. If she had sinned, she had been more sinned against than sinning, and it was not his part to judge her. He had yielded to a sentimental weakness in deciding upon this trip to Patesville. A matter of business had brought him within a day's journey of the town, and an over-mastering impulse had compelled him to seek the mother who had given him birth and the old town where he had spent the earlier years of his life. No one would have acknowledged sooner than he the folly of this visit. Men who have elected to govern their lives by principles of abstract right and reason, which happen, perhaps, to be at variance with what society considers equally right and reasonable, should, for fear of complications, be careful about descending from the lofty heights of logic to the common level of impulse and affection. Many years before, Warwick, when a lad of eighteen, had shaken the dust of the town from his feet, and with it, he fondly thought, the blight of his inheritance, and had achieved elsewhere a worthy career. But during all these years of absence he had cherished a tender feeling for his mother, and now again found himself in her house, amid the familiar surroundings of his childhood. His visit had brought joy to his mother's heart, and was now to bring its shrouded companion, sorrow. His mother had lived her life, for good or ill. A wider door was open to his sister—her mother must not bar the entrance.

"She may go," the mother repeated sadly, drying her tears. "I'll give her up for her good."

"The table's ready, mamma," said Rena, coming to the door.

The lunch was spread in the kitchen, a large unplastered room at the rear, with a wide fireplace at one end. Only yesterday, it seemed to Warwick, he had sprawled upon the hearth, turning sweet potatoes before the fire, or roasting groundpeas in the ashes; or, more often, reading, by the light of a blazing pine-knot or lump of resin, some volume from the bookcase in the hall. From Bulwer's novel, he had read the story of Warwick the Kingmaker, and upon leaving home had chosen it for his own. He was a new man, but he had the blood of an old race, and he would select for his own one of its worthy names. Overhead loomed the same smoky beams, decorated with what might have been, from all appearances, the same bunches of dried herbs, the same strings of onions and red peppers. Over in the same corner stood the same spinning-wheel, and through the open door of an adjoining room he saw the old loom, where in childhood he had more than once thrown the shuttle. The kitchen was different from the stately dining-room of the old colonial mansion where he now lived; but it was homelike, and it was familiar. The sight of it moved his heart, and he felt for the moment a sort of a blind anger against the fate which made it necessary that he should visit the home of his childhood, if at all, like a thief in the night. But he realized, after a moment, that the thought was pure sentiment, and that one who had gained so much ought not to complain if he must give up a little. He who would climb the heights of life must leave even the pleasantest valleys behind.

"Rena," asked her mother, "how'd you like to go an' pay yo'r brother John a visit? I guess I might spare you for a little while."

The girl's eyes lighted up. She would not have gone if her mother had wished her to stay, but she would always have regarded this as the lost opportunity of her life.

"Are you sure you don't care, mamma?" she asked, hoping and yet doubting.

"Oh, I'll manage to git along somehow or other. You can go an' stay till you git homesick, an' then John'll let you come back home."

But Mis' Molly believed that she would never come back, except, like her brother, under cover of the night. She must lose her daughter as well as her son, and this should be the penance for her sin. That her children must expiate as well the sins of their fathers, who had sinned so lightly, after the manner of men, neither she nor they could foresee, since they could not read the future.

The next boat by which Warwick could take his sister away left early in the morning of the next day but one. He went back to his hotel with the understanding that the morrow should be devoted to getting Rena ready for her departure, and that Warwick would visit the household again the following evening; for, as has been intimated, there were several reasons why there should be no open relations between the fine gentleman at the hotel and the women in the house behind the cedars, who, while superior in blood and breeding to the people of the neighborhood in which they lived, were yet under the shadow of some cloud which clearly shut them out from the better society of the town. Almost any resident could have given one or more of these reasons, of which any one would have been sufficient to most of them; and to some of them Warwick's mere presence in the town would have seemed a bold and daring thing.

Critcal Eye

FOR DISCUSSION

a. How significant is it that Warwick has taken "a man's chance in life" to his success? Could his sister, Rena, have taken the same chance alone?

b. Why can't Warwick risk taking his mother into his White world, too? What does his leaving her behind signify?

c. The fact that Warwick has decided to pass as a White person has led him to great Success, as he is now respected and revered by all persons. Has he made the right choice? Said differently, is being a part of the majority—the ruling class by birth—worth denouncing one's true heritage?

REAPPROACHING THE LITERATURE

How would Warwick's life be different if he had not chosen to Pass?

WRITING ASSIGNMENT

Imagine a circumstance where you would denounce your ethnicity and leave behind your family and, for that matter, all that you know. For a chance at the best education and social status, would you walk away from everything and everyone? Or, can you imagine a circumstance where you would give up the advantages afforded one based on skin color, religion, or social grouping—realities that provide ethnic privilege at birth—and willingly become part of another group?

Scott Gold

Little to Reclaim
in the Lower 9th

The sun was still burning off the fog Thursday morning when 88-year-old Nelson Meyers climbed five stairs onto a concrete porch he had built four decades ago. The railing was there. The house was gone.

The 25-foot wall of water that burst through the levee forming the western boundary of New Orleans' Lower 9th Ward after Hurricane Katrina lifted the home off its foundation. The house landed in the neighbor's yard, on top of a car, caked in mud, its lacy curtains shredded into filthy ribbons.

"A man's home is his castle," Meyers said. "And this is what we've got."

Currently living with 28 other relatives in Florida, Meyers and three family members drove to New Orleans to take up Mayor C. Ray Nagin on his offer to sift through the wreckage, to salvage what they could.

The Lower 9th had been closed since the flooding, and residents had grown agitated over not being able to get to their property. Nagin relented, cautioning that the neighborhood—probably the pocket of the city hit the hardest—was not stable enough for people to move back. But, he said: "Everybody can get their stuff."

So for two hours, Meyers and his family rumbled through the Lower 9th in a small convoy, stopping at four family homes that dated back five generations. They all had their wish lists: the lovely picture of Meyers and his wife enjoying a picnic, taken in the '40s. The family Bible. Birth certificates.

They came away with nothing.

Like hundreds of other families, they did not—could not—salvage a single item.

Little more than three months ago, few outside of New Orleans had heard of the 9th Ward. Today, the neighborhood remains a singular testament to the wrath of Katrina's flood, a mind-boggling heap of splintered houses, upside-down cars, refrigerators stuck on rooftops and, across Jourdan

From _Los Angeles Times,_ December 5, 2005. Reprinted by permission of Los Angeles Times.

Avenue, a massive barge that floated through the levee breach and settled atop a school bus.

The mayor's "look and leave" program could do little to stem the pain—or to extinguish the anger among many residents, who feel that they were forgotten even as politicians' promises were echoing off the deserted streets.

"We heard so many words," said Linda Garth Llopis, 60, as she stood outside her partially collapsed home on Deslonde Street. "Our president said he was going to help. Everybody said they were going to help. We are citizens of the United States. And we've just been thrown away."

It is popular in New Orleans these days to remind people that they should feel blessed to have survived, that material possessions can be replaced. But such reassurances sounded empty Thursday to those who had lost everything.

Llopis is living in a hotel, with no job and no hope for rebuilding. At her feet was a small pile of belongings that her husband was able to retrieve from their home—a handful of costume jewelry, a batch of his heart medicine, most likely ruined.

"We had a nice life," she said. "We had marble countertops. I had a mink hat for church."

She and many of her neighbors say they are fighting the conventional wisdom that the 9th isn't worth saving, that it was dirty and crime-ridden anyway, that the storm's silver lining was that it washed away the city's blight.

Like most poor neighborhoods, the 9th had its troubles. But it was a community, said Barbara Ponder, 50, who had never lived anywhere but the 1900 block of Deslonde. Just about everybody owned their home; there were very few renters. There was a preschool down the street from Ponder's house. Several nearby houses had been remodeled in recent years.

Ponder lived a few hundred feet from the levee lining the Inner Harbor Navigational Canal. Her daughter used to play there, often skidding down its sloped, grassy bank on flattened cardboard boxes.

On Thursday, Ponder stood on a flattened lot. There was no sign of her house. The few remnants of life where her home once stood—some dishes, a bashed-in stove, a flyswatter—were not hers. They had floated in from elsewhere.

She had made her final mortgage payment in July.

"We had our crimes and everything—car thefts and things—but this was my home," she said. "Now it's gone. My whole life, everything I owned, everything I have ever accomplished, has vanished."

Much of the destruction in New Orleans, particularly in the Central Business District, was brought by a slow, seeping flood. That was not true in the Lower 9th, much of which was crushed instantly by a wave of water when an 800-foot-wide section of the levee collapsed early in the storm. Close to the canal, entire blocks are gone. Even a mile or so east, houses have been reduced to rubble, as if a giant stomped through town.

Here, the notion of rebuilding seems faint at best. Almost all of the houses above Claiborne Avenue—an 11-by 25-square-block area—will be demolished. Most were below sea level, and it is far from certain that the neighborhood will ever be rebuilt.

Nelson Meyers and his relatives knew it was going to be bad. But, he said, they were not prepared for what they found Thursday.

They began at a single-story home on Caffin Avenue, where his daughter, 58-year-old Patricia Meyers Washington, lived. Five generations of the family had lived in that house. Washington's grandmother had lived there for years, until she died recently at 105. The garden she had tended to was still there—tomato plants and turnip greens.

"It was beautiful," Washington said. "There were flowers everywhere."

With nothing to recover, the relatives hopped in their cars. Their next stop was a relative's four-bedroom home in the 1800 block of Lizardi Street, five blocks southwest, or "Upriver," as they say around here. Washington leapt out of the car.

"It's gone," she said.

It was a vacant lot. A blue jacket and a pair of pink tennis shoes belonging to Washington's granddaughter were the only reminders that the family had ever lived there—until Dewitt Lucas, another relative, spotted the home about 200 feet away.

"There it is!" he said, pointing and standing on the bumper of a car. "That looks like the front door over there."

The house had collapsed on itself. They couldn't get inside, and didn't need to bother anyway.

They hung a right on North Derbigny Street, past the skeletal remains of a couple of businesses—"Po Boys and Hot Plates," one sign read—and a house where rescuers had spray-painted "POSSIBLE BODY" on an outside wall. They headed to another home owned by Washington, where more relatives had lived. She had decorated and maintained the house, and it contained a slew of her possessions, including antique tables and a painting she had bought in the French Quarter.

They pulled up. Someone's shed had been carried into the yard. Lucas squeezed inside the blown-out front door as Washington stood on the porch and peered in behind him. Thick, dried mud coated the floors and walls. She pointed to items that she thought she might be able to save as Lucas climbed over the jumbled furniture, including a picture of her grandson, Cornell.

Lucas handed her the small gold frame. Inside, the picture was curdled and faded.

"This was a picture of my baby," Washington said with a smile. "It was taken on Easter, when he was 2. There was an Easter Bunny down there." She pointed to a large white blob in the corner of the photo.

"What about those picture books, the albums?" she asked, pointing to a bookcase that was still standing. Lucas climbed across the room.

"No, Pat," he said. "I'm sorry."

Their last stop held their greatest hope. It was on the 1600 block of Gordon Street, farther east of the levee breach.

Like the first house they stopped at, which had floated off its foundation, Meyers built this one himself, in 1952, and he had raised five children there. Meyers had added storm braces to the walls—2-by-4s crisscrossed inside the walls—and they had done their job. The house was still standing, though the walls were beginning to separate from the floor.

The mud, however, had gotten inside. The dining room table was upside down, though there were still bills dating back to August on top of the television. Meyers dispatched Lucas into a back bedroom to retrieve two boxes containing the family's papers, birth certificates, deeds and the like. But the floor of the attic had collapsed, burying the room in debris, so he couldn't get there.

Everyone went outside except for Washington, who was desperate to come away with some token of what had been their lives. She lingered for a few minutes, pawing at framed photos, scraping away slime and mold to see if any could be saved. No luck. In the corner, she spotted the thick family Bible. It had been around for as long as anyone could remember. Important dates—birthdays, weddings—had been written on the inside cover.

"Daddy! I found your Bible," she shouted.

Critical Eye

FOR DISCUSSION

a. Given the slow government response, why should the people interviewed in the article believe anything their government says? How does one move forward when everything is lost and the government sworn to protect its citizens abandons them?

b. How do Class and racial matters play into the role of rebuilding? Why has New Orleans still not been rebuilt?

REAPPROACHING THE TEXT

Consider the fact that most of the residents in the lower 9th owned their homes, a reality that is indicative of the American dream. How, after losing everything—alongside being displaced and seemingly forgotten by their government—should these citizens view their place in society? Juxtapose your response with Alan Parker's *Mississippi Burning* and Spike Lee's documentary about the hurricane and its aftermath, *When the Levees Broke.*

WRITING ASSIGNMENT

Historically speaking, Blacks have been treated, following slavery, as second class citizens. In an age of change, how do the events of Katrina speak to the growing alarm for Black people in America? Keeping in mind that the promise of "40 acres and a mule" has never been fulfilled, what options—socially, politically, economically—do those who feel like "other" in society really have?

1 2 3 4 **5**

Religion

When I was kid I used to pray every night for a new bicycle. Then I realized that the
Lord doesn't work that way so I stole one and asked him to forgive me.
Emo Phillips

Now, now my good man, this is no time for making enemies.
Voltaire, on his deathbed, to a priest asking that he renounce Satan.

Religion is generally perceived as a belief in and, arguably—maybe more
importantly—a reverence for a supernatural power or powers regarded as
both the creator and governing body of the universe. A subtler notion of
religion is defined as a cause, activity, or principle that is undertaken with
conscientious devotion. Almost every person walking the planet has either
embraced or been touched by the broad hand of a higher being and the
tradition that governs it. While all humans may not believe or follow, none
are unaffected by the influence and power of religion. Oddly enough,
religion is, like taxes, inescapable.

Historically, religion has appeared in the embracing words and arms
of the church; at the same time, at least in some cases, our faiths have
harmed as many as they have helped. For some, religion, faith, and
spiritual matters provide support for the people. Yet, too often have our
faith-based beliefs become blurred with our worldly views on power and
dominance. This blending of religion with politics, power, and—as we
see as clearly in the 21st century as ever before—"intolerance" demands a
converting with the snap of a merciless whip that appears as fanatical as it
is blind. Which is accurate? What is the real face of our world's churches,
synagogues, mosques, temples, and meeting places where people gather
to worship? What happens when the "word" of deities is played out and
manipulated by flawed humans who manipulate religious doctrines
to fit their own vision of the world? And, moreover, what happens
when religious mandates become vexing to the point of oppression?
Undoubtedly, the fact that we have various religions is a blessing. But,

the judgment that seems to follow—the worldwide bickering that one interpretation of a higher power is better than others—seems as absurd as it is contradictory. Surely the purpose of faith is to bring a sense of reconciliation that humankind cannot explain. As such, if spirituality is an elevation from our secular lives to a higher sense of being, then shouldn't those who so wholeheartedly claim to "believe" denounce the shallow views of politics, financial compensation, rivalry—as well as mores and rules that seem painfully outdated—in an attempt to heal our damaged world?

The selections in this chapter touch different parts of the world and brazenly cross gender lines. For some, faith not only guarantees salvation but also provides the individual with patience and fortitude in a trying world. For others, faith is neither black nor white, but, as we recognize now more than ever before, varied shades of gray that are so very difficult to muddle through.

G.E. Moore

The Indefinability of Good

"Good" Is a Simple Notion

. . . What, then, is good? How is good to be defined? Now, it may be thought that this is a verbal question. A definition does indeed often mean the expressing of one word's meaning in other words. But this is not the sort of definition I am asking for. Such a definition can never be of ultimate importance in any study except lexicography. If I wanted that kind of definition I should have to consider in the first place how people generally used the word "good," but my business is not with its proper usage, as established by custom. I should, indeed, be foolish, if I tried to use it for something which it did not usually denote: if, for instance, I were to announce that, whenever I used the word "good," I must be understood to be thinking of that object which is usually denoted by the word "table." I shall, therefore, use the word in the sense in which I think it is ordinarily used; but at the same time I am not anxious to discuss whether I am right in thinking that it is so used. My business is solely with that object or idea, which I hold rightly or wrongly, that the word is generally used to stand for. What I want to discover is the nature of the object or idea, and about this I am extremely anxious to arrive at an agreement.

But, if we understand the question in this sense, my answer to it may seem a very disappointing one. If I am asked "What is good?" my answer is that good is good, and that is the end of the matter. Or if I am asked "How is good to be defined?" my answer is that it cannot be defined, and that is all I have to say about it. But disappointing as these answers may appear they are of the very last importance. To readers who are familiar with philosophic terminology, I can express their importance by saying that they amount to this: That propositions about the good are all of them synthetic and never analytic; and that is plainly no trivial matter. And the same thing may be expressed more popularly, by saying that, if I am right, then nobody can foist upon us such an axiom as that "Pleasure is the only good" or that "The good is the desired" on the pretence that this is the very meaning of the word.

Let us, then, consider this position. My point is that "good" is a simple notion, just as "yellow" is a simple notion; that, just as you cannot, by any manner of means, explain to any one who does not already know it, what yellow is, so you cannot explain what good is. Definitions of the kind that I was asking for, definitions which describe the real nature of the object or notion denoted by a word, and which do not merely tell us what the word is used to mean, are only possible when the object or notion in question is something complex. You can give a definition of a horse, because a horse has many different properties and qualities, all of which you can enumerate. But when you have enumerated them all, when you have reduced a horse to his simplest terms, then you can no longer define those terms. They are simply something which you think of or perceive, and to any one who cannot think of or perceive them, you can never, by any definition, make their nature known. It may perhaps be objected to this that we are able to describe to others, objects which they have never seen or thought of. We can, for instance, make a man understand what a chimaera is, although he has never heard of one or seen one. You can tell him that it is an animal with a lionesshead and body, with a goat's head growing from the middle of its back, and with a snake in place of a tail. But here the object which you are describing is a complex object; it is entirely composed of parts, with which we are all perfectly familiar—a snake, a goat, a lioness; and we know, too, the manner in which those parts are to be put together, because we know what is meant by the middle of a lioness's back, and where her tail is wont to grow. And so it is with all objects, not previously known, which we are able to define; they are all complex; all composed of parts, which may themselves, in the first instance be capable of similar definition, but which must in the end be reducible to simplest parts, which can no longer be defined. But yellow and good, we say, are not complex; they are notions of that simple kind, out of which definitions are composed and with which the power of further defining ceases.

When we say, as Webster says, "The definition of horse is a 'hoofed quadruped of the genus Equus,'" we may, in fact, mean three different things. (1) We may mean merely: "When I say 'horse,' you are to understand that I am talking about a hoofed quadruped of the genus Equus." This might be called the arbitrary verbal definition: and I do not mean that good is indefinable in that sense. (2) We may mean, as Webster ought to mean: "When most English people say 'horse,' they mean a hoofed quadruped of the genus Equus." This may be called the verbal definition proper, and I do not say that good is indefinable in this sense either; for it is certainly possible to discover how people use a word: otherwise, we could never have known that "good" may be translated by "gut" in German and by "bon" in French. But (3) we may, when we define horse, mean something much more important. We may mean that a certain object, which we all of us know, is composed in a certain manner; that it has four legs, a head, a heart, a liver, etc., etc., all of them arranged in definite relations to one another. It is in this sense that I deny good to be definable. I say that it is not composed of any parts, which we can substitute for it in our minds when we are thinking of it. We might think just as clearly and correctly about a horse, if we thought of all its parts and their arrangement instead of thinking of the whole: we could, I say, think how a horse differed from a donkey just as well, just as truly, in this way, as now we do, only not so easily; but there is nothing whatsoever which we could so substitute for good; and that is what I mean, when I say that good is indefinable.

But I am afraid I have still not removed the chief difficulty which may prevent acceptance of the proposition that good is indefinable. I do not mean to say that *the* good, that which is good, is thus indefinable; if I did think so, I should not be writing on Ethics, for my main object is to help towards discovering that definition. It is just because I think there will be less risk of error in our search for a definition of "the good," that I am now insisting that *good* is indefinable. I must try to explain the difference between these two. I suppose it may be granted that "good" is an adjective. Well "the good," "that which is good," must therefore be the substantive to which the adjective "good" will apply: it must be the whole of that to which the adjective will apply, and the adjective must *always* truly apply to it. But if it is that to which the adjective will apply, it must be something different from that adjective itself; and the whole of that something different, whatever it is, will be our definition of *the* good. Now it may be that this something will have other adjectives, besides "good," that will apply to it. It may be full of pleasure, for example; it may be intelligent; and if these two adjectives are really part of its definition, then it will certainly be true, that pleasure and intelligence are good. And many people appear to think that, if we say "Pleasure and intelligence are good," or if we say "Only pleasure and intelligence are good," we are defining "good." Well, I cannot deny that propositions of this nature may sometimes be called definitions; I do not know well enough how the word is generally used to decide upon this point. I only wish it to be understood that that is not what I mean when I say there is no possible definition of good, and that I shall not mean this if I use the word again. I do most fully believe that some true proposition of the form "Intelligence is good and intelligence alone is good" can be found; if none could be found, our definition of *the* good would be impossible. As it is, I believe *the* good to be definable; and yet I still say that good itself is indefinable.

"Good," then, if we mean by it that quality which we assert to belong to a thing, when we say that the thing is good, is incapable of any definition, in the most important sense of that word. The most important sense of "definition" is that in which a definition states what are the parts which invariably compose a certain whole; and in this sense "good" has no definition because it is simple and has no parts. It is one of those innumerable objects of thought which are themselves incapable of definition, because they are the ultimate terms by reference to which whatever *is* capable of definition must be defined. That there must be an indefinite number of such terms is obvious, on reflection; since we cannot define anything except by analysis, which, when carried as far as it will go, refers us to something, which is simply different from anything else, and which by that ultimate difference explains the peculiarity of the whole which we are defining: for every whole contains some parts which are common to other wholes also. There is, therefore, no intrinsic difficulty in the contention that "good" denotes a simple and indefinable quality. There are many other instances of such qualities.

Consider yellow, for example. We may try to define it, by describing its physical equivalent; we may state what kind of light-vibrations must stimulate the normal eye, in order that we may perceive it. But a moment's reflection is sufficient to show that those light-vibrations are not themselves what we mean by yellow. *They* are not what we perceive. Indeed we should never have been able to discover their existence, unless we had first been struck by the patent difference of quality between the different colours. The most we can be entitled to say of those vibrations is that they are what corresponds in space to the yellow which we actually perceive.

Yet a mistake of this simple kind has commonly been made about "good." It may be true that all things which are good are *also* something else, just as it is true that all things which are yellow produce a certain kind of vibration in the light. And it is a fact, that Ethics aims at discovering what are those other properties belonging to all things which are good. But far too many philosophers have thought that when they named those other properties they were actually defining good; that these properties, in fact, were simply not "other," but absolutely and entirely the same with goodness.

Critical Eye

FOR DISCUSSION

a. Is there any such thing as a "good" person?

b. Why must the individual strive for goodness?

c. Is goodness a religious or social construct?

REAPPROACHING THE LITERATURE

Ralph Waldo Emerson would argue that "good" is doing what is true for the individual self and that which would be good for all mankind. How does this theory work alongside Moore's argument?

WRITING ASSIGNMENT

Often our leaders tell us that they are making decisions for the overall "greater good" of our society. Do you agree with this practice? Use examples from history to support your claims.

Audrey Smedly

Race in North America

The Backing of God and Other Justifications for Conquest

From the very beginnings of English excursions into overseas exploration and trade, the rationale most frequently expressed was that the venture was sanctioned by God. John Hawkins, the earliest and most successful of the English slave traders, once led an expedition of slave ships with names such as *Jesus of Lubeck* and *John the Baptist* (Wright 1965, 9). Not only were ships commonly given names with biblical references, but virtually all also had clerics aboard to bless the expedition. Leaders of expeditions invariably referred to the Lord's blessings and special care for them, his children, in their ships' logs.

Without question, military dominance of the English and their success in ultimately destroying the Indians and their cultures were seen as God's will, no matter how brutal and insensitive the actions and no matter the innocence of the Indian victims. A high degree of self-righteousness and arrogance characterized the religious beliefs, particularly of the Puritans. Offshoots of the Protestant Reformation, they had evolved a sharply focused sense of the nature of salvation and what was needed to achieve it. Their theology relinquished the vast majority of souls on earth to be damned forever. Only the select few would ultimately enter the glorious kingdom of God. These were individuals who adhered strictly to Puritan ideals of proper behavior and laid claims to personal salvation through faith. Knowledge of Christ, including a personal relationship to him, were prerequisites. In their strict division of the world into the saved and the damned, there was no explicit, or intrinsic, requirement for tolerance and understanding of others. Nor was there any commitment to humanistic values that might have inhibited or curtailed the excessive cruelty dispensed to the damned. Instead, the Puritans developed the very convenient belief that all sinners, witches, and savages who opposed the word of God deserved the atrocities inflicted upon them. They were a fitting retribution for their opposition to the civilizing efforts of Christianity.

From *Race in North America* by Audrey Smedley. Copyright © 1998 by Westview Press, Member of Perseus Books Group. Reprinted by permission of Westview Press, member of Perseus Books L.L.C.

In the New England area, many settlers rejoiced at the extraordinary reduction of the Indian population from epidemic diseases. John Winthrop, who led the colony in the 1630s, wrote that the smallpox epidemic of 1617 was God's way of "thinning out" the Indian population "to make room for the Puritans." Later, he recorded that the Indians "are neere all dead of the small Poxe, so the Lord hathe cleared our title to what we possess" (quoted in Nash 1972, 136).

According to Louis B. Wright (1965), it was the preachers of England who "induced in public consciousness a sense of mission, a feeling often not put into words but nonetheless strong, that Englishmen had a destiny overseas" (151). These preachers, both Anglican and Puritan, had a powerful influence on the colonization process. From their pulpits and in their publications, they exhorted the public to become involved in the colonization of the New World, a region seen as a new Canaan. And the commercial companies and promoters of colonization encouraged the clergy to advertise their schemes.

The English clergy themselves were motivated by a number of considerations, all of which were highly publicized at the time. Chief among these was their desire to thwart the further spread of Catholicism. The success of Spanish proselytizing in the New World was well known; and nothing irked the Protestants so much as the idea of Spain winning the battle for new souls. Economic and political competition with the Spanish intensified these feelings of religious antagonism. The defeat of the Spanish Armada had made the planting of English colonies all the more pressing.

Another important reason for ministerial preachments had to do with the increasingly large numbers of the poor and unemployed who roamed the streets and byways of English cities. Several lines of reasoning led clergymen to advocate the exportation of these "vagabonds" to the new colonies. As educated men, they concluded that England was facing a problem of overpopulation, and there was a need to do something about this demographic situation. Moreover, unemployment was acute in many areas, and existing charitable institutions were hard pressed to provide sufficient services to an expanding impoverished class. The clergy saw colonization as a way of siphoning off an excess of able-bodied workers and putting them to useful labor in the plantations overseas.

Exhortations to send the poor and unemployed off to the colonies should be understood within a wider framework of English, and specifically, Puritan beliefs. Seventeenth-century preachers, we are told, "looked upon idleness and consequent poverty as moral iniquities" (Wright 1965, 152). Those virtues most valued in the Puritan life-style were work, sobriety, thrift, diligence, and honesty. An idle or lazy person would be lacking in all of these traits. Thus, poverty, immorality, and sloth were bound together in the Puritan mind as evils that had to be overcome, if necessary by forced labor. Hoover claims that the Puritans created a new class of evil people, the poor who were seen as "being wicked and outside the bonds of society" (1976, 31). So colonization would not only relieve the poverty at home, but, by putting sinful, idle men and women to work, it would also restore them to the true and proper values of religion and improve their characters.

Finally, Wright (1965) argues that many English clergymen, who "were almost unanimous in supporting colonization in America," (86) were motivated by a sincere desire to save the souls of the heathens of America. They were convinced, and convinced others, that God had commanded them to go forth and preach the gospel. There was no better setting in which to do this than among the indigenes of newly discovered lands. However, this missionary zeal peaked in the early stages of settlement, as we have seen. The Puritans and their church leaders soon concluded that if the savages could not be saved from themselves, their extermination would be a worthy enterprise in the sight of the Lord. This notion of a God-given right to mistreat others, especially for private gain, runs through much of Western culture, and after the emergence of capitalism it became especially acute in North America.

When they were not invoking God's blessings or permission for their mistreatment of the Indians, the colonizers had other rational and pragmatic arguments of particular use for co-opting native lands. One was that the Indians did not make proper use of the land "and thus could be justly deprived of it by the more enterprising English" (Canny 1973, 596). Such an argument, we have seen, was invoked to force the Irish off their lands. A more pervasive argument was the ancient one of the right of conquest. This was often linked to the religious position and rationalized that since God had chosen the English to find these new shores, he must have wanted them to possess such bountiful land. Conquest was thus God's ordained plan; it was he who had led them thence. The Puritans as God's "chosen people" were responsible merely for carrying out his will.

Though God's supposed will should have been enough, an even more secular and philosophical argument was also proposed, one that derived from some knowledge of the codes of laws of the ancients. John Winthrop expressed this in his reasoning on the Englishman's rights to land. There are, he declared, two types of rights that God has given mankind: natural rights and civil rights. Natural rights were held by all men including those who lived in a state of nature, holding land and resources in common.

But when some men began to enclose parcels of land and hold them separate from others, to have a settled habitation on it, and to use domesticated cattle to improve the land, then they acquired civil rights to the land. Since the Indians had not done these things, they gained no civil rights but retained only natural ones. And, since clearly the English had developed superior modes of utilizing land, they enjoyed lawful civil rights that inevitably took precedence over natural rights. Under this argument, superior "civilized" people had legitimate cause to seize land, as long as they left sufficient areas for the "uncivilized" to exercise their natural rights (Thomas 1975).

Partly because of the myths of origin that Americans created for themselves, too few of us have sufficiently noted the cruel and barbaric treatment that the English imposed on the Indians, although the evidence, largely from the pens of the colonists themselves, is overwhelming. The incidents described above—in no way exceptional—attest to extreme and callous brutality and to a policy of treachery and deceit that seems hardly consonant with the English history of concern for the rights of mankind, and even less with England's image of itself as the most "civilized" of the European nations.

Some historians have labored hard to explain this seeming paradox. Although we might accept Nash's psychologically oriented argument that the dehumanization of the Indian was "one means of justifying one's own inhumanity" (1972, 137), this is a somewhat circular or teleological explication that does not reveal much as to underlying causes. Nicholas P. Canny's (1973) explanation follows in a similar vein and is very close to that of Winthrop Jordan (1968). Both refer to the insecurities and uncertainties of the English, and of their need to know who they were in a rapidly changing society and in a setting in which they constantly felt threatened. More evident than such psychological needs, however, were the drives to achieve power and control, to establish and maintain political, economic, and social dominance, all of which arose from an English sense of moral and cultural superiority. The Indians, said Morgan, "presented a challenge . . . to their image of themselves, to their self-esteem, to their conviction of their own superiority over foreigners, and especially over barbarous foreigners like the Irish and the Indians" (1975, 89).

Christian values regarding humane behavior (the Sermon on the Mount, the Golden Rule, the Ten Commandments) had little impact on the minds, the morals, and the consciences of the settlers. Jordan gives a brief analysis of the kind of Christianity that developed among the English after the Protestant Reformation. He shows that it was "altered in the direction of Biblicism, personal piety, individual judgment, and more intense self-scrutiny and internalized control" (1968, 40). The English came to evaluate and judge themselves according to their own individual interpretations of the scriptures. The older institutional and external constraints of Catholicism were replaced with a less certain and more nebulous sense of personal responsibility and control.

Such inner controls, however, were virtually antithetical to the spirits of adventurism and greed for wealth that characterized the English in the seventeenth century and later. English colonists were caught up in a dilemma that might have evoked massive ambivalence, leading to a catatonic inability to take action. Instead, or perhaps because of this, too many of them in the New World opted for the path of moral and ethical duplicity, hypocrisy, and the priority of aggrandizing wealth at no matter what cost. A self-serving moral order had replaced the constraints once exercised by the institutions of family, kinship, class, community, and church. It was not merely self-control that the new settlers sought, it was control over others and over potentially advantageous situations and resources. Jordan's (1968) discussion of an age driven by the twin spirits of adventure and of control euphemistically glosses over this reality. But Morgan's (1975) description of the ruthless, cold-hearted, and avaricious men who led or participated in the Virginia colony leaves us little room for doubt.

Critical Eye

FOR DISCUSSION

a. When one group conquers or dominates another, is it wrong to impose one's religious or spiritual practices?

b. Can religion really be used as a form of subjugation?

REAPPROACHING THE TEXT

Go back through the author's argument. How well does she substantiate her claims?

WRITING ASSIGNMENT

Outside of religion, what other means can a country use to insert its way of life on others outside or inside of its community?

Barbara Grizzuti Harrison

Growing Up Apocalyptic

"The trouble with you," Anna said, in a voice in which compassion, disgust, and reproach fought for equal time, "is that you can't remember what it was like to be young. And even if you could remember—well, when you were my age, you were in that crazy Jehovah's Witness religion, and you probably didn't even play spin the bottle."

Anna, my prepubescent eleven-year-old, feels sorry for me because I did not have "a normal childhood." It has never occurred to her to question whether her childhood is "normal" . . . which is to say, she is happy. She cannot conceive of a life in which one is not free to move around, explore, argue, flirt with ideas and dismiss them, form passionate alliances and friendships according to no imperative but one's own nature and volition; she regards love as unconditional, she expects nurturance as her birthright. It fills her with terror and pity that anyone—especially her mother—could have grown up any differently—could have grown up in a religion where love was conditional upon rigid adherence to dogma and established practice . . . where approval had to be bought from authoritarian sources . . . where people did not fight openly and love fiercely and forgive generously and make decisions of their own and mistakes of their own and have adventures of their own.

"Poor Mommy," she says. To have spent one's childhood in love with/ tyrannized by a vengeful Jehovah is not Anna's idea of a good time—nor is it her idea of goodness. As, in her considered opinion, my having been a proselytizing Jehovah's Witness for thirteen years was about as good a preparation for real life as spending a commensurate amount of time in a Skinner box on the North Pole, she makes allowances for me. And so, when Anna came home recently from a boy-girl party to tell me that she had kissed a boy ("interesting," she pronounced the experiment), and I heard my mouth ask that atavistic mother-question, "And what else did you do?" Anna was inclined to be charitable with me: "Oh, for goodness' sake, what do you think we did, screw? The trouble with you is . . ." And then she explained to me about spin the bottle.

"Growing Up Apocalyptic" from *Off Center* by Barbara Grizzuti Harrison. Copyright © 1980 by Barbara Grizzuti Harrison. Reprinted by permission of Georges Borchardt, Inc., on behalf of the author.

I do worry about Anna. She is, as I once explained drunkenly to someone who thought that she might be the better for a little vigorous repression, a teleological child. She is concerned with final causes, with ends and purposes and means; she would like to see evidence of design and order in the world; and all her adventures are means to that end. That, combined with her love for the music, color, poetry, ritual, and drama of religion, might, I think, if she were at all inclined to bow her back to authority—and if she didn't have my childhood as an example of the perils thereof—have made her ripe for conversion to an apocalyptic, messianic sect.

That fear may be evidence of my special paranoia, but it is not an entirely frivolous conjecture. Ardent preadolescent girls whose temperament tends toward the ecstatic are peculiarly prone to conversion to fancy religions.

I know. My mother and I became Jehovah's Witnesses in 1944, when I was nine years old. I grew up drenched in the dark blood-poetry of a fierce messianic sect. Shortly after my conversion, I got my first period. We used to sing this hymn: "Here is He who comes from Eden/all His raiment stained with blood." My raiments were stained with blood, too. But the blood of the Son of Man was purifying, redemptive, cleansing, sacrificial. Mine was filthy—proof of my having inherited the curse placed upon the seductress Eve. I used to "read" my used Kotexes compulsively, as if the secret of life—or a harbinger of death—were to be found in that dull, mysterious effluence.

My brother, at the time of our conversion, was four. After a few years of listlessly following my mother and me around in our door-to-door and street-corner proselytizing, he allied himself with my father, who had been driven to noisy, militant atheism by the presence of two female religious fanatics in his hitherto patriarchal household. When your wife and daughter are in love with God, it's hard to compete—particularly since God is good enough not to require messy sex as proof or expression of love. As a child, I observed that it was not extraordinary for women who became Jehovah's Witnesses to remove themselves from their husband's bed as a first step to getting closer to God. For women whose experience had taught them that all human relationships were treacherous and capricious and frighteningly volatile, an escape from the confusions of the world into the certainties of a fundamentalist religion provided the illusion of safety and of rest. It is not too simple to say that the reason many unhappily married and sexually embittered women fell in love with Jehovah was that they didn't have to go to bed with Him.

Apocalyptic religions are, by their nature, antierotic. Jehovah's Witnesses believe that the world—or, as they would have it, "this evil system under Satan the Devil"—will end in our lifetime. After the slaughter Jehovah has arranged for his enemies at Armageddon, say the Witnesses, this quintessentially masculine God—vengeful in battle, benevolent to survivors—will turn the earth into an Edenic paradise for true believers. I grew up under the umbrella of the slogan, "Millions Now Living Will Never Die," convinced that 1914 marked "the beginning of the times of the end." So firmly did Jehovah's Witnesses believe this to be true that there were those who, in 1944, refused to get their teeth filled, postponing all care of their bodies until God saw to their regeneration in His New World, which was just around the corner.

Some corner.

Despite the fact that their hopes were not immediately rewarded, Jehovah's Witnesses have persevered with increasing fervor and conviction, and their attitude toward the world remains the same: because all their longing is for the future, they are bound to hate the present—the material, the sexual, the flesh. It's impossible, of course, truly to savor and enjoy the present, or to bend one's energies to shape and mold the world into the form of goodness, if you are only waiting for it to be smashed by God. There is a kind of ruthless glee in the way in which Jehovah's Witnesses point to earthquakes, race riots, heroin addiction, the failure of the United Nations, divorce, famine, and liberalized abortion laws as proof of the nearest Armageddon.

The world will end, according to the Witnesses, in a great shaking and rending and tearing of unbelieving flesh, with unsanctified babies swimming in blood—torrents of blood. They await God's Big Bang—the final orgasmic burst of violence, after which all things will come together in a cosmic orgasm of joy. In the meantime, they have disgust and contempt for the world; and freedom and spontaneity, even playfulness, in sex are explicitly frowned upon.

When I was ten, it would have been more than my life was worth to acknowledge, as Anna does so casually, that I knew what *screwing* was. (Ignorance, however, delivered me from that grave error.) Once, having read somewhere that Hitler had a mistress, I asked my mother what a mistress was. (I had an inkling that it was some kind of sinister superhousekeeper, like Judith Anderson in *Rebecca*.) I knew from my mother's silence, and from her cold, hard, and frightened face, that the question was somehow a grievous offense. I knew that I had done something terribly wrong, but as usual, I didn't know what. The fact was that I never knew how to buy God's—or my mother's—approval. There were sins I consciously and knowingly committed. That was bad, but it was bearable. I could always pray to God to forgive me, say, for reading the Bible for its "dirty parts" (to prefer the Song of Solomon to all the begats of Genesis was proof absolute of the sinfulness of my nature). But the offenses that made me most cringingly guilty were those I had committed unconsciously; as an imperfect human being descended from the wretched Eve, I was bound—so I had been taught—to offend Jehovah seventy-seven times a day without my even knowing what I was doing wrong.

I knew that good Christians didn't commit "unnatural acts"; but I didn't know what "unnatural acts" were. I knew that an increase in the number of rapes was one of the signs heralding the end of the world, but I didn't know what rape was. Consequently, I spent a lot of time praying that I was not committing unnatural acts or rape.

My ignorance of all things sexual was so profound that it frequently led to comedies of error. Nothing I've ever read has inclined me to believe that Jehovah has a sense of humor, and I must say that I consider it a strike against Him that He wouldn't find this story funny: One night shortly after my conversion, a visiting elder of the congregation, as he was avuncularly tucking me in bed, asked me if I were guilty of performing evil practices with my hands under the covers at night. I was puzzled. He was persistent. Finally, I thought I understood. And I burst into wild tears of self-recrimination: What I did under the covers at night was bite my cuticles—a practice which, in fact, did afford me a kind of sensual pleasure. I didn't learn about masturbation—which the Witnesses call "idolatry" because "the masturbator's affection is diverted away from the Creator and is bestowed upon a coveted object . . . his genitals"—until much later. So, having confessed to a sin that I didn't even know existed, I was advised of the necessity of keeping one's body pure from sin; cold baths were recommended, I couldn't see the connection between cold baths and my cuticles, but no one ever questioned the imperatives of an elder. So I subjected my impure body, in midwinter, to so many icy baths that I began to look like a bleached prune. My mother thought I was demented. But I couldn't tell her that I'd been biting my cuticles, because to have incurred God's wrath—and to see the beady eye of the elder steadfastly upon me at every religious meeting I went to—was torment enough. There was no way to win.

One never questioned the imperatives of an elder. I learned as a very small child that it was my primary duty in life to "make nice." When I was little, I was required to respond to inquiries about my health in this manner: "Fine and dandy, just like sugar candy, thank you." And to curtsy. If that sounds like something from a Shirley Temple movie, it's because it is. Having been brought up to be the Italian working-class Shirley Temple from Bensonhurst, it was not terribly difficult for me to learn to "make nice" for God and the elders. Behaving well was relatively easy. The passionate desire to win approval guaranteed my conforming. But behaving well never made me feel good. I always felt as if I were a bad person.

I ask myself why it was that my brother was not hounded by the obsessive guilt and the desperate desire for approval that informed all my actions. Partly, I suppose, luck, and an accident of temperament, but also because of the peculiarly guilt-inspiring double message girls received. Girls were taught that it was their nature to be spiritual, but paradoxically that they were more prone to absolute depravity than were boys.

In my religion, everything beautiful and noble and spiritual and good was represented by a woman; and everything evil and depraved and monstrous was represented by a woman. I learned that "God's organization," the "bride of Christ," or His 144,000 heavenly co-rulers were represented by a "chaste virgin." I also learned that "Babylon the Great," or "false religion," was "the mother of the abominations or the 'disgusting things of the earth' . . . She likes to get drunk on human blood. . . . Babylon the Great is . . . pictured as a woman, an international harlot."

Young girls were thought not to have the "urges" boys had. They were not only caretakers of their own sleepy sexuality but protectors of boys' vital male animal impulses as well. They were thus doubly responsible, and, if they fell, doubly damned. Girls were taught that, simply by existing, they were provoking male sexuality . . . which it was their job then to subdue.

To be female, I learned, was to be Temptation; nothing short of death—the transformation of your atoms into a lilac bush—could change that, (I used to dream deliciously of dying, of being as inert—and as unaccountable—as the dust I came from.) Inasmuch as males naturally "wanted it" more, when a female "wanted it" she was doubly depraved, unnatural as well as sinful. She was the receptacle for male lust, "the weaker vessel." If the vessel, created by God for the use of males, presumed to have desires of its own, it was perforce consigned to the consuming fires of God's wrath. If then, a woman were to fall from grace, her fall would be mighty indeed—and her willful nature would lead her into that awful abyss where she would be deprived of the redemptive love of God and the validating love of man. Whereas, were a man to fall, he would be merely stumbling over his own feet of clay.

(Can this be accident? My brother, when he was young, was always falling over his own feet. I, on the other hand, to this day sweat with terror at the prospect of going down escalators or long flights of stairs. I cannot fly; I am afraid of the fall.)

I spent my childhood walking a religious tightrope, maintaining a difficult dizzying balance. I was, for example, expected to perform well at school, so that glory would accrue to Jehovah and "His organization." But I was also made continually aware of the perils of falling prey to "the wisdom of this world which is foolishness to God." I had constantly to defend myself against the danger of trusting my own judgment. To question or to criticize God's "earthly representatives" was a sure sign of "demonic influence"; to express doubt openly was to risk being treated like a spiritual leper, I was always an honor student at school; but this was hardly an occasion for unqualified joy. I felt, rather, as if I were courting spiritual disaster: while I was congratulated for having "given a witness" by virtue of my academic excellence, I was, in the next breath, warned against the danger of supposing that my intelligence could function independently of God's. The effect of all this was to convince me that my intelligence was like some kind of tricky, predatory animal, which, if it were not kept firmly reined, would surely spring on and destroy me.

"Vanity, thy name is woman." I learned very early what happened to women with "independent spirits" who opposed the will and imperatives of male elders. They were disfellowshipped (excommunicated) and thrown into "outer darkness." Held up as an example of such perfidious conduct was Maria Frances Russell, the wife of Charles Taze Russell, charismatic founder of the sect.

Russell charged his wife with "the same malady which has smitted others—*ambition.*" Complaining of a "female conspiracy" against the Lord's organization, he wrote: "The result was a considerable stirring up of slander and misrepresentation, for of course it would not suit (her) purposes to tell the plain unvarnished truth, that Sister Russell was ambitious. . . . When she desired to come back, I totally refused, except upon a promise that she should make reasonable acknowledgment of the wrong course she had been pursuing." Ambition in a woman was, by implication, so reprehensible as to exact from Jehovah the punishment of death.

(What the Witnesses appeared less eager to publicize about the Russell's spiritual-cum-marital problems is that in April, 1906, Mrs. Russell, having filed suit for legal separation, told a jury that her husband had once remarked to a young orphan woman the Russells had reared: "I am like a jellyfish. I float around here and there. I touch this one and that one, and if she responds I take her to me, and if not I float on to others." Mrs. Russell was unable to prove her charge.)

I remember a line in A *Nun's Story:* "Dear God," the disaffected Belgian nun anguished, "forgive me. I will never be able to love a Nazi." I, conversely, prayed tormentedly for many years, "Dear God, forgive me, I am not able to hate what you hate. I love the world." As a Witness I was taught that "friendship with the world" was "spiritual adultery." The world was crawling with Satan's agents. But Satan's agents—evolutionists, "false religionists," and all those who opposed, or were indifferent to, "Jehovah's message"—often seemed like perfectly nice, decent, indeed lovable people to me. (They were certainly interesting.) As I went from door to door, ostensibly to help the Lord divide the "goats" from the "sheep," I found that I was more and more listening to *their* lives; and I became increasingly more tentative about telling them that I had *The* Truth. As I grew older, I found it more and more difficult to eschew their company, I entertained fantasies, at one time or another, about a handsome, ascetic Jesuit priest I had met in my preaching work and about Albert Schweitzer, J.D. Salinger, E.B. White, and Frank Sinatra; in fact, I was committing "spiritual adultery" all over the place. And then, when I was fifteen, I fell in love with an "unbeliever."

If I felt—before having met and loved Arnold Horowitz, English 31, New Utrecht High School—that life was a tightrope, I felt afterward that my life was perpetually being lived on a high wire, with no safety net to catch me. I was obliged, by every tenet of my faith, to despise him: to be "yoked with an unbeliever," an atheist and an intellectual . . . the pain was exquisite.

He was the essential person, the person who taught me how to love, and how to doubt. Arnold became interested in me because I was smart; he loved me because he thought I was good. He nourished me. He nurtured me. He paid me the irresistible compliment of totally comprehending me. He hated my religion. He railed against the sect that would rather see babies die than permit them to have blood transfusions, which were regarded as unscriptural; he had boundless contempt for my overseers, who would not permit me to go to college—the "Devil's playground," which would fill my head with wicked, ungodly nonsense; he protested mightily, with the rage that springs from genuine compassion, against a religion that could tolerate segregation and apartheid, sneer at martyred revolutionaries, dismiss social reform and material charity as "irrelevant," a religion that—waiting for God to cure all human ills—would act by default to maintain the status quo, while regarding human pain and struggle without pity and without generosity. He loathed the world view that had been imposed on me, a black-and-white view that allowed no complexities, no moral dilemmas, that disdained metaphysical or philosophical or psychological inquiry; he loathed the bloated simplicities that held me in thrall. But he loved *me*. I had never before felt loved unconditionally.

This was a measure of his love: Jehovah's Witnesses are not permitted to salute the flag. Arnold came, unbidden, to sit with me at every school assembly, to hold my hand, while everyone else stood at rigid salute. We were very visible; and I was very comforted. And this was during the McCarthy era. Arnold had a great deal to lose, and he risked it all for me. Nobody had ever risked anything for me before. How could I believe that he was wicked?

We drank malteds on his porch and read T.S. Elliot and listened to Mozart. We walked for hours, talking of God and goodness and happiness and death. We met surreptitiously. (My mother so feared and hated the man who was leading me into apostasy that she once threw a loaf of Arnold bread out the window; his very name was loathsome to her.) Arnold treated me with infinite tenderness; he was the least alarming man I had ever known. His fierce concentration on me, his solicitous care uncoupled with sexual aggression, was the gentlest—and most thrilling— love I had ever known. He made me feel what I had never felt before— valuable, and good.

It was very hard. All my dreams centered around Arnold, who was becoming more important, certainly more real to me, than God. All my dreams were blood-colored. I would fantasize about Arnold's being converted and surviving Armageddon and living forever with me in the New World. Or I would fantasize about my dying with Arnold, in fire and flames, at Armageddon. I would try to make bargains with God—my life for his. When I confessed my terrors to the men in charge of my spiritual welfare—when I said that I knew I could not rejoice in the destruction of the "wicked" at Armageddon—I was told that I was presuming to be "more compassionate than Jehovah," the deadliest sin against the holy spirit. I was reminded that, being a woman and therefore weak and sentimental, I would have to go against my sinful nature and listen to their superior wisdom, which consisted of my never seeing Arnold again. I was also reminded of the perils of being over-smart: if I hadn't been such a good student, none of this would have happened to me.

I felt as if I were leading a double life, as indeed I was. I viewed the world as beautifully various, as a blemished but mysteriously wonderful place, as savable by humans, who were neither good nor bad but imperfectly wise; but I *acted* as if the world were fit for nothing but destruction, as if all human efforts to purchase happiness and goodness were doomed to failure and deserving of contempt, as if all people could be categorized as "sheep" or "goats" and herded into their appropriate destinies by a judgmental Jehovah, the all-seeing Father who knew better than His children what was good for them.

As I had when I was a little girl, I "made nice" as best I could. I maintained the appearance of "goodness," that is, of religiosity, although it violated my truest feelings. When I left high school, I went into the full-time preaching work. I spent a minimum of five hours a day ringing doorbells and conducting home Bible studies. I went to three religious meetings a week. I prayed that my outward conformity would lead to inner peace. I met Arnold very occasionally, when my need to see him overcame my elders' imperatives and my own devastating fears. He was always accessible to me. Our meetings partook equally of misery and of joy. I tried, by my busyness, to lock all my doubts into an attic of my mind.

And for a while, and in a way, it "took." I derived sustenance from communal surges of revivalist fervor at religious conventions and from the conviction that I was united, in a common cause, with a tiny minority of persecuted and comradely brothers and sisters whose approval became both my safety net and the Iron Curtain that shut me off from the world. I felt that I had chosen Jehovah, and that my salvation, while not assured, was at least a possibility; perhaps He would choose me. I vowed finally never to see Arnold again, hoping, by this sacrifice, to gain God's approval for him as well as for me.

I began to understand that for anyone so obviously weak and irresponsible as I, only a life of self-sacrifice and abnegation could work. I wanted to be consumed by Jehovah, to be locked so closely into the straitjacket of His embrace that I would be impervious to the devilish temptations my irritable, independent intelligence threw up in my path.

I wished to be eaten up alive; and my wish was granted. When I was nineteen, I was accepted into Bethel, the headquarters organization of Jehovah's Witnesses, where I worked and lived, one of twelve young women among two hundred and fifty men, for three years. "Making nice" had paid off. Every minute of my waking life was accounted for; there was no leisure in which to cultivate vice or reflection. I called myself happy. I worked as a housekeeper for my brothers, making thirty beds a day, sweeping and vacuuming and waxing and washing fifteen rooms a day (in addition to proselytizing in my "free time"); I daily washed the bathtub thirty men had bathed in. In fact, the one demural I made during those years was to ask—I found it so onerous—if perhaps the brothers, many of whom worked in the Witnesses' factory, could not clean out their own bathtub (thirty layers of grease is a lot of grease). I was told by the male overseer who supervised housekeepers that Jehovah had assigned me this "privilege." And I told myself I was lucky.

I felt myself to be even luckier—indeed, blessed—when, after two years of this servant's work, one of Jehovah's middlemen, the president of the Watch Tower Bible and Tract Society, told me that he was assigning me to proofread Watch Tower publications. He accompanied this benediction with a warning: this new honor, I was told, was to be a test of my integrity—"Remember in all things to defer to the brothers; you will have to guard your spirit against pride and vanity. Satan will try now to tempt you as never before."

And defer I did. There were days when I felt literally as if my eternal destiny hung upon a comma: if the brother with whom I worked decided a comma should go out where I wanted to put one in, I prayed to Jehovah to forgive me for that presumptuous comma. I was perfectly willing to deny the existence of a split infinitive if that would placate my brother. I denied and denied—commas, split infinitives, my sexuality, my intelligence, my femaleness, my yearning to be part of the world—until suddenly with a great silent shifting and shuddering, and with more pain than I had ever experienced or expect to experience again, I broke. I woke up one morning, packed my bags, and walked out of that place. I was twenty-two; and I had to learn how to begin to live. It required a great deal of courage; I do not think I will ever be capable of that much courage again.

The full story of life in that institution and the ramifications of my decision to leave it is too long to tell here; and it will take me the rest of my life to understand fully the ways in which everything I have ever done since has been colored and informed by the guilt that was my daily bread for so many dry years, by the desperate need for approval that allowed me to be swallowed up whole by a devouring religion, by the carefully fostered desire to "make nice" and to be "a good girl," by the conviction that I was nothing and nobody unless I served a cause superior to that of my own necessities.

Arnold, of course, foresaw the difficulty; when I left religion, he said, "Now you will be just like the rest of us." With no guiding passion, he meant; uncertain, he meant, and often muddled and confused, and always struggling. And he wept.

Critical Eye

FOR DISCUSSION

a. Is Harrison's issue with organized religion, or with the way she feels religion was used to make her feel? Is there really a difference?

b. Why did her father and brother become atheists?

c. What is the cause of Harrison's disassociation from her church?

REAPPROACHING THE TEXT

In his essay "Self-Reliance," Emerson suggests that individuals must be true to themselves, honoring what they truly believe in order to be whole. Reading Emerson alongside Harrison, determine whether or not the pieces share any similarities.

WRITING ASSIGNMENTS

In the end, Harrison's text is about finding your own way even though it may conflict with what you have been taught all your life—especially when those choices put you at odds with those who are important to you. Taking this into consideration, why is it important for the individual to carve out his or her own path?

Bharati Mukherjee

A Father

One Wednesday morning in mid-May Mr. Bhowmick woke up as he usually did at 5:43 A.M., checked his Rolex against the alarm clock's digital readout, punched down the alarm (set for 5:45), then nudged his wife awake. She worked as a claims investigator for an insurance company that had an office in a nearby shopping mall. She didn't really have to leave the house until 8:30, but she liked to get up early and cook him a big breakfast. Mr. Bhowmick had to drive a long way to work. He was a naturally dutiful, cautious man, and he set the alarm clock early enough to accommodate a margin for accidents.

While his wife, in a pink nylon negligee she had paid for with her own Master-Card card, made him a new version of French toast from a clipping ("Eggs-cellent Recipes!") Scotchtaped to the inside of a kitchen cupboard, Mr. Bhowmick brushed his teeth. He brushed, he gurgled with the loud, hawking noises that he and his brother had been taught as children to make in order to flush clean not merely teeth but also tongue and palate.

After that he showered, then, back in the bedroom again, he recited prayers in Sanskrit to Kali, the patron goddess of his family, the goddess of wrath and vengeance. In the pokey flat of his childhood in Ranchi, Bihar, his mother had given over a whole bedroom to her collection of gods and goddesses. Mr. Bhowmick couldn't be that extravagant in Detroit. His daughter, twenty-six and an electrical engineer, slept in the other of the two bedrooms in his apartment. But he had done his best. He had taken Woodworking I and II at a nearby recreation center and built a grotto for the goddess. Kali-Mata was eight inches tall, made of metal and painted a glistening black so that the metal glowed like the oiled, black skin of a peasant woman. And though Kali-Mata was totally nude except for a tiny gilt crown and a garland strung together from sinners' chopped off heads, she looked warm, cozy, *pleased,* in her makeshift wooden shrine in Detroit. Mr. Bhowmick had gathered quite a crowd of admiring, fellow woodworkers in those final weeks of decoration.

"Hurry it up with the prayers," his wife shouted from the kitchen. She was an agnostic, a believer in ambition, not grace. She frequently complained

"A Father" by Bharati Mukherjee. Copyright © 1985 by Bharati Mukherjee. Originally published in *Darkness*. Reprinted with permission of the author.

that his prayers had gotten so long that soon he wouldn't have time to go to work, play duplicate bridge with the Ghosals, or play the tabla in the Bengali Association's one-Sunday-per-month musical soirees. Lately she'd begun to drain him in a wholly new way. He wasn't praying, she nagged; he was shutting her out of his life. There'd be no peace in the house until she hid Kali-Mata in a suitcase.

She nagged, and he threatened to beat her with his shoe as his father had threatened his mother: it was the thrust and volley of marriage. There was no question of actually taking off a shoe and applying it to his wife's body. She was bigger than he was. And, secretly, he admired her for having the nerve, the agnosticism, which as a college boy in backward Bihar he too had claimed.

"I have time," he shot at her. He was still wrapped in a damp terry towel.

"You have time for everything but domestic life."

It was the fault of the shopping mall that his wife had started to buy pop psychology paperbacks. These paperbacks preached that for couples who could sit down and talk about their "relationship," life would be sweet again. His engineer daughter was on his wife's side. She accused him of holding things in.

"Face it, Dad," she said. "You have an affect deficit."

But surely everyone had feelings they didn't want to talk about or talk over. He definitely did not want to blurt out anything about the sick-in-the-guts sensations that came over him most mornings and that he couldn't bubble down with Alka-Seltzer or smother with Gas-X. The women in his family were smarter than him. They were cheerful, outgoing, more American somehow.

How could he tell these bright, mocking women that in the 5:43 A.M. darkness, he sensed invisible presences: gods and snakes frolicked in the master bedroom, little white sparks of cosmic static crackled up the legs of his pajamas. Something was out there in the dark, something that could invent accidents and coincidences to remind mortals that even in Detroit they were no more than mortal. His wife would label this paranoia and dismiss it. Paranoia, premonition: whatever it was, it had begun to undermine his composure.

Take this morning. Mr. Bhowmick had woken up from a pleasant dream about a man taking a Club Med vacation, and the postdream satisfaction had lasted through the shower, but when he'd come back to the shrine in the bedroom, he'd noticed all at once how scarlet and saucy was the tongue that Kali-Mata stuck out at the world. Surely he had not lavished such alarming detail, such admonitory colors on that flap of flesh.

Watch out, ambulatory sinners. Be careful out there, the goddess warned him, and not with the affection of Sergeant Esterhaus,[1] either.

"French toast must be eaten hot-hot," his wife nagged. "Otherwise they'll taste like rubber."

Mr. Bhowmick laid the trousers of a two-trouser suit he had bought on sale that winter against his favorite tweed jacket. The navy stripes in the trousers and the small, navy tweed flecks in the jacket looked quite good together. So what if the Chief Engineer had already started wearing summer cottons?

"I am coming, I am coming," he shouted back. "You want me to eat hot-hot, you start the frying only when I am sitting down. You didn't learn anything from Mother in Ranchi?"

"Mother cooked French toast from fancy recipes? I mean French Sandwich Toast with complicated filling?"

He came into the room to give her his testiest look. "You don't know the meaning of complicated cookery. And mother had to get the coal fire of the *chula* going first."

His daughter was already at the table. "Why don't you break down and buy her a microwave oven? That's what I mean about sitting down and talking things out." She had finished her orange juice. She took a plastic measure of Slim-Fast out of its can and poured the powder into a glass of skim milk. "It's ridiculous."

Babli was not the child he would have chosen as his only heir. She was brighter certainly than the sons and daughters of the other Bengalis he knew in Detroit, and she had been the only female student in most of her classes at Georgia Tech, but as she sat there in her beige linen business suit, her thick chin dropping into a polka-dotted cravat, he regretted again that she was not the child of his dreams. Babli would be able to help him out moneywise if something happened to him, something so bad that even his pension plans and his insurance policies and his money market schemes wouldn't be enough. But Babli could never comfort him. She wasn't womanly or tender the way that unmarried girls had been in the wistful days of his adolescence. She could sing Hindi film songs, mimicking exactly the high, artificial voice of Lata Mungeshkar, and she had taken two years of dance lessons at Sona Devi's Dance Academy in Southfield, but these accomplishments didn't add up to real femininity. Not the kind that had given him palpitations in Ranchi.

Mr. Bhowmick did his best with his wife's French toast. In spite of its filling of marshmallows, apricot jam and maple syrup, it tasted rubbery. He drank two cups of Darjeeling tea, said, "Well, I'm off," and took off.

All might have gone well if Mr. Bhowmick hadn't fussed longer than usual about putting his briefcase and his trenchcoat in the backseat. He got in behind the wheel of his Oldsmobile, fixed his seatbelt and was just about to turn the key in the ignition when his neighbor, Al Stazniak, who was starting up his Buick Skylark, sneezed. A sneeze at the start of a journey brings bad luck. Al Stazniak's sneeze was fierce, made up of five short bursts, too loud to be ignored.

Be careful out there! Mr. Bhowmick could see the goddess's scarlet little tongue tip wagging at him.

He was a modern man, an intelligent man. Otherwise he couldn't have had the options in life that he did have. He couldn't have given up a good job with perks in Bombay and found a better job with General Motors in Detroit. But Mr. Bhowmick was also a prudent enough man to know that some abiding truth lies bunkered within each wanton Hindu superstition. A sneeze was more than a sneeze. The heedless are carried off in ambulances. He had choices to make. He could ignore the sneeze, and so challenge the world unseen by men. Perhaps Al Stazniak had hay fever. For a sneeze to be a potent omen, surely it had to be unprovoked and terrifying, a thunderclap cleaving the summer skies. Or he could admit the smallness of mortals, undo the fate of the universe by starting over, and go back inside the apartment, sit for a second on the sofa, then restart his trip.

Al Stazniak rolled down his window. "Everything okay?"

Mr. Bhowmick nodded shyly. They weren't really friends in the way neighbors can sometimes be. They talked as they parked or pulled out of their adjacent parking stalls. For all Mr. Bhowmick knew, Al Stazniak had no legs. He had never seen the man out of his Skylark.

He let the Buick back out first. Everything was okay, yes, please. All the same he undid his seatbelt. Compromise, adaptability, call it what you will. A dozen times a day he made these small trade-offs between new-world reasonableness and old-world beliefs.

While he was sitting in his parked car, his wife's ride came by. For fifty dollars a month, she was picked up and dropped off by a hard up, newly divorced woman who worked at a florist's shop in the same mall. His wife came out the front door in brown K-Mart pants and a burgundy windbreaker. She waved to him, then slipped into the passenger seat of the florist's rusty Japanese car.

He was a metallurgist. He knew about rust and ways of preventing it, secret ways, thus far unknown to the Japanese.

Babli's fiery red Mitsubishi was still in the lot. She wouldn't leave for work for another eight minutes. He didn't want her to know he'd been undone by a sneeze. Babli wasn't tolerant of superstitions. She played New Wave music in her tapedeck. If asked about Hinduism, all she'd ever said to her American friends was that "it's neat." Mr. Bhowmick had heard her on the phone years before. The cosmos balanced on the head of a snake was like a beachball balanced on the snout of a circus seal. "This Hindu myth stuff," he'd heard her say, "is like a series of super graphics."

He'd forgiven her. He could probably forgive her anything. It was her way of surviving high school in a city that was both native to her, and alien.

There was no question of going back where he'd come from. He hated Ranchi. Ranchi was no place for dreamers. All through his teenage years, Mr. Bhowmick had dreamed of success abroad. What form that success would take he had left vague. Success had meant to him escape from the constant plotting and bitterness that wore out India's middle class.

Babli should have come out of the apartment and driven off to work by now. Mr. Bhowmick decided to take a risk, to dash inside and pretend he'd left his briefcase on the coffee table.

When he entered the living room, he noticed Babli's spring coat and large vinyl pocketbook on the sofa. She was probably sorting through the junk jewelry on her dresser to give her business suit a lift. She read hints about dressing in women's magazines and applied them to her person with seriousness. If his luck held, he could sit on the sofa, say a quick prayer and get back to the car without her catching on.

It surprised him that she didn't shout our from her bedroom, "Who's there?" What if he had been a rapist?

Then he heard Babli in the bathroom. He heard unladylike squawking noises. She was throwing up, A squawk, a spitting, then the horrible gurgle of a waterfall.

A revelation came to Mr. Bhowmick. A woman vomiting in the privacy of the bathroom could mean many things. She was coming down with the flu. She was nervous about a meeting. But Mr. Bhowmick knew at once that his daughter, his untender, unloving daughter whom he couldn't love and hadn't tried to love, was not, in the larger world of Detroit, unloved. Sinners are everywhere, even in the bosom of an upright, unambitious family like the Bhowmicks. It was the goddess sticking out her tongue at him.

The father sat heavily on the sofa, shrinking from contact with her coat and pocketbook. His brisk, bright engineer daughter was pregnant. Someone had taken time to make love to her. Someone had thought her tender, feminine. Someone even now was perhaps mooning over her. The idea excited him. It was so grotesque and wondrous. At twenty-six Babli had found the man of her dreams; whereas at twenty-six Mr. Bhowmick had given up on truth, beauty . . .

Mr. Bhowmick's tweed-jacketed body sagged against the sofa cushions. Babli would abort, of course. He knew his Babli. It was the only possible option if she didn't want to bring shame to the Bhowmick family. All the same, he could see a chubby baby boy on the rug, crawling to his granddaddy. Shame like that was easier to hide in Ranchi. There was always a barren womb sanctified by marriage that could claim sudden fructifying by the goddess Parvati. Babli would do what she wanted. She was headstrong and independent and he was afraid of her.

Babli staggered out of the bathroom. Damp stains ruined her linen suit, was the first time he had seen his daughter look ridiculous, quite unprofessional. She didn't come into the living room to investigate the noises he'd made. He glimpsed her shoeless stockinged feet flip-flop on collapsed arches down the hall to her bedroom.

"Are you all right?" Mr. Bhowmick asked, standing in the hall. "Do you need Sinutab?"

She wheeled around. "What're you doing here?"

He was the one who should be angry. "I'm feeling poorly too," he said. "I'm taking the day off."

"I feel fine, "Babli said.

Within fifteen minutes Babli had changed her clothes and left. Mr. Bhowmick had the apartment to himself all day. All day for praising or cursing the life that had brought him along with its other surprises an illegitimate grandchild.

It was his wife that he blamed. Coming to America to live had been his wife's idea. After the wedding, the young Bhowmicks had spent two years in Pittsburgh on his student visa, then gone back home to Ranchi for nine years. Nine crushing years. Then the job in Bombay had come through. All during those nine years his wife had screamed and wept. She was a woman of wild, progressive ideas—she'd called them her "American" ideas—and she'd been martyred by her neighbors for them. American *memsahib. Markin mem, Markin mem.* In bazaars the beggar boys had trailed her and hooted. She'd done provocative things. She'd hired a *chamar* woman who by caste rules was forbidden to cook for higher caste families, especially for widowed mothers of decent men. This had caused a blowup in the neighborhood. She'd made other, lesser errors. While other wives shopped and cooked every day, his wife had cooked the whole week's menu on weekends.

"What's the point of having a refrigerator, then?" She'd been scornful of the Ranchi women.

His mother, an old-fashioned widow, had accused her of trying to kill her by poisoning. "You are in such a hurry? You want to get rid of me quick-quick so you can go back to the States?"

Family life had been turbulent.

He had kept aloof, inwardly siding with his mother. He did not love his wife now, and he had not loved her then. In any case, he had not defended her. He felt some affection, and he felt guilty for having shunned her during those unhappy years. But he had thought of it then as revenge. He had wanted to marry a beautiful woman. Not being a young man of means, only a young man with prospects, he had had no right to yearn for pure beauty. He cursed his fate and after a while, settled for a barrister's daughter, a plain girl with a wide, flat plank of a body and myopic eyes. The barrister had sweetened the deal by throwing in an all-expenses-paid two years' study at Carnegie Tech to which Mr. Bhowmick had been admitted. Those two years had changed his wife from pliant girl to an ambitious woman.

It was his wife who had forced him to apply for permanent resident status in the U.S. even though he had a good job in Ranchi as a government engineer. The putting together of documents for the immigrant visa had been a long and humbling process. He had had to explain to a chilly clerk in the Embassy that, like most Indians of his generation, he had no birth certificate. He had to swear out affidavits, suffer through police checks, bribe orderlies whose job it was to move his dossier from desk to desk. The decision, the clerk had advised him, would take months, maybe years. He hadn't dared hope that merit might be rewarded. Merit could collapse under bad luck. It was for grace that he prayed.

While the immigration papers were being processed, he had found the job in Bombay. So he'd moved his mother in with his younger brother's family, and left his hometown for good. Life in Bombay had been lighthearted, almost fulfilling. His wife had thrown herself into charity work with the same energy that had offended the Ranchi women. He was happy to be in a big city at last. Bombay was the Rio de Janeiro of the East; he'd read that in a travel brochure. He drove out to Nariman Point at least once a week to admire the necklace of municipal lights, toss coconut shells into the dark ocean, drink beer at the Oberoi-Sheraton where overseas Indian girls in designer jeans beckoned him in sly ways. His nights were full. He played duplicate bridge, went to the movies, took his wife to Bingo nights at his club. In Detroit he was a lonelier man.

Then the green card had come through. For him, for his wife, and for the daughter who had been born to them in Bombay. He sold what he could sell, and put in his brother's informal trust what he couldn't to save on taxes. Then he had left for America, and one more start.

All through the week, Mr. Bhowmick watched his daughter. He kept furtive notes on how many times she rushed to the bathroom and made hawking, wrenching noises, how many times she stayed late at the office, calling her mother to say she'd be taking in a movie and pizza afterwards with friends.

He had to tell her that he knew. And he probably didn't have much time. She shouldn't be on Slim-Fast in her condition. He had to talk things over with her. But what would he say to her? What position could he take? He had to choose between public shame for the family, and murder.

For three more weeks he watched her and kept his silence. Babli wore shifts to the office instead of business suits, and he liked her better in those garments. Perhaps she was dressing for her young man, not from necessity. Her skin was pale and blotchy by turn. At breakfast her fingers looked stiff, and she had trouble with silverware.

Two Saturdays running, he lost badly at duplicate bridge. His wife scolded him. He had made silly mistakes. When was Babli meeting this man? Where? He must be American; Mr. Bhowmick prayed only that he was white. He pictured his grandson crawling to him, and the grandson was always fat and brown and buttery-skinned, like the infant Krishna. An American son-in-law was a terrifying notion. Why was she not mentioning men, at least, preparing the way for the major announcement? He listened sharply for men's names, rehearsed little lines like, "Hello, Bob, I'm Babli's old man," with a cracked little laugh. Bob, Jack, Jimmy, Tom. But no names surfaced. When she went out for pizza and a movie it was with the familiar set of Indian girls and their strange, unpopular, American friends, all without men. Mr. Bhowmick tried to be reasonable. Maybe she had already gotten married and was keeping it secret. "Well, Bob, you and Babli sure had Mrs. Bhowmick and me going there, heh-heh," he mumbled one night with the Sahas and Ghosals, over cards. "Pardon?" asked Pronob Saha. Mr. Bhowmick dropped two tricks, and his wife glared. "Such stupid blunders," she fumed on the drive back. A new truth was dawning; there would be no marriage for Babli. Her young man probably was not so young and not so available. He must be already married. She must have yielded to passion or been raped in the office. His wife seemed to have noticed nothing. Was he a murderer, or a conspirator? He kept his secret from his wife; his daughter kept her decision to herself.

Nights, Mr. Bhowmick pretended to sleep, but as soon as his wife began her snoring—not real snores so much as loud, gaspy gulpings for breath—he turned on his side and prayed to Kali-Mata.

In July, when Babli's belly had begun to push up against the waistless dress she'd bought herself, Mr. Bhowmick came out of the shower one weekend morning and found the two women screaming at each other. His wife had a rolling pin in one hand. His daughter held up a *National Geographic* as a shield for her head. The crazy look that had been in his wife's eyes when she'd shooed away beggar kids was in her eyes again.

"Stop it!" His own boldness overwhelmed him. "Shut up! Babli's pregnant so what? It's your fault, you made us come to the States."

Girls like Babli were caught between rules, that's the point he wished to make. They were too smart, too impulsive for a backward place like Ranchi, but not tough nor smart enough for sex-crazy places like Detroit.

"My fault?" his wife cried. "I told her to do hanky-panky with boys? I told her to shame us like this?"

She got in one blow with the rolling pin. The second glanced off Babli's shoulder and fell on his arm which he had stuck out for his grandson's sake.

"I'm calling the police," Babli shouted. She was out of the rolling pin's range "This is brutality. You can't do this to me."

"Shut up! Shut your mouth, foolish woman." He wrenched the weapon from his wife's fist. He made a show of taking off his shoe to beat his wife on the face.

"What do you know? You don't know anything." She let herself down slowly on a dining chair. Her hair, curled overnight, stood in wild whorls around her head. "Nothing."

"And you do!" He laughed. He remembered her tormentors, and laughed again. He had begun to enjoy himself. Now *he* was the one with the crazy, progressive ideas.

"Your daughter is pregnant, yes," she said, "any fool knows that. But ask her the name of the father. Go, ask."

He stared at his daughter who gazed straight ahead, eyes burning with hate, jaw clenched with fury.

"Babli?"

"Who needs a man?" she hissed. "The father of my baby is a bottle and a syringe. Men louse up your lives. I just want a baby. Oh, don't worry—he's a certified fit donor. No diseases, college graduate, above average, and he made the easiest twenty-five dollars of his life—"

"Like animals," his wife said. For the first time he heard horror in her voice. His daughter grinned at him. He saw her tongue, thick and red, squirming behind her row of perfect teeth.

"Yes, yes, yes," she screamed, "like livestock. Just like animals. You should be happy—that's what marriage is all about, isn't it? Matching bloodlines, matching horoscopes, matching castes, matching, matching, matching . . ." and it was difficult to know if she was laughing or singing, or mocking and like a madwoman.

Mr. Bhowmick lifted the rolling pin high above his head and brought it down hard on the dome of Babli's stomach. In the end, it was his wife who called the police.

(1985)

Critical Eye

FOR DISCUSSION

a. In what way(s) is the father's traditional role in his house being undermined?

b. The father looks out upon the women in his house and finds them to be what he terms "more American." Why is this problematic for him? What is he suggesting has been lost?

c. Why is the father moved to violence by the end of the story? What is he angry about?

REAPPROACHING THE TEXT

How is this story about the difficulties immigrants experience once they arrive in America? How are their traditions challenged? What are they expected to surrender?

WRITING ASSIGNMENT

As much as this is a story about the father's moment of truth, in what ways is this story about the daughter taking her life into her own hands? Is this defining moment traumatic for most parents? If so, why?

Mohammed Naseehu Ali

Mallam Sile

He was popularly known as *mai tea,* or the tea seller. His shop was situated right in the navel of Zongo Street—a stone's throw from the chief's assembly shed and adjacent to the kiosk where Mansa BBC, the town gossip, sold her provisions. Along with fried eggs and white butter bread, Mallam Sile carried all kinds of beverages: regular black tea, Japanese green tea, Milo, Bournvita, cocoa drink, instant coffee. But on Zongo Street all hot beverages were referred to just as tea, and it was common, therefore, to hear people say, "Mallam Sile, may I have a mug of cocoa tea?" or "Sile, may I have a cup of coffee tea?"

The tea shop had no windows. It was built of *wawa,* a cheap wood easily infested by termites. The floor was uncemented, and heaps of dust rose in the air whenever a customer walked in. Sile protected his merchandise from the dust by keeping everything in plastic bags. An enormous wooden "chop box," the top of which he used as a serving table, covered most of the space in the shop. There was a tall chair behind the chop box for Sile, but he never used it, preferring instead to stand on his feet even when the shop was empty. There were also three benches that were meant to be used only by those who bought tea, though the idle gossips who crowded the shop and never spent any money occupied the seats most of the time.

Old Sile had an irrational fear of being electrocuted and so he'd never tapped electricity into his shack, as was usually done on Zongo Street. Instead, he used kerosene lanterns, three of which hung from the low wooden ceiling. Sile kept a small radio in the shop, and whenever he had no customers he listened, in meditative silence, to the English programs on GBC 2, as though he understood what was being said. Mallam Sile was fluent only in his northern Sisaala tongue, though he understood Hausa—the language of the street's inhabitants—and spoke just enough pidgin to be able to conduct his business.

The mornings were usually slow for the tea seller, as a majority of the street folks preferred the traditional breakfast of *kókó da mása,* or corn porridge with rice cake. But, come evening, the shop was crowded with the street's young men and women, who gossiped and talked about the

"Mallam Sile" [pp. 149–68] from *The Prophet of Zongo Street* by Mohammad Nasseehu Ali. Copyright © 2005 by Mohammed Naseehu Ali. Reprinted by permission of HarperCollins Publishers, Amistad Press.

"latest news" in town. Some came to the shop just to meet their loved ones. During the shop's peak hours—from eight in the evening until around midnight—one could hardly hear oneself talk because of the boisterous chattering that went on. But anytime Mallam Sile opened his mouth to add to a conversation people would say, "Shut up, Sile, what do you know about this?" or "Close your beak, Sile, who told you that?" The tea seller learned to swallow his words, and eventually spoke only when he was engaged in a transaction with a customer. But nothing said or even whispered in the shop escaped his sharp ears.

Mallam Sile was a loner, without kin on the street or anywhere else in the city. He was born in Nanpugu, a small border town in the north. He left home at age sixteen, and, all by himself, journeyed more than nine hundred miles in a cow truck to find work down south in Kumasi—the capital city of Ghana's gold-rich Ashanti region.

Within a week of his arrival in the city, Sile landed a job as a house servant. Although his monthly wages were meagre, he sent a portion of them home to his ailing parents, who lived like paupers in their drought-stricken village. Even so, Sile's efforts were not enough to save his parents from the claws of Death, who took them away in their sleep one night. They were found clinging tightly to each other, as if one of them had seen what was coming and had grabbed onto the other so that they could go together.

The young Sile received the news of his parents' death with mixed emotions. He was sad to lose them, of course, but he saw it as a well-deserved rest for them, as they both had been ill and bedridden for many months. Though Sile didn't travel up north to attend their funeral, he sent money for a decent burial. With his parents deceased, Sile suddenly found himself with more money in his hands. He quit his house-servant job and found another, selling iced *kenkey* in Kumasi's central market. Sile kept every pesewa he earned, and two years later he was able to use his savings to open a tea business. It was the first of such establishments on Zongo Street, and would remain the only one for many years to come.

Mallam Sile was short—so short, in fact, that many claimed he was a Pygmy. He stood exactly five feet one inch tall. Although he didn't have the broad, flat nose, poorly developed chin, and round head of the Pygmies, he was stout and hairy all over, as they were. A childhood illness that had caused Sile's vision to deteriorate had continued to plague him throughout his adult life. Yet he refused to go to the hospital and condemned any form of medication, traditional or Western. "God is the one who brings illness, and he is the only true healer"—this was Sile's simple, if rather mystical, explanation.

Sile's small face was covered with a thick, long beard. The wrinkles on his dark forehead and the moistness of his soft, squinted eyes gave him the appearance of a sage, one who had lived through and conquered many adversities in his life. His smile, which stretched from one wrinkled cheek to the other, baring his kola-stained teeth, radiated strength, wisdom, and self-confidence.

Sile wore the same outfit every day: a white polyester djellabah and its matching *wando,* a loose pair of slacks that tied with strings at the waist. He had eight of these suits, and wore a different one each day of the week. Also, his head was perpetually shaved, and he was never without his white embroidered Mecca hat—worn by highly devout Muslims as a reflection of their submission to Allah. Like most of the street's dwellers, Sile owned just one pair of slippers at a time, and replaced them only when they were worn out beyond repair. An unusual birth defect that caused the tea seller to grow an additional toe on each foot had made it impossible for him to find footwear that fit him properly; special slippers were made for him by Anaba the cobbler, who used discarded car tires for the soles of the shoes he made. The rascals of Zongo Street, led by Samadu, the street's most notorious bully, poked at Sile's feet and his slippers, which they called *kalabilwala,* a nonsensical term that no one could understand, let alone translate.

At forty-six, Mallam Sile was still a virgin. He routinely made passes at the divorcées and widows who came to his shop, but none showed any interest in him whatsoever. "What would I do with a dwarf?" the women would ask, feeling ashamed of having had passes made at them by Sile. A couple of them seemed receptive to tea seller Sile's advances, but everyone knew that they were flirting with him only in order to get free tea.

Eventually, Sile resigned himself to his lack of success with women. He was convinced that he would die a virgin. Yet late at night, after all the customers, idlers, and rumormongers had left the shop to seek refuge in their shanties and on their bug-ridden grass mattresses, Sile could be heard singing love songs, hoping that a woman somewhere would respond to his passionate cries:

> A beautiful woman, they say,
> Is like an elephant's meat.
> And only the man with the sharpest knife
> Can cut through.
> That's what they say.
> Young girl, I have no knife,
> I am not a hunter of meat.

And I am not savage.
I am only looking for love.
This is what I say.
Up north where I am from,
Young girls are not what they are here.
Up north where I am from,
People don't judge you by your knife.
They look at the size of your heart.
Young girl, I don't know what you look like.
I don't know where to look for you.
I don't even know who you are, young girl.
All I know is: my heart is aching.
Oh, oh, oh! My heart is aching for you.

Sile's voice rang with melancholy when he sang his songs. But still the rascals derided him. "When are you going to give up, Sile?" they would say. "Can't you see that no woman would marry you?"

"I have given up on them long, long ago," he would reply. "But I am never going to give up on myself!" "You keep fooling yourself," they told him, laughing.

The rascals' mocking didn't end there. Knowing that Mallam Sile couldn't see properly, they often used fake or banned cedi notes to purchase tea from him at night. The tea seller pinned the useless bills to the walls of his shop as if they were good-luck charms. He believed that it was hunger—and not mischief—that had led the rascals to cheat him. And, since he considered it inhuman to refuse a hungry person food, Mallam Sile allowed them to get away with their frauds.

To cool off the hot tea for his customers, Sile poured the contents of one mug into another, raising one over the other. The rascals would push Sile in the middle of this process, causing the hot liquid to spill all over his arms. The tea seller was never angered by such pranks. He merely grinned and, without saying a word, wiped off the spilled tea and continued to serve his customers. And when the rascals blew out the lanterns in the shop, so as to steal bread and Milo while he was trying to rekindle the light, Sile accepted that, too. He managed to rid his heart of any ill feelings. He would wave his short arms to anyone who walked past his shop, and shout, by way of greeting, "How are the heavens with you, boy?" Sile called everyone "boy," including women and older people, and he hardly ever uttered a sentence without referring to the heavens.

He prided himself on his hard work, and smiled whenever he looked in the mirror and saw his dwarfish body and ailing eyes, two abnormalities that he had learned to love. A few months before the death of his parents, he had come to the conclusion that if Allah had made him any differently he would not have been Mallam Sile—and Mallam Sile was an individual whom Sile's heart, mind, and spirit had come to accept and respect. This created within him a peace that made it possible for him not only to tolerate the rascals' ill treatment but also to forgive them. Though in their eyes Sile was only a buffoon.

One sunny afternoon during the dry season, Mallam Sile was seen atop the roof of his shack with hammers, saws, pliers, and all kinds of building tools. He lingered there all day long like a stray monkey, and by dusk he had dismantled all the aluminum roofing sheets that had once sheltered him and his business. He resumed work early the following morning, and by about one-thirty, before *azafar,* the first of the two afternoon prayers, Sile had no place to call either home or tea shop—he had demolished the shack down to its dusty floor.

At three-thirty, after *la-asar,* the second afternoon worship, Mallam Sile moved his personal belongings and all his tea paraphernalia to a room in the servants' quarters of the chiefs' palace. The room had been arranged for him by the chief's wazir, or right-hand man, who was sympathetic to the tea seller.

During the next two days, Mallam Sile ordered plywood and planks of *odum,* a wood superior to the *wawa* used for the old shop. He also ordered a few bags of cement and truckloads of sand and stones, and immediately began building a new shack, much bigger than the first.

The street folks were shocked by Sile's new building—they wondered where he had got the money to embark on such an enterprise. Sile was rumored to be constructing a mini-market store to compete with Alhaji Saifa, the owner of the street's provision store. (And though the tea seller denied the rumor, it rapidly spread up and down the street, eventually creating bad blood between Sile and Alhaji Saifa.)

It took three days for Mallam Sile to complete work on the new shop's foundation, and an additional three weeks for him to erect the wooden walls and the aluminum roofing sheets. While Sile was busy at work, passersby would call out, "How is the provision store coming?" or "*Mai tea,* how is the mansion coming?" Sile would reply simply, "It is coming well, boy. It will be completed soon, *Inshallah.*" He would grin his usual wide grin and wave his short hairy arms, and then return to his work.

Meanwhile, as the days and weeks passed, the street folks grew impatient and somewhat angry at the closing of Sile's shop. The nearest tea shack was three hundred metres away, on Zerikyi Road—and not only that but the owner of the shack, Abongo, was generally abhorred. And for good reason. Abongo, also a northerner, was quite unfriendly even to his loyal customers. He maintained a rigid no-credit policy, and made customers pay him even before they were served. No one was an exception to this policy—even if he or she was dying of hunger. And, unlike Sile, Abongo didn't tolerate idlers or loud conversation in his shop. If a customer persisted in chatting, Abongo reached for the customer's mug, poured the contents in a plastic basin, and refunded his money. He then chased the customer out of the shop, brandishing his bullwhip and cursing after him, "If your mama and papa never teach you manners, I'll teach you some! I'll sew those careless lips of yours together, you bastard son of a bastard woman!"

As soon as work on the shop was completed, Sile left for his home town. Soon afterward, yet another rumor surfaced: it was said that the tea seller had travelled up north in search of "black medicine" for his bad eyesight.

Sile finally returned one Friday evening, some six weeks after he'd begun work on the shop, flanked by a stern woman who looked to be in her late thirties and was three times larger than the tea seller. The woman, whose name was Abeeba, turned out to be Mallam Sile's wife. She was tall and massive, with a face as gloomy as that of someone mourning a dead relative. Like her husband, Abeeba said very little to people in or out of the shop. She, too, grinned and waved her huge arms whenever she greeted people, though, unlike the tea seller, she seemed to have something harder lurking behind her cheerful smile. Abeeba carried herself with the grace and confidence of a lioness, and covered her head and part of her face with an Islamic veil, a practice that had been dropped by most of the married women on Zongo Street.

The rascals asked Sile, when they ran into him at the market, "From where did you get this elephant? Better not get on her bad side; she'll sit on you till you sink into the ground." To this, the tea seller did not say a word.

Exactly one week after Sile's return from his village, he and his wife opened the doors of the new shop to their customers. Among the most talked-about features were the smooth concrete floor and the bright gas lantern that illuminated every corner. In a small wooden box behind the counter, Sile and his wife burned *tularen mayu,* or witches' lavender, a strong yet sweet-smelling incense that doubled as a jinx repellent—to drive bad spirits away from the establishment.

On the first night, the tea shop was so crowded that some customers couldn't find a seat, even with the twelve new metal folding chairs that Sile had bought. The patrons sang songs of praise to the variety of food on the new menu, which included meat pies, brown bread, custard, and Tom

Brown, an imported grain porridge. Some of the patrons even went so far as to thank Sile and his wife for relieving them of "Abongo's nastiness." But wise old Sile, who was as familiar with the street folks' cynicism as he was with the palms of his hands, merely nodded and grinned his sheepish grin. He knew that, despite their praise, and despite the smiles they flashed his way, some customers were at that very moment thinking of ways to cheat him.

While Sile prepared the tea and food, Abeeba served and collected the money. Prior to the shop's reopening, Abeeba had tried to convince her husband that they, too, should adopt Abongo's no-credit policy. Sile had quickly frowned upon the idea, claiming that it was inhumane to do such a thing.

The tea seller and his wife debated the matter for three days before they came to a compromise. They agreed to extend credit, but only in special cases and also on condition that the debtor swear by the Koran to pay on time; if a debtor didn't make a payment, he or she would not be given any credit in the future. But, even with the new policy in place, it wasn't long before some of the customers reverted to their old habits and began skipping payments. Then an encounter between Abeeba and one of the defaulters changed everything.

What took place was this: Samadu, the pugnacious sixteen-year-old whose fame had reached every corner of the city, was the tough guy of Zongo Street. He was of medium height, muscular, and a natural-born athlete. For nine months running, no one in the neighborhood had managed to put Samadu's back to the ground in the haphazard wrestling contests held beside the central market's latrine. Samadu's "power" was such that parents paid him to protect their children from other bullies at school. He was also known for having tortured and even killed the livestock of the adults who denounced him.

If they didn't have pets or domestic animals, he harassed their children for several days until he was appeased with cash or goods. Some parents won Samadu's friendship for their children by bribing him with gifts of money, food, or clothing.

Samadu, of course, was deeply in debt to Mallam Sile—he owed him eighty cedis, about four dollars. Early one Tuesday morning, Mallam Sile's wife showed up at Samadu's house to collect the money. Abeeba had tried to collect the debt amicably, but after her third futile attempt she had suggested to Sile that they use force to persuade the boy to pay. Sile had responded by telling his wife, "Stay out of that boy's way—he is dangerous. If he has decided not to pay, let him keep it. He will be the loser in the end."

"But, Mallam, it is an insult what he is doing," Abeeba argued. "I think people to whom we have been generous should only be generous in return. I am getting fed up with their ways, and the sooner the folks here know that even the toad gets sick of filling his belly with the same dirty pond water every day, the better!" Though Sile wasn't sure what his wife meant, he let the matter drop.

When Abeeba arrived at Samadu's house, a number of housewives and young women were busily doing their morning chores in and around the compound—some sweeping and stirring up dust, others fetching water from the tap in the compound's center or lighting up charcoal pots to warm the food left over from the previous night. Abeeba greeted them politely and asked to be shown to the tough guy's door. The women tried to turn Abeeba away, as they feared that Samadu would humiliate her in some way. But Abeeba insisted that she had important business with him, and so the housewives reluctantly directed her to Samadu's room, which, like all the young men's rooms, was situated just outside the main compound.

The usual tactic that the street's teen-age boys used when fighting girls or women was to strip them of the wrapper around their waist, knowing that they would be reluctant to continue fighting half-naked. But Abeeba had heard young boys in the shop discussing Samadu's bullying ways and had come prepared for anything. She wore a sleeveless shirt and a pair of tight-fitting khaki shorts, and, for the first time ever, she had left her veil at home.

"You rogue! If you call yourself a man, come out and pay your debt!" Abeeba shouted, as she pounded on Samadu's door.

"Who do you think you are, ruining my sleep because of some useless eighty cedis?" Samadu screamed from inside.

"The money may be useless, but it is certainly worthier than you, and that's why you haven't been able to pay, you rubbish heap of a man!" Abeeba's voice was coarse and full of menace. The veins on her neck stood out, like those of the *juju* fighters at the annual wrestling contest. Her eyes moved rapidly inside her head, as though she were having a fit of some sort.

One of the onlookers, a famished-looking housewife, pleaded with the tea seller's wife, "Go back to your house, woman. Don't fight him, he will disgrace you in public." Another woman in the background added, "What kind of a woman thinks she can fight a man? Be careful, oh!"

Abeeba didn't pay any attention to the women's admonitions. Just then, a loud bang was heard inside the room. The door swung open, and Samadu stormed out, his face red with anger. "No one gets away with insulting me. No one!" he shouted. There was a line of dried drool on his right cheek, and whitish mucus had gathered in the corners of his eyes. "You ugly elephant-woman. After I am done with you today, you'll learn a lesson or two about why women don't grow beards!"

"Ha, you teach me a lesson? You?" Abeeba said. "I, too, will educate you about the need to have money in your pocket before you flag the candy man!" With this, she lunged at Samadu.

The women placed their palms on their breasts, and their bodies shook with dread. "Where are the men on the street? Come and separate the fight, oh! Men, come out, oh!" they shouted. The children in the compound, though freshly aroused from sleep, hopped about excitedly, as if they were watching a ritual. Half of them called out, *"Piri pirin-pi,"* while the other half responded, *"Wein son!,"* as they chanted and cheered for Samadu.

Samadu knew immediately that if he engaged Abeeba in a wrestling match she would use her bulky mass to force him to the ground. His strategy, therefore, was to throw punches and kicks from a safe distance, thereby avoiding close contact. But Abeeba was a lot quicker than he imagined, and she managed to dodge the first five punches he threw. He threw a sixth punch, and missed. He stumbled over his own foot when he tried to connect the seventh, and landed inches from Abeeba. With blinding quickness, she seized him by the sleeping wrapper tied around his neck and began to punch him. The exuberant crowd was hushed by this unexpected turn of events.

But Samadu wasn't heralded as the street's tough guy for nothing. He threw a sharp jab at Abeeba's stomach and succeeded in releasing himself from her grip by deftly undoing the knot of his sleeping cloth. He was topless now, clad only in a pair of corduroy knickers. He danced on his feet, swung his arms, and moved his torso from side to side, the way true boxers do. The crowd got excited again and picked up the fight song, *"Piri pirin-pi, Wein son! Piri pirin-pi, Wein son!"* Some among them shouted "Ali! Ali! Ali!" as Samadu danced and pranced, carefully avoiding Abeeba, who watched his movements with the keenness of a hungry lioness.

The women in the crowd went from holding their breasts to slapping their massive thighs. They jumped about nervously, moving their bodies in rhythm to the chants. The boys booed Abeeba, calling her all sorts of names for the beasts of the jungle. "Destroy that elephant!" they shouted.

The harder the crowd cheered for Samadu, the fancier his footwork became. He finally threw a punch that landed on Abeeba's left shoulder, though she seemed completely unfazed and continued to chase him around the small circle created by the spectators. When Samadu next threw his fist, Abeeba anticipated it. She dodged, then grabbed his wrist and twisted his arm with such force that he let out a high-pitched cry: "*Wayyo* Allah!" The crowd gasped as the tough guy attempted to extricate himself from Abeeba's grip. He tightened all the muscles in his body and craned his neck. But her strength was just too much for him.

The crowd booed, "Wooh, ugly rhinoceros." Then, in a sudden, swift motion, Abeeba lifted the tough guy off the ground, raised him above her head (the crowd booed louder), and dumped him back down like a sack of rice. She then jumped on top of him and began to whack him violently.

The women, now frantic, shouted, "Where are the men in this house?" Men, come out, oh! There is a fight!"

A handful of men came running to the scene, followed by many more a few minutes later.

Meanwhile, with each punch Abeeba asked, "Where is our money?"

"I don't have it, and wouldn't pay even if I did!" Samadu responded. The men drew nearer and tried to pull Abeeba off, but her grip on Samadu's waistband was too firm. The men pleaded with Abeeba to let go. "I will not release him until he pays us back our money!" she shouted. "And if he doesn't I'll drag his ass all the way to the Zongo police station."

On hearing this, an elderly man who lived in Samadu's compound ran inside the house; he returned a few minutes later with eighty cedis, which he placed in the palm of Abeeba's free hand. With one hand gripping Samadu's waistband, she used the fingers of the other to flip and count the money. Once she was sure the amount was right, she released the boy, giving him a mean, hard look as she left. The crowd watched silently, mouths agape, as though they had just witnessed something from a cinema reel.

Mallam Sile was still engaged in his morning *zikhr*, or meditation, when Abeeba returned to the shack. He, of course, had no inkling of what had taken place. Later, when Abeeba told him that Samadu had paid the money he owed, the tea seller, though surprised, didn't think to ask how this had happened. In his naïveté, he concluded that Samadu had finally been entered by the love and fear of God. Abeeba's news therefore confirmed Mallam Sile's long-standing belief that every man was capable of goodness, just as he was capable of evil.

The tea seller's belief was further solidified when he ran into Samadu a fortnight later. The tough guy greeted him politely, something he had never done before. When Mallam Sile related this to his wife, she restrained herself from telling him the truth. Abeeba knew that Sile would be quite displeased with her methods. Just a week ago, he had spoken to her about the pointlessness of using fire to put out fire, of how it "worsens rather than extinguishes the original flame." Abeeba prayed that no one else would tell her husband about her duel with Samadu, although the entire city seemed to know about it by now. Tough guys from other neighborhoods came to the tea shop just to steal a glance at the woman who had conquered the tough guy of Zongo Street.

Then one night during the fasting month of Ramadan, some two months after the fight, a voice in Mallam Sile's head asked, "Why is everyone calling my wife 'the man checker'? How come people I give credit to suddenly pay me on time? Why am I being treated with such respect, even by the worst and most stubborn rascals on the street?" Sile was lying in bed with his wife when these questions came to him. But, in his usual fashion, he didn't try to answer them. Instead, he drew in a deep breath and began to pray. He smiled and thanked Allahu-Raheemu, the Merciful One, for curing the street folks of the prejudice they had nursed against him for so long. Mallam Sile also thanked Allah for giving his neighbors the will and the courage to finally accept him just as he was created. He flashed a grin in the darkness and moved closer to his slumbering wife. He buried his small body in her massive, protective frame and soon fell into a deep, dreamless sleep.

Critical Eye

FOR DISCUSSION

a. What commentary is the author making about relying on faith and taking a situation into one's own hands?

b. If Mallam had come to know the truth about why everyone's treatment toward him changed so drastically, could he still consider himself a man?

c. Indeed men hold the power throughout many lands worldwide, but why is it that Mallam, although a man by birthright, is treated with so little respect?

REAPPROACHING THE TEXT

Considering that, generally, women are not celebrated for aggressive or overly "manish" behavior, make the argument that Mallam's wife has overstepped her boundary as a woman.

WRITING ASSIGNMENT

Is it important for a man to assert himself physically in order to be taken seriously?

The Sermon on the Mount

5

And seeing the multitudes, he went up into a mountain: and when he was set, his disciples came unto him:

2 And he opened his mouth, and taught them, saying,

3 Blessed *are* the poor in spirit: for theirs is the kingdom of heaven.

4 Blessed *are* they that mourn: for they shall be comforted.

5 Blessed *are* the meek: for they shall inherit the earth.

6 Blessed *are* they which do hunger and thirst after righteousness: for they shall be filled.

7 Blessed *are* the merciful: for they shall obtain mercy.

8 Blessed *are* the pure in heart: for they shall see God.

9 Blessed *are* the peacemakers: for they shall be called the children of God.

10 Blessed *are* they which are persecuted for righteousness' sake: for theirs is the kingdom of heaven.

11 Blessed are ye, when *men* shall revile you, and persecute *you,* and shall say all manner of evil against you falsely, for my sake.

12 Rejoice, and be exceedingly glad: for great is your reward in heaven: for so persecuted they the prophets which were before you.

13 Ye are the salt of the earth: but if the salt have lost his savor, wherewith shall it be salted? It is thenceforth good for nothing, but to be cast out, and to be trodden under foot of men.

14 Ye are the light of the world. A city that is set on a hill cannot be hid.

15 Neither do men light a candle, and put it under a bushel, but on a candlestick; and it giveth light unto all that are in the house.

16 Let your light so shine before men, that they may see your good works, and glorify your Father which is in heaven.

17 Think not that I am come to destroy the law, or the prophets: I am not come to destroy, but to fulfil.

18 For verily I say unto you, Till heaven and earth pass, one jot or one tittle shall in no wise pass from the law, till all be fulfilled.

19 Whosoever therefore shall break one of these least commandments, and shall teach men so, he shall be called the least in the kingdom of heaven: but whosoever shall do and teach *them,* the same shall be called great in the kingdom of heaven.

20 For I say unto you, That except your righteousness shall exceed *the righteousness* of the scribes and Pharisees, ye shall in no case enter into the kingdom of heaven.

21 Ye have heard that it was said by them of old time, Thou shalt not kill; and whosoever shall kill shall be in danger of the judgment:

22 But I say unto you, That whosoever is angry with his brother without a cause shall be in danger of the judgment: and whosoever shall say to his brother, Raca, shall be in danger of the council: but whosoever shall say, Thou fool, shall be in danger of hell fire.

23 Therefore if thou bring thy gift to the altar, and there rememberest that thy brother hath aught against thee;

24 Leave there thy gift before the altar, and go thy way; first be reconciled to thy brother, and then come and offer thy gift.

25 Agree with thine adversary quickly, while thou art in the way with him; lest at any time the adversary deliver thee to the judge, and the judge deliver thee to the officer, and thou be cast into prison.

26 Verily I say unto thee, Thou shalt by no means come out thence, till thou hast paid the uttermost farthing.

27 Ye have heard that it was said by them of old time, Thou shall not commit adultery:

28 But I say unto you, That whosoever looketh on a woman to lust after her hath committed adultery with her already in his heart.

29 And if thy right eye offend thee, pluck it out, and cast *it* from thee: for it is profitable for thee that one of thy members should perish, and not *that* thy whole body should be cast into hell.

30 And if thy right hand offend thee, cut it off, and cast *it* from thee: for it is profitable for thee that one of thy members should perish, and not *that* thy whole body should be cast into hell.

31 It hath been said, Whosoever shall put away his wife, let him give her a writing of divorcement:

32 But I say unto you, That whosoever shall put away his wife, saving for the cause of fornication, causeth her to commit adultery: and whosoever shall marry her that is divorced committeth adultery.

33 Again, ye have heard that it hath been said by them of old time, Thou shall not forswear thyself, but shalt perform unto the Lord thine oaths:

34 But I say unto you, Swear not at all; neither by heaven; for it is God's throne:

35 Nor by the earth; for it is his footstool: neither by Jerusalem; for it is the city of the great King.

36 Neither shalt thou swear by thy head, because thou canst not make one hair white or black.

37 But let your communication be, Yea, yea; Nay, nay: for whatsoever is more than these cometh of evil.

38 Ye have heard that it hath been said, An eye for an eye, and a tooth for a tooth:

39 But I say unto you, That ye resist not evil: but whosoever shall smite thee on thy right cheek, turn to him the other also.

40 And if any man will sue thee at the law, and take away thy coat, let him have *thy* cloak also.

41 And whosoever shall compel thee to go a mile, go with him twain.

42 Give to him that asketh thee, and from him that would borrow of thee turn not thou away.

43 Ye have heard that it hath been said, Thou shalt love thy neighbor, and hate thine enemy.

44 But I say unto you, Love your enemies, bless them that curse you, do good to them that hate you, and pray for them which despitefully use you, and persecute you;

45 That ye may be the children of your Father which is in heaven: for he maketh his sun to rise on the evil and on the good, and sendeth rain on the just and on the unjust.

46 For if ye love them which love you, what reward have ye? do not even the publicans do the same?

47 And if ye salute your brethren only, what do ye more *than others?* do not even the publicans so?

48 Be ye therefore perfect, even as your Father which is in heaven is perfect.

6

Take heed that ye do not do your alms before men, to be seen of them: otherwise ye have no reward of your Father which is in heaven.

2 Therefore when thou doest *thine* alms, do not sound a trumpet before thee, as the hypocrites do in the synagogues and in the streets, that they may have glory of men. Verily I say unto you, They have their reward.

3 But when thou doest alms, let not thy left hand know what thy right hand doeth:

4 That thine alms may be in secret: and thy Father which seeth in secret himself shall reward thee openly.

5 And when thou prayest, thou shalt not be as the hypocrites *are:* for they love to pray standing in the synagogues and in the corners of the streets, that they may be seen of men. Verily I say unto you, They have their reward.

6 But thou, when thou prayest, enter into thy closet, and when thou hast shut thy door, pray to thy Father which is in secret, and thy Father which seeth in secret shall reward thee openly.

7 But when ye pray, use not vain repetitions, as the heathen *do:* for they think that they shall be heard for their much speaking.

8 Be not ye therefore like unto them: for your Father knoweth what things ye have need of, before ye ask him.

9 After this manner therefore pray ye: Our father which art in heaven, Hallowed be thy name.

10 Thy kingdom come. Thy will be done in earth, as it *is* in heaven.

11 Give us this day our daily bread.

12 And forgive us our debts, as we forgive our debtors.

13 And lead us not into temptation, but deliver us from evil: For thine is the kingdom, and the power, and the glory, for ever. Amen.

14 For if ye forgive men their trespasses, your heavenly Father will also forgive you:

15 But if ye forgive not men their trespasses, neither will your Father forgive your trespasses.

16 Moreover when ye fast, be not, as the hypocrites, of a sad countenance: for they disfigure their faces, that they may appear unto men to fast. Verily I say unto you, They have their reward.

17 But thou, when thou fastest, anoint thine head, and wash thy face;

18 That thou appear not unto men to fast, but unto thy Father which is in secret: and thy Father which seeth in secret shall reward thee openly.

19 Lay not up for yourselves treasures upon earth, where moth and rust doth corrupt, and where thieves break through and steal:

20 But lay up for yourselves treasures in heaven, where neither moth nor rust doth corrupt, and where thieves do not break through nor steal:

21 For where your treasure is, there will your heart be also.

22 The light of the body is the eye: if therefore thine eye be single, thy whole body shall be full of light.

23 But if thine eye be evil, thy whole body shall be full of darkness. If therefore the light that is in thee be darkness, how great is that darkness!

24 No man can serve two masters: for either he will hate the one, and love the other; or else he will hold to the one, and despise the other. Ye cannot serve God and mammon.

25 Therefore I say unto you, Take no thought for your life, what ye shall eat, or what ye shall drink; nor yet for your body, what ye shall put on. Is not the life more than meat, and the body than raiment?

26 Behold the fowls of the air: for they sow not, neither do they reap, nor gather into barns; yet your heavenly Father feedeth them. Are ye not much better than they?

27 Which of you by taking thought can add one cubit unto his stature?

28 And why take ye thought for raiment? Consider the lilies of the field, how they grow; they toil not, neither do they spin:

29 And yet I say unto you, That even Solomon in all his glory was not arrayed like one of these.

30 Wherefore, if God so clothe the grass of the field, which today is, and tomorrow is cast into the oven, *shall he* not much more *clothe* you, O ye of little faith?

31 Therefore take no thought, saying, What shall we eat? or, What shall we drink? or, Wherewithal shall we be clothed?

32 (For after all these things do the Gentiles seek:) for your heavenly Father knoweth that ye have need of all these things.

33 But seek ye first the kingdom of God, and his righteousness; and all these things shall be added unto you.

34 Take therefore no thought for the morrow: for the morrow shall take thought for the things of itself. Sufficient unto the day *is* the evil thereof.

7

Judge not, that ye be not judged.

2 For with what judgment ye judge, ye shall be judged: and with what measure ye mete, it shall be measured to you again.

3 And why beholdest thou the mote that is in thy brother's eye, but considerest not the beam that is in thine own eye?

4 Or how wilt thou say to thy brother, Let me pull out the mote out of thine eye; and, behold, a beam *is* in thine own eye?

5 Thou hypocrite, first cast out the beam out of thine own eye; and then shalt thou see clearly to cast out the mote out of thy brother's eye.

6 Give not that which is holy unto the dogs, neither cast ye your pearls before swine, lest they trample them under their feet, and turn again and rend you.

7 Ask, and it shall be given you; seek, and ye shall find; knock, and it shall be opened unto you:

8 For every one that asketh receiveth; and he that seeketh findeth; and to him that knocketh it shall be opened.

9 Or what man is there of you, whom if his son ask bread, will he give him a stone?

10 Or if he ask a fish, will he give him a serpent?

11 If ye then, being evil, know how to give good gifts unto your children, how much more shall your Father which is in heaven give good things to them that ask him?

12 Therefore all things whatsoever ye would that men should do to you, do ye even so to them: for this is the law and the prophets.

13 Enter ye in at the strait gate: for wide *is* the gate, and broad *is* the way, that leadeth to destruction, and many there be which go in thereat:

14 Because strait *is* the gate, and narrow *is* the way, which leadeth unto life, and few there be that find it.

15 Beware of false prophets, which come to you in sheep's clothing, but inwardly they are ravening wolves.

16 Ye shall know them by their fruits. Do men gather grapes of thorns, or figs of thistles?

17 Even so every good tree bringeth forth good fruit; but a corrupt tree bringeth forth evil fruit.

18 A good tree cannot bring forth evil fruit, neither *can* a corrupt tree bring forth good fruit.

19 Every tree that bringeth not forth good fruit is hewn down, and cast into the fire.

20 Wherefore by their fruits ye shall know them.

21 Not every one that saith unto me, Lord, Lord, shall enter into the kingdom of heaven; but he that doeth the will of my Father which is in heaven.

22 Many will say to me in that day, Lord, Lord, have we not prophesied in thy name? and in thy name have cast out devils? and in thy name done many wonderful works?

23 And then will I profess unto them, I never knew you: depart from me, ye that work iniquity.

24 Therefore whosoever heareth these sayings of mine, and doeth them, I will liken him unto a wise man, which built his house upon a rock:

25 And the rain descended, and the floods came, and the winds blew, and beat upon that house; and it fell not: for it was founded upon a rock.

26 And every one that heareth these sayings of mine, and doeth them not, shall be likened unto a foolish man, which built his house upon the sand:

27 And the rain descended, and the floods came, and the winds blew, and beat upon that house; and it fell: and great was the fall of it.

28 And it came to pass, when Jesus had ended these sayings, the people were astonished at his doctrine:

29 For he taught them as *one* having authority, and not as the scribes.

Critical Eye

FOR DISCUSSION

a. One goal of this speech is to promise a sense of judgment and justice. To whom are the judgment and justice promised, and why were these images so important to convey?

b. Why is it so very important for human beings to believe that there is another world that is better than this one?

REAPPROACHING THE TEXT

Read this text alongside the selection from the Koran. What are the similarities?

WRITING ASSIGNMENT

What would be the value of people using their diverging faiths to bring them together as opposed to keeping them separate?

The Prophet Mohammed

From
The Koran

THE BELIEVER

In the Name of God, the Compassionate, the Merciful

Hāmōn. This Book is revealed by God, the Mighty One, the All-knowing, who forgives sin and accepts repentance.

His punishment is stern, and His bounty infinite. There is no god but Him. All shall return to Him.

None but the unbelievers dispute the revelations of God. Do not be deceived by their prosperous dealings in the land. Long before them the people of Noah denied Our revelations, and so did the factions after them. Every nation strove to slay their apostle, seeking with false arguments to refute the truth; but I smote them, and how stern was My punishment! Thus shall the word of your Lord be fulfilled concerning the unbelievers: they are the heirs of the Fire.

Those who bear the Throne and those who stand around it give glory to their Lord and believe in Him. They implore forgiveness for the faithful, saying: "Lord, you embrace all things with Your mercy and Your knowledge. Forgive those that repent and follow Your path. Shield them from the scourge of Hell. Admit them, Lord, to the gardens of Eden which You have promised them, together with all the righteous among their fathers, their spouses, and their descendants. You are the Almighty, the Wise One. Deliver them from all evil. He whom You will deliver from evil on that day will surely earn Your mercy. That is the supreme triumph."

But to the unbelievers a voice will cry: "God's abhorrence of you is greater than your hatred of yourselves. You were called to the Faith, but you denied it."

They shall say: "Lord, twice have You made us die, and twice have You given us life. We now confess our sins. Is there no way out?"

"The Believer" from *The Koran* translated by N. J. Dawood (Penguin Classics 1956, Fifth revised edition 1990). Copyright © N. J. Daewood, 1956, 1959, 1966, 1968, 1974, 1990, 1993, 1997, 1999, 2003. Reproduced by permission of Penguin Books Ltd.

They shall be answered: "This is because when God was invoked alone, you disbelieved; but when you were bidden to serve other gods besides Him you believed in them. Today judgement rests with God, the Most High, the Supreme One."

It is He who reveals His signs to you, and sends down sustenance from the sky for you. Yet none takes heed except the repentant. Pray, then, to God and worship none but Him, however much the unbelievers may dislike it.

Exalted and throned on high, He lets the Spirit descend at His behest on those of His servants whom He chooses, that He may warn them of the day when they shall meet Him; the day when they shall rise up from their graves with nothing hidden from God. And who shall reign supreme on that day? God, the One, the Almighty.

On that day every soul shall be paid back according to what it did. On that day none shall be wronged. Swift is God's reckoning.

Forewarn them of the approaching day, when men's hearts will leap up to their throats and choke them; when the wrongdoers will have neither friend nor intercessor to be heard. He knows the furtive look and the secret thought. God will judge with fairness, but the idols to which they pray besides Him can judge nothing. God alone hears all and observes all.

Have they never journeyed through the land and seen what was the end of those who have gone before them, nations far greater in prowess and in splendour? God scourged them for their sins, and from God they had none to protect them. That was because their apostles had come to them with clear revelations and they denied them. So God smote them. Mighty is God, and stern His retribution.

We sent forth Moses with Our signs and with clear authority to Pharaoh, Haman, and Korah. But they said: "A sorcerer, a teller of lies."

And when he brought them the Truth from Ourself, they said: "Put to death the sons of those who share his faith, and spare only their daughters." Futile were the schemes of the unbelievers.

Pharaoh said: "Let me slay Moses, and then let him invoke his god! I fear that he will change your religion and spread disorder in the land."

Moses said: "I take refuge in my Lord and in your Lord from every tyrant who denies the Day of Reckoning."

But one of Pharaoh's kinsmen, who in secret was a true believer, said: "Would you slay a man merely because he says: 'My Lord is God'?" He has brought you evident signs from your Lord. If he is lying, may his lie be on his head; but if he is speaking the truth, a part at least of what he threatens will smite you. God does not guide the lying transgressor. Today you are the masters, my people, illustrious throughout the earth. But who will save us from the might of God when it bears down upon us?"

Pharaoh said: "I have told you what I think. I will surely guide you to the right path."

He who was a true believer said: "I warn you, my people, against the fate which overtook the factions: the people of Noah, 'Ad, and Thamūd, and those that came after them. God does not seek to wrong His servants.

"I warn you, my people, against the day when men will cry out to one another, when you will turn and flee, with none to defend you against God. He whom God confounds shall have none to guide him. Long before this, Joseph came to you with veritable signs, but you never ceased to doubt them; and when he died you said: 'After him God will never send another apostle.' Thus God confounds the doubting transgressor. Those who dispute God's revelations, with no authority vouchsafed to them, are held in deep abhorrence by God and by the faithful. Thus God seals up the heart of every scornful tyrant."

Pharaoh said to Haman: "Build me a tower that I may reach the highways—the very highways—of the heavens, and look upon the god of Moses. I am convinced that he is lying."

Thus was Pharaoh seduced by his foul deeds, and he was turned away from the right path. Pharaoh's cunning led to nothing but perdition.

He who was a true believer said: "Follow me, my people, that I may guide you to the right path. My people, the life of this world is a fleeting comfort, but the life to come is an everlasting mansion. Those that do evil shall be rewarded with like evil; but those that have faith and do good works, both men and women, shall enter the gardens of Paradise and therein receive blessings without number.

"My people, how is it that I call you to salvation, while you call me to the Fire? You bid me deny God and serve other gods I know nothing of; while I exhort you to serve the Almighty, the Benignant One. Indeed, the gods to whom you call me can be invoked neither in this world nor in the hereafter. To God we shall return. The transgressors are the heirs of the Fire.

"Bear in mind what I have told you. To God I commend myself. God is cognizant of all His servants."

God delivered him from the evils which they planned, and a grievous scourge encompassed Pharaoh's people. They shall be brought before the

Fire morning and evening, and on the day the Hour strikes, a voice will cry: "Mete out to the people of Pharaoh the sternest punishment!"

And when they argue in the Fire, the humble will say to those who deemed themselves mighty: "We have been your followers: will you now ward off from us some of these flames?" But those who deemed themselves mighty will reply: "Here are all of us now. God has judged His servants."

And those in the Fire will say to the keepers of Hell: "Implore your Lord to relieve our torment for one day!"

"But did your apostles not come to you with undoubted signs?" they will ask.

"Yes," they will answer. And their keepers will say: "Then offer your prayers." But vain shall be the prayers of the unbelievers.

We shall help Our apostles and the true believers both in this world and on the day when the witnesses rise to testify. On that day no excuse will avail the guilty. The Curse shall be their lot, and the scourge of the hereafter.

We gave Moses Our guidance and the Israelites the Book to inherit: a guide and an admonition to men of understanding. Therefore have patience; God's promise is surely true. Implore forgiveness for your sins, and celebrate the praise of your Lord evening and morning.

As for those who dispute the revelations of God, with no authority vouchsafed to them, they nurture in their hearts ambitions they shall never attain. Therefore seek refuge in God; it is He that hears all and observes all.

Surely, the creation of the heavens and the earth is greater than the creation of man; yet most men have no knowledge.

The blind and the seeing are not equal, nor are the wicked the equal of those that have faith and do good works. Yet do you seldom give thought.

The Hour of Doom is sure to come: of this there is no doubt; and yet most men do not believe.

Your Lord has said: "Call on me and I will answer you. Those that disdain My service shall enter Hell with all humility."

It was God who made for you the night to rest in and the day to give you light. God is bountiful to men, yet most men do not give thanks.

Such is God your Lord, the Creator of all things. There is no god but Him. How then can you turn away from Him? Yet even thus the men who deny God's revelations turn away from Him.

It is God who has made the earth a dwelling-place for you, and the sky a ceiling. He has moulded your bodies into a comely shape and provided you with good things.

Such is God, your Lord. Blessed be God, Lord of the Universe.

He is the Living One; there is no god but Him. Pray to Him, then, and worship none besides Him. Praise be to God, Lord of the Universe!

Say: "I am forbidden to serve your idols, now that clear proofs have been given me from my Lord. I am commanded to surrender myself to the Lord of the Universe."

It was He who created you from dust, then from a little germ, and then from a clot of blood. He brings you infants into the world; you reach manhood, then decline into old age (though some of you die young), so that you may complete your appointed term and grow in wisdom.

It is He who ordains life and death. If He decrees a thing, He need only say: "Be," and it is.

Do you not see how those who dispute the revelations of God turn away from the right path? Those who have denied the Book and the message We sent through Our apostles shall realize the truth hereafter: when, with chains and shackles round their necks, they shall be dragged through scalding water and burnt in the fire of Hell.

They will be asked: "Where are the gods whom you have served besides God?"

"They have forsaken us," they will reply. "Indeed, they were nothing, those gods to whom we prayed." Thus God confounds the unbelievers.

And they will be told: "That is because on earth you took delight in falsehoods, and led a wanton life. Enter the gates of Hell and stay therein for ever. Evil is the home of the arrogant."

Therefore have patience: God's promise is surely true. Whether We let you[1] glimpse in some measure the scourge We threaten them with, or call you back to Us before We smite them, to Us they shall return.

We sent forth other apostles before your time; of some We have already told you, of others We have not yet told you. None of those apostles could bring a sign except by God's leave. And when God's will was done, justice prevailed and there and then the disbelievers lost.

It is God who has provided you with beasts, that you may ride on some and eat the flesh of others. You put them to many uses; they take you where you wish to go, carrying you by land as ships carry you by sea.

He reveals to you His signs. Which of God's signs do you deny?

Have they never journeyed through the land and seen what was the end of those who have gone before them? More numerous were they in the land, and far greater in prowess and in splendour; yet all their labours proved of no avail to them.

When their apostles brought them veritable signs they proudly boasted of their own knowledge; but soon the scourge at which they scoffed encompassed them. And when they beheld Our might they said: "We now believe in God alone. We deny the idols which We served besides Him."

But their new faith was of no use to them, when they beheld Our might: such being the way of God with His creatures; and there and then the unbelievers lost.

Critical Eye

FOR DISCUSSION

a. Are there any similarities between Islam and Christianity?

b. How important is faith to an individual's development?

REAPPROACHING THE TEXT

For nations where Islam is the dominant religion there is no separation between the ruling/political body or the faith that governs the land. How does that compare with a country such as the United States, where we have a separation between church and state?

WRITING ASSIGNMENT

Why, in your opinion, does there appear to be such conflict between Islam and other faiths?

Thomas Paine

Age of Reason

Part I

Luxembourg, 8th Pluviose, Second Year of the French Republic, one and indivisible. January 27, O. S. 1794.

To My Fellow-Citizens of the United States of America:

> *I put the following work under your protection. It contains my opinions upon Religion. You will do me the justice to remember, that I have always strenuously supported the Right of every Man to his own opinion, however different that opinion might be to mine. He who denies to another this right, makes a slave of himself to his present opinion, because he precludes himself the right of changing it.*
>
> *The most formidable weapon against errors of every kind is Reason. I have never used any other, and I trust I never shall.*
>
> *Your affectionate friend and fellow-citizen,*
>
> *Thomas Paine*

It has been my intention, for several years past, to publish my thoughts upon religion. I am well aware of the difficulties that attend the subject, and from that consideration, had reserved it to a more advanced period of life. I intended it to be the last offering I should make to my fellow-citizens of all nations, and that at a time when the purity of the motive that induced me to it, could not admit of a question, even by those who might disapprove the work.

The circumstance that has now taken place in France, of the total abolition of the whole national order of priesthood, and of everything appertaining to compulsive systems of religion, and compulsive articles of faith, has not only precipitated my intention, but rendered a work of this kind exceedingly necessary, lest in the general wreck of superstition, of false systems of government, and false theology, we lose sight of morality, of humanity, and of the theology that is true.

As several of my colleagues, and others of my fellow-citizens of France have given me the example of making their voluntary and individual profession of faith, I also will make mine; and I do this with all that sincerity and frankness with which the mind of man communicates with itself.

I believe in one God, and no more; and I hope for happiness beyond this life.

I believe in the equality of man; and I believe that religious duties consist in doing justice, loving mercy, and endeavoring to make our fellow-creatures happy.

But, lest it should be supposed that I believe many other things in addition to these, I shall, in the progress of this work, declare the things I do not believe, and my reasons for not believing them.

I do not believe in the creed professed by the Jewish church, by the Roman church, by the Greek church, by the Turkish church, by the Protestant church, nor by any church that I know of. My own mind is my own church.

All national institutions of churches, whether Jewish, Christian or Turkish, appear to me no other than human inventions set up to terrify and enslave mankind, and monopolize power and profit.

I do not mean by this declaration to condemn those who believe otherwise; they have the same right to their belief as I have to mine. But it is necessary to the happiness of man, that he be mentally faithful to himself. Infidelity does not consist in believing, or in disbelieving; it consists in professing to believe what he does not believe.

It is impossible to calculate the moral mischief, if I may so express it, that mental lying has produced in society. When a man has so far corrupted and prostituted the chastity of his mind, as to subscribe his professional belief to things he does not believe, he has prepared himself for the commission of every other crime. He takes up the trade of a priest for the sake of gain, and in order to qualify himself for that trade, he begins with a perjury. Can we conceive any thing more destructive to morality than this?

Soon after I had published the pamphlet Common Sense, in America, I saw the exceeding probability that a revolution in the system of government would be followed by a revolution in the system of religion. The adulterous connection of church and state, wherever it had taken place, whether Jewish, Christian, or Turkish, had so effectually prohibited by pains and penalties, every discussion upon established creeds, and upon first principles of religion, that until the system of government should be changed, those subjects could not be brought fairly and openly before the world; but that whenever this should be done, a revolution in the system of religion would follow. Human inventions and priestcraft would be detected; and man would return to the pure, unmixed and unadulterated belief of one God, and no more.

Every national church or religion has established itself by pretending some special mission from God, communicated to certain individuals. The Jews have their Moses; the Christians their Jesus Christ, their apostles and saints; and the Turks their Mahomet, as if the way to God was not open to every man alike.

Each of those churches shows certain books, which they call revelation, or the word of God. The Jews say that their word of God was given by God to Moses, face to face; the Christians say, that their word of God came by divine inspiration; and the Turks say, that their word of God (the Koran) was brought by an angel from Heaven. Each of those churches accuses the other of unbelief; and for my own part, I disbelieve them all.

As it is necessary to affix right ideas to words, I will, before I proceed further into the subject, offer some observations on the word revelation. Revelation, when applied to religion, means something communicated immediately from God to man.

No one will deny or dispute the power of the Almighty to make such a communication, if he pleases. But admitting, for the sake of a case, that something has been revealed to a certain person, and not revealed to any other person, it is revelation to that person only. When he tells it to a second person, a second to a third, a third to a fourth, and so on, it ceases to be a revelation to all those persons. It is revelation to the first person only, and hearsay to every other, and consequently they are not obliged to believe it.

It is a contradiction in terms and ideas, to call anything a revelation that comes to us at second-hand, either verbally or in writing. Revelation is necessarily limited to the first communication—after this, it is only an account of something which that person says was a revelation made to him; and though he may find himself obliged to believe it, it cannot be incumbent on me to believe it in the same manner; for it was not a revelation made to me, and I have only his word for it that it was made to him.

When Moses told the children of Israel that he received the two tables of the commandments from the hand of God, they were not obliged to believe him, because they had no other authority for it than his telling them so; and I have no other authority for it than some historian telling me so. The commandments carrying no internal evidence of divinity with them; they contain some good moral precepts, such as any man qualified to be a lawgiver, or a legislator, could produce himself, without having recourse to supernatural intervention.*

> *It is, however, necessary to except the declamation which says that God visits the sins of the fathers upon the children it is contrary to every principle of moral justice.

When I am told that the Koran was written in Heaven, and brought to Mahomet by an angel, the account comes too near the same kind of hearsay evidence and second-hand authority as the former. I did not see the angel myself, and, therefore, I have a right not to believe it.

When also I am told that a woman, called the Virgin Mary, said, or gave out, that she was with child without any cohabitation with a man, and that her betrothed husband, Joseph, said that an angel told him so, I have a right to believe them or not; such a circumstance required a much stronger evidence than their bare word for it; but we have not even this—for neither Joseph nor Mary wrote any such matter themselves—it is only reported by others that they said so—it is hearsay upon hearsay, and I do not chose to rest my belief upon such evidence.

It is, however, not difficult to account for the credit that was given to the story of Jesus Christ being the son of God. He was born when the heathen mythology had still some fashion and repute in the world, and that mythology had prepared the people for the belief of such a story. Almost all the extraordinary men that lived under the heathen mythology were reputed to be the sons of some of their gods. It was not a new thing, at that time, to believe a man to have been celestially begotten; the intercourse of gods with women was then a matter of familiar opinion. Their Jupiter, according to their accounts, had cohabited with hundreds: the story, therefore, had nothing in it either new, wonderful, or obscene; it was conformable to the opinions that then prevailed among the people called Gentiles, or Mythologists, and it was those people only that believed it. The Jews who had kept strictly to the belief of one God, and no more, and who had always rejected the heathen mythology, never credited the story.

It is curious to observe how the theory of what is called the Christian Church sprung out of the tail of the heathen mythology. A direct incorporation took place in the first instance, by making the reputed founder to be celestially begotten. The trinity of gods that then followed was no other than a reduction of the former plurality, which was about twenty or thirty thousand; the statue of Mary succeeded the statue of Diana of Ephesus; the deification of heroes changed into the canonization of saints; the Mythologists had gods for everything; the Christian Mythologists had saints for everything; the church became as crowded with the one, as the Pantheon had been with the other, and Rome was the place of both. The Christian theory is little else than the idolatry of the ancient Mythologists, accommodated to the purposes of power and revenue; and it yet remains to reason and philosophy to abolish the amphibious fraud.

Nothing that is here said can apply, even with the most distant disrespect, to the real character of Jesus Christ. He was a virtuous and an amiable man. The morality that he preached and practiced was of the most benevolent kind; and though similar systems of morality had been preached by Confucius, and by some of the Greek philosophers, many years before; by the Quakers since; and by many good men in all ages, it has not been exceeded by any.

Jesus Christ wrote no account of himself, of his birth, parentage, or anything else; not a line of what is called the New Testament is of his writing. The history of him is altogether the work of other people; and as to the account given of his resurrection and ascension, it was the necessary counterpart to the story of his birth. His historians having brought him into the world in a supernatural manner, were obliged to take him out again in the same manner, or the first part of the story must have fallen to the ground.

The wretched contrivance with which this latter part is told exceeds every thing that went before it. The first part, that of the miraculous conception, was not a thing that admitted of publicity; and therefore the tellers of this part of the story had this advantage, that though they might not be credited, they could not be detected. They could not be expected to prove it, because it was not one of those things that admitted of proof, and it was impossible that the person of whom it was told could prove it himself.

But the resurrection of a dead person from the grave, and his ascension through the air, is a thing very different as to the evidence it admits of, to the invisible conception of a child in the womb. The resurrection and ascension, supposing them to have taken place, admitted of public and ocular demonstration, like that of the ascension of a balloon, or the sun at noon-day, to all Jerusalem at least. A thing which everybody is required to believe, requires that the proof and evidence of it should be equal to all, and universal; and as the public visibility of this last related act was the only evidence that could give sanction to the former part, the whole of it falls to the ground, because that evidence never was given. Instead of this, a small number of persons, not more than eight or nine, are introduced as proxies for the whole world, to say they saw it, and all the rest of the world are called upon to believe it. But it appears that Thomas did not believe the resurrection, and, as they say, would not believe without having ocular and manual demonstration himself. So neither will I, and the reason is equally as good for me, and for every other person, as for Thomas.

It is in vain to attempt to palliate or disguise this matter. The story, so far as relates to the supernatural part, has every mark of fraud and imposition stamped upon the face of it. Who were the authors of it is as impossible for us now to know, as it is for us to be assured that the books in which the account is related were written by the persons whose names they bear; the best surviving evidence we now have respecting this affair is the Jews. They are regularly descended from the people who lived in the times this resurrection and ascension is said to have happened, and they say, it is not true. It has long appeared to me a strange inconsistency to cite the Jews as a proof of the truth of the story. It is just the same as if a man were to say, I will prove the truth of what I have told you, by producing the people who say it is false.

That such a person as Jesus Christ existed, and that he was crucified, which was the mode of execution at that day, are historical relations strictly within the limits of probability. He preached most excellent morality, and the equality of man; but he preached also against the corruptions and avarice of the Jewish priests, and this brought upon him the hatred and vengeance of the whole order of priesthood. The accusation which those priests brought against him was that of sedition and conspiracy against the Roman government, to which the Jews were then subject and tributary; and it is not improbable that the Roman government might have some secret apprehensions of the effects of his doctrine, as well as the Jewish priests; neither is it improbable that Jesus Christ had in contemplation the delivery of the Jewish nation from the bondage of the Romans. Between the two, however, this virtuous reformer and revolutionist lost his life. It is upon this plain narrative of facts, together with another case I am going to mention, that the Christian Mythologists, calling themselves the Christian Church, have erected their fable, which, for absurdity and extravagance, is not exceeded by anything that is to be found in the mythology of the ancients.

The ancient Mythologists tell us that the race of Giants made war against Jupiter, and that one of them threw a hundred rocks against him at one throw; that Jupiter defeated him with thunder, and confined him afterwards under Mount Etna, and that every time the Giant turns himself Mount Etna belches fire.

It is here easy to see that the circumstance of the mountain, that of its being a volcano, suggested the idea of the fable; and that the fable is made to fit and wind itself up with that circumstance.

The Christian mythologists tell us that their Satan made war against the Almighty, who defeated him, and confined him afterward, not under a mountain, but in a pit. It is here easy to see that the first fable suggested the idea of the second; for the fable of Jupiter and the Giants was told many hundred years before that of Satan. Thus far the ancient and the Christian Mythologists differ very little from each other. But the latter have contrived to carry the matter much farther. They have contrived to connect the fabulous part of the story of Jesus Christ with the fable originating from Mount Etna; and in order to make all the parts of the story tie together, they have taken to their aid the traditions of the Jews; for the Christian mythology is made up partly from the ancient mythology and partly from the Jewish traditions.

The Christian Mythologists, after having confined Satan in a pit, were obliged to let him out again to bring on the sequel of the fable. He is then introduced into the Garden of Eden in the shape of a snake or a serpent, and in that shape he enters into familiar conversation with Eve, who is no way surprised to hear a snake talk; and the issue of this tete-a-tete is that he persuades her to eat an apple, and the eating of that apple damns all mankind.

After giving Satan this triumph over the whole creation, one would have supposed that the Church Mythologists would have been kind enough to send him back again to the pit; or, if they had not done this, that they would have put a mountain upon him (for they say that their faith can remove a mountain), or have put him under a mountain, as the former mythologists had done, to prevent his getting again among the women and doing more mischief. But instead of this they leave him at large, without even obliging him to give his parole—the secret of which is, that they could not do without him; and after being at the trouble of making him, they bribed him to stay. They promised him ALL the Jews, ALL the Turks by anticipation, nine-tenths of the world beside, and Mahomet into the bargain. After this, who can doubt the bountifulness of the Christian Mythology?

Having thus made an insurrection and a battle in Heaven, in which none of the combatants could be either killed or wounded—put Satan into the pit—let him out again—giving him a triumph over the whole creation—damned all mankind by the eating of an apple, these Christian Mythologists bring the two ends of their fable together. They represent this virtuous and amiable man, Jesus Christ, to be at once both God and

Man, and also the Son of God, celestially begotten, on purpose to be sacrificed, because they say that Eve in her longing had eaten an apple.

Putting aside everything that might excite laughter by its absurdity, or detestation by its profaneness, and confining ourselves merely to an examination of the parts, it is impossible to conceive a story more derogatory to the Almighty, more inconsistent with his wisdom, more contradictory to his power, than this story is. In order to make for it a foundation to rise upon, the inventors were under the necessity of giving to the being whom they call Satan, a power equally as great, if not greater, than they attribute to the Almighty. They have not only given him the power of liberating himself from the pit, after what they call his fall, but they have made that power increase afterward to infinity. Before this fall they represent him only as an angel of limited existence, as they represent the rest. After his fall, he becomes, by their account, omnipresent. He exists everywhere, and at the same time. He occupies the whole immensity of space.

Not content with this deification of Satan, they represent him as defeating, by stratagem, in the shape of an animal of the creation, all the power and wisdom of the Almighty. They represent him as having compelled the Almighty to the direct necessity either of surrendering the whole of the creation to the government and sovereignty of this Satan, or of capitulating for its redemption by coming down upon earth, and exhibiting himself upon a cross in the shape of a man.

Had the inventors of this story told it the contrary way, that is, had they represented the Almighty as compelling Satan to exhibit himself on a cross, in the shape of a snake, as a punishment for his new transgression, the story would have been less absurd—less contradictory. But instead of this, they make the transgressor triumph, and the Almighty fall.

That many good men have believed this strange fable, and lived very good lives under that belief (for credulity is not a crime), is what I have no doubt of. In the first place, they were educated to believe it, and they would have believed anything else in the same manner. There are also many who have been so enthusiastically enraptured by what they conceived to be the infinite love of God to man, in making a sacrifice of himself, that the vehemence of the idea has forbidden and deterred them from examining into the absurdity and profaneness of the story. The more unnatural anything is, the more is it capable of becoming the object of dismal admiration.

But if objects for gratitude and admiration are our desire, do they not present themselves every hour to our eyes? Do we not see a fair creation prepared to receive us the instant we are born—a world furnished to our hands, that cost us nothing? Is it we that light up the sun, that pour down the rain, and fill the earth with abundance? Whether we sleep or wake, the vast machinery of the universe still goes on. Are these things, and the blessings they indicate in future, nothing to us? Can our gross feelings be excited by no other subjects than tragedy and suicide? Or is the gloomy pride of man become so intolerable, that nothing can flatter it but a sacrifice of the Creator?

I know that this bold investigation will alarm many, but it would be paying too great a compliment to their credulity to forbear it on that account; the times and the subject demand it to be done. The suspicion that the theory of what is called the Christian Church is fabulous is becoming very extensive in all countries; and it will be a consolation to men staggering under that suspicion, and doubting what to believe and what to disbelieve, to see the subject freely investigated. I therefore pass on to an examination of the books called the Old and the New Testament.

These books, beginning with Genesis and ending with Revelation (which, by the by, is a book of riddles that requires a revelation to explain it) are, we are told, the word of God. It is, therefore, proper for us to know who told us so, that we may know what credit to give to the report. The answer to this question is, that nobody can tell, except that we tell one another so. The case, however, historically appears to be as follows:

When the church mythologists established their system, they collected all the writings they could find, and managed them as they pleased. It is a matter altogether of uncertainty to us whether such of the writings as now appear under the name of the Old and New Testament are in the same state in which those collectors say they found them, or whether they added, altered, abridged, or dressed them up.

Be this as it may, they decided by vote which of the books out of the collection they had made should be the WORD OF GOD, and which should not. They rejected several; they voted others to be doubtful, such as the books called the Apocrypha; and those books which had a majority of votes, were voted to be the word of God. Had they voted otherwise, all the people, since calling themselves Christians, had believed otherwise—for the belief of the one comes from the vote of the other. Who the people were that did all this, we know nothing of; they called themselves by the general name of the Church and this is all we know of the matter.

As we have no other external evidence or authority for believing these books to be the word of God than what I have mentioned, which is no evidence or authority at all, I come, in the next place, to examine the internal evidence contained in the books themselves. In the former part of this Essay, I have spoken of revelation; I now proceed further with that subject, for the purpose of applying it to the books in question.

Revelation is a communication of something which the person to whom that thing is revealed did not know before. For if I have done a thing, or seen it done, it needs no revelation to tell me I have done it, or seen it, nor to enable me to tell it, or to write it.

Revelation, therefore, cannot be applied to anything done upon earth, of which man is himself the actor or the witness; and consequently all the historical and anecdotal parts of the Bible, which is almost the whole of it, is not within the meaning and compass of the word revelation, and, therefore, is not the word of God.

When Samson ran off with the gate-posts of Gaza, if he ever did so (and whether he did or not is nothing to us), or when he visited his Delilah, or caught his foxes, or did any thing else, what has revelation to do with these things? If they were facts, he could tell them himself or his secretary, if he kept one, could write them, if they were worth either telling or writing; and if they were fictions, revelation could not make them true; and whether true or not, we are neither the better nor the wiser for knowing them. When we contemplate the immensity of that Being who directs and governs the incomprehensible WHOLE, of which the utmost ken of human sight can discover but a part, we ought to feel shame at calling such paltry stories the word of God.

As to the account of the Creation, with which the Book of Genesis opens, it has all the appearance of being a tradition which the Israelites had among them before they came into Egypt; and after their departure from that country they put it at the head of their history, without telling (as it is most probable) that they did not know how they came by it. The manner in which the account opens, shows it to be traditionary. It begins abruptly; it is nobody that speaks; it is nobody that hears; it is addressed to nobody; it has neither first, second, nor third person; it has every criterion of being a tradition; it has no voucher. Moses does not take it upon himself by introducing it with the formality that he uses on other occasions, such as that of saying, "The Lord spake unto Moses, saying."

Why it has been called the Mosaic account of the Creation, I am at a loss to conceive. Moses, I believe, was too good a judge of such subjects to put his name to that account. He had been educated among the Egyptians, who were a people as well skilled in science, and particularly in astronomy, as any people of their day; and the silence and caution that Moses observes, in not authenticating the account, is a good negative evidence that he neither told it nor believed it. The case is, that every nation of people has been world-makers, and the Israelites had as much right to set up the trade of world-making as any of the rest; and as Moses was not an Israelite, he might not chose to contradict the tradition. The account, however, is harmless; and this is more than can be said for many other parts of the Bible.

Whenever we read the obscene stories, the voluptuous debaucheries, the cruel and torturous executions, the unrelenting vindictiveness, with which more than half the Bible is filled, it would be more consistent that we called it the word of a demon, than the word of God. It is a history of wickedness, that has served to corrupt and brutalize mankind; and, for my own part, I sincerely detest it, as I detest everything that is cruel.

We scarcely meet with anything, a few phrases excepted, but what deserves either our abhorrence or our contempt, till we come to the miscellaneous parts of the Bible. In the anonymous publications, the Psalms, and the Book of Job, more particularly in the latter, we find a great deal of elevated sentiment reverentially expressed of the power and benignity of the Almighty; but they stand on no higher rank than many other compositions on similar subjects, as well before that time as since.

The Proverbs which are said to be Solomon's, though most probably a collection (because they discover a knowledge of life which his situation excluded him from knowing), are an instructive table of ethics. They are inferior in keenness to the proverbs of the Spaniards, and not more wise and economical than those of the American Franklin.

All the remaining parts of the Bible, generally known by the name of the Prophets, are the works of the Jewish poets and itinerant preachers, who mixed poetry,* anecdote, and devotion together—and those works still retain the air and style of poetry, though in translation.

> *As there are many readers who do not see that a composition is poetry unless it be in rhyme, it is for their information that I add this note. Poetry consists principally in two things—imagery and composition. The composition of poetry differs from that of prose in the manner of mixing long and short syllables together. Take a long syllable out of a line of poetry, and put a short one in the room of it, or put a long syllable where a short one should be, and that line will lose its poetical harmony. It will have an effect upon the line like that of misplacing a note in a song. The imagery in these books, called the Prophets, appertains altogether to poetry. It is fictitious, and often extravagant, and not admissible in any other kind of writing than poetry. To show that these writings are composed in poetical numbers, I will take ten syllables, as they stand in the book, and make a line of the same number of syllables, (heroic measure) that shall rhyme with the last word. It will then be

seen that the composition of those books is poetical measure. The instance I shall first produce is from Isaiah:

"Hear, O ye heavens, and give ear, O earth"
Tis God himself that calls attention forth.

Another instance I shall quote is from the mournful Jeremiah, to which I shall add two other lines, for the purpose of carrying out the figure, and showing the intention of the poet:

"O! that mine head were waters and mine eyes"
Were fountains flowing like the liquid skies;
Then would I give the mighty flood release
And weep a deluge for the human race.

There is not, throughout the whole book called the Bible, any word that describes to us what we call a poet, nor any word that describes what we call poetry. The case is, that the word prophet, to which latter times have affixed a new idea, was the Bible word for poet, and the word 'prophesying' meant the art of making poetry. It also meant the art of playing poetry to a tune upon any instrument of music.

We read of prophesying with pipes, tabrets, and horns—of prophesying with harps, with psalteries, with cymbals, and with every other instrument of music then in fashion. Were we now to speak of prophesying with a fiddle, or with a pipe and tabor, the expression would have no meaning or would appear ridiculous, and to some people contemptuous, because we have changed the meaning of the word.

We are told of Saul being among the prophets, and also that he prophesied; but we are not told what they prophesied, nor what he prophesied. The case is, there was nothing to tell; for these prophets were a company of musicians and poets, and Saul joined in the concert, and this was called prophesying.

The account given of this affair in the book called Samuel is, that Saul met a company of prophets; a whole company of them! coming down with a psaltery, a tabret, a pipe and a harp, and that they prophesied, and that he prophesied with them. But it appears afterwards, that Saul prophesied badly; that is, he performed his part badly; for it is said that an "evil spirit from God"* came upon Saul, and he prophesied.

*As those men who call themselves divines and commentators, are very fond of puzzling one another, I leave them to contest the meaning of the first part of the phrase, that of an evil spirit from God. I keep to my text—I keep to the meaning of the word prophesy.

Now, were there no other passage in the book called the Bible than this, to demonstrate to us that we have lost the original meaning of the word prophesy, and substituted another meaning in its place, this alone would be sufficient; for it is impossible to use and apply the word prophesy, in the place it is here used and applied, if we give to it the sense which latter times have affixed to it. The manner in which it is here used strips it of all religious meaning, and shows that a man might then be a prophet, or he might prophesy, as he may now be a poet or a musician, without any regard to the morality or the immorality of his character. The word was originally a term of science, promiscuously applied to poetry and to music, and not restricted to any subject upon which poetry and music might be exercised.

Deborah and Barak are called prophets, not because they predicted anything, but because they composed the poem or song that bears their name, in celebration of an act already done. David is ranked among the prophets, for he was a musician, and was also reputed to be (though perhaps very erroneously) the author of the Psalms. But Abraham, Isaac, and Jacob are not called prophets; it does not appear from any accounts we have that they could either sing, play music, or make poetry.

We are told of the greater and the lesser prophets. They might as well tell us of the greater and the lesser God; for there cannot be degrees in prophesying consistently with its modern sense. But there are degrees in poetry, and therefore the phrase is reconcilable to the case, when we understand by it the greater and the lesser poets.

It is altogether unnecessary, after this, to offer any observations upon what those men, styled propliets, have written. The axe goes at once to the root, by showing that the original meaning of the word has been mistaken and consequently all the inferences that have been drawn from those books, the devotional respect that has been paid to them, and the labored commentaries that have been written upon them, under that mistaken meaning, are not worth disputing about. In many things, however, the writings of the Jewish poets deserve a better fate than that of being bound up, as they now are with the trash that accompanies them, under the abused name of the word of God.

If we permit ourselves to conceive right ideas of things, we must necessarily affix the idea, not only of unchangeableness, but of the utter impossibility of any change taking place, by any means or accident whatever, in that which we would honor with the name of the word of God; and therefore the word of God cannot exist in any written or human language.

The continually progressive change to which the meaning of words is subject, the want of a universal language which renders translation necessary, the errors to which translations are again subject, the mistakes of copyists and printers, together with the possibility of willful alteration, are of themselves evidences that the human language, whether in speech or in print, cannot be the vehicle of the word of God. The word of God exists in something else.

Did the book called the Bible excel in purity of ideas and expression all the books now extant in the world, I would not take it for my rule of faith, as being the word of God, because the possibility would nevertheless exist of my being imposed upon. But when I see throughout the greatest part of this book scarcely anything but a history of the grossest vices and a collection of the most paltry and contemptible tales, I cannot dishonor my Creator by calling it by his name.

Thus much for the Bible; I now go on to the book called the New Testament. The new Testament! that is, the new will, as if there could be two wills of the Creator.

Had it been the object or the intention of Jesus Christ to establish a new religion, he would undoubtedly have written the system himself, or procured it to be written in his life-time. But there is no publication extant authenticated with his name. All the books called the New Testament were written after his death. He was a Jew by birth and by profession; and he was the son of God in like manner that every other person is—for the Creator is the Father of All.

The first four books, called Matthew, Mark, Luke, and John, do not give a history of the life of Jesus Christ, but only detached anecdotes of him. It appears from these books that the whole time of his being a preacher was not more than eighteen months; and it was only during this short time that these men became acquainted with him. They make mention of him at the age of twelve years, sitting, they say, among the Jewish doctors, asking and answering questions. As this was several years before their acquaintance with him began, it is most probable they had this anecdote from his parents. From this time there is no account of him for about sixteen years. Where he lived, or how he employed himself during this interval, is not known. Most probably he was working at his father's trade, which was that of a carpenter. It does not appear that he had any school education, and the probability is, that he could not write, for his parents were extremely poor, as appears from their not being able to pay for a bed when he was born.

It is somewhat curious that the three persons whose names are the most universally recorded, were of very obscure parentage. Moses was a foundling; Jesus Christ was born in a stable; and Mahomet was a mule driver. The first and the last of these men were founders of different systems of religion; but Jesus Christ founded no new system. He called men to the practice of moral virtues, and the belief of one God. The great trait in his character is philanthropy.

The manner in which he was apprehended shows that he was not much known at that time; and it shows also, that the meetings he then held with his followers were in secret; and that he had given over or suspended preaching publicly. Judas could no otherwise betray him than by giving information where he was, and pointing him out to the officers that went to arrest him; and the reason for employing and paying Judas to do this could arise only from the causes already mentioned, that of his not being much known and living concealed.

The idea of his concealment, not only agrees very ill with his reputed divinity, but associates with it something of pusillanimity; and his being betrayed, or in other words, his being apprehended, on the information of one of his followers, shows that he did not intend to be apprehended, and consequently that he did not intend to be crucified.

The Christian Mythologists tell us, that Christ died for the sins of the world, and that he came on purpose to die. Would it not then have been the same if he had died of a fever or of the small-pox, of old age, or of anything else?

The declaratory sentence which, they say, was passed upon Adam, in case he eat of the apple, was not, that thou shalt surely be crucified, but thou shalt surely die—the sentence of death, and not the manner of dying. Crucifixion, therefore, or any other particular manner of dying, made no part of the sentence that Adam was to suffer, and consequently, even upon their own tactics, it could make no part of the sentence that Christ was to suffer in the room of Adam. A fever would have done as well as a cross, if there was any occasion for either.

This sentence of death, which they tell us was thus passed upon Adam must either have meant dying naturally, that is, ceasing to live, or have meant what these Mythologists call damnation; and, consequently, the act of dying on the part of Jesus Christ, must, according to their system, apply as a prevention to one or other of these two things happening to Adam and to us.

That it does not prevent our dying is evident, because we all die; and if their accounts of longevity be true, men die faster since the crucifixion than before: and with respect to the second explanation (including with it the natural death of Jesus Christ as a substitute for the eternal death or damnation of all mankind), it is impertinently representing the Creator as coming off, or revoking the sentence, by a pun or a quibble upon the word death. That manufacturer of quibbles, St. Paul, if he wrote the books that bear his name, has helped this quibble on by making another quibble upon the word Adam. He makes there to be two Adams; the one who sins in fact, and suffers by proxy; the other who sins by proxy, and suffers in fact. A religion thus interlarded with quibble, subterfuge, and pun has a tendency to instruct its professors in the practice of these arts. They acquire the habit without being aware of the cause.

If Jesus Christ was the being which those Mythologists tell us he was, and that he came into this world to suffer, which is a word they sometimes use instead of to die, the only real suffering he could have endured would have been to live. His existence here was a state of exilement or transportation from Heaven, and the way back to his original country was to die. In finè, everything in this strange system is the reverse of what it pretends to be. It is the reverse of truth, and I become so tired of examining into its inconsistencies and absurdities, that I hasten to the conclusion of it, in order to proceed to something better.

How much or what parts of the books called the New Testament, were written by the persons whose names they bear, is what we can know nothing of; neither are we certain in what language they were originally written. The matters they now contain may be classed under two heads— anecdote and epistolary correspondence.

The four books already mentioned, Matthew, Mark, Luke, and John, are altogether anecdotal. They relate events after they had taken place. They tell what Jesus Christ did and said, and what others did and said to him; and in several instances they relate the same event differently. Revelation is necessarily out of the question with respect to those books; not only because of the disagreement of the writers, but because revelation cannot be applied to the relating of facts by the person who saw them done, nor to the relating or recording of any discourse or conversation by those who heard it. The book called the Acts of the Apostles (an anonymous work) belongs also to the anecdotal part.

All the other parts of the New Testament, except the book of enigmas, called the Revelations, are a collection of letters under the name of epistles; and the forgery of letters has been such a common practice in the world, that the probability is at least equal, whether they are genuine or forged. One thing, however, is much less equivocal, which is, that out of the matters contained in those books, together with the assistance of some old stories, the Church has set up a system of religion very contradictory to the character of the person whose name it bears. It has set up a religion of pomp and of revenue, in pretended imitation of a person whose life was humility and poverty.

The invention of a purgatory, and of the releasing of souls therefrom by prayers bought of the church with money; the selling of pardons, dispensations, and indulgences, are revenue laws, without bearing that name or carrying that appearance. But the case nevertheless is, that those things derive their origin from the paroxysm of the crucifixion and the theory deduced therefrom, which was that one person could stand in the place of another, and could perform meritorious services for him. The probability, therefore, is, that the whole theory or doctrine of what is called the redemption (which is said to have been accomplished by the act of one person in the room of another) was originally fabricated on purpose to bring forward and build all those secondary and pecuniary redemptions upon; and that the passages in the books, upon which the idea or theory of redemption is built, have been manufactured and fabricated for that purpose. Why are we to give this Church Credit when she tells us that those books are genuine in every part, any more than we give her credit for everything else she has told us, or for the miracles she says she had performed? That she could fabricate writings is certain, because she could write; and the composition of the writings in question, is of that kind that anybody might do it; and that she did fabricate them is not more inconsistent with probability than that she could tell us, as she has done, that she could and did work miracles.

Since, then no external evidence can, at this long distance of time, be produced to prove whether the Church fabricated the doctrines called redemption or not (for such evidence, whether for or against, would be subject to the same suspicion of being fabricated), the case can only be referred to the internal evidence which the thing carries of itself; and this affords a very strong presumption of its being a fabrication. For the internal evidence is that the theory or doctrine of redemption has for its basis an idea of pecuniary Justice, and not that of moral Justice.

If I owe a person money, and cannot pay him, and he threatens to put me in prison, another person can take the debt upon himself, and pay it for me; but if I have committed a crime, every circumstance of the case is changed; moral Justice cannot take the innocent for the guilty, even if the innocent would offer itself. To suppose Justice to do this, is to destroy the principle of its existence, which is the thing itself; it is then no longer Justice, it is indiscriminate revenge.

This single reflection will show, that the doctrine of redemption is founded on a mere pecuniary idea corresponding to that of a debt which another person might pay; and as this pecuniary idea corresponds again with the system of second redemption, obtained through the means of money given to the Church for pardons, the probability is that the same persons fabricated both the one and the other of those theories; and that, in truth there is no such thing as redemption—that it is fabulous, and that man stands in the same relative condition with his Maker he ever did stand since man existed, and that it is his greatest consolation to think so.

Let him believe this, and he will live more consistently and morally than by any other system; it is by his being taught to contemplate himself as an outlaw, as an outcast, as a beggar, as a mumper, as one thrown, as it were, on a dunghill at an immense distance from his Creator, and who must make his approaches by creeping and cringing to intermediate beings, that he conceives either a contemptuous disregard for everything under the name of religion, or becomes indifferent, or turns what he calls devout. In the latter case, he consumes his life in grief, or the affectation of it; his prayers are reproaches; his humility is ingratitude; he calls himself a worm, and the fertile earth a dunghill; and all the blessings of life by the thankless name of vanities; he despises the choicest gift of God to man, the GIFT OF REASON; and having endeavored to force upon himself the belief of a system against which reason revolts, he ungratefully calls it human reason, as if man could give reason to himself.

Yet, with all this strange appearance of humility and this contempt for human reason, he ventures into the boldest presumptions; he finds fault with everything; his selfishness is never satisfied; his ingratitude is never at an end. He takes on himself to direct the Almighty what to do, even in the government of the universe; he prays dictatorially; when it is sunshine, he prays for rain, and when it is rain, he prays for sunshine; he follows the same idea in everything that he prays for; for what is the amount of all his prayers, but an attempt to make the Almighty change his mind, and act otherwise than he does? It is as if he were to say: Thou knowest not so well as I.

But some, perhaps will say: Are we to have no word of God—no revelation? I answer, Yes; there is a word of God; there is a revelation.

THE WORD OF GOD IS THE CREATION WE BEHOLD and it is in this word, which no human invention can counterfeit or alter, that God speaketh universally to man.

Human language is local and changeable, and is therefore incapable of being used as the means of unchangeable and universal information. The idea that God sent Jesus Christ to publish, as they say, the glad tidings to all nations, from one end of the earth unto the other, is consistent only with the ignorance of those who knew nothing of the extent of the world, and who believed, as those world-saviours believed, and continued to believe for several centuries (and that in contradiction to the discoveries of philosophers and the experience of navigators), that the earth was flat like a trencher, and that a man might walk to the end of it.

But how was Jesus Christ to make anything known to all nations? He could speak but one language; which was Hebrew and there are in the world several hundred languages. Scarcely any two nations speak the same language, or understand each other; and as to translations, every man who knows anything of languages knows that it is impossible to translate from one language into another, not only without losing a great part of the original, but frequently of mistaking the sense; and besides all this, the art of printing was wholly unknown at the time Christ lived.

It is always necessary that the means that are to accomplish any end be equal to the accomplishment of that end, or the end cannot be accomplished. It is in this that the difference between finite and infinite power and wisdom discovers itself. Man frequently fails in accomplishing his ends, from a natural inability of the power to the purpose, and frequently from the want of wisdom to apply power properly. But it is impossible for infinite power and wisdom to fail as man faileth. The means it useth are always equal to the end; but human language, more especially as there is not a universal language, is incapable of being used as a universal means of unchangeable and uniform information, and therefore it is not the means that God useth in manifesting himself universally to man.

It is only in the CREATION that all our ideas and conceptions of a word of God can unite. The Creation speaketh a universal language, independently of human speech or human language, multiplied and various as they may be. It is an ever-existing original, which every man can read. It cannot be forged; it cannot be counterfeited; it cannot be lost; it cannot be altered; it cannot be suppressed. It does not depend upon the will of man whether it shall be published or not; it publishes itself from one end of the earth to the other. It preaches to all nations and to all worlds; and this word of God reveals to man all that is necessary for man to know of God.

Do we want to contemplate his power? We see it in the immensity of the Creation. Do we want to contemplate his wisdom? We see it in the unchangeable order by which the incomprehensible whole is governed! Do we want to contemplate his munificence? We see it in the abundance with which he fills the earth. Do we want to contemplate his mercy? We see it in his not withholding that abundance even from the unthankful. In finè, do we want to know what God is? Search not the book called the Scripture, which any human hand might make, but the Scripture called the Creation.

The only idea man can affix to the name of God is that of a first cause, the cause of all things. And incomprehensible and difficult as it is for a man to conceive what a first cause is, he arrives at the belief of it from the tenfold greater difficulty of disbelieving it. It is difficult beyond description to conceive that space can have no end; but it is more difficult to conceive an end. It is difficult beyond the power of man to conceive an eternal duration of what we call time; but it is more impossible to conceive a time when there shall be no time.

In like manner of reasoning, everything we behold carries in itself the internal evidence that it did not make itself. Every man is an evidence to himself that he did not make himself; neither could his father make himself, nor his grandfather, nor any of his race; neither could any tree, plant, or animal make itself; and it is the conviction arising from this evidence that carries us on, as it were, by necessity to the belief of a first cause eternally existing, of a nature totally different to any material existence we know of, and by the power of which all things exist; and this first cause man calls God.

It is only by the exercise of reason that man can discover God. Take away that reason, and he would be incapable of understanding anything; and in this case it would be just as consistent to read even the book called the Bible to a horse as to a man. How then is it that those people pretend to reject reason?

Almost the only parts in the book called the Bible that convey to us any idea of God, are some chapters in Job, and the 19th Psalm; I recollect no other. Those parts are true deistical compositions, for they treat of the Deity through his works. They take the book of Creation as the word of God, they refer to no other book, and all the inferences they make are drawn from that volume.

I insert in this place the 19th Psalm, as paraphrased into English verse by Addison. I recollect not the prose, and where I write this I have not the opportunity of seeing it.

> "The spacious firmament on high,
> With all the blue ethereal sky,
> And spangled heavens, a shining frame,
> Their great original proclaim.
> The unwearied sun, from day to day,
> Does his Creator's power display;
> And publishes to every land
> The work of an Almighty hand.

"Soon as the evening shades prevail,
The moon takes up the wondrous tale,
And nightly to the list'ning earth
Repeats the story of her birth;
Whilst all the stars that round her burn,
And all the planets, in their turn,
Confirm the tidings as they roll,
And spread the truth from pole to pole.

"What though in solemn silence all
Move round this dark terrestrial ball?
What though no real voice, or sound,
Amidst their radiant orbs be found
In reason's ear they all rejoice
And utter forth a glorious voice,
Forever singing, as they shine,
THE HAND THAT MADE US IS DIVINE."

What more does man want to know, than that the hand or power that made these things is divine, is omnipotent? Let him believe this with the force it is impossible to repel, if he permits his reason to act, and his rule of moral life will follow of course.

The allusions in Job have, all of them, the same tendency with this Psalm; that of deducing or proving a truth that would be otherwise unknown, from truths already known.

I recollect not enough of the passages in Job to insert them correctly; but there is one that occurs to me that is applicable to the subject I am speaking upon. "Canst thou by searching find out God? Canst thou find out the Almighty to perfection?"

I know not how the printers have pointed this passage, for I keep no Bible; but it contains two distinct questions that admit of distinct answers.

First,—Canst thou by searching find out God? Yes; because, in the first place, I know I did not make myself, and yet I have existence; and by searching into the nature of other things, I find that no other thing could make itself; and yet millions of other things exist; therefore it is, that I know, by positive conclusion resulting from this search, that there is a power superior to all those things, and that power is God.

Secondly,—Canst thou find out the Almighty to perfection? No; not only because the power and wisdom He has manifested in the structure of the Creation that I behold is to me incomprehensible, but because even this manifestation, great as it is, is probably but a small display of that immensity of power and wisdom by which millions of other worlds, to me invisible by their distance, were created and continue to exist.

It is evident that both of these questions were put to the reason of the person to whom they are supposed to have been addressed; and it is only by admitting the first question to be answered affirmatively, that the second could follow. It would have been unnecessary and even absurd, to have put a second question, more difficult than the first, if the first question had been answered negatively. The two questions have different objects; the first refers to the existence of God, the second to his attributes; reason can discover the one, but it falls infinitely short in discovering the whole of the other.

I recollect not a single passage in all the writings ascribed to the men called apostles, that conveys any idea of what God is. Those writings are chiefly controversial; and the subjects they dwell upon, that of a man dying in agony on a cross, is better suited to the gloomy genius of a monk in a cell, by whom it is not impossible they were written, than to any man breathing the open air of the Creation. The only passage that occurs to me, that has any reference to the works of God, by which only his power and wisdom can be known, is related to have been spoken by Jesus Christ, as a remedy against distrustful care. "Behold the lilies of the field, they toil not, neither do they spin." This, however, is far inferior to the allusions in Job and in the 19th Psalm; but it is similar in idea, and the modesty of the imagery is correspondent to the modesty of the man.

As to the Christian system of faith, it appears to me as a species of Atheism—a sort of religious denial of God. It professes to believe in a man rather than in God. It is a compound made up chiefly of Manism with but little Deism, and is as near to Atheism as twilight is to darkness. It introduces between man and his Maker an opaque body, which it calls a Redeemer, as the moon introduces her opaque self between the earth and the sun, and it produces by this means a religious, or an irreligious, eclipse of light. It has put the whole orbit of reason into shade.

The effect of this obscurity has been that of turning everything upside down, and representing it in reverse, and among the revolutions it has thus magically produced, it has made a revolution in theology.

That which is now called natural philosophy, embracing the whole circle of science, of which astronomy occupies the chief place, is the study of the works of God, and of the power and wisdom of God in his works, and is the true theology.

As to the theology that is now studied in its place, it is the study of human opinions and of human fancies concerning God. It is not the study of

God himself in the works that he has made, but in the works or writings that man has made; and it is not among the least of the mischiefs that the Christian system has done to the world, that it has abandoned the original and beautiful system of theology, like a beautiful innocent, to distress and reproach, to make room for the hag of superstition.

The Book of Job and the 19th Psalm, which even the Church admits to be more ancient than the chronological order in which they stand in the book called the Bible, are theological orations conformable to the original system of theology. The internal evidence of those orations proves to a demonstration that the study and contemplation of the works of creation, and of the power and wisdom of God, revealed and manifested in those works, made a great part of the religious devotion of the times in which they were written; and it was this devotional study and contemplation that led to the discovery of the principles upon which what are now called sciences are established; and it is to the discovery of these principles that almost all the arts that contribute to the convenience of human life owe their existence. Every principal art has some science for its parent, though the person who mechanically performs the work does not always, and but very seldom, perceive the connection.

It is a fraud of the Christian system to call the sciences human inventions; it is only the application of them that is human. Every science has for its basis a system of principles as fixed and unalterable as those by which the universe is regulated and governed. Man cannot make principles, he can only discover them.

For example: Every person who looks at an almanac sees an account when an eclipse will take place, and he sees also that it never fails to take place according to the account there given. This shows that man is acquainted with the laws by which the heavenly bodies move. But it would be something worse than ignorance, were any Church on earth to say that those laws are a human invention. It would also be ignorance, or something worse, to say that the scientific principles by the aid of which man is enabled to calculate and foreknow when an eclipse will take place, are a human invention. Man cannot invent any thing that is eternal and immutable; and the scientific principles he employs for this purpose must be, and are of necessity, as eternal and immutable as the laws by which the heavenly bodies move, or they could not be used as they are to ascertain the time when, and the manner how, an eclipse will take place.

The scientific principles that man employs to obtain the foreknowledge of an eclipse, or of anything else relating to the motion of the heavenly bodies, are contained chiefly in that part of science that is called trigonometry, or the properties of a triangle, which, when applied to the study of the heavenly bodies, is called astronomy; when applied to direct the course of a ship on the ocean, it is called navigation; when applied to the construction of figures drawn by a rule and compass, it is called geometry; when applied to the construction of plans of edifices, it is called architecture; when applied to the measurement of any portion of the surface of the earth, it is called land-surveying. In finè, it is the soul of science; it is an eternal truth; it contains the mathematical demonstration of which man speaks, and the extent of its uses are unknown.

It may be said that man can make or draw a triangle, and therefore a triangle is a human invention.

But the triangle, when drawn, is no other than the image of the principle; it is a delineation to the eye, and from thence to the mind, of a principle that would otherwise be imperceptible. The triangle does not make the principle, any more than a candle taken into a room that was dark makes the chairs and tables that before were invisible. All the properties of a triangle exist independently of the figure, and existed before any triangle was drawn or thought of by man. Man had no more to do in the formation of those properties or principles, than he had to do in making the laws by which the heavenly bodies move; and therefore the one must have the same Divine origin as the other.

In the same manner, as it may be said, that man can make a triangle, so also, may it be said, he can make the mechanical instrument called a lever; but the principle by which the lever acts is a thing distinct from the instrument, and would exist if the instrument did not; it attaches itself to the instrument after it is made; the instrument, therefore, cannot act otherwise than it does act; neither can all the efforts of human invention make it act otherwise; that which, in all such cases, man calls the effect is no other than the principle itself rendered perceptible to the senses.

Since, then, man cannot make principles, from whence did he gain a knowledge of them, so as to be able to apply them, not only to things on earth, but to ascertain the motion of bodies so immensely distant from him as all the heavenly bodies are? From whence, I ask, could he gain that knowledge, but from the study of the true theology?

It is the structure of the universe that has taught this knowledge to man. That structure is an ever-existing exhibition of every principle upon which every part of mathematical science is founded. The offspring of this science is mechanics; for mechanics is no other than the principles of science applied practically. The man who proportions the several parts of a mill, uses the same scientific principles as if he had the power of constructing a universe; but as he cannot give to matter that invisible agency by which all the component parts of the immense machine of the universe have influence upon each other, and act in motional unison together, without any apparent contact, and to which man has given the name of attraction, gravitation, and repulsion, he supplies the place of that agency by the humble imitation of teeth and cogs. All the parts of man's microcosm must visibly touch; but could he gain a knowledge of that agency, so as to be able to apply it in practice, we might then say that another canonical book of the Word of God had been discovered.

If man could alter the properties of the lever, so also could he alter the properties of the triangle: for a lever (taking that sort of lever which is called a steelyard, for the sake of explanation) forms, when in motion, a triangle. The line it descends from (one point of that line being in the fulcrum), the line it descends to, and the chord of the arc which the end of the lever describes in the air, are the three sides of a triangle. The other arm of the lever describes also a triangle; and the corresponding sides of those two triangles, calculated scientifically, or measured geometrically, and also the sines, tangents, and secants generated from the angles, and geometrically measured, have the same proportions to each other, as the different weights have that will balance each other on the lever, leaving the weight of the lever out of the case.

It may also be said, that man can make a wheel and axis; that he can put wheels of different magnitudes together, and produce a mill. Still the case comes back to the same point, which is, that he did not make the principle that gives the wheels those powers. This principle is as unalterable as in the former case or rather it is the same principle under a different appearance to the eye.

The power that two wheels of different magnitudes have upon each other, is in the same proportion as if the semi-diameter of the two wheels were joined together and made into that kind of lever I have described, suspended at the part where the semi-diameters join; for the two wheels, scientifically considered, are no other than the two circles generated by the motion of the compound lever.

It is from the study of the true theology that all our knowledge of science is derived, and it is from that knowledge that all the arts have originated.

The Almighty Lecturer, by displaying the principles of science in the structure of the universe, has invited man to study and to imitation. It is as if He had said to the inhabitants of this globe that we call ours, "I have made an earth for man to dwell upon, and I have rendered the starry heavens visible, to teach him science and the arts. He can now provide for his own comfort, AND LEARN FROM MY MUNIFICENCE TO ALL, TO BE KIND TO EACH OTHER."

Of what use is it, unless it be to teach man something, that his eye is endowed with the power of beholding to an incomprehensible distance, an immensity of worlds revolving in the ocean of space? Or of what use is it that this immensity of worlds is visible to man? What has man to do with the Pleiades, with Orion, with Sirius, with the star he calls the North Star, with the moving orbs he has named Saturn, Jupiter, Mars, Venus, and Mercury, if no uses are to follow from their being visible? A less power of vision would have been sufficient for man, if the immensity he now possesses were given only to waste itself, as it were, on an immense desert of space glittering with shows.

It is only by contemplating what he calls the starry heavens, as the book and school of science, that he discovers any use in their being visible to him, or any advantage resulting from his immensity of vision. But when be contemplates the subject in this light, he sees an additional motive for saying, that nothing was made in vain; for in vain would be this power of vision if it taught man nothing.

As the Christian system of faith has made a revolution in theology, so also bas it made a revolution in the state of learning. That which is now called learning, was not learning originally. Learning does not consist, as the schools now make it consist, in the knowledge of languages, but in the knowledge of things to which language gives names.

The Greeks were a learned people, but learning with them did not consist in speaking Greek, any more than in a Roman's speaking Latin, or a Frenchman's speaking French, or an Englishman's speaking English. From what we know of the Greeks, it does not appear that they knew or studied any language but their own, and this was one cause of their becoming so learned: it afforded them more time to apply themselves to better studies. The schools of the Greeks were schools of science and philosophy, and not of languages; and it is in the knowledge of the things that science and philosophy teach, that learning consists.

Almost all the scientific learning that now exists came to us from the Greeks, or the people who spoke the Greek language. It, therefore, became necessary for the people of other nations who spoke a different language that some among them should learn the Greek language, in order that the learning the Greeks had, might be made known in those nations, by translating the Greek books of science and philosophy into the mother tongue of each nation.

The study, therefore, of the Greek language (and in the same manner for the Latin) was no other than the drudgery business of a linguist; and the language thus obtained, was no other than the means, or as it were the tools, employed to obtain the learning the Greeks had. It made no part of the learning itself, and was so distinct from it, as to make it exceedingly probable that the persons who had studied Greek sufficiently to translate those works, such, for instance as Euclid's Elements, did not understand any of the learning the works contained.

As there is now nothing new to be learned from the dead languages, all the useful books being already translated, the languages are become useless, and the time expended in teaching and in learning them is wasted. So far as the study of languages may contribute to the progress and communication of knowledge, (for it has nothing to do with the creation of knowledge), it is only in the living languages that new knowledge is to be found; and certain it is that, in general, a youth will learn more of a living language in one year, than of a dead language in seven, and it is but seldom that the teacher knows much of it himself. The difficulty of learning the dead languages does not arise from any superior abstruseness in the languages themselves, but in their being dead, and the pronunciation entirely lost. It would be the same thing with any other language when it becomes dead. The best Greek linguist that now exists does not understand Greek so well as a Grecian plowman did, or a Grecian milkmaid; and the same for the Latin, compared with a plowman or a milkmaid of the Romans; it would therefore be advantageous to the state of learning to abolish the study of the dead languages, and to make learning consist, as it originally did, in scientific knowledge.

The apology that is sometimes made for continuing to teach the dead languages is, that they are taught at a time when a child is not capable of exerting any other mental faculty than that of memory; but that is altogether erroneous. The human mind has a natural disposition to scientific knowledge, and to the things connected with it. The first and favourite amusement of a child, even before it begins to play, is that of imitating the works of man. It builds houses with cards or sticks; it navigates the little ocean of a bowl of water with a paper boat, or dams the stream of a gutter and contrives something which it calls a mill; and it interests itself in the fate of its works with a care that resembles affection. It afterwards goes to school, where its genius is killed by the barren study of a dead language, and the philosopher is lost in the linguist.

But the apology that is now made for continuing to teach the dead languages, could not be the cause, at first, of cutting down learning to the narrow and humble sphere of linguistry; the cause, therefore, must be sought for elsewhere. In all researches of this kind, the best evidence that can be produced, is the internal evidence the thing carries with itself, and the evidence of circumstances that unites with it; both of which, in this case, are not difficult to be discovered.

Putting then aside, as a matter of distinct consideration, the outrage offered to the moral justice of God by supposing him to make the innocent suffer for the guilty, and also the loose morality and low contrivance of supposing him to change himself into the shape of a man, in order to make an excuse to himself for not executing his supposed sentence upon Adam—putting, I say, those things aside as a matter of distinct consideration, it is certain that what is called the Christian system of faith, including in it the whimsical account of the creation—the strange story of Eve—the snake, and the apple—the amphibious idea of a man-god—the corporeal idea of the death of a god—the mythological idea of a family of gods, and the christian system of arithmetic, that three are one, and one is three, are all irreconcilable, not only to the divine gift of reason that God, has given to man, but to the knowledge that man gains of the power and wisdom of God by the aid of the sciences and by studying the structure of the universe that God has made.

The setters-up, therefore, and the advocates of the Christian system of faith could not but foresee that the continually progressive knowledge that man would gain, by the aid of science, of the power and wisdom of God, manifested in the structure of the universe and in all the works of Creation, would militate against, and call into question, the truth of their system of faith; and therefore it became necessary to their purpose to cut learning down to a size less dangerous to their project, and this they effected by restricting the idea of learning to the dead study of dead languages.

They not only rejected the study of science out of the Christian schools, but they persecuted it, and it is only within about the last two centuries that the study has been revived. So late as 1610, Galileo, a Florentine, discovered and introduced the use of telescopes, and by applying them to observe the motions and appearances of the heavenly bodies, afforded additional means for ascertaining the true structure of the universe. Instead of being esteemed for these discoveries, he was sentenced to renounce them, or the opinions resulting from them, as a damnable heresy. And, prior to that time, Virgilius was condemned to be burned for asserting the antipodes, or in other words that the earth was a globe, and habitable in every part where there was land; yet the truth of this is now too well known even to be told.

If the belief of errors not morally bad did no mischief, it would make no part of the moral duty of man to oppose and remove them. There was no moral ill in believing the earth was flat like a trencher, any more than there was moral virtue in believing it was round like a globe; neither was there any moral ill in believing that the Creator made no other world than this, any more than there was moral virtue in believing that he made millions, and that the infinity of space is filled with worlds. But when a system of religion is made to grow out of a supposed system of creation that is not true, and to unite itself therewith in a manner almost inseparable therefrom, the case assumes an entirely different ground. It is then that errors not morally bad become fraught with the same mischiefs as if they were. It is then that the truth, though otherwise indifferent itself, becomes an essential by becoming the criterion that either confirms by corresponding evidence, or denies by contradictory evidence, the reality of the religion itself. In this view of the case it is the moral duty of man to obtain every possible evidence that the structure of the heavens, or any other part of creation affords, with respect to systems of religion. But this, the supporters or partisans of the Christian system, as if dreading the result, incessantly opposed, and not only rejected the sciences, but persecuted the professors. Had Newton or Descartes lived three or four hundred years ago, and pursued their studies as they did, it is most probable they would not have lived to finish them; and had Franklin drawn lightning from the clouds at the same time, it would have been at the hazard of expiring for it in flames.

Later times have laid all the blame upon the Goths and Vandals; but, however unwilling the partisans of the Christian system may be to believe or to acknowledge it, it is nevertheless true, that the age of ignorance commenced with the Christian system. There was more knowledge in the world before that period than for many centuries afterwards; and as to religious knowledge, the Christian system, as already said was only another species of mythology, and the mythology to which it succeeded was a corruption of an ancient system of theism.*

> *It is impossible for us now to know at what time the heathen mythology began; but it is certain, from the internal evidence that it carries, that it did not begin in the same state or condition in which it ended. All the gods of that mythology, except Saturn, were of modern invention. The supposed reign of Saturn was prior to that which is called the heathen mythology, and was so far a species of theism, that it admitted the belief of only one God. Saturn is supposed to have abdicated the government in favor of his three sons and one daughter, Jupiter, Pluto, Neptune, and Juno; after this, thousands of other Gods and demi-gods were imaginarily created, and the calendar of gods increased as fast as the calendar of saints and the calendar of courts have increased since. All the corruptions that have taken place, in theology and in religion, have been produced by admitting of what man calls revealed religion. The Mythologists pretended to more revealed religion

than the Christians do. They had their oracles and their priests, who were supposed to receive and deliver the word of God verbally, on almost all occasions. Since, then, all corruptions, down from Moloch to modem predestinarianism, and the human sacrifices of the heathens to the Christian sacrifice of the Creator, have been produced by admitting of what is called revealed religion, the most effectual means to prevent all such evils and impositions is not to admit of any other revelation than that which is manifested in the book of creation, and to contemplate the creation as the only true and real word of God that ever did or ever will exist; and everything else called the word of God, is fable and imposition.

It is owing to this long interregnum of science, and to no other cause, that we have now to look back through a vast chasm of many hundred years to the respectable characters we call the ancients. Had the progression of knowledge gone on proportionably with the stock that before existed, that chasm would have been filled up with characters rising superior in knowledge to each other; and those ancients we now so much admire would have appeared respectably in the background of the scene. But the Christian system laid all waste; and if we take our stand about the beginning of the sixteenth century, we look back through that long chasm, to the times of the ancients, as over a vast sandy desert, in which not a shrub appears to intercept the vision to the fertile hills beyond.

It is an inconsistency scarcely possible to be credited, that any thing should exist, under the name of a religion, that held it to be irreligious to study and contemplate the structure of the universe that God has made. But the fact is too well established to be denied. The event that served more than any other to break the first link in this long chain of despotic ignorance is that known by the name of the Reformation by Luther. From that time, though it does not appear to have made any part of the intention of Luther, or of those who are called reformers, the sciences began to revive, and liberality, their natural associate, began to appear. This was the only public good the Reformation did; for with respect to religious good, it might as well not have taken place. The mythology still continued the same, and a multiplicity of National Popes grew out of the downfall of the Pope of Christendom.

Having thus shown from the internal evidence of things the cause that produced a change in the state of learning, and the motive for substituting the study of the dead languages in the place of the sciences, I proceed, in addition to the several observations already made in the former part of this work, to compare, or rather to confront, the evidence that the structure of the universe affords with the Christian system of religion; but, as I cannot begin this part better than by referring to the ideas that occurred to me at an early part of life, and which I doubt not have occurred in some degree to almost every other person at one time or other, I shall state what those ideas were, and add thereto such other matter as shall arise out of the subject, giving to the whole, by way of preface, a short introduction.

My father being of the Quaker profession, it was my good fortune to have an exceedingly good moral education, and a tolerable stock of useful learning. Though I went to the grammar school,* I did not learn Latin, not only because I had no inclination to learn languages, but because of the objection the Quakers have against the books in which the language is taught. But this did not prevent me from being acquainted with the subjects of all the Latin books used in the school.

> *The same school, Thetford In Norfolk that the present Counsellor Mingay went to and under the same master.

The natural bent of my mind was to science. I had some turn, and I believe some talent for poetry; but this I rather repressed than encouraged, as leading too much into the field of imagination. As soon as I was able I purchased a pair of globes, and attended the philosophical lectures of Martin and Ferguson, and became afterwards acquainted with Dr. Bevis, of the society called the Royal Society, then living in the Temple, and an excellent astronomer.

I had no disposition for what was called politics. It presented to my mind no other idea than is contained in the word Jockeyship. When therefore I turned my thoughts toward matters of government, I had to form a system for myself that accorded with the moral and philosophic principles in which I had been educated. I saw, or at least I thought I saw, a vast scene opening itself to the world in the affairs of America, and it appeared to me that unless the Americans changed the plan they were then pursuing with respect to the government of England, and declared themselves independent, they would not only involve themselves in a multiplicity of new difficulties, but shut out the prospect that was then offering itself to mankind through their means. It was from these motives that I published the work known by the name of Common Sense, which is the first work I ever did publish; and so far as I can judge of myself, I believe I should never have been known in the world as an author, on any subject whatever, had it not been for the affairs of America. I wrote Common Sense the latter end of the year 1775, and published it the first of January, 1776. Independence was declared the fourth of July following.

Any person who has made observations on the state and progress of the human mind, by observing his own, can not but have observed that there are two distinct classes of what are called thoughts—those that we produce in ourselves by reflection and the act of thinking, and those that bolt into the mind of their own accord. I have always made it a rule to treat those voluntary visitors with civility, taking care to examine, as well as I was able, if they were worth entertaining, and it is from them I have acquired almost all the knowledge that I have. As to the learning that any person gains from school education, it serves only, like a small capital, to put him in the way of beginning learning for himself afterward. Every person of learning is finally his own teacher, the reason of which is that principles, being of a distinct quality to circumstances, cannot be impressed upon the memory; their place of mental residence is the understanding and they are never so lasting as when they begin by conception. Thus much for the introductory part.

From the time I was capable of conceiving an idea and acting upon it by reflection, I either doubted the truth of the Christian system or thought it to be a strange affair; I scarcely knew which it was, but I well remember, when about seven or eight years of age, hearing a sermon read by a relation of mine, who was a great devotee of the Church, upon the subject of what is called redemption by the death of the Son of God. After the sermon was ended, I went into the garden, and as I was going down the garden steps (for I perfectly recollect the spot) I revolted at the recollection of what I had heard, and thought to myself that it was making God Almighty act like a passionate man, that killed his son when he could not revenge himself any other way, and as I was sure a man would be hanged that did such a thing, I could not see for what purpose they preached such sermons. This was not one of those kind of thoughts that had anything in it of childish levity; it was to me a serious reflection, arising from the idea I had that God was too good to do such an action, and also too almighty to be under any necessity of doing it. I believe in the same manner to this moment; and I moreover believe, that any system of religion that has anything in it that shocks the mind of a child, cannot be a true system.

It seems as if parents of the Christian profession were ashamed to tell their children anything about the principles of their religion. They sometimes instruct them in morals, and talk to them of the goodness of what they call Providence, for the Christian mythology has five deities—there is God the Father, God the Son, God the Holy Ghost, the God Providence, and the Goddess Nature. But the Christian story of God the Father putting his son to death, or employing people to do it (for that is the plain language of the story) cannot be told by a parent to a child; and to tell him that it was done to make mankind happier and better is making the story still worse—as if mankind could be improved by the example of murder;

and to tell him that all this is a mystery is only making an excuse for the incredibility of it.

How different is this to the pure and simple profession of Deism! The true Deist has but one Deity, and his religion consists in contemplating the power, wisdom, and benignity of the Deity in his works, and in endeavouring to imitate him in everything moral, scientific, and mechanical.

The religion that approaches the nearest of all others to true Deism, in the moral and benign part thereof, is that professed by the Quakers; but they have contracted themselves too much, by leaving the works of God out of their system. Though I reverence their philanthropy, I cannot help smiling at the conceit, that if the taste of a Quaker could have been consulted at the creation, what a silent and drab-colored creation it would have been! Not a flower would have blossomed its gayeties, nor a bird been permitted to sing. Quitting these reflections, I proceed to other matters. After I had made myself master of the use of the globes, and of the orrery,* and conceived an idea of the infinity of space, and of the eternal divisibility of matter, and obtained at least a general knowledge of what was called natural philosophy, I began to compare, or, as I have before said, to confront, the internal evidence those things afford with the Christian system of faith.

> *As this book may fall into the bands of persons who do not know what an orrery is, it is for their information I add this note, as the name gives no idea of the uses of the thing. The orrery has its name from the person who invented it. It is a machinery of clock-work, representing the universe in miniature, and in which the revolution of the earth round itself and round the sun, the revolution of the moon round the earth, the revolution of the planets round the sun, their relative distances from the sun, as the centre of the whole system, their relative distances from each other, and their different magnitudes, are represented as they really exist in what we call the heavens.

Though it is not a direct article of the Christian system that this world that we inhabit is the whole of the habitable creation, yet it is so worked up therewith, from what is called the Mosaic account of the Creation, the story of Eve and the apple, and the counterpart of that story, the death of the Son of God, that to believe otherwise, that is, to believe that God created a plurality of worlds, at least as numerous as what we call stars, renders the Christian system of faith at once little and ridiculous, and scatters it in the mind like feathers in the air. The two beliefs cannot be held together in the same mind, and he who thinks that be believes both, has thought but little of either.

Though the belief of a plurality of worlds was familiar to the ancients, it is only within the last three centuries that the extent and dimensions of this globe that we inhabit have been ascertained. Several vessels, following the tract of the ocean, have sailed entirely round the world, as a man may march in a circle, and come round by the contrary side of the circle to the spot he set out from. The circular dimensions of our world, in the widest part, as a man would measure the widest round of an apple, or a ball, is only twenty-five thousand and twenty English miles, reckoning sixty-nine miles and a half to an equatorial degree, and may be sailed round in the space of about three years.*

> *Allowing a ship to sail, on an average, three miles in an hour, she would sail entirely round the world in less than one year, if she could sail in a direct circle; but she is obliged to follow the course of the ocean.

A world of this extent may, at first thought, appear to us to be great; but if we compare it with the immensity of space in which it is suspended, like a bubble or a balloon in the air, it is infinitely less in proportion than the smallest grain of sand is to the size of the world, or the finest particle of dew to the whole ocean, and is therefore but small; and, as will be hereafter shown, is only one of a system of worlds of which the universal creation is composed.

It is not difficult to gain some faint idea of the immensity of space in which this and all the other worlds are suspended, if we follow a progression of ideas. When we think of the size or dimensions of a room, our ideas limit themselves to the walls, and there they stop; but when our eye or our imagination darts into space, that is, when it looks upward into what we call the open air, we cannot conceive any walls or boundaries it can have, and if for the sake of resting our ideas, we suppose a boundary, the question immediately renews itself, and asks, what is beyond that boundary? and in the same manner, what is beyond the next boundary? and so on till the fatigued imagination returns and says, There is no end. Certainly, then, the Creator was not pent for room when he made this world no larger than it is, and we have to seek the reason in something else.

If we take a survey of our own world, or rather of this, of which the Creator has given us the use as our portion in the immense system of creation, we find every part of it—the earth, the waters, and the air that surround it—filled and, as it were crowded with life, down from the largest animals that we know of to the smallest insects the naked eye can behold, and from thence to others still smaller, and totally invisible without the assistance of the microscope. Every tree, every plant, every leaf, serves not only as a habitation but as a world to some numerous race, till animal existence becomes so exceedingly refined that the effluvia of a blade of grass would be food for thousands.

Since, then, no part of our earth is left unoccupied, why is it to be supposed that the immensity of space is a naked void, lying in eternal waste? There is room for millions of worlds as large or larger than ours, and each of them millions of miles apart from each other.

Having now arrived at this point, if we carry our ideas only one thought further, we shall see, perhaps, the true reason, at least a very good reason for our happiness, why the Creator, instead of making one immense world extending over an immense quantity of space, has preferred dividing that quantity of matter into several distinct and separate worlds, which we call planets, of which our earth is one. But before I explain my ideas upon this subject, it is necessary (not for the sake of those that already know, but for those who do not) to show what the system of the universe is.

That part of the universe that is called the solar system (meaning the system of worlds to which our earth belongs, and of which Sol, or in English language, the Sun, is the centre) consists, besides the Sun, of six distinct orbs, or planets, or worlds, besides the secondary called the satellites or moons, of which our earth has one that attends her in her annual revolution round the Sun, in like manner as the other satellites or moons attend the planets or worlds to which they severally belong, as may be seen by the assistance of the telescope.

The Sun is the centre round which those six worlds or planets revolve at different distances therefrom, and in circles concentric to each other. Each world keeps constantly in nearly the same track round the Sun, and continues, at the same time, turning round itself in nearly an upright position, as a top turns round itself when it is spinning on the ground, and leans a little sideways.

It is this leaning of the earth (23.5 degrees) that occasions summer and winter, and the different length of days and nights. If the earth turned round itself in a position perpendicular to the plane or level of the circle it moves in a round the Sun, as a top turns round when it stands erect on the ground, the days and nights would be always of the same length, twelve hours day and twelve hours night, and the season would be uniformly the same throughout the year.

Every time that a planet (our earth for example) turns round itself, it makes what we call day and night; and every time it goes entirely round the Sun it makes what we call a year; consequently our world turns three hundred and sixty-five times round itself, in going once round the Sun.*

> *Those who supposed that the sun went round the earth every 24 hours made the same mistake in idea that a cook would do in fact, that should make the fire go round the meat, instead of the meat turning round itself toward the fire.

The names that the ancients gave to those six worlds, and which are still called by the same names, are Mercury, Venus, this world that we call ours, Mars, Jupiter, and Saturn. They appear larger to the eye than the stars, being many million miles nearer to our earth than any of the stars are. The planet Venus is that which is called the evening star, and sometimes the morning star, as she happens to set after or rise before the Sun, which in either case is never more than three hours.

The Sun as before said, being the centre, the planet or world nearest the Sun is Mercury; his distance from the Sun is thirty-four million miles, and he moves round in a circle always at that distance from the Sun, as a top may be supposed to spin round in the track in which a horse goes in a mill. The second world is Venus; she is fifty-seven million miles distant from the Sun, and consequently moves round in a circle much greater than that of Mercury. The third world is this that we inhabit, and which is eighty-eight million miles distant from the Sun, and consequently moves round in a circle greater than that of Venus. The fourth world is Mars; he is distant from the Sun one hundred and thirty-four million miles, and consequently moves round in a circle greater than that of our earth. The fifth is Jupiter; he is distant from the Sun five hundred and fifty-seven million miles, and consequently moves round in a circle greater than that of Mars. The sixth world is Saturn; he is distant from the Sun seven hundred and sixty-three million miles, and consequently moves round in a circle that surrounds the circles, or orbits, of all the other worlds or planets.

The space, therefore, in the air, or in the immensity of space, that our solar system takes up for the several worlds to perform their revolutions in round the Sun, is of the extent in a straight line of the whole diameter of the orbit or circle, in which Saturn moves round the Sun, which being double his distance from the Sun, is fifteen hundred and twenty-six million miles, and its circular extent is nearly five thousand million, and its globular contents is almost three thousand five hundred million times three thousand five hundred million square miles.*

> *If it should be asked, how can man know these things? I have one plain answer to give, which is, that man knows how to calculate an

eclipse, and also how to calculate to a minute of time when the planet Venus, in making her revolutions round the sun, will come in a straight line between our earth and the sun, and will appear to us about the size of a large pea passing across the face of the sun. This happens but twice in about a hundred years, at the distance of about eight years from each other, and has happened twice in our time, both of which were foreknown by calculation. It can also be known when they will happen again for a thousand years to come, or to any other portion of time. As therefore, man could not be able to do these things if he did not understand the solar system, and the manner in which the revolutions of the several planets or worlds are performed, the fact of calculating an eclipse, or a transit of Venus, is a proof in point that the knowledge exists; and as to a few thousand, or even a few million miles, more or less, it makes scarcely any sensible difference in such immense distances.

But this, immense as it is, is only one system of worlds. Beyond this, at a vast distance into space, far beyond all power of calculation, are the stars called the fixed stars. They are called fixed, because they have no revolutionary motion, as the six worlds or planets have that I have been describing. Those fixed stars continue always at the same distance from each other, and always in the same place, as the Sun does in the centre of our system. The probability, therefore, is, that each of those fixed stars is also a Sun, round which another system of worlds or planets, though too remote for us to discover, performs its revolutions, as our system of worlds does round our central Sun.

By this easy progression of ideas, the immensity of space will appear to us to be filled with systems of worlds, and that no part of space lies at waste, any more than any part of our globe of earth and water is left unoccupied.

Having thus endeavoured to convey, in a familiar and easy manner, some idea of the structure of the universe, I return to explain what I before alluded to, namely, the great benefits arising to man in consequence of the Creator having made a plurality of worlds, such as our system is, consisting of a central Sun and six worlds, besides satellites, in preference to that of creating one world only of a vast extent.

It is an idea I have never lost sight of, that all our knowledge of science is derived from the revolutions (exhibited to our eye and from thence to our understanding) which those several planets or worlds of which our system is composed make in their circuit round the Sun.

Had, then, the quantity of matter which these six worlds contain been blended into one solitary globe, the consequence to us would have been, that either no revolutionary motion would have existed, or not a sufficiency of it to give us the ideas and the knowledge of science we now have; and it is from the sciences that all the mechanical arts that contribute so much to our earthly felicity and comfort are derived.

As, therefore, the Creator made nothing in vain, so also must it be believed that he organized the structure of the universe in the most advantageous manner for the benefit of man; and as we see, and from experience feel, the benefits we derive from the structure of the universe formed as it is, which benefits we should not have had the opportunity of enjoying, if the structure, so far as relates to our system, had been a solitary globe—we can discover at least one reason why a plurality of worlds has been made, and that reason calls forth the devotional gratitude of man, as well as his admiration.

But it is not to us, the inhabitants of this globe, only, that the benefits arising from a plurality of worlds are limited. The inhabitants of each of the worlds of which our system is composed enjoy the same opportunities of knowledge as we do. They behold the revolutionary motions of our earth, as we behold theirs. All the planets revolve in sight of each other, and, therefore, the same universal school of science presents itself to all.

Neither does the knowledge stop here. The system of worlds next to us exhibits, in its revolutions, the same principles and school of science to the inhabitants of their system, as our system does to us, and in like manner throughout the immensity of space.

Our ideas, not only of the almightiness of the Creator, but of his wisdom and his beneficence, become enlarged in proportion as we contemplate the extent and the structure of the universe. The solitary idea of a solitary world, rolling or at rest in the immense ocean of space, gives place to the cheerful idea of a society of worlds, so happily contrived as to administer, even by their motion, instruction to man. We see our own earth filled with abundance, but we forget to consider how much of that abundance is owing to the scientific knowledge the vast machinery of the universe has unfolded.

But, in the midst of those reflections, what are we to think of the Christian system of faith, that forms itself upon the idea of only one world, and that of no greater extent, as is before shown, than twenty-five thousand miles. An extent which a man walking at the rate of three miles an hour, for twelve hours in the day, could he keep on in a circular direction, would walk entirely round in less than two years. Alas! what is this to the mighty ocean of space, and the almighty power of the Creator?

From whence, then, could arise the solitary and strange conceit that the Almighty, who had millions of worlds equally dependent on his protection, should quit the care of all the rest, and come to die in our world, because, they say, one man and one woman had eaten an apple? And, on the other hand, are we to suppose that every world in the boundless creation had an Eve, an apple, a serpent, and a redeemer? In this case, the person who is irreverently called the Son of God, and sometimes God himself, would have nothing else to do than to travel from world to world, in an endless succession of deaths, with scarcely a momentary interval of life.

It has been by rejecting the evidence that the word or works of God in the creation affords to our senses, and the action of our reason upon that evidence, that so many wild and whimsical systems of faith and of religion, have been fabricated and set up. There may be many systems of religion that, so far from being morally bad, are in many respects morally good; but there can be but ONE that is true; and that one necessarily must, as it ever will, be in all things consistent with the ever-existing word of God that we behold in his works. But such is the strange construction of the Christian system of faith that every evidence the Heavens affords to man either directly contradicts it or renders it absurd.

It is possible to believe, and I always feel pleasure in encouraging myself to believe it, that there have been men in the world who persuade themselves that what is called a pious fraud might, at least under particular circumstances, be productive of some good. But the fraud being once established, could not afterwards be explained, for it is with a pious fraud as with a bad action, it begets a calamitous necessity of going on.

The persons who first preached the Christian system of faith, and in some measure combined with it the morality preached by Jesus Christ, might persuade themselves that it was better than the heathen mythology that then prevailed. From the first preachers the fraud went on to the second, and to the third, till the idea of its being a pious fraud became lost in the belief of its being true; and that belief became again encouraged by the interest of those who made a livelihood by preaching it.

But though such a belief might by such means be rendered almost general among the laity, it is next to impossible to account for the continual persecution carried on by the Church, for several hundred years, against the sciences and against the professors of science, if the Church had not some record or tradition that it was originally no other than a pious fraud, or did not foresee that it could not be maintained against the evidence that the structure of the universe afforded.

Having thus shown the irreconcileable inconsistencies between the real word of God existing in the universe, and that which is called the Word of God, as shown to us in a printed book that any man might make, I proceed to speak of the three principal means that have been employed in all ages, and perhaps in all countries, to impose upon mankind.

Those three means are Mystery, Miracle, and Prophecy, The first two are incompatible with true religion, and the third ought always to be suspected.

With respect to mystery, everything we behold is, in one sense, a mystery to us. Our own existence is a mystery; the whole vegetable world is a mystery. We cannot account how it is that an acorn, when put into the ground, is made to develop itself and become an oak. We know not how it is that the seed we sow unfolds and multiplies itself, and returns to us such an abundant interest for so small a capital.

The fact, however, as distinct from the operating cause, is not a mystery, because we see it, and we know also the means we are to use, which is no other than putting the seed in the ground. We know, therefore, as much as is necessary for us to know; and that part of the operation that we do not know, and which, if we did, we could not perform, the Creator takes upon himself and performs it for us. We are, therefore, better off than if we had been let into the secret, and left to do it for ourselves.

But though every created thing is, in this sense, a mystery, the word mystery cannot be applied to moral truth, any more than obscurity can be applied to light. The God in whom we believe is a God of moral truth, and not a God of mystery or obscurity. Mystery is the antagonist of truth. It is a fog of human invention, that obscures truth, and represents it in distortion. Truth never invelops itself in mystery, and the mystery in which it is at any time enveloped is the work of its antagonist, and never of itself.

Religion, therefore, being the belief of a God, and the practice of moral truth, cannot have connection with mystery. The belief of a God, so far from having any thing of mystery in it, is of all beliefs the most easy, because it arises to us, as is before observed, out of necessity. And the practice of moral truth, or, in other words, a practical imitation of the moral goodness of God, is no other than our acting toward each other as he acts benignly toward all. We cannot serve God in the manner we serve those who cannot do without such service; and, therefore, the only idea we can have of serving God, is that of contributing to the happiness of the living creation that God has made. This cannot be done by retiring ourselves from the society of the world and spending a recluse life in selfish devotion.

The very nature and design of religion, if I may so express it, prove even to demonstration that it must be free from every thing of mystery, and unencumbered with everything that is mysterious. Religion, considered as a duty, is incumbent upon every living soul alike, and, therefore, must be on a level to the understanding and comprehension of all. Man does not learn religion as he learns the secrets and mysteries of a trade. He learns the theory of religion by reflection. It arises out of the action of his own mind upon the things which he sees, or upon what he may happen to hear or to read, and the practice joins itself thereto.

When men, whether from policy or pious fraud, set up systems of religion incompatible with the word or works of God in the creation, and not only above, but repugnant to human comprehension, they were under the necessity of inventing or adopting a word that should serve as a bar to all questions, inquiries and speculations. The word mystery answered this purpose, and thus it has happened that religion, which is in itself without mystery, has been corrupted into a fog of mysteries.

As mystery answered all general purposes, miracle followed as an occasional auxiliary. The former served to bewilder the mind, the latter to puzzle the senses. The one was the lingo, the other the legerdemain.

But before going further into this subject, it will be proper to inquire what is to be understood by a miracle.

In the same sense that everything may be said to be a mystery, so also may it be said that everything is a miracle, and that no one thing is a greater miracle than another. The elephant, though larger, is not a greater miracle than a mite, nor a mountain a greater miracle than an atom. To an almighty power, it is no more difficult to make the one than the other, and no more difficult to make a millions of worlds than to make one. Everything, therefore, is a miracle, in one sense, whilst in the other sense, there is no such thing as a miracle. It is a miracle when compared to our power and to our comprehension; if not a miracle compared to the power that performs it; but as nothing in this description conveys the idea that is affixed to the word miracle, it is necessary to carry the inquiry further.

Mankind have conceived to themselves certain laws, by which what they call nature is supposed to act; and that a miracle is something contrary to the operation and effect of those laws; but unless we know the whole extent of those laws, and of what are commonly called the powers of nature, we are not able to judge whether any thing that may appear to us wonderful or miraculous be within, or be beyond, or be contrary to, her natural power of acting.

The ascension of a man several miles high into the air would have everything in it that constitutes the idea of a miracle, if it were not known that a species of air can be generated, several times lighter than the common atmospheric air, and yet possess elasticity enough to prevent the balloon in which that light air is enclosed from being compressed into as many times less bulk, by the common air that surrounds it. In like manner, extracting flashes or sparks of fire from the human body, as visible as from a steel struck with a flint, and causing iron or steel to move without any visible agent, would also give the idea of a miracle, if we were not acquainted with electricity and magnetism. So also would many other experiments in natural philosophy, to those who are not acquainted with the subject. The restoring persons to life who are to appearance dead as is practised upon drowned persons, would also be a miracle, if it were not known that animation is capable of being suspended without being extinct.

Besides these, there are performances be slight-of-hand, and by persons acting in concert, that have a miraculous appearance, which when known are thought nothing of. And besides these, there are mechanical and optical deceptions. There is now an exhibition in Paris of ghosts or spectres, which, though it is not imposed upon the spectators as a fact, has an astonishing appearance. As, therefore, we know not the extent to which either nature or art can go, there is no criterion to determine what a miracle is, and mankind, in giving credit to appearances, under the idea of their being miracles, are subject to be continually imposed upon.

Since, then, appearances are so capable of deceiving, and things not real have a strong resemblance to things that are, nothing can be more inconsistent than to suppose that the Almighty would make use of means such as are called miracles, that would subject the person who performed them to the suspicion of being an impostor, and the person who related them to be suspected of lying, and the doctrine intended to be supported thereby to be suspected as a fabulous invention.

Of all the modes of evidence that ever were invented to obtain belief to any system or opinion to which the name of religion has been given, that of miracle, however successful the imposition may have been, is the most inconsistent. For, in the first place, whenever recourse is had to show, for the purpose of procuring that belief, (for a miracle, under any idea of the word, is a show), it implies a lameness or weakness in the doctrine that is preached. And, in the second place, it is degrading the Almighty into the character of a showman, playing tricks to amuse and make the people stare and wonder. It is also the most equivocal sort of evidence that can be set up; for the belief is not to depend upon the thing called a miracle, but upon the credit of the reporter who says that he saw it; and, therefore, the thing, were it true, would have no better chance of being believed than if it were a lie.

Suppose I were to say, that when I sat down to write this book, a hand presented itself in the air, took up the pen, and wrote every word that is herein written; would anybody believe me? Certainly they would not. Would they believe me a whit the more if the thing had been a fact? Certainly they would not. Since, then, a real miracle, were it to happen, would be subject to the same fate as the falsehood, the inconsistency becomes the greater of supposing the Almighty would make use of means that would not answer the purpose for which they were intended, even if they were real.

If we are to suppose a miracle to be something so entirely out of the course of what is called nature, that she must go out of that course to accomplish it, and we see an account given of such a miracle by the person who said he saw it, it raises a question in the mind very easily decided, which is, is it more probable that nature should go out of her course, or that a man should tell a lie? We have never seen, in our time, nature go out of her course; but we have good reason to believe that millions of lies have been told in the same time; it is therefore, at least millions to one, that the reporter of a miracle tells a lie.

The story of the whale swallowing Jonah, though a whale is large enough to do it, borders greatly on the marvellous; but it would have approached nearer to the idea of a miracle, if Jonah had swallowed the whale. In this, which may serve for all cases of miracles, the matter would decide itself, as before stated, namely, is it more probable that a man should have swallowed a whale or told a lie?

But suppose that Jonah had really swallowed the whale, and gone with it in his belly to Nineveh, and to convince the people that it was true, had cast it up in their sight, of the full length and size of a whale, would they not have believed him to have been the devil, instead of a prophet? Or if the whale had carried Jonah to Nineveh, and cast him up in the same public manner, would they not have believed the whale to have been the devil, and Jonah one of his imps?

The most extraordinary of all the things called miracles, related in the New Testament, is that of the devil flying away with Jesus Christ, and carrying him to the top of a high mountain, and to the top of the highest pinnacle of the temple, and showing him and promising to him all the kingdoms of the World. How happened it that he did not discover America, or is it only with kingdoms that his sooty highness has any interest?

I have too much respect for the moral character of Christ to believe that he told this whale of a miracle himself; neither is it easy to account for what purpose it could have been fabricated, unless it were to impose upon the connoisseurs of Queen Anne's farthings and collectors of relics and antiquities; or to render the belief of miracles ridiculous, by outdoing miracles, as Don Quixote outdid chivalry; or to embarrass the belief of miracles, by making it doubtful by what power, whether of God or of the devil, anything called a miracle was performed. It requires, however, a great deal of faith in the devil to believe this miracle.

In every point of view in which those things called miracles can be placed and considered, the reality of them is improbable and their existence unnecessary. They would not, as before observed, answer any useful purpose, even if they were true; for it is more difficult to obtain belief to a miracle, than to a principle evidently moral without any miracle. Moral principle speaks universally for itself. Miracle could be but a thing of the moment, and seen but by a few; after this it requires a transfer of faith from God to man to believe a miracle upon man's report. Instead, therefore, of admitting the recitals of miracles as evidence of any system of religion being true, they ought to be considered as symptoms of its being fabulous. It is necessary to the full and upright character of truth that it rejects the crutch, and it is consistent with the character of fable to seek the aid that truth rejects. Thus much for mystery and miracle.

As mystery and miracle took charge of the past and the present, prophecy took charge of the future and rounded the tenses of faith. It was not sufficient to know what had been done, but what would be done. The supposed prophet was the supposed historian of times to come; and if he happened, in shooting with a long bow of a thousand years, to strike within a thousand miles of a mark, the ingenuity of posterity could make it point-blank; and if he happened to be directly wrong, it was only to suppose, as in the case of Jonah and Nineveh, that God had repented himself and changed his mind. What a fool do fabulous systems make of man!

It has been shown, in a former part of this work, that the original meaning of the words prophet and prophesying has been changed, and that a prophet, in the sense of the word as now used, is a creature of modern invention; and it is owing to this change in the meaning of the words, that the flights and metaphors of the Jewish poets, and phrases and expressions now rendered obscure by our not being acquainted with the local circumstances to which they applied at the time they were used, have been erected into prophecies, and made to bend to explanations at the will and whimsical conceits of sectaries, expounders, and commentators. Everything unintelligible was prophetical, and everything insignificant was typical. A blunder would have served for a prophecy, and a dish-clout for a type.

If by a prophet we are to suppose a man to whom the Almighty communicated some event that would take place in the future, either there were such men or there were not. If there were, it is consistent to believe that the event so communicated would be told in terms that could be understood, and not related in such a loose and obscure manner as to be out of the comprehension of those that heard it, and so equivocal as to fit almost any circumstance that might happen afterward. It is conceiving very irreverently of the Almighty, to suppose he would deal in this jesting manner with mankind, yet all the things called prophecies in the book called the Bible come under this description.

But it is with prophecy as it is with miracle; it could not answer the purpose even if it were real. Those to whom a prophecy should be told, could not tell whether the man prophesied or lied, or whether it had been revealed to him, or whether he conceited it; and if the thing that he prophesied, or intended to prophesy, should happen, or something like it, among the multitude of things that are daily happening, nobody could again know whether he foreknew it, or guessed at it, or whether it was accidental. A prophet, therefore, is a character useless and unnecessary; and the safe side of the case is to guard against being imposed upon by not giving credit to such relations.

Upon the whole, mystery, miracle, and prophecy are appendages that belong to fabulous and not to true religion. They are the means by which so many Lo, heres! and Lo, theres! have been spread about the world, and religion been made into a trade. The success of one impostor gave encouragement to another, and the quieting salvo of doing some good by keeping up a pious fraud protected them from remorse.

Having now extended the subject to a greater length than I first intended, I shall bring it to a close by abstracting a summary from the whole.

First—That the idea or belief of a word of God existing in print, or in writing, or in speech, is inconsistent in itself for the reasons already assigned. These reasons, among many others, are the want of a universal language; the mutability of language; the errors to which translations are subject; the possibility of totally suppressing such a word; the probability of altering it, or of fabricating the whole, and imposing it upon the world.

Secondly—That the Creation we behold is the real and ever-existing word of God, in which we cannot be deceived. It proclaimeth his power, it demonstrates his wisdom, it manifests his goodness and beneficence.

Thirdly—That the moral duty of man consists in imitating the moral goodness and beneficence of God manifested in the creation toward all his creatures. That seeing, as we daily do, the goodness of God to all men, it is an example calling upon all men to practise the same toward each other; and, consequently, that everything of persecution and revenge between man and man, and everything of cruelty to animals, is a violation of moral duty.

I trouble not myself about the manner of future existence. I content myself with believing, even to positive conviction, that the Power that gave me existence is able to continue it, in any form and manner he pleases, either with or without this body; and it appears more probable to me that I shall continue to exist hereafter, than that I should have had existence, as I now have, before that existence began.

It is certain that, in one point, all nations of the earth and all religions agree—all believe in a God; the things in which they disagree, are the redundancies annexed to that belief; and therefore, if ever an universal religion should prevail, it will not be believing anything new, but in getting rid of redundancies, and believing as man believed at first. Adam, if ever there was such a man, was created a Deist; but in the meantime, let every man follow, as he has a right to do, the religion and worship he prefers.

Critical Eye

FOR DISCUSSION

a. Paine claims "my own mind is my own church?" What exactly does he mean? Is this assertion important?

b. Many viewed Paine's work as following early eighteenth century British Deism. What does this approach outline? Do you think it is an appropriate way to approach religion, or is it, as many claim, blasphemy?

REAPPROACHING THE TEXT

Many claim that religion is the foundation of any civilized society; as such, how does Paine's approach to religion speak to his juxtaposition of "common sense" and spirituality?

WRITING ASSIGNMENT

Researching Paine's life, how does the treatment he received—social expulsion, prison, not allowing his body to be buried on American soil—speak to religious indignation? Are Americans overly-religious and, as a result, intolerant, or have we truly evolved into a country where a person can worship however they choose without fear of repercussions?

6 7 8

Gender, Sex, and Sexuality

Being Powerful is like being a lady. If you have to tell people you are, you aren't.
Margaret Thatcher

Whether women are better than men I cannot say—but I can say they are certainly no worse.
Golda Meir

Why can't they have gay people in the army? Personally, I think they are just afraid of a thousand guys with m16s going, "who'd you call a faggot?"
John Stewart

We live in a world of only two genders. As the 21st century progresses, societies continue to explore and define what a male and female's roles should be. Within the confines of our respective cultures, we embrace, expect, and exclude members based on these expectations of whom and, just as importantly, what its members should represent. Understanding how people should behave and look, as well as who we should become as citizens of nations, or, for that matter, who we can be intimate with, are mandates—either codified in law or unsaid but understood—that allow us to not only embrace our partners and neighbors, but punish them as well. Understanding how powerful sex is, how personally and socially defining it is—within the confines of our homes, schools, and religions—remains one of the most influential issues our world continues to grapple with.

Perhaps what is most perplexing about the issue of gender is that, in many ways, we are still holding fast to stereotypes that stagnate our identities. Should we still, in the 21st century, be arguing that men were born to do one thing and women another? Are we at a point where one's sexuality or sexual orientation can be viewed separately and distinctly from what makes them male or female? Moreover, should we consider that our sexual stereotyping is placing lives in danger?

The works presented here should help navigate the global ramifications of gender, sex, and sexuality in an attempt to help readers determine whether the old adage holds any truth. In short, "have we really come a long way, baby?"

Louie Crew

Thriving as an Outsider, Even as an Outcast, in Smalltown America

From 1973 to 1979, my spouse and I lived in Fort Valley, a town of 12,000 people, the seat of Peach County, sixty miles northeast of Plains, right in the geographic center of Georgia. I taught English at a local black college and my spouse was variously a nurse, hairdresser, choreographer for the college majorettes, caterer, and fashion designer.

The two of us have often been asked how we survived as a gay, racially integrated couple living openly in that small town. We are still perhaps too close to the Georgia experience and very much caught up in our similar struggles in central Wisconsin to offer a definite explanation, but our tentative conjectures should interest anyone who values the role of the dissident in our democracy.

Survive we did. We even throve before our departure. Professionally, my colleagues and the Regents of the University System of Georgia awarded me tenure, and the Chamber of Commerce awarded my spouse a career medal in cosmetology. Socially, we had friends from the full range of the economic classes in the community. We had attended six farewell parties in our honor before we called a halt to further fetes, especially several planned at too great a sacrifice by some of the poorest folks in the town. Furthermore, I had been away only four months when the college brought me back to address an assembly of Georgia judges, majors, police chiefs, and wardens. We are still called two to three times a week by scores of people seeking my spouse's advice on fashion, cooking, or the like.

It was not always so. In 1974 my spouse and I were denied housing which we had "secured" earlier before the realtor saw my spouse's color. HUD documented that the realtor thought that "the black man looked like a criminal." Once the town was up in arms when a bishop accused the two of us of causing a tornado which had hit the town early in 1975, an accusation which appeared on the front page of the newspaper. "This is

"Thriving as an Outsider, even as an Outcast, in Smalltown America," by Louie Crew. Used by permission of the author.

the voice of God. The town of Fort Valley is harboring Sodomists. Would one expect God to keep silent when homosexuals are tolerated? We remember what He did to Sodom and Gomorrah" (*The Macon Herald*, March 20, 1975; 1). A year later my Episcopal vestry asked me to leave the parish, and my own bishop summoned me for discipline for releasing to the national press correspondence related to the vestry's back-room maneuvers. Prompted in part by such officials, the local citizens for years routinely heckled us in public, sometimes threw rocks at our apartment, trained their children to spit on us from their bicycles if we dared to jog, and badgered us with hate calls on an average of six to eight times a week.

One such episode offers a partial clue to the cause of our survival. It was late summer, 1975 or 1976. I was on my motorcycle to post mail at the street-side box just before the one daily pickup at 6:00 P.M. About fifty yards away, fully audible to about seventy pedestrians milling about the court house and other public buildings, a group of police officers, all men, began shouting at me from the steps of their headquarters: "Louise! Faggot! Queer!"

Anyone who has ever tried to ease a motorcycle from a still position without revving the engine knows that the feat is impossible: try as I did to avoid the suggestion, I sounded as if I were riding off in a huff. About half-way up the street, I thought to myself, "I'd rather rot in jail than feel the way I do now." I turned around, drove back—the policemen still shouting and laughing—and parked in the lot of the station. When I walked to the steps, only the lone black policeman remained.

"Did you speak to me?" I asked him.

"No, sir," he replied emphatically.

Inside I badgered the desk sergeant to tell her chief to call me as soon as she could locate him, and I indicated that I would press charges it necessary to prevent a recurrence. I explained that the police misconduct was an open invitation to more violent hoodlums to act out the officers' fantasies with impunity in the dark. Later, I persuaded a black city commissioner and a white one, the latter our grocer and the former our mortician, to threaten the culprits with suspension if ever such misconduct occurred again.

Over a year later, late one Friday after his payday, a black friend of my spouse knocked at our door to offer a share of his Scotch to celebrate his raise—or so he said. Thus primed, he asked me, "You don't recognize me, do you?"

"No," I admitted.

"I'm the lone black policeman that day you were heckled. I came by really because I thought you two might want to know what happened inside when Louie stormed up to the sergeant."

"Yes," we said.

"Well, all the guys were crouching behind the partition to keep you from seeing that they were listening. Their eyes bulged when you threatened to bring in the K.B.I. and such. Then when you left, one spoke for all when he said, 'But sissies aren't supposed to do things like that!'"

Ironically, I believe that a major reason for our thriving on our own terms of candor about our relationship has been our commitment to resist the intimidation heaped upon us. For too long lesbians and gay males have unwillingly encouraged abuses against ourselves by serving advance notice to any bullies, be they the barnyard-playground variety, or the Bible-wielding pulpiteers, that we would whimper or run into hiding when confronted with even the threat of exposure. It is easy to confuse sensible nonviolence with cowardly nonresistance.

In my view, violent resistance would be counter-productive, especially for lesbians and gays who are outnumbered 10 to 1 by heterosexuals, according to Kinsey's statistics. Yet our personal experience suggests that special kinds of creative nonviolent resistance are a major source of hope if lesbians and gay males are going to reverse the physical and mental intimidation which is our daily portion in this culture.

Resistance to oppression can be random and spontaneous, as in part was my decision to return to confront the police hecklers, or organized and sustained, as more typically has been the resistance by which my spouse and I have survived. I believe that only organized and sustained resistance offers much hope for long-range change in any community. The random act is too soon forgotten or too easily romanticized.

Once we had committed ourselves to one another, my spouse and I never gave much thought for ourselves to the traditional device most gays have used for survival, the notorious "closet" in which one hides one's identity from all but a select group of friends. In the first place, a black man and a white man integrating a Georgia small town simply cannot be inconspicuous. More importantly, the joint checking account and other equitable economies fundamental to the quality of our marriage are public, not private acts. Our denial of the obvious would have secured closet space only for our suffocation; we would have lied, "We are ashamed and live in secret."

All of our resistance stems from our sense of our own worth, our conviction that we and our kind do not deserve the suffering which heterosexuals continue to encourage or condone for sexual outcasts. Dr. Martin Luther King used to say, "Those who go to the back of the bus, deserve the back of the bus."

Our survival on our own terms has depended very much on our knowing and respecting many of the rules of the system which we resist. We are not simply dissenters, but conscientious ones.

For example, we are both very hard workers. As a controversial person, I know that my professionalism comes under far more scrutiny than that of others. I learned early in my career that I could secure space for my differences by handling routine matters carefully. If one stays on good terms with secretaries, meets all deadlines, and willingly does one's fair share of the busy work of institutions, one is usually already well on the way towards earning collegial space, if not collegial support. In Georgia, I routinely volunteered to be secretary for most committees on which I served, thereby having enormous influence in the final form of the groups' deliberations without monopolizing the forum as most other molders of policy do. My spouse's many talents and sensibilities made him an invaluable advisor and confidante to scores of people in the community. Of course, living as we did in a hairdresser's salon, we knew a great deal more about the rest of the public than that public knew about us.

My spouse and I are fortunate in the fact that we like the enormous amount of work which we do. We are not mere opportunists working hard only as a gimmick to exploit the public for lesbian and gay issues. Both of us worked intensely at our professional assignments long before we were acknowledged dissidents with new excessive pressures to excel. We feel that now we must, however unfairly, be twice as effective as our competitors just to remain employed at all.

Our survival has also depended very much on our thorough knowledge of the system, often knowledge more thorough than that of those who would use the system against us. For example, when my bishop summoned me for discipline, I was able to show him that his own canons give him no authority to discipline a lay person except by excommunication. In fact, so hierarchical have the canons of his diocese become, that the only laity who exist worthy of their mention are the few lay persons on vestries.

Especially helpful has been our knowledge of communication procedures. For example, when an area minister attacked lesbians and gays on a TV talk show, I requested actual time; so well received was my response that for two more years I was a regular panelist on the talk show, thereby reaching most residents of the entire middle Georgia area as a known gay person, yet one speaking not just to sexual issues, but to a full range of religious and social topics.

When I was occasionally denied access to media, as in the parish or diocese or as on campus when gossip flared, I knew the value of candid explanations thoughtfully prepared, xeroxed, and circulated to enough folks to assure that the gossips would have access to the truthful version. For example, the vestry, which acted in secret, was caught by surprise when I sent copies of their hateful letter to most other parishioners, together with a copy of a psalm which I wrote protesting their turning the House of Prayer into a Court House. I also was able to explain that I continued to attend, not in defiance of their withdrawn invitation, but in obedience to the much higher invitation issued to us all by the real head of the Church. In January, 1979, in the first open meeting of the parish since the vestry's letter of unwelcome three years earlier, the entire parish voted to censure the vestry for that action and to extend to me the full welcome which the vestry had tried to deny. Only three voted against censure, all three of them a minority of the vestry being censured.

My spouse and I have been very conscious of the risks of our convictions. We have viewed our credentials—my doctorate and his professional licenses—not as badges of comfortable respectability, but as assets to be invested in social change. Dr. King did not sit crying in the Albany jail, "Why don't these folk respect me? How did his happen? What am I doing here?" When my spouse and I have been denied jobs for which we were the most qualified applicants, we have not naively asked how such things could be, nor have we dwelled overly long on self-pity, for we have known in advance the prices we might have to pay, even if to lose our lives. Our realism about danger and risk has helped us to preserve our sanity when everyone about us has seemed insane. I remember the joy which my spouse shared with me over the fact that he had just been fired for his efforts to organize other black nurses to protest their being treated as orderlies by the white managers of a local hospital.

Never, however, have we affirmed the injustices. Initially, we simply cannot be surprised by any evil and are thus less likely to be intimidated by it. Hence, we find ourselves heirs to a special hybrid of courage, a form of courage too often ignored by the heterosexual majority, but widely manifest among sexual outcasts, not the courage of bravado on battlegrounds or sportsfields, but the delicate courage of the lone person who patiently waits out the stupidity of the herd, the cagey courage that has operated many an underground railway station.

Our survival in smalltown America has been helped least, I suspect, by our annoying insistence that potential friends receive us not only in our own right, but also as members of the larger lesbian/gay and black communities of which we are a part. Too many whites and heterosexuals are prepared to single us out as "good queers" or "good niggers," offering us thereby the "rewards" of their friendship only at too great a cost to our integrity. My priest did not whip up the vestry against me the first year we lived openly together. He was perfectly happy to have one of his "clever queers" to dress his wife's hair and the other to help him write his annual report. We became scandalous only when the two of us began to organize the national group of lesbian and gay-male Episcopalians, known as INTEGRITY; then we were no longer just quaint. We threatened his image of himself as the arbiter of community morality, especially as he faced scores of queries from brother priests elsewhere.

Many lesbians and gay males are tamed by dependencies upon carefully selected heterosexual friends with whom they have shared their secret, often never realizing that in themselves alone, they could provide far more affirmation and discover far more strength than is being cultivated by the terms of these "friendships." Lesbians and gay males have always been taught to survive on the heterosexuals' terms, rarely on one's own terms, and almost never on the terms of a community shared with other lesbians and gay males.

Heterosexuals are often thus the losers. The heterosexual acquaintances close to us early on when we were less visible who dropped us later as our notoriety spread were in most cases folks of demonstrably much less character strength than those heterosexuals who remained our friends even as we asserted our difference with thoughtful independence.

My spouse and I have never been exclusive nor aspired to move to any ghetto. In December, 1978, on the night the Macon rabbi and I had successfully organized the area's Jews and gays to protest a concert by Anita Bryant, I returned home to watch the videotape of the march on the late news in the company of eight house guests invited by my spouse for a surprise party, not one of them gay (for some strange reason nine out of ten folks are not), not one of them obligated to be at the earlier march, and not one of them uneasy, as most of our acquaintances would have been a few years earlier before we had undertaken this reeducation together.

Folks who work for social change need to be very careful to allow room for it to happen, not to allow realistic appraisals of risks to prevent their cultivation of the very change which they germinate.

Our survival has been helped in no small way by our candor and clarity in response to rumor and gossip, which are among our biggest enemies. On my campus in Georgia, I voluntarily spoke about sexual issues to an average of 50 classes per year outside my discipline. Initially, those encounters sharpened my wits for tougher national forums, but long after I no longer needed these occasions personally for rehearsal, I continued to accept the invitations, thereby reaching a vast majority of the citizens of the small town where we continued to live. I used to enjoy the humor of sharing with such groups facts which would make my day-to-day life more pleasant. For example, I routinely noted that when a male student is shocked at my simple public "Hello," he would look both ways to see who might have seen him being friendly with the gay professor. By doing this he is telling me and all other knowledgeable folks far more new information about his own body chemistry than he is finding out about mine. More informed male students would reply, "Hello" when greeted. With this method I disarmed the hatefulness of one of their more debilitating weapons of ostracism.

All personal references in public discussions inevitably invade one's privacy, but I have usually found the invasion a small price to pay for the opportunity to educate the public to the fact that the issues which most concern sexual outcasts are not genital, as the casters-out have so lewdly imagined, but issues of justice and simple fairness.

Resistance is ultimately an art which no one masters to perfection. Early in my struggles, I said to a gay colleague living openly in rural Nebraska, "We must stamp on every snake." Wisely he counseled, "Only if you want to get foot poisoning." I often wish I had more of the wisdom mentioned in *Ecclesiastes*, the ability to judge accurately, "The time to speak and the time to refrain from speaking." Much of the time I think it wise to pass public hecklers without acknowledging their taunts, especially when they are cowardly hiding in a crowd. When I have faced bullies head-on, I have tried to do so patiently, disarming them by my own control of the situation. Of course, I am not guaranteed that their violence can thus be aborted every time.

Two major sources of our survival are essentially very private—one, the intense care and love my spouse and I share, and the other, our strong faith in God as Unbounding Love. To these we prefer to make our secular witness, more by what we do than by what we say.

I am not a masochist. I would never choose the hard lot of the sexual outcast in small-town America. Had I the choice to change myself but not the world, I would return as a white male heterosexual city-slicker millionaire, not because whites, males, heterosexuals, city-slickers, and millionaires are better, but because they have it easier.

Yet everyone faces a different choice: accept the world the way you find it, or change it. For year after year I dissented, right in my own neighborhood.

America preserves an ideal of freedom, although it denies freedom in scores of instances. My eighth-grade civics teacher in Alabama did not mention the price I would have to pay for the freedom of speech she taught me to value. I know now that the docile and ignorant dislike you fiercely when you speak truth they prefer not to hear. But I had a good civics class, one that showed me how to change our government. I rejoice.

Sometimes I think it society's critics must appreciate the society far more than others, for the critics typically take very seriously the society's idle promises and forgotten dreams. When I occasionally see them, I certainly don't find many of my heterosexual eighth-grade classmates probing much farther than the issues of our common Form 1040 headaches and the issues as delivered by the evening news. Their lives seem often far duller than ours and the main adventures in pioneering they experience come vicariously, through television, the movies, and for a few, through books. In defining me as a criminal, my society may well have hidden a major blessing in its curse by forcing me out of lethargy into an on-going, rigorous questioning of the entire process. Not only do I teach *The Adventures of Huckleberry Finn,* my spouse and I have in an important sense had the chance to be Huck and Jim fleeing a different form of slavery and injustice in a very real present.

Critical Eye

FOR DISCUSSION

a. Despite Crew's civil right to live as he pleases, did the town have the right to express their views about his lifestyle? And, at the same time, what right does a religious community have to impose their religious views on others?

b. Can you ask someone to adjust his or her faith in order to accommodate someone else's lifestyle?

c. Can/should a faith that strictly forbids someone's lifestyle still embrace the individual?

REAPPROACHING THE LITERATURE

Imagine that Crew is telling the story from the viewpoint of a Muslim. Would the account be worse or the same?

WRITING ASSIGNMENT

Crew asserts that those who discriminate are often bullies who need to be confronted. Is this notion true or false? Furthermore, what are the dangers of challenging bullies in this day and age?

David Sedaris

Hejira

It wasn't anything I had planned on, but at the age of twenty-two, after dropping out of my second college and traveling across the country a few times, I found myself back in Raleigh, living in my parents' basement. After six months spent waking at noon, getting high, and listening to the same Joni Mitchell record over and over again, I was called by my father into his den and told to get out. He was sitting very formally in a big, comfortable chair behind his desk, and I felt as though he were firing me from the job of being his son.

I'd been expecting this to happen, and it honestly didn't bother me all that much. The way I saw it, being kicked out of the house was just what I needed if I was ever going to get back on my feet. "Fine," I said, "I'll go. But one day you'll be sorry."

I had no idea what I meant by this. It just seemed like the sort of thing a person should say when he was being told to leave.

My sister Lisa had an apartment over by the university and said that I could come stay with her as long as I didn't bring my Joni Mitchell record. My mother offered to drive me over, and after a few bong hits I took her up on it. It was a fifteen-minute trip across town, and on the way we listened to the rebroadcast of a radio call-in show in which people phoned the host to describe the various birds gathered around their backyard feeders. Normally the show came on in the morning, and it seemed strange to listen to it at night. The birds in question had gone to bed hours ago and probably had no idea they were still being talked about. I chewed this over and wondered if anyone back at the house was talking about *me*. To the best of my knowledge, no one had ever tried to imitate my voice or describe the shape of my head, and it was depressing that I went unnoticed while a great many people seemed willing to drop everything for a cardinal.

My mother pulled up in front of my sister's apartment building, and when I opened the car door she started to cry, which worried me, as she normally didn't do things like that. It wasn't one of those "I'm going to

"Hejira" from *Dress Your Family in Courduroy and Denim* by David Sedaris. Copyright © 2004 by David Sedaris. By permission of Little, Brown and Co., Inc.

miss you" things, but something sadder and more desperate than that. I wouldn't know it until months later, but my father had kicked me out of the house not because I was a bum but because I was gay. Our little talk was supposed to be one of those defining moments that shape a person's adult life, but he'd been so uncomfortable with the most important word that he'd left it out completely, saying only, "I think we both know why I'm doing this." I guess I could have pinned him down, I just hadn't seen the point. "Is it because I'm a failure? A drug addict? A sponge? Come on, Dad, just give me one good reason."

Who wants to say that?

My mother assumed that I knew the truth, and it tore her apart. Here was yet another defining moment, and again I missed it entirely. She cried until it sounded as if she were choking, "I'm sorry," she said, "I'm sorry, I'm sorry, I'm sorry."

I figured that within a few weeks I'd have a job and some crummy little apartment. It didn't seem insurmountable, but my mother's tears made me worry that finding these things might be a little harder than I thought. Did she honestly think I was that much of a loser?

"Really," I said, "I'll be fine."

The car light was on and I wondered what the passing drivers thought as they watched my mother sob. What kind of people did they think we were? Did they think she was one of those crybaby moms who fell apart every time someone chipped a coffee cup? Did they assume I'd said something to hurt her? Did they see us as just another crying mother and her stoned gay son, sitting in a station wagon and listening to a call-in show about birds, or did they imagine, for just one moment, that we might be special?

Critical Eye

FOR DISCUSSION

a. What does the father gain by not having a conversation about the true reason his son is being asked to leave the house? Why might the conversation be too difficult for him?

REAPPROACHING THE TEXT

Consider "A Conversation with My Father" (download) by Grace Paley alongside Sedaris's short story. What do they share in common? Have the troubles and expectations of parents and children lessened over the past sixty years?

WRITING ASSIGNMENT

Despite politics, sexual orientation, economic stability, or other life choices, how much input should a parent have in the lives of their adult children?

James Baldwin

From
Giovanni's Room

The person who appeared, and whom I did not know very well, was a girl named Sue, blonde and rather puffy, with the quality, in spite of the fact that she was not pretty, of the girls who are selected each year to be Miss Rheingold. She wore her curly blond hair cut very short, she had small breasts and a big behind, and in order, no doubt, to indicate to the world how little she cared for appearance or sensuality, she almost always wore tight blue jeans. I think she came from Philadelphia and her family was very rich. Sometimes, when she was drunk, she reviled them, and, sometimes, drunk in another way, she extolled their virtues of thrift and fidelity. I was both dismayed and relieved to see her. The moment she appeared I began, mentally, to take off all her clothes.

'Sit down,' I said. 'Have a drink.'

'I'm glad to *see* you,' she cried, sitting down, and looking about for the waiter. 'You'd rather dropped out of sight. How've you been?'— abandoning her search for the waiter and leaning forward to me with a friendly grin.

'I've been fine,' I told her. 'And you?'

'Oh, *me!* Nothing ever happens to me.' And she turned down the corners of her rather predatory and also vulnerable mouth to indicate that she was both joking and not joking. 'I'm built like a brick stone wall.' We both laughed. She peered at me. 'They tell me you're living way out at the end of Paris, near the zoo.'

'I found a maid's room out there. Very cheap.'

'Are you living alone?'

I did not know whether she knew about Giovanni or not. I felt a hint of sweat on my forehead. 'Sort of,' I said.

'Sort of? What the hell does *that* mean? Do you have a monkey with you, or something?'

From *Giovanni's Room* by James Baldwin, copyright © 1956 by James Baldwin. Used by permission of Doubleday, a division of Random House, Inc.

I grinned, 'No. But this French kid I know, he lives with his mistress, but they fight a lot and it's really *his* room so sometimes, when his mistress throws him out, he bunks with me for a couple of days.'

'Ah!' she sighed. '*Chagrin d'amour!*'

'He's having a good time,' I said. 'He loves it.' I looked at her. 'Aren't you?

'Stone walls,' she said, 'are impenetrable.'

The waiter arrived. 'Doesn't it,' I dared, 'depend on the weapon?'

'What are you buying me to drink?' she asked.

'What do you want?' We were both grinning. The waiter stood above us, manifesting a kind of surly *joie de vivre*.

'I believe I'll have'—she batted the eyelashes of her tight blue eyes—'*un ricard*. With a hell of a lot of ice.'

'*Deux ricards,*' I said to the waiter '*avec beaucoup de la glace.*'

'*Oui, monsieur.*' I was sure he despised us both. I thought of Giovanni and of how many times in an evening the phrase, *Oui, monsieur* fell from his lips. With this fleeting thought there came another, equally fleeting: a new sense of Giovanni, his private life and pain, and all that moved like a flood in him when we lay together at night.

'To continue,' I said.

'To continue?' She made her eyes very wide and blank. 'Where were we?' She was trying to be coquettish and she was trying to be hard-headed. I felt that I was doing something very cruel.

But I could not stop. 'We were talking about stone walls and how they could be entered.'

'I never knew,' she simpered, 'that you had any interest in stone walls.'

'There's a lot about me you don't know.' The waiter returned with our drinks. 'Don't you think discoveries are fun?'

She stared discontentedly at her drink. 'Frankly,' she said, turning toward me again, with those eyes, 'no.'

'Oh, you're much too young for that,' I said. '*Everything* should be a discovery.'

She was silent for a moment. She sipped her drink. 'I've made,' she said, finally, 'all the discoveries that I can stand.' But I watched the way her thighs moved against the cloth of her jeans.

'But you can't just go on being a brick stone wall forever.'

'I don't see why not,' she said. 'Nor do I see *how* not.'

'Baby,' I said, 'I'm making you a proposition.'

She picked up her glass again and sipped it, staring straight outward at the boulevard. 'And what's the proposition?'

'Invite me for a drink. *Chez toi.*'

'I don't believe,' she said, turning to me, 'that I've got anything in the house.'

'We can pick up something on the way,' I said.

She stared at me for a long time. I forced myself not to drop my eyes. 'I'm sure that I shouldn't,' she said at last.

'Why not?'

She made a small, helpless movement in the wicker chair. 'I don't know. I don't know what you want.'

I laughed. 'If you invite me home for a drink,' I said, 'I'll show you.'

'I think you're being impossible,' she said, and for the first time there was something genuine in her eyes and voice.

'Well,' I said, 'I think *you* are.' I looked at her with a smile which was, I hoped, both boyish and insistent. 'I don't know what I've said that's so impossible. I've put all my cards on the table. But you're still holding yours. I don't know why you should think a man's being impossible when he declares himself attracted to you.'

'Oh, please,' she said, and finished her drink, 'I'm sure it's just the summer sun.'

'The summer sun,' I said, 'has nothing to do with it.' And when she still made no answer, 'All you've got to do,' I said desperately, 'is decide whether we'll have another drink here or at your place.'

She snapped her fingers abruptly but did not succeed in appearing jaunty. 'Come along,' she said. 'I'm certain to regret it. But you really will have to buy something to drink. There *isn't* anything in the house. And that way,' she added, after a moment, 'I'll be sure to get something out of the deal.'

It was I, then, who felt a dreadful holding back. To avoid looking at her, I made a great show of getting the waiter. And he came, as surly as ever, and I paid him, and we rose and started walking towards the rue de Sèvres, where Sue had a small apartment.

Her apartment was dark and full of furniture. 'None of it is mine,' she said. 'It all belongs to the French lady of a certain age from whom I rented it, who is now in Monte Carlo for her nerves.' She was very nervous, too, and I saw that this nervousness could be, for a little while, a great help to me. I had bought a small bottle of cognac and I put it down on her marble-topped table and took her in my arms. For some reason I was terribly aware that it was after seven in the evening, that soon the sun would have disappeared from the river, that all the Paris night was about to begin, and that Giovanni was now at work.

She was very big and she was disquietingly fluid—fluid without, however, being able to flow. I felt a hardness and a constriction in her, a grave distrust, created already by too many men like me ever to be conquered now. What we were about to do would not be pretty.

And, as though she felt this, she moved away from me. 'Let's have a drink' she said. 'Unless, of course, you're in a hurry. I'll try not to keep you any longer than absolutely necessary.'

She smiled and I smiled, too. We were as close in that instant as we would ever get—like two thieves. 'Let's have several drinks.' I said.

'But not *too* many,' she said, and simpered again suggestively, like a broken-down movie queen facing the cruel cameras again after a long eclipse.

She took the cognac and disappeared into her corner of a kitchen. 'Make yourself comfortable,' she shouted out to me. 'Take off your shoes. Take off your socks. Look at my books—I often wonder what I'd do if there weren't any books in the world.'

I took off my shoes and lay back on her sofa. I tried not to think. But I was thinking that what I did with Giovanni could not possibly be more immoral than what I was about to do with Sue.

She came back with two great brandy snifters. She came close to me on the sofa and we touched glasses. We drank a little, she watching me all the while, and then I touched her breasts. Her lips parted and she put her glass down with extraordinary clumsiness and lay against me. It was a gesture of great despair and I knew that she was giving herself, not to me, but to that lover who would never come.

And I—I thought of many things, lying coupled with Sue in that dark place. I wondered if she had done anything to prevent herself from becoming pregnant; and the thought of a child belonging to Sue and me, of my being trapped that way—in the very act, so to speak, of trying to escape—almost precipitated a laughing jag. I wondered if her blue jeans had been thrown on top of the cigarette she had been smoking. I wondered if anyone else had a key to her apartment, if we could be heard through the inadequate walls, how much in a few moments, we would hate each other. I also approached Sue as though she were a job of work, a job which it was necessary to do in an unforgettable manner. Somewhere, at the very bottom of myself, I realized that I was doing something awful to her and it became a matter of my honor not to let this fact become too obvious. I tried to convey, through this grisly act of love, the intelligence, at least, that it was not her, not *her* flesh, that I despised—it would not be her I could not face when we became vertical again. Again, somewhere at the bottom of me, I realized that my fears had been excessive and groundless and, in effect, a lie: it became clearer every instant that what I had been afraid of had nothing to do with my body. Sue was not Hella and she did not lessen my terror of what would happen when Hella came: she increased it, she made it more real than it had been before. At the same time, I realized that my performance with Sue was succeeding even too well, and I tried not to despise her for feeling so little what her laborer felt. I travelled through a network of Sue's cries, of Sue's tom-tom fists on my back, and judged by means of her thighs, by means of her legs, how soon I could be free. Then I thought, *The end is coming soon,* her sobs became even higher and harsher, I was terribly aware of the small of my back and the cold sweat there, I thought, *Well, let her have it for Christ sake, get it over with;* then it was ending and I hated her and me, then it was over, and the dark, tiny room rushed back. And I wanted only to get out of there.

She lay still for a long time. I felt the night outside and it was calling me. I leaned up at last and found a cigarette.

'Perhaps,' she said, 'we should finish our drinks.'

She sat up and switched on the lamp which stood beside her bed. I had been dreading this moment. But she saw nothing in my eyes—she stared at me as though I had made a long journey on a white charger all the way to her prison house. She lifted her glass.

'*À la votre,*' I said.

'*À la* votre?' She giggled. '*À la* tienne, *chéri!*' She leaned over and kissed me on the mouth. Then, for a moment, she felt something; she leaned back and stared at me, her eyes not quite tightening yet; and she said, lightly, 'Do you suppose we could do this again sometime?'

'I don't see why not,' I told her, trying to laugh. 'We carry our own equipment.'

She was silent. Then: 'Could we have supper together—tonight?'

'I'm sorry,' I said. 'I'm really sorry, Sue, but I've got a date.'

'Oh. Tomorrow, maybe?'

'Look, Sue. I hate to make dates. I'll just surprise you.'

She finished her drink. 'I doubt that,' she said.

She got up and walked away from me. 'I'll just put on some clothes and come down with you.'

She disappeared and I heard the water running. I sat there, still naked, but with my socks on, and poured myself another brandy. Now I was afraid to go out into that night which had seemed to be calling me only a few moments before.

When she came back she was wearing a dress and some real shoes, and she had sort of fluffed up her hair. I had to admit she looked better that way, really more like a girl, like a school-girl. I rose and started putting on my clothes. 'You look nice,' I said.

There was a great many things she wanted to say, but she forced herself to say nothing. I could scarcely bear to watch the struggle occurring in her face, it made me so ashamed. 'Maybe you'll be lonely again,' she said, finally. 'I guess I won't mind if you come looking for me.' She wore the strangest smile I had ever seen. It was pained and vindictive and humiliated, but she inexpertly smeared across this grimace a bright, girlish gaiety—as rigid as the skeleton beneath her flabby body. If fate ever allowed Sue to reach me, she would kill me with just that smile.

'Keep a candle,' I said, 'in the window'—and she opened her door and we passed out into the streets.

Critical Eye

FOR DISCUSSION

a. In what way is the character dealing with his own self-hatred as he tries to reach out for human contact?

b. Is this text condemning casual sex or revealing a kind of enlightenment that comes as a result of it?

REAPPROACHING THE TEXT

While we are not made aware of it in this section, the text reveals that the main character is a homosexual. How does that impact your reading of this section?

WRITING ASSIGNMENT

In what ways are we all leading two lives? Is it almost necessary to do so in order to protect ourselves from the scrutiny and abuse of others?

David Mura

How America Unsexes the Asian Male

The Japanese-American actor Marc Hayashi once said to me: "Every culture needs its eunuchs. And we're it. Asian-American men are the eunuchs of America." I felt an instant shock of recognition.

To my chagrin, I came close to being one such eunuch on screen in the Coen brothers' movie "Fargo."

The call for the role seemed perfect: a Japanese-American man, in his late 30's, a bit portly, who speaks with a Minnesota accent.

I am a sansei, a third-generation Japanese-American. I've lived in Minnesota for 20 years. Though not portly, I'm not thin. A writer and a performance artist, I had done one small film for PBS.

After I passed the first two readings, my wife and I talked about what other parts might follow and even joked about moving to Hollywood. But in the end, the Coens found another Asian-American actor.

But when I saw the much-acclaimed "Fargo," I said to myself, "Thank God I didn't get the part." The character I would have played is Mike Yanagita, a Japanese-American who speaks with a thick Minnesota accent and awkwardly attempts a pass at an old high school friend, Marge Gunderson, a rural police chief who is visibly pregnant.

He then tells of marrying a mutual acquaintance from high school and of her recent death from cancer. A few scenes later, Marge learns that his marriage was fiction: the acquaintance is not only alive, but has also complained to the police that Mike has been harassing her.

The Japanese-American character has no relevance to Margie's investigation. He is there mainly for humor. The humor is based on his derangement and his obvious illusions that Marge or their acquaintance would ever find him attractive.

I recognized this character as only the latest in a long line of Asian and Asian-American male nerds. Often, as in "Fargo," such a character will

"How America Unsexes the Asian Male" by David Mura. Reprinted by permission of the author.

pant after white women, ridiculous in his desires. In the movies, as in the culture as a whole, Asian-American men seem to have no sexual clout. Or sexual presence.

Americans rarely talk about race and sex together. It's still taboo. Yet, I often wonder what people make of me and my wife, who is three-quarters WASP and one-quarter Hungarian Jew. Recently we went shopping with my sister Linda and our children. Several people, all white, mistook Linda for the wife, the mother. Was that because many whites find it difficult to picture an Asian-American man with a white woman?

In fiction, when East meets West, it is almost always a Western man meeting an Asian woman. There is constant reinforcement for the image of the East as feminine and the stereotype of Asian women as exotic, submissive and sensual. From "Madame Butterfly" to "The Karate Kid, Part II" and "Miss Saigon," the white man who falls in love with an Asian woman has been used to proffer the view that racial barriers cannot block the heart's affections.

But such pairings simply place while men at the screen's center and reinforce a hierarchy of power and sexual attractiveness. They play on the stereotype of the East as feminine. And where does that leave Asian men?

A salient feature of the play "M. Butterfly" is that it affirms this feminine view of Asian men. In it, a French diplomat conducts a lengthy love affair with someone he believes is a woman but is actually a Chinese transvestite. The affair proves that Asian manhood is indeed difficult to find, at least for white Westerners. And when the "mistress" strips to a highly buffed and masculine body, it is not just the diplomat who gasps, but the audience as well.

And the stereotypes continue. In the sitcom "All-American Girl," Margaret Cho played a hip Korean-American who dated white boys in defiance of her mother's wishes. The brother was a studious, obsequious geek who dated no one.

Asian and Asian-American men are simply not seen as attractive or sexual beings by the mainstream culture. What could be attractive about the horny, thick-glassed, nerdy Asian guy, ridiculous in his desires for white women?

How little things change. As a boy I watched Mickey Rooney as the Japanese buffoon neighbor in "Breakfast at Tiffany's" and knew I never wanted to be associated with this snarling, bucktoothed creature who shouted at Audrey Hepburn, "Miss Gorrightry, Miss Gorrightry," and panted when she offered to let him photograph her; I identified with John Wayne against the Japs; in "Have Gun Will Travel," I was a cowboy like Paladin, not the Chinese messenger who ran into the hotel lobby shouting, "Terragram for Mr. Paradin."

To me as a child, Asian features, Asian accents—these were all undesirable. They weren't part of my image of a real all-American boy.

For a while this seemed to work. My parents, interned during World War II, wanted to distance themselves from their ethnic roots. We lived in an all-white suburb, where I generally felt like one of the crowd. Then came adolescence, and my first boy-girl party. As usual, I was the only Asian-American and person of color in the room. But when we began to play spin the bottle, I felt a new sense of difference from the others. And then the bottle I'd spun pointed to a girl I had a crush on, and she refused to kiss me.

Did that have to do with race? I had no language to express how race factored into the way the others perceived me, nor did they. But if the culture had told me Asian men were nerds or goofy houseboys, the white kids at the party must have received the same message.

In college, in the early 1970's, my reaction to the sexual place assigned to me took the form of compulsive sexuality: rampant promiscuity with white women and an obsession with pornography. There was definitely a racial component to it: my desires focused specifically on white women. I thought if I was with a white woman, then I would be as "good" as a white guy.

It took me years to figure out what was going on. It helped to read Frantz Fanon, the great Caribbean author and psychiatrist. In "Black Skin, White Masks," he writes of how the black man who constantly sleeps with white women has the illusion that his feelings of inferiority will somehow be erased by this act.

Gradually, I began to ask questions about how I learned what was sexually attractive and what images the culture gave me of myself.

How, for instance, does race factor in attraction? A popular way around such questions is to say that love sees no color.

I don't believe that. We are taught to see and process race early on. Race may not be the sole determinant in interracial relationships, but it is a factor. When I look at my wife, for example, I'm aware my desires for her cannot be separated from the ways the culture has inculcated me with standards of white beauty.

And when I told Alexs Pate, an African-American novelist, about Marc Hayashi's comment about the eunuchization of Asian-American men, he replied, "And black men are the sexual demons."

One is undersexed, the other, oversexed. Everyone knows who possesses a normal, healthy sense of sexuality.

Recently, after a panel discussion on "identity art," an elderly white man came up and complimented me on a performance I'd appeared in with my friend Alexs. Then he asked, "Weren't you in 'Fargo,' too?"

"No," I replied. "That wasn't me."

Critical Eye

a. The author posits that being stereotyped sexually is just as offensive and prejudiced as any form of racism. Why might this be true?

b. Would you argue that the images of what can be construed as "attractive," "beautiful," or "normal" are received from television and film and that these images in turn affect how we view those who are outside of these constructs?

c. What other myths have we constructed about Asian people, and how have these images come about?

REAPPROACHING THE LITERATURE

Mura's assertion is that America, as a whole, has a fixed viewpoint of all Asian men as eunichs and all Asian women as exotic. Has he presented enough information to substantiate his claims?

WRITING ASSIGNMENT

Think of other ethnic groups in this country who have undergone some form of racial/ethnic stereotyping. Is what any of these groups has endured any different than what Mura writes about?

Junot Diaz

Fiesta 1980

Mami's youngest sister—my tía Yrma—finally made it to the United States that year. She and tío Miguel got themselves an apartment in the Bronx, off the Grand Concourse and everybody decided that we should have a party. Actually, my pops decided, but everybody—meaning Mami, tía Yrma, tío Miguel and their neighbors—thought it a dope idea. On the afternoon of the party Papi came back from work around six. Right on time. We were all dressed by then, which was a smart move on our part. If Papi had walked in and caught us lounging around in our underwear, he would have kicked our asses something serious.

He didn't say nothing to nobody, not even my moms. He just pushed past her, held up his hand when she tried to talk to him and headed right into the shower. Rafa gave me the look and I gave it back to him; we both knew Papi had been with that Puerto Rican woman he was seeing and wanted to wash off the evidence quick.

Mami looked really nice that day. The United States had finally put some meat on her; she was no longer the same flaca who had arrived here three years before. She had cut her hair short and was wearing tons of cheap-ass jewelry which on her didn't look too lousy. She smelled like herself, like the wind through a tree. She always waited until the last possible minute to put on her perfume because she said it was a waste to spray it on early and then have to spray it on again once you got to the party.

We—meaning me, my brother, my little sister and Mami—waited for Papi to finish his shower. Mami seemed anxious, in her usual dispassionate way. Her hands adjusted the buckle of her belt over and over again. That morning, when she had gotten us up for school, Mami told us that she wanted to have a good time at the party. I want to dance, she said, but now, with the sun sliding out of the sky like spit off a wall, she seemed ready just to get this over with.

Rafa didn't much want to go to no party either, and me, I never wanted to go anywhere with my family. There was a baseball game in the parking lot outside and we could hear our friends, yelling, Hey, and, Cabrón,

"Fiesta 1980," from *Drown* by Junot Diaz, copyright © 1996 by Junot Diaz. Used by permission of Riverhead Books, an imprint of Penguin Group (USA) Inc.

to one another. We heard the pop of a ball as it sailed over the cars, the clatter of an aluminum bat dropping to the concrete. Not that me or Rafa loved baseball; we just liked playing with the local kids, thrashing them at anything they were doing. By the sounds of the shouting, we both knew the game was close, either of us could have made a difference. Rafa frowned and when I frowned back, he put up his fist. Don't you mirror me, he said.

Don't you mirror me, I said.

He punched me—I would have hit him back but Papi marched into the living room with his towel around his waist, looking a lot smaller than he did when he was dressed. He had a few strands of hair around his nipples and a surly closed-mouth expression, like maybe he'd scalded his tongue or something.

Have they eaten? he asked Mami.

She nodded. I made you something.

You didn't let him eat, did you?

Ay, Dios mío, she said, letting her arms fall to her side.

Ay, Dios mío is right, Papi said.

I was never supposed to eat before our car trips, but earlier, when she had put out our dinner of rice, beans and sweet platanos, guess who had been the first one to clean his plate? You couldn't blame Mami really, she had been busy—cooking, getting ready, dressing my sister Madai. I should have reminded her not to feed me but I wasn't that sort of son.

Papi turned to me. Coño, muchacho, why did you eat?

Rafa had already started inching away from me. I'd once told him I considered him a low-down chickenshit for moving out of the way every time Papi was going to smack me.

Collateral damage, Rafa had said. Ever heard of it?

No.

Look it up.

Chickenshit or not, I didn't dare glance at him. Papi was old-fashioned; he expected your undivided attention when you were getting your ass whupped. You couldn't look him in the eye either—that wasn't allowed. Better to stare at his belly button, which was perfectly round and immaculate. Papi pulled me to my feet by my ear.

If you throw up—

I won't, I cried, tears in my eyes, more out of reflex than pain.

Ya, Ramón, ya. It's not his fault, Mami said.

They've known about this party forever. How did they think we were going to get there? Fly?

He finally let go of my ear and I sat back down. Madai was too scared to open her eyes. Being around Papi all her life had turned her into a major-league wuss. Anytime Papi raised his voice her lip would start trembling, like some specialized tuning fork. Rafa pretended that he had knuckles to crack and when I shoved him, he gave me a *Don't start* look. But even that little bit of recognition made me feel better.

I was the one who was always in trouble with my dad. It was like my God-given duty to piss him off, to do everything the way he hated. Our fights didn't bother me too much. I still wanted him to love me, something that never seemed strange or contradictory until years later, when he was out of our lives.

By the time my ear stopped stinging Papi was dressed and Mami was crossing each one of us, solemnly, like we were heading off to war. We said, in turn, Bendición, Mami, and she poked us in our five cardinal spots while saying, Que Dios te bendiga.

This was how all our trips began, the words that followed me every time I left the house.

None of us spoke until we were inside Papi's Volkswagen van. Brand-new, lime-green and bought to impress. Oh, we were impressed, but me, every time I was in that VW and Papi went above twenty miles an hour, I vomited. I'd never had trouble with cars before—that van was like my curse. Mami suspected it was the upholstery. In her mind, American things—appliances, mouthwash, funny-looking upholstery—all seemed to have an intrinsic badness about them. Papi was careful about taking me anywhere in the VW, but when he had to, I rode up front in Mami's usual seat so I could throw up out a window.

¿Cómo te sientas? Mami asked over my shoulder when Papi pulled onto the turnpike. She had her hand on the base of my neck. One thing about Mami, her palms never sweated.

I'm OK, I said, keeping my eyes straight ahead. I definitely didn't want to trade glances with Papi. He had this one look, furious and sharp, that always left me feeling bruised.

Toma. Mami handed me four mentas. She had thrown three out her window at the beginning of our trip, an offering to Eshú; the rest were for me.

I took one and sucked it slowly, my tongue knocking it up against my teeth. We passed Newark Airport without any incident. If Madai had been awake she would have cried because the planes flew so close to the cars.

How's he feeling? Papi asked.

Fine, I said. I glanced back at Rafa and he pretended like he didn't see me. That was the way he was, at school and at home. When I was in trouble, he didn't know me. Madai was solidly asleep, but even with her face all wrinkled up and drooling she looked cute, her hair all separated into twists.

I turned around and concentrated on the candy. Papi even started to joke that we might not have to scrub the van out tonight. He was beginning to loosen up, not checking his watch too much. Maybe he was thinking about that Puerto Rican woman or maybe he was just happy that we were all together. I could never tell. At the toll, he was feeling positive enough to actually get out of the van and search around under the basket for dropped coins. It was something he had once done to amuse Madai, but now it was habit. Cars behind us honked their horns and I slid down in my seat. Rafa didn't care; he grinned back at the other cars and waved. His actual job was to make sure no cops were coming. Mami shook Madai awake and as soon as she saw Papi stooping for a couple of quarters she let out this screech of delight that almost took off the top of my head.

That was the end of the good times. Just outside the Washington Bridge, I started feeling woozy. The smell of the upholstery got all up inside my head and I found myself with a mouthful of saliva. Mami's hand tensed on my shoulder and when I caught Papieye, he was like, No way. Don't do it.

The first time I got sick in the van Papi was taking me to the library, Rafa was with us and he couldn't believe I threw up. I was famous for my steel-lined stomach. A third-world childhood could give you that. Papi was worried enough that just as quick as Rafa could drop off the books we were on our way home. Mami fixed me one of her honey-and-onion concoctions and that made my stomach feel better. A week later we tried the library again and on this go-around I couldn't get the window open in time. When Papi got me home, he went and cleaned out the van himself, an expression of askho on his face. This was a big deal, since Papi almost never cleaned anything himself. He came back inside and found me sitting on the couch feeling like hell.

It's the car, he said to Mami. It's making him sick.

This time the damage was pretty minimal, nothing Papi couldn't wash off the door with a blast of the hose. He was pissed, though; he jammed his finger into my cheek, a nice solid thrust. That was the way he was with his punishments: imaginative. Earlier that year I'd written an essay in school called "My Father the Torturer," but the teacher made me write a new one. She thought I was kidding.

We drove the rest of the way to the Bronx in silence. We only stopped once, so I could brush my teeth. Mami had brought along my toothbrush and a tube of toothpaste and while every car known to man sped by us she stood outside with me so I wouldn't feel alone.

Tío Miguel was about seven feet tall and had his hair combed up and out, into a demi-fro. He gave me and Rafa big spleen-crushing hugs and then kissed Mami and finally ended up with Madai on his shoulder. The last time I'd seen Tío was at the airport, his first day in the United States. I remembered how he hadn't seemed all that troubled to be in another country.

He looked down at me. Carajo, Yunior, you look horrible!

He threw up, my brother explained.

I pushed Rafa. Thanks a lot, ass-face.

Hey, he said. Tío asked.

Tío clapped a bricklayer's hand on my shoulder. Everybody gets sick sometimes, he said. You should have seen me on the plane over here. Dios mio! He rolled his Asian-looking eyes for emphasis. I thought we were all going to die.

Everybody could tell he was lying. I smiled like he was making me feel better.

Do you want me to get you a drink? Tío asked. We got beer and rum.

Miguel, Mami said. He's young.

Young? Back in Santo Domingo, he'd be getting laid by now.

Mami thinned her lips, which took some doing.

Well, it's true, Tío said.

So, Mami, I said. When do I get to go visit the D.R.?

That's enough, Yunior.

Its the only pussy you'll ever get, Rafa said to me in English.

Not counting your girlfriend, of course.

Rafa smiled. He had to give me that one.

Papi came in from parking the van. He and Miguel gave each other the sort of handshakes that would have turned my fingers into Wonder bread.

Coño, compa'i, ¿cómo va todo? they said to each other.

Tía came out then, with an apron on and maybe the longest Lee Press-On Nails I've ever seen in my life. There was this one guru motherfucker in the *Guinness Book of World Records* who had longer nails, but I tell you, it was close. She gave everybody kisses, told me and Rafa how guapo we were—Rafa, of course, believed her—told Madai how bella she was, but when she got to Papi, she froze a little, like maybe she'd seen a wasp on the tip of his nose, but then kissed him all the same.

Mami told us to join the other kids in the living room. Tío said, Wait a minute, I want to show you the apartment. I was glad Tía said, Hold on, because from what I'd seen so far, the place had been furnished in Contemporary Dominican Tacky. The less I saw, the better. I mean, I liked plastic sofa covers but damn, Tío and Tía had taken it to another level. They had a disco ball hanging in the living room and the type of stucco ceilings that looked like stalactite heaven. The sofas all had golden tassels dangling from their edges. Tía came out of the kitchen with some people I didn't know and by the time she got done introducing everybody, only Papi and Mami were given the guided tour of the four-room third-floor apartment. Me and Rafa joined the kids in the living room. They'd already started eating. We were hungry, one of the girls explained, a pastelito in hand. The boy was about three years younger than me but the girl who'd spoken, Leti, was my age. She and another girl were on the sofa together and they were cute as hell.

Leti introduced them: the boy was her brother Wilquins and the other girl was her neighbor Mari. Leti had some serious tetas and I could tell that my brother was going to gun for her. His taste in girls was predictable. He sat down right between Leti and Mari and by the way they were smiling at him I knew he'd do fine. Neither of the girls gave me more than a cursory one-two, which didn't bother me. Sure, I liked girls but I was always too terrified to speak to them unless we were arguing or I was calling them stupidos, which was one of my favorite words that year. I turned to Wilquins and asked him what there was to do around here. Mari, who had the lowest voice I'd ever heard, said, He can't speak.

What does that mean?

He's mute.

I looked at Wilquins incredulously. He smiled and nodded, as if he'd won a prize or something.

Does he understand? I asked.

Of course he understands, Rafa said. He's not dumb.

I could tell Rafa had said that just to score points with the girls. Both of them nodded. Low-voice Mari said, He's the best student in his grade.

I thought, Not bad for a mute. I sat next to Wilquins. After about two seconds of TV Wilquins whipped out a bag of dominos and motioned to me. Did I want to play? Sure. Me and him played Rafa and Leti and we whupped their collective asses twice, which put Rafa in a real bad mood. He looked at me like maybe he wanted to take a swing, just one to make him feel better. Leti kept whispering into Rafa's ear, telling him it was OK.

In the kitchen I could hear my parents slipping into their usual modes. Papi's voice was loud and argumentative; you didn't have to be anywhere near him to catch his drift. And Mami, you had to put cups to your ears to hear hers. I went into the kitchen a few times—once so the tíos could show off how much bullshit I'd been able to cram in my head the last few years; another time for a bucket-sized cup of soda. Mami and Tía were frying tostones and the last of the pastelitos. She appeared happier now and the way her hands worked on our dinner you would think she had a life somewhere else making rare and precious things. She nudged Tía every now and then, shit they must have been doing all their lives. As soon as Mami saw me though, she gave me the eye. Don't stay long, that eye said. Don't piss your old man off.

Papi was too busy arguing about Elvis to notice me. Then somebody mentioned María Montez and Papi barked, María Montez? Let me tell *you* about María Montez, compa'i.

Maybe I was used to him. His voice—louder than most adults'—didn't bother me none, though the other kids shifted uneasily in their seats. Wilquins was about to raise the volume on the TV, but Rafa said, I wouldn't do that. Muteboy had balls, though. He did it anyway and then sat down. Wilquins's pop came into the living room a second later, a bottle of Presidente in hand. That dude must have had Spider-senses or something. Did you raise that? he asked Wilquins and Wilquins nodded.

Is this your house? his pops asked. He looked ready to beat Wilquins silly but he lowered the volume instead.

See, Rafa said. You nearly got your *ass kicked*.

I met the Puerto Rican woman right after Papi had gotten the van. He was taking me on short trips, trying to cure me of my vomiting. It wasn't really working but I looked forward to our trips, even though at the end of each one I'd be sick. These were the only times me and Papi did anything together. When we were alone he treated me much better, like maybe I was his son or something.

Before each drive Mami would cross me.

Bendición, Mami, I'd say.

She'd kiss my forehead. Que Dios te bendiga. And then she would give me a handful of mentas because she wanted me to be OK. Mami didn't think these excursions would cure anything, but the one time she had brought it up to Papi he had told her to shut up, what did she know about anything anyway?

Me and Papi didn't talk much. We just drove around our neighborhood. Occasionally he'd ask, How is it?

And I'd nod, no matter how I felt.

One day I was sick outside of Perth Amboy. Instead of taking me home he went the other way on Industrial Avenue, stopping a few minutes later in front of a light blue house I didn't recognize. It reminded me of the Easter eggs we colored at school, the ones we threw out the bus windows at other cars.

The Puerto Rican woman was there and she helped me clean up. She had dry papery hands and when she rubbed the towel on my chest, she did it hard, like I was a bumper she was waxing. She was very thin and had a cloud of brown hair rising above her narrow face and the sharpest blackest eyes you've ever seen.

He's cute, she said to Papi.

Not when he's throwing up, Papi said.

What's your name? she asked me. Are you Rafa?

I shook my head.

Then it's Yunior, right?

I nodded.

You're the smart one, she said, suddenly happy with herself. Maybe you want to see my books?

They weren't hers. I recognized them as ones my father must have left in her house. Papi was a voracious reader, couldn't even go cheating without a paperback in his pocket.

Why don't you go watch TV? Papi suggested. He was looking at her like she was the last piece of chicken on earth.

We got plenty of channels, she said. Use the remote if you want.

The two of them went upstairs and I was too scared of what was happening to poke around. I just sat there, ashamed, expecting something big and fiery to crash down on our heads. I watched a whole hour of the news before Papi came downstairs and said, Let's go.

About two hours later the women laid out the food and like always nobody but the kids thanked them. It must be some Dominican tradition or something. There was everything I liked—chicharrones, fried chicken, tostones, sancocho, rice, fried cheese, yuca, avocado, potato salad, a meteor-sized hunk of pernil, even a tossed salad which I could do without—but when I joined the other kids around the serving table, Papi said, Oh no you don't, and took the paper plate out of my hand. His fingers weren't gentle.

What's wrong now? Tía asked, handing me another plate.

He ain't eating, Papi said. Mami pretended to help Rafa with the pernil.

Why can't he eat?

Because I said so.

The adults who didn't know us made like they hadn't heard a thing and Tío just smiled sheepishly and told everybody to go ahead and eat. All the kids—about ten of them now—trooped back into the living room with their plates a-heaping and all the adults ducked into the kitchen and the dining room, where the radio was playing loud-ass bachatas. I was the only one without a plate. Papi stopped me before I could get away from him. He kept his voice nice and low so nobody else could hear him.

If you eat anything, I'm going to beat you. ¿Entiendes?

I nodded.

And if your brother gives you any food, I'll beat him too. Right here in front of everybody. ¿Entiendes?

I nodded again. I wanted to kill him and he must have sensed it because he gave my head a little shove.

All the kids watched me come in and sit down in front of the TV.

What's wrong with your dad? Leti asked.

He's a dick, I said.

Rafa shook his head. Don't say that shit in front of people.

Easy for you to be nice when you're eating, I said.

Hey, if I was a pukey little baby, I wouldn't get no food either.

I almost said something back but I concentrated on the TV. I wasn't going to start it. No fucking way. So I watched Bruce Lee beat Chuck Norris into the floor of the Colosseum and tried to pretend that there was no food anywhere in the house. It was Tía who finally saved me. She came into the living room and said, Since you ain't eating, Yunior, you can at least help me get some ice.

I didn't want to, but she mistook my reluctance for something else.

I already asked your father.

She held my hand while we walked; Tía didn't have any kids but I could tell she wanted them. She was the sort of relative who always remembered your birthday but who you only went to visit because you had to. We didn't get past the first-floor landing before she opened her pocketbook and handed me the first of three pastelitos she had smuggled out of the apartment.

Go ahead, she said. And as soon as you get inside make sure you brush your teeth.

Thanks a lot, Tía, I said.

Those pastelitos didn't stand a chance.

She sat next to me on the stairs and smoked her cigarette. All the way down on the first floor and we could still hear the music and the adults and the television. Tía looked a ton like Mami; the two of them were both short and light-skinned. Tía smiled a lot and that was what set them apart the most.

How is it at home, Yunior?

What do you mean?

How's it going in the apartment? Are you kids OK?

I knew an interrogation when I heard one, no matter how sugar-coated it was. I didn't say anything. Don't get me wrong, I loved my tía, but something told me to keep my mouth shut. Maybe it was family loyalty, maybe I just wanted to protect Mami or I was afraid that Papi would find out—it could have been anything really.

Is your mom all right?

I shrugged.

Have there been lots of fights?

None, I said. Too many shrugs would have been just as bad as an answer. Papi's at work too much.

Work, Tía said, like it was somebody's name she didn't like.

Me and Rafa, we didn't talk much about the Puerto Rican woman. When we ate dinner at her house, the few times Papi had taken us over there, we still acted like nothing was out of the ordinary. Pass the ketchup, man. No sweat, bro. The affair was like a hole in our living room floor, one we'd gotten so used to circumnavigating that we sometimes forgot it was there.

By midnight all the adults were crazy dancing. I was sitting outside Tía's bedroom—where Madai was sleeping—trying not to attract attention. Rafa had me guarding the door; he and Leti were in there too, with some of the other kids, getting busy no doubt. Wilquins had gone across the hall to bed so I had me and the roaches to mess around with.

Whenever I peered into the main room I saw about twenty moms and dads dancing and drinking beers. Every now and then somebody yelled, Quisqueya! And then everybody else would yell and stomp their feet. From what I could see my parents seemed to be enjoying themselves.

Mami and Tía spent a lot of time side by side, whispering, and I kept expecting something to come of this, a brawl maybe. I'd never once been out with my family when it hadn't turned to shit. We weren't even theatrical or straight crazy like other families. We fought like sixth-graders, without any real dignity. I guess the whole night I'd been waiting for a blowup, something between Papi and Mami. This was how I always figured Papi would be exposed, out in public, where everybody would know.

You're a cheater!

But everything was calmer than usual. And Mami didn't look like she was about to say anything to Papi. The two of them danced every now and then but they never lasted more than a song before Mami joined Tía again in whatever conversation they were having.

I tried to imagine Mami before Papi. Maybe I was tired, or just sad, thinking about the way my family was. Maybe I already knew how it would all end up in a few years, Mami without Papi, and that was why I did it.

Picturing her alone wasn't easy. It seemed like Papi had always been with her, even when we were waiting in Santo Domingo for him to send for us.

The only photograph our family had of Mami as a young woman, before she married Papi, was the one that somebody took of her at an election party that I found one day while rummaging for money to go to the arcade. Mami had it tucked into her immigration papers. In the photo, she's surrounded by laughing cousins I will never meet, who are all shiny from dancing, whose clothes are rumpled and loose. You can tell it's night and hot and that the mosquitos have been biting. She sits straight and even in a crowd she stands out, smiling quietly like maybe she's the one everybody's celebrating. You can't see her hands but I imagined they're knotting a straw or a bit of thread. This was the woman my father met a year later on the Malecón, the woman Mami thought she'd always be.

Mami must have caught me studying her because she stopped what she was doing and gave me a smile, maybe her first one of the night. Suddenly I wanted to go over and hug her, for no other reason than I loved her, but there were about eleven fat jiggling bodies between us. So I sat down on the tiled floor and waited.

I must have fallen asleep because the next thing I knew Rafa was kicking me and saying, Let's go. He looked like he'd been hitting those girls off; he was all smiles. I got to my feet in time to kiss Tía and Tío good-bye. Mami was holding the serving dish she had brought with her.

Where's Papi? I asked,

He's downstairs, bringing the van around. Mami leaned down to kiss me.

You were good today, she said.

And then Papi burst in and told us to get the hell downstairs before some pendejo cop gave him a ticket. More kisses, more handshakes and then we were gone.

I don't remember being out of sorts after I met the Puerto Rican woman, but I must have been because Mami only asked me questions when she thought something was wrong in my life. It took her about ten passes but finally she cornered me one afternoon when we were alone in the apartment. Our upstairs neighbors were beating the crap out of their kids, and me and her had been listening to it all afternoon. She put her hand on mine and said, Is everything OK, Yunior? Have you been fighting with your brother?

Me and Rafa had already talked. We'd been in the basement, where our parents couldn't hear us. He told me that yeah, he knew about her.

Papi's taken me there twice now, he said.

Why didn't you tell me? I asked.

What the hell was I going to say? *Hey, Yunior, guess what happened yesterday? I met Papi's sucia!*

I didn't say anything to Mami either. She watched me, very very closely. Later I would think, maybe if I had told her, she would have confronted him, would have done something, but who can know these things? I said I'd been having trouble in school and like that everything was back to normal between us. She put her hand on my shoulder and squeezed and that was that.

We were on the turnpike, just past Exit 11, when I started feeling it again. I sat up from leaning against Rafa. His fingers smelled and he'd gone to sleep almost as soon as he got into the van. Madai was out too but at least she wasn't snoring.

In the darkness, I saw that Papi had a hand on Mami's knee and that the two of them were quiet and still. They weren't slumped back or anything; they were both wide awake, bolted into their seats. I couldn't see either of their faces and no matter how hard I tried I could not imagine their expressions. Neither of them moved. Every now and then the van was filled with the bright rush of somebody else's headlights. Finally I said, Mami, and they both looked back, already knowing what was happening.

Critical Eye

FOR DISCUSSION

a. Why, in your opinion, does the father seem comfortable flaunting his secret in front of his sons?

b. Can the way the father treats his son be construed as child abuse or discipline?

REAPPROACHING THE TEXT

Examine Cheever's "The Reunion" alongside Diaz's story. Are the two sons suffering from similar burdens?

WRITING ASSIGNMENT

Should a child still love and respect a parent, even after discovering something shameful about the adult who is supposed to stand as a shining example of how to live?

Julian Williams

The New Breed

A few days ago, I found myself engaged in an awkward conversation with a group of people I continuously encounter at a neighborhood bar on what seems like every Thursday. We meet with no planned invitation, and there are no official announcements about the next meeting. Now that I think about it, we—in true New York fashion—never meet for dinner or visit each other's apartments before or after drinks. And no, we do not communicate via email. We are simply a group of casual drunks who, for well over a year, seem to find themselves in familiar proximity of each other on the same day of every week. On this night, we were spaced out comfortably, having beaten the after-work-rush, discussing the ever-puzzling yet seemingly simplistic phenomenon known as parenting.

One of our more vocal members is a woman named Nicole. She is a former Wall Street analyst who consciously, going on ten years, opted to become a fulltime housewife. She is a woman whose stinging and frequently derisive views have exposed her as a resentful babysitter with too much education and no one around during the day to really notice. In retrospect, she is a relatively young, married White woman who drinks far too much. Looking at her, Nicole has a decent figure—which, given that she can stay home and exercise all day, she should—yet she is not nearly as cute as she thinks. During our abbreviated time together she tends to speak very loudly and exudes a smug and patronizing demeanor, which everyone whispers about when she leaves to go outside for one of her many smoking breaks. While unintentional on her part, Nicole is often abrupt and haughty in her demeanor—and, uh, when she talks to you, she can be a little condescending when she is attempting to appear insightful. "My husband always says . . ." or "Our place upstate. . ." or "When I was in charge of the Hershman account—you know Hershman, don't you? Hello, the billionaire developer. Anyway. . . ." Not unlike her deluded perception regarding her looks, her discernment on matters of life and living are rudimentary and overly opinionated. I am not uncomfortable around Nicole—and am not denying her acumen with numbers—but, well, I believe she needs to learn that over-talking other people while engaging in social conversation is rude.

It was Nicole who introduced the topic of parenting, just as she had guided us towards a discussion on the true nature of Islam the week before. I'm sure I am not the only one who wonders if she picks a focus ahead of time and prepares herself so that she can appear more insightful than the rest of us. "Well, actually, from the oasis cities of Makkah and Madinah in the Arabian desert—centuries before the Turks embraced it— Islam spread with electrifying speed within a half century of the Prophet's death. If I'm not mistaken, and I'm sure I'm not, this was during the 6th century," she explained off-handedly, after Simone had simply asked if anyone knew where the best place to get Middle Eastern food was.

On tonight's topic she claimed that when it comes to raising kids, "parents are the first line of defense." "It's the job of a mother and father to make sure that their kids grow up to be productive members of society," she asserted. In a somewhat disinterested tone, I asked her, "Well what sacrifice does that entail for the parent?" Tilting her head, she eyed me as if I had asked if her own kids—two supposedly "adorable" tots, one male, the other not, of five and seven years—were well-adjusted and, if not, they would like to come and live with me. Her response was—in her special, condescending way—quick and brief. She said, "everything."

The others, who were now eager to become involved in the discussion, nodded and agreed, even though out of the seven people present, only one other was a parent. I pressed the issue.

"Well, what exactly is everything?"

The room was now a-buzz. This is just the type of discussion people of a certain age in these types of settings—those past twenty-five with a drink nearby—hope to find on a Thursday after work which, in New York, actually begins the weekend. This gathering, like so many others in bars across the city, provides an outlet where those who often feel unappreciated at work or home can now assert themselves in a conversation where they can be witty and droll without fear of know-it-all spouses or bosses.

As Elif—our heavily accented Romanian chain smoker—arrived, they caught her up on the discussion. While she ordered a drink and expressed how thankful she was that she hadn't missed much, I caught a glimpse of something that I had, until that moment, never really noticed—something that I'm now sure is a constant during our talks: Elif, like the rest of them, was sitting directly facing me. From my vantage point, I now sat alone. This was fine, I guess, especially since no one ever really seems too eager to take-up my argument. Yet, as I reflect on our past conversations, I now see that, at some point, I usually become odd member out. By asking my simple questions, I somehow position myself as the Thursday night nitwit—the antagonist who never seems to quite agree with the rest. As I scanned the reactions of the group—the eyes rolled upward, brows creased, lips twisted—I knew as I have always known, that these people don't think I'm as bright as they are.

Feeling a little played, I asked again, "Well, what the hell does everything mean?" John, a male flight attendant who insists on always wearing several silver arm bangles of various sizes that are far too feminine for my taste but, otherwise, a seemingly good guy, responded through a chuckle, "Well, everything means everything."

In my mind's eye, it was here that I should have recognized we had arrived at my stop. I should have pressed the buzzer, exited, happy to dismount the conversation. Instead . . .

"I'm still not sure what 'everything' entails," I said. "Do you mean that parents should have no lives other than their children; that from the moment the child plops outta the mother and gulps its first thankful breath, the parents should resign to quit their jobs, turn over their gym memberships, and send out 'gone til child can fend for self' notices?" I asked.

"Is this the 'everything' you mean?" I inquired, face frowning, distaste written all over my brow.

At the time I wasn't really sure why I was becoming worked-up about this issue, but I began to feel as if I was presenting the air of one who has been insulted. Yet, when I think back, their faces showed no sign of worry—not regarding my questioning or their understanding of the matter. See, this group is a mixture of seemingly intelligent—at the very least educated— and somewhat successful drinkers who consider themselves well-versed in many different areas of, both, fact and trivia. In other words, these are people who know what they know. And in our year of sharing stories and opinions, they have come to know that I am joker, a kidder, a sarcastic satirist who couldn't possibly think half the stuff I express. Quite simply, our time together has made them believe they have insight into my person.

What I often find interesting are the types of relationships we have with people. This gathered group of Thursday night warriors know me, but don't really know me. They are merely acquaintances that, over time, assume they have figured me out. They are like the people we work with but never associate with outside of work. They call you friend and, probably in their limited minds, actually believe that is what you are. But the reality is different. These are individuals who you would never share real secrets with or talk about anything of importance late into the night; you would never invite them to hang out where you're actually from, nor would you allow them to see what you look like away from the office.

My Thursday group has heard me speak of fatherhood, children, the state of the union, and have giggled or waved a dismissive hand at me—as if I were too intellectually inept to comprehend their more insightful views on the ways of family, politics, or religion—time and again. Yet, as this night's conversation matured and I became more and more agitated, I could see in the faces of a few that they were beginning to wonder if some of my biting commentary on these subjects had not merely been banter for laughs and shock value.

"C'mon. Y'all talk a good game, but I mean—c'mon. Really now, it takes more to raise little monsters than just some empty concept—a bit of 'everything,' " I said drolly.

One of our motley crew is a very short, extremely small-breasted woman with an unusually wide nose and an overbite that borders on buck-toothedness. For the life of me, I can never remember her name. When this happens to me, and it happens often, I tend to reference people, at least to myself, based upon some physical trait.

She is lil' Bucky.

Lil' Bucky's eyes started at my feet and eventually rested on my forehead. Once she'd scanned me completely, she snickered, "You weren't kidding when you said you don't like kids." I didn't really see how that comment was a fitting response. Not that it is not true or that I haven't said it a million times. It just wasn't timed right. Timing is everything, no?

As I was preparing my witty retort, the hot Dominican bartender, whose breasts couldn't possibly sit up or out like that without the help of a better than average bra or a surgeon's skillful hand, came, took drink orders, and chimed in as if this was a discussion open to the public, saying "I know what you all mean. I do everything wit' my kids. If you don't, you lose dem to the streets. I mean, hell, you got ta' watch em' all de time—watchem' like hawks. If you don't, errested or molested, I always say." High fives were exchanged. Laughs turned to bellows. Both men and women agreed. After thinking about what she had said, I rose and looked behind the bar, then towards the back and then towards the front. After surveying the premises, I looked the bartender in her big blue eyes which, I'd guess, had to be colored contacts, and asked, "If that's true, where are your kids now?"

One day I'll stop, I swear.

Looking at me as if I'd asked "does that thong ride up your back only when you bend over or are you just high-hipped?" she went on to pour our drinks. Dana, the motherless mother hen of the group asked me "why do you have to be so crass?" I didn't actually think I was being crass. Rude?

Maybe. Insensitive? I could argue for or against. Nosey? I could see. But crass? C'mon. If I had said "If that's true, seems like yo sexy lil ass should be with your kids instead of shaking those melons and pouring drinks for dollar bills," now that, that would have been crass.

After wet napkins were thrown and boos were lauded my way, Jan and Amir, the married couple of our outing, piped up: "I mean, you can't be with them twenty-four-seven. You gotta have a life," Amir claimed. Jan added, "Yeah, hell, what are grandparents for?" Taking his cue as only a couple that spends too much time together can, Amir—a one cosmopolitan drunk if ever there was one—slurred, "When we have our kids, they'll be with us as much as possible. Dana will take the first two years off and stay home but, after that, we've got to go on living." Slapping Amir's groping hand off her shoulder with a shocked and somewhat flushed look on her face, one that indicated a late night conversation about the sexist views from "the man I married," Dana said, with a pitch of annoyance, "Uh, yeah. The point is you have to get a support system until you eventually drop them off at school. You gotta have help. You'd go crazy if you didn't get away from them sometimes." Hoisting her drink in the air, Nicole screamed "Ain't that the truth, girl."

Turning to face Nicole, I drooped my shoulders, presented a confused and defeated posture, and said "But I thought you said that the sacrifice entailed 'everything.' " Staring me straight in the face, Nicole—who I noticed for the first time is a wee bit cross-eyed—said to me, and I quote, "well, I didn't mean E VER Y thing. What I meant was, well, everything." To her comment they all nodded in some form of agreement. To Nicole's assessment I, too, acted as if I understood—as if her simple words had shined a holy light upon my sinning eyes. But what I understood and what they thought I understood was vastly different. My nodding was more of an inner conversation, a self-confirming clarity on their final concord, which was just what I had assumed when I pressed the issue. Their opinions on the matter were just what I thought they would be.

Before leaving my Thursday night bunch with my knickers in a bunch, having switched to bottled beer from my staple of Kettle One on the rocks because I was afraid I might get a special and unwanted mystery taste courtesy of the bartender—who, consequently, I left a big tip—I summed up what these people, either parents or hoping-to-be-parents-as-soon-as-it-fits, had told me. Apparently, what must happen before and after having kids is a knowledge they all seemed of one mind about: A. You must sacrifice ev. . .er. . .ythin. . .g, but not everything; B. Kids need constant love and affection, but parents need to breathe sometimes, too; C. There needs to be a good babysitting connection, and grandparents work best;

D. School is the eventual day care center that they can't wait to drop their children off at, leaving the kids attended to during the day and giving the grandparents a much needed break; E. There is no I in team, and, when kids arrive, there is no longer a me either until. . . . Walking down Lexington Ave, I was overwhelmed by the contradictions, the hypocrisy of it all. The opinions or supposed thinking of this drunken bunch were, for me, another sobering nod for birth control.

Honestly, Lil' Bucky was right. In my routine, throughout the course of any given day, I am liable to say aloud that I do not like children. One of my favorite quips is "the only thing I hate worse than kids are teenagers." Men often think I say this to shock people, but that it couldn't possibly be a trueism; women think my sentiment is actually a twisted code for "I really want kids, but I'm too insecure and embarrassed to express my real nature." But those who know me, the real me, understand that my slant on the subject comes from years of thoughtful observation. More than anything, as a student of human behavior, I have come to realize that what keeps psychiatrists and psychologists in overpriced offices on Fifth Ave. and lavish summer homes in the Hamptons is what my compadres had all just confirmed: today's generation of parents don't know shit.

Four days later, I was on the train headed to Queens.

Twice a week—because I must prostitute my only marketable skill to make ends meet—I am forced to ride the E train, which connects on the East Side at 51 Street, to teach an Art history course entitled Greece, Mythology, and the Artistry of an Empire. As a supposed academic, riding these trains to teach these types of classes seems to be my fate. This course is not even in my field, but, as the saying goes, "beggars can't be choosers—so they just keep begging." In order to get to the college, I have to ride a train I hate more than most with people I despise wholeheartedly. While walking through the tunnel from the no. 6 train to the E—on my consistently monotonous quest to make the donuts—I actually feel my body undergo a physical change: my ass tightens, my teeth become tight, and my out-on-the-street scowl grows more fearsome looking.

This transformation is because I know that they are there, waiting, hyperly looking forward to the presence of those they can intimidate, disrespect, or shock. As I trod towards the down escalator, dragging my feet like an insolent child approaching the dentist's office, I see many of them. I recognize them instantly. They are my greatest nemeses next to the state lottery people who refuse to acknowledge me as the rightful winner of all those millions I deserve. They are horribly loathsome creatures, and I would love to have a mass killing of them all—an organized shoving onto the tracks, a strangling, one by one, as the rest wait patiently in line. The way they smell. The way they move. The aggressive nature of these pubescent misfits makes my journey to Queens one that is as uncomfortable as it is unfortunate.

It's 2:30 PM. The bell has rung. The beasts have been released from their cages.

After waiting on the crowded platform, the E pulls into the station. I have positioned myself so that I am on the last car or, when put into perspective, the first car to exit at Jamaica Center, the final stop. When the doors open, a few enter with me. The car is crowded, always crowded, and we are all forced to stand. The surrounding hellions who have entered the car with me make noise and entertain themselves. This assembly atmosphere resembles a flock of cackling ducks whose soul purpose is to disrupt those either reading or trying to catch a quick nap. At any moment you expect someone to yell "shut the fuck up!"—to assert their right to peace and quiet during their journey. But alas, these flapping mongrels are allowed to continue. There presence is, in reality, not that bad—not overwhelming. They are the tamed beasts, the ones who are wearing uniforms. They do not represent the threat to come. These are the private school irritants, with high-pitched voices, blue and checkered prints, knee socks and black shoes. They are a part of the world I despise, but they are more grating than anything.

"I mean, man, like, I hate Jennifer," the blond with the pink barrettes and severely red lipstick declares. "I know," her Asian confidant responds, "I know. She su-ha-bitch."

Lord, they have corrupted the Asians, the last hope for their kind.

These types of conversations make you want to catch their eye and mouth a threatening "quiet, child" followed-up with a look that says, "hey, don't make me have to come over there and straighten you out." Luckily, a maternal browbeating is unnecessary. This bunch is basically benign to the rest of us because, while their actions contain maddening manners, there is no real malice. But then we approach the Roosevelt Ave. station, and the sense that they are coming, the terrible ones, builds. Head down, reading my book, I hear them enter before I see them. They rush the door before it fully opens, brushing aggressively past anyone exiting the train. To a novice, they immediately reflect their "fuck you, we rule" attitude. But to an experienced rider, a veteran of this war, it is more than that. These are students of dark skin, Black teenagers—with a sprinkling of Puerto Rican and Dominican here and there—whose message is "We'll gather as a group and stomp anyone who doesn't like what we are saying, what we stand for. Just look us in the eye if you dare!" Growling, they walk slumped and crooked, bouncing up and down the length of the car. One of them is in possession of a radio that is as big as an adult torso—a monstrosity covered in lights and dials that must run on no less than fifty dollars worth of batteries. He is blaring a song by some ignorant misogynist, an individual whose main lyrics seem to be about "riding" and "dropping it."

New York is funny. It is the only place I know where people without skateboards or sandy beaches still carry boom boxes in this age of MP3 players, I-pods, and the CD disc-man.

As music fills the car, the savage ones rant and rave, hoop and holler, pacing between cars as if high on some drug that's main jolts are surges of stupidity and profanity. As the frantic pounding continues, people still act as if they are reading. But as I know—a pretender myself—this is no longer really possible.

I try not to stare, make no eye contact. I look away or keep my head low. I do this not because I am afraid, but, moreso, because I am—maybe I am afraid. As I skim the car between moments of feigning as if I'm reading the lines on my now lifeless book's pages, I notice the most horrific and outrageous conversation—the one which spews hatred and overflows with recognizable anger and vileness that is appalling, yet no longer surprising—is coming from a group near the door across from me. This loud and profanely despicable monologue is led as a vulgar donation to the rest of us by the most vicious of the creatures. Clearly, the tone emanating is different than the rest. Yelling at a fevers-pitch, we cannot not hear this discourse. We are all—those of us who were dumb enough to have not run for, if not our lives, our tender sensibilities—witnesses to the unrehearsed production of what has emerged in the past years as the most untamed, shrewdest, and dangerous of the bunch. Speaking is the predator to be watched most closely, truly the most despicable of their kind—a new breed of animal.

She is around 5′4. Her hair is pulled back in braids and she is wearing too much makeup. Her skin is riddled with poc-marks, as if she were in the habit of bursting pimples as soon as they arrive and flicking off the morning scabs, leaving a pink mark blending in with her other darker ones. She is of a dark complexion, with a huge behind and small breasts. She is wearing what appear to be calf-length pink high top sneakerish type shoes—with pump heels? I try not to look anymore, but its like a car wreck—and everybody has to look at a wreck. As I continue to slyly take the measure of my captor, I note that she has black with white tipped painted fingernails that, if I'm not mistaken, seem to have a picture of her own face superimposed on the thumbs. Noticing all this as I covertly examine her person, I am ever leery to any sudden moves she might make. As she continues to roar, I note that her teeth are not so much yellow as sepia in coloring, and her breath, though I cannot smell it, is most assuredly foul. She is neither large in stature nor bearing any apparent weapons, but, like the pack leading hyena, she is dangerous—undeniably dangerous.

As I look over, I note that her bag is on the floor, leaning heavily against the leg of a nervous looking Indian woman coming from or going to work. My only hope is that this is not the woman's first trip with these filthy mammals, for it is a scarring adventure for the faint of heart.

"I woulda' cut dat bitch. I will fuck that hoe and her fat ass sista up. Let them hoes come round tomorrow. Shit, you know I don't care. Fuck, fuck, fuck," she roared. And then came the threat.

As if her stomach was rumbling and she was desperate to relieve herself, the loathsome creature said, "Ooooooooooo, I 'ma haveta smack me a muthafucka before I see dem hoes. Shit, I gotta get this out." Slowly shifting my head from side to side, I'm sure I wasn't the only person wondering whom exactly she might choose to express herself upon.

Slowly as I turned back toward her, it seemed, at least for a moment, that she was staring at me with an annoyed yet wondering look.

The rest of the pack lauded her on, and she gathered explosive energy from their combinations of sweat, fear, and docile—animus is the word that comes to mind. For though she seems to lead this group of hooligans or, at the very least, she is the voice that represents the twisted pragmatism of her peers, they cannot like or respect her. I refuse to believe that possible. There has to be something else that links those obviously less vocal to her.

Fear is an interesting factor to come to grips with. Some people are afraid of bugs. For some, it's animals. Some, it's heights. Some people are, I've heard, afraid of success. But most people are afraid of confrontation. It is not an unwise course of awareness, this fear, because there are many angry, crazed folks out there, hoping that you're not insightful enough to know that you should look away. It is, however, not fear of imminent physical danger that makes this bunch so bad. What is worse than being afraid of anyone, let alone a group of anyones, is when you catch yourself behaving timidly and unsure around people who are so much younger, so much dumber, and, often, who look similar—though horribly evolved—to pictures in the photo albums located in your own parents' home. This awakening is, undeniably, humiliating.

As the young carnivore scanned the car sniffing and snorting, possibly sending warning signals or mating calls to her kind, you could actually see in her face how she reveled in the environment she was creating. The creatures that resembled her but were from another world—those who had boarded the train earlier—clearly found the monster and her minions amusing. As I looked to the other end of the train where they were, I noted how they giggled, snickered, and nodded their approval at the scene the more barbarous members of their species performed. Having observed both groups extensively, I knew, at that very moment, that these privileged teens had so much and nothing at all in common with these terrorists of a darker hue. In a sense, the private school kids were like White kids who dress Black and imitate Black trends in clothes and speech. While thinking it is cool to rail and offend the majority, they have a buried knowledge in their subconscious, a sense of knowing that betrays their jovial mood, their defiant body language. Inevitably, this insight will appear like a wise specter in the coming years and whisper, "this act was cute at one point, but it is time to step away from this silliness, straighten up, and assume your rightful role as productive and respectful citizen." Once they actually reach this realization, they can cut their hair, remove their gaudy earrings, cover their tattoos, pull up their pants, put on a suit or a knee-length skirt, and then presto-changeo—like it never happened.

I don't know which group I hate worse.

As the music blared about bitches and cars, and how bitches like cars, and about how much crissy and bling and bitches can be ridden inside cars, the walls shrank inward and those who were not part of this spectacle were smushed together against the windows looking as if they were contemplating breaking the glass and leaping onto the safety of the tracks. Refusing to move and bracing any of the encroaching hostage takers with my evil stare, I—standing erect, back to door, chest poked forward—stood amid a few of the braver souls. While not reading the book I was desperately trying to read, I noticed that the young female . . . thing—I really don't know what to call her at this point, her behavior so repulsive, her presence so offensive—had adjusted her position so that she would be the first-line, the welcoming party standing in front of the opening doors to meet and greet any new passengers. Many straphangers opted to run and enter another car. Some eventually gathered their belongings and walked through the connecting doors. And then there were those who squeezed past the menacing gauntlet, either aggressively pushing forward and showing little dread or giving off the sent of coward and thus having to put up with the subjective whims of this gang of hoodlums led by a girl gone wild and ugly.

It was a tense thirty-minute ride, one that often made me consider changing cars. But being a man of full height and body weight—a least as full of size as my 5'7, 160 pounds will ever reach—I stood my ground and waited for it to get worse. Somehow, I never expected what was to come. With eyes lowered, I saw the whole disgusting act. It was the moment when she proved herself—this leader, this monster—to me, us all, what she thought of life.

"I can't wait to get to da crib and light up. I need something to drink cus my mouth is dry as hell," she said. "Dog, my . . ." was the sentence she didn't complete. The words seemed to catch in her throat, and the hope that maybe she had swallowed her tongue and was going to strangle on her own vomit became a dream too pleasing to share. Instead she hocked and, as she extended her chin forward, looking down towards the tiled floor, her discolored incisors extending as she pursed her lips— parting them some—she spit, or is it spat, on the train's floor.

Well I'll be damned.

I gawked at the result, waiting for the alien's acid laced saliva to burn a hole through the floor of the car down onto the tracks.

And then I waited.

I waited for the police to come and drag her away because, I'm almost positive, spitting on the train is a crime. I waited for someone to reach out and smack her face, to let her know that this was not the act of a human being on a train—at least not an act performed in the company of other human beings. But mostly I waited for her to at least seem abashed in some way—to wipe her mouth and offer an apology, head held low, to those of us who were witnesses to this atrocious behavior. Luckily the train ride was almost over, because if forced to ride any further, since she obviously had no sense of what is done where and when, her next trick might have been a dropping of trough accompanied by a solid bowel movement.

Mouth opened, I slowly raised my head and shamefully locked eyes with a White woman sitting across from me. Her look was one that pleaded with me to act, to speak, to pull out a weapon and slay the beast before it could breed. "Kill her! Lynch the griffin while it is unaware. Slay the Chimera, now!" her eyes begged. But I simply lowered my eyes, embarrassed that this girl would reduce me to this sense of cultural shame, that her behavior would bring the pity and rage of those around us who somehow automatically grouped me as—if no longer one of them—one who had been one of them.

As the train pulled into Jamaica Center the people disembarked, most leaving through a different door, or circling a wide ark around the yellowish phlegm that was gelling precariously on the floor. Taking my time as to avoid any further interaction with the savage brutes, I hung back, allowing the car to empty out. When I exited, I saw them all hoopin' and hollarin', led by this new breed of teenager—who was now minus the unacknowledged support from her uniformed conspirators who had exited at an earlier stop, retreating to homes and, possibly, meals prepared by hand. Thinking of this contrast as I rode the escalator up to exit the station, I found that I was more than my usually perturbed self. This was definitely a different sensation, not like the daily irritation I usually feel due to the offending presence of those who keep riding the train talking, eating, laughing—breathing. What I felt this time was a strange sense of sadness, and this led to me reflecting on the conversation I'd had with my fellow Thursday night drunkards. Thinking about our conversation on parenting, I began to earnestly reflect on that word—the one that now hung in my mind like an impenetrable mushroom cloud— which all of my cronies kept repeating, as if the term had a power all its own: "everything."

Had this young girl—for surely, before mutating into the thing she had become, she had to have been an innocent, one who wanted nothing more than to be read bedtime stories and who blushed at those who said "well aren't you pretty"—been given "everything?" As I thought about that, my curiosity peaked. I really began to consider if the person who for that last half-hour had been the very bane of my existence, had received the "everything" that Nicole and the others had so snootily carried on about?

Was she loved and cared for? Fed at all hours? Spoiled endlessly with toys and affection? Had she been given airplane spins on the flats of a parent's feet? Had she been helped with her homework?

As I shuffled past the resident platform Jesus Freak, the man holding his worn Bible, screaming at people about how the Lord was coming and how disgusted he was going to be with us heathens, I wondered about the creature—the girl—that had already exited the station.

Had anyone told her that, no matter what, everything was going to be okay? Was there someone in her life who looked her in the eye and promised that, no matter what, they would be there for her? Had she been given direction; taught discretion; punished when insolent and hugged just for being? Was there a party who represented her interests during parent/teacher conferences—someone who was actually stressed about how she was performing in school? Surely there was a person, once upon a time, who cared if she was learning?

Certainly someone taught her to bathe, that brushing prevents gingivitis, and that proper hygiene is important—the whole cleanliness/ Godliness spiel. Someone must have shown her how to insert a tampon; or the best types of pads to buy; or explained, at the very least, to never wear white on those uncomfortable days—or, for that matter, after Labor Day. Of course there was a hand that showed her how to cook, how to clean, and how by simply lighting a match in the bathroom the air becomes more breathable and the rest of the house is spared one's most personal smell.

As I strolled off the escalator, I wondered more.

Wasn't there a trust fund set up to bring her comfort in her latter years? Wouldn't she grow up and strive to find her own voice, even though her family would want her to join the legacy that was their empire? Wouldn't she fight to find a love all her own, instead of the young man from the prestigious family her parents had been hoping she would wed—possibly heir to a shipping fortune? Was this all just a cruel fantasy—one that a person like her could never truly fancy?

At the very least, surely there had to be a figure at home who pressed her about test scores and reminded her that college was a necessity.

But if all of this were true, didn't someone tell her how to carry herself, how to behave?

Didn't someone tell her not to spit on the train?

"Everything." In thirty minutes, this hopelessly angry and ill- mannered misanthrope had confirmed why I was so pessimistic and defensive about the naïve responses of those who tossed around the word as if it was the solution to a life of balance and success. "Everything?" What the hell is it? Who can actually provide it? Is it even possible? While a great notion, a wonderful fantasy, it seems to be impossible. Or, am I simply so bitter about the world that I can no longer even see how something like "everything" can exist?

Now my curiosity began to bubble my buried resentment. I mean, could they—those who dismissed me as the jaded guy who one day would probably be alone and bitter—actually offer "everything?" No, surely the reality remains the same. Of course they can't. They just as well had admitted it that night. They contradicted themselves left and right.

"You have to guide them and be firm about stuff. I read this book about silence as discipline. I think it's the approach I'll take," Elif declared.

"I'm not sure how I'll tell my kid not to do drugs—as much dope as I smoked when I was a teenager? Shit. Just tell em' not to do it and hope for the best," was Joel's solution.

But it was Nicole who summed it up best, who had really poked her finger in my eye that night: "Just buy them the best stuff and get them the best help. If I decide to go back to work, I wanna be sure they have the best of everything. Please, I'm just trying to get them to leave the house more, get off those damn computers in their rooms, and get outta my face!" she laughed.

Computers? Rooms? Plural? Wow.

Did the terror of the E-line have a computer in her home, I now pondered? Did she even have a room of her own, a space where she could be private with her own thoughts? Hell, for that matter, I wondered if both her parents were in her life. I wonder if she even knows who her father is.

Does she have a sense of privilege about anything?

Maybe that's why she behaved the way she did. Maybe harassing a trainload of people was her way of saying "hey, nobody ever gave me shit. I ain't got nuthin and ain't gonna be nuthin."

I wondered if she ever thought about what it would be like to have someone even discussing her and the silliness of "everything" in the same breath. I bet she would have liked to see somebody at least fail at the effort. Maybe subjecting the rest of us to her diatribe of anger and disdain was as close to feeling apart of the world as she could reach.

As I walked past two transit policemen who were talking way too familiarly with a couple of tight jean wearing teenagers, I'm pretty sure I know why I became so sensitive last week. It was because I know, having come from a world not completely dissimilar than the misguided monsters', that there is no such thing as "everything." And, for some, there is nothing that even comes close. For the poor, the under-educated, the ones that can never escape the stigmas and stereotypes of their culture—overcome them, maybe, but never escape them—isn't "everything" as ridiculous an illusion to low-income people of color as those White co-workers who return every Monday declaring they have just had a "great weekend?"

Maybe I'd gotten a little heated the previous Thursday because I knew— know—that the "everything" my typically heterogeneous Manhattan group, people who are only urban because they live in a major metropolis, not because they have lived the veiled and coded "urban" life, was more of a possibility than I'd ever known—than this angry young woman would ever be privy. Was I upset because the people who were talking last Thursday were like those privileged private school kids? Was I upset because I know that they all had or might have a chance, an actual real live chance, to provide their kids with so much stuff, so many advantages, that it might actually resemble "everything?" See, my Thursday night crew could never understand that the real reason I have opted never to have children directly correlates with my own failure to conceive of the reality of our topic, all while grasping the utter importance of it.

Or, maybe I got mad because I think that the opposite of everything—no matter how much you give—is sometimes nothing at all.

As I lumbered towards the school, my head throbbed and I felt despondent beyond words. Just as I was beginning to really feel sorry for the girl who society had robbed of a childhood, of opportunities, of love, I heard someone call me. Well, I assume that I was the addressee only because "say, bitch" was shouted so loudly in my direction that it snapped me out of my haze. As I looked around, I saw her—along with about ten of her devilish minions—step out from under the viaduct near the college. If I didn't know any better, I'd have to think they had been laying in wait for me. As I smelled the remnants of marijuana smoke filtering the air, I was shocked more than frightened. More than anything, I was quickly reminded why I hate this group more than any other social irritant in New York—a place overrun with homeless beggars, cons, freaks and deviants.

Looking her in the face, I could see the rage in her dilated pupils. "You was looking all crazy at me and shit like you had beef. We gotta a problem, mutherfucka?" As she said these things to me, her flippant behavior and exaggerated movements brought oooos and aahhhhhs from her peers. Not being a peer, I found myself less than amused. At first, I could not figure out my next move. While not a physically imposing man—and being one who hasn't had a fistfight since the eighth grade—I was extremely nervous about tussling with a group of teenagers who, obviously, were bold enough to accost me in broad daylight. Now, at the same time, I am also a grown ass man, and I'm pretty sure I'd find it more than difficult to live with myself if I allowed a teenager—a girl, no less—to strip away my manhood. As she hopped around, dancing and flailing herself about for her friends' amusement, I decided to act like an adult and walk through the gauntlet they had made. Whatever was going to happen was going to happen. I mean lets be real. What was she going to do, hit me?

As I took two steps toward the future leaders of our country—our great youthful braintrust—I felt her move quickly, beseeched, I must assume, by the drug she had recently smoked coupled with her crazed attitude.

In a blink, she had swung upward, trying to snatch off my—as she put it "lil hoe ass hat." Before I realized what I was doing, I had pivoted on one foot and pushed her off with my left hand. Falling back as if she couldn't believe I had laid hands on her—as if I was the one bothering her person—her face changed to one of pure and irrational fury, contorting and transforming the way a housecat hunches its back and bares its pointy little teeth, hissing angrily as if to remind its owner that it is the descendent of a long line of warrior felines. As she lunged forward the crowd backed away, almost as if they were going to let the two of us go head-to-head without any interference. Like we were two men arguing outside a bar near a deserted truck stop.

Well, nobody ever said this new breed was bright. My punch landed flush, right above her left eye—splitting the skin instantly. Because she had charged forward, she was already off balance. The punch plus her own momentum sent her spiraling downward. When she hit the ground her face actually scraped the concrete, removing a nice patch of skin from her forehead.

Shit.

Just as a few of her friends were trying to decide if they would take up the battle, I heard the wailing of a siren barreling toward us. As the crowd dispersed, the two police officers came charging over to find me standing over a bleeding teenage girl. As they helped her to her feet, her curses grew more fearsome and the officers actually had to restrain her as she wildly kicked and clawed her way at me, screaming through a foaming mouth about how she was going kill me.

When they questioned me, my mind and my mouth could not seem to gather pace with one another. I was in the mist of telling the cops how she and her friends were waiting for me and I was just defending myself when I began to sweat uncontrollably. And the more and more I said, the more my nerves frayed.

And then I lost it.

I rambled off about how she had held the train hostage. I told them how I was an adult and how she was a dirty train spitter. I tried to tell them how nobody cared about her and how she was just lashing out and that this wasn't my fault. I mean, her fault. I tried to tell them how she was unloved and poor and under-educated and how no one cared and how she shared a room with several siblings and how no one had ever spun her on their feet and how she shouldn't wear white after Labor Day and. . . .

Whoa. Listening to myself, I now see that what I had done was nothing more than stereotype this young savage's life to suit my own need to make her actions somehow justifiable. My words were actually nothing more than imaginative, self-deluding drivel. So much so, my goings-on even made the girl shut-up, tilt her head, and scrunch her face with one of those "what the hell are you talking about?" looks. At that moment, I must have looked as crazy as she did. Was I really so desperate to justify my reactions last Thursday that I made up a life story for this hateful little ogre? Maybe I need counseling.

I tried to explain to the police—but I was nervous and angry, so the last forty minutes came out in a flood of emotion. As the ambulance pulled onto the sidewalk to take her away, the police handcuffed me and placed me in the back of the patrol car. I wanted to ask them if they would be so kind as to go and tell my class I wasn't going to make it, but I figured I should probably be quiet for a little while. As we drove off—away from the school, the college where I teach, as a professor, with an office and everything—I had to assume I was going to jail. I had to guess that I, too, had been stereotyped, and that these officers looked at me, at us, as a product of Black beastiality run-a-muck in the streets of NY, once again. Or, maybe I'd been arrested because I'd just cold-cocked a sixteen-year old female. Tomato, tomatoe.

However, after traveling around the corner, the cops pulled into what appeared to be a car impound right off Jamaica Ave. near Guy Brewer Blvd.

Shit.

As I was becoming more and more afraid—a sense of dread that I have not experienced since that time last summer when I was almost killed by a M-103 bus that jumped the curve and sent me diving before crushing the bus pole that I was standing near—I could sense that soon, not yet, but soon, I might actually shed a tear. I was sure that another stereotype was getting ready to play out—and that this one was really going to be painful. Opening the door, the officers stood me up. As I braced myself, hoping, that at the very least, I would not piss myself, one of the officers spun me around. And removed my cuffs. Although a little surprised, this was nothing in the realm of the unexpected—not when you consider what happened next. Before I could open my mouth, the taller of the two officers opened his arms and, before I could react, squeezed me into a bear hug. His partner, a small pug of a woman, reached in and hugged me too. I can only imagine what a sight we must have been. After the embrace was broken, they applauded me for, how did she put it, "letting that group of filthy savages know that they do not own the world." Her partner, who was shaking me like a proud father, said, "Hell yeah. We're forced to watch them act like animals everyday around this time. We break em up, make em disperse, but they just flip us the bird and talk about their rights—like we ain't the cops! Bet they go out and buy a can of respect for next time!" he bellowed. Laughing themselves teary-eyed, they then proceeded to shake my hand. I was too stunned. As they drove away, I could see them holding their hands over their heads, shaking their heads. Before they turned the corner, she, the partner, actually leaned out of the window, bowing at me as if I had just announced a scholarship fund for police officers. Really. I couldn't make this stuff up.

Picking my mouth up off the ground, I didn't know if I was happy or disgusted. I mean, really, I'd just assaulted a young girl. I had hit a female on the street. I had just assaulted someone and, simply because they didn't like her and friends, they let me go. Where was the justice? Where was the humanity? Where was Al Sharpton? As I walked back to the college I felt exhausted. After all that, after running the gambit of emotions—anticipation, apprehension, disgust, pity, wrath and, ultimately, fear—all I knew for sure was that I needed a drink. Looking over my shoulder, in case there were any other young beast girls that needed a good beat down, I knew that while I understood how a monster like that was made—madcap stereotyping, if I do say—it doesn't matter. Bad manners, threatening posturing, overbearing behavior would no longer be tolerated. I would forever more defend my space—and the space of the weaker. Maybe I'd become like a superhero fighting against rude and intolerable behavior—smacking young girls everywhere I went.

Okay, maybe not.

Well, one thing is for sure. Tonight's class is going to be canceled. I wonder if any of the gang ever shows up at the bar on Mondays. Hell, at this point, I wonder if any of my students would like to go get a cocktail.

Critical Eye

FOR DISCUSSION

a. How valid is the "cultural shame" the narrator says he experiences while on the train? In short, is it ever possible to feel ashamed of the race or culture one descends from? Moreover, at what point do we cease being responsible for the sins committed by people who "look" like us?

b. While in the bar, the author learns that children must have "everything" in order to become functional adults. But, can we argue that today's children have way too much of everything at their disposal and, as a result, have become spoiled beyond measure?

c. Is parenting a skill, or is it merely a game of trial and error in which most parents simply hope for the best?

REAPPROACHING THE TEXT

How is this story a manifesto against having children?

WRITING ASSIGNMENT

In the text, the author makes a clear distinction between the "good kids" and the "bad kids." The "good kids" he asserts, take on the appearance, vernacular, and sometimes the culture of other groups but will one day shrug off these characteristics and become functional members of society. The so-called "good kids," he suggests, are perhaps worse than the "bad kids." How valid is this assumption?

T. Coraghessan Boyle

The Love of My Life

They wore each other like a pair of socks. He was at her house, she was at his. Everywhere they went—to the mall, to the game, to movies and shops and the classes that structured their days like a new kind of chronology—their fingers were entwined, their shoulders touching, their hips joined in the slow triumphant sashay of love. He drove her car, slept on the couch in the family room at her parents' house, played tennis and watched football with her father on the big, thirty-six-inch TV in the kitchen. She went shopping with his mother and hers, a triumvirate of tastes, and she would have played tennis with his father, if it came to it, but his father was dead. "I love you," he told her, because he did, because there was no feeling like this, no triumph, no high—it was like being immortal and unconquerable, like floating. And a hundred times a day she said it, too: "I love you. I love you."

They were together at his house one night when the rain froze on the streets and sheathed the trees in glass. It was her idea to take a walk and feel it in their hair and on the glistening shoulders of their parkas, an other-worldly drumming of pellets flung down out of the troposphere, alien and familiar at the same time, and they glided the length of the front walk and watched the way the power lines bellied and swayed. He built a fire when they got back, while she towelled her hair and made hot chocolate laced with Jack Daniel's. They'd rented a pair of slasher movies for the ritualized comfort of them—"Teens have sex," he said, "and then they pay for it in body parts"—and the maniac had just climbed out of the heating vent, with a meat hook dangling from the recesses of his empty sleeve, when the phone rang.

It was his mother, calling from the hotel room in Boston where she was curled up—shacked up?—for the weekend with the man she'd been dating. He tried to picture her, but he couldn't. He even closed his eyes a minute, to concentrate, but there was nothing there. Was everything all right? she wanted to know. With the storm and all? No, it hadn't hit Boston yet, but she saw on the Weather Channel that it was on its way. Two seconds after he hung up—before she could even hit the Start button on the VCR—the phone rang again, and this time it was her mother.

"The Love of My Life," from *After the Plague* by T. Coraghessan Boyle, copyright © 2001 by T. Coraghessan Boyle. Used by permission of Viking Penguin, a division of Penguin Group (USA) Inc.

Her mother had been drinking. She was calling from the restaurant, and China could hear a clamor of voices in the background. "Just stay put," her mother shouted into the phone. "The streets are like a skating rink. Don't you even think of getting in that car."

Well, she wasn't thinking of it. She was thinking of having Jeremy to herself, all night, in the big bed in his mother's room. They'd been having sex ever since they started going together at the end of their junior year, but it was always sex in the car or sex on a blanket or the lawn, hurried sex, nothing like she wanted it to be. She kept thinking of the way it was in the movies, where the stars ambushed each other on beds the size of small planets and then did it again and again until they lay nestled in a heap of pillows and blankets, her head on his chest, his arm flung over her shoulder, the music fading away to individual notes plucked softly on a guitar and everything in the frame glowing as if it had been sprayed with liquid gold. That was how it was supposed to be. That was how it was going to be. At least for tonight.

She'd been wandering around the kitchen as she talked, dancing with the phone in an idle slow saraband, watching the frost sketch a design on the window over the sink, no sound but the soft hiss of the ice pellets on the roof, and now she pulled open the freezer door and extracted a pint box of ice cream. She was in her socks, socks so thick they were like slippers, and a pair of black leggings under an oversize sweater. Beneath her feet, the polished floorboards were as slick as the sidewalk outside, and she liked the feel of that, skating indoors in her big socks. "Uh-huh," she said into the phone. "Uh-huh. Yeah, we're watching a movie." She dug a finger into the ice cream and stuck it in her mouth.

"Come on," Jeremy called from the living room, where the maniac rippled menacingly over the Pause button. "You're going to miss the best part."

"O.K., Mom, O.K.," she said into the phone, parting words, and then she hung up. "You want ice cream?" she called, licking her finger.

Jeremy's voice came back at her, a voice in the middle range, with a congenital scratch in it, the voice of a nice guy, a very nice guy who could be the star of a TV show about nice guys: "What kind?" He had a pair of shoulders and pumped up biceps, too, a smile that jumped from his lips to his eyes, and close-cropped hair that stood up straight off the crown of his head. And he was always singing—she loved that—his voice so true he could do any song, and there was no lyric he didn't know, even on the oldies station. She scooped ice cream and saw him in a scene from last summer, one hand draped casually over the wheel of his car, the radio throbbing, his voice raised in perfect synch with Billy Corgan's, and the night standing still at the end of a long dark street overhung with maples.

"Chocolate. Swiss-chocolate almond."

"O.K.," he said, and then he was wondering if there was any whipped cream, or maybe hot fudge—he was sure his mother had a jar stashed away somewhere, *Look behind the mayonnaise on the top row*—and when she turned around he was standing in the doorway.

She kissed him—they kissed whenever they met, no matter where or when, even if one of them had just stepped out of the room, because that was love, that was the way love was—and then they took two bowls of ice cream into the living room and, with a flick of the remote, set the maniac back in motion.

It was an early spring that year, the world gone green overnight, the thermometer twice hitting the low eighties in the first week of March. Teachers were holding sessions outside. The whole school, even the halls and the cafeteria, smelled of fresh-mowed grass and the unfolding blossoms of the fruit trees in the development across the street, and students—especially seniors—were cutting class to go out to the quarry or the reservoir or to just drive the backstreets with the sunroof and the windows open wide. But not China. She was hitting the books, studying late, putting everything in its place like pegs in a board, even love, even that. Jeremy didn't get it. "Look, you've already been accepted at your first-choice school, you're going to wind up in the top ten G.P.A.-wise, and you've got four years of tests and term papers ahead of you, and grad school after that. You'll only be a high-school senior once in your life. Relax. Enjoy it. Or at least *experience* it."

He'd been accepted at Brown, his father's alma mater, and his own G.P.A. would put him in the top ten percent of their graduating class, and he was content with that, skating through his final semester, no math, no science, taking art and music, the things he'd always wanted to take but never had time for—and Lit., of course, A.P. History, and Spanish 5. *"Túeres el amor de mi vida,"* he would tell her when they met at her locker or at lunch or when he picked her up for a movie on Saturday nights.

"Y tútambién," she would say, "or is it *'yo también'?"*—French was her language. "But I keep telling you it really matters to me, because I know I'll never catch Margery Yu or Christian Davenport, I mean they're a lock for val and salut, but it'll kill me if people like Kerry Sharp or Jalapy Seegrand finish ahead of me—you should know that, you of all people—"

It amazed him that she actually brought her books along when they went backpacking over spring break. They'd planned the trip all winter and through the long wind tunnel that was February, packing away freeze-dried entrées, PowerBars, Gore-Tex windbreakers, and matching sweatshirts, weighing each item on a handheld scale with a dangling hook at the bottom of it. They were going up into the Catskills, to a lake he'd found on a map, and they were going to be together, without interruption, without telephones, automobiles, parents, teachers, friends, relatives, and pets, for five full days. They were going to cook over an open fire, they were going to read to each other and burrow into the double sleeping bag with the connubial zipper up the seam he'd found in his mother's closet, a relic of her own time in the lap of nature. It smelled of her, of his mother, a vague scent of her perfume that had lingered there dormant all these years, and maybe there was the faintest whiff of his father, too, though his father had been gone so long he didn't even remember what he looked like, let alone what he might have smelled like. Five days. And it wasn't going to rain, not a drop. He didn't even bring his fishing rod, and that was love.

When the last bell rang down the curtain on Honors Math, Jeremy was waiting at the curb in his mother's Volvo station wagon, grinning up at China through the windshield while the rest of the school swept past with no thought for anything but release. There were shouts and curses, T-shirts in motion, slashing legs, horns bleating from the seniors' lot, the school buses lined up like armored vehicles awaiting the invasion—chaos, sweet chaos—and she stood there a moment to savor it. "Your mother's car?" she said, slipping in beside him and laying both arms over his shoulders to pull him to her for a kiss. He'd brought her jeans and hiking boots along, and she was going to change as they drove, no need to go home, no more circumvention and delay, a stop at McDonald's, maybe, or Burger King, and then it was the sun and the wind and the moon and the stars. Five days. Five whole days.

"Yeah," he said, in answer to her question, "my mother said she didn't want to have to worry about us breaking down in the middle of nowhere—"

"So she's got your car? She's going to sell real estate in your car?"

He just shrugged and smiled. "Free at last," he said, pitching his voice down low till it was exactly like Martin Luther King's. "Thank God Almighty, we are free at last."

It was dark by the time they got to the trailhead, and they wound up camping just off the road in a rocky tumble of brush, no place on earth less likely or less comfortable, but they were together, and they held each other through the damp whispering hours of the night and hardly slept at all. They made the lake by noon the next day, the trees just coming into leaf, the air sweet with the smell of the sun in the pines. She insisted on setting up the tent, just in case—it could rain, you never knew—but all he wanted to do was stretch out on a gray neoprene pad and feel the sun on his face. Eventually, they both fell asleep in the sun, and when they woke they made love right there, beneath the trees, and with the wide blue expanse of the lake giving back the blue of the sky. For dinner, it was étouffée and rice, out of the foil pouch, washed down with hot chocolate and a few squirts of red wine from Jeremy's bota bag.

The next day, the whole day through, they didn't bother with clothes at all. They couldn't swim, of course—the lake was too cold for that—but they could bask and explore and feel the breeze out of the south on their bare legs and the places where no breeze had touched before. She would remember that always the feel of that, the intensity of her motions, the simple unrefined pleasure of living in the moment. Wood smoke. Duelling flashlights in the night. The look on Jeremy's face when he presented her with the bag of finger-size crayfish he'd spent all morning collecting.

What else? The rain, of course. It came midway through the third day, clouds the color of iron filings, the lake hammered to iron, too, and the storm that crashed through the trees and beat at their tent with a thousand angry fists. They huddled in the sleeping bag, sharing the wine and a bag of trail mix, reading to each other from a book of Donne's love poems (she was writing a paper for Mrs. Masterson called "Ocular Imagery in the Poetry of John Donne") and the last third of a vampire novel that weighed eighteen-point-one ounces.

And the sex. They were careful, always careful—*I will never, never be like those breeders that bring their puffed-up squalling little red-faced babies to class,* she told him, and he agreed, got adamant about it, even, until it became a running theme in their relationship, the breeders overpopulating an overpopulated world and ruining their own lives in the process—but she had forgotten to pack her pills and he had only two condoms with him, and it wasn't as if there were a drugstore around the corner.

In the fall—or the end of August, actually—they packed their cars separately and left for college, he to Providence and she to Binghamton. They were separated by three hundred miles, but there was the telephone, there was e-mail, and for the first month or so there were Saturday nights in a motel in Danbury, but that was a haul, it really was, and they both agreed that they should focus on their course work and cut back to every second or maybe third week. On the day they'd left—and no, she didn't want her parents driving her up there, she was an adult and she could take care of herself—Jeremy followed her as far as the Bear Mountain Bridge and they pulled off the road and held each other till the sun fell down into the trees. She had a poem for him, a Donne poem, the saddest thing he'd ever heard. It was something about the moon. *More than moon,* that was it, lovers parting and their tears swelling like an ocean till the girl—the woman, the female—had more power to raise the tides than the moon itself, or some such. More than moon. That's what he called her after that, because she was white and round and getting rounder, and it was no joke, and it was no term of endearment.

She was pregnant. Pregnant, they figured, since the camping trip, and it was their secret, a new constant in their lives, a fact, an inescapable fact that never varied no matter how many home-pregnancy kits they went through. Baggy clothes, that was the key, all in black, cargo pants, flowing dresses, a jacket even in summer. They went to a store in the city where nobody knew them and she got a girdle, and then she went away to school in Binghamton and he went to Providence. "You've got to get rid of it," he told her in the motel room that had become a prison. "Go to a clinic." he told her for the hundredth time, and outside it was raining—or, no, it was clear and cold that night, a foretaste of winter. "I'll find the money—you know I will."

She wouldn't respond. Wouldn't even look at him. One of the *Star Wars* movies was on TV, great flat thundering planes of metal roaring across the screen, and she was just sitting there on the edge of the bed, her shoulders hunched and hair hanging limp. Someone slammed a car door—two doors in rapid succession—and a child's voice shouted, "Me! Me first!"

"China," he said. "Are you listening to me?"

"I can't," she murmured, and she was talking to her lap, to the bed, to the floor. "I'm scared. I'm so scared." There were footsteps in the room next door, ponderous and heavy, then the quick tattoo of the child's feet and a sudden thump against the wall. "I don't want anyone to know," she said.

He could have held her, could have squeezed in beside her and wrapped her in his arms, but something flared in him. He couldn't understand it. He just couldn't. "What are you thinking? Nobody'll know. He's a doctor, for Christ's sake, sworn to secrecy, the doctor-patient compact and all that. What are you going to do, keep it? Huh? Just show up for English 101 with a baby on your lap and say, 'Hi, I'm the Virgin Mary'?"

She was crying. He could see it in the way her shoulders suddenly crumpled and now he could hear it, too, a soft nasal complaint that went right through him. She lifted her face to him and held out her arms and he was there beside her, rocking her back and forth in his arms. He could feel the heat of her face against the hard fibre of his chest, a wetness there, fluids, her fluids. "I don't want a doctor," she said.

And that colored everything, that simple negative: life in the dorms, roommates, bars, bullshit sessions, the smell of burning leaves and the way the light fell across campus in great wide smoking bands just before dinner, the unofficial skateboard club, films, lectures, pep rallies, football—none of it mattered. He couldn't have a life. Couldn't be a freshman. Couldn't wake up in the morning and tumble into the slow steady current of the world. All he could think of was her. Or not simply her—her and him, and what had come between them. Because they argued now, they wrangled and fought and debated, and it was no pleasure to see her in that motel room with the queen-size bed and the big color TV and the soaps and shampoos they made off with as if they were treasure. She was pig-headed, stubborn, irrational. She was spoiled, he could see that now, spoiled by her parents and their standard of living and the socioeconomic expectations of her class—of his class—and the promise of life as you like it, an unscrolling vista of pleasure and acquisition. He loved her. He didn't want to turn his back on her. He would be there for her no matter what, but why did she have to be so *stupid*?

Big sweats, huge sweats, sweats that drowned and engulfed her, that was her campus life, sweats and the dining hall. Her dorm mates didn't know her, and so what if she was putting on weight? Everybody did. How could you shovel down all those carbohydrates, all that sugar and grease and the puddings and nachos and all the rest, without putting on ten or fifteen pounds the first semester alone? Half the girls in the dorm were waddling around like the Doughboy, their faces bloated and blotched with acne, with crusting pimples and whiteheads fed on fat. So she was putting on weight. Big deal. "There's more of me to love," she told her roommate, "and Jeremy likes it that way. And, really, he's the only one that matters." She was careful to shower alone, in the early morning, long before the light had begun to bump up against the windows.

On the night her water broke—it was mid-December, almost nine months, as best as she could figure—it was raining. Raining hard. All week she'd been having tense rasping sotto-voce debates with Jeremy on phone—arguments, fights—and she told him that she would die, creep out into the woods like some animal and bleed to death, before she'd go to a hospital. "And what am I supposed to do?" he demanded in a high childish whine, as if he were the one who'd been knocked up, and she didn't want to hear it, she didn't.

"Do you love me?" she whispered. There was a long hesitation, a pause you could have poured all the affirmation of the world into.

"Yes," he said finally, his voice so soft and reluctant it was like the last gasp of a dying old man.

"Then you're going to have to rent the motel."

"And then what?"

"Then—I don't know." The door was open, her roommate framed there in the hall, a burst of rock and roll coming at her like an assault. "I guess you'll have to get a book or something."

By eight, the rain had turned to ice and every branch of every tree was coated with it, the highway littered with glistening black sticks, no moon, no stars, the tires sliding out from under her, and she felt heavy, big as a sumo wrestler, heavy and loose at the same time. She'd taken a towel from the dorm and put it under her, on the seat, but it was a mess, everything was a mess. She was cramping. Fidgeting with her hair. She tried the radio, but it was no help, nothing but songs she hated, singers that were worse. Twenty-two miles to Danbury and the first of the contractions came like a seizure, like a knife blade thrust into her spine. Her world narrowed to what the headlights would show her.

Jeremy was waiting for her at the door to the room, the light behind him a pale rinse of nothing, no smile on his face, no human expression at all. They didn't kiss—they didn't even touch—and then she was on the bed, on her back, her face clenched like a fist. She heard the rattle of the sleet at the window, the murmur of TV: *I can't let you go like this*, a man protested, and she could picture him, angular and tall, a man in a hat and overcoat in a black-and-white world that might have been another planet, *I just can't*. "Are you—?" Jeremy's voice drifted into the mix, and then stalled. "Are you ready? I mean, is it time? Is it coming now?"

She said one thing then, one thing only, her voice as pinched and hollow as the sound of the wind in the gutters: "Get it out of me."

It took a moment, and then she could feel his hands fumbling with her sweats.

Later, hours later, when nothing had happened but pain, a parade of pain with drum majors and brass bands and penitents crawling on their hands and knees till the streets were stained with their blood, she cried out and cried out again. "It's like *Alien*," she gasped, "like that thing in *Alien* when it, it—"

"It's O.K.," he kept telling her, "it's O.K.," but his face betrayed him. He looked scared, looked as if he'd been drained of blood in some evil experiment in yet another movie, and a part of her wanted to be sorry for him, but another part, the part that was so commanding and fierce it overrode everything else, couldn't begin to be.

He was useless, and he knew it. He'd never been so purely sick at heart and terrified in all his life, but he tried to be there for her, tried to do his best, and when the baby came out, the baby girl all slick with blood and mucus and the lumped white stuff that was like something spilled at the bottom of a garbage can, he was thinking of the ninth grade and how close he'd come to fainting while the teacher went around the room to prick their fingers one by one so they each could smear a drop of blood across a slide. He didn't faint now. But he was close to it, so close he could feel the room dodging away under his feet. And then her voice, the first intelligible thing she'd said in an hour: "Get rid of it. Just get rid of it."

Of the drive back to Binghamton he remembered nothing. Or practically nothing. They took towels from the motel and spread them across the seat of her car, he could remember that much . . . and the blood, how could he forget the blood? It soaked through her sweats and the towels and even the thick cotton bathmat and into the worn fabric of the seat itself. And it all came from inside her, all of it, tissue and mucus and the shining bright fluid, no end to it, as if she'd been turned inside out. He wanted to ask her about that, if that was normal, but she was asleep the minute she slid out from under his arm and dropped into the seat. If he focused, if he really concentrated, he could remember the way her head lolled against the doorframe while the engine whined and the car rocked and the slush threw a dark blanket over the windshield every time a truck shot past in the opposite direction. That and the exhaustion. He'd never been so tired, his head on a string, shoulders slumped, his arms like two pillars of concrete. And what if he'd nodded off? What if he'd gone into a skid and hurtled over an embankment into the filthy gray accumulation of the worst day of his life? What then?

She made it into the dorm under her own power, nobody even looked at her, and, no, she didn't need his help. "Call me," she whispered, and they kissed, her lips so cold it was like kissing a steak through the plastic wrap, and then he parked her car in the student lot and walked to the bus station. He made Danbury late that night, caught a ride out to the motel, and walked right through the "Do Not Disturb" sign on the door. Fifteen minutes. That was all it took. He bundled up everything, every trace, left the key in the box at the desk, and stood scraping the ice off the windshield of his car while the night opened up above him to a black glitter of sky. He never gave a thought to what lay discarded in the Dumpster out back, itself wrapped in plastic, so much meat, so much cold meat.

He was at the very pinnacle of his dream, the river dressed in its currents, the deep hole under the cutbank, and the fish like silver bullets swarming to his bait, when they woke him—when Rob woke him, Rob Greiner, his roommate, Rob with a face of crumbling stone and two policemen there at the door behind him and the roar of the dorm falling away to a whisper. And that was strange, policemen, a real anomaly in that setting, and at first—for the first thirty seconds, at least—he had no idea what they were doing there. Parking tickets? Could that be it? But then they asked him his name, just to confirm it, joined his hands together behind his back, and fitted two loops of naked metal over his wrists, and he began to understand. He saw McCaffrey and Tuttle from across the hall staring at him as if he were Jeffrey Dahmer or something, and the rest of them, all the rest, every head poking out of every door up and down the corridor, as the police led him away.

"What's all this about?" he kept saying, the cruiser nosing through the dark streets to the station house, the man at the wheel and the man beside him as incapable of speech as the seats or the wire mesh or the gleaming black dashboard that dragged them forward into the night. And then it was up the steps and into an explosion of light, more men in uniform, stand here, give me your hand, now the other one, and then the cage and the questions. Only then did he think of that thing in the garbage sack and the sound it had made—its body had made—when he flung it into the Dumpster like a sack of flour and the lid slammed down on it. He stared at the walls, and this was a movie, too. He'd never been in trouble before, never been inside a police station, but he knew his role well enough, because he'd seen it played out a thousand times on the tube: deny everything. Even as the two detectives settled in across from him at the bare wooden table in the little box of the overlit room he was telling himself just that *Deny it, deny it all.*

The first detective leaned forward and set his hands on the table as if he'd come for a manicure. He was in his thirties, or maybe his forties, a tired-looking man with the scars of the turmoil he'd witnessed gouged into the flesh under his eyes. He didn't offer a cigarette ("I don't smoke," Jeremy was prepared to say, giving them that much at least), and he didn't smile or soften his eyes. And when he spoke his voice carried no freight at all, not outrage or threat or cajolery—it was just a voice, flat and tired. "Do you know a China Berkowitz?" he said.

And she. She was in the community hospital, where the ambulance had deposited her after her roommate had called 911 in a voice that was like a bone stuck in the back of her throat, and it was raining again. Her parents were there, her mother red-eyed and sniffling, her father looking like an actor who has forgotten his lines, and there was another woman there, too, a policewoman. The policewoman sat in an orange plastic chair in the corner, dipping her head to the knitting in her lap. At first, China's mother had tried to be pleasant to the woman, but pleasant wasn't what the circumstances called for, and now she ignored her, because the very unpleasant fact was that China was being taken into custody as soon as she was released from the hospital.

For a long while no one said anything—everything had already been said, over and over, one long flood of hurt and recrimination—and the antiseptic silence of the hospital held them in its grip while the rain beat at the windows and the machines at the foot of the bed counted off numbers. From down the hall came a snatch of TV dialogue, and for a minute China opened her eyes and thought she was back in the dorm. "Honey," her mother said, raising a purgatorial face to her, "are you all right? Can I get you anything?"

"I need to—I think I need to pee."

"Why?" her father demanded, and it was the perfect non sequitur. He was up out of the chair, standing over her, his eyes liked cracked porcelain. "Why didn't you tell us, or at least tell your mother—or Dr. Fredman? Dr. Fredman, at least. He's been—he's like a family member, you know that, and he could have, or he would have . . . What were you *thinking*, for Christ's sake?"

Thinking? She wasn't thinking anything, not then and not now. All she wanted—and she didn't care what they did to her, beat her, torture her, drag her weeping through the streets in a dirty white dress with "Baby Killer" stitched over her breast in scarlet letters—was to see Jeremy. Just that. Because what really mattered was what he was thinking.

The food at the Sarah Barnes Cooper Women's Correctional Institute was exactly what they served at the dining hall in college, heavy on the sugars, starches, and bad cholesterol, and that would have struck her as ironic if she'd been there under other circumstances—doing community outreach, say, or researching a paper for sociology class. But given the fact that she'd been locked up for more than a month now, the object of the other girls' threats, scorn, and just plain *nastiness*, given the fact that her life was ruined beyond any hope of redemption, and every newspaper in the country had her shrunken white face plastered across its front page under a headline that screamed "MOTEL MOM," she didn't have much use for irony. She was scared twenty-four hours a day. Scared of the present, scared of the future, scared of the reporters waiting for the judge to set bail so that they could swarm all over her the minute she stepped out the door. She couldn't concentrate on the books and magazines her mother brought her, or even on the TV in the rec room. She sat in her room—it was a room, just like a dorm room, except that they locked you in at night—and stared at the walls, eating peanuts, M&M's, sunflower seeds by the handful, chewing for the pure animal gratification of it. She was putting on more weight, and what did it matter?

Jeremy was different. He'd lost everything—his walk, his smile, the muscles of his upper arms and shoulders. Even his hair lay flat now, as if he couldn't bother with a tube of gel and a comb. When she saw him at the arraignment, saw him for the first time since she'd climbed out of the car and limped into the dorm with the blood wet on her legs, he looked like a refugee, like a ghost. The room they were in—the courtroom—seemed to have grown up around them, walls, windows, benches, lights, and radiators already in place, along with the judge, the American flag, and the ready-made spectators. It was hot. People coughed into their fists and shuffled their feet, every sound magnified. The judge presided, his arms like bones twirled in a bag, his eyes searching and opaque as he peered over the top of his reading glasses.

China's lawyer didn't like Jeremy's lawyer, that much was evident, and the state prosecutor didn't like anybody. She watched him—Jeremy, only him—as the reporters held their collective breath and the judge read off the charges and her mother bowed her head and sobbed into the bucket of her hands. And Jeremy was watching her, too, his eyes locked on hers as if he defied them all, as if nothing mattered in the world but her, and when the judge said *First-degree murder* and *Murder by abuse or neglect* he never flinched.

She sent him a note that day—"I love you, will always love you no matter what, More than Moon"—and in the hallway, afterward, while their lawyers fended off the reporters and the bailiffs tugged impatiently at them, they had a minute, just a minute, to themselves. "What did you tell them?" he whispered. His voice was a rasp, almost a growl; she looked at him, inches away, and hardly recognized him.

"I told them it was dead."

"My lawyer—Mrs. Teagues?—she says they're saying it was alive when we, when we put it in the bag." His face was composed, but his eyes were darting like insects trapped inside his head.

"It was dead."

"It looked dead," he said, and already he was pulling away from her and some callous shit with a camera kept annihilating them with flash after flash of light, "and we certainly didn't—I mean, we didn't slap it or anything to get it breathing. . . ."

And then the last thing he said to her, just as they were pulled apart, and it was nothing she wanted to hear, nothing that had any love in it, or even the hint of love: "You told me to get rid of it."

There was no elaborate name for the place where they were keeping him. It was known as Drum Hill Prison, period. No reform-minded notions here, no verbal gestures toward rehabilitation or behavior modification, no benefactors, mayors, or role models to lend the place their family names, but then who in his right mind would want a prison named after him anyway? At least they kept him separated from the other prisoners, the gangbangers and dope dealers and sexual predators and the like. He was no longer a freshman at Brown, not officially, but he had his books and his course notes and he tried to keep up as best he could Still, when the screams echoed through the cell block at night and the walls dripped with the accumulated breath of eight and a half thousand terminally angry sociopaths, he had to admit it wasn't the sort of college experience he'd bargained for.

And what had he done to deserve it? He still couldn't understand. That thing in the Dumpster—and he refused to call it human, let alone a baby—was nobody's business but his and China's. That's what he'd told his attorney, Mrs. Teagues, and his mother and her boyfriend, Howard, and he'd told them over and over again: *I didn't do anything wrong.* Even if it was alive, and it was, he knew in his heart that it was, even before the state prosecutor presented evidence of blunt-force trauma and death by asphyxiation and exposure, it didn't matter, or shouldn't have mattered. There was no baby. There was nothing but a mistake, a mistake clothed in blood and mucus. When he really thought about it, thought it through on its merits and dissected all his mother's pathetic arguments about where he'd be today if she'd felt as he did when she was pregnant herself, he hardened like a rock, like sand turning to stone under all the pressure the planet can bring to bear. Another unwanted child in an overpopulated world? They should have given him a medal.

It was the end of January before bail was set—three hundred and fifty thousand dollars his mother didn't have—and he was released to house arrest. He wore a plastic anklet that set off an alarm if he went out the door, and so did she, so did China, imprisoned like some fairy-tale princess at her parents' house. At first, she called him every day, but mostly what she did was cry—"I want to see it," she sobbed. "I want to see our daughter's *grave.*" That froze him inside. He tried to picture her—her now, China, the love of his life—and he couldn't. What did she look like? What was her face like, her nose, her hair, her eyes and breasts and the slit between her legs? He drew a blank. There was no way to summon her the way she used to be or even the way she was in court, because all he could remember was the thing that had come out of her, four limbs and the equipment of a female, shoulders rigid and eyes shut tight, as if she were a mummy in a tomb . . . and the breath, the shuddering long gasping rattle of a breath he could feel ringing inside her even as the black plastic bag closed over her face and the lid of the Dumpster opened like a mouth.

He was in the den, watching basketball, a drink in his hand (7UP mixed with Jack Daniel's in a ceramic mug, so no one would know he was getting shit-faced at two o'clock on a Sunday afternoon), when the phone rang. It was Sarah Teagues. "Listen, Jeremy," she said in her crisp, equitable tones, "I thought you ought to know—the Berkowitzes are filing a motion to have the case against China dropped."

His mother's voice on the portable, too loud, a blast of amplified breath and static: "On what grounds?"

"She never saw the baby, that's what they're saying. She thought she had a miscarriage."

"Yeah, right," his mother said.

Sarah Teagues was right there, her voice as clear and present as his mother's. "Jeremy's the one that threw it in the Dumpster, and they're saying he acted alone. She took a polygraph test day before yesterday."

He could feel his heart pounding like it used to when he plodded up that last agonizing ridge behind the school with the cross-country team, his legs sapped, no more breath left in his body. He didn't say a word. Didn't even breathe.

"She's going to testify against him."

Outside was the world, puddles of ice clinging to the lawn under a weak afternoon sun, all the trees stripped bare, the grass dead, the azalea under the window reduced to an armload of dead brown twigs. She wouldn't have wanted to go out today anyway. This was the time of year she hated most, the long interval between the holidays and spring break, when nothing grew and nothing changed—it didn't even seem to snow much anymore. What was out there for her anyway? They wouldn't let her see Jeremy, wouldn't even let her talk to him on the phone or write him anymore, and she wouldn't be able to show her face at the mall or even the movie theater without somebody shouting out her name as if she were a freak, as if she were another Monica Lewinsky or Heidi Fleiss. She wasn't China Berkowitz, honor student, not anymore—she was the punch line to a joke, a footnote to history.

She wouldn't mind going for a drive, though—that was something she missed, just following the curves out to the reservoir to watch the way the ice cupped the shore, or up to the turnout on Route 9 to look out over the river where it oozed through the mountains in a shimmering coil of light. Or to take a walk in the woods, just that. She was in her room, on her bed, posters of bands she'd out-grown staring down from the walls, her high-school books on two shelves in the corner, the closet door flung open on all the clothes she'd once wanted so desperately she could have died for each individual pair of boots or the cashmere sweaters that felt so good against her skin. At the bottom of her left leg, down there at the foot of the bed, was the anklet she wore now, the plastic anklet with the transmitter inside, no different, she supposed, than the collars they put on wolves to track them across all those miles of barren tundra or the bears sleeping in their dens. Except that hers had an alarm on it.

For a long while she just lay there gazing out the window, watching the rinsed-out sun slip down into the sky that had no more color in it than a TV tuned to an unsubscribed channel, and then she found herself picturing things the way they were an eon ago, when everything was green. She saw the azalea bush in bloom, the leaves knifing out of the trees, butterflies—or were they cabbage moths?—hovering over the flowers. Deep green. That was the color of the world. And she was remembering a night, summer before last, just after she and Jeremy started going together, the crickets thrumming, the air thick with humidity, and him singing along with the car radio, his voice so sweet and pure it was as if he'd written the song himself, just for her. And when they got to where they were going, at the end of that dark lane overhung with trees, to a place where it was private and hushed and the night fell in on itself as if it couldn't support the weight of the stars, he was as nervous as she was. She moved into his arms and they kissed, his lips groping for hers in the dark, his fingers trembling over the thin yielding silk of her blouse. He was Jeremy. He was the love of her life. And she closed her eyes and clung to him as if that were all that mattered. [2000]

Critical Eye

FOR DISCUSSION

a. How is this story about how we idealize love when we are young but often find the emotion lacking once it is confronted with real life issues like the one's Jeremy and China confront?

b. How do (C)lass and gender come into play after Jeremy and China are taken into custody. In short, why are their outcomes so different even though they both took part in the event?

REAPPROACHING THE TEXT

Keeping in mind that both Jeremy and China are very young and that young people tend to make mistakes in their youth that they would never make as adults, can their lapse in judgment be understood and forgiven?

WRITING ASSIGNMENT

Using specific examples from the text, make the claim that Jeremy was treated more harshly because he was a man. Discuss how perhaps our perceptions of what men are expected to do as the dominant gender was used to cast China as the victimized and weak woman.

J. California Cooper

Vanity

I'm sittin here thinking, ponderin, over life. I hear my radio playin music softly round me. Beautiful full religious music bout God and what he does. I am listenin . . . and I am thinkin . . . about this life. Even death.

Sometimes you get something in life and you don't know you got it, so you don't do nothin with it. Then sometime you get something and you know you got it and you want everybody else to know it too. You be just done got lucky, even got something you can share, like beauty. But some people turn a gift into a weapon and use it on everybody. Sometimes, they think they be goin up, up . . . but they ain't. They be goin down, down . . . and taking people with em! Two fools. Fool for doin it, and a fool for goin down with it. One thing I do know, life is like a bank sometime. You ain't gonna get no more out of it than you put in it! Tho it do look like some people do . . . in the end, they don't.

Some people say everybody got a Guardian Angel looks over you. I ain't sure God got that kind of labor to waste on some people, but if he do, I don't envy the one was watchin over Vanity.

My mind is turned to these thoughts by death. A strange death, ugh!, of a woman I knew. A friend? I don't know was she a friend or not. She might'a tried, I don't know. I was her friend tho. I do know that. Vanity. Vanity is her name.

I knew her well. Very well. I am a little older than she was. I used to keep her, sit with her for her mama when Vanity was little. She was grown then, in a little way. She talk to me all her life. She thought I was her friend . . . well I was, but I was a little scared of her. I was. She didn't seem to have nothin in her heart for nobody but herself. I watched her think, listened to her talk.

Just listen what she said to me a year or so ago, when her trouble started. Another kind of trouble she didn't understand. See, she didn't have no women friends for too long. They didn't like her for long. But she never cared no way. She get lonely she just come find me. I knew all her secrets. I think. Just listen what she said to me when we be sittin on the front porch, laughin, talkin softly. She be drinkin champagne. She drink enough to keep even a Guardian Angel high.

From *The Matter is Life* by J. California Cooper, copyright © 1991 by J. California Cooper. Used by permission of Doubleday, a division of Random House, Inc.

She say, "I was always very beautiful. You may not believe that, but it's true. I know. I am still beautiful.

"I knew I was beautiful the day I was born. You may not believe that either, that a newborn could know that, but I did. The doctor did not want to slap me, the nurses looked at me with envy and hate. My mother was elated. She was . . . uncomely. But I let that pass. ME. I was the important one . . . and . . . as I said I was beautiful. But bored . . . from birth.

"Bored! Do you know how long I had to wait to walk? To speak? To buy things, beautiful clothes, to enhance my beauty? Several years. But I used the time well.

"I studied my father. I wrapped his heart around all my fingers. Many times he slept, holding me, instead of my mother. That became a problem, but I don't wish to talk about that now. But . . . I was practicing, yes, practicing for my future. When I spoke, I spoke in question marks. 'Will you buy that for me? May I have that? Do you think this is right for me? Don't you want me to have that? Does this look good on me, compliment me?' Oh yes, I knew what to do with me, my beauty.

"I wanted to goooo somewhere. Beeee somebody. Doooo something with what I had. I was born decided not to be a victim. Determined. And I had the greatest tool I know in life. Beauty.

"At five, ten, twelve, fifteen years of age, I knew, I knew, just by looking at people looking at me. I knew I was superb . . . that I could acquire things and people in proportion to my beauty. The world lets you know they are fools because they love beauty no matter how empty it is. However, I was not empty. I was full of thoughts. Of myself. Well . . . what better? Who should you be thinking of? See?" She said and laughed, "I'm still into question marks?

"Reasons, causes and effects, results . . . that's what I studied on. Hard. But not too hard . . . it wasn't necessary . . . for all. Boys and then men became monotonous, always telling me of their love. What did they think I thought? Didn't I know they would love me? Want me? I was delicious to look upon. Ask my father. He gave me everything! He loved to touch me, assure himself I was his. My mother had very little, she didn't need it anyway. She had her chosen man . . . who really belonged to me after I was born. She had us. She had him anyway. I was there I guess. But only I had me.

"Many, many hours were spent, me with myself, alone. The sun rose and shone on ME, sent its warmth into my soul. Flowers bent when I passed, God knew. Everyone, anyone, who looked on me, their heart beat and throbbed with the thoughts of love and possession. Men and some women too. Desire . . . ahhhh, desire, the crux of the whole life matter.

"I was young . . . innocent, in a way, in my body, not my mind. I was sad because I had to wait for life, get older. Wait for the joy of being a woman. A beautiful woman. To get my due. I said prayers. After all, God was, is, greater than I, at least." (I know her Guardian Angel almost choked!)

"So many loves came into my life, before my eyes. I was always smiling, happy. At peace with my self and my glory. I cared, oh!, I cared for myself because when I first looked at me, I loved, loved me.

"At twelve years old, I washed, creamed and smoothed my body. I brushed, combed my luxuriant hair that it might nestle on my lovely soft shoulders and be a cape of beauty for others to enjoy. Yes, I thought of others, sometime. I loved my arms, my waist, my legs, so full and smooth, beautiful . . . and mine.

"You know I loved clothes! To sheath my body! Let them be expensive! Let my father struggle to do what he had to do to afford them for me. Wasn't I his child? Wasn't he supposed to do for me? Getting anything I needed? I needed beauty. As I grew older, I HAD to have lovely, beautiful, costly things. Wasn't I ME!? Mama had had her time and got him . . . and me . . . now it was my turn. Practicing, practicing. My hands, my nails, my shoulders, my breast, beautiful. My legs, my thighs, my feet . . . all of me, I oiled, creamed, smoothed and loved. And I felt joy. Anything that made me look like me . . . beautiful . . . I loved. Not people . . . just things.

"The only thing that bothered me was time. TIME. Always moving, passing, getting away. But too slow for me. I had to wait, wait and waste those early years I needed, to be admired and loved. I got up early, mornings, to have more time to be admired. I have sat looking out my windows, hours and hours, weeks and weeks, just waiting for someone new to come along, pass by, to look upon me and know . . . I was beautiful. I watched their eyes.

"Seasons meant nothing to me. All were mine. Except, I learned I must stay out of the sun. Ahhh, and it was such a spotlight.

"One day after school graduation, after all the shit I had to go through to get to my life, my freedom, I said to myself, 'I'm not beautiful enough.' You see, I had seen others then, that might come close to me. And I wished, tho I looked better than all others, that all, ALL pretty women, even cute women, would die, DIE. And leave me to have all the men, all the adulation, my choice, anybody I wanted . . . to love me.

"Somebody special to love me. It was now at the time when loving myself was not enough . . . not enough. I began to know fear. Fear is a low, low, sad feeling. But it was into me. I couldn't help it. Of course, I should have known better. What had fear to do with me? YET . . . I feared. Somehow I knew . . . I might not . . . might not . . . have everything. Oh! my lord, ME!?

"Now! It was now time. I was eighteen. Through with high school. My parents could not afford college where I might have found my true future, my love to love me as I should be loved. Riches, position, everything! No . . . I had to work with what I had. Well, it was quite a bit. But, still, all by myself. Only, only?, my beauty to help me. And it did. Don't you make the mistake that men will not let anything go for a beautiful thing to look at. In the morning, the evening, especially the night. Men are fools. Good grand fools. Don't let me mislead you, they are alright. Are they not rich sometimes? I still believe the world belongs to a woman, but only because it belongs to men and they give it to her! Just fools for beauty. Is it beauty? Or is it body? Hmmmm. But . . . I was always just like a lady, a real lady. A beautiful, beautiful Lady."

Yessss, chile! All those things Vanity said to me . . . and more. I can't remember everything now, my mind is mixed up with death . . . and life.

I'ma tell you something, bout this life I done found out. Sometimes from the birthstone to the tombstone ain't nothing but a few steps. High ones, low ones. Don't matter. And sometime you don't even know you been walking on the road of time, think you been standin still and you been flyin with your feet. Laughin, having a good time, even cryin, having a bad time. Then, one day, you look up and you way, way up the road. One day you twenty, overnight, you thirty, one movin year . . . forty, one afternoon . . . fifty. After that, it pass by like hours, minutes! All the time you thought you was spending only money, you been spending time. TIME. Chile, time. The most valuable thing you got! Or ever gonna have!

Now, if you ain't there where you think you ought to be when you think you oughta be THERE, and you done spent time til you broke and you ain't even enjoyed gettin to where you are! If you don't understand what I'm sayin, I do, I just maybe ain't sayin it right for you to understand. Try.

There was no lie about it! Vanity was a beautiful thing, a beautiful woman to see. Not to know. Just to see. Her Guardian Angel had a JOB!

But, back to her family, her dear mother saw the love transferred away from her. She wasn't no longer the center of the home. She just waned and drifted to the background with the second daughter she had, Mega. The father often slept with Vanity cause she said she had bad dreams, holdin her, pettin her, kissin her. As she grew older, them kisses grew lower and lower until she was kissed by father all over her body. It was like a form of worship to her. If it is true some men had their own daughters way, way back there in them cavemen days without feelin shame nor fear, that is still in some men. I don't blive he went that far with her tho. Just fondles, touches. But she grew to expect, and get, the same thing from most all her men the rest of her life. Her Guardian Angel musta shuddered.

Then, when Mega was born the father expected to have another great beauty to show off. He smiled and waited. But, as she grew, her beauty was neat, plain, sweet. He might could'a grew to understand those was also wonderful things to love, but Vanity always movin between them, pullin on his arms when he played with Mega, wrappin herself round his head to shield his eyes from Mega. In time, he centered on Vanity again. The mother cried awhile, then smiled thru her tears and took Mega to herself. Mega grew up affectionate, patient, sweet and, I guess, just normally normal. The mother refused to have any more children. So they each had one!

But these things tells on a woman who loves her husband. She loved her husband, had dreamed of the perfect home. Her love grieved, her spirit grieved. She was alone in her home, in her marriage, in her life. She was a sad, sad heartbroken woman, whose daughter had stolen her husband, with a smile. A beautiful smile. A Guardian Angel grieved, I know.

In time, when Vanity was seventeen, Mega fifteen, the parents divorced. The mother could take no more, could not watch Mega's confusion no more. The family had been divided too often and too long by Vanity's demands on her father. The mother took Mega, naturally, and because I don't have time to tell just everything, I'll just tell you they did well. Mega had a normal life, I guess. She wondered, from time to time, about the family ways. She loved them all. She was patient with them all. Just like a real little lady. Her time passed that way, and she grew up strong in spite of all of them.

All this time Vanity was runnin after hearts . . . anybody's. Had great pleasure in takin the heart of a boy, or man, who seemed to love another girl, or woman. Even her closest friends' beaus. Of course she ended up with no friends! But Vanity didn't care, she was havin a good time. Just like a lady (she thought). And time passed. Don't it always.

Her father bought her everything. Sometime being late, very late, with payments for Mega. Vanity explained that away to him by saying she gave Mega all her cast-off clothing and things, that Mega didn't need as much right at that time of her life.

Also, at that time of Vanity's life, she was twenty or twenty-one then, dancin, laughin, always goin out, riding, playin. Life was gettin dull to her. Same old crowd, growing smaller. Some gettin married. Women shyin away from her. Men already been burnt by her, keepin a distance. No magic around for her to play with. She turned her lofty head to look over the horizon for fresh life and dreams. Her Guardian Angel was in dread.

Vanity loved picture shows. Lookin at one, one day, she decided she had always wanted to be a movie star. She knew she looked as good as those up on that screen. She prepared her father a good meal (in her gloves). Set a beautiful table, candles and all, just for her father and her. His eyes just sparkled, he was so proud of his daughter and happy she had decided to stay home with him an evenin. Vanity didn't waste no time tho, she just came right out and told him almost soon as he sat down to eat.

"Daddy, I need some money. I've made up my mind what I want to be, at last. I'm going to Los Angeles to seek my fame . . . and my fortune. I know I will be successful. All they want is beauty! So . . . I am prepared." She laughed, he frowned, started to say something. She thought she anticipated him. "You always wanted me to be serious about something. Now, I'm ready."

He sighed. They argued awhile. He lost, again.

He said, as he sighed, "Well . . . if that's what you really want. I'll transfer my job . . . and we'll move."

She pursed her beautiful lips. "Noooo. I want to . . . I need to go alone. I'm over twenty-one now. I want to be on my own. Just send me some money. But I want to be alone." She thought of allll the men there. And Dad was gettin old and showing it. Ugly comin. She didn't like ugly.

He was hurt . . . and feared loneliness. "You'd leave me? You'd go alone? So far from me?"

She turned her beautiful lips down, and snapped, "What do you expect me to do? Be here under . . . with you the rest of my life?"

He stammered, "No . . . no . . . I . . . I thought . . ."

She stopped his thought. "Well, I am grown. I will go alone. You can't be with me forever! I have to have my own life! I am your daughter . . . NOT your wife." He groaned and twisted in his seat, dinner, candles forgotten. She continued. "You'll . . . you'll still have Mega . . . and Mama, if you can get her to leave her new husband and come back to you! But I . . ."

He bent his dumb head. "Your mother will never leave that man. He loves her . . . and Mega." He looked up suddenly, angry. "He better not be doing anything to my child!" He looked sad again. "Let me get a house there and we . . ."

She threw him a disdainful look. "Dad. I . . . am . . . grown. I have to go alone." Her tone softened, "I have to see if I can make it on my own. So you will be proud of me. Just a little money to help me til I am rich and can make it on my own." She smiled brightly, beautifully. "Then I will send for you to come . . . visit me sometime."

Anyway . . . she got her way. Her Guardian Angel shook its head . . . and waited.

Vanity went to Los Angeles expecting to have heads and hearts rolling in the streets. Instead she found so many beautiful women everywhere she went to seek a job. Everywhere she walked, ate, sat, looked. She got nervous and was throwing up every night. Got sick even, but didn't get a job in films. Men had so much pretty to look upon. She was just one of them. Beauty was five feet deep in Los Angeles. Talent wasn't. Vanity didn't have much talent. In two months she called home for a ticket back. Back to safety and some kind of throne. In Los Angeles they didn't even know she was gone, cause they hardly knew she was there.

Her daddy smiled sadly, gladly sent the money, borrowed money. He had been sending her so much to keep her in the style she thought she had to have, to keep her happy, he was most broke. But he was happy he was gonna have his "baby" back! Her Guardian Angel must have smiled with relief cause a whole lotta things wait for pretty girls in them big busy cities.

She returned to her little three-legged throne. Told everybody she didn't like it in L.A. because the people had no class. But she read that writin on the back of that throne, looked at the horizon again, saw "marriage."

Now . . . one man, Robert, really worshipped Vanity. You know right there he was a lightweight fool. He had done gone to college and had a future, but the future wasn't there yet, so he was still in the strugglin stage. He sure knew how to talk tho. And he could kiss her from the feet up . . . she had to have that! He wrote her poems. Sent her flowers. Kissed her feet. Used his eyes as mirrors for her. Since she saw herself so much in his eyes, and thought he had a future, she married him. Her daddy surely did go into BIG debt for that weddin. I blive he still owe some on it and he dead and gone now!

The mother and Mega came. The mother lookin sad, Mega smiling with joy for her sister. She wasn't asked to be in the weddin. She was married now, with one child. Vanity said she needed a pretty matron of honor with some money so she could get a better present from her. She seemed to understand Vanity, didn't seem to mind, but I knew she was hurt cause she was a family person. She cared. She knew how to love people for real reasons.

Anyway, the Guardian Angel must have held its breath, but the marriage lasted only three years. Til Vanity was twenty-five. Turned out Robert's struggle was lastin too long . . . and the kisses didn't last long enough, cause they got borin and all tied up with cookin (in gloves) and eatin, going to the bathroom and snorin, his dirty clothes, underwear and all, and blowin noses and payin bills (she made). He be tired and she need another dose of worship. She took to leavin him snorin and going out to get what worship she needed, in them expensive clothes she charged on him. Her daddy was still payin for some of her clothes too, she sure could spend money on herself. He was still livin then, poor fool. She never did buy nobody else nothin!

Now, Vanity didn't go too far out. Not very much adultry, cause that wasn't what she was after. Just more love and worship. A few times she did commit adultry was cause her worship bank was low and she couldn't get that worship no other way. She ended up have two abortions for two reasons. One, she didn't quite know whose baby it was. Two, she was never gonna mess her body up with nothin! Her husband never knew. Her daddy never knew. Even her hairdresser never knew. Just her and the one who gave her the pills and things, and me, cause I had to help her, care for her.

Now that took a little toll on her looks, but it didn't show right then at the time. That little bit of drinkin, she loved champagne, didn't do much harm, but it did some. She liked to smoke cause it made her look classy, she thought. That took a toll, too. But you couldn't see it cause she made-up and dressed-up so good. But . . . she still got bored after awhile. Her Guardian Angel used to whisper things to her conscience to make her life fuller, more satisfying to all. But it found nothin there to listen to it.

She got divorced. She didn't get no job tho. She lived off the money from her father and what she could get out of her ex-husband. She could work with that money. Somebody else's! Cause she wouldn't work FOR it.

Then she made friends with a wealthy older woman, Snity. Snity spelled her name "$nity." Her new friend was almost just like her, so $nity didn't let Vanity round her husband too much. Snity did go all the way with her admirers. She was growin old and losin her beauty from livin so hard and much. She did introduce her to other wealthy men tho.

Vanity was a good catcher for $nity and was used as such for a long time, til she was thirty or thirty-one. She got to travel, go places she never could have gone before. She was lonely, so she was sleepin around a bit. But you had to give her some money then, cause she needed clothes to keep up with $nity. Her Guardian Angel weeped.

Finally a older man came along who $nity didn't want. Name Edward. The man had some little sense cause he had made a lotta money. But, between $nity talkin him into it and Vanity bein so beautiful (still), he asked Vanity to be his wife. Vanity opened her arms wide, showin all her beauty at once, and flew to his side like a Condor jet! Guardian Angel held its breath again.

As life would have it, Edward got bored early with the kissin from the feet up. Wanted hisself kissed from the feet up. But mostly he wanted someone to share his mind with. He took a clear, longer look inside his beautiful wife and . . . HE got bored!

The man still had some sense, so he took the good from the marriage. Vanity was a good hostess, handled his business meetings at home well. Could socialize successfully. He kept her. And she kept him. In time, tho, she became bored, less men paid attention to her. She became lonely. Edward wasn't often interested in makin love and worship to her. He became lonely. No one to really talk to in his home. She didn't care for his grown children. They were uncomfortable, so they just gradually stayed away. He had to visit them. He was welcome, but it wasn't like bein at his own home. Guardian Angel shook its head in sorrow.

Edward liked Mega, even did some business with her husband who was moving right along with his business, using elbow grease and brains. But even Mega didn't come round much cause she had three children that Vanity didn't like.

No, Vanity didn't seem to like children at all. Edward didn't know it, but Vanity had already had one abortion with him. It was his child and he sure would have loved it. The child would have tied them closer, into a family. Guardian Angel wept again.

Another thing Edward didn't know, Vanity was workin with a doctor to plan a appendix operation which was really goin to be a historectory. She told me she could not keep up them abortions. She had got real sick from the last time and thought Edward might find out why, for real, if it happened again.

She looked over at me, over that glass of champagne she had brought over to my house and said, "I simply cannot afford to ruin my body. Not for any baby, nor any man! My body is all I have, and I am not sharing it! The baby will end up with all my looks and all I will have is a 'baby.' "

The woman was a lonely woman, very lonely inside all her beauty and didn't know how much a baby, her own child, could mean. But the baby might have been lucky not to have been born, after all. I don't know, cause I don't know everything. So, historectory it was.

When Vanity got to be round thirty-five she was runnin round like she was crazy. Going to every party, every show, every night club, about every night. Driven dissipation. She was desperately trying to be rich and happy. Sometimes her despondence and dissipation was pitiful. She cried. But not too long, cause it made you ugly. Her tears musta been champagne cause she drank it all the time. Carried a bottle in her car. Opened. Guardian Angel asked to be relieved of its duty. Devil grinned cause he likes destruction and confusion.

She kept that up til she was round thirty-eight years old. Beauty goin cause beauty ain't somethin you can beat to death every night. Edward was so bored, disgusted, tired of everything so empty, he was in pain. When I say, "bored," don't take that word lightly. "Bored" can be miserable, miserable. That is what he was, miserable. And each month the bills were higher. He was payin plenty to be miserable. Divorce came on his mind, naturally, cause he never was a real stone-fool.

Mega's husband died round that time, too. She was broken nearly to pieces by his death. She truly loved him. Theirs was a good marriage. She had the children tho, and he left her pretty well fixed. Edward, of course, went to console her. In her innocence, he was consoled. She looked healthy and warm, too. And her house had lots of love in it.

Vanity's and Mega's father died round bout then. Death comes like that sometime. In threes, people say. His heart was probly broken, cause it sure was starved. Vanity didn't never have no time for him in her fast life. He was like some child she didn't want to be bothered with. She was in New York partyin at the time. Called and told Mega to decide everything and take care everything, see bout the insurance money. That she would TRY to get back in time for the funeral. Guardian Angel tried to quit.

I was her friend, but I got mad at her then, and didn't know whether I'd keep on bein her friend or not! I could see how she might do me one day! Or anybody! Her father did everything she ever wanted! She never paid no time to her mother either, but that old woman made it so she didn't need Vanity. She had her Mega and grandchildren. I know she would have loved to be closer to her daughter Vanity tho. You know mothers.

She did make it to the funeral . . . late. Mega did all the work need to be done. Mega cried the most. The mother too. Vanity cried, with a glass of champagne in her hands all through the funeral, what was left when she got there. Edward was disgusted . . . again. He had his arms round Mega, consoling her, more than he had em round Vanity.

Well, now . . . Vanity had all the money she needed, but them admirers was fadin away. Edward was fadin away. Vanity was lonely, unhappy. Her beauty was really fadin away too. She decided to go in for all that plastic surgery stuff. Edward put his foot down, then he put his marriage down. They got a divorce. Now, she really was alone. Lotsa friends don't last long sometime. Vanity was very, very lonely with only herself. But that was the main person she had loved.

Everything happened so fast. Edward and Vanity divorced and we looked up and Edward was marryin Mega, who probably saw in him the father she never had. He was good to the children too! Neither one was marryin for money cause they both had some. He older, but they still together and it look like they happy to me. That whole family! His kids is welcome now to his home.

Vanity like to died, sure nuff! when they got married. She said Mega had always tried to take everything from her she ever wanted. Lied. She consoled herself by trying to take every dime she could from him. She told everybody her sister had broken up her happy home. Lied. Friends (?) smiled and turned away. Guardian Angel had a sore neck from shaking it.

Vanity was thirty-nine years old then. She spent plenty money on that face surgery. It did some good. Then her mother died. She said she couldn't let herself cry like she felt, cause her operation was too new, it would ruin it. But even with them operations, she was beginnin to look like her mother. She had mirrors all over her house. She would see herself all day, wherever she moved. Sometimes she just scream, break out in tears and run jump in the middle of her sumptuous bed and cry, tryin to hold her face straight.

Vanity went into retreat. Wouldn't come out for nothin. Ordered everything brought in. Chile, the woman was somethin! Layin out there in that big ole house with all the rich stuff in it. Lonely and unhappy . . . and scared. She had never lived like that before, and she didn't know what to do. Everybody who would help her was gone . . . or dead. She was alone. No mama, no daddy, no close sister, no child. Alone, chile.

Mega who was nowhere near her in looks had her husband. Vanity knew something was wrong. The men were gone. She was free, divorced, and the men weren't rushing in. It must be her beauty. She really stayed out of the sun. Spent hundreds of dollars on lotions and creams, magic formulas. Like a lady, she thought. Her Guardian Angel looked over the world, saw the starving, the sick, and cried. That was the saddest angel!

So . . . she lived her life alone. Retreated from all her "friends" and "admirers" for, to her, the reason for their admiration was fadin away. She wanted to be remembered as the most beautiful. The most beautiful lady ever in their world. Yea . . . so she retreated from the world. Like a lady. Her Guardian Angel took a deep breath, sighed and rested in defeat, but hope.

But . . . no matter what you do or how you hide, this world, life, is not going to let you get away without livin. Long as you breathin, something is going to happen to you!

Her life proceeded in a quiet way. All her days was spent alone. She might talk on the phone just to keep up with what was goin on in her old world. She didn't want any company. Maybe $nity, but $nity didn't want to come nowhere dark and quiet. She was old, but she thought she was still goin strong, tho now, she was givin the men her money.

Vanity told $nity, "You are a fool! Givin somebody all that money you have worked hard lyin, layin and marrying for! A man wouldn't know how to fix his lips to ask me for any of my money! I'll never get that old and need any loving from anybody who expects something for it other than my time and my beautiful body!" She laughed. "I don't need anybody, or anything that bad! A man coming into my life better bring something with him!"

After long days, bathing, drinkin, creaming her body, wearin her lovely delicate negligies, drinkin, eating, lookin at TV, staring out in space through the curtains of her huge windows, drinkin, listenin to records, starin into mirrors, drinkin again, she was bored and restless, but did not want to go out where people were. She actually thought she was gettin ugly, but she really wasn't ugly. Older, naturally, but, she didn't look bad as she seem to think.

She lay in bed at night, lonely, longing. Staring at the mirror over her bed. Wishing for someone. Her first husband . . . no. Her second husband . . . maybe. Rainy nights were the hardest. She played blues records and, yes, sometimes she cried. She felt sorry for herself that everyone had left behind, somehow. They say the blues ain't nothin but a woman cryin for her man. Well, she just didn't exactly know who her man was. He had to be in her past. Sure didn't look like he was in her future.

Sometimes . . . she felt just like the dogs she could hear howling at night. Oh! Lord! They sure must have the blues, to sound so, so sad. So blue. Even lost, deserted. So lonely . . . in the darkness of the night . . . in the rain . . . in the quiet. Sometime she would cut off all sound, music and TV, in the house and lay and listen to the sound of dogs callin to each other. Mating calls. Sad longing songs that sounded full of need and painful feelings. Alone. In need. Alone.

Her life was so quiet, she began to look forward to orderin things somebody had to bring. The groceries was the most likely thing, cause she did like to eat good food. The liquor store, too, was the most regular delivery.

The man who delivered the liquor was very mannerable, respectful, quiet, youngish . . . bout thirty-eight or thirty-nine years old. Always smiling. Gentle, smooth, smart. Knew how to do a million things around the house that always need doing and always did a few before he left. Hang a plant different, move a table, a large chair. Fix a small pipe, see why a light didn't work. All those kinds of things. You know. All the things some women wish a man was around the house for.

He never touched her. Even accidently. No, no. He remained mannerable, never familiar, never out of line. Didn't even curse a little bit. Just never did anything wrong. You know. Like I say, the kind some women wish was around the house. He was good-lookin too. Bright, youngish face. Hell, he wasn't old anyway.

He liked good music. It got to where she always searched for something new to play for him . . . to hold him a little longer. Then it got to where she had something fixed for him, something he had said he liked to eat. He drank very little. She ordered so much liquor to get him over there, she could have stocked a speakeasy. She liked to see him. He was just about perfect. Her Guardian Angel became alarmed. Because, you see, the angel knew.

Yes, he was almost perfect. He had practiced a long time. He had several older women he always delivered to. A few with money, they had to have money, had even become what they thought was "his woman." He made love to them. Good love. He was gentle sometimes, rough sometimes, but always only just enough. He never did anything too much. With them.

He had a nice life. Just deliver liquor. His customers bought so much, the owner let him handle just the ones he wanted to deliver to. He could do something extra if he wanted to. He had wanted to deliver to Vanity. He had watched her for several years. She hadn't seen him. Until she was alone.

He wouldn't live with any woman. Wanted to be alone, free. Wanted everything he wanted and all he could get of it. He really didn't want for nothin, not with them ladies he had. He dressed, always in good taste, very expensively. He liked hats and he sure looked good in em!

He knew when not to see someone. He was a bit cruel. He could ignore either one of his "women" for a week or two. Send someone else with the order. Not call for two or three days. You know. They always end up givin him what he wanted. He never asked, just mentioned. And he only mentioned once. So you better remember what he said and hurry up and get it if you wanted him comin back.

Vanity came to expect him. To count on him. Even to love him . . . a little, and he had never touched her. Yet. Her Guardian Angel whispered to her, but she really couldn't hear the angel I guess.

His name was Jody. Jody was born, I think, with something left out of his soul. The ability to love somebody, anybody, but himself.

Yea, he came into her life. Yes, chile. Ain't it the way life is? Just keep foolin round with it . . . it will fool back with you!

Jody had all the charm, all the manners, all the look-like concern and care for the female race they needed. He was warm and affectionate with his voice. Color of a sunny Hershey bar, lookin just as rich and sweet. Warm, admiring eyes and a gentleman to the hundredth degree. Six feet tall, large shoulders, played football and basketball in school and college. Yes, he went to college and still just a delivery boy. He wore bikini underwear. Don't ask me how I know! He, also, had five children he claimed were all not his.

In two months, they were close, old friends. Watchin the results of all they had done in the garden at night. Vanity would only come out at night. He smiled that warm, sweet smile and started workin with her. He had to build some new shelves on his day off, for all the liquor she had bought. He never asked for a dime. Never accepted a dime. Anyway, that started him spendin most his days off with her. One of em anyway, she didn't know he had all of em off if he wanted to.

Then, his television broke. He could fix everything, but he couldn't fix his own stuff. Naturally they spent several evenings, just friends, lookin at TV. Somehow Vanity mentioned, in a laughin voice of confidence between friends, how she loved to make love in the mornings, and when it rained, when it stormed, when it thundered. You know?

One day, when the weather report said "rain, storm," he came by that night, to check on her, of course. She sat down and lay back, in one of them flimsy rich gowns and looked at him. He was quiet, but he knew how to look back. He looked so good, so big, so strong. Vanity squirmed, crossed her legs back and forth, all them things we do. She finally jumped up when the programs was finished, news, weather and all. Jumped up and said, "Go! Please go! I . . . I . . . I don't know what's wrong with me! Please go."

He smiled a warm intimate smile, said, "Talk to me. Tell me what the matter is."

She couldn't.

He said, "Am I your friend? I guess I'm not. And I . . . I feel so much for you. I want you to like me. But . . . I know you can't." He looked down into his drink, then back at her, deeply. "You are so beautiful. So beautiful. You could talk to, or have anyone you want in the world." He stood, as if to go. Vanity raised from her seat, but she didn't stand, just sat up. He went on talkin, "I am only me. So . . . I understand. I'm not . . . something enough for you."

Vanity slowly got to her feet, reached one hand out to him. "Oh!" Her other hand touched her throat. "Oh, you are everything wonderful to me. You are my friend. The only one I have. Do I really look beautiful to you?"

Jody reached out to her slowly, with that warm hand. Took her arm that had brushed against him so regularly lately, pulled her to his side. She buried her face in his shoulder. He used his chin to nudge her head around til their lips met . . . then he kissed the shit out of that woman.

Moments later, with heavy breathin from both of them, he said, "I better go . . . I'm only a man . . . and you are a beautiful woman. I won't be able to control myself." And he left, even tho she was holdin him and pullin on that man for all she was worth. He left. And she longed.

Vanity went to the phone, ordered more liquor. A big order. Then she went to her dressin table, made up her face. Perfumed her body. Soon the deliver came, Jody brought it. Not long after, she came. Jody brought it.

His time had come. The next time she saw him he said, "I am ashamed to have taken such a liberty with such a beautiful woman of whom I am not worthy." You ever seen or listened to a woman convince a man he is worthy of her? Well, all I can say is her Guardian Angel wept for her.

Vanity told him he was worthy of her when she came again . . . and he went away, satisfied. She came . . . he went . . . and that ain't the same thing. You know it! But Vanity fell asleep, satisfied. Like a lady?

When she woke up the next day, everything else did too. Passion, love, need. All for a man whose address and telephone number she didn't even know. A man she didn't even know what his dreams was. A smiling man she didn't know, who brought her liquor when she ordered and paid for it. A stranger. Maybe we are all strangers, but, Lord, help a woman at such a time in life where she will put her heart in strange hands full of blood and tears. Lord, help the men, too, cause it's all kinds of strangers out here.

Jody didn't come back with the next order . . . nor the next. A young, young boy did. Vanity like to died. All her morning had been about getting ready for him. She called the store and asked for him . . . he was not there. She had nowhere else to call and the store owner could not give her his number, he didn't know it. Finally, in a few days, he just dropped in about 11:00 at night. Her heart bloomed, opened, screamed out at the sight of him. He had come again! And so did she. But this time there was fear in the coming and she did not sleep so soundly satisfied when he left at 1:00 in the morning. The heart that had blossomed, had wilted with a little hurt pain. He gave her no number, no address. Said he had no phone and was never hardly home anyway. Always lookin for a job to do. He had huge bills to pay. "But, no, don't worry, I will make it." He said, "I don't want your money." She had offered, of course. She loved him and his painful beauty.

The next week passed. No call. No visit. When, finally, he did come, all the anger she had planned, vanished. She loved him who loved her beauty. For the first time, he had brought her something . . . a lovely golden mirror. "A magic mirror" he said. "So you can see your beauty framed by me." Vanity looked into that mirror all the time. All the time. Like a fairy princess . . . preparing for her prince.

In the following months they kinda had a relationship, least a year and a half. He still came to her at his will. She was always ready because he took so long. Sometime, when he and his regular girl were on the outs, yea, you know he had one, he would stay a day or two. Til he and his regular girl were together again. The regular girl woulda missed him for the two days and be eager to mend things. He would have lain around, eaten, watched TV, made love once, slept . . . and thought. He would then have to go see about his other regular old ladies, also.

Sometimes he would come to Vanity and sleep only on top of the covers, while she lay beneath them, body smoldering, longing for him to enter her. But he would not get into bed . . . let lone into her, tho she begged.

Jody did not kiss her from the feet up. For the first time she longed to kiss him from the feet up, but was afraid her beauty would not look good from that distance. He kissed her lips . . . when she asked him, or when she seemed to be gettin tired of longing for him, ready to quit her grief. He would not see her for five, six, seven, eight days at a time. Let her suffer.

He made dates with her. Then she would do a lot of cleaning. Herself! Cooking, setting the table, puttin out flowers, all of it. Then, looking out the window, sittin, waitin for him. . . . He did not come. Then . . . she looking into that magic mirror . . . to see what was wrong. She saw lines, wrinkles that were not there. In that mirror, when he did not come, and she could not . . . her beauty faded, faded.

She began to buy him clothes, lay them all out on the bed. If he didn't come . . . she would want to throw them all away, give them away. But, she never did, because she had the good sense to know she really wanted this man and would need something to lure him. She "forced" money on him, which he never asked for, just needed, but he took. He folded away, smiling, hundreds of dollars that disappeared deep into his pockets, never to be seen again.

Valentine's Day. No card. He didn't call.

Birthday. No card first year. Only a card the next year . . . late.

Christmas. The second time. A handkerchief. Not wrapped.

Easter. No card. No eggs. Not even his.

Thanksgiving. Said he had to work, needed the money. She cried, again, for she had cooked a full, good meal . . . for him. She couldn't eat.

All the time, he was having a good time with the money from his other little old ladies and his woman. Yet . . . he really was with nobody in his heart. Nobody at all. Vanity spent so much money on him to ease the worry he said was on his mind, made me sick! I mean, really sick, I got ill.

Vanity asked that man to marry her. Marry her! She wanted a lifetime of all that pain. That's what she was askin for! He said he had never planned to marry. He didn't trust women to be true to him. Now! She tried to convince him of her love and faithfulness. He thought about that, a long, long time. Sometimes, he looked into that golden mirror he had given Vanity. Looking at his own beauty. Thinking of marryin Vanity. Of livin in the dark, cause Vanity kept her house darkened. She thought she looked better that way.

Once or twice, when he had come to Vanity, he had been a little sick. She cared for him better than anyone else he knew. Vanity! Caring for somebody else! In a day or so, he always felt better and left with some money.

When she spoke to him of marriage again, he thought a moment, then asked for the use of the little roomette she had in her yard in the back. She gladly gave it to him, tho she said he could stay in the house with her til he decided. Til HE decided. Her Guardian Angel just stayed quiet and grieved all the time now.

He took the roomette, but did not LIVE in it. He used it a lot. He liked to be alone, he said, so she often just looked out at the little house, glad he was out there, close. She would cook and take him food. Sometimes he didn't let her in, said he would be on in her house, later.

Often, when he did come in later, he would be so shinin and sweet to her. He kissed a lot and spoke much of her beauty. But he didn't make love much. He sure talk to her tho!

"My lord! You are so beautiful! So beautiful to me! How do I deserve you? You could have anyone in the world you want you are so beautiful."

Vanity's answer, always, was, "But I only want you."

She began to pester him about lettin her come visit him in the little house. "What did he do there? Couldn't she be with him? She would be quiet, not bother him. He wouldn't have to make love to her. She wouldn't ask him or touch him." Can you magin a woman sayin that to her man?

She told him one day, "I always look so beautiful to you when you come out of your hideaway. If I was in there with you, and I was quiet, I could look beautiful to you longer. In there."

He said no, and no, and no, no, so many times. Til he looked at her one night, thoughtfully. She was sittin there with little tears in her still lovely eyes, waiting, waiting for any little sign he loved her. I hate to think she was such a fool!, but I don't know bout this kinda love!

He answered, touching her cheek, "Soon."

"Soon" came one night when he needed some money and asked for it for the first time. She hesitated, cause she thought that would help him leave. He read her mind, said, "I will let you come with me to my hideaway." She gave him the money. He left. He was back soon this time.

He looked at her another long time. Then sighed, and said, "Give me one half hour, then come."

She did. Her Guardian Angel cried aloud, screamed to her, "Beware!" then wept again.

The little hideaway was darkened. Persian type blankets and carpets covered everything. A small, low table on the floor was draped, covered with little saucers and things. He sat her down beside it, smiled down at her, warily. He then picked up a pipe. A pipe he used for free-basing cocaine.

The Guardian Angel could not come in, but he pounded at the door and screamed for Vanity to hear. She did not hear. She was looking at the man she loved, smiling. Just like a lady.

Jody fixed the pipe. Used a lighter to heat the stem til he reached the rock inside and melted it. Drew the first breath, blew it out. Took another breath, closed his eyes and held it in. Opened his eyes, smiled, and handed the pipe to her. Said, "Do what I do."

His hand reached out, slowly. His beautiful, powerful, strong hand that had held her, stroked her, seemed to love her. He held that hand out to her with the cocaine-rock, crack, in the pipe. She already loved that hand. She remembered only the pleasure it had held for her. Her eyes, lovely tho wrinkled around, misted, than clung to his smiling face.

She took the hand, that then gently removed itself from the pipe, leaving it in her once lovelier hand, then gently raising it to her once lovelier lips. Her eyes held to his own. Just like a lady.

Then? Then . . . she slowly finished lifting the pipe to her lips, closed her eyes with the imprint of his smiling face in them, pursed her lips and drew her first breath from the pipe. The magic pipe. She opened her eyes, the smoke wafting slowly through her body, inundating her brain, while looking at this gorgeous man. Then she smiled, raised her beautiful head, parted her lips . . . and blew . . . her . . . life . . . and all her beauty . . . away. Forever.

Just like a fool.

The devil slapped his knee, leaned back and laughed.

The Guardian Angel gave up. On its knees, beside the garden house door, it wept. The angel's voice was silenced by the golden pipe, the golden man. The golden pipe had a new voice to whisper in her ears. The Guardian Angel could only come back if she sought it. It will wait, even for nothing.

So . . . I'm just sittin here, lookin into this magic golden mirror Vanity has gave me because she could not hear to look into it anymore. She could not see the self she sought. The golden pipe has lied.

PLUS, I know she needed the money I pressed into her thin little hands. Almost all her beautiful things are gone . . . sold for that wisp of smoke. And that man she can never have for her own.

I am ponderin . . . ahhh, ponderin . . . thinkin about life . . . and death. Love.

Ahhhh, but so much happened. So much I didn't know about til way much later. My heart aches for her, but . . . it was HER choice, HER life.

In tryin to understand what had happened to my friend's mind, her life, I searched, asked questions of them people who knew her then, were her friends. Friends? I will tell you what I found out. It was pitiful. And if you got youngsters, you better listen to this first, then decide do you want them to hear this truth. This is just one day in the later life of Vanity, just fore she died from a heart attack, a broken, busted-heart attack.

Early one wintry morning after bein out all night til bout 5:00 A.M. . . . Vanity went inside the shell of her large, once beautiful house, empty now. Everything being sold, piece by piece. First, by Jody, then, at last, when her need was great and she started doin crack without Jody, she sold her own things, her own self. So the house was empty now.

The house note hadn't been paid in thirteen months and was soon to be foreclosed on. Gone. All her usta-be dreams. Gone.

The lectric company had turned off the lights. The gas company had done turned off the gas . . . and it was cold, cold, cold in that house. The water was the only thing on cause Jody knew how to turn it back on after the water company turned it off. So Vanity could drink water out a paper cup or a leftover tin can. Didn't need no water for cookin cause wasn't nothin to cook. She didn't have no appetite anyway for nothin but more crack . . . them bumps, them hits of rock. She was thin, thin, thin. Skin and bones. Somehow, she managed to keep her phone workin, cause she had to be able to get them calls from them fellows who might give her a bump. A Bump!

This particular night, and I know now there were lots of these kinda nights, she had been workin for that crack. She didn't call it "workin," but I do.

Jody was no longer the only man in her life. Now, she had had all kinds of men. All kinds. Kinds she wouldn't even use to spit on! Them "Bumps" had sucked and bumped all her pride out of her brain. That shit must be some powerful, cause you remember how full of pride she was!

Now . . . from the lowest person in a garbage can, man or woman, to the crack dealer who was the highest she could get, even they only wanted to use her for a half-hour or hour. Not even them so much anymore cause they had all already tore her down, stripped whatever little dignity she mighta had left. Yes, the bottom was as high as Vanity could go now. Them old days was gone. Like her beauty. Like her health. Like her life. Gone. No future to it. Nothin meant nothin to her now but that next bump, that next rock. Low-life crack users called her a "Rock Star," laughin and graspin their crotches. I heard about em!

See, she had a big reputation, well deserved, they say. She was known, far and wide, as the best "head" in the city . . . and anything else you wanted you could get from her if she needed that crack! Her! Can you magin?! Her?

Anyway, she had come into that empty house that dark wintry morning. She closed the door, leanin back against it. Tired. Worn. She looked at the phone tho. It wasn't ringin. Then she felt her hunger. She hadn't eaten in bout five days. She didn't have no energy. Her mouth tasted like sex from goin down on eight men in the last ten hours. Two others had refused her head, preferred anal sex. So, besides her mouth feeling used, stretched and bad, her rectum was bleedin a little.

Little pains shot through it now and again, cause of the huge . . . organ . . . one man had smashed into her, hard. She had cried out, but he laughed and stuck his chest out in front of the other men (yes, chile, they do it in front of everybody!) and thrust harder. She wanted to scream and tell him to stop!, BUT she wanted that rock he had promised her. That crack. If this is what it cost, well, she didn't have no money, so . . . this is what it cost!

When he, finally, finished and it was time to give her her reward, her bump, he decided to tease her . . . and degrade her even more. He melted the crack on a pipe, took him a big deep puff of it, blew the smoke at her to make her want it more. He was smart, he knew what he was doin. He leaned toward her, offering the pipe with the crack to her then, pullin back when she reached for it. She loooooooonnnggggeeed for that pipe.

Involuntary, she snarled and lunged to snatch the pipe. He saw her comin . . . He caught her in the top of her long, used-to-be-pretty, hair and pulled her face down to his penis what was still coated from that anal sex they had just finished.

He told her, "Lick it clean."

That stopped her a moment, brought her back to some ooold reality, the times before she ever thought about crack. When she was beautiful and only dealt with the best of people. She felt disgust. She started to say "No!" and shake his hand from her head. BUT . . . then . . . her eyes fell upon that pipe in his hand. As he knew they would. She remembered that big rock he had just melted in that pipe. All thoughts of disgust just flew away. She closed her eyes . . . leaned over into the man's lap . . . and cleaned him with her tongue . . . her mouth that sits right in her face.

When he had had another orgasm, this time in her mouth making her swallow it, he let go her hair he had been pullin. She raised her head, lookin down at the large, limp penis . . . for the rough spots that felt like sores to her tongue. They were there. She wiped the back of her hand across her mouth and almost gagged. But didn't. She wouldn't allow herself to think about the sores now. She needed that pipe now.

She sat up, didn't even pull her clothes straight fore she asked, "Give me my hit now?"

He, that piece of cancer sore, looked down at her with contempt, looked at the other fellows with laughter. He sank back comfortably, flicked his bic and heated his pipe stem, moving the fire to the end where the cocaine-rock was, then he took a pull, a hit. He thought it was a real good one, so he kicked back and let the death hidden inside the good feeling reach into his body and brain, chippin away at what was left of his sanity. He did not know that in six months he would be dyin from just what he was doin now . . . and from them sores. He would be slave to the King Crack then. He was already, just didn't blive it, but he would do anything for it too!

But, now, he just laughed, and thought how he had got over on her. Humped her from the behind and then stuck it in her mouth to clean it! All them users had the same aim, like he did. They was so low they just wanted to degrade, humiliate other people, specially women. Then, too, it was because she was so beautiful once, it still showed. He had never ever even talked to anyone who had been so pretty and almost rich. He knew she would never have been looked his way, if she had not become this . . . thing . . . called a rock star. They would do the same thing to a ugly woman, but they wouldn't enjoy it so much, or gone so far . . . maybe.

He looked down into Vanity's pleading eyes, waved the pipe in front of her face and said, "Bitch, I ain't givin you nothin! The best thing you can do is get your funky, dirty ass out of here!"

She cried out, "You promised me!" Wiped her mouth again with the back of her hand, "Give me my bump!?"

He looked at the other fellows, laughed, said, "You just got your bumpin! Get the fuck out of my face, ho!" (That's short for whore.)

Another fellow there felt a little sorry for her. He didn't really like to see people dogged, til it was his turn. He wanted to speak up, but he owed the crack dealer some money and he wanted some more crack hisself, so he didn't want to mess up his own game. So he sat back and let it all happen. He laughed a little too. He thought to himself, since he felt sorry for her and knew she was walkin, that he would give her a ride home. Then she could clean herself up. Maybe . . . even give him a little head fore he went home. He didn't want nothin else from her cause he knew how many men she had to go through to get some crack and he didn't want no disease to take home to his wife and kids. He musta not known you can catch a disease from a mouth too!

Vanity never did get her bump, her hit. They put her out instead. The man hurried and begged up on his rock then rushed out to catch up with Vanity fore she found somewhere else to go beggin for crack and he lost her. He wanted that head! He drove and caught up with her, offerin her a ride home. Fore he got her to her house he told her they would look for some crack. He got his head. But he pulled to the curb front of her house and put her out, sayin, "Let's try later, baby. I'll try to get hold of some money. You try to get hold of some too. I'll call you." Then . . . he drove off with his crack deep down in his pocket. His own wife didn't know he was a user. Or that he already had that bug in his blood that would kill both of them . . . just from makin love. That's all his wife did to get it, make love to him, her husband. Chile, chile.

Anyway . . . Vanity was home. Home? Her back against her door. Hungry, wet, cold, dirty, stinkin and sick. She never had got that bump. They had just used her, again.

Her body wanted to sleep, but she couldn't get that bump, that feeling she wanted, out of her mind. Her brain raced, trying to think of somewhere, someone, she could get some money from. Sell some head to. She thought briefly of Mega, but Mega had loaned her so much in the beginning, never gettin it back. Now Mega watched her so carefully when Vanity was in her house because she had lost so many small valuable things that Vanity could put in her brassiere or under her dress. Couldn't go there. The early mornin time never entered her mind cause when she wanted some dope, she didn't care bout no inconvenience to nobody else.

Sellin some of her head came back into her mind. Vanity's mind snapped back to the man who had had anal sex with her then made her clean him with her mouth. She remembered the sores on his penis. She worried: AIDS? Syphilis? Gonorrhea? Herpes? What? She pulled her tired back away from the door, went to wash her mouth out with the peroxide Jody kept there for when she made oral sex to him. After she did other people in front of him sometimes to get both of them a bump, he didn't like her to do him without washing her mouth out. Jody never wanted her body anymore. That is, when she did get to see him. She couldn't see him noway less she had some crack to share.

She rinsed her mouth. She didn't think of the fact she had swallowed everything and that peroxide couldn't reach it. Then she lay her tired, abused body across the old, dirty quilt thrown on her bedroom floor. She fell asleep . . . for awhile.

The phone rang! She jumped awake to answer it. It was a fellow saying he had a rock he would share with her . . . for a little fun. She told him to come on over.

He said, "No, we . . . I rather ride awhile."

She quickly answered, "Okey, I'll be outside waitin."

They came. There was two of them, fellows. One got out to let her get in the middle and they drove off, sayin they was goin to somebody's house. They had the rock.

She asked, "How we all gonna use one rock?"

They laughed, answered, "Ahhh, we share all things all the time."

But they drove too long, too far. She became afraid. The feelin in the car was not good. The men were groping over her legs, her breast. She kept pushin their hands away.

She asked, "Where we goin? Where is the rock?"

They laughed and turned off the highway. Who needs to tell it all?

They finally stopped. Pale, early mornin. Deserted woods. They made her get out, go down, lay down, then go down again. She cried all through everything. Mad cause they had fooled her and there was no rock. Then they talked awhile to decide should they take her home or not.

One, the "nice" one, said, "It's kinda dark, man, and cold. Let's take her back into town anyway." So they did that. But they never did give her a bump or puff from their pipe. Why should they? They had had all the fun they wanted anyway. Well, at least they didn't beat her too. Yes, they did that to her sometimes.

Vanity still ain't had no food.

She didn't have enough clothes on, she was frozen almost.

She ain't had no real sleep for almost four, five days.

Her body is stinkin and dirty, again.

But her brain still wouldn't think of nothin but that dope. That bump. That puff from a pipe. What kind of stuff must that be that can strip you, make you do ANYTHING to get it? Take everything away from you? House, furniture, automobile, bank account, clothes; yours and everybody else's you can get your hands on!? Takes your honor, your dignity, your pride in yourself. Your very life! I wouldn't even want to SEE it, much less use it! It scares me to death!

Well, she came to my house. She looked so bad, so sad, my heart broke for her. She wanted to "borrow" some of my little, hard-earned money. She already owed me plenty fore I got wise that she wasn't gonna buy food or nothin she needed. Just dope.

I fed her. Ran bath water, gave her some clean clothes. All mine was better than all hers now, and I really didn't have nothin special. She lay down and slept. I took advantage of that to wash her clothes and run to the store to get somethin better for her to eat and to cash a small check to give her a few dollars of my small money.

When I came back . . . she was gone. So was my watch I was stupid enough to leave layin on my dresser. My only watch what had belonged to my mother. I loved that watch! I cried. I know that crack took my watch, not her, but it was gone right on.

Vanity didn't stop to pawn my watch, I mighta got it back if she did. She took it straight to the crack dealer and got her three rocks for my beautiful watch. Then she went home and blew my watch away . . . in a hour and a half. Just like that!

At last, her body just dragged her down to sleep. And even while sleep she waited for that phone to ring. When it did ring, she went out again . . . and everything started all over again.

All over again. All her whole life now, given up for a bump, a hit, a puff, a feeling. A little piece of death . . . that had such a hold on her mind that only a full death is stronger. Or God. But she wasn't likely to run into Him. Her Guardian Angel wasn't allowed to go into the places she went into. Her Guardian Angel just sat over her and wept sometimes when she was home waitin for a call. It did that til she died, then they parted forever, and it went to its home, sadly sayin, "I hope I never have to go to Earth again."

Five years is all it took. Five years of days just like the one I'm tellin you about. She lived all that, every day, over and over and over again. And, surely, some worse ones I don't know about.

I couldn't do it, couldn't take it. I don't want nothin that strong to kill my life and me! Do you? Would you?

So . . . I am sittin here ponderin . . . ahhh, ponderin . . . thinkin about life . . . and death.

Love.
And Vanity.
Lord, Lord.

Critical Eye

FOR DISCUSSION

a. In what way(s) does Vanity use her beauty as a weapon? Was she trained or encouraged by society and her immediate environment to do so? Is she merely mimicking what women have been expected to do for generations?

b. Emerson tells us that the great danger for us is conformity. If the story took place within a college/high-school setting, how popular would Vanity be? Why would it be easy for people to flock to her side simply because of what she represents—the chance to be popular? How real would those relationships/friendships be? How real are they in the story?

c. What do Vanity's actions reveal about men/boys? Does the story seem to discuss the idea that we have socialized men to behave in a way that encourages sexist or overly sexualized behavior towards women? According to the text, what do men really want from women?

REAPPROACHING THE TEXT

Outside of the lessons about addiction and bad behavior, this story is also about mothers and daughters. Keeping this in mind, consider the following: did the mother sacrifice her daughter in order to maintain her lifestyle? Did she somehow assuage her guilt by doting on Mega? Does the story move beyond the theories about the Oedipus and Antigone complexes, suggesting that all mothers secretly despise their daughters?

WRITING ASSIGNMENT

How is this short story meant to discuss the ways in which we are our own worst enemy? How does the story align itself with what Emerson says about the ways in which we undermine our own power and intelligence?

6 **7** 8

Fork in the Road

One day Alice came to a fork in the road and saw a Cheshire cat in a tree.
Which road do I take? she asked. Where do you want to go? was his response.
I don't know, Alice answered. Then, said the cat, it doesn't matter.

Lewis Carroll

The Fish Trap exists because of the fish. Once you've gotten the fish, you can forget the trap. The
rabbit snare exists because of the rabbit. Once you've gotten the rabbit, you can forget the snare.
Words exist because of meaning. Once you've got the meaning, you can forget the words. Where
can I find a man who has forgotten words so I can talk to him?

Chuang Tzu

Who am I? What should I do with my life? How did I get to this point?
These are the questions that fill our lives—those often unanswered
life evaluations that beg to be addressed. And, as we go through life
wondering, hoping for more, we find ourselves pondering the prolific
utterance that Jack Nicholson's movie made famous, "Is this as good as it
gets?"

The average preteen has already discovered that life is tough, and that
it, all too frequently, is unfair. If you ask teenagers about love, marriage,
or adulthood in general, they will explain to you that one day they plan
to get married, get a good job, have children, buy a home, and become
productive members of their communities. If you talk with them further,
these same young, maturing people will explain how they anticipate being
unhappy with their chosen careers, that marriage and children are "hard
work," and that some level of misery is to be expected.

Apparently, living our lives is a paved road filled with potholes, sometimes
even landmines that appear primed to explode. As a result, we find
ourselves going through life desperately trying to figure out how to make
sense of our socioeconomic status, our complex home environments, love,
death, education, work, and, yes, even where and how to vacation—all

the while looking for that path that will shine a light into our shaded eyes. So many of us hope for a better way of being. So many of us want to break a cycle and rise up, evolve, and display that we are better than before—stronger, smarter, capable of leaping where we once stumbled. So many of us look at the way the world divides the "have" and the "have nots," leaving us moored to a fixed post. Summed up, so many of us want things to change. Yet, at some point, many of us trip over the "fork"—the opening pathway that signals that a new day, be it cognizant recognition or physical transformation, is offering a new opportunity; the owe that, when recognized, will change everything.

Clearly, one point remains a constant: No matter how you slice it, the proverbial "fork in the road" and the choices one makes upon it end up being character definers. As you read these selected works, you will note the following: Some people do not like what they find out about themselves; others welcome the challenge, and may find that those around them—whom they consider "constant"—fail them at every turn.

Richard Selzer

What I Saw at the Abortion

I am a surgeon. Particularities of sick flesh is everyday news. Escaping blood, all the outpourings of disease—phlegm, pus, vomitus, even those occult meaty tumors that terrify—I see as blood, disease, phlegm, and so on. I touch them to destroy them. But I do not make symbols of them.

What I am saying is that I have seen and I am used to seeing. We are talking about a man who has a trade, who has practiced it long enough to see no news in any of it. Picture this man, then. A professional. In his forties. Three children. Lives in a university town—so, necessarily, well—enlightened? Enough, anyhow. Successful in his work, yes. No overriding religious posture. Nothing special, then, your routine fellow, trying to do his work and doing it well enough. Picture him, this professional, a sort of scientist, if you please, in possession of the standard admirable opinions, positions, convictions, and so on—on this and that matter—on *abortion,* for example.

All right.

Now listen.

It is the western wing of the fourth floor of a great university hospital. I am present because I asked to be present. I wanted to see what I had never seen. An abortion.

The patient is Jamaican. She lies on the table in that state of notable submissiveness I have always seen in patients. Now and then she smiles at one of the nurses as though acknowledging a secret.

A nurse draws down the sheet, lays bare the abdomen. The belly mounds gently in the twenty-fourth week of pregnancy. The chief surgeon paints it with a sponge soaked in red antiseptic. He does this three times, each time a fresh sponge. He covers the area with a sterile sheet, an aperture

"What I Saw at the Abortion," from *Mortal Lessons: Notes on the Art of Surgery* by Richard Selzer. Copyright © 1974, 1975, 1976, 1987 by Richard Selzer. Reprinted by permission of Georges Borchardt, Inc., on behalf of the author.

in its center. He is a kindly man who teaches as he works, who pauses to reassure the woman.

He begins.

A little pinprick, he says to the woman.

He inserts the point of a tiny needle at the midline of the lower portion of her abdomen, on the downslope. He infiltrates local anesthetic into the skin, where it forms a small white bubble.

The woman grimaces.

That is all you will feel the doctor says. Except for a little pressure. But no more pain.

She smiles again. She seems to relax. She settles comfortably on the table. The worst is over.

The doctor selects a three-and-one-half-inch needle bearing a central stylet. He places the point at the site of the previous injection. He aims it straight up and down, perpendicular. Next he takes hold of her abdomen with his left hand, palming the womb, steadying it. He thrusts with his right hand. The needle sinks into the abdominal wall.

Oh, says the woman quietly.

But I guess it is not pain that she feels. It is more a recognition that the deed is being done.

Another thrust and he has spread the uterus.

We are in, he says.

He has felt the muscular wall of the organ gripping the shaft of his needle. A further slight pressure on the needle advances it a bit more. He takes his left hand from the woman's abdomen. He retracts the filament of the stylet from the barrel of the needle. A small geyser of pale yellow fluid erupts.

"We are in the right place, says the doctor. Are you feeling any pain? he says.

She smiles, shakes her head. She gazes at the ceiling.

In the room we are six: two physicians, two nurses, the patient, and me.

The participants are busy, very attentive. I am not at all busy—but I am no less attentive. I want to see.

I see something!

It is unexpected, utterly unexpected, like a disturbance in the earth, a tumultuous jarring. I see something other than what I expected here. I see a movement—a small one. But I have seen it.

And then I see it again. And now I see that it is the hub of the needle in the woman's belly that has jerked. First to one side. Then to the other side. Once more it wobbles, is *tugged,* like a fishing line nibbled by a sunfish.

Again! And I *know!*

It is the *fetus* that worries thus. It is the fetus struggling against the needle. Struggling? How can that be? I think: *that cannot be.* I think: the fetus feels no pain, cannot feel fear, has no *motivation.* It is merely reflex.

I point to the needle.

It is a reflex, says the doctor.

By the end of the fifth month, the fetus weighs about one pound, is about twelve inches long. Hair is on the head. There are eyebrows, eyelashes. Pale pink nipples show on the chest. Nails are present, at the fingertips, at the toes.

At the beginning of the sixth month, the fetus can cry, can suck, can make a fist. He kicks, he punches. The mother can feel this, can *see* this. His eyelids, until now closed, can open. He may look up, down, sideways. His grip is very strong. He could support his weight by holding with one hand.

A reflex, the doctor says.

I hear him. But I saw something. I saw *something* in that mass of cells *understand* that it must bob and butt. And I see it again! I have an impulse to shove to the table— it is just a step—seize that needle, pull it out.

We are not six, I think. I think we are *seven.*

Something strangles *there.* An effort, its effort, binds me to it.

I do not shove to the table. I take no little step. It would be . . . well, madness. Everyone here wants the needle where it is. Six do. No, *five* do.

I close my eyes. I see the inside of the uterus. It is bathed in ruby gloom. I see the creature curled upon itself. Its knees are flexed. Its head is bent upon its chest. It is in fluid and gently rocks to the rhythm of the distant heartbeat.

It resembles . . . a sleeping infant.

Its place is entered by something. It is sudden. A point coming. A needle!

A spike of *daylight* pierces the chamber. Now the light is extinguished. The needle comes closer in the pool. The point grazes the thigh, and I, stir. Perhaps I wake from dozing. The light is there again. I twist and straighten. My arms and legs *push*. My hand finds the shaft—grabs! I *grab*. I bend the needle this way and that. The point probes, touches on my belly. My mouth opens. Could I cry out? All is a commotion and a churning. There is a presence in the pool. An activity! The pool colors, reddens, darkens.

I open my eyes to see the doctor feeding a small plastic tube through the barrel of the needle into the uterus. Drops of pink fluid overrun the rim and spill onto the sheet. He withdraws the needle from around the plastic tubing. Now only the little tube protrudes from the woman's body. A nurse hands the physician a syringe loaded with a colorless liquid. He attaches it to the end of the tubing and injects it.

Prostaglandin, he says.

Ah, well, prostaglandin—a substance found normally in the body. When given in concentrated dosage, it throws the uterus into vigorous contraction. In eight to twelve hours, the woman will expel the fetus.

The doctor detaches the syringe but does not remove the tubing.

In case we must do it over, he says.

He takes away the sheet. He places gauze pads over the tubing. Over all this he applies adhesive tape.

I know. We cannot feed the great numbers. There is no more room. I know, I know. It is woman's right to refuse the risk, to decline the pain of childbirth. And an unwanted child is a very great burden. An unwanted child is a burden to himself. I know.

And yet . . . there is the flick of that needle. I *saw* it. I saw . . . I *felt*—in that room, a pace away, life prodded, life fending off, I saw life avulsed—swept by flood, blackening—then *out*.

There says the doctor, It's all over. It wasn't too bad, was it? he says to the woman.

She smiles. It is all over. Oh, yes.

And who would care to imagine that from a moist and dark commencement six months before there would ripen the cluster and globule, the sprout and pouch of man?

And who would care to imagine that trapped within the laked pearl and a dowry of yolk would lie the earliest stuff of dream and memory?

It is a persona carried here as well as person, I think. I think it is a signed piece, engraved with a hieroglyph of human genes.

I did not think this until I saw. The flick. The fending off.

We leave the room, the three of us, the doctors.

"Routine procedure," the chief surgeon says.

"All right," I say.

"Scrub nurse says first time you've seen one, Dick. First look at a purge," the surgeon says.

"That's right," I say. "First look."

"Oh, well," he says, "I guess you've seen everything else."

"Pretty much," I say.

"I'm not prying, Doctor," he says, "but was there something on your mind? I'd be delighted to field any questions . . ."

"No," I say. "No, thanks. Just simple curiosity."

"Okay," he says, and we all shake hands, scrub, change, and go to our calls.

I know, I know. The thing is normally done at sixteen weeks. "Well, I've seen it performed at that stage, too. And seen . . . the flick. But I also know that in the sovereign state of my residence it is hospital policy to warrant the procedure at twenty-four weeks. And that in the great state that is adjacent, policy is enlarged to twenty-eight weeks.

Does this sound like argument? I hope not. I am not trying to argue. I am only saying I've *seen*. The flick. "Whatever else may be said in abortion's defense, the vision of that other defense will not vanish from my eyes.

What I saw I saw as that: a *defense*, a motion *from*, an effort *away*. And it has happened that you cannot reason with me now. For what can language do against the truth of what I saw?

Critical Eye

FOR DISCUSSION

a. Why is the doctor unable to reconcile the issues surrounding the right to choose and issues of overpopulation with what he witnesses during the procedure?

b. Why would a doctor who faces life and death every day wish to witness an abortion?

REAPPROACHING THE TEXT

Consider the events that led up to the legalization of abortion. How do these issues factor in with the doctor's argument? Does his argument become more or less relevant?

WRITING ASSIGNMENT

While our society is indeed split on the issue of abortion, is it important, as a matter of civil rights, that "the choice" still remain?

Frances A. Althaus

Female Circumcision: Rite of Passage or Violation of Rights?

Female circumcision, the partial or total cutting away of the external female genitalia, has been practiced for centuries in parts of Africa, generally as one element of a rite of passage preparing young girls for womanhood and marriage. Often performed without anesthetic under septic conditions by lay practitioners with little or no knowledge of human anatomy or medicine, female circumcision can cause death or permanent health problems as well as severe pain. Despite these grave risks, its practitioners look on it as an integral part of their cultural and ethnic identity, and some perceive it as a religious obligation.

Opponents of female genital cutting, however, emphasize that the practice is detrimental to women's health and well-being. Some consider female circumcision a ritualized form of child abuse and violence against women, a violation of human rights.

The debate over female circumcision is relatively recent. The practice was rarely spoken of in Africa and little known in the West until the second half of this century. In the 1950s and 1960s, however, African activists and medical practitioners brought the health consequences of female circumcision to the attention of international organizations such as the United Nations and the World Health Organization (WHO). Still, it was not until 1979 that any formal policy statement was made: A seminar organized by WHO in Khartoum to address traditional practices affecting the health of women and children issued recommendations that governments work to eliminate the practice.

During the following decade, the widespread silence surrounding female circumcision was broken. After African women's organizations met in Dakar, Senegal, in 1984 to discuss female circumcision and other detrimental cultural practices, the Inter African Committee Against Harmful Traditional Practices (IAC) was formed. With national

"Female circumcision: right of passage or violation of rights?" by Frances A. Althaus, *International Family Planning Perspectives*, 1997, 23(3): 130–133. Reprinted by permission of The Alan Guttmacher Institute.

committees in more than 20 countries, the IAC has been important in bringing the harmful effects of female circumcision to the attention of African governments. In addition, other African women's networks and organizations that had focused primarily on such issues as reproductive health, women's rights and legal justice became involved in working against the practice. Such groups as Mandalaeo Ya Wanawake in Kenya, NOW in Nigeria and New Woman in Egypt now include the elimination of female circumcision among their goals.

In part because these groups brought fresh perspectives to the issue, the emphasis in discussions of female circumcision shifted to encompass women's human and reproductive rights as well as their health. International consensus statements and treaties such as the Convention to Eliminate All Forms of Discrimination Against Women, the Convention on the Rights of the Child and the African Charter on the Rights and Welfare of the Child began to include language applicable to female circumcision. These documents, however, did not directly mention the practice, focusing instead on broad categories such as detrimental practices, violence and rights violations."

With shifts in emphasis came new language: Although activists and clinicians continued to refer to female circumcision when working directly with women in the community, policy statements and other documents began to use the term "female genital mutilation." That term was used in the first international document to specifically address the practice, the Programme of Action adopted by the International Conference on Population and Development in Cairo in 1994. The Program refers to female genital mutilation as a "basic rights violation" and urges governments to "prohibit and urgently stop the practice . . . wherever it exists."

In the Platform of the Fourth World Conference on Women, held in Beijing in 1995, female genital mutilation was cited as both a threat to women's reproductive health and a violation of their human rights. In addition to making general recommendations, the Platform specifically called on governments to "enact and enforce legislation against the perpetrators of practices and acts of violence against women, such as female genital mutilation. . . ." Notably, the drive to include language specifically condemning female genital mutilation in the Platform was led by Africans.

Against this background of activity and changing emphasis, the plight of Fauziya Kassindja, a 17-year-old woman from Togo, focused public attention in the United States on female circumcision. More important, her case was instrumental in redefining the practice as gender-based violence that could be grounds for the granting of political asylum. Kassindja, who fled her homeland in October 1994 to avoid an arranged marriage and the genital cutting that would be part of the marriage rites, was placed in a detention center after arriving in the United States under a false passport and asking for asylum. She was released a year and a half later and granted asylum after intensive media coverage of her situation.

Prevalence

Female circumcision is currently practiced in at least 28 countries stretching across the center of Africa north of the equator; it is not found in southern Africa or in the Arabic-speaking nations of North Africa, with the exception of Egypt. Female circumcision occurs among Muslims, Christians, animists and one Jewish sect, although no religion requires it.

The availability of reliable figures on the prevalence of female circumcision has increased greatly in recent years: National data have now been collected in the Demographic and Health Survey (DHS) program for six countries—the Central African Republic. Côte d'Ivoire, Egypt, Eritrea, Mali and Sudan. In these countries, from 43% to 97% of reproductive-age women have been circumcised. Within countries, prevalence may vary across ethnic groups; in Mali, for example, where the overall proportion of women who have undergone circumcision is 94%, only 17% of women of Tamachek ethnicity have been circumcised.

Estimates for other countries are generally based on local surveys or anecdotal information. The estimated proportion of women who have undergone circumcision in these countries ranges from 5% in Uganda and the Congo (formerly Zaire) to 98% in Djibouti and Somalia. Both because of wide variations in prevalence across social and demographic subgroups and because of data limitations, these figures should be interpreted with caution.

Types of Circumcision

Although circumcision may be performed during infancy, during adolescence or even during a woman's first pregnancy, the procedure is usually carried out on girls between ages four and 12. In the countries for which DHS data are available, the median age at excision ranges from less than two months in Eritrea to about six years in Mali and almost 10 years in Egypt. The operation is generally performed by a traditional birth attendant or an *exciseuse,* an elder village woman.

There are three basic types of genital excision, although practices vary widely. In the first type, clitoridectomy, part or all of the clitoris is amputated, while in the second (often referred to as excision), both the clitoris and the labia minora are removed. Infibulation, the third type, is the most severe: After excision of the clitoris and the labia minora, the labia majora are cut or scraped away to create raw surfaces, which are held in contact until they heal, either by stitching the edges of the wound or by tying the legs together. As the wounds heal, scar tissue joins the labia and covers the urethra and most of the vaginal orifice, leaving an opening that may be as small as a matchstick for the passage of urine and menstrual blood.

The overall proportion of women who have undergone each type of circumcision is not known, although clitoridectomy appears to be by far the most common procedure. It is estimated that about 15% of all circumcised women have been infibulated, although an estimated 80–90% of all circumcisions in Djibouti, Somalia and the Sudan are of this type.

Consequences of Excision

In the conditions under which female circumcision is generally performed in Africa, even the less extensive types of genital cutting can lead to potentially fatal complications, such as hemorrhage, infection and shock. The inability to pass urine because of pain, swelling and inflammation following the operation may lead to urinary tract infection. A woman may suffer from abscesses and pain from damaged nerve endings long after the initial wound has healed.

Infibulation is particularly likely to cause long-term health problems. Because the urethral opening is covered, repeated urinary tract infections are common, and stones may form in the urethra and bladder because of obstruction and infection. If the opening is very small, menstrual flow may be blocked, leading to reproductive tract infections and lowered fertility or sterility. One early study estimated that 20–25% of cases of sterility in northern Sudan can be linked to infibulation.

Without deinfibulation before childbirth, obstructed labor may occur, causing life-threatening complications for both mother and infant. Because birthrates are high in many countries where infibulation is practiced, a woman's infibulation scar may be cut and resewn many times during her reproductive years.

In addition, the amputation of the clitoris and other sensitive tissue reduces a woman's ability to experience sexual pleasure. For infibulated women, the consummation of marriage is likely to be painful because of the small vaginal opening and the lack of elasticity in the scar tissue that forms it. Tearing and bleeding may occur, or the infibulation scar may have to be cut open to allow penetration.

Infibulation may make intercourse unsatisfying for men as well as women: In a study of 300 polygynous Sudanese men, each of whom had one wife who had been infibulated and one or more who had not, 266 expressed a definite sexual preference for the uninfibulated wife; in addition, 60 said they had married a second, uninfibulated wife because of the penetration difficulties they experienced with their first wife, whose scarred vaginal opening became progressively more inelastic after each birth. Under such conditions, marital dissolution may occur, especially if a woman's fertility is affected. In Sudan, for example, one study found that infibulated women are almost twice as likely as other women to have lower fertility and more than twice as likely to be divorced. Thus, a practice that is justified as making girls marriageable and safeguarding their fertility may actually increase the risk of marital dissolution and subfertility.

Given the medical complications and related consequences of female circumcision, why does the practice continue? First, it is unclear how frequently such problems occur, for few data exist and those that are available come from small studies or are based on self-reports. Second, in societies in which few women remain uncircumcised, problems arising from female circumcision are likely to be seen as a normal part of a woman's life and may not even be associated with circumcision. The most important reasons, however, probably lie in the social and economic conditions of women's lives.

Social Context

Female circumcision is an integral part of the societies that practice it, where patriarchal authority and control of female sexuality and fertility are givens. In communities where a person's place in society is determined by lineage traced through fathers, female circumcision reduces the uncertainty surrounding paternity by discouraging or preventing women's sexual activity outside of marriage. Although the societies that practice circumcision vary in many ways, most girls receive little education and are valued primarily for their future role as sources of labor and producers of children. In some communities, the prospective husband's family pays a brideprice to the family of the bride, giving his family the right to her labor and her children; she herself has no right to or control over either.

A girl's virginity may be considered essential to her family's ability to arrange her marriage and receive a brideprice, as well as to family honor.

In Somalia, for example, a prospective husband's family may have the right to inspect the bride's body prior to marriage, and mothers regularly check their infibulated daughters to ensure that they are still "closed." In this context, parents see both infibulation and early marriage as means of ensuring that their daughter remains "pure" and thus worthy of the brideprice.

In many cultures, considerable social pressure is brought to bear on families who resist conforming to the tradition of female circumcision. In Man, a town in the interior of Côte d'Ivoire, a Yacouba girl who has not been circumcised is not considered marriageable. Among the Samburu of Kenya, who consider uncircumcised girls unclean, promiscuous and immature, girls are generally circumcised at age 14 or 15, usually just before they are married. A girl with a younger brother may undergo circumcision if she remains unmarried by her late teens, since custom dictates that a boy with an uncircumcised older sister may not be initiated into the warrior class.

Girls' desires to conform to peer norms may make them eager to undergo circumcision, since those who remain uncut may be teased and looked down on by their age mates. In addition, the ritual cutting is often embedded in ceremonies in which the girls are feted and showered with presents and their families are honored. A girl's wishes, in any case, are often irrelevant; it is her family—often the father or elder female relatives—who decide whether she will undergo circumcision. According to one Yacouba father, "[My daughter] has no choice. I decide. Her viewpoint is not important."

Indeed, girls have very little choice. Given their age and their lack of education and resources, they are dependent on their parents, and later on their husband, for the basic necessities of life. Those who resist may be cut by force. If they remain uncircumcised and their families are therefore unable to arrange a marriage, they may be cast out without any means of subsistence.

Because of their lack of choice and the powerful influence of tradition, many girls accept circumcision as a necessary, and even natural part of life, and adopt the rationales given for its existence. Of the five countries for which DHS data are available on women's opinions toward excision, the Central African Republic is the only one in which the majority favor discontinuation. A variety of justifications are given by DHS respondents who favor continuation of the practice, including preservation of virginity before marriage, fidelity after marriage, enhancement of the husband's sexual pleasure, enhancement of fertility, prevention of infant and child mortality, cleanliness and religious requirements, but tradition is by far the most commonly mentioned reason.

As these data show, women themselves are involved in perpetuating the practice of female genital cutting. Data on the attitudes of men have been collected only in Eritrea and Sudan. DHS data for Eritrea show that men are slightly more likely than women to favor discontinuation, and that men who believe the practice should be stopped are about twice as likely as their female counterparts to cite medical complications and lack of sexual satisfaction as reasons. In Sudan, a 1981 study found that men are somewhat more likely than women to believe female genital cutting should continue, but are less than half as likely as women to prefer infibulation.

Working for Change

Efforts to eliminate female circumcision have often been unsuccessful because opponents of the practice ignored its social and economic context. In some cases, external intervention has strengthened the resolve of communities to continue their genital cutting rituals as a way of resisting what they perceive as cultural imperialism.

During the era of colonial rule in Africa, some governments attempted to ban female circumcision and met with resistance. In Sudan, when a law banning infibulation was about to be proclaimed in 1946, many parents rushed to midwives to have their daughters infibulated in case it should become impossible later on. When some midwives were arrested for performing circumcision, anticolonial protests broke out. The British colonial government, fearing a massive nationalist revolt such as those that had occurred in Egypt and Kenya, eventually let the law go unenforced.

More recently, calls to action by Western feminists and human rights activists have provoked similar negative reactions. African women have perceived many of these efforts as condescending and derogatory toward their culture. In the words of one infibulated Somali woman. "If Somali women change, it will be a change done by us, among us. When they order us to stop, tell us what we must do, it is offensive to the black person or the Muslim person who believes in circumcision. To advise is good, but not to order."

In many Western publications dealing with female circumcision, one anthropologist observes, "African women are . . . depicted as aberrant, while intact Western women have their sexuality affirmed as the norm." Yet, as Nahid Toubia points out, Western women also subject themselves to medically unnecessary, hazardous procedures, such as cosmetic surgery and the insertion of breast implants, to increase their sexual desirability.

The strong reactions against depictions of cultures practicing female circumcision as savage, violent and abusive of women and children have led to new ways of approaching the issue. Some international organizations working against the practice are supporting local activist groups with funding, training and technical expertise rather than choosing direct involvement. Numerous projects have been mounted to eliminate female circumcision, although none have included rigorous evaluations to determine their success. The following approaches are typical:

- *Community education.* A nationwide study conducted in 1985–1986 by the National Association of Nigerian Nurses and Midwives found that female circumcision was practiced in all states and that in five of the then 11 states at least 90% of the women had been cut. In response to this information, the organization designed an eradication campaign with support from Population Action International and the Program for Appropriate Technology in Health. The project trained health workers to teach individuals about the harmful effects of female circumcision and to work through religious organizations, women's organizations and social clubs to mobilize communities against the practice.
- *Alternative rituals.* The organization Maendeleo Ya Wanawake carried out a pilot project in the Meru district of Kenya in 1996 to develop an alternative initiation ritual. Some 25 mother-daughter pairs participated in a six-day training session that included information on the consequences of female circumcision and how to defend the decision not to be cut. The session culminated in a coming-of-age celebration planned by the community, excluding circumcision but including gifts and special T-shirts for the initiates, skits, and "books of wisdom" prepared by the parents of each girl.
- *Drama.* In Burkina Faso, the director of a local theater group developed a play, based on the experience of his niece, on the consequences of female circumcision; the play is aimed particularly at men. A grant from the Research Action and Information Network for Bodily Integrity of Women (RAINBO) enabled him to videotape the play and show it throughout the region.

Prospects for the Future

The available data provide little evidence that the practice of female circumcision will decline substantially in the near future. The Central African Republic, where prevalence is moderate, is the only country in which steady decline seems to be occurring. Young women in Côte d'Ivoire, Egypt, Eritrea and Mali appear to be no less likely than older women to have undergone circumcision. In Sudan, the sole country for which longitudinal comparisons can be made, prevalence appears to have declined slightly, from 96% to 89%, between the 1978–1979 Sudan Fertility Survey and the 1989–1990 Sudan DHS. Nevertheless, the DHS data do not indicate any differences between younger and older women.

Despite the overall lack of change in the percentages of girls who undergo circumcision, changes in attitudes and practices seem to be occurring in some countries. In Eritrea, for example, women and men younger than 25 are much more likely than those in their 40s to believe that the tradition should be discontinued. In Sudan, where the great majority of women have traditionally been infibulated, there appears to be a small shift toward clitoridectomy.

Given the lack of enforcement of most laws against female circumcision, it is unclear whether a purely legal approach is effective in itself. While legislation may be enforceable in countries where only a small minority adhere to the practice, that is unlikely to be the case when the majority follow the tradition. As Toubia points out, "Clear policy declarations by government and professional bodies are essential to send a strong message of disapproval, but if the majority of the society is still convinced that female genital mutilation serves the common good, legal sanctions that incriminate practitioners and families may be counterproductive." In such countries, she suggests, public information campaigns and counseling of families about the effects of the practice on children may be more useful.

Substantial change is likely to occur only with improvements in the status of women in society. According to Rogaia Abusharaf. "To get married and have children, which on the surface fulfills gender expectations and the reproductive potential of females, is, in reality, a survival strategy in a society plagued with poverty, disease, and illiteracy. . . . The socio economic dependency of women on men affects their response to female circumcision."

This view is born out by the DHS data: In most countries, women with higher levels of education and those who have income of their own are less likely than other women to have been circumcised and are also less likely to have had their daughters circumcised. As Toubia comments, "this one violation of women's rights cannot [be abolished] without placing it firmly within the context of efforts to address the social and economic injustice women face the world over. If women are to be considered as equal and responsible members of society, no aspect of their physical, psychological or sexual integrity can be compromised."

Critical Eye

FOR DISCUSSION

a. If every cultural practice can be questioned and changed, what is the purpose of tradition?

b. How can female circumcision be justified/viewed as a rite of passage?

REAPPROACHING THE TEXT

In what ways can those African nations that still practice female circumcision see outside interference/concern as a disregard for a culture westerners fail to understand?

WRITING ASSIGNMENT

Overt sexism, racism, and discrimination against the disabled are practices that America has engaged in. In your opinion, what other American practices need to be questioned in order to create reform and change?

Elizabeth Nunez

From
Beyond the Limbo Silence

CHAPTER 3

September is the saddest time of the year to leave Trinidad. Like April of the country I would soon journey to, September ushered in new life from the destruction of the old. Out of the hurricane-whipped foliage rotted into the damp earth burst fresh-dressed greenery: new growths of delicate lime and dazzling emerald shimmering against the bold olive of trees that survived the hurricanes, coconut palms shaking hurricane waters from the spaces in their fronds, poui and immortelle disentangling themselves from the smothering grip of dead vines. Mango trees flowered: tiny white buds folded between new green leaves. The flamboyant spread out its thick brown arms and sprouted flames of fire, red and yellow, from its branches.

On the Sunday before I left Trinidad, already feeling nostalgia for the landscape that I would not see for years, my father drove me through the mountains north of Port-of-Spain to Maracas Bay, on the other side of the island. He wanted to say his good-byes to me, give me his last words of advice on the price of gifts.

Along the road he reminded me that this, too, the freshly paved road on which we traveled, was a gift from the Americans to the Trinidad colonial government.

"They built it after the war," he said, spitting out the word *war* between clenched teeth, as he always did, as if merely voicing the word threatened to release an anger in him he had chosen to stifle. His older brother, George, obsessed by a sense of obligation to his mother country and deluding himself perhaps into believing that as a British subject he was a British person, had enlisted in that war.

Sometimes my father would boast about how his brother had learned to fly the British bomber planes in sixth months. "Just imagine," he would say in wonder, "one day before that, he'd never ever been in the insides of a regular plane."

From *Beyond the Limbo Silence* by Elizabeth Nunez. Copyright © 1998 by Elizabeth Nunez. Reprinted by permission of Seal Press.

. times my father would grow morose and speak bitterly of the war ₐad taken his brother's life and the lives of the best of the young men ₁he colonies, and had given nothing back. But not so the Americans, he would tell me. They knew how to repay debts.

By then, I knew more about the Americans than I had as a child, and America had already begun to lose its fairy tale quality. A military air base at Waller Field stretched across central Trinidad; the farmers just rolled their belongings into bundles and left their lands when the British told them to move. And the naval base in Chaguaramus: the fishermen simply had to find new waters, and there would be no more family picnics on Sundays on the beach at Teteron Bay. All for fifty battered American destroyers when the mother country was afraid Germany would become their father country. And no one asked us anything, my father would shout.

Now I was barely listening to him, smelling the wind full of the sea, fishy and salty. Now my mind spun circles. Could I live without this in Wisconsin? Could I live on prairie lands whose borders touched only land and more land thousands of miles from the sea?

I pressed my face against the car window, greedy for the forests of fat-trunked trees, the clutter of leaves and vines on their tops, sifting the sun, the sudden surprise of precipices that plunged from dizzying heights at the edge of the road as we curled around the tight bends up the mountain to the sea. "For ninety-nine years," my father was saying to me. I shut off his words with the roar of the white surf crashing onto the huge rocks below us. I didn't want to feel his anger, not then, not when I was etching in my mind, for Wisconsin, white, frothy mists hugging mountain peaks, sparkling jewels reflected in the sun.

"Even the Americans knew that they had taken too much," my father said, and then mercifully, like me, he grew quiet, silenced by the beauty of the landscape.

I knew the rest of what he would have said. Even the Americans realized that the best seaports in Trinidad, Sunday picnic beaches, acres of cocoa fields and farmlands and anything else they wanted on the other islands, were too much to pay for fifty old destroyers when no one asked the people if they minded paying. And for ninety-nine years. It was too much. But when our car skated down the last stretch of road from the mountaintop and the bay appeared shimmering blue against the sunlit sky, its edges skirted with cotton white surf and then ivory brown sand, I was ready to forget. The road the Americans had built, giving Maracas Bay to us—though only to those of us in the middle class who had cars—eased the resentment of ninety-nine years. I was ready to filter out my father's words, his anger about discarded fuel and debris snaking down from the huge military ships in Chaguaramus, soiling our waters in Carenage Bay. Fishermen's sons, naked and brown like the earth, splashing in oil-drenched waters, wondering later about the eczemas that grew on their legs, pustulant and ugly.

On the beach my father made me peel my eyes off the sunlit sea. He wanted to warn me, as he had said before when we left Port-of-Spain, about the cost of gifts. I wanted to turn away from him, to keep my etching intact for Wisconsin, but he held my shoulders firmly and looked deeply into my eyes. He had something important to tell me, he said. Eric Williams had come back from America and he had learned a lot from him.

"When you get to that college in America," he said, "I want you to be careful. Don't let America fool you with its righteous words. Freedom, independence, the right to choose, justice—these are for them alone. Americans are sentimental. They cry and weep at the movies, at make-believe—but don't think real life moves them. Be careful, Sara. To them, you owe them everything. They owe you nothing. Your, scholarship? They have paid for your silence and your friendship."

He spoke in generalities and I fought to understand him, abandoning the sea." Not every smile is a smile," he said. "And you can lie with your face and keep your heart."

The sun blazed down on my back and burned the sand, and I remembered, and too late tried to erase the image of the other burning my father was pressing me to recall." Not every smile is a smile." I knew what he wanted me to understand were his own smiles to Captain McNeil.

My back grew hotter and I placed my hand on the nape of my neck and felt my perspiration, hot and steamy as the water that rolled off the tool shed my father had burned, the tool shed full of Captain McNeil's gifts. He wanted me to remember the fire. To understand his smiles after he had accepted the Salk vaccine from Captain McNeil, to know why he accepted the other gifts that came after that, each one perversely less expensive than the other, each one larger and more cumbersome: a box of perfume for my mother, then a stack of towels, a carton of beans, bags of flour; cufflinks for my father, then a case of beer, cans of sodas, fertilizer for our lawn, chewing gum. Afterward my father would store the presents quietly in the tool shed, and his mood would darken and he would drift like a shadow through the house.

Each day I saw him grow more sullen and fall more deeply into a silence that even my mother could not break. Then another American, Paul

Robeson, came to our island. Captain McNeil invited my father to a concert Robeson was giving at the base on Christmas Eve. It was the only gift my father ever truly accepted. Later, when he returned from the concert, my father set the tool shed on fire.

Our neighbors grieved for us: who would do such a heartless thing on Christmas Eve? My mother, uncanny, hiding our secret, fanned their sympathies. "All our Christmas gifts had been stored there," she said.

Her lie allowed for catharsis and permitted us to admit, while concealing the horrible truth, that my father had stored the gifts from the Americans there. It released the humiliation we had endured, the guilt we had not acknowledged, even to ourselves, when we accepted our vaccines in silence and watched helplessly as polio ravaged the children of our neighbors.

What price had my father paid for my life? The fire consumed the need to know, to give voice to the question. It eradicated from my memory, or so I thought at eleven years of age, my father's silent acceptance of the gifts from the Americans. Yet it left in its ashes suspicions that never died. Now, sitting in the sun on the beach at Maracas Bay, my father was to fuse forever the memory of that fire with the beauty of the landscape I did not want to forget.

"Just be careful what you accept from them, that's all. Just be careful what you take."

I would wonder later, why, in spite of what he knew, he let me go to America.

My mother also had her special good-byes to me. No more advice on how I could be transformed into a swan. No hair straighteners, food to make curves where I was all angles, clothes that would never make me look like her. I was leaving Trinidad, taking with me the embarrassment of her failure. Nor did she need to warn me of the price of gifts from the Americans. The fire had relieved her of guilt and she had chosen to forget. Now she could say, without betraying my father, that the Americans were angels. Yet something troubled her about the physical appearance of the American priest who brought the gift of my scholarship, and she wanted to protect me.

There should have been no reason for her to distrust Father Jones. He looked like us. Not that he resembled my family directly, but he could have been any one of the hundreds of Trinidadians who walked up and down Frederick Street in Port-of-Spain. He was about five feet seven, his skin the fresh, ruddy brown color of the rain-washed sides of a clay mountain, his hair, short and nappy, cut close to his head. He had a sturdy nose bridge with a matter-of-fact nose, open nostrils to draw in the air— attractive on a man of his complexion—high cheekbones and an expressive, generous mouth. He talked with his hands. Our instinct was to trust him. In one respect only did his physical features differ dramatically from ours. But this feature so dominated his face that, in spite of the similarity of the rest of his body to people's on my island, it filled us with an uneasiness that fought against our natural inclination to accept him as one of us. His eyes were the clearest blue, the color of the early morning sky.

Perhaps that was what troubled my mother most about Father Jones, though she never said so. Her final good-byes to me the night before I left were as enigmatic as my father's. She gave me a medal of St. Jude, the patron saint of impossible cases, and a bag of herbs. "Put it away and never use it," she said, pressing the bag of herbs into the palm of my hand and folding my fingers over it. "Never, unless you have to, and you'll know when that is." Father Jones, she said, was like us and not like us. More like Captain McNeil than like us. Yet, in the long run, she'd trust Father Jones first. But I should remember that, colored or white, all Americans were the same. When push came to shove, they would band together. Still, if she were me and she got into any trouble while she was in America, she'd ask the colored people for help first. She'd trust them first, but only after she'd prayed to St. Jude and put the bag of herbs in her bath water.

September in New York, six hours from Piarco Airport in Port-of-Spain, frightened me with its absence of greenery, its dead brown and gold leaves clutching desperately to dry branches, chilly winds plucking off withering stems, swirling brittle leaves into debris strewn by passersby, dirty yellow grass sprouting between broken concrete pavements, brown dirt hills in fields that would be richly green on the island I had just left. The woman who had come to meet me at the airport, a friend of my grandfather's murdered brother, was not unsympathetic. She kept her silence and let me stare gloomily through the car window at the dismal landscape on the drive from Idlewild Airport to her home in Jamaica, Queens. But when the taxi turned into her street of red-brick faced houses, she became impatient with my unhappiness.

"Look," she said, "some people would give their right eye to have the chance you have now."

My despair made me brazen. I didn't think the States would be so ugly. "My grandmother did not want me to come," I said. "She said America killed my great-uncle."

"Monkey chaser." The words hissed from her lips like venom from a cobra.

"What?" The muscles in my throat contracted.

"You. You, monkey chasers from the banana bush."

"Me? I?"

"Yes. You, monkey chasers from the banana bush think you know everything. Well, you don't know anything. Monkey chasers!"

The violence in her voice and the anger that flared from her eyes released the tears I had stoically dammed behind my wall of silence during that drive to Queens, and now they rushed down my cheeks uncontrollably. I had arrived in the country of the Americans, the fabled place of money, big cars and beautiful mansions, and all I saw around me was clutter—the clutter of brick houses leaning against each other, broken-down cars, twisted metal lining the pavement, people huddled at the corners of treeless streets. And now she had called me a monkey chaser, and my beautiful island home, the banana bush. Father Jones had made no mistake when he told my mother that he had come to Trinidad to find raw talent in the primitive world. That was how this woman saw my world, too. I was primitive, my island was primitive. She widened that gap between us—between her people, black and white, and me—to such a distance that I experienced an isolation for which even my self-imposed exile into a world of books had not prepared me. The strangeness of the place, the cool, detached weather, the lifeless trees, the squalor of concrete and brick and the brown and gold landscape triggered a longing in me for the radiant greenery I had left, and a sense of loss and regret for my folly, for my careless acceptance of the beauty that had once surrounded me, my easy willingness to give it all up.

Before I left Trinidad I had begun to miss the landscape. Now I knew that I would miss even more than that. Although I had accepted the priest's offer of a scholarship to a Catholic college in Wisconsin because I wanted to escape my mother's pitying eyes and the guilt I felt for the unhappiness my existence caused her, now I knew I would miss her more than I had dreamed possible. I would miss my father, my cousins, my aunts, my uncles, all those who loved me. I would miss the people I looked down my nose at, the ones who had seemed insignificant to me because I thought, from the books I read, that the world of the big countries was filled with people more civilized, more sophisticated—kinder. I never could have imagined this utter feeling of isolation into which

Mrs. Clancy's words, spoken to me in the cavernous shadows of the back seat of a taxi, now plunged me, a feeling of being completely severed from the human race.

My mother had arranged for me to stay with Mrs. Clancy for three days. She was to take me shopping to purchase winter clothes. My mother thought that as I had never seen winter clothes before, I should not try to buy them by myself. She had prepared me to recognize Mrs. Clancy. Skin your color, she had said. Her words were meant to comfort me, to make me feel safe. But Mrs. Clancy was hard and jagged, sinewy muscles and bones, blackness without luster. In her eyes was a pained expression that forced me to turn away or look down when she faced me. She was my great-uncle's friend, my father said. His last lover before he made his trip to Georgia.

She took me into her living room in silence and gave me a box of tissues. I could see in that gesture, in the way she placed the box gently in my hands, that she felt remorse for what she had said, but her words continued to pain me, to keep the gulf wide between us.

"Dry your eyes and sit down," she said. "Catch your breath. I'll put your suitcase in the bedroom for you."

She came back offering me a glass of lemonade. "I shouldn't have said those words to you," she said, her voice gentler than I could ever have imagined it. "But it's best you learn now to be tough. I hope these are the hardest words anyone says to you while you're here. Contrary to what I said back there in the taxi, this is no bed of roses you fell into, child."

The lilting way she pronounced the word *child* began to chip away at the isolation I had felt minutes ago. The familiar cadence of her speech comforted me and I smiled at her. We were seated facing each other on two enormous couches that crowded her living room. Thick red draperies embossed with white flowers fell from high white ceilings onto a dark red carpet and shrouded the room. It had already grown dark. The faint glimmer of the streetlights at the end of the block filtered through the white diaphanous curtains hanging limply between the parted drapes. Mrs. Clancy rose and turned on what seemed to be a showroom of lights. Still, the room felt close and I longed for the airy, light spaces of my mother's open living room with its many windows, wicker furniture and wood-beamed floors.

"You hear the accent, eh? Came here when I was a child, thirty years ago. Could fool some people though. Like your great-uncle Thomas." A vague softness crossed her face. "Thomas didn't know until it was too late that, like him, I came from the bush. He was so busy making it the American way. Didn't want to have anything to do with bush people."

She knew the words offended me. "I say bush people," she said, "but I don't mean anything bad by it, the way Thomas did. Sometimes the bush is better than all this concrete we have here"

I began to feel warmer toward her, the gap narrowing, the isolation less intense. She was my great-uncle's friend. Family almost. Curiosity finally broke down the remaining traces of my resentment.

"What happened to him?" I asked.

"Who?"

"My great-uncle Thomas."

"Didn't your grandmother tell you? He died."

"How?" I asked.

"How? How do people die?"

"My grandmother said he was murdered, Lynched."

"Lynched? Lynched? Where did she ever hear that?"

"Well, was he?"

She narrowed her eyes. The muscles on her face moved up and down as if she were chewing something hard. "Lynched?" She looked away. "I didn't think they heard that news in the bush." Her voice was barely above a whisper.

"What happened?" I asked.

"He forgot the rules."

"My mother said they shot him in a bar in Georgia, then they lynched him." I mixed my grandmother's version of the story with my mother's.

She laughed. "They don't lynch you when you dead, child. They lynch you so you can feel the lynching. So they can see the fear in your eyes telling them they have the power. Thomas was in the wrong place. He always thought he could go anywhere. I told him, a drop of black blood make you black, Thomas, He thought all you had to have was white skin. He came out different from your grandfather, you know. Same mother, same father. Portuguese and African, but Thomas took the white skin. He thought that made him white."

"And they lynched him for that?" I asked incredulously.

"Something like that. They're real hard on you here when you start thinking you're white. Thomas was a big-time New York dentist. He owned an apartment building in Harlem. He drove a Cadillac. He put his money in the bank on Madison Avenue. Big shot, But he didn't look where he was going. He didn't follow the rules."

I thought of my grandmother's words: *America is like the sea. You think it's good. You think you can swim in it and you'll be safe.*

"Did he rape those five girls?" I asked.

Mrs. Clancy threw back her head and laughed. "Rape five girls? Thomas? My Thomas? He was a gentleman, my Thomas." She stopped laughing. "I mean a gentle kind of man. A cultured man. That's what those rednecks hated the most. That's why they strung him up. My Thomas wouldn't hurt a fly. He opened doors for women and walked with them on the street side of the pavement. They probably knew he thought he was better than them. He probably called himself doctor. They wanted to put him in his place. All they saw was the bush. I don't mean Trinidad bush. Africa. All they saw was the jungle. To them we were animals. No, Thomas was in the wrong place at the wrong time. Here, if you're the wrong race, that can mean serious problems. Those are the rules."

I was to discover later, in June of the following year precisely, when three young men, two white and one black, passed through the town of Philadelphia, Mississippi, seeking answers for the senseless burning of a black church in Longdale, that being in the wrong place at the wrong time in the United States of America was a crime so heinous it was punishable by death. Even in a town named for brotherly love.

But Mrs. Clancy had her rules, too, her way of preparing me for America. I had to give her a dime for every call I made on her phone. The cash box was on the table next to the phone. Nothing is free in America, she wanted me to know, not even clean air. I also had to pay her the fifteen-dollar fare for the cab that brought me to her house, and five dollars for the one she called to take me shopping for winter clothes, She disregarded my downcast face and pocketed the money, reminding me that I was going to be all alone in Wisconsin—no mother, father, aunt, uncle or neighbor to help me out, to give me a dollar.

"How much money did you bring with you?" she asked me.

I lied, making it one hundred more than I had. "Three hundred dollars."

"And what do you expect to get with that?"

"My winter clothes," I said.

She laughed. "A warm coat, boots and a pair of gloves, the most. But that's not all the winter clothes you'll need. We'll spend two hundred here.

You can take one hundred with you to Wisconsin. They plan to give you pocket money on that scholarship you have?"

I had not thought of pocket money.

"Well," she said, "you write your parents and tell them send you some, and soon as you get to that school of yours, you find a job. Hear me?"

On the last day I stayed with Mrs. Clancy I had five dollars left in my wallet. As far as Mrs. Clancy knew, I had one hundred and five. She came to help me pack clothes that were strange to me—a pair of long, gray knit underpants, two undershirts, a gray woolen scarf, a pair of black knit gloves, a black knit hat, thick gray socks and an ugly brown-and-black-tweed coat. She was pushing aside my thin, pastel-colored clothes from Trinidad to make room for the new drab winter garments she had told me to buy, when her fingers brushed against the bag of herbs my mother had placed between the folds of my nightgown. She pulled the bag out and brought it close to her nose.

"For protection?"

"Oh no," I said quickly. "My mother must have put it there by mistake."

"By mistake?" She peered into my eyes. "Don't lose yourself so fast, child."

I tried to explain again and she stopped me.

"When you get to Wisconsin, child, don't let them make you forget who you are. All a person has is who they know they are." She replaced the bag of herbs in my suitcase.

I wanted to tell her that the herbs had nothing to do with who I was or who my mother was, either. It was just a custom, a habit, a sort of extra protection, like the St. Jude medal I wore. We didn't really believe in it. At least, I didn't believe in it.

"Well, you're lucky, child. Many a day I wished I had my mojo bag."

The word made me cringe. "It's not a mojo bag," I said.

"You forgetting already?" Her eyes pierced mine. They were hard, condemning. "It's dangerous when you forget."

On the airplane to Oshkosh I opened my wallet to count my money again. Five dollars, I did not know how I would survive. Then, opening the section that held the change, I found a fifty-dollar bill. Mrs, Clancy had put it there—her extra protection for me in Wisconsin. She, like my mannish grandmother who refused to cry, wore a mask of toughness.

And so I arrived at that tiny airport in Oshkosh, burdened with words of advice, warnings, dismal predictions, feelings of isolation and desolation and a yearning to return to the familiar—to the sounds, smells and warmth I had left behind in Trinidad three short days ago. When the tiny propeller plane I had boarded in Chicago touched down on chat barren landing strip, my imagination was aflame with all that had been said to me about America. The warnings, disassociated in a new setting from the persons who had spoken them and the incidents that had given rise to them, stripped of almost any human, sympathetic context, became cold, objective realities that I was certain I would encounter. I began to fear that I, too, could end up like my great-uncle Thomas, that my face would be so unknown, my identity so unremarkable, that someone would come out of the dark, an authorized official of the law, and shoot me down, or lynch me, as they had lynched my great-uncle, because in this great big place to which I'd willfully gone merely to hide from my mother's pity, there would be no one who would know me, who could say I went to school with her, or she was my neighbor's daughter, or I knew her mother or her family, or I was a good person, a young woman who would not hurt a fly.

My head also swirled with my father's warnings about the price of gifts. Would the nuns make me pay for my scholarship the way Captain McNeil made my father pay for the vaccine that saved my life, in secretive little installments that would strip me of my self-respect and pride? And could I withstand the cold of winter?

Once, in the sweltering heat of the August hurricane season, I tried to trick myself into believing the stories in the English books I had read: winter was nicer than the sultry heat of the tropics. I rubbed cold bottles of ice water up and down my arms and legs and basked in the pleasant sensation of the soothing cold against my hot, sticky skin. But my mother broke the spell I had woven.

"If you really want to know, put your arm in the freezer and keep it there for ten minutes. Then you'll have an idea of winter,"

She would know. She'd been to England three times before I was four years old.

At first there was only the tingling chill on my arm that cooled the rest of my body, and then the prickly sensation that comes with touching something hot. But finally I felt the pain—brutal and burning. It seared through the bones in my fingers and enclosed my wrists. I could not endure ten minutes. Three was all I could withstand with my hand in the freezer. I had a glimpse of a nightmare then: the unbearable pain in the joints of my fingers multiplied when it spread to every bone in my body.

No one came to meet me at the airport. I was somewhat prepared for this because my plane was delayed three hours in Chicago. I was grateful, though, for the time to be alone. It gave me the chance to disguise my fear, to put on a smile, to reassure myself I had done the right thing. Wisconsin was not Georgia. The nuns would be kind to me.

I decided I would use the fifty dollars Mrs. Clancy had left in my wallet to take a taxi from the airport to the college. All along the ten-mile trip I could see the driver looking at me through his rear-view mirror.

"Going to work for the Sisters?" he asked me finally.

"I'm going to college," I said.

"Is that so?" The words blended into each other. *Izzatso*. The curiosity in his voice was edged with anger. He lapsed into silence.

I looked out the window less out of interest in the landscape than to avoid meeting his eyes in the mirror. Once we had passed a few concrete buildings, we entered vast open spaces of acres and acres of grain that flooded me with memories of the sugar cane fields that lined the road on the way to the airport in Trinidad. How familiar this now seemed. How beautiful. It was about four in the afternoon. It could have been morning. The sun was stretched out over the tops of the grain. Was it corn? It could have been maize or wheat. I would not have known the difference, but the sea of green it made, rippling right and left with the wind, shimmering against a backdrop of blue hills that merged with the sky so engaged me, so absorbed me that my fears about my isolation, my feelings of strangeness in this new country began to melt away with each mile on our approach to the college.

"Did you say you're going to college?" The driver spoke again and shattered my reverie. His emphasis on *college* was pronounced with such disbelief that it immediately triggered my defenses.

"I have a scholarship," I said, tearing my eyes away from the grain field. "The nuns are expecting me."

He looked at me through the rear-view mirror. Only his eyes were visible. Ice blue.

"How'd you get that?"

I didn't think blue could be so hard. Blue, I saw in the soft sky in Trinidad. Blue, in the warm turquoise sea. "The nuns gave it to me."

"What'd you do? Take some exam for it or something?"

"No, I just got it."

"Just so. Just got it. That's all."

I could hear the growing irritation in his voice and I clutched my handbag tightly. I didn't know what he meant, what it was that bothered him.

"They gave it to me," I said.

"What kind of English is that you're speaking?"

Ice blue again in the rear-view mirror.

"I don't understand," I said.

"Your English. Your accent. Where you from?"

I took a deep breath and forced myself to relax. "Trinidad."

"And Where's that?"

"In the West Indies."

"And they went all the way out there and gave you a scholarship?" He took off his cap and whistled long and loudly. There was no music in the sound. "All the way down there?"

"I was lucky," I said, forcing a smile.

"For nothing? They gave it to you for nothing?"

"Father Jones," I began. "He said the nuns were looking for . . ." I couldn't finish my sentence. Primitive, people with raw talent, Father Jones had said. "The nuns were looking for someone to help in my country." I tried again, groping for the right words.

"I have three sons myself," he said. He put his cap back on his head. His voice was quiet now. Distant. "The oldest one goes to college in Milwaukee. Works thirty-five hours a week like me, driving a cab. Goes to school at night. Nobody came up to him or me to give him a scholarship. Not like we live far away like you. Just right down the road a few miles ahead. Wisconsin-bred and Wisconsin-born."

I felt a need to apologize. "I have to work, also," I said, the lie coming rapidly to my lips. "To pay for my scholarship."

His ice blue eyes caught and held mine. "Then that's no scholarship, lady."

I pulled away. "Well, it's part of a scholarship. I work and they let me go to college free."

"What kind of work?" His question came swiftly, challenging my answer.

I looked down at my hands. "Cook," I said. Miraculously, I had chosen the right word.

He grinned, brushed back strands of dirty blond hair that had fallen on his forehead and leaned back against his seat. "Thought so," he said. "Thought so." A satisfied smile crossed his lips. He didn't speak again until we arrived at the college.

All the nuns had come out to meet me on the front lawn. I saw them against the backdrop of a huge, dark building, their long white skirts and veils billowing out behind them in the sudden gusts of wind that accompanied my arrival. One of them broke off from the rest in a slight trot as the taxi pulled up against the curb. The Mother Superior, I correctly guessed, for she had been standing at the head of the open triangle they had formed. When the taxi came to a halt, she grasped the door handle and yanked open the door. In seconds I was folded into mounds of white cotton, my right cheek pressed painfully against the metal crucifix on her chest.

"We are all so sorry, so sorry." She tightened her embrace. "They told us you'd be here by six. Those commuter planes are always off schedule. We called. They told us the plane would be late, just by chance Sister Agnes called again at four to make sure there wasn't another change, and there it was, you were already in and on your way here." She released me. "Come, come out. Welcome, welcome." She guided me out of the taxi. "Sister Agnes! Sister Maryann! Come, come."

The other nuns crowded around me, "Isn't she brave?" Mother Superior tightened her grasp around my shoulders. "Isn't she smart? How'd you know how to take a taxi? Of course it was the right thing to do. But all by yourself the first time in a new country? That was brave."

The smile I painted on my lips warmed them to me.

"What a face," one said.

"What hair."

"So thin." I heard another clucking her tongue and once again I was folded into mounds of white.

Mother Superior clapped her hands, "Sisters, sisters, don't crowd her." She pulled me away from the arms of the one who had called me thin. "My, my," she said. "My, my." Her eyes surveyed me.

The taxi driver came up behind us and tapped my shoulder. "Now, miss, who's going to pay the fare?"

Mother Superior turned to him. "Shame on you, Charlie. This is a special visitor from Trinidad. Miss Sara Edgehill. Miss Edgehill, this is Charlie. He does the regular runs from the airport into town."

Charlie shifted his eyes to the ground and mumbled, "Errands. I have a lot to do."

"So you have, Charlie. But the suitcases?" Mother Superior placed some folded dollar bills in the palm of his hand.

Charlie flashed me a look of pure hatred. It stung my eyes.

He went to the trunk of the taxi and pulled out my suitcases. "Here," he said. He dropped them at my feet.

"Aren't you going to bring them in?" Mother Superior looked at him, but something in the way he stepped backward toward the car, rubbing his hands against his thighs and shaking his head, warned her not to press him further. "That's okay, Charlie," she said. "Leave them here. We'll take them inside."

He drove off with such speed that the car wheels skidded against the concrete pavement.

"What happened that evening is still blurred in my mind. I remember the shock of looking into a sea of white faces drowned in white cotton. I had never before seen so many white people, so white, all crowded in one room. I had been taught by nuns in the Catholic high school I attended in Trinidad, many of them from Ireland, some from southern European countries. All had been in the Caribbean so long that by the time I met them their faces were permanently tanned. Occasionally a new nun would arrive at the school and we would ogle at her whiteness, but she would be one, an oddity. Before we really got to make jokes about her "It's a good thing Mother Angela has eyes or you'd think she has no face at all"—the nun would look like all the rest. There were some who couldn't tan but then their faces were covered in freckles. "It's a good-thing Mother Perpetua has freckles or she'd have to hang a sign on her face." But I had never seen such whiteness gathered in one place. It frightened me.

At dinner my fear intensified. I began to feel this new, colorless world close in on me. Perhaps this feeling was triggered by the food which, coincidentally, was without color: white steam rising from mounds of fluffy white mashed potatoes topped with a pat of pale melting butter, white baked fish covered in a white sauce and slices of white bread served on white plates on top of a white linen tablecloth. Not even the tiny beads of green peas or the shredded lettuce broke the vast stretches of whiteness before me. Gradually the nuns merged one into the other, their faces lost in the voluminous folds of their habits, each growing increasingly indistinguishable from the other. I could feel them pressing me with more kindness, and then I was sucked down into a vortex of bottomless whiteness, my legs flailing limply from my body. White clouds, strangely ponderous and heavy, now converged upon me, enveloping me, smothering me. I gasped for breath and the clouds entered my lungs and expanded my chest further and further outward until I exploded and my body broke up into tiny fragments of white paper that gently floated up out of the vortex and hovered along the four corners of the ceiling. I saw the nuns raise their crucifixes upward and I felt myself grow lighter until tiny bits of me sprinkled down like the noonday drizzle. The nuns cupped their hands and caught me, and when they each had a little fragment of me, they clamped their palms together like the shells of an oyster and trapped me in the shelter of their goodness.

Critical Eye

FOR DISCUSSION

a. Can the taxi driver's feelings be justified, and, to a larger extent, do we feel exactly the same way right now, in 21st-century America, about those who migrate here?

b. America holds promise for many who wish to "change their lives." Why is this so? And, moreover, why is the transplant so very traumatic?

REAPPROACHING THE LITERATURE

Compare this text with Ana Lisa Raya's, "It's Hard Enough Being Me." These two women are generations apart, but has anything changed?

WRITING ASSIGNMENT

Why it is important to step outside one's cultural comfort zone?

John Cheever

Reunion

The last time I saw my father was in Grand Central Station. I was going from my grandmother's in the Adirondacks to a cottage on the Cape that my mother had rented, and I wrote my father that I would be in New York between trains for an hour and a half, and asked if we could have lunch together. His secretary wrote to say that he would meet me at the information booth at noon, and at twelve o'clock sharp I saw him coming through the crowd. He was a stranger to me—my mother divorced him three years ago and I hadn't been with him since—but as soon as I saw him I felt that he was my father, my flesh and blood, my future and my doom. I knew that when I was grown I would be something like him; I would have to plan my campaigns within is limitations. He was a big, good-looking man, and I was terribly happy to see him again. He struck me on the back and shook my hand. "Hi, Charlie," he said. "Hi, boy. I'd like to take you up to my club, but it's in the Sixties, and if you have to catch an early train I guess we'd better get something to eat around here." He put his arm around me, and I smelled my father the way my mother sniffs a rose. It was a rich compound of whiskey, after-shave lotion, shoe polish, woolens, and the rankness of a mature male. I hoped that someone would see us together. I wished that we could be photographed. I wanted some record of our having been together.

We went out of the station and up a side street to a restaurant. It was still early, and the place was empty. The bartender was quarreling with a delivery boy, and there was one very old waiter in a red coat down by the kitchen door. We sat down, and my father hailed the waiter in a loud voice. "*Kellner!*" he shouted. "*Garçon! Cameriere! You!*" His boisterousness in the empty restaurant seemed out of place. "Could we have a little service here!" he shouted. "Chop-chop." Then he clapped his hands. This caught the waiter's attention, and he shuffled over to our table.

"Were you clapping your hands at me?" he asked.

"Calm down, calm down, *sommelier*," my father said. "If it isn't too much to ask of you—if it wouldn't be too much above and beyond the call of duty, we would like a couple of Beefeater Gibsons."

"Reunion" from *The Stories of John Cheever* by John Cheever, copyright © 1978 by John Cheever. Used by permission of Alred A. Knopf, a division of Random House, Inc.

"I don't like to be clapped at," the waiter said.

"I should have brought my whistle," my father said. "I have a whistle that is audible only to the ears of old waiters. Now, take out your little pad and your little pencil and see if you can get this straight: two Beefeater Gibsons. Repeat after me: two Beefeater Gibsons."

"I think you'd better go somewhere else," the waiter said quietly.

"That," said my father, "is one of the most brilliant suggestions I have ever heard. Come on, Charlie, let's get the hell out of here!"

I followed my father out of that restaurant into another. He was not so boisterous this time. Our drinks came, and he cross-questioned me about the baseball season. He then struck the edge of his empty glass with his knife and began shouting again. "*Garçon! Kellner! Cameriere! You!* Could we trouble you to bring us two more of the same."

"How old is the boy?" the waiter asked.

"That," my father said, "is none of your God-damned business."

"I'm sorry, sir," the waiter said, "but I won't serve the boy another drink."

"Well, I have some news for you," my father said. "I have some very interesting news for you. This doesn't happen to be the only restaurant in New York. They've opened another on the corner. Come on, Charlie."

He paid the bill, and I followed him out of that restaurant into another. Here the waiters wore pink jackets like hunting coats, and there was a lot of horse tack on the walls. We sat down, and my father began to shout again. "Master of the hounds! Tallyhoo and all that sort of thing. We'd like a little something in the way of a stirrup cup. Namely, two Bibson Geefeaters."

"Two Bibson Geefeaters?" the waiter asked, smiling.

"You know damned well what I want," my father said angrily. "I want two Beefeater Gibsons, and make it snappy. Things have changed in jolly old England. So my friend the duke tells me. Let's see what England can produce in the way of a cocktail."

"This isn't England," the waiter said.

"Don't argue with me," my father said. "Just do as you're told."

"I just thought you might like to know where you are," the waiter said.

"If there is one thing I cannot tolerate," my father said, "it is an impudent domestic. Come on, Charlie."

The fourth place we went to was Italian. "*Buon giorno,*" my father said. "*Per favore, possiamo avere due cocktail americani, forti, forti. Molto gin, poco vermut.*"[1]

"I don't understand Italian," the waiter said.

"Oh, come off it," my father said. "You understand Italian, and you know damned well you do. *Vogliamo due cocktail americani. Subito.*"

The waiter left us and spoke with the captain, who came over to our table and said, "I'm sorry, sir, but this table is reserved."

"All right," my father said. "Get us another table."

"All the tables are reserved," the captain said.

"I get it," my father said. "You don't desire our patronage. Is that it? Well, the hell with you. *Vada all' inferno.* Let's go, Charlie."

"I have to get my train," I said.

"I'm sorry, sonny," my father said. "I'm terribly sorry." He put his arm around me and pressed me against him. "I'll walk you back to the station. If there had only been time to go up to my club."

"That's all right, Daddy," I said.

"I'll get you a paper," he said. "I'll get you a paper to read on the train."

Then he went up to a newsstand and said, "Kind sir, will you be good enough to favor me with one of your God-damned, no-good, ten-cent afternoon papers?" The clerk turned away from him and stared at a magazine cover. "Is it asking too much, kind sir," my father said, "is it asking too much for you to sell me one of your disgusting specimens of yellow journalism?"

"I have to go, Daddy," I said. "It's late."

"Now, just wait a second, sonny," he said. "Just wait a second. I want to get a rise out of this chap."

"Goodbye, Daddy," I said, and I went down the stairs and got my train, and that was the last time I saw my father.

—1962

Critical Eye

FOR DISCUSSION

a. How is this a text about failed expectations for the father and the son?

b. Why does the father feel that power/strength comes from humiliation?

REAPPROACHING THE TEXT

Examine Cheever's text alongside Sedaris' "Hejira." Is there any difference between the father/son and mother/son dynamic?

WRITING ASSIGNMENT

We often hear about fathers feeling disappointed in their sons, but what is at stake when a son is disappointed in his father?

Jonathan Kozol

The Human Cost
of an Illiterate Society

Precautions, Read Before Using.
Poison; Contains sodium hydroxide (caustic soda-lye).
Corrosive: Causes severe eye and skin damage, may cause blindness.
Harmful or fatal if swallowed.
If swallowed, give large quantities of milk or water.
Do not induce vomiting.
Important: Keep water out of can at all times to prevent
contents from violently erupting. . . .
—*Warning on a can of Drano*

Questions of literacy, in Socrates' belief, must at length be judged as matters of morality. Socrates could not have had in mind the moral compromise peculiar to a nation like our own. Some of our Founding Fathers did, however, have this question in their minds. One of the wisest of those Founding Fathers (one who may not have been most compassionate but surely was more prescient than some of his peers) recognized the special dangers that illiteracy would pose to basic equity in the political construction that he helped to shape.

"A people who mean to be their own governors," James Madison wrote, "must arm themselves with the power knowledge gives. A popular government without popular information or the means of acquiring it, is but a prologue to a farce or a tragedy, or perhaps both."

Tragedy looms larger than farce in the United Stares today. Illiterate citizens seldom vote. Those who do are forced to cast a vote of questionable worth. They cannot make informed decisions based on serious print information. Sometimes they can be alerted to their interests by aggressive voter education. More frequently, they vote for a face, a smile, or a style, not for a mind or character or body of beliefs.

The number of illiterate adults exceeds by 16 million the entire vote cast for the winner in the 1980 presidential contest. If even one third of all illiterates could vote, and read enough and do sufficient math to vote

"The Human Cost of an Illiterate Society," from *Illiterate America* by Jonathan Kozol, copyright © 1985 Jonathan Kozol. Used by permission of Doubleday, a division of Random House, Inc.

in their self-interest, Ronald Reagan would not likely have been chosen president. There is, of course, no way to know for sure. We do know this; Democracy is a mendacious term when used by those who are prepared to countenance the forced exclusion of one third of our electorate. So long as 60 million people are denied significant participation, the government is neither of nor for, nor by, the people. It is a government, at best, of those two thirds whose wealth, skin color, or parental privilege allows them opportunity to profit from the provocation and instruction of the written word.

The undermining of democracy in the United States is one "expense" that sensitive Americans can easily deplore because it represents a contradiction that endangers citizens of all political positions. The human price is not so obvious at first.

Since I first immersed myself within this work I have often had the following dream: I find that I am in a railroad station or a large department store within a city that is utterly unknown to me and where I cannot understand the printed words. None of the signs or symbols is familiar. Everything looks strange: like mirror writing of some kind. Gradually I understand that I am in the Soviet Union. All the letters on the walls around me are Cyrillic. I look for my pocket dictionary but I find that it has been mislaid. Where have I left it? Then I recall that I forgot to bring it with me when I packed my bags in Boston. I struggle to remember the name of my hotel. I try to ask somebody for directions. One person stops and looks at me in a peculiar way. I lose the nerve to ask. At last I reach into my wallet for an ID card. The card is missing. Have I lost it? Then I remember that my card was confiscated for some reason, many years before. Around this point, I wake up in a panic.

This panic is not so different from the misery that millions of adult illiterates experience each day within the course of their routine existence in the U.S.A.

Illiterates cannot read the menu in a restaurant.

They cannot read the cost of items on the menu in the *window* of the restaurant before they enter.

Illiterates cannot read the letters that their children bring home from their teachers. They cannot study school department circulars that tell them of the courses that their children must be taking if they hope to pass the SAT exams. They cannot help with homework. They cannot write a letter to the teacher. They are afraid to visit in the classroom. They do not want to humiliate their child or themselves.

Illiterates cannot read instructions on a bottle of prescription medicine. They cannot find out when a medicine is past the year of safe consumption; nor can they read of allergenic risks, warnings to diabetics, or the potential sedative effect of certain kinds of nonprescription pills. They cannot observe preventive health care admonitions. They cannot read about "the seven warning signs of cancer" or the indications of blood-sugar fluctuations or the risks of eating certain foods that aggravate the likelihood of cardiac arrest.

Illiterates live, in more than literal ways, an uninsured existence. They cannot understand the written details on a health insurance form. They cannot read the waivers that they sign preceding surgical procedures. Several women I have known in Boston have entered a slum hospital with the intention of obtaining a tubal ligation and have emerged a few days later after having been subjected to a hysterectomy. Unaware of their rights, incognizant of jargon, intimidated by the unfamiliar air of fear and atmosphere of ether that so many of us find oppressive in the confines even of the most attractive and expensive medical facilities, they have signed their names to documents they could not read and which nobody, in the hectic situation that prevails so often in those overcrowded hospitals that serve the urban poor, had even bothered to explain.

Childbirth might seem to be the last inalienable right of any female citizen within a civilized society. Illiterate mothers, as we shall see, already have been cheated of the power to protect their progeny against the likelihood of demolition in deficient public schools and, as a result, against the verbal servitude within which they themselves exist. Surgical denial of the right to bear that child in the first place represents an ultimate denial, an unspeakable metaphor, a final darkness that denies even the twilight gleamings of our own humanity. What greater violation of our biological, our biblical, our spiritual humanity could possibly exist than that which takes place nightly, perhaps hourly these days, within such overburdened and benighted institutions as the Boston City Hospital? Illiteracy has many costs; few are so irreversible as this.

Even the roof above one's head, the gas or other fuel for heating that protects the residents of northern city slums against the threat of illness in the winter months become uncertain guarantees. Illiterates cannot read the lease that they must sign to live in an apartment which, too often, they cannot afford. They cannot manage check accounts and therefore seldom pay for anything by mail. Hours and entire days of difficult travel (and the cost of bus or other public transit) must be added to the real cost of whatever they consume. Loss of interest on the check accounts they do not have, and could not manage if they did, must be regarded as another of the excess costs paid by the citizen who is excluded from the common instruments of commerce in a numerate society.

"I couldn't understand the bills," a woman in Washington, D.C., reports, "and then I couldn't write the checks to pay them. We signed things we didn't know what they were."

Illiterates cannot read the notices that they receive from welfare offices or from the IRS. They must depend on word-of-mouth instruction from the welfare worker—or from other persons whom they have good reason to mistrust. They do not know what rights they have, what deadlines and requirements they face, what options they might choose to exercise. They are half-citizens. Their rights exist in print but not in fact.

Illiterates cannot look up numbers in a telephone directory. Even if they can find the names of friends, few possess the sorting skills to make use of the yellow pages; categories are bewildering and trade names are beyond decoding capabilities for million of nonreaders. Even the emergency numbers listed on the first page of the phone book—"Ambulance," "Police," and "Fire"—are too frequently beyond the recognition of nonreaders.

Many illiterates cannot read the admonition on a pack of cigarettes. Neither the Surgeon General's warning nor its reproduction on the package can alert them to the risks. Although most people learn by word of mouth that smoking is related to a number of grave physical disorders, they do not get the chance to read the detailed stories which can document this danger with the vividness that turns concern into determination to resist. They can see the handsome cowboy or the slim Virginia lady lighting up a filter cigarette; they cannot heed the words that tell them that this product is (not "may be") dangerous to their health. Sixty million men and women are condemned to be the unalerted, high-risk candidates for cancer.

Illiterates do not buy "no-name" products in the supermarkets. They must depend on photographs or the familiar logos that are printed on the packages of brand-name groceries. The poorest people, therefore, are denied the benefits of the least costly products.

Illiterates depend almost entirely upon label recognition. Many labels, however, are not easy to distinguish. Dozens of different kinds of Campbell's soup appear identical to the nonreader. The purchaser who cannot read and does not dare to ask for help, out of the fear of being stigmatized (a fear which is unfortunately realistic), frequently comes home with something which she never wanted and her family never tasted.

Illiterates cannot read instructions on a pack of frozen food. Packages sometimes provide an illustration to explain the cooking preparations; but illustrations are of little help to someone who must "boil water, drop the food—*within* its plastic wrapper—in the boiling water, wait for it to simmer, instantly remove."

Even when labels are seemingly clear, they may be easily mistaken. A woman in Detroit brought home a gallon of Crisco for her children's dinner. She thought that she had bought the chicken that was pictured on the label. She had enough Crisco now to last a year—but no more money to go back and buy the food for dinner.

Recipes provided on the packages of certain staples sometimes tempt a semiliterate person to prepare a meal her children have not tasted. The longing to vary the uniform and often starchy content of low-budget meals provided to the family that relies on food stamps commonly leads to ruinous results. Scarce funds have been wasted and the food must be thrown out. The same applies to distribution of food-surplus produce in emergency conditions. Government inducements to poor people to "explore the ways" by which to make a tasty meal from tasteless noodles, surplus cheese, and powdered milk are useless to nonreaders. Intended as benevolent advice, such recommendations mock reality and foster deeper feelings of resentment and of inability to cope. (Those, on the other hand, who cautiously refrain from "innovative" recipes in preparation of their children's meals must suffer the opprobrium of "laziness," "lack of imagination. . . .")

Illiterates cannot travel freely. When they attempt to do so, they encounter risks that few of us can dream of. They cannot read traffic signs and, while they often learn to recognize and to decipher symbols, they cannot manage street names which they haven't seen before. The same is true for bus and subway stops. While ingenuity can sometimes help a man or woman to discern directions from familiar landmarks, buildings, cemeteries, churches, and the like, most illiterates are virtually immobilized. They seldom wander past the streets and neighborhoods they know. Geographical paralysis becomes a bitter metaphor for their entire existence. They are immobilized in almost every sense we can imagine. They can't move up. They can't move out. They cannot see beyond. Illiterates may take an oral test for drivers' permits in most sections of America. It is a questionable concession. Where will they go? How will they get there? How will they get home? Could it be that some of us might like it better if they stayed where they belong?

Travel is only one of many instances of circumscribed existence. Choice, in almost all its facets, is diminished in the life of an illiterate adult. Even the printed TV schedule, which provides most people with the luxury of preselection, does not belong within the arsenal of options in illiterate existence. One consequence is that the viewer watches only what appears at moments when he happens to have time to turn the switch. Another consequence, a lot more common, is that the TV set remains in operation night and day. Whatever the program offered at the hour when he walks into the room will be the nutriment that he accepts and swallows. Thus, to passivity, is added frequency—indeed, almost uninterrupted continuity. Freedom to select is no more possible here than in the choice of home or surgery or food.

"You don't choose," said one illiterate woman. "You take your wishes from somebody else." Whether in perusal of a menu, selection of highways, purchase of groceries, or determination of affordable enjoyment, illiterate Americans must trust somebody else; a friend, a relative, a stranger on the street, a grocery clerk, a TV copywriter.

"All of our mail we get, it's hard for her to read. Settin' down and writing a letter, she can't do it. Like if we get a bill . . . we take it over to my sister-in-law. . . . My sister-in-law reads it."

Billing agencies harass poor people for the payment of the bills for purchases that might have taken place six months before. Utility companies offer an agreement for a staggered payment schedule on a bill past due. "You have to trust them," one man I said. Precisely for this reason, you end up by trusting no one and suspecting everyone of possible deceit. A submerged sense of distrust becomes the corollary to a constant need to trust. "They are cheating me . . . I have been tricked . . . I do not know . . ."

Not knowing: This is a familiar theme. Not knowing the right word for the right thing at the right time is one form of subjugation. Not knowing the world that lies concealed behind those words is a more terrifying feeling. The longitude and latitude of one's existence are beyond all easy apprehension. Even the hard, cold stars within the firmament above one's head begin to mock the possibilities for self-location. Where am I? Where did I come from? Where will I go?

"I've lost a lot of jobs," one man explains. "Today, even if you're a janitor, there's still reading and writing. . . . They leave a note saying, 'Go to room so-and-so . . .' You can't do it. You can't read it. You don't know."

"The hardest thing about it is that I've been places where I didn't know where I was. You don't know where you are. . . . You're lost."

"Like I said: I have two kids. What do I do if one of my kids starts choking? I go running to the phone . . . I can't look up the hospital phone number.

That's if we're at home. Out on the street, I can't read the sign. I get to a pay phone. Okay, tell us where you are. We'll send an ambulance.' I look at the street sign. Right there, I can't tell you what it says. I'd have to spell it out, letter for letter. By that time, one of my kids would be dead. . . . These are the kinds of fears you go with, every single day . . ."

"Reading directions, I suffer with. I work with chemicals. . . . That's scary to begin with . . ."

"You sit down. They throw the menu in front of you. Where do you go from there? Nine times out of ten you say, 'Go ahead. Pick out something for the both of us.' I've eaten some weird things, let me tell you!"

Menus. Chemicals. A child choking while his mother searches for a word she does not know to find assistance that will come too late. Another mother speaks about the inability to help her kids to read; "I can't read to them. Of course that's leaving them out of something they should have. Oh, it matters. You *believe* it matters! I ordered all these books. The kids belong to a book club. Donny wanted me to read a book to him. I told Donny: 'I can't read.' He said: 'Mommy, you sit down. I'll read it to you.' I tried it one day, reading from the pictures. Donny looked at me. He said, 'Mommy, that's not right.' He's only five. He knew I couldn't read . . .'"

A landlord tells a woman that her lease allows him to evict her if her baby cries and causes inconvenience to her neighbors. The consequence of challenging his words conveys a danger which appears, unlikely as it seems, even more alarming than the danger of eviction. Once she admits that she can't read, in the desire to maneuver for the time in which to call a friend, she will have defined herself in terms of an explicit impotence that she cannot endure. Capitulation in this case is preferable to self-humiliation. Resisting the definition of oneself in terms of what one cannot do, what others take for granted, represents a need so great that other imperatives (even one so urgent as the need to keep one's home in winter's cold) evaporate and fall away in face of fear. Even the loss of home and shelter, in this case, is not so terrifying as the loss of self.

"I come out of school. I was sixteen. They had their meetings. The directors meet. They said that I was wasting their school paper. I was wasting pencils . . ."

Another illiterate, looking back, believes she was not worthy of her teacher's time. She believes that it was wrong of her to take up space within her school. She believes that it was right to leave in order that somebody more deserving could receive her place.

Children choke. Their mother chokes another way: on more than chicken bones.

People eat what others order, know what others tell them, struggle not to see themselves as they believe the world perceives them. A man in California speaks about his own loss of identity, of self-location, definition:

"I stood at the bottom of the ramp. My car had broke down on the freeway. There was a phone. I asked for the police. They was nice. They said to tell them where I was. I looked up at the signs. There was one that I had seen before. I read it to them: ONE WAY STREET. They thought it was a joke. I told them I couldn't read. There was other signs above the ramp. They told me to try. I looked around for somebody to help. All the cars was going by real fast. I couldn't make them understand that I was lost. The cop was nice. He told me: 'Try once more.' I did my best. I couldn't read. I only knew the sign above my head. The cop was trying to be nice. He knew that I was trapped. 'I can't send out a car to you if you can't tell me where you are.' I felt afraid. I nearly cried. I'm forty-eight years old. I only said: 'I'm on a one-way street, . . .'"

The legal problems and the courtroom complications that confront illiterate adults have been discussed above. The anguish that may underlie such matters was brought home to me this year while I was working on this book. I have spoken, in the introduction, of a sudden phone call from one of my former students, now in prison for a criminal offense. Stephen is not a boy today. He is twenty-eight years old. He called to ask me to assist him in his trial, which comes up next fall. He will be on trial for murder. He has just knifed and killed a man who first enticed him to his home, then cheated him, and then insulted him—as "an illiterate subhuman."

Stephen now faces twenty years to life. Stephen's mother was illiterate. His grandparents were illiterate as well. What parental curse did not destroy was killed off finally by the schools. Silent violence is repaid with interest. It will cost us $25,000 yearly to maintain this broken soul in prison. But what is the price that has been paid by Stephen's victim? What is the price that will be paid by Stephen?

Perhaps we might slow down a moment here and look at the realities described above. This is the nation that we live in. This is a society that most of us did not create but which our President and other leaders have been willing to sustain by virtue of malign neglect. Do we possess the character and courage to address a problem which so many nations, poorer than our own, have found it natural to correct?

The answers to these questions represent a reasonable test of our belief in the democracy to which we have been asked in public school to swear allegiance.

Critical Eye

FOR DISCUSSION

a. Are we deeply concerned with the illiteracy of others, or do we believe it to be "their" problem?

b. The author paints a rather apocalyptic view for those who are outside of the literacy construct. Is it really that devastating?

c. In order to combat this issue what must we do? In essence, who bares the most responsibility?

REAPPROACHING THE TEXT

The author suggests that those most in danger of falling into the illiteracy hole are those who do not speak English. Do we make it difficult for the immigrant to succeed? In short, are we patient and helpful with their "assimilation"?

WRITING ASSIGNMENT

Does President Bush's No Child Left Behind Act help the situation of illiteracy in this country?

Ernesto Quiñonez

From
Bodega Dreams

Round 2
Willie Bodega

In the eighth grade I applied to the High School of Art and Design on Fifty-seventh Street and Second Avenue. When I was accepted a lot of things seemed possible. I now left East Harlem every day and without my quite knowing it, the world became new.

Little by little the neighborhood's petty street politics became less important. I started to hang out less with Sapo, who had already dropped out. When we did meet on the street it was like we were long-lost brothers who hadn't seen each other in years. Regardless of the distance created, I did know that he was still my *pana,* my main-mellow-man. I knew that if I went to Sapo and said some guys wanted to jump me, he'd round up a crew for me, a clique from 112th and Lex or from another block. Sapo knew a lot of blocks. He knew just about all the guys that lived in the neighborhood. Most of them owed Sapo one thing or another, or were just scared of him and would do as he said, no questions asked.

In my senior year at Art and Design, I learned about the Futurists. I wanted to do something like they had done. The Futurists had been a malcontent group of artists at the beginning of the century who loved speed and thought war was good, the "hygiene of humanity." To them it was important to begin again. Culture was dead and it was time for something new. Burn all the museums! Burn all the libraries! Let's begin from scratch! were some of their battle cries, and although most of them were, like their leader, Marinetti, from upper-middle-class backgrounds and not from the slums like myself, I liked them because I could relate to their anger. I realized that by reinventing culture, they were reinventing themselves. I wanted to reinvent myself too; I no longer wanted the world to be just my neighborhood anymore. Blanca thought the same, and when we started going out we would talk about this all the time.

From *Bodega Dreams* by Ernesto Quinonez, copyright © 2000 by Ernesto Quinonez. Used by permission of Vintage Books, a division of Random House, Inc.

"Julio, don't you hate it when people from the neighborhood who somehow manage to leave change their names? Instead of Juan, they want to be called John."

"I see your point. But what's in a name, anyway? A Rivera from Spanish Harlem by any other name would still be from Spanish Harlem."

Blanca laughed and called me stupid. Then she said, "I have an aunt named Veronica. When she married this rich guy from Miami, she changed her name to Vera."

"That's wack," I said.

"I'm not going to do that. I'm going to keep my name, Nancy Saldivia, and my friends can always call me Blanca. The only time I'll change my name is when I get married."

I could have married Blanca right then and there. Instead we enrolled at Hunter College, because we knew we needed school if we were ever going to change ourselves. We got married the following year. Those were the days when all conversations seemed as important as a cabinet crisis. We'd always talk about graduating and saving up to buy a house. About children who looked like me and slept like her. With Blanca next to me, El Barrio seemed less dirty, life less hard, God less unjust. Those were the good days, when Blanca and I worked hard to invent new people. It was important to have someone help you as you grew and changed.

That's what it was always about. Shedding your past. Creating yourself from nothing. Now I realize that that's what attracted me to Willie Bodega. Willie Bodega didn't just change me and Blanca's life, but the entire landscape of the neighborhood. Bodega would go down as a representation of all the ugliness in Spanish Harlem and also all the good it was capable of being. Bodega placed a mirror in front of the neighborhood and in front of himself. He was street nobility incarnated in someone who still believed in dreams. And for a small while, those dreams seemed as palpable as that dagger Macbeth tried to grab. From his younger days as a Young Lord to his later days as Bodega, his life had been triggered by a romantic ideal found only in those poor bastards who really wanted to be poets but got drafted and sent to the front lines. During that time Bodega would create a green light of hope. And when that short-lived light went supernova, it would leave a blueprint of achievement and desire for anyone in the neighborhood searching for new possibilities.

It was always about Bodega and nobody else but Bodega and the only reason I began with Sapo was because to get to Bodega, you first had to go through Sapo.

Anyway, it was Sapo who introduced me. Sapo would knock at my door at crazy hours of the night.

"Yo, Chino, man, whass up? You know yo'r my *pana,* right? And like, you know yo'r the only guy I can trust, right? I mean, we go way back." He'd rattle out credentials as if I might deny him the favor. Then after recapping our friendship from the fourth grade to the adult present he would say, "So, *mira,* I have this package here and bein' that yo'r the only guy I can trust, you know, can I leave it here wi'choo, Chino?" Of course I knew what was in the paper bag. Blanca did too, and she had fits.

"You know he's bad news. Always has been. I don't want you around Enrique."

"What are you, my mother?"

"He's a drug dealer, Julio."

"Man, you're brilliant, Blanca. What could have possibly given him away?" The honeymoon had been over for months.

"What is your problem? You know, Julio, I married you because I thought you had brains. I thought you had more brains than most of the f-f-fucks in this neighborhood." When Blanca cursed, I knew she was mad. Even when she was angry I could detect some hesitation, a stutter before the curse. Blanca measured her curses very carefully. She didn't waste too many.

"Just look at Enrique," she continued. "He has all these women who sleep with him hoping to rip him off when he falls asleep. So he brings his dope here so you, my idiot husband, can guard it while he has a great time!"

"So what's wrong with that? It's not like we have to change it and make a bottle for it."

"*Dios mío!* Enrique might have some money and drive a BMW but he still lives in the same roach-infested buildings that we do. He can't leave because his money is only good here. You don't see him living on Eighty-sixth Street with the *blanquitos,* do you?"

"Did you figure all this out by yourself, Blanca?" I acted more interested in looking for the remote, so I could switch on the television.

"Did it ever occur to you," I said after finding it under the sofa cushions, "that maybe Sapo likes it here? Maybe, like a pig, Sapo likes the mud. Not everybody wants to go to college, Blanca." I switched on the TV and began to surf. "Not everyone wants to save up. Buy a little house in the Bronx. Raise some brats. You think everyone wants what you want?"

"What we want, Julio, what we want." She pointed at the two of us,

"Blanca, I hate that supermarket job and I've no classes tonight so don't ask me right now what I want. Right now just let me watch *Jeopardy*, okay?" She went over to switch the television off. She stood in between the remote and the television so that I couldn't turn it back on from the sofa.

"I don't like that receptionist desk, either." Blanca stepped forward and snatched the remote from my hand. "But unlike you, I'm almost finished at Hunter. Maybe if you would stop hanging around with Sapo, you could finish up before the baby arrives. Wegoing to need real money, real jobs."

"Ahh, Blanca, this is all reruns. It's all been said before. Come on. You may know what to do when you get that degree; me, I don't care. I'm getting it because I like books and all that stuff. Give me the remote." Blanca sat down on the edge of the sofa next to me. She was calm, staring straight ahead, avoiding any possibility of eye contact. When she did this, I knew a little speech was coming.

"Julio, I know how you feel about your studies. I do. But I'm only thinking about the baby. I would have preferred to have waited a year or two after we graduated, but it didn't work out that way."

"Oh, so it's my fault, right?"

"It's no one's fault. Look, I don't intend to keep badgering you about finishing school. And who knows what you'll do when you finish. I wish you'd talk to me about it." Her tone changed, a bit more angry. "But if you're up to something, something stupid with Sapo that's going to get you in some trouble, I want to hear about it. I want to hear it from you." Blanca faced me. Her hazel eyes stared fiercely into mine. I blinked. She didn't. She poked a finger in my chest. "I want to hear it, understand? From you and not from someone else's mouth. From you. So I can decide if I'm going to stay with you or not. I want to know. At least give me that. One hundred percent of that. If you are up to something illegal, you tell me. Let me decide for myself if I want to stay with you, if I'm going to be one of those wives whose husbands are in jail. I'm willing to put up with a lot, but I want to be told. If you keep me in the dark it's like insulting me. And you know Enrique is trouble."

"Blanca, I'm here with you, right? Have I ever been in any trouble? I'm here, right?"

"But what if one day Enrique doesn't tell you where he is taking you and actually takes you somewhere bad? What if the police bust him and since you were with him you get in trouble too? That happens a lot, you know."

"Sapo would never do that to me."

"How do you know?"

"Because I know."

"Julio, when we were teenagers at Julia de Burgos, I knew guys had to play this macho game and I knew you didn't really want to play but you had to. Even though you were this kid who just wanted to paint. I liked you even back then."

"I liked you too—"

"No, let me say this, okay?"

"Okay."

"I remember when they would call you on the loudspeaker to go down to the office and paint this for Mrs. So-and-So, or paint a mural for an assembly. It happened a lot. Sometimes you would miss all eight periods because you were painting something for some teacher. I remember how cool you thought it was that you were singled out and had this special privilege. But I knew you were being ruined by those terrible teachers. You were just a kid. You should have been in a classroom and they didn't care about you, they only wanted you to make their assemblies look good."

"So what are you getting at, Blanca?"

"Listen, I know this neighborhood, Julio. Just because I go to church doesn't mean I don't know this neighborhood. Here it only matters what they can break, take, or steal from you. I know that Sapo is your friend. I know that. But his friends are not your friends. His friends don't have friends." I saw her point. It was a good one. But I just played it off as if she was wrong and told her to go to sleep. Without saying another word Blanca handed the remote back and slowly walked into the bedroom. I guess she'd had her say and was leaving it up to me.

But the fights with Blanca over Sapo only got worse. Finally, during her second trimester, Blanca didn't even bother, more out of preoccupation with the baby than out of hopelessness. When she knew I was going to hang with Sapo, she would throw her hands up in disgust and ask the Lord for forgiveness. To forgive me, that is, never her. Always me. This also meant I couldn't touch her. I was impure and her body, round as the moon, was still the temple.

I can't say I blamed her. When I asked her to marry me, her pastor, Miguel Vasquez, had warned her that if she married me—a worldly person, a mundane—she'd lose the privilege of playing the tambourine in front of the congregation. That meant a lot to Blanca. At times she'd beg me to convert so she could be in good grace again. Besides, she hated going to church by herself. Now I know about wanting some sort of recognition, of wanting to have some sort of status, but when I think about yelling things like *Cristo salva!* I get the heebie-jeebies. You don't know what it's like inside a Pentecostal church full of Latinos. They really get down to some serious worshiping, with tambourines here, tambourines there, some guy beginning to wiggle on the floor because he has the Holy Ghost in him. The pastor gives his speech, yelling about Christ coming, every week Christ is coming. *Christo viene pronto! Arrepiéntete! Arrepiéntete!* Then an entire band goes to the platform and begins to jam on some of that religious salsa. It's like a circus for Christians. But the one thing you could never make fun of about Pentecostals was their girls. They had the prettiest church girls in the neighborhood. You knew their beauty was real because they didn't wear any makeup and still looked good. And I had married one of the prettiest. Like with Sapo while I was growing up, I needed Blanca with me so I could feel valuable. No, I didn't want to mess that up.

Then one day when I came home from work and was getting my books to go and meet Blanca at Hunter, I got a call from Sapo.

"Yo, Chino, whass up?"

"Whass up, man."

"So like, can you do me a solid? Like, you my *pana*, right? You know, like the day Mario DePuma jumped yo' ass at school? Who was there to save you from that fucken Italian horse? I mean, I know you didn't back down and shit but, like, he was fuckin' you up pretty bad."

"Sapo, I'm in a rush. Are you gettin' somewhere or just swimmin' laps?"

"Yo, I hear that. All right, you know that taped-up paper bag I left wi'choo lass night?"

"Yeah, but if you picking that up you gonna have to wait, bro. Because I have to go to class and meet Blanca."

"Oh, I'm touched, Jane and Joe Night School. How sweet."

"Whatever, bro. Look, I have to get off."

"*Pero, bro, no corra,* I call to ask ya if, like, could you drop it off for me?"

"What the fuck! Sapo, you think I was fucken born yesterday? Yo, I'm not going to do your dirty work, what the fuck. Me letting you keep that shit in my place is one thing, taking it around is another—"

"Hold your *caballos*, bro, like I wouldn't be askin' ya unless I knew it was somethin' easy and not out of your way."

"Yeah, well it's way out of my way. I have to go to class, man, I'll see you around." I was ready to hang up.

"Nah, wait! Bro, that's the beauty of it. You'd be droppin' those fucks right at Hunta. Yo, I swera-ma-mahthah. There's a guy in the library. You know where the library at Hunta is, don'cha?"

"Yeah, so?"

"Well, just put the bag in a backpack and he'll take it. It's no big deal. You'll lose the backpack but it's a cheap fucken bag anyway. My bro, you even know the dude. Tweety, remember him? Tweety from Julia de Burgos? Later on everyone started calling him Sylvester b'cause when he talked he gave you the weather. Remember him?"

"Ho, shit, that guy still alive?"

"Alive and spitting. Yeah, so Chino, come on. Some rich white nigga on Sixty-eighth Street ordered all this shit for a party in one of those penthouses by Park."

"I don't know, Sapo." I was afraid. Not of the cops but of Blanca.

"Yo, come on, man, one last favor for your *pana,* Sapo. You be just taking the sack to Tweety, bro. He's the one who's gonna be doing the real thing."

"So why don't you take it to Tweety? Look, I'll wait for you here to come pick—"

"I'm in the Bronx, Chino! You think I would've called you if I coulda come by? Fuck, man, you go to school or what?"

So, without telling Blanca, I did as Sapo had asked.

The next night Sapo knocked at my door and handed me fifty dollars, just for taking something to where I was already headed.

"Compliments of Willie Bodega, my man. For your backpack." Sapo slapped the crisp bill in my hand.

And that's when I heard the name Willie Bodega for the first time.

"Willie wha'?" I thought it was a funny name.

"Willie Bodega? You nevah heard of him? He's like the big Taino in this neighborhood, you know? Although only a few have seen his face."

It's important for me to remember that night, because once I heard that name it was never about Blanca or Sapo. As important as they were to me, it was always about Bodega. We were all insignificant, dwarfed by what his dream meant to Spanish Harlem. And in obtaining it, he took shortcuts and broke some laws, leaving crumbs along the way in hopes of one day turning around and finding his way back to dignity.

Round 3
Willie Bodega Don't Sell Rocks.
Willie Bodega Sells Dreams.

It was a night like any other. Blanca was laboring at the computer writing a paper for one of her classes and I wasn't. I was reading a book that had nothing to do with any of the classes I was taking. I knew that Blanca would soon get up from the computer and ask me why I wasn't writing my paper. I was ready.

"We only have one computer."

"I'm finished for tonight."

"So fast?" I thought I had it covered.

"Fast? I been at this paper for over a week. When are you going to start your work?"

"I'm researching even as we speak, see?" I showed her my book.

Blanca squinted at the title. She had her suspicions but let it go. Then someone knocked at our door. I went to answer it. It was Sapo.

"Yo, Chino, Bodega wants ta speak with ya." As always Sapo was Sapo and he said this not caring that Blanca could hear him. She strode to the door and stared at me, waiting to see what I was going to say.

"What does he want?"

"Bro, are you coming or not?" Sapo asked impatiently as if I was taking up his valuable time. He didn't look at Blanca and Blanca didn't look at Sapo.

Blanca pulled me away from the door, "Julio, who is this Bodega guy?" she asked, letting the door slam. Sapo waited in the hallway. He hated Blanca and he knew Blanca hated him right back.

"A friend."

"A friend of Enrique's, you mean?"

"A friend of Sapo is a friend of mine," I said, and Blanca shot me an evil look, then pointedly clasped her rounded belly.

"Blanca, please, I'll only be gone an hour or two. It's not like you're going to give birth any minute, you got months to go."

"Julio, we've gone through this already. When you leave with him," she loudly whispered, "I get these feelings, *Dios me salve.*"

"Blanca, no Christ right now, all right?" This upset her.

"What about your work?" Her voice got louder. "Weren't you studying or something?"

"I just finished." I don't know why I said those things to Blanca sometimes when I knew she could see right through me.

"You mean you want to hang with Sapo." She sighed and waved her hand dismissively. "Forget it *Vete.* Act like a single man." She stormed into the bedroom to get on the phone with her sister, Deborah. Blanca called her sister only when she wanted to hear gossip or to complain about me. Deborah was the complete opposite of Blanca. She wasn't as pretty, wasn't Pentecostal, she cursed, drank Budweiser from the can, and got into fights. She was so much the opposite of her kid sister that from the time Blanca was ten and Deborah twelve, everyone called her Negra.

After the skirmish with Blanca I grabbed my denim jacket and headed out the door. When I came out, I saw Sapo waiting impatiently in the hallway. When he saw me he smiled, his big lips uncovering all his teeth. He was happy, as if he had won some duel.

"Let me tell you, bro, I always knew you were gonna marry that girl. And that's all right cuz she's fine, but you got to admit she's a bitch sometimes." His hand landed on my shoulder and he said, "Bodega is nice, man. You'll like the guy."

"What does he want with me?" I asked again.

"He didn't say. He just wants ta speak with you, thass all." We headed toward the stairs and Sapo squeezed my shoulder and then stopped. He took his hand off me, turned, and looked in my eyes to make sure I was listening.

"Bodega wants something from you, man. That shit don't happen often. Know what I'm sayin'?"

I nodded, and we walked down the stairs.

"Where does does Bodega live?"

"Bodega? Bodega lives in a lotta places. He has apartments all over the neighborhood. You got to have many places and juggle your place of dwellin' in order to create confusion. Only your closest of *panas* can know your exact whereabouts. All I know is he said he wanted to speak with ya and that he was goin' to be at his place on top of Casablanca. You know where Casasblanca is, don' cha? That fucken meat market."

"Yeah, I know," I said, and we walked out to the street.

From my place in the Schomburg projects on 111th and Fifth to Casablanca the *carnicería* on 110th between Lexington and Park is only four blocks. Regardless, Sapo led me to his parked BMW and we drove the short distance.

"There's this retard at the door yo'r going to meet, He's Bodega's cousin. Thass the only reason why Bodega has him around, b'cause you can't fire your own family. But the nigga is stupid, bro. So when we get there he is going to open the door and that nigga, bro, that nigga talks in songs. Like, he fucken grew up on radio. *Ese tipo está craquiado.*"

When we arrived Sapo parked the car right next to a fire hydrant. Outside the walkup some men had set up a table and were sitting on milk crates, drinking Budweisers in paper bags and playing dominoes. They had a small radio at their feet tuned to an old love song, "*Mujer, si puedes tu con Dios hablar pregúntale si yo alguna vez te he dejado de adorar.*" Across the street, on the entrance wall of a project building, was an altar, meaning someone had just died. There were flowers, a forty-ounce Miller, pictures of saints, and pictures of the deceased, with six large candles burning in the form of a cross. Sapo led me inside the old tenement where the storefront butcher shop Casablanca had been been serving up meat to the neighborhood for years. We walked up three flights. Inside the tenement the walls were torn up, the stairs creaked, the smell was of old and decay; the only thing worse than the smell of a tenement is a pissed-up elevator in a project. If you look at the floors of an old tenement, you'll see layers upon layers of linoleum from different years. All in different colors. Sapo stopped at a steel door that looked like it was imported from Rikers Island.

A tall, big man with a baby's face and the shoulders of a bear opened the door. He was Bodega's cousin. He was slow, but only in intelligence. Later on I would find out that he was actually light on his feet, like a feeding grizzly. I guessed he was in his forties and was stronger than he knew. I mean, this guy could hug you and not know he was killing you. He was a child of AM radio's Top Forty heyday. Word had it he started to talk in song years ago, when AM radio broke his heart by going all talk. I figured Bodega kept him as someone to watch his back or at least to watch the door.

"*Oye, como va. Bueno pa gozar,*" Nene said to Sapo, who then introduced me.

"This is my main-mellow-man Chino. Yo'r cus asked for him."

"Chino, yeah, bro." Nene looked at me and extended his hand. I met it. "Hey, it's cool, bro. You a businessman, I take?" Nene asked me. I just shrugged. "You cool, Chino, because *any businessman can come and drink my wine. Come and dig my earth.*" And he let us inside. Sapo just shook his head and muttered curses under his breath every time Nene used a piece of a song. It was something Sapo had to tolerate, a clause he had to accept if he was going to work for Bodega.

Inside was nothing. Just bare rooms. I had never gone to Sapo's place, but I'd heard it was the same way. It had to do with not owning too many things because you never knew when you had to disappear for a while. You had to travel light and easy. Nene led us into a room with a desk, two chairs, and an old, dirty sofa with a *Playboy* magazine stuck in between the cushions. Standing behind the desk was a man in his forties with a goatee and the droopy eyes of an ex-heroin addict. His hair was curly and he was about five feet ten. He was talking on a cellular phone and when he saw Sapo and me he quickly smiled, cut off the conversation, hung up the phone, and motioned to me to take the seat in front of him. Sapo sat on the dirty sofa and pulled out the *Playboy.*

"Sapito, this is your friend?" Bodega asked.

"Yeah, this is my main-mellow-man, Chino. He's smart, Willie, yo he's smart. I useta copy off him when we were in school. Till I got tired of that shit." Sapo was excited. He was happy that I was there, as if he wanted me to be part of some crew. I saw Bodega scope me out and shake his head, as if he was disappointed. As if he had expected someone else.

"You a friend of Sapo, right?" He asked, knowing full well that I was.

"Yeah," I said, not really knowing how to answer.

"So check it out, Sapito tells me you go to college. That true?"

"What kinda question is that?" I said laughing, playing it off because I was a little nervous. I would have been scared, but Sapo was there with me and I knew nothing would happen to me.

"Yeah, man, I go to a public college, nothing big and fancy—"

"Yo, college is college and thass all that maras." Bodega then eyed me again up and down, then nodded his head, snapped his fingers, and pointed at me all in the same motion.

"You all right," he said, as if he finally approved. "So, check it out, Chino, right? It was Chino?"

"Yeah."

"So, check it out, Chino, you evah heard of Edwin Nazario?"

"Edwin Nazario? Is he related to the boxer who was going to fight Rosario, el Chapo?"

"Nah, same last name, no relation."

"Don't know him. Who is he?"

"He's a lawyer."

"I don't like lawyers, they're prostitutes in suits," I said, trying to be cool.

"Not my man Nazario. He's my brothuh, we share the same vision." Bodega pointed at his eyes as if he could see whatever it was he was going to tell me. As if it were there in front of him.

"I hear you," I said. I always say "I hear you" when I don't understand things or have nothing to add.

"Nazario, he's amazin'. Chino, he knows the law inside out, like a reversible coat. And thass just the beginnin'. With Nazario I intend to own this neighborhood and turn El Barrio into my sandbox." His cellular phone rang and he picked it up.

"I can't talk right now," he hissed, his droopy eyes flashing, "I'm in the middle of somethin', yeah . . . yeah, no no, at the botanica, *que pendejos son,* yeah . . . yeah . . . at the botanica." He put the phone down on the desk and looked at me.

"Like I was tellin' you, Chino, check it out, Nazario and I know that we are livin' in the most privileged of times since the nineteen-twenties, since Prohibition." I saw that Bodega was in no rush to get to where he was going. That night when I met him I didn't like him. It wasn't because he was some drug lord. Nah, to me that was no different than some Wall Street executive who makes a million dollars by destroying some part of the world. I didn't like him because he was a loudmouth who couldn't cut to the chase. Bodega was the type of guy who, if he was going to show you how to make paper airplanes, would first tell you how trees had to be cut down in order to make paper.

"B'cause men that made this country, men that built this country were men from the street. Men like me, men like you, men like Sapito there." He pointed at Sapo, who had his nose in the *Playboy*. "Men that used whatever moneymakin' scheme they could, and made enough money to clean their names by sending their kids to Harvard. Did you see that special on the Kennedys, on channel thirteen, Chino?"

"You watch channel thirteen?" I was surprised.

"Yeah, I watch channel thirteen. What you think, only kids and white people watch public television?"

"Nah, I ain't saying that. It's just that *eso está* heavy duty, thass all."

"Not only do I watch it but I'm even a member. So did you see that special on the Kennedys, Chino?"

"Nah, must have missed it."

"Yeah, well, that shit told the truth, Yo, *ese tipo era un raquetero.* Joe Kennedy was no different from me. He already had enough money in the twenties but he still became a rumrunner. Alcohol is a drug, right? Kennedy sold enough booze to kill a herd of rhinos. Made enough money from that to launch other, legal schemes. Years later he fucken bought his kids the White House. Bought it. Yeah, he broke the law. Like I'm breaking the law, but I get no recognition because I am no Joe Kennedy."

I wanted to ask Bodega what he was talking about but I just nodded my head and let him talk.

"Because, Chino, this country is ours as much as it is theirs. Puerto Rican limbs were lost in the sands of Iwo Jima, in Korea, in Nam. You go to D.C. and you read that wall and you'll also see our names: Rivera, Ortega, Martinez, Castillo. Those are our names there along with Jones and Johnson and Smith. But when you go fill out a job application you get no respect. You see a box for Afro-American, Italian-American, Irish-American but you don't see Puerto Rican-American, you just see one box, Hispanic. Now, you don't want to consider me an American, I got no beef with that. You want to keep me a bastard child, I got no beef with that, either. But when the spoils of the father are being divided, I better get some or I'll have to take the booty by force. East Harlem, East LA, South Bronx, South Central, South Chicago, Overtown down in Miami, they're all the same bastard ghetto."

He paused for about a second and looked at me. For the first time I saw his eyes were a strange shade of pale brown, as if they had been dulled by some deep sadness that the years had turned into anger.

"I hear you," I said again. I was ready to excuse myself. At the first opportunity I was going to tell Bodega that I had to go home to Blanca because she was pregnant. That I hoped he would understand. That I would love to hang with him but I couldn't. But right that minute, Bodega slid open a drawer and pulled out a Ziploc bag the size of a Bible and said the magic words that kept me there that night.

"Yo, smoke with me, Chino."

I settled myself down and looked at the weed. That shit must be real good, I thought. When he opened the plastic bag, the aroma was like coffee and the seeds were as big as *quenepas*. Bodega then zipped the bag back up and flung it to Sapo.

"Sapito, roll us some."

Sapo smiled his huge smile and brought out his own *bambú*. He opened the bag, grabbed a handful of pot, and spilled it all over the *Playboy* on his lap. He closed the bag and began to unseed the handful he had spilled on the magazine. "Ho, shit, I just realized," Sapo said, laughing, "I spilled all this pot on Bo Derek's face. Man, that bitch is still fine, she like forty and shit."

"Nah, she's wack. She was hot once, not anymore," I said, happy that the conversation with Bodega was stalled. As I watched Sapo, I hoped that Bodega would get down to the point. I wanted Bodega to just tell me what this had to do with me. But right then, it didn't matter as much because a nice joint was coming my way and since the day I had married Blanca, I hadn't had a good smoke.

"Nah, Bo Derek is still usable," Sapo said.

"Not like when she had those little *trensitas*. You know, when she had those little braids like Stevie Wonder. Back then she was fine. That shit should come back. White girls look fine with their hair like that," I said.

Sapo continued to smile. "You know, Iris Chacón in huh prime never posed for *Playboy*. Thass a fucken shame," he said.

"Now that," I agreed, "would have been worth paying for." Iris Chacón was my wet dream, as she was for many. When she danced, she prostituted your blood, masturbated your soul. She was a gift from the mother island to remind us of the women that were left behind, the girls that were not brought over to Nueva York and were left waving goodbye near *las olas del mar, en mi viejo San Juan*.

"But I don't care," Sapo said. "Iris Chacón or not, *yo las cojo a to'a'*. I take 'em all, from eight to eighty. Blind, crippled, and crazy," I laughed with him. Sapo hammed it up. "If they know how to crawl, they're in the right position."

I laughed. "Nigga, you're crazy."

"If they can play with Fisher-Price"—Sapo was on a roll, grabbed his crotch "they can play with this device."

"Dude, shut up, get help," I said, laughing.

Just when Sapo was about to crack another snap—"If they watch *Sesame Street* they can"—Bodega came back to life. "So, Chino, like I was telling you . . ."

Sapo quieted down and I let out a deep sigh because I wanted to talk about something else. Even hearing Sapo's mad crazy snaps would have been a welcome relief. Bodega picked upon my boredom, smiled, and went right to the point.

"Nazario needs help. It would be good if he had you. You know, a smart guy, like an assistant, Chino."

"Hey, man, it's cool but I'm not interested in this business."

"Did I say anything about pushing rocks?" Bodega looked insulted. His voice sailed a notch. "I told you Nazario is a lawyer."

"Look man, I know you gotta do what you gotta do," I said. "I got nothin' against you or what you're doin'. I don't believe in this 'Just say no' shit because there ain't too many things to say 'Yes' to in this fucken place. But I can't."

"Nah, hear me out, Chino. Hear me out, don't interrupt me. Check it out. You know those three buildings on 111th between Lexington and Park, right in back of us and right in front of P.S. 101, you know, those newly renovated tenements?"

"Yeah, so wha'?"

"Those shits are mine."

"Yours?" I didn't believe him and looked at Sapo for confirmation. Sapo nodded.

"Those shits were condemned but look at them now," Sapo said. "Its like the fat girl no one wanted until someone took a chance on the bitch and put her on a diet, and now everybody's sweatin' her."

"But thass not all, Chino," Bodega continued, "I got a line of them that are being renovated on 119th and Lexington. And Nazario is working with his contacts in City Hall on getting me more. Housing. Housing, Chino. Thass how I'm going to do it. Thass the vision." The phone rang. He cursed at the air and answered it.

"Yeah . . . What botanica? You mean you fucks don't know what botanica? San Lázaro y las Siele Vueltas, what other botanica do you think? Now go!" Bodega hung up, shook his head. "Like children," he whispered to himself, "like fucken children."

Sapo kept rolling. Sapo could roll real good. A joint from him looked like it came out of a pack of Camels. I looked back at Bodega, who was still shaking his head. He muttered something to God or maybe to himself and continued.

"Like I was telling you, Chino, when Nazario acquired the first buildin', the cops would drive by and see Puerto Ricans workin' on tryin' to renovate a building. The cops would laugh. They said we had no ingenuity because we were Puerto Ricans. They would say things like, you guys ain't Incas, you have no Machu Picchus in San Juan; you guys aren't Aztecs, there ain't no pyramids in Mayaguez. You guys are Tainos, dumb mothafuckas. There ain't no ancient ruins on that island of yours cuz you guys can't build shit."

Bodega stopped, and held his index finger in front of his eyes. "But Nazario, he saw. He knew. He knew better." He moved his finger to his temple. "He's a lawyer, but he hustled. He can still hustle because he never forgot he is street. Me hustled like all of us who started stealin' a hubcap here and a radio there until we owned the car. Nazario was hustlin'." Bodega cupped his hands around his mouth as if he was going to shout.

"'Yo! Anybody knows someone who's an electrician? A plasterer? A plumber?'" He dropped his hands and continued. "Nazario was in the street hustlin'. In Loisaida and in East Harlem. 'Yo I'm tryin' to renovate a buildin' here! You know anybody who would do it for the love of his brother or at least for cheap?' And soon, the community answered him. 'Yeah, my brother is an electrician, he'll help out; yeah, my sister is a plumber; my cousin does roofin'.' And then, Chino, a blue plastic chute dropped down the side of the buildin'. Bricks began to fall. Pipes were cut. The roof was stripped. The buildin' was gutted. Like a fucken fish, it was gutted. And the cops stopped laughin'. And then Nazario was hustlin' again. Only this time it was with the fire marshal at City Hall. 'We haven't broken any fire codes. This building is safe. You can come see for yourselves." And they came and they checked. And they declared the buildin' safe. And the fire department backed off. And you know what I did?"

"What'?"

"I placed fourteen families in the buildin', cheap rent, too. You know what that means, Chino?"

"You a sweetheart?" I said, smiling.

"Yeah, that too. But what it means is fourteen families that would riot for Bodega. Fourteen families that would take a bullet for Bodega. Yeah, they ain't stupid, they know where the money is comin' from. They know who their real landlord is. They know what he does. But they're getting a slice, right? See, Chino, I see it as a grant. Just like IBM issues grants, like Mobil issues grants. Do those places really want to give money away? I don't think so. But it helps their image, it's tax deductible, and the government backs off some. In order for me to keep my slice, I also got to issue grants. But I take care of the community and the community will take care of me. They must, because their shelter depends on me." Bodega banged a fist on the table, then pointed a finger at the wall as if he were pointing at the people outside. As if he were pointing at the neighborhood.

"So if Doña Ramonita can't pay her rent, I take care of it. The community center needs a new pool table, I take care of it. Casita Maria's Peewee League needs new uniforms, I take care of it, bro. They all come to Bodega. The word is out. It's out all over El Barrio. Baby needs a new pair of shoes, go speak ta Willie Bodega. My daughter is getting married, and I need a big cake from Valencia, go see Bodega. My *fritura* stand in La Marqueta burned down, go see Willie Bodega, he'll help ya. Any shit like that. What I ask for is their loyalty. If something happens to me, people will take to the streets. Bro, there will be Latinos from 125th Street to 96th Street with congas and timbales twenty-four hours a day stopping traffic, overturning cars, setting fires, yelling, 'Free William Irizarry! Free that brother, that sweet, sweet brother! Free Willie Irizarry and lock up some fucken stockbroker!' I'm talkin' major riots here. Do you see what I'm talking about?"

As he asked me this I looked at Sapo again. He had finished rolling two joints. They were lovely: long, thin, white, like the fingers of a model. It seemed a shame to light them, but Sapo lit one up anyway. Toked it. Got up from the dirty sofa and handed it to me. I followed.

"One problem, Bodega," I said, holding the smoke in my lungs.

"Yeah?"

"Yo'r sellin' that stuff"—releasing the smoke "to your own people."

"Fuck that!" He banged a fist on the desk again, only this time it was hard. I just ignored it and passed the joint to him.

"Nah, enjoy." He waved the joint away. "*To'a' pa' ti,*" he said, so I knew he couldn't be too mad.

"See, Chino, any Puerto Rican or any of my Latin brothers and sisters who are stupid enough to buy that shit . . ." He motioned with his fingers for me to come closer as if he was going to tell me a secret. I leaned toward him. Then he whispered, repeating, "Any Puerto Rican or any of my Latin brothers who are stupid enough to buy that shit," don't belong in my Great Society."

I wanted to laugh. Who did he think he was, Lyndon Johnson?

Back then, that night, to me he was a joke. I was surprised he had come this far. But I knew it couldn't have been pure luck. No one gets this far on luck. I was to discover that I was living in a rare moment when a personality becomes so interlocked with the era that it can't be spoken of in different sentences. Bodega was a lost relic from a time when all things seemed possible. When young people cared about social change. He had somehow brought that hope to my time. It was hard to define it at first because I thought no one could possibly believe any of that, not anymore. But Bodega didn't just believe it, he was actually practicing it. He had learned from the past and knew change couldn't just come from free love, peace, and brotherhood. Extreme measures would have to be taken, and all you could hope for was that the good would outweigh the bad.

"Great Society?" I repeated after him, shaking my head. "I don't know, Willie, that sounds like something out of the sixties, know what I'm sayin'? Something about declaring war on poverty and Spanish Harlem being a prisoner of war. Now, I don't know when that war ended, all I know is they never came looking to free us." I toked the joint again, laughing. I was about to get up and pass it to Sapo but I saw Sapo had lit his own joint. So I guessed this one was all mine. I smiled.

"Yeah, well I'm a throwback, m'man." Bodega returned my smile. "I'm glad you picked up on that, Chino." He was beaming. "You were just a puppy, Sapo was just a tadpole when the neighborhood was a joy. It was a joy because there was pride and anger and identity. The Black Panthers in Harlem were yellin', 'Power to the People!' Us here in El Barrio saw what they were doing up in Harlem. We began to ask ourselves, why can't we do some shit like that here? Somethin' had to be done, otherwise we were goin' to kill one another. So then came Cha Cha Jimenez, a cat from Chicago. He started speakin' about Puerto Rican nationalism and soon formed the Young Lords. Us here in East Harlem took that movement and ran with it." Bodega began to pace the room with excitement. "The Young Lords were beautiful, Chino, El Barrio was full of hope and revolution was in the air. We wanted jobs, real jobs. We wanted education, real education, for our little brothers and sisters, b'cause it was too late for us. We wanted lead paint out of our buildings, window guards so our babies wouldn't go flying after pigeons, we wanted to be heard. But first we knew we had to get the community on our side. So what did we Young Lords do?"

"Wha'?"

"We cleaned the streets. Everybody, Chino, went home and got a broom, bought bags, rakes, Comet and Ajax for the graffiti walls, trash cans, and soon the community was for us. Soon they were cleaning the streets with us. No one feared us. They all loved us. Later we said to ourselves, hey, we didn't start the Lords to fuckin' clean the street. So one day we all put on our Sunday best and ambushed Gracie Mansion. To talk with Mayor Lindsay about jobs, education, housing, training programs. When we arrived at the gates of Gracie, Lindsay's aide said to us, 'Any complaints must be filed at City Hall.' We said, 'We're not here to complain, we're here to talk.' But Lindsay wouldn't see us. He could not believe that there were hoods in suits out by the gates who were not stabbing each other. Who weren't there to rob his house. Who had organized to make their neighborhood better. He couldn't understand that East Harlem, only a mile away from where he lived, had the capacity to see itself in the mirror and say, 'We need a change. Let's go and see the man.' Eventually, Chino, we all went home and did what Lindsay's aide had said. The next day we went to City Hall and filed our demands. And you know what happened the next month, Chino?"

"Nah, tell me," I said, knowing he was going to anyway.

"The next month, they hiked the subway fare from twenty-five cents to thirty-five cents." He shrugged. "So we waited, and we waited, and we filed and we filed. Finally, when we knew our demands weren't going to be met, when we knew Lindsay wouldn't get back to us, the sanitation department wouldn't even lend us brooms to clean our streets, we had no choice but to take over the streets of East Harlem." Bodega's cool was betrayed by excitement. "Those were the East Harlem garbage riots of sixty-nine. We used garbage cans and thrown-out furniture to blockade 116th Street from Fifth Avenue to First. And Mayor Lindsay, the biggest fraud this fucken city has ever known, but with enough charisma to charm Hitler, sent his fucken city officials and his police goons after us. So we started stackin' guns inside a church we took over by 111th Street and Lex. Thass right, inside a fucken church. And we began preaching Que Pasa Power." Bodega kept pacing around the room with the energy of a shadow boxer. "All over the neighborhood, Que Pasa Power! Even old ladies started to smuggle things for us, b'cause Mayor Lindsay's dogs would never think of frisking them. Old ladies, Chino. Old ladies would do this for us b'cause they knew, they knew where we were comin' from. Yo, it was remarkable. Que Pasa Power was what was happenin'. *Pa'lante* was our horse, a newspaper we pushed our ideas with." Bodega stopped pacing and returned to his dirty desk. He sat down, facing me. "But just like now, there was the eternal hustle." He looked at me quietly for a second. The sadness had returned, mixed with anger. "The eternal hustle, Chino. The decision to either be a pimp or a whore, thass all you can be in this world. You work for someone else or you work for yourself. And when the Young Lords got too high and mighty they began to bicker among themselves. Later they even changed their agenda and became somethin' else. I was broken. Chino, bro, I left and knew that the only way for me was to hustle. So I hustled enough heroin to knock out all the elephants in Africa. And then I met ma man Nazario. He was just gettin' out of Brooklyn Law School back then. And from those days on, Nazario and me—" I saw some light in his eyes as if hope had returned. He then joined his two fingers as if they were glued together. "—Nazario and me, brothers. *Panas*. And now we've got bigger things in mind. You see," he continued, "you either make money with me or you make money for me. Thass what I tell my boys. Either way I win."

Bodega pointed at his eyes again. Then he laughed a little laugh. "It's all a matter of where yo'r standing, where you comin' from. Willie Bodega don't sell rocks. Willie Bodega sells dreams."

At that moment Sapo got up. He stuffed the *Playboy* in his back pocket, dropped the joint he had been smoking, carefully killed it with his sneaker, picked it up, and put the roach in his wallet.

"Yo, I'm going down to the bodega to get some beer," he said. "Anybody wan'anythin'?"

Critical Eye

FOR DISCUSSION

a. How important is "street-cred," and is it more important for boys/men or girls/women?

b. How important are the rules of the street, and should we hold those who follow them to a different standard?

c. Why is it that sometimes those who try to leave their impoverished neighborhoods are viewed as "sell-outs"?

REAPPROACHING THE LITERATURE

Could we exist as a society that allows the so-called "underworld" of the streets to flourish as long as it does not infect the larger society?

WRITING ASSIGNMENT

When individuals try to start over, does society ever let them forget their criminal past? Should they?

6 7 **8**

Comprehension through Charts and Graphs

During the course of our students' academic lives, they will inevitably encounter an array of source material: poetry, fiction, plays, essays, newspaper articles, journal articles, and a bevy of online material. "Read this," we say to them, "and then tell me what you think." But the learning does not stop there. The following selections not only ask students to read but to also place what they have read in context with a series of graphs and charts that are meant to further illustrate the authors' meanings. Readings such as these are becoming even more crucial for our students because they are now being included alongside more traditional staples of writings and questions presented in many college/university testing packages. The reality is that, more and more across the country, our students are being tested by way of entrance and exit exams that have become requirements for graduation and certification. The following selections are meant to assess levels of reading comprehension and further develop the cognitive learning process.

Crime in America

Violent and irrational—and that's just the Policy

Recent falls in America's crime rate have led policy-makers round
the world to look admiringly at the country's get-tough policies. They should not.
American criminal-justice policy is misconceived and dangerous.

Remember serial killers? A few years ago, these twisted creatures haunted
not just the American imagination but, it seemed, America's real streets
and parks: an official of the Justice Department was widely reported
as saying that 4,000 of America's annual 24,000-or-so murders were
attributable to serial killers.

America loves its myths—and that was pretty much what the "wave of
serial killings" turned out to be: 4,000 people are not victims of serial
murderers; 4,000 murders remain unsolved each year. According to cool-
headed academic research, maybe 50 people a year are victims of serial
murderers; the figure has been stable for 20 years.

Serial murderers obviously form a bizarre and special category of criminal.
People might well believe extraordinary things about them. But about
crime in general, surely ordinary folk have a better understanding—don't
they? Well, consider two widely-held beliefs:

"America has experienced a crime wave in the past 20 years." No.
According to the National Crime Victimisation Survey, violent crime fell
in the first half of the 1980s, rose in the second half, and has been falling
in the 1990s. Over the past two decades, it has fallen slightly. Non-violent
property crimes (theft, larceny and burglary) have followed similar
patterns. So has murder: its peak was in 1980 (see chart that follows).

"America is more criminal than other countries." Again, no. According
to an International Crime Survey, carried out by the Ministry of Justice
in the Netherlands in 1992, America is not obviously more criminal than

Reprinted with permission from *The Economist,* June 8, 1996, pp. 23–25. © 1996 by The
Economist, Ltd. Distributed by The New York Times Special Features.
"Crime in America: Violent and Irrational—and that's just the Policy" from *The Economist,*
June 8, 1996. © 1996 The Economist Newspaper Ltd. All rights reserved. Reprinted with
permission. Further reproduction prohibited. www.economist.com.

anywhere else. You are more likely to be burgled in Australia or New Zealand. You are more likely to be robbed with violence in Spain; you are more likely to be robbed without violence in Spain, Canada, Australia and New Zealand. You are more likely to be raped or indecently assaulted in Canada, Australia or western Germany. And so on.

American misconceptions raise two questions. First, why are Americans so afraid of crime? (As according to Gallup polls, they are: in recent years Americans have put crime either first or second in their list of problems facing the country; in Britain, crime limps along between second and sixth in people's priorities.) Second, why should Americans be so punitive in their attitude to criminals? (As they also seem to be: when asked by the International Crime Survey what should happen to a young burglar who has committed more than one offence, 53% of Americans reckoned he should go to prison, compared with 37% of English, and Welsh, 22% of Italians, and 13% of Germans and French.)

One possible explanation is that Americans are irrational in their attitudes to crime. But that cannot be right: crime imposes huge costs on the country and has helped turn parts of American inner cities into nightmares of violence. Given that, it is hardly surprising that Americans should fear the spread of crime. But it remains surprising that American public attitudes should be so different from those in other countries which also have dangerous inner cities. No, there seems to be something else feeding Americans' fear and loathing of criminals. More probably, two things: the violence of American crime, and its irrationality. And it is with these that America's real crime-policy problems begin.

Murder as Public Choice

America tops the developed-country crime league only in one category: murder. While you are more likely to be burgled in Sydney than in Los Angeles, you are 20 times more likely to be murdered in Los Angeles than you are in Sydney.

American crime is not only more violent; it is also irrational in its violence. Think about a person held up at gunpoint who fails to co-operate with a robber. "Since both the risk of apprehension and the potential punishment escalate when the victim is killed," says Franklin Zimring, a criminologist at the University of California, Berkeley, "the rational robber would be well advised to meet flight or refusal by avoiding conflict and seeking another victim." Yet Americans commonly get killed in these circumstances, and it is the irrationality of such violence that terrifies.

There is nothing odd or surprising in the observation that America is more violent than other countries, that Americans are more afraid of crime, and they are therefore more punitive. But the problem with America's criminal-justice policy lies in that sequence of thought. By eliding violence and crime, Americans fail to identify the problem that sets them apart from the rest of the rich world, which is violence, rather than crime generally. Americans are right to think they have a special problem of violence. They are wrong to think their country is being overwhelmed by crime of every sort. Yet because many people do think that, they are throwing their weight behind indiscriminate policies which, at huge cost, bludgeon crime as a whole but fail to tackle the problem of violence.

America now imprisons seven times as many people (proportionately) as does the average European country, largely as a result of get-tough-on-crime laws. These are the laws other countries are now studying with admiration.

First came mandatory sentencing laws, requiring courts to impose minimum sentences on offenders for particular crimes. Michigan, for instance, has a mandatory life sentence for an offender caught with 650 grams of cocaine. A federal law condemns anybody convicted of possession of more than five grams of crack to a minimum of five years in prison.

Then came "three-strike laws", supported by Bill Clinton and adopted by 20-odd states and the federal government. These impose a mandatory life sentence on anybody convicted of a third felony. The seriousness of the felony, and therefore the impact of the law, varies from state to state. In California, in the most celebrated case, a man who stole a pizza as his third felony got life. His case was extreme, but not unique: another man got life after stealing three steaks.

Three Steaks and You're Out

Now, the fashion is for "truth-in-sentencing". Such laws require the criminal to spend most of his sentence (usually 85%) in prison, rather than making him eligible for parole after, say, four to six years of a ten-year sentence. There is much to be said for a system that does not leave the public feeling cheated about what sentences actually amount to. But, by imposing the 85% average on all offenders, "truth in sentencing" makes it impossible to discriminate between people who seem genuinely remorseful and might be let out early and the more dangerous types who should serve the whole of their sentence.

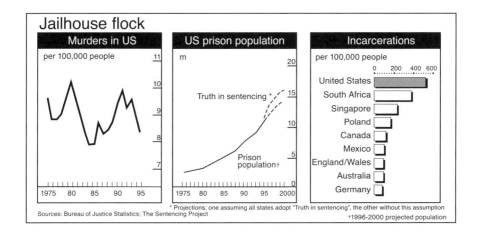

Jailhouse flock

| Murders in US | US prison population | Incarcerations |

Sources: Bureau of Justice Statistics; The Sentencing Project

* Projections: one assuming all states adopt "Truth in sentencing", the other without this assumption

†1996-2000 projected population

Since the early 1970s, when the first tough-sentencing laws were introduced, the prison population has risen from 200,000 to 1.1m. If that increase were made up mostly of the violent people that have engendered America's crime panic, that could be counted as a blow against violent crime. But it is not: the biggest increase is in non-violent drug offenders.

Between 1980 and now, the proportion of those sentenced to prison for non-violent property crimes has remained about the same (two-fifths). The number of those sentenced for drugs has soared (from one-tenth to over one-third). The share sentenced for violent crimes has fallen from half to under one-third.

And so what, you might ask? Non-violent crime still matters. Even if America's crime panic is related to violence, it is right and proper that the system should be seeking to minimize all crime. The prison population is going up. The crime figures are going down. Let 'em rot. As the right says: "Prison works."

Or does it? That depends on what you mean by "works". To many people, prison can strongly influence the trend in the crime rate: putting a lot of people in prison, they believe, can achieve a long-term reversal of rising crime. This must be doubtful. Yes, crime is falling now. But it also fell in the early 1980s, rose in the late 1980s and fell again in the early 1990s. The prison population rose through the whole period.

If there is any single explanation for these changes, it would seem to lie in demographics. Young men commit by far and away the largest number of crimes, so when there are more of them around, proportionately, the crime rate goes up. That was what happened in the 1960s, the period of the big, sustained post-war rise in the crime rate. Demography also tells you that there will be more young men around in ten years' time to commit more crimes.

But demographics cannot be the only explanation. If it were, crime would have fallen in the second half of the 1980s, when there were fewer teenagers. In fact, it rose.

Why? The answer is probably drugs. What seems to have happened is that the appearance of crack in late 1985 shook up the drugs-distribution business. The number of dealers increased, kids with no capital got into the business and gangs competed murderously for market share.

This theory would account for the decline in homicides in the 1990s. Crack consumption seems to be falling—possibly just because drugs go in and out of fashion, possibly because teenagers have seen how bad the stuff is. And the market has matured as well as declined. Policemen and researchers say territories have been carved out, boundaries set. With competition less rife, murders have declined.

The significance of all this is that it loosens the connection between the rise in the prison population and the fall in the crime rate. Crime might have fallen anyway. A combination of demographic and social explanations, rather than changes in the prison population, seems to account for much of the changing pattern of crime.

Vox Populi, Vox Dei, Vox Dementiae

That said, there might still be a justification for putting more people in prison: if by doing so you lowered the overall level of crime by taking criminals out of circulation. Indeed, if a small number of young men commit a disproportionately large number of crimes, then locking up this particular group might depress crime a lot.

Liberal criminologists sometimes appear to doubt this. "It seems," says John Dilulio, the right-wing's favourite thinker on crime, "that you need a PHD in criminology to doubt the proposition that putting criminals in prison will keep down crime." Of course, the proposition is self-evidently true. If you banged up for life anyone who had ever committed a crime, however trivial, crime would plummet. But the question is: is this sensible, even if it does work?

To many ordinary Americans, it is and politicians are happy to oblige the voters by promising to get ever tougher on crime. But what is the evidence about whether prison is an effective way of reducing crime?

Looking across the states' different crime rates and imprisonment rates, there is no correlation between the two. True, you would not necessarily expect one: states are different and tough-sentencing laws might be a reaction to a high crime rate as much as a way of bringing it down. But more sophisticated analyses confirm there is no link. Mr Zimring took the adult and juvenile crime rates in California and studied what happened over the period when tough laws were being introduced for adults, but not for juveniles. No relationship is detectable: for most crimes, offences committed by juveniles either fell or rose significantly less than did those committed by adults.

And, just as there is no convincing argument that prison effectively reduces the level of crime, nor does there seem to be a convincing cost-benefit argument in favour of prison. The problem lies in costing crime. One often-used estimate, which monetizes intangibles like pain and suffering, calculates the annual costs of crime at $450 billion. This makes prison look a bargain: its annual bill is $35 billion, while the criminal-justice system, including police and courts, costs $100 billion. But if you calculate the costs of crime on the basis of physical damage—hospital bills or the cost of replacing stolen goods—the figure comes out at a mere $18 billion a year. The moral is that, while the cost of crime must be high, no one has any real idea what it is.

What you can say is that, out of the range of options for dealing with criminals, prison is among the most expensive. One currently popular alternative is the "drugs court". Under this system, people charged with possession or small dealing may opt to go through a drugs-treatment programme rather than stand trial. Treatment costs $3,500–15,000 a year, depending on whether it is residential or not; prison costs $22,000. There is also some evidence that these courts are better than prisons at discouraging reoffending, though, since they are relatively new, the evidence is not conclusive.

Of course, get-tough policies raise questions other than that of efficacy. One is moral. Is it right to lock somebody up for life for stealing a pizza? Another is racial. These concerns have not, it seems, made much of an impact on public opinion. According to Mr. Dilulio, "Americans have lost interest in the Anglo-Saxon, innocent-until-proven-guilty model of justice. They want to get the bad guys."

Yet even by this measure, the get-tough policies are misfiring. Around 100,000 people go to prison for the 6m-odd violent crimes committed a year. The system is not getting the bad guys. What it is getting is a great many drug-taking, drug-dealing, small-time thieves. Conservatives argue that most people in prison are either violent or repeat offenders.

True, but many or the repeat offenders are addicts financing their habit through drug dealing or burglary. Nobody suggests that they are unfortunates for whom one should merely be sorry; but it is not clear that sending a crack-user to prison for five years is a rational solution to America's violent-crime problem.

America is awash with academics, judges, commissioners and policemen who know and study crime. The Justice Department's research arm, the National Institute of Justice, spent $53m last year on research of a higher standard, and in a larger quantity, than goes on anywhere else in the world.

Almost all of this stuff doubts the efficacy of what is going on in criminal justice, and fears for the consequences. Almost all the professionals agree that America's problem is violence, and that the way to reduce violence is to restrict access to guns. And on this—though the point is rarely noticed—the public agrees: 62%, according to a recent Gallup poll, favour stricter gun control.

Yet none of it makes much difference to public policy. The administration promotes a three-strike policy even though it knows that the main effect of three-strike laws is to bung up the prison system with people long past crime-committing age.

American crime policy seems to have become an area where the arguments—admittedly often complex and finely balanced—take second place to the lobbying power of special-interest groups. The effectiveness of one, the National Rifle Association, has been well-documented. A less familiar one is the prison-building lobby.

Prisons have been likened to the defence industry as a government subsidy to the white working class. For areas hit by the end of the cold war, and by the ups and downs of agriculture, prisons provide attractively recession-proof employment. As the flier for the American Jail Association last year said, "Jails are BIG BUSINESS." Towns compete to get them.

The prison guards' union has also become a powerful voice. According to a study of campaign contributions in California in 1991–92, the local version, the California Correctional Peace Officers' Association, was the second-largest donor in the state. It spends around $1m on political contributions for the governorship and the legislature in each electoral cycle.

But more important than the lobbying, and more worrying, is the failure of public debate on prison, its costs, and the alternatives. According to Bobby Scott, a Democratic congressman opposed to tough-sentencing laws, "When you call for more incarceration, you do not have to explain yourself; when you argue for effective alternatives, you do. And in politics, when you start explaining, you've lost." If that is true—and it sounds painfully accurate—something has gone badly wrong not just with American crime policy, but with America's capacity for reasoned public debate.

One-third and Rising

Blacks are more likely to commit crimes than are whites. Around 45% of those arrested for serious crimes are black. But they are also more harshly treated. Numberless studies have shown that the criminal-justice system is not colour blind. There are more unfounded arrests of blacks. Blacks pay on average twice as much bail as whites. They are more likely to be jailed before trial and get heavier sentences for the same crime.

Since the "war on drugs", the bias seems to have got worse. Blacks make up 12% of the American population, and, according to government surveys, 13% of those who say they have used drugs in the past month. But they account for 35% of arrests for drug possession, 55% of convictions and 74% of prison sentences.

Partly, that is because drug laws implicitly target blacks. Crack is a drug favoured by blacks. The mandatory federal penalty for possessing five grams of crack (a couple of days' supply for an addict) is five years in jail. Cocaine is principally a white person's drug. To get the same sentence a cocaine user has to have half a kilo in his possession.

The implementation of anti-drug laws also affects blacks disproportionately. Partly that is because the police raid black areas, not nice white suburbs, but that is not the full explanation. A study of sentencing in the 1980s, which divided blacks between "underclass" and "non-underclass", concluded that the biggest increase in the prison population was among "non-underclass" blacks convicted for drug offences.

The figures on blacks in the criminal-justice system are shocking. According to the Sentencing Project, a Washington-based penal-reform group, one-third of 20–29-year-old black men are on probation on parole or in prison. As the prison population rises, that share will increase yet further. Think about that.

People who have been in prison have a slim chance of regular employment on release. Their families are therefore poorer than others. Their children are fatherless while they are inside. Prison becomes the norm; "normal" life abnormal. America is on a dangerous course.

Critical Eye

WRITING ASSIGNMENT

a. According to the article, America appears to be a culture dominated by fear—one that has a special desire to combat crime at every level, in order to possess the illusion of safety. Why is this an unrealistic goal?

b. The initial argument asserts that studies were hasty in their determinations about just how many crimes are committed by serial killers each year. What is gained by "adjusting" the numbers to arrive at the conclusion that citizens are in immediate danger from these kinds of criminals?

LEARNING THROUGH CHARTS AND GRAPHS

Examine the charts that accompany this article. Each seeks to explore the rate of crime in America alongside that of other countries. What appears to be the determining factor as to why America leads all of the represented nations when it comes to incarceration?

Men

Tomorrow's Second Sex

The signs are everything in America and Europe: more women at work; girls doing better in school; debate about "feminisation" in America's politics; its "million-man march" last year. This article summaries the evidence of a growing social problem: uneducated, unmarried, unemployed men

ARTICLE 17

These four pages nail the following arguments to the door of debate:

- that boys are doing worse than girls at every age in school, except university where girls are narrowing the gap;
- that women dominate the jobs that are growing, while men (especially those with the least education) are trapped in jobs that are declining;
- that, for some reason, men are not even trying to do "women's work;"
- that there is a loose connection between work and marriage: joblessness reduces the attractiveness of men as marriage partners;
- that men do not necessarily adopt "social behaviour" (obeying the law; looking after women and children) if left to themselves; rather, they seem to learn it through some combination of work and marriage (this is a matter of anthropological observation rather than statistical proof);
- and hence, putting these claims together, that men pose a growing problem. They are failing at school, at work and in families. Their failure shows up in crime and unemployment figures. The problem seems to be related in some way to male behaviour and instincts. It is more than merely a matter of economic adjustment. And (considering the growth in "knowledge-based" employment) it is likely to get worse.

The problem is already far worse in some areas than others. Over the past 30 years, professional men have been less badly affected by economic change than their unskilled brethren. And (to the limited extent

"Men: Tomorrow's Second Sex" from *The Economist,* September 29, 1996. © 1996 The Economist Newspaper Ltd. All rights reserved. Reprinted with permission. Further reproduction prohibited. www.economist.com.

they want to) some have added so-called "New Man" attitudes to their traditional breadwinning role. They have adjusted reasonably well to social and economic change. But unskilled men have lost on both counts. Traditional family values—husband winning the bread, wife watching the bairns—tend to be strongest (at least in theory) at the poorer end of the labour market. But American working-class men are increasingly unable (or unwilling) to support families; in Europe, high unemployment has fallen on such men disproportionately. And because providing for a family has been central to men's social role, finding a substitute for steady work will be an immensely hard—conceivably an impossible—task.

Trouble in Class

The trouble with men appears early: at school. Though men take up half or more university places in most countries (America is an exception), at primary and secondary school girls are increasingly outperforming boys. In England and Wales, for example, girls score higher than boys in tests conducted at seven, nine, eleven and—which is less often realised—at five. In America, boys are much more likely than girls to be held back a grade and twice as likely to drop out of high school.

Both the reasons for this discrepancy and its true extent are hotly debated. In some subjects at some ages boys still do better than girls (for example, mathematics at 16). Traditionally, boys have done less well than girls before puberty but used to catch up afterwards. What is new now is that boys are no longer catching up. English and Welsh 16-year-olds take a series of tests known as GCSES. A standard measurement is the percentage of children who achieve grades A, B, or C in five or more subjects; 48.1% of girls achieve this, compared with 39% of boys. In some of Britain's poorer areas, the disparity is greater. In Hackney, a poor part of east London, for example, a mere 14.9% of boys reached this standard, compared with 30.2% of girls.

The pattern is repeated all over Europe. In 1995, in the European Union, 124 girls got general leaving certificates to every 100 boys. The boys, narrow lead in vocational certificates—they took 5% more—does not close the gap. Girls also tend to stay in school longer: Austria and Switzerland apart, in every West-European country, more girls than boys stay on in education beyond school-leaving age (though the boys who do stay are slightly more likely to go to university, taking 51% of places).

Trouble at Work

Because jobs are increasingly "knowledge-based", this disparity in educational attainment is bound to be reflected in employment once today's schoolchildren become adults. This does not necessarily mean that girls have better job prospects than boys; other factors, including sex discrimination at work, may intervene. But it does mean that girls are improving their job prospects relative to boys. Moreover, the job market is already moving the girls' way.

Between 1980 and 1992, women accounted for three-fifths of the increase in the American workforce and two-thirds of the increase in the European one. Between 1990 and 1993, in ten of the then 12 EU members, women's share of unemployment fell.

But the problem for men is not just that women are taking more jobs; it is that a significant proportion of men are dropping out of the job market altogether as women enter it. In the 1960s, almost all men worked and less than half of women. Not so now. The percentage of working-age men in the EU outside the labour force rose from just 8% in 1968 to 22% in 1993. For women, the trend was reversed, falling from 58% to 44% over the same period.

In America, the pattern is slightly different: while women's labour-force participation has risen from 43% in 1970 to about 60% now, men's has dropped relatively little from 80% to 75% (though there is an important exception: male high-school dropouts—those completing fewer than 12 years of school; in 1970, 86% were either working or looking for work; by 1993, only 72% were). If its employment trends continue, America will be employing nearly as many women as men by 2005.

Overall, then, the picture in the West is as follows: the labour market is increasingly friendly to women (though men still make more money and are more likely to be in work); but there are growing numbers of men outside the labour market in a way that women have been accustomed to but men are not.

The future for men looks bleaker, even if you disregard what is going on in schools. Western occupational surveys show that for the foreseeable future new job-growth will be in work typically done by women. America's Bureau of Labour, for example, forecasts that the five fastest-growing kinds of work between now and 2002 will be residential care, computer and data processing, health services, child care, and business services.

Boys and girls at school

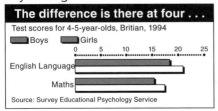

The difference is there at four . . .

Test scores for 4-5-year-olds, Britian, 1994

■ Boys   ■ Girls

0   5   10   15   20   25

English Language

Maths

Source: Survey Educational Psychology Service

. . . eleven . . .

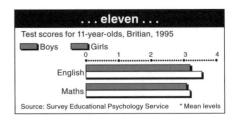

Test scores for 11-year-olds, Britian, 1995

■ Boys   ■ Girls

0   1   2   3   4

English

Maths

Source: Survey Educational Psychology Service   * Mean levels

. . . and sixteen

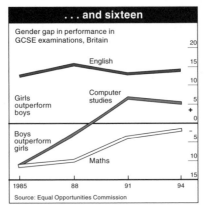

Gender gap in performance in GCSE examinations, Britain

20

English

15

10

Computer studies

5

Girls outperform boys

+

0

Boys outperform girls

–

5

Maths

10

15

1985   88   91   94

Source: Equal Opportunities Commission

Men and women at work

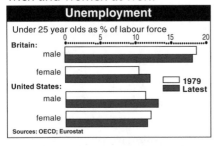

Unemployment

Under 25 year olds as % of labour force

0   5   10   15   20

Britain:

male

female

United States:

□ 1979
■ Latest

male

female

Sources: OECD; Eurostat

Wages

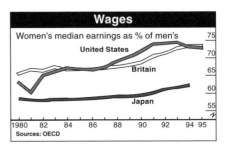

Women's median earnings as % of men's

75

United States

70

Britain

65

60

Japan

55

1980   82   84   86   88   90   92   94 95

Sources: OECD

Employment in Nordic countries

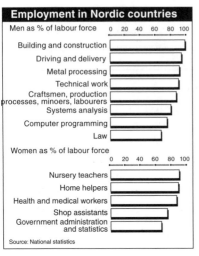

Men as % of labour force

0   20   40   60   80   100

Building and construction

Driving and delivery

Metal processing

Technical work

Craftsmen, production processes, minoers, labourers

Systems analysis

Computer programming

Law

Women as % of labour force

0   20   40   60   80   100

Nursery teachers

Home helpers

Health and medical workers

Shop assistants

Government administration and statistics

Source: National statistics

US labour force

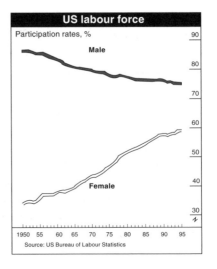

Participation rates, %

90

Male

80

70

60

50

Female

40

30

1950   55   60   65   70   75   80   85   90   95

Source: US Bureau of Labour Statistics

Women dominate all these activities: their share of employment in them is respectively: 79%, 68%, 70%, 70% and 51%. In contrast, the five sectors declining fastest will be footwear, ammunition-making, shipbuilding, leather-working and photographic supplies. They are man's work. Men account for at least two-thirds of the workforce in all the categories.

There are numerous explanations for female success in growing businesses: women tend to be better educated; they stay in jobs longer (especially women with children); low-paid jobs are growing quickly and women are readier to accept them than men, who still see themselves as a family's breadwinner; women tend to have the social skills needed for jobs in services (though whether because of nature or nurture is disputed).

For men, the obvious response to such economic shifts would be to move into the bits of the economy which are expanding. But they are not doing this. Social theorists may like to claim that concepts like "men's work" or "women's work" are outmoded. The choices people make in the labour force tell a different story. Even in Nordic countries, which have made sexual neutrality a principle of national policy, sex segregation is the norm. Local government, state-run day-care centres, schools and social services are run by women. Men weld cars and take out the rubbish. The pattern is unchanging. In America's "administrative services" (ie, office work) men accounted for only 19.8% of the workforce in 1985 and 20.5% in 1995.

Why should this be? Part of the explanation no doubt lies in the advantages that women have in the workforce—especially their willingness to accept lower-paid jobs. But there seems to be more to it than that. Men continue to spurn even well-paid work that is dominated by women. Less than 5% of America's registered nurses, for example, are men, though the average starting salary of a registered nurse is a comfortable $30,000–35,000. Women account for 96% of America's licensed practical nurses, a responsible but not especially highly-skilled job that pays a full-time worker about $23,000.

The picture is similar in Europe. In Britain, the proportion of men in nursing, 11.6%, has budged little since 1984, when it was 10.2%. As the EU noted in a report on "Occupational Segregation of Women and Men in the European Community", male manual workers are "willing to undertake low-paid and low-skilled jobs provided they are not feminised." In Spain, the share of male office clerks has dropped by a third since 1980—even though this has been a fast-growing field at a time of high unemployment; women, meanwhile, have withdrawn from the textile and footwear industries. In these areas, job separation seems to have increased.

Blue-collar Blues

So women are catching up with men for economic reasons ("women's jobs" are growing faster than men's) and social ones (men won't do "women's work"). Both reasons hit unskilled and ill-educated men disproportionately hard.

Jobs that require some tertiary education or training are growing faster than those that require no qualifications. In America's ten largest cities, the number of jobs requiring less than a high-school education has fallen by half since 1970; two-thirds of new jobs created in America since 1989 have been professional and managerial. Germany's Ministry of Labour estimates that by 2010, only 10% of German jobs will be appropriate for unskilled workers. In 1976, the proportion was 35%. In 1970, there were more blue-collar workers than white-collar ones in more than half the OECD countries; by 1990, that was true only in Spain.

In principle, unskilled men could accept these changes and kiss their wives goodbye on the doorstep as the little woman goes off to work at the nursing home. In reality, that is not happening. Despite huge social change during the past 30 years, traditional sexual attitudes retain a stubborn hold. A survey for the EU found that more than two-thirds of Europeans (ranging from 85% in Germany to 60% in Denmark) thought it better for the mother of a young child to stay at home than the father. Mothers, said this survey, should take care of nappies, clothes and food; fathers are for money, sport and punishment.

Trouble at Home

Among the poor, this combination of traditional sexual attitudes and male unemployment has been deadly to two groups: men in general in high unemployment areas and, especially, young unemployed men there. The reason is that the combination has set off a spiral of harmful and sometimes uncontrollable consequences which is tearing the web that ties together work, family and law-abiding behaviour.

Consider for a moment a neighbourhood in which most working-age women are not in paid jobs. This may conjure up a picture of tidy homes, children at play and gossip. Now think of a neighbourhood in which most men are jobless. The picture is more sinister. Areas of male idleness are considered, and often are, places of deterioration, disorder and danger. Non-working women are mothers; non-working men, a blight.

Men tend to commit most crimes. In America, they commit 81% of all crime and 87% of violent crime. Adolescent boys are the most volatile and violent of all. Those under 24 are responsible for half of America's violent crime; those under 18 commit a quarter. The figures for most western countries are comparable.

Now ask yourself what restrains such behaviour? The short answer is: a two-parent home. Without belabouring the complexity of family policies, two-parent families are demonstrably better at raising trouble-free children than one-parent ones. Fatherless boys commit more crimes than those with father at home; a study of repeat juvenile offenders by the Los Angeles Probation Department found that they were much more likely to come from one-parent backgrounds than either the average child or than juvenile criminals who offended once only.

Having a man in the house (preferably the biological father) is, it seems, more important than any other single factor. William Galston and Elaine Kamarck, two social scientists who worked in the Clinton administration, argue that the connection between crime and having a father at home "is so strong that [it] erases the relationship between race and crime and between low income and crime." That is why is is a worry that, in America in 1994, just 50.8% of children lived in traditional nuclear families (families where both parents were present and the children were the biological offspring of both parents). Among Hispanics, the figure was 38%; among blacks, 27%.

But family is not the end of the matter. Work also plays a part, both in its own right and as a means of keeping men tied to families. In 1949, Margaret Mead, an eminent anthropologist, argued that

> In every known human society, everywhere in the world, the young male learns that when he grows up, one of the things which he must do in order to be a full member of society is to provide food for some female and her young. . . Every known human society rests firmly on the learned nurturing behaviour of men.

When men find it impossible to provide, they also seem to find it difficult to learn the nurturing bits. They may retreat into fundamentalist masculinity—the world of gangs which provide for their members a kind of rule-based behaviour that boys do not get elsewhere. For everyone else (and, in the long run, for boys too), the effects of failing to learn nurturing are universally bad.

For an extreme example of this dynamic, take the studies by William Julius Wilson of mass male joblessness in American inner cities*. Here, for the first time in the West, most men are not working and women are the breadwinners (partly because they are working more than ever and partly because welfare cheques go to them). Mr. Wilson argues that

The social consequences of men

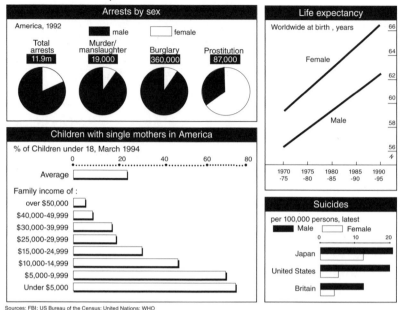

Sources: FBI; US Bureau of the Census; United Nations; WHO

joblessness, especially among young men, not poverty is a prime cause of the disintegration of inner cities: "high rates of neighbourhood poverty are less likely to trigger problems of social organisation if the residents are working." Mass unemployment, he claims, destroys the institutions that enforce social behaviour—small firms, clubs, informal networks and, above all, the family.

Mr. Wilson demonstrates that, for men, employment is strongly linked to marriage and fatherhood; for a woman, children and work are separate (often competing) worlds. Men who cannot support a family are much less likely to form one; their attractiveness as a marriage partner sags. Among the inner-city blacks in Chicago whom he studied, almost 60% of those aged 18–44 have never been married and marriage rates are even lower among jobless black fathers than among employed black fathers. And this is true in America as a whole. Black men born in the early 1940s, who came of age during an era of full employment, were more than twice as likely to marry as those born since the late 1950s, who joined the workforce at a time when blue-collar jobs were falling.

So, in the language of social science, "The uncertainties in the labour market are carrying over into uncertainties in the marriage market," as John Ermisch of Britain's Economic and Social Research Centre puts it. Work, it seems, helps determine other aspects of men's lives.

Obviously, the impact upon a neighbourhood of large numbers of jobless single men is influenced by other factors, especially the prevalence of sophisticated deadly weapons. Europe has nothing like Chicago's South Side, the so-called "black belt" that is Mr. Wilson's particular area of study. Compared with the South Side, drug use is lower in European cities; gun ownership is much lower; crime is lower; fear of crime is lower. The living standards of the poorest are generally higher. Schools do not have metal detectors.

All the same, if male joblessness is the crucial factor in neighbourhood decline (as Mr. Wilson claims), then Europe faces similar problems, though they may be bottled up. Not only is average unemployment more than twice as high as in America, but a jobless European stays that way longer. Of Europe's 19m unemployed, more than half have been out of work for a year or more, compared with about 10% of Americans. And young people make up a disproportionate share of Europe's unemployed (except in Germany) and take even longer to get a job. In France, unemployment among under 25-year-old is 27%, compared with a national average of 12.5%. More than 60% of European youths who are long-term unemployed have never had work; 40% will take two years or more to find their first job. You do not need a sociology degree to worry about the effects of so many young men with nothing to do.

The Japanese Solution? No, Thanks

There is one rich country that does not have these problems; where just 1% of children are born to single mothers; where crime is low; where marriage rates are relatively high—and where the labour market is rigged in favour of men. This is Japan. In any recession, the "office flowers" are made redundant first. Women are expected to give up jobs on marriage. In the professions, there is not so much a glass ceiling as a concrete one: hard to miss, painful to hit.

The trouble is that the West is unlikely to copy such a system, which is showing cracks in Japan, too. Just because men—or some of them—are struggling in work and at home, women are not about to stride back to the past, accepting the kitchen and nursery as their allotted spheres.

That is all to the good. But there has been a loser in women's march to something closer to equality and that is the man in the blue-collar uniform. Many of the gains that the West has made through enhancing the economic position of women will be tarnished if the male labourer is pushed to the margins. Once known as the salt of the earth, at the moment his troubles are making countries lose their savour.

Critical Eye

WRITING ASSIGNMENT

a. According to the article, written in 1996, if the disparities between men and women are not addressed, the amount of women and men in the workforce will be equal by the year 2005. Taking into consideration what the article offers as well as additional research, has the article's hypothesis come true? Are we, in fact, a nation in which the role of man as the "breadwinner" is declining? Have the indicating factors the article speaks of worsened, and what new contributing determiners have arisen?

b. Is this article merely rehashing what we have come to know as "natural selection?" Is it merely time for women to reign?

LEARNING THROUGH CHARTS AND GRAPHS

a. Doing research, have the numbers shifted or are men in even more danger of losing their footing as the dominant providers?

b. According to the charts/graphs, the phenomenon of men struggling is not limited to America. Examining the information provided in each, which country appears to have the most in common with the United States, and what may be the cause?

Dania Rajendra

Big Disparities in UFS Survey

How satisfied are you?

The results of the University Faculty Senate survey of full-time CUNY faculty are in, and survey coordinator Dean Savage says that one thing stands out. "The real message of this survey is that there are astonishing differences by campus," said Savage, who chairs the sociology department at Queens College. "It's quite spectacular."

On many questions, Savage told *Clarion,* it was not uncommon to see the share of respondents who were very or somewhat satisfied range from 80% at one campus down to 20% at another.

Baruch was the campus that showed the most widespread satisfaction: on 83% of the survey's 47 questions, its responses were above the CUNY-wide mean. Dissatisfaction was widest at Medgar Evers and City College—on both of those campuses, only 17% of questions drew responses above the CUNY mean.

Discontent

Results often showed a large number of campuses bunched in the middle, and a relatively high level of discontent CUNY-wide. On half of the questions, 40% or more said they were very or somewhat dissatisfied,

"CUNY-wide, the overall level of satisfaction was especially low for faculty influence on college policies, effectiveness of shared governance, access to information about the budget, support for intellectual life, and enforcement of health and safety regulations," said PSC First Vice President Steve London.

UFS Chair Susan O'Malley said she hoped CUNY administrators would look to the survey results to identify and promote best practices within CUNY. "We're thinking about doing a UFS conference on this in the

"Big disparities in UFS survey" by Dania Rajendra, *Clarion,* January 2006. www.psc-cuny .org/communication.htm. Reprinted by permission.

Spring," O'Malley said. "It's important to understand why one college does so well on a certain topic, while at another college the level of satisfaction is 60 points less." For example, on th effectiveness of shared governance, satisfaction ranged from a high of 69% at Queensborough to a low of 12% at City College.

The survey results have been most thoroughly analyzed for the questions on "college culture," O'Malley said. On a majority of CUNY campuses, the faculty were mainly dissatisfied with their influence over college policies and with the effectiveness of shared governance. On respect for faculty shown by college administration, discontent outweighed satisfaction on seven campuses: CCNY, Medgar Evers, LaGuardia, BMCC, John Jay, York and Hunter. (Except for John Jay and York, the same colleges were also in the bottom seven on shared governance and faculty influence on college policy. The survey was conducted before York's new president took office.)

No Respect

At City College, 73% of respondents said they were dissatisfied with the level of respect shown to faculty by the CCNY administration. "If you look at the way that City scored, you'll notice a whole series of items on the relationship between faculty and the administration," said George Brandon, acting chair. "Some of this, I think, relates to the way the provost's office has gotten a lot more power than it used to have. I was at a labor- management meeting once, [where] it became apparent that the provost thought nobody else cared about faculty governance, that the idea was passé."

National Trends

The problems at CCNY reflect national trends, Brandon said "There's the corporate thrust in university management," he said, which affects how decisions are made. "There's a generalized pressure on state-funded colleges and universities, which leads towards viewing education and knowledge as commodities. People sense that, and for many of them it is a devaluing of the work that they're dedicated to."

PSC chapter chair Jay Appleman credits Queensborough President Eduardo Marti with much of the faculty satisfaction on his campus. "We have a good administrator who is working cooperatively with us, not against us. It's more of a relationship of equals, and that's an extremely important factor." He noted that Marti is himself a former CUNY faculty member who worked for years as a professor of biology at BMCC.

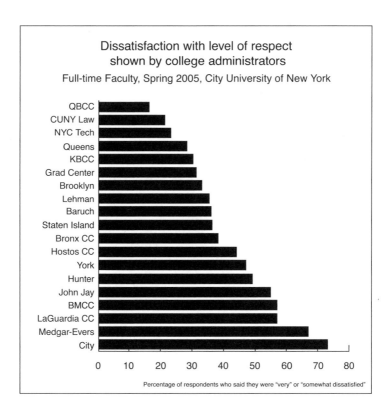

Dissatisfaction with level of respect
shown by college administrators

Full-time Faculty, Spring 2005, City University of New York

Percentage of respondents who said they were "very" or "somewhat dissatisfied"

Full-time faculty at Queensborough were almost as broadly satisfied as those at Baruch: on 76% of the questions, they expressed more satisfaction than the CUNY-wide mean. But the sources of satisfaction at the two colleges were notably different.

At Baruch, the five issues where satisfaction was the highest above the CUNY mean were classroom space, office space, restrooms, audio-visual equipment and maintenance of physical plants. At Queensborough, the top five were shared governance, respect shown to faculty, support for intellectual life, enforcement of health and safety regulations—and parking. QCC actually fared poorly on office space and class size, scoring below the CUNY mean.

Results from a number of questions pointed to an important conclusion, commented Savage: "You may not have a lot of money at CUNY, but it's still possible to treat the faculty with respect," At QCC, 83% of respondents expressed satisfaction with the level of respect from college administrators, while at CCNY the picture was almost the reverse—73% were dissatisfied.

Tami Gold, PSC chapter chair at Hunter, said that these issues were important not only to faculty, but also to students. "When you have a workforce that feels valued and feels that it's part of a community, then people work better," she told *Clarion*. "If you have people rushing to get home at the end of the day because they don't like being here, then it's not an environment which is good for our mission—which is to educate our students. These statistics need to be taken seriously."

The survey was distributed to 6,200 full-time faculty, and more than 2,000 forms were returned. Survey forms were also distributed to several hundred adjunct faculty in a pilot study, Savage told *Clarion*, but the response rate was low. Since the overall study was "exploratory" and the first such UFS effort, he said, there was no provision for follow-up work to increase the response rate and therefore the full survey focused on full-time faculty. But part-timers should be included in future research, Savage said: "They're the majority of the people who teach [at CUNY], and they need to have a voice, too."

Analysis Continues

Much of the data is still being analyzed, Savage said, including response rate by college. "However, with such huge percentage differences, I can't imagine that even if we had an 80% response rate that is would eliminate the very large campus-by-campus differentials, " he said.

O'Malley noted that many of the questions came from an existing national study, and that the UFS plans to repeat its survey every two years. Thus, she said, CUNY's results can be compared to those other universities and also analyzed over time.

"Administrators in general are not evaluated in such a public way," said Savage. "Now they have been evaluated by a significant number of their full-time faculty, and evaluated in a forum that is quite public. Some, but not all, of them will be paying attention." He paused. "Man, how can there be such big differences? A lot of this stuff is free—you just have to be nice!"

Critical Eye

WRITING ASSIGNMENT

a. The article assumes that a large number of faculty across CUNY campuses are concerned with the level of respect they receive from administration. As you see it, what kinds of problems arise when faculty feel that they are undervalued? How essential is it to the success of the school and its graduates for the professors to be happy?

b. Are educators merely in a thankless job? Should they accept feeling underappreciated as a condition of the career they have chosen?

LEARNING THROUGH CHARTS AND GRAPHS

According to the graph, is there a clear disparity between the level of dissatisfaction experienced at two-year colleges as compared to that of four-year colleges? If so, why?

Index